PERSONAL GROWTH AND BEHAVIOR 98/99

Eighteenth Edition

Editor

Karen G. Duffy

SUNY College, Geneseo

Karen G. Duffy holds a doctorate in psychology from Michigan State University and is currently a professor of psychology at SUNY at Geneseo. She sits on the executive board of the New York State Employees Assistance Program and is a certified community and family mediator. She is a member of the American Psychological Society and the Eastern Psychological Association.

A Library of Information from the Public Press

Dushkin/McGraw·Hill

Sluice Dock, Guilford, Connecticut 06437

Visit us on the Internet—http://www.dushkin.com/

The Annual Editions Series

ANNUAL EDITIONS, including GLOBAL STUDIES, consist of over 70 volumes designed to provide the reader with convenient, low-cost access to a wide range of current, carefully selected articles from some of the most important magazines, newspapers, and journals published today. ANNUAL EDITIONS are updated on an annual basis through a continuous monitoring of over 300 periodical sources. All ANNUAL EDITIONS have a number of features that are designed to make them particularly useful, including topic guides, annotated tables of contents, unit overviews, and indexes. For the teacher using ANNUAL EDITIONS in the classroom, an Instructor's Resource Guide with test questions is available for each volume. GLOBAL STUDIES titles provide comprehensive background information and selected world press articles on the regions and countries of the world.

VOLUMES AVAILABLE

ANNUAL EDITIONS
Abnormal Psychology
Accounting
Adolescent Psychology
Aging
American Foreign Policy
American Government
American History, Pre-Civil War
American History, Post-Civil War
American Public Policy
Anthropology
Archaeology
Astronomy
Biopsychology
Business Ethics
Child Growth and Development
Comparative Politics
Computers in Education
Computers in Society
Criminal Justice
Criminology
Developing World
Deviant Behavior
Drugs, Society, and Behavior
Dying, Death, and Bereavement
Early Childhood Education
Economics
Educating Exceptional Children
Education
Educational Psychology
Environment
Geography
Geology
Global Issues
Health
Human Development
Human Resources
Human Sexuality
International Business
Macroeconomics
Management
Marketing
Marriage and Family
Mass Media
Microeconomics
Multicultural Education
Nutrition
Personal Growth and Behavior
Physical Anthropology
Psychology
Public Administration
Race and Ethnic Relations
Social Problems
Social Psychology
Sociology
State and Local Government
Teaching English as a Second Language
Urban Society
Violence and Terrorism
Western Civilization, Pre-Reformation
Western Civilization, Post-Reformation
Women's Health
World History, Pre-Modern
World History, Modern
World Politics

GLOBAL STUDIES
Africa
China
India and South Asia
Japan and the Pacific Rim
Latin America
Middle East
Russia, the Eurasian Republics, and Central/Eastern Europe
Western Europe

Cataloging in Publication Data
Main entry under title: Annual Editions: Personal growth and behavior. 1998/99.
    1. Personality—Periodicals. 2. Adjustment (Psychology)—Periodicals. I. Duffy, Karen G., comp. II. Title: Personal growth and behavior.
ISBN 0-697-39175-2
155'.2'05   75-20757   ISSN 0732-0779

© 1998 by Dushkin/McGraw-Hill, Guilford, CT 06437, A Division of The McGraw-Hill Companies.

Copyright law prohibits the reproduction, storage, or transmission in any form by any means of any portion of this publication without the express written permission of Dushkin/McGraw-Hill and of the copyright holder (if different) of the part of the publication to be reproduced. The Guidelines for Classroom Copying endorsed by Congress explicitly state that unauthorized copying may not be used to create, to replace, or to substitute for anthologies, compilations, or collective works.

Annual Editions® is a Registered Trademark of Dushkin/McGraw-Hill, A Division of The McGraw-Hill Companies.

Eighteenth Edition

Cover image © 1997 PhotoDisc, Inc.

Printed in the United States of America

Editors/Advisory Board

Members of the Advisory Board are instrumental in the final selection of articles for each edition of ANNUAL EDITIONS. Their review of articles for content, level, currentness, and appropriateness provides critical direction to the editor and staff. We think that you will find their careful consideration well reflected in this volume.

EDITOR

Karen G. Duffy
SUNY College, Geneseo

ADVISORY BOARD

Sonia L. Blackman
California State Polytechnic University

Stephen S. Coccia
Orange County Community College

Linda Corrente
Community College of Rhode Island

Robert DaPrato
Solano Community College

Jack S. Ellison
University of Tennessee

Mark J. Friedman
Montclair State University

Roger Gaddis
Gardner-Webb University

Don Hamachek
Michigan State University

Richard A. Kolotkin
Moorhead State University

Angela J. C. LaSala
Community College of Southern Nevada

David M. Malone
Duke University

Donald McGuire
Dalhousie University

Karla K. Miley
Black Hawk College

Terry F. Pettijohn
Ohio State University Marion

Victor L. Ryan
University of Colorado Boulder

Pamela E. Stewart
Northern Virginia Community College

Leora C. Swartzman
University of Western Ontario

Kenneth L. Thompson
Central Missouri State University

Robert S. Tomlinson
University of Wisconsin Eau Claire

Charmaine Wesley
Modesto Junior College

Lois J. Willoughby
Miami Dade Community College Kendall

Staff

Ian A. Nielsen, Publisher

EDITORIAL STAFF

Roberta Monaco, Developmental Editor
Dorothy Fink, Associate Developmental Editor
Addie Raucci, Administrative Editor
Cheryl Greenleaf, Permissions Editor
Deanna Herrschaft, Permissions Assistant
Diane Barker, Proofreader
Lisa Holmes-Doebrick, Program Coordinator

PRODUCTION STAFF

Brenda S. Filley, Production Manager
Charles Vitelli, Designer
Shawn Callahan, Graphics
Lara M. Johnson, Graphics
Laura Levine, Graphics
Mike Campbell, Graphics
Joseph Offredi, Graphics
Juliana Arbo, Typesetting Supervisor
Jane Jaegersen, Typesetter
Marie Lazauskas, Word Processor
Kathleen D'Amico, Word Processor
Larry Killian, Copier Coordinator

To the Reader

In publishing ANNUAL EDITIONS we recognize the enormous role played by the magazines, newspapers, and journals of the *public press* in providing current, first-rate educational information in a broad spectrum of interest areas. Many of these articles are appropriate for students, researchers, and professionals seeking accurate, current material to help bridge the gap between principles and theories and the real world. These articles, however, become more useful for study when those of lasting value are carefully *collected, organized, indexed,* and *reproduced* in a *low-cost format,* which provides easy and permanent access when the material is needed. That is the role played by ANNUAL EDITIONS. Under the direction of each volume's *academic editor,* who is an expert in the subject area, and with the guidance of an *Advisory Board,* each year we seek to provide in each ANNUAL EDITION a current, well-balanced, carefully selected collection of the best of the public press for your study and enjoyment. We think that you will find this volume useful, and we hope that you will take a moment to let us know what you think.

Have you ever watched children on a playground? Some children are reticent; watching the other children play, they sit demurely and shun becoming involved in the fun. Some children readily and happily interact with their playmates. They take turns, share their toys, and follow the rules of the playground. Other children are bullies who brazenly taunt the playing children and aggressively take others' possessions. What makes each child so different? Do childhood behaviors forecast adult behaviors? Can children's (or adults') antisocial behaviors be changed?

These questions are not new. Lay persons and social scientists alike have always been curious about human nature. The answers to our questions, though, are incomplete, because attempts to address these issues are relatively new or just developing. Psychology, the science that can and should answer questions about individual differences and that is the primary focus of this book, has existed for just over one hundred years. That may seem old to you, but it is young when other disciplines are considered. Mathematics, medicine, and philosophy are thousands of years old.

By means of psychology and related sciences, this anthology will help you explore the issues of individual differences and their origins, methods of coping, personality change, and other matters of human adjustment. The purpose of this anthology is to compile the newest, most complete, and readable articles that examine individual behavior and adjustment as well as the dynamics of personal growth and interpersonal relationships. The readings in this book offer interesting insights into both the everyday and scientific worlds, a blend welcomed by most of today's specialists in human adjustment.

This anthology is revised each year to reflect both traditional viewpoints and emerging perspectives about people's behavior. Thanks to the editorial board's valuable advice, the present edition has been completely revised and includes a large number of new articles representing the latest thinking in the field.

Annual Editions: Personal Growth and Behavior 98/99 comprises six units, each of which serves a distinct purpose. The first unit is concerned with issues related to self-identity. For example, one theory, humanism, hypothesizes that self-concept, our feelings about who we are and how worthy we are, is the most valuable component of personality. This unit includes articles that supplement the theoretical articles by providing applications of, or alternate perspectives on, popular theories about individual differences and human adjustment. These include all of the classic and major theories of personality: humanistic, behavioral, psychoanalytic, and trait theories.

The second unit provides information on how and why a person develops in a particular way—in other words, what factors determine or direct individual growth: physiology, heredity, experience, or some combination. The third unit pertains to problems commonly encountered in the different stages of development: infancy, childhood, adolescence, and adulthood.

The fourth and fifth units are similar in that they address problems of adjustment—problems that occur in interpersonal relationships and problems that are created for individuals by the prevailing social environment or our culture. Unit 4 concerns topics such as competition, love, and friendship, while unit 5 discusses racism, trends in violent crime, and the rapid increase in the use of technology in America. The final unit focuses on adjustment, or on how most people cope with some of these and other issues.

Annual Editions: Personal Growth and Behavior 98/99 will challenge you and interest you in a variety of topics. It will provide you with many answers, but it will also stimulate many questions. Perhaps it will inspire you to continue your study of the burgeoning field of psychology, which is responsible for exploring personal growth and behavior. As has been true in the past, your feedback on this edition would be valuable for future revisions. Please take a moment to fill out and return the postage-paid *article rating form* on the last page. Thank you.

Karen Groves Duffy

Karen G. Duffy
Editor

Contents

To the Reader	iv
Topic Guide	2
Selected World Wide Web Sites	4

UNIT 1

Becoming a Person: Seeking Self-Identity

Four selections discuss the psychosocial development of an individual's personality. Attention is given to values, emotions, lifestyles, and self-concept.

Overview — 6

1. **The Last Interview of Abraham Maslow,** Edward Hoffman, *Psychology Today,* January/February 1992. — 8
   Although initially "sold on behaviorism," Abraham Maslow became one of the founders of a comprehensive human psychology or *humanistic psychology.* In an important last interview, Maslow shares his philosophy on the nature of human beings and of the potential for world peace and understanding.

2. **Evolutionary Necessity or Glorious Accident? Biologists Ponder the Self,** Natalie Angier, *New York Times,* April 22, 1997. — 13
   Are infants born with a *self-concept*? Biologists suggest that perhaps they are and that the self serves as a tool to advance the individual's interest among peers.

3. **How Useful Is Fantasy?** Paul M. Insel, *Healthline,* March 1995. — 17
   Daydreams can be adaptive. They can prepare us for future events, substitute for impulsive behavior, and get us past anger. Paul Insel explores these and other aspects of *fantasy* life.

4. **The Stability of Personality: Observations and Evaluations,** Robert R. McCrae and Paul T. Costa Jr., *Current Directions in Psychological Science,* December 1994. — 19
   There is substantial evidence for the *stability of personality* as well as for *individual differences* in personality traits. The authors review research on personality that supports their view, and they critique research that does not.

UNIT 2

Determinants of Behavior: Motivation, Environment, and Physiology

Nine articles examine the effects of culture, genes, and emotions on an individual's behavior.

Overview — 22

5. **Is It Nature or Nurture?** Marc Peyser and Anne Underwood, *Newsweek,* Special Issue, Spring/Summer 1997. — 24
   A *gene* may be only a probability for a given trait—not a guarantee. Researchers are finding that, with the right *environment,* children's *personalities* can be reprogrammed. This article provides a general overview of the *nature-nurture* controversy.

6. **Politics of Biology,** Wray Herbert, *U.S. News & World Report,* April 21, 1997. — 26
   How can a bank robbery be rooted in DNA? Wray Herbert develops the premise that the *nature-nurture* debate is a heated one with vast implications for psychology and for public policy. She researches ramifications for such interesting areas as *crime, mental illness, alcoholism,* and *homosexuality.*

The concepts in bold italics are developed in the article. For further expansion please refer to the Topic Guide, the Glossary, and the Index.

7. **Nature's Clones,** Jill Neimark, *Psychology Today,* July/August 1997.   31
   Twins are nature's mysteries and offer scientists the opportunity to tease apart the effects of ***nature and nurture.*** Jim Neimark looks carefully at the controversies surrounding the results of twin studies.

8. **Forget Money; Nothing Can Buy Happiness, Some Researchers Say,** Daniel Goleman, *New York Times,* July 16, 1996.   38
   There may be a ***set point*** for ***happiness*** that varies from individual to individual. Thus, the ***brain*** may be wired to a preset level of well-being that is different in each person.

9. **Revealing the Brain's Secrets,** Kathleen Cahill Allison, *Harvard Health Letter,* January 1996.   41
   Discoveries in molecular biology and ***genetics*** are unlocking the mysteries of Alzheimer's disease, depression, and other ***brain disorders.*** From these discoveries, scientists hope to find new forms of ***treatment*** for such disabling neuronal problems.

10. **Violence and the Brain,** Norbert Myslinski, *The World & I,* May 1997.   45
    This essay helps us to understand the ***brain*** by means of a disorder. ***Episodic dysfunction*** is a disorder in which individuals have violent attacks of rage. It is probably the result of brain injury or biochemical imbalance. Today, such individuals are treatable through surgery or medicine.

11. **Man's World, Woman's World? Brain Studies Point to Differences,** Gina Kolata, *New York Times,* February 28, 1995.   50
    The use of functional ***Magnetic Resonance Imaging*** provides scientists with a noninvasive technique to study the ***brain.*** Using resting and active images, scientists are uncovering some interesting cognitive, behavioral, and emotional differences in the brain functioning of ***men*** and ***women.***

12. **Studies Show Talking with Infants Shapes Basis of Ability to Think,** Sandra Blakeslee, *New York Times,* April 17, 1997.   54
    Research shows that when caretakers talk to infants, the ***talking*** provides the neurological foundations for reasoning and problem solving later in life. The ***environment,*** therefore, is a powerful influence, just as are genes and other biological bases of behavior.

13. **Faith & Healing,** Claudia Wallis, *Time,* June 24, 1996.   57
    Faith healers have frequented various cultures at various points in history. Some medical studies demonstrate that faith indeed leads to better ***health*** and faster recovery; however, more evidence exists of a ***mind-body connection.***

UNIT 3

Problems Influencing Personal Growth

Nine articles consider aging, development, self-image, depression, and social interaction and their influences on personal growth.

Overview   60

14. **Clipped Wings,** Lucile F. Newman and Stephen L. Buka, *American Educator,* Spring 1991.   62
    A report for the Education Commission of the States is excerpted here. Details of research compilations demonstrate that *prenatal exposure* to drugs, alcohol, and nicotine hampers *children's development,* especially their *learning.*

15. **Invincible Kids,** *U.S. News & World Report,* November 11, 1996.   68
    Some children survive *trauma* and, in fact, thrive. Psychologists are studying these *resilient children* to determine how this happens, who these children are, and what factors enhance their development despite the children's ordeals.

16. **Students Want More Discipline, Disruptive Classmates Out,** Lyric Wallwork Winik, *American Educator,* Fall 1996.   72
    American schools are being disrupted more and more by unruly and sometimes *violent students.* Lyric Wallwork Winik explores why this is occurring and what schools and classmates are doing to bring a modicum of control back into the *educational system.*

17. **Kids & Pot,** Lance Morrow, and **High Times at New Trier High,** James L. Graff, *Time,* December 9, 1996.   75
    Marijuana use among *teens* is rising, and baby-boomer parents do not know what to do about it although they, themselves, may also have used drugs. Lance Morrow discusses why the rise is occurring and among whom. Then, James Graff reveals how one Illinois high school is handling its teen drug use problem.

18. **Rethinking Puberty: The Development of Sexual Attraction,** Martha K. McClintock and Gilbert Herdt, *Current Directions in Psychological Science,* December 1996.   80
    Puberty and *first sexual attraction* are psychosocial and physiological *adolescent* phenomena. New research demonstrates that these are two distinct *stages,* not just one, and should be treated as such in the psychological literature.

19. **A World of Half-Adults,** Robert Bly, *Utne Reader,* May/June 1996.   85
    Robert Bly contends that as *adults* we have created a sibling *social order* in which we tolerate no one above us and have no concern for anyone below us. We need to behave more like adults so that we do not disenfranchise *preadults.*

20. **Older, Longer,** Jill Smolowe, *Time,* Fall 1996.   89
    Researchers are finding more ways to prevent *aging,* but how long can we live? How long should we live? Jill Smolowe looks at these questions as well as at other thorny issues such as what determines how we age—heredity or environment.

21. **The Mystery of Suicide,** David Gelman, *Newsweek,* April 18, 1994.   92
    Through analysis of the suicide of rock singer Kurt Cobain, David Gelman helps the reader understand the *frequency* and *causes* of *suicide* and the *interventions* used with those individuals who attempt suicide.

22. **Is There Life after Death?** Brendan I. Koerner, *U.S. News & World Report,* March 31, 1997.   95
    Near-death experiences have remarkable personal effects. The psychology and physiology behind these experiences are not yet well understood, but scientists continue to study this *paranormal phenomenon.*

UNIT 4

Relating to Others

Nine articles examine some of the dynamics involved in relating to others. Topics discussed include friendship, love, the importance of family ties, and self-esteem.

Overview   98

23. **The EQ Factor,** Nancy Gibbs, *Time,* October 2, 1995.   100
    Emotional intelligence, our ability to understand our own and others' *emotions,* may be more important to success than cognitive intelligence. But emotional intelligence (EQ) may be as useless as IQ is without a *moral* compass. Nancy Gibbs explores psychological research that investigates how these concepts relate to one another and how emotional intelligence develops.

24. **The Enduring Power of Friendship,** Susan Davis, *American Health,* July/August 1996.   105
    Adult friendships are not studied as often as are adult romances or childhood friendships. Research indicates that most adult friendships end due to *life transitions* and that they dissolve with a whimper, unlike some of our romantic relationships.

25. **Born to Be Good?** Celia Kitzinger, *New Internationalist,* April 1997.   108
    Social scientists have long pondered the origins and purposes of *morality.* Newer conceptualizations are more inclusive of women and minorities and suggest that *self-interest* alone is not at the root of helpful behavior toward others.

26. **Are You Shy?** Bernardo J. Carducci with Philip G. Zimbardo, *Psychology Today,* November/December 1995.   110
    Shy people suffer not just from *shyness* but also from the inability to think clearly in the presence of others, from the perception by others that they are snobbish, and from an overall lack of success. The *social, cultural, and physiological causes* of shyness are elaborated here.

27. **Hotheads and Heart Attacks,** Edward Dolnick, *Health,* July/August 1995.   117
    The Type H (for hostility) theory is replacing the concept of the Type A personality. Type A's are competitive, hostile, and deadline-oriented. It is *hostility,* especially when acted upon, that may be the real culprit in *heart attack proneness.*

The concepts in bold italics are developed in the article. For further expansion please refer to the Topic Guide, the Glossary, and the Index.

28. **Go Ahead, Say You're Sorry,** Aaron Lazare, *Psychology Today,* January/February 1995. 123
Apologies are important for restoring self-esteem and *interpersonal relationships.* Apologies, however, are antithetical to our values of winning, success, and perfection. Aaron Lazare describes the content of a successful apology.

29. **The Biology of Beauty,** Geoffrey Cowley, *Newsweek,* June 3, 1996. 126
Why are we attracted to another person? We are beginning to study *physical attractiveness* and the answers are yielding surprising results. For example, part of what makes an individual attractive includes *facial symmetry* and *ideal proportions.*

30. **The Future of Love,** Barbara Graham, *Utne Reader,* November/December 1996. 131
Barbara Graham contends that we have overglamorized and idealized *love* so that it is improbable that anyone will be satisfied with an *intimate relationship.* We need to take pressure off our close relationships and view them as a way for people to grow.

31. **Was It Good for Us?** David Whitman, *U.S. News & World Report,* May 19, 1997. 135
A somewhat surprising fact is that more babies are born out of wedlock to *adults* than to teens. Why do we hear so little about these *pregnancies* and about the negative social consequences of adult premarital sex? The answers are developed in this informative article.

UNIT 5

Dynamics of Personal Adjustment: The Individual and Society

Five selections discuss some of the problems experienced by individuals as they attempt to adjust to society.

Overview 140

32. **Psychopathy, Sociopathy, and Crime,** David T. Lykken, *Society,* November/December 1996. 142
David Lykken takes a look at what causes *crime* in American *society.* He examines several theories and trends in order to dismiss arguments suggesting that the propensity for crime is inherited. Instead, he lays blame for increases in crime squarely on the shoulders of *parents.*

33. **Mixed Blood,** Jefferson M. Fish, *Psychology Today,* November/December 1995. 152
The American concept of *race* is quite different from that concept in other cultures; thus, the American concept is just one of many "folk taxonomies." Because race as construed by Americans does not exist, discussions of *racial differences in IQ* are moot, according to Jefferson Fish.

34. **Media, Violence, Youth, and Society,** Ray Surette, *The World & I,* July 1994. 157
Violence is a cultural product. Years of research have linked violence on our streets to *mass media.* Other reasons for our epidemic of violence, as well as solutions for decreasing violence, are suggested.

35. **The Evolution of Despair,** Robert Wright, *Time,* August 28, 1995. 164
Evolutionary psychologists suggest that our modern lives are at odds with our ancestral past. Specifically, *modern technology* isolates us, when in order to spread our genes through the *gene pool* we need to be more, not less, *social*.

36. **The Lure of the Cult,** Richard Lacayo, *Time,* April 7, 1997. 168
Cults and *cult suicide* seem to have become a way of life in the United States. As the year 2000 approaches, more people will turn to cults and the tragedy that they often entail.

UNIT 6

Enhancing Human Adjustment: Learning to Cope Effectively

Nine selections examine some of the ways an individual learns to cope successfully within today's society. Topics discussed include therapy, depression, stress, and interpersonal relations.

Overview 170

37. **What You Can Change and What You Cannot Change,** Martin E. P. Seligman, *Psychology Today,* May/June 1994. 172
Americans seem to be on constant *self-improvement* kicks, many of which fail. Martin Seligman explains which attempts to change are a waste of time and which are worthwhile. He discusses *diets* and *psychological disorders* in particular.

38. **No More Bells and Whistles,** Scott Miller, Mark Hubble, and Barry Duncan, *Family Therapy Networker,* March/April 1995. 179
The authors claim that it is neither the *type of therapy* used nor which theory underlies the therapy that determines whether therapy is effective. It is, rather, the match between therapist and client, the *therapeutic relationship*, that predicts whether or not therapy will work.

39. **Targeting the Brain,** Judith Hooper, *Time,* Special Issue, Fall 1996. 188
Many forms of *mental illness* that were previously thought to be caused by trauma or psychological distress are now known to be caused by *chemical imbalances*. Several disorders and the new *psychoactive drugs* used to treat them are reviewed in this article.

40. **Upset? Try Cybertherapy,** Kerry Hannon, *U.S. News & World Report,* May 13, 1996. 191
More psychologists are offering *computerized or electronic consultation* for fees. *Ethical standards* lag behind the growth of Web sites. This article lists several legitimate sites for finding psychological information, including therapy.

41. **Defeating Depression,** Nancy Wartik, *American Health,* December 1993. 193
Millions of people are afflicted with *depression*. Scientists believe that a combination of *genetics, personality structure,* and *life events* triggers major depression. A self-assessment quiz is included as well as a discussion of a variety of all-important interventions.

The concepts in bold italics are developed in the article. For further expansion please refer to the Topic Guide, the Glossary, and the Index.

42. **Addicted,** J. Madeleine Nash, *Time,* May 5, 1997. **199**
What do sex, chocolate, and cocaine addiction have in common? All stimulate a powerful *neurotransmitter*—dopamine. Researchers are just beginning to understand the effect of *dopamine* and, therefore, *addiction*. Better understanding may lead to better treatments.

43. **Don't Face Stress Alone,** Benedict Carey, *Health,* April 1997. **203**
Many Americans are competitive, so they prefer to face *stress* alone. Research, however, is demonstrating how beneficial *social support,* or talking to others, can be in times of distress.

44. **Personality Disorders: Coping with the Borderline,** Patrick Perry, *The Saturday Evening Post,* July/August 1997. **206**
Individuals with *borderline personalities* destroy close *personal relationships* and then blame the other person. How to diagnose, recognize, and *cope* with someone who has this disorder is revealed in this detailed article.

45. **On the Power of Positive Thinking: The Benefits of Being Optimistic,** Michael F. Scheier and Charles S. Carver, *Current Directions in Psychological Science,* February 1993. **213**
Two psychologists discuss *optimism* and its relationship to *psychological and physical well-being* and to other psychological constructs such as *self-efficacy*.

Glossary 217
Index 225
Article Review Form 228
Article Rating Form 229

The concepts in bold italics are developed in the article. For further expansion please refer to the Topic Guide, the Glossary, and the Index.

Topic Guide

This topic guide suggests how the selections in this book relate to topics of traditional concern to students and professionals involved with the study of personal growth and behavior. It is useful for locating articles that relate to each other for reading and research. The guide is arranged alphabetically according to topic. Articles may, of course, treat topics that do not appear in the topic guide. In turn, entries in the topic guide do not necessarily constitute a comprehensive listing of all the contents of each selection. **In addition, relevant Web sites, which are annotated on the next two pages, are noted in bold italics under the topic articles.**

TOPIC AREA	TREATED IN	TOPIC AREA	TREATED IN
Abuse	15. Invincible Kids (13, 15, 17)	Death	21. Mystery of Suicide 22. Is There Life after Death? (19)
Addiction	17. Kids & Pot/High Times 42. Addicted (15, 16, 17, 18, 31, 32)	Depression	41. Defeating Depression (16, 30, 31, 32)
Adolescents	17. Kids & Pot/High Times 18. Rethinking Puberty (4, 10, 13, 14, 15, 17)	Development	14. Clipped Wings 15. Invincible Kids 16. Students Want More Discipline 17. Kids & Pot/High Times 18. Rethinking Puberty 19. World of Half Adults 20. Older, Longer (1, 4, 7, 13, 14, 15, 20)
Adults	19. World of Half Adults 20. Older, Longer (15, 16, 18)		
Apologies	28. Go Ahead, Say You're Sorry (34)	Education/ Schools	16. Students Want More Discipline (17)
Brain	8. Forget Money; Nothing Can Buy Happiness 9. Revealing the Brain's Secrets 10. Violence and the Brain 11. Man's World, Woman's World? 12. Talking with Infants 39. Targeting the Brain (2, 7, 8, 9, 11, 12)	Emotional Intelligence	23. EQ Factor (21, 22)
		Evolution	35. Evolution of Despair (1, 7, 11, 12, 29, 31, 32)
		Fantasy	3. How Useful Is Fantasy? (3, 4, 5, 6)
Children	12. Talking with Infants 14. Clipped Wings 15. Invincible Kids (7, 9, 11, 12, 13)	Friends/ Friendship	24. Enduring Power of Friendship (20)
		Gender	11. Man's World, Woman's World? (7, 8, 9, 11, 12)
Computers	40. Upset? Try Cybertherapy (35, 36)	Genes	5. Is It Nature or Nurture? 7. Nature's Clones 9. Revealing the Brain's Secrets 35. Evolution of Despair (7, 8, 9, 11, 12)
Crime	32. Psychopathy, Sociopathy, and Crime (20, 23, 26)		
Cults	36. Lure of the Cult (24, 25)	Health	13. Faith & Healing (7, 11, 12)

TOPIC AREA	TREATED IN	TOPIC AREA	TREATED IN
Humanistic Psychology	1. Last Interview with Abraham Maslow	Prenatal Life	14. Clipped Wings *(13, 18)*
Love	30. Future of Love *(20)*	Psychopharma-cology	39. Targeting the Brain *(7, 8, 9, 11, 12)*
Maslow, Abraham	1. Last Interview with Abraham Maslow	Psychotherapy	37. What You Can Change and What You Cannot Change 38. No More Bells and Whistles 40. Upset? Try Cybertherapy *(29, 30, 31, 32, 35, 36)*
Media	34. Media, Violence, Youth, and Society *(26, 27, 28)*	Self	2. Evolutionary Necessity or Glorious Accident? *(3, 4, 5, 6)*
Mind/Body	13. Faith & Healing *(7, 11, 12)*	Self-Improvement	37. What You Can Change and What You Cannot Change *(29, 30, 31, 32, 33)*
Morality	25. Born to Be Good? *(23, 26, 29)*	Sex/Sexuality	31. Was It Good for Us?
Nature/Nurture Issue	5. Is It Nature or Nurture? 6. Politics of Biology 7. Nature's Clones *(8, 11, 12)*	Shyness	26. Are You Shy? *(20, 23)*
Near-Death Experience	22. Is There Life after Death?	Stress	43. Don't Face Stress Alone *(30, 34)*
Optimism	45. On the Power of Positive Thinking	Suicide	21. Mystery of Suicide *(19)*
Personality	4. Stability of Personality 5. Is It Nature or Nurture? *(11, 23)*	Television/Media	34. Media, Violence, Youth, and Society *(26, 27)*
Personality Disorders	44. Coping with the Borderline *(29, 31, 32)*	Twins	7. Nature's Clones
Physical Attractiveness	29. Biology of Beauty *(13, 14, 15, 33)*	Type A/Type H Behavior	27. Hotheads and Heart Attacks *(21, 22, 23)*
Prejudice	33. Mixed Blood *(26, 27, 28)*	Violence	16. Students Want More Discipline 34. Media, Violence, Youth, and Society *(20, 26, 27)*

Selected World Wide Web Sites for AE: *Personal Growth and Behavior*

All of these Web sites are hot-linked through the *Annual Editions* home page: http://www.dushkin.com/annualeditions (just click on a book). In addition, these sites are referenced by number and appear where relevant in the Topic Guide on the previous two pages.

Some Web sites are continually changing their structure and content, so the information listed may not always be available.

General Sources

1. National Institute of Child Health and Human Development—*http://www.nih.gov/nichd/home2_home.html*—The NICHD conducts and supports research on the reproductive, neurobiologic, developmental, and behavioral processes that determine and maintain the health of children, adults, families, and populations.

2. Psychnet—*http://www.apa.org/psychnet/*—Get information on psychology from this Web site through the site map or by using the search engine. Access APA Monitor, the American Psychological Association newspaper, APA Books on a wide range of topics, PsychINFO, an electronic database of abstracts on over 1,350 scholarly journals, and HelpCenter for information on dealing with modern life problems.

Becoming a Person

3. Abraham A. Brill Library—*http://plaza.interport.net/nypsan/service.html*—The Abraham A. Brill Library, perhaps the largest psychoanalytic library in the world, contains data on over 40,000 books, periodicals, and reprints in psychoanalysis and related fields. Its holdings span literature of psychoanalysis from its beginning to the present day.

4. Adolescence—Age of Change—*http://www.getnet.com/~davidp/article2.html*—Here is an interesting article on the psychological and biological changes that occur in the transition from childhood to adolescence.

5. JungWeb—*http://www.onlinepsych.com/jungweb/*—Dedicated to the work of Carl Jung, this site is a comprehensive resource for Jungian psychology. Links to Jungian psychology, reference materials, graduate programs, dreams, multilingual sites, and related Jungian themes are available.

6. Sigmund Freud and the Freud Archives—*http://plaza.interport.net/nypsan/freudarc.html*—Internet resources related to Sigmund Freud can be accessed through this site. A collection of libraries, museums, and biographical materials, as well as the Brill Library archives, can be found here.

Determinants of Behavior

7. American Psychological Society (APS)—*http://psych.hanover.edu/APS/*—APS membership includes a diverse group of the world's foremost scientists and academics working to expand basic and applied psychological science knowledge. The APS is dedicated to advancing the best of scientific psychology in research, application, and the improvement of human conditions. Links to teaching, research, and graduate studies resources are available.

8. Federation of Behavioral, Psychological, and Cognitive Science—*http://www.am.org/federation/*—The Federation's mission is fulfilled through three classes of activity: legislative and regulatory advocacy, education, and information dissemination to the scientific community. It is possible to hotlink to the National Institutes of Health's medical database, government links to public information on mental health, a social psychology network, and the Project on the Decade of the Brain.

9. Max Planck Institute for Psychological Research—*http://www.mpipf-muenchen.mpg.de/BCD/bcd_e.htm*—Several behavioral and cognitive development research projects are available on this site.

10. The Opportunity of Adolescence—*http://www.winternet.com/~webpage/adolescencepaper.html*—This paper calls adolescence the turning point, after which the future is redirected and confirmed, and goes on to discuss the opportunities and problems of this period to the individual and society, using quotations from Erik Erikson, Jean Piaget, and others.

11. Psychology Research on the Net—*http://psych.hanover.edu/APS/exponnet.html*—Psychologically related experiments on the Internet can be found at this site. Biological psychology/neuropsychology, clinical psychology, cognition, developmental psychology, emotions, general issues, health psychology, personality, sensation/perception, and social psychology are just some of the areas addressed.

12. Serendip—*http://serendip.brynmawr.edu/serendip/*—Organized into five subject areas (brain and behavior, complex systems, genes and behavior, science and culture, and science education), Serendip contains interactive exhibits, articles, links to other resources, and a forum area for comments and discussion.

Problems Influencing Personal Growth

13. Ask NOAH About: Mental Health—*http://www.noah.cuny.edu/illness/mentalhealth/mental.html*—This enormous resource contains information about child and adolescent family problems, mental conditions and disorders, suicide prevention, and much more, all organized in a clickable outline form.

14. Biological Changes in Adolescence—*http://www.personal.psu.edu/faculty/n/x/nxd10/biologic2.htm*—This site offers a discussion of puberty, sexuality, biological changes, cross-cultural differences, and nutrition for adolescents, including obesity and its effects on adolescent development.

15. Facts for Families—*http://www.aacap.org/web/aacap/factsFam/*—The American Academy of Child and Adolescent Psychiatry here provides concise, up-to-date information on issues that affect teenagers and their families. Fifty-six fact sheets include issues of teenagers, such as coping with life, sad feelings, inability to sleep, getting involved with drugs, or not getting along with family and friends.

16. Mental Health Infosource: Disorders—*http://www.mhsource.com/disorders/*—This no-nonsense page lists hotlinks to psychological disorders pages, including anxiety, panic, phobic disorders, schizophrenia, and violent/self-destructive behaviors.

17. Mental Health Risk Factors for Adolescents—*http://education.indiana.edu/cas/adol/mental.html*—This collection of Web resources is useful for parents, educators, researchers, health practitioners, and teens. It covers a great deal, including abuse, conduct disorders, stress, and support.

18. National Women's Resource Center—*http://www.nwrc.org/*—Site contains bibliographic databases with current citations to literature related to women's substance abuse and mental illness.

19. Suicide Awareness: Voices of Education—*http://www.save.org/*—This is the most popular suicide site on the Internet. It is very thorough, with information on dealing with suicide (both before and after), along with material from the organization's many education sessions.

Relating to Others

20. CYFERNET-Youth Development—*http://www.cyfernet.mes.umn.edu/youthdev.html*—Excellent source of many articles on youth development, including a statement on the concept of normal adolescence and impediments to healthy development.

21. Hypermedia, Literature, and Cognitive Dissonance—*http://www.uncg.edu/~rsginghe/metastat.htm*—This article, subtitled *The Heuristic Challenges of Connectivity*, discusses EQ (emotional intelligence) in adults and offers an interactive study, the Metatale Paradigm, which is linked to story sources. Click on *http://www.uncg.edu/~rsginghe/metatext.htm* for access.

22. International Society of Applied Emotional Intelligence—*http://www.swiftsite.com/isaei#welcome*—The ISAEI is an organization dedicated to the promotion of emotional intelligence through education, training, events, and special activities. Their mission is to promote the principles of applied emotional intelligence by teaching people specific principles and skills to empower them to realize their full potential.

23. The Personality Project—*http://fas.psych.nwu.edu/personality.html*—The Personality Project of William Revelle, director of the Graduate Program in Personality at Northwestern University, is meant to guide those interested in personality theory and research to the current personality research literature.

Dynamics of Personal Adjustment

24. A–Z of Cults—*http://www.guardian.co.uk/observer/cults/a-z-cults/index.html*—Here is a clickable list of cults, along with comments about the definition and meaning of cults at this time in the world's history.

25. AFF Cult Group Information—*http://www.csj.org/index.html*—Information about cults, cult groups, and psychological manipulation is available at this page sponsored by the secular, not-for-profit, tax-exempt research center and educational orgainization, American Family Foundation.

26. Explanations of Criminal Behavior—*http://www.uaa.alaska.edu/just/just110/crime2.html*—An excellent outline of the causes of crime, including major theories, which was prepared by Darryl Wood at the University of Alaska Anchorage.

27. National Clearinghouse for Alcohol and Drug Information—*http://www.health.org/*—This is an excellent general site for information on drug and alcohol facts that might relate to adolescence and the issues of peer pressure and youth culture. Resources, referrals, research and statistics, databases, and related Internet links are among the options available at this site.

28. Schools Health Education Unit (SHEU)—*http://www.ex.ac.uk/~dregis/sheu.html*—SHEU is a research unit that offers survey, research, and evaluation services on health and social development for young people.

Enhancing Human Adjustment

29. Clinical Psychology Resources—*http://www.psychologie.uni-bonn.de/kap/links_20.htm*—This page contains Internet resources for clinical and abnormal psychology, behavioral medicine, and mental health.

30. Health Information Resources—*http://nhic-nt.health.org/Scripts/Tollfree.cfm*—Here is a long list of toll-free numbers that provide health-related information. None offer diagnosis and treatment, but some do offer recorded information; others provide personalized counseling, referrals, and/or written materials.

31. Knowledge Exchange Network (KEN)—*http://www.mentalhealth.org/about/index.htm*—The CMHS National Mental Health Services Exchange Network (KEN) provides information about mental health via toll-free telephone services, an electronic bulletin board, and publications. It is a one-stop source for information and resources on prevention, treatment, and rehabilitation services for mental illness, with many links to related sources.

32. Mental Health Net—*http://www.cmhc.com/*—Comprehensive guide to mental health online, featuring more than 6,300 individual resources. Covers information on mental disorders, professional resources in psychology, psychiatry, and social work, journals, and self-help magazines.

33. Mental Health Net: Eating Disorder Resources—*http://www.cmhc.com/guide/eating.htm*—This is a very complete list of Web references on eating disorders, including anorexia, bulimia, and obesity.

34. Mind Tools—*http://www.gasou.edu/psychweb/mtsite/smpage.html*—Useful information on stress management can be found at this Web site.

35. NetPsychology—*http://netpsych.com/index.htm*—This site explores the uses of the Internet to deliver mental health services. This is a basic cybertherapy resource site.

36. Shareware Psychological Consultation—*http://netpsych.com/share/index.htm*—Here is an example of a cybertherapy site. The consulting psychologist is Leonard Holmes, who offers his credentials and explains how a session with him would work, and what it would cost.

We highly recommend that you review our Web site for expanded information and our other product lines. We are continually updating and adding links to our Web site in order to offer you the most usable and useful information that will support and expand the value of your Annual Editions. You can reach us at: *http://www.dushkin.com/annualeditions/*.

Becoming a Person: Seeking Self-Identity

A baby sits in front of a mirror and looks at himself. A chimpanzee sorts through photographs while its trainer carefully watches its reactions. A college student answers a survey on how she feels about herself. What do each of these events share in common? All are examples of techniques used to investigate self-concept.

That baby in front of the mirror has a red dot on his nose. Researchers watch to see if the baby reaches for the dot in the mirror or touches his own nose. Recognizing the fact that the image he sees in the mirror is his own, the baby touches his real nose, not the nose in the mirror.

The chimpanzee has been trained to sort photographs into two piles—human pictures or animal pictures. If the chimp has been raised with humans, the researcher wants to know into which pile (animal or human) the chimp will place its own picture. Is the chimp's concept of itself animal or human? Or does the chimp have no concept of self at all?

The college student taking the self-survey answers questions about her body image, whether or not she thinks she is fun to be with, whether or not she spends large amounts of time in fantasy, and what her feelings are about her personality and intelligence.

These research projects are designed to investigate how self-concept develops and steers our behaviors and thoughts. Most psychologists believe that people develop a personal identity or a sense of self, which is a sense of who we are, our likes and dislikes, our characteristic feelings and thoughts, and an understanding of why we behave as we do. *Self-concept* is our knowledge of our gender, race, and age, as well as our sense of self-worth and more. Strong positive or negative feelings are usually attached to this identity. Psychologists are studying how and when this sense of self develops. Most psychologists do not believe that infants are born with a sense of self but rather that children slowly develop self-concept as a consequence of their experiences.

This unit delineates some of the popular viewpoints regarding how sense of self and personality develop and how, or if, they guide behavior. This knowledge of how self develops provides an important foundation for the rest of the units in this book. This unit explores three major theories or forces in psychology: self or humanistic, psychoanalytic, and trait theories. For each theory, related research, applications, or concepts are examined in companion articles.

The first two articles are related to the school of psychology with a strong interest in self-concept, humanistic psychology. In fact, many of the humanistic theorists also are called self-theorists. In "The Last Interview of Abraham Maslow," one of the founders of humanistic psychology discusses the evolution of his theory. In the interview, Maslow talks about his philosophy of human nature and its potential for peaceful living and other positive outcomes for humans. Natalie Angier discusses the purpose of self. Biologists suggest that we are predestined to develop a sense of self. On the other hand, self might just be an accident. If biologists are correct, self serves as a vehicle by which we advance our own self-interests.

The next essay relates to psychoanalysis, a theory and form of therapy to which humanism was a reaction. The main proponent of psychoanalysis was Sigmund Freud, who believed that individuals possess a dark, lurking unconscious that often motivates negative behaviors such as guilt and defensiveness. This essay explores Freudian concepts. In "How Useful Is Fantasy?" fantasies are examined. Freud claimed that the unconscious expresses itself in our fantasies. Thus, to know more about the unconscious, all we need to do is understand or interpret our fantasies. This piece will help you to understand what fantasies mean and what their value is in everyday life.

The last article in the unit offers a contrasting viewpoint of human nature, known as the trait or dispositional approach. Trait theories in general hold that our personalities comprise various traits that are possibly tied together by our self-concept. This review of relevant research claims that most personality traits remain constant over time, a view that is in sharp contrast especially with the growth theory of Abraham Maslow and the psychoanalytic stage theory of Freud.

UNIT 1

Looking Ahead: Challenge Questions

What does Abraham Maslow propose about self in his theory? How can his humanistic theory help us produce a more peaceful world and strengthen positive human attributes?

Do you think that the development of self is driven by biology? Why or why not? What else do you think prompts the development of self-concept? Do you believe that self is utilized only to promote our own selfish interests in competition with others? Defend your answer.

Does the sense of self develop the same way in each individual? What, if any, aspects of self, such as gender, develop faster than other aspects? Can one type of experience influence identity more than another experience? How and when does self-concept influence us?

How and when do you think children develop a sense of self? How do people show others that they have a sense of self? Do children understand their own behavior first or others' behavior first? Which word, "yes" or "no," is usually added first to the child's vocabulary? What impact does this have on the child's development of self-concept?

Is self-concept stable, or does it seem to change regularly? What events create change? How could an individual change his or her self-concept? Is psychotherapy the best or only way to create change? Why or why not? Can people change spontaneously or as a result of a growth experience? Explain.

Is self-concept the only guide for our behaviors? Do individuals have a number of selves and show different ones to different people? If so, is this normal, or does it signal some kind of maladjustment? Defend your answer.

Do you believe in the unconscious? Why or why not? If yes, give examples from your own life of its influence. What scientific evidence exists that demonstrates the potential of the unconscious? What other concepts are important to Sigmund Freud's concept of humans? Define and give examples of each. Discuss whether or not dreams reveal unconscious wishes. What do various fantasies mean to you? To Freudians? Why do people fantasize? Are fantasies and dreams the same? Explain.

Do you think personality traits remain stable over a lifetime? From where do personality traits come? Are they biological or learned? Do traits remain stable across situations: are they carried from church to school, for example? Do traits collectively comprise self-concept or does self comprise more than traits?

Which theory of human personality (humanistic, psychoanalytic, or trait) do you think is best and why?

The Last Interview of ABRAHAM MASLOW

Edward Hoffman, Ph.D.

When Abraham Maslow first shared his pioneering vision of a "comprehensive human psychology" in this magazine in early 1968, he stood at the pinnacle of his international acclaim and influence.

About the author: Edward Hoffman received his doctorate from the University of Michigan. A clinical psychologist on New York's Long Island, he is the author of several books, including The Right to be Human: A Biography of Abraham Maslow *(Tarcher).*

HIS ELECTION AS PRESIDENT OF THE AMERIcan Psychological Association some months before capped an illustrious academic career spanning more than 35 productive years, during which Maslow had steadily gained the high regard—even adulation— of countless numbers of colleagues and former students. His best-known books, *Motivation and Personality* and *Toward a Psychology of Being*, were not only being discussed avidly by psychologists, but also by professionals in fields ranging from management and marketing to education and counseling. Perhaps even more significantly, Maslow's iconoclastic concepts like peak experience, self-actualization, and synergy had even begun penetrating popular language.

Nevertheless, it was a very unsettling time for him: Recovering from a major heart attack, the temperamentally restless and ceaselessly active Maslow was finding forced convalescence at home to be almost painfully unbearable. Suddenly, his extensive plans for future research, travel, and lecturing had to be postponed. Although Maslow hoped for a speedy recovery, frequent chest pains induced a keen sense of his own mortality. As perhaps never before, he began to ponder his career's accomplishments and his unrealized goals.

In 1968 PSYCHOLOGY TODAY was a precocious one-year-old upstart, but such was its prestige that it was able to attract perhaps the country's most famous psychologist for an interview.

Maslow likely regarded the PT interview as a major opportunity to outline his "comprehensive human psychology" and the best way to actualize it. At 60, he knew that time permitted him only to plant seeds (in his own metaphor) of research and theory—and hope that later generations would live to see the flowering of human betterment. Perhaps most prescient at a time of global unrest is Maslow's stirring vision of "building a psychology for the peace table." It was his hope that through psychological research, we might learn how to unify peoples of differing racial and ethnic origins, and thereby create a world of peace.

Although the complete audiotapes of the sessions, conducted over three days, disappeared long ago under mysterious circumstances, the written condensation that remains provides a fascinating and still-relevant portrait of a key thinker at the height of his prowess. Intellectually, Maslow was decades ahead of his time; today the wide-ranging ideas he offers here are far from outdated. Indeed, after some twenty-odd years, they're still on the cutting edge of American psychology and social science. Emotionally, this interview is significant for the rare—essentially unprecedented—glimpse it affords into Maslow's personal history and concerns: his ancestry and upbringing; his mentors and ambitions; his courtship, marriage, and fatherhood; and even a few of his peak experiences.

Maslow continued to be puzzled and intrigued by the more positive human phenomenon of self-actualization. He was well aware that his theory about the "best of humanity" suffered from methodological flaws. Yet he had become ever more convinced of its intuitive validity, that self-actualizers provide us with clues to our highest innate traits: love and compassion, creativity and aesthetics, ethics and spirituality. Maslow longed to empirically verify this lifelong hunch.

In the two years of his life that remained, this gifted psychologist never wrote an autobiography, nor did he ever again bare his soul in such a public and wide-ranging way. It may have been that Maslow regarded this unusually personal interview as a true legacy. More than 20 years later, it remains a fresh and important document for the field of psychology.

Mary Harrington Hall, for PSYCHOLOGY TODAY: A couple of William B. Yeats's lines keep running through my head: "And in my heart, the daemons and the gods wage an eternal battle and I feel the pain of wounds, the labor of the spear." How thin is the veneer of civilization, and how can we understand and deal with evil?

Abraham H. Maslow: It's a psychological puzzle I've been trying to solve for years. Why are people cruel and why are they nice? Evil people are rare, but you find evil behavior in the majority of people. The next thing I want to do with my life is to study evil and understand it.

PT: By evil here, I think we both mean destructive action without remorse. Racial prejudice is an evil in our society which we must deal with. And soon. Or we will go down as a racist society.

> All the goals of objectivity, repeatability, and preplanned experimentation are things we have to move toward. The more reliable you make knowledge, the better it is.

Maslow: You know, when I became A.P.A. president, the first thing I wanted to do was work for greater recognition for the Negro psychologists. Then I found that there were no Negroes in psychology, at least not many. They don't major in psychology.

PT: Why should they? Why would I think that psychology would solve social problems if I were a Negro living in the ghetto, surrounded by despair?

Maslow: Negroes have really had to take it. We've given them every possible blow. If I were a Negro, I'd be fighting, as Martin Luther King fought, for human recognition and justice. I'd rather go down with my flag flying. If you're weak or crippled, or you can't speak out or fight back in some way, then people don't hesitate to treat you badly.

PT: Could you look at evil behavior in two ways: evil from below and evil from above? Evil as a sickness and evil as understood compassionately?

Maslow: If you look at evil from above, you can be realistic. Evil exists. You don't give it quarter, and you're a better fighter if you can understand it. You're in the position of a psychotherapist. In the same way, you can look at neurosis. You can see neurosis from below—as a sickness—as most psychiatrists see it. Or you can understand it as a compassionate man might: respecting the neurosis as a fumbling and inefficient effort toward good ends.

PT: You can understand race riots in the same way, can't you?

Maslow: If you can only be detached enough, you can feel that it's better to riot than to be hopeless, degraded, and defeated. Rioting is a childish way of trying to be a man, but it takes time to rise out of the hell of hatred and frustration and accept that to be a man you don't have to riot.

PT: In our society, we see all behavior as a demon we can vanquish and banish, don't we? And yet good people do evil things.

Maslow: Most people are nice people. Evil is caused by ignorance, thoughtlessness, fear, or even the desire for popularity with one's gang. We can cure many such causes of evil. Science is progressing, and I feel hope that psychology can solve many of these problems. I think that a good part of evil behavior bears on the behavior of the normal.

PT: How will you approach the study of evil?

Maslow: If you think only of evil, then you become pessimistic and hopeless like Freud. But if you think there is no evil, then you're just one more deluded Pollyanna. The thing is to try to understand and realize how it's possible for people who are capable of being angels, heroes, or saints to be bastards and killers. Sometimes, poor and miserable people are hopeless. Many revenge themselves upon life for what society has done to them. They enjoy hurting.

PT: Your study of evil will have to be subjective, won't it? How can we measure evil in the laboratory?

Maslow: All the goals of objectivity, repeatability, and preplanned experimentation are things we have to move toward. The more reliable you make knowledge, the better it is. If the salvation of man comes out of the advancement of knowledge—taken in the best sense—then these goals are part of the strategy of knowledge.

PT: What did you tell your own daughters, Ann and Ellen, when they were growing up?
Maslow: Learn to hate meanness. Watch out for anybody who is mean or cruel. Watch out for people who delight in destruction.
PT: How would you describe yourself? Not in personality, because you're one of the warmest and sweetest men I've ever met. But who are you?
Maslow: I'm someone who likes plowing new ground, then walking away from it. I get bored easily. For me, the big thrill comes with the discovering.
PT: Psychologists all love Abe Maslow. How did you escape the crossfire?
Maslow: I just avoid most academic warfare. Besides, I had my first heart attack many years ago, and perhaps I've been unconsciously favoring my body. So I may have avoided real struggle. Besides, I only like fights I know I can win, and I'm not personally mean.
PT: Maybe you're just one of the lucky few who grew up through a happy childhood without malice.
Maslow: With my childhood, it's a wonder I'm not psychotic. I was the little Jewish boy in the non-Jewish neighborhood. It was a little like being the first Negro enrolled in the all-white school. I grew up in libraries and among books, without friends.

Both my mother and father were uneducated. My father wanted me to be a lawyer. He thumbed his way across the whole continent of Europe from Russia and got here at the age of 15. He wanted success for me. I tried law school for two weeks. Then I came home to my poor father one night after a class discussing "spite fences" and told him I couldn't be a lawyer. "Well, son," he said, "what do you want to study?" I answered: "Everything." He was uneducated and couldn't understand my passion for learning, but he was a nice man. He didn't understand either that at 16, I was in love.
PT: All 16-year-olds are in love.
Maslow: Mine was different. We're talking about my wife. I loved Bertha. You know her. Wasn't I right? I was extremely shy, and I tagged around after her. We were too young to get married. I tried to run away with her.
PT: Where did you run?
Maslow: I ran to Cornell for my sophomore year in college, then to Wisconsin. We were married there when I was 20 and Bertha was 19. Life didn't really start for me until I got married.

I went to Wisconsin because I had just discovered John B. Watson's work, and I was sold on behaviorism. It was an explosion of excitement for me. Bertha came to pick me up at New York's 42nd Street library, and I was dancing down Fifth Avenue with exuberance. I embarrassed her, but I was so excited about Watson's behaviorist program. It was beautiful. I was confident that here was a real road to travel: solving one problem after another and changing the world.
PT: A clear lifetime with built-in progress guaranteed.
Maslow: That was it. I was off to Wisconsin to change the world. I went there to study with psychologist Kurt Koffka, biologist Hans Dreisch, and philosopher Alexander Meiklejohn. But when I showed up on the campus, they weren't there. They

---

> I've devoted myself to developing a theory of human nature that could be tested by experiment and research. I wanted to prove that humans are capable of something grander than war, prejudice, and hatred.

---

had just been visiting professors, but the lying catalog had included them anyway.

Oh, but I was so lucky, though. I was young Harry Harlow's first doctoral graduate. And they were angels, my professors. I've always had angels around. They helped me when I needed it, even fed me. Bill Sheldon taught me how to buy a suit. I didn't know anything of amenities. Clark Hull was an angel to me, and later, Edward L. Thorndike.
PT: You're an angelic man. I've heard too many stories to let you deny it. What kind of research were you doing at Wisconsin?
Maslow: I was a monkey man. By studying monkeys for my doctoral dissertation, I found that dominance was related to sex, and to maleness. It was a great discovery, but somebody had discovered it two months before me.
PT: Great ideas always go in different places and minds at the same time.
Maslow: Yes, I worked on it until the start of World War II. I thought that working on sex was the easiest way to help mankind. I felt if I could discover a way to improve the sexual life by even one percent, then I could improve the whole species.

One day, it suddenly dawned on me that I knew as much about sex as any man living—in the intellectual sense. I knew everything that had been written; I had made discoveries with which I was pleased; I had done therapeutic work. This was about 10 years before the Kinsey report came out. Then I suddenly burst into laughter. Here was I, the great sexologist, and I had never seen an erect penis except one, and that was from my own bird's-eye view. That humbled me considerably.
PT: I suppose you interviewed people the way Kinsey did?
Maslow: No, something was wrong with Kinsey. I really don't think he liked women, or men. In my research, I interviewed 120 women with a new form of interview. No notes. We just talked until I got some feeling for the individual's personality, then put sex against that background. Sex has to be considered in regard to love, otherwise it's useless. This is because behavior can be a defense—a way of hiding what you feel—particularly regarding sex.

I was fascinated with my research. But I gave up interviewing men. They were useless because they boasted and lied about sex. I also planned a big research project involving prostitutes. I thought we could learn a lot about men from them, but the research never came off.
PT: You gave up all your experimental research in these fields.
Maslow: Yes, around 1941 I felt I must try to save the world, and to prevent the horrible wars and the awful hatred and prejudice. It happened very suddenly. One day just after Pearl Harbor, I was driving home and my car was stopped by a poor, pathetic parade. Boy Scouts and old uniforms and a flag and someone playing a flute off-key.

As I watched, the tears began to run down my face. I felt we didn't understand—not Hitler, nor the Germans, nor Stalin, nor the Communists. We didn't understand any of them. I felt that if we could understand, then we could make progress. I had a vision of a peace table, with people sitting around it, talking about human nature and hatred, war and peace, and brotherhood.

I was too old to go into the army. It was at that moment I realized that the rest of my life must be devoted to discovering a psychology for the peace table. That moment changed my whole life. Since then, I've devoted myself to developing a theory of human nature that could be tested by experiment and research. I wanted to prove that humans are capable of something grander than war, prejudice, and hatred. I wanted to make science consider all the people: the best specimen of mankind I could find. I found that many of them reported having something like mystical experiences.

PT: Your work with "self-actualizing" people is famous. You have described some of these mystical experiences.

Maslow: Peak experiences come from love and sex, from aesthetic moments, from bursts of creativity, from moments of insight and discovery, or from fusion with nature.

I had one such experience in a faculty procession here at Brandeis University. I saw the line stretching off into a dim future. At its head was Socrates. And in the line were the ones I love most. Thomas Jefferson was there. And Spinoza. And Alfred North Whitehead. I was in the same line. Behind me, that infinite line melted into the dimness. And there were all the people not yet born who were going to be in the same line.

I believe these experiences can be studied scientifically, and they will be.

PT: This is all part of your theory of metamotivation, isn't it?

Maslow: But not all people who are metamotivated report peak experiences. The "nonpeakers" are healthy, but they lack poetry and soaring flights of the imagination. Both peakers and nonpeakers can be self-actualized in that they're not motivated by basic needs, but by something higher

PT: Real self-actualization must be rare. What percentage of us achieve it?

Maslow: I'd say only a fraction of one percent.

PT: People whose basic needs have been met, then, will pursue life's ultimate values?

Maslow: Yes, the ultimate happiness for man is the realization of pure beauty and truth, which are the ultimate values. What we need is a system of thought—you might even call it a religion—that can bind humans together. A system that would fit the Republic of Chad as well as the United States: a system that would supply our idealistic young people with something to believe in. They're searching for something they can pour all that emotion into, and the churches are not much help.

PT: This system must come.

Maslow: I'm not alone in trying to make it. There are plenty of others working toward the same end. Perhaps their efforts, aided by the hundreds of youngsters who are devoting their lives to this, will develop a new image of man that rejects the chemical and technological views. We've technologized everything.

PT: The technologist is the person who has fallen in love with a machine. I suppose that has also happened to those in psychology?

Maslow: They become fascinated with the machine. It's almost a neurotic love. They're like the man who spends Sundays polishing his car instead of stroking his wife.

> **Good psychology should include all the methodological techniques, without having loyalty to one method, one idea, or one person.**

PT: In several of your papers, you've said that you stopped being a behaviorist when your first child was born.

Maslow: My whole training at Wisconsin was behaviorist. I didn't question it until I began reading some other sources. Later, I began studying the Rorschach test.

At the same time, I stumbled into embryology and read Ludwig von Bertalanffy's *Modern Theories of Development*. I had already become disillusioned with Bertrand Russell and with English philosophy generally. Then, I fell in love with Alfred North Whitehead and Henri Bergson. Their writings destroyed behaviorism for me without my recognizing it.

1. Abraham Maslow

When my first baby was born, that was the thunderclap that settled things. I looked at this tiny, mysterious thing and felt so stupid. I felt small, weak, and feeble. I'd say that anyone who's had a baby couldn't be a behaviorist.

PT: As you propose new ideas, and blaze new ground, you're bound to be criticized, aren't you?

Maslow: I have worked out a lot of good tricks for fending off professional attacks. We all have to do that. A good, controlled experiment is possible only when you already know a hell of a lot. If I'm a pioneer by choice and I go into the wilderness, how am I going to make careful experiments? If I tried to, I'd be a fool. I'm not against careful experiments. But rather, I've been working with what I call "growing tip" statistics.

With a tree, all the growth takes place at the growing tips. Humanity is exactly the same. All the growth takes place in the growing tip: among that one percent of the population. It's made up of pioneers, the beginners. That's where the action is.

PT: You were the one who helped publish Ruth Benedict's work on synergy. What's it about?

Maslow: That it's possible to set up social institutions that merge selfishness and unselfishness, so that you can't benefit yourself without benefiting others. And the reverse.

PT: How can psychology become a stronger force in our society?

Maslow: We all should look at the similarities within the various disciplines and think of enlarging psychology. To throw anything away is crazy. Good psychology should include all the methodological techniques, without having loyalty to one method, one idea, or one person.

PT: I see you as a catalyst and as a bridge between many disciplines, theories, and philosophies.

Maslow: My job is to put them all together. We shouldn't have "humanistic psychology." The adjective should be unnecessary. I'm not antibehaviorist. I'm antidoctrinaire.

PT: Abe, when you look back on your own education, what kind would you recommend for others?

Maslow: The great educational experiences of my life were those that taught me most. They taught me what kind of a person I was. These were experiences that drew me out and strengthened me. Psychoanalysis was a big thing for me. And getting married. Marriage is a school itself. Also, having children. Becoming a father changed my whole life. It taught me as if by revelation. And reading particular books. William Graham Sumner's *Folkways* was a Mount Everest in my life: It changed me.

My teachers were the best in the world. I sought them out: Erich Fromm, Karen

Horney, Ruth Benedict, Max Wertheimer, Alfred Adler, David Levy, and Harry Harlow. I was there in New York City during the 1930s when the wave of distinguished émigrés arrived from Europe.

PT: Not everyone can have such an illustrious faculty.

Maslow: It's the teacher who's important. And if this is so, then what we are doing with our whole educational structure—with credits and the idea that one teacher is as good as another? You look at the college catalog and it says English 342. It doesn't even bother to tell you the instructor's name, and that's insane. The purpose of education—and of all social institutions—is the development of full humaneness. If you keep that in mind, all else follows. We've got to concentrate on goals.

PT: It's like the story about the test pilot who radioed back home: "I'm lost, but I'm making record time."

Maslow: If you forget the goal of education, then the whole thing is lost.

PT: If a rare, self-actualizing young psychologist came to you today and said, "What's the most important thing I can do in this time of crisis?" what advice would you give?

Maslow: I'd say: Get to work on aggression and hostility. We need the definitive book on aggression. And we need it now. Only the pieces exist: the animal stuff, the psychoanalytic stuff, the endocrine stuff. Time is running out. A key to understanding the evil which can destroy our society lies in this understanding.

There's another study that could be done. I'd like to test the whole, incoming freshman class at Brandeis University in various ways: psychiatric interviews, personality tests, everything. I want to follow them for four years of college. For a beginning, I want to test my theory that emotionally healthy people perceive better.

PT: You could make the college study only a preliminary, and follow them through their whole life span, the way Lewis Terman did with his gifted kids.

Maslow: Oh yes! I'd like to know: How good a father or mother does this student become? And what happens to his/her children? This kind of long-term study would take more time than I have left. But that ultimately doesn't make any difference. I like to be the first runner in the relay race. I like to pass on the baton to the next person.

Evolutionary Necessity or Glorious Accident? Biologists Ponder the Self

NATALIE ANGIER

THE self is like an irritating television jingle: you cannot get it out of your head. Whatever you do on this blue planet with your allotted three score and ten, whatever you taste, embrace, learn or create, all will be filtered through the self. Even sleep offers no escape, for who is it that struts through the center of every dream but you, yourself and id?

Call it self-awareness, self-identity, mind, consciousness, or even soul, but the sense of self, of being a particular individual set apart from others, seems intrinsic to the human condition. After all, Homo sapiens have large brains, and they are awfully good at taking stock of their surroundings. Sooner or later, they were bound to notice themselves, and the impermeable physical barrier between themselves and others. The

> For people, and other mammals, 'Know thyself' may be the key to living in a group.

invention of personal pronouns, philosophy and large-pore illuminating mirrors was bound to follow.

Yet as natural and inevitable as human self-awareness may seem, evolutionary biologists and psychologists do not take its existence for granted. Instead, they are asking deceptively simple questions that cut to the core of selfhood. Among them: What good is the self, anyway? Has self-awareness been selected by evolutionary pressures, or is it, to borrow a phrase from Stephen Jay Gould, a "glorious accident," the by-product of a large intelligence that allows humans to build tools and otherwise manipulate their environment? Might humans not fare just as well operating like computers, which, cyberfantasy notwithstanding, do their jobs without mulling over why they are here?

The quest to understand the evolution of the self is part of the much larger and very fashionable study of

1. ❖ BECOMING A PERSON: SEEKING SELF-IDENTITY

consciousness, which has spawned enough scientific symposiums, Web sites and books to render even the most diligent student unconscious. But most consciousness research focuses on so-called proximate mechanisms, the question of how the brain knows itself and which neural pathways and patterns of synaptic firings might underlie self-awareness. Evolutionary researchers concern themselves with ultimate mechanisms, the whys and wherefores of self. They are taking a phylogenetic approach, seeking to understand when self-awareness arose in the evolutionary past, whether other species have a sense of self, and if so, how it can be demonstrated.

The researchers are aided in their efforts by recent advances in the study of infants, and improved tools for asking questions of subjects that lack language skills. The new work indicates that an infant's sense of self, once thought to develop only gradually over the first couple of years of life, may arise prenatally. Those insights, in turn, suggest that self-awareness is not limited to the species capable of growling, "I want to be alone."

A number of biologists now suspect that a robustly articulated sense of self, far from being an afterthought of abundant cortical tissue, is very much the point of the human brain. They propose that consciousness allows humans to manipulate the most important resource of all—themselves—and to use the invented self as a tool to advance their own interests among their peers. This theory, in turn, suggests that the sense of self, of being set apart like an island afloat in a dark cosmic sea, paradoxically may have arisen because humans evolved in a highly interdependent group—because, in fact, no human is an island.

The rudiments of selfhood are as ancient as the plasma membrane, the greasy coating that separates one single-celled organism from another. "Even something as simple as an amoeba has a boundary between the self and the outside world," said Dr. David Darling, a former computer researcher and author of "Soul Search" (Villard Books, 1995) about the nature of self-consciousness. "That physical and chemical border is the beginning of some kind of self." Most creatures are sufficiently self-aware to place themselves first on their list. "It would be unlikely for an insect to start grooming a neighbor's foot," said Dr. May R. Berenbaum, an entomologist at the University of Illinois in Urbana-Champaign and author of "Bugs in the System" (Addison-Wesley, 1995). 'You wouldn't want to waste energy promoting the well-being of somebody else."

Two-month-old babies may already have a sense of self and other.

But it is one thing to have a foot-jerk preference for No. 1, and another to be conscious of that preference, or to have some sense of the self's relationship to others. Dr. Stephen W. Porges, a neurobiology researcher at the University of Maryland in College Park, defines a sense of self as essentially self-actualization, of acting upon the world rather than being acted on. He sees the emergence of self-awareness reflected in the neuroanatomical differences between the reptilian and mammalian brains. Reptiles are sit-and-wait feeders, he explains, and their primary neural structures, the brainstem and hypothalamus, are driven by their viscera. "When there's food available, they eat," Dr. Porges said. "When there isn't, their brain reduces their metabolic demands and slows everything up." Moreover, reptiles must react defensively to fine-tune their physiology; for example, by moving into the shade to cool themselves, or into the sun for warmth. For the cold-bloods, Dr. Porges said, life is a perpetual case of matter over mind, and there is no room for mindfulness.

Mammals, by comparison, are dynamic foragers and explorers of their environment. Regardless of external circumstances, their core body temperature and metabolism are maintained stably by the brainstem and hypothalamus, thus freeing up neural circuits to permit an active as opposed to reactive stance in the world. With the development of the cortex, mammals, particularly primates, gained the ability to engage with others, vocalize, display facial expressions and otherwise show evidence of emotions, all of which Dr. Porges counts as aspects of self-awareness.

In describing the transition from the reptilian to the primate brain, Dr. Porges uses the metaphor of emergence from the Garden of Eden. "In the garden, food is available, but there is no awareness of self," he said. "When we leave the garden, we must search for food, and we are aware of self. That is the forbidden knowledge."

Many mammals give signs that they know themselves, at least well enough to know their place. A spotted hyena, for example, learns shortly after birth where it stands in the hierarchy of its clan, a position determined by its mother's status, and it behaves accordingly, bullying its subordinates and groveling up to its superiors. Yet many researchers are reluctant to attribute that sort of bureaucratic behavior to genuine consciousness. They seek evidence that an animal is aware of its individuality—that it has an internal life.

One classic method for testing an animal's degree of self-awareness is the mirror self-recognition test, which has been mainly used in primate studies. In the experiment, a researcher sees how an animal reacts when confronted with its image in a mirror, and whether it recognizes that, for example, a bit of paint has been daubed on its face.

The initial results of such tests seemed to indicate an intellectual divide between the monkeys and the great apes, the primate group most closely related to humans, which includes chimpanzees, gorillas and orangutans. Apes were said to be able to recognize themselves in the mirror, while monkeys were not, supposed evidence that only apes have self-awareness. But recently, Dr. Marc D. Hauser, an associate professor of psychology and anthropology at Harvard University, and his colleagues showed that cotton-top tamarins, a South American monkey, can indeed recognize themselves in the mirror, staring in fascination after their shock of white hair had been dyed a punkish neon color. Yet Dr. Hauser and others dispute whether the results of this or any other mirror test are all that revealing. "The mirror test is not the be-all and end-all of self-recognition," he said. "People have been relying on it too much. What we need are a battery of tests to look at many aspects of self-awareness."

To that end, Dr. Hauser has lately borrowed a page from child development studies and begun subjecting nonhuman primates to the so-called false-belief test, a measure of how well one individual can appreciate that another individual might have a mental geography that differs from one's own. In a hypothetical example of such tests, three monkeys might be allowed to watch a trainer put a banana into a box. Two of the monkeys are then taken away, just long enough for the remaining monkey to see the trainer moving the banana from the box to a basket. Dr. Hauser's question: when its two fellows are returned to the training area, will the observing monkey show signs that it recognizes they now hold a false belief about the banana's location? Preliminary results with tamarins suggest that the monkeys do have something approaching a theory of mind: the observing monkey will look at the box seemingly in full expectation that the fooled monkeys will hunt for the banana there.

In this regard, at least, nonhuman primates seem to be like 3-year-old children, who show with their eye gaze that they, too, recognize another's false belief. Interestingly, though, when 3-year-olds are asked, as in the above example, where the

---

As psychology tests reveal, most people have a slightly inflated image of themselves and their talents.

---

benighted individuals will look, they say, "The basket." "Their eyes look at the right place, but they can't yet express their awareness of the deception," Dr. Hauser said. "They have implicit rather than explicit knowledge." By 4, the children make the correct response with language as well as with eye gaze.

Assuming that some nonhuman species have an implicit self-awareness, researchers expect that such intelligence is likely to be limited to, or at least most prominent in, highly social animals like primates, and possibly dolphins and a sprinkling of others. All research points to the importance of the group in giving birth to the self, and nowhere is the link more clearly seen than in humans. "Even before a baby is born, it has an identity, a place in the social hierarchy," said Dr. Roy F. Baumeister, a professor of psychology at Case Western Reserve University in Cleveland. "It may be given a name, a Social Security number, even a bank account, long before it has consciousness." The earliest contents of self-description are categorical ones, Dr. Baumeister said. By the age of 15 months or so, children identify themselves by their family, their sex and the fact that they are children rather than adults.

Dr. Alan Fogel of the University of Utah in Salt Lake City, who studies the development of the self in children, proposes that an infant first understands itself relationally, by registering its impact on others. Contrary to old notions that a young baby knows no distinction between itself and its mother, he said, recent work suggests that even newborns can tell the difference between when they move or touch themselves and when they are being moved or touched by others.

Dr. Fogel has found that babies see themselves as part of a "relational field," which they can alter with their behavior. For example, he said, it a mother smiles and coos at a 2-month-old, the baby will smile and gurgle in response, a seamless exchange of delight. But if the mother suddenly turns stony-faced, the baby will stop, turn away and then look back with a smile, as though trying to reinitiate the exchange. If that fails, the baby eventually turns away, apparently dejected.

"Some people argue that, well, it is just because the baby's expectations were upset," Dr. Fogel said. "But I argue that the baby has a sense of itself and its role in the relationship, as shown by the fact that the baby tries to re-establish communication. It doesn't wither away and do nothing at all."

In seeing itself as dependent on yet distinct from the mother, and in

1. ❖ BECOMING A PERSON: SEEKING SELF-IDENTITY

seeking to manipulate the relationship with its behavior, a baby demonstrates, on a small scale, the benefits of self-awareness and offers insight into why humans are so full of themselves. Dr. Steven Pinker, professor of cognitive science at the Massachusetts Institute of Technology and author of "How the Mind Works," a book to be published this fall by W. W. Norton, points out that humans are the most elaborately social of all species, possibly as a result of environmental conditions pitting early humans against other hominids and apes. Self-awareness helps an individual maximize the benefits that he or she can reap from the group.

"Our fate depends on what other people think of us," Dr. Pinker said. "It would make sense to apply our intelligence to assuring that social interactions come out in our favor."

For example, he said, people want to form alliances with those they deem brave, honest and trustworthy. "It's to our advantage to be seen as brave, trustworthy, kind and so forth," Dr. Pinker said. "We have the ability to float above ourselves and look down at ourselves, to play back tapes of our own behavior to evaluate and manipulate it. Knowing thyself is a way of making thyself as palatable as possible to others."

Certain oddities of self-awareness support the theory that it has adaptive value, Dr. Pinker said. Self-deception is one of them. As psychology tests reveal, most people have a slightly inflated image of themselves and their talents. "There may be an advantage to believing that one is kinder, smarter and more in control than you really are," he said. "To the extent that all of us are at least occasional liars, the best liar is one who believes his own lies." Those with low self-esteem, then, may be the most truthful members of the tribe, but somehow that sort of honesty will not win you allies or a date on Saturday night.

HOW USEFUL IS

Daydreams can help us prepare for future events by keeping us aware of unfinished business

Paul M. Insel, Ph.D.

Dr. Insel, Editor-in-chief of HEALTHLINE, is Clinical Associate Professor of Psychiatry at the Stanford University School of Medicine.

EVERYONE DAYDREAMS, ESPECIALLY THOSE of us who are fantasy-prone, and particularly at times when we are tired of focusing on tasks that are tedious or intense. Daydreaming, or fantasizing, can be adaptive: it can help prepare us for future events. It can also substitute for impulsive behavior and help us get past a frustrating or anger-provoking experience.

Here's an example of one use of fantasy: Ralph Thomas, a mild-mannered bank clerk, pulls into the parking lot at work and finds that his parking space is taken by one of the senior bank managers, who is both aggressive and unfriendly. Instead of confronting the manager, Ralph fantasizes about walking up to him, grabbing him by the scruff of the neck in front of admiring onlookers, and yelling at him about his inconsiderate and callous behavior. Although he never says a thing to the manager, he nevertheless feels better about the situation, at least for the moment. If it happens again he still is unlikely to assertively confront the manager, but he may be prompted to at least mention his frustration to the manager or another employee.

Through extensive interviews and questionnaires, psychologist Jerome Singer has found that almost everyone has daydreams, or waking fantasies, every day—on the train, on the job, in the elevator, or walking down the street; in fact, we daydream almost anywhere, at any time. Young adults spend more time daydreaming and admit to more sexual fantasies than do older adults.

In *The Secret Life of Walter Mitty*, a classic story by James Thurber, Mitty seasons a rather bland life with heroic fantasies, imagining himself as the hero in a variety of scenes played out in his mind's eye. He returns triumphant at the head of an army to the acclaim of the crowd. As he drives past a hospital, Dr. Mitty astounds renowned specialists with his surgical skill. In one fantasy after another he is courageous and valiant, reaching unending pinnacles of heroism.

Not all fantasy is escapist or dramatic. Mostly people daydream about the details of their lives, such as imagining an alternative approach to a task they are performing, picturing themselves explaining to the boss why they are late, or replaying "mind tapes" about personal encounters they either savor or wish had gone differently.

According to one study, close to 4 percent of the population has fantasy-prone personalities. As children, they had enjoyed intense make-believe play with their dolls, stuffed animals, or imaginary companions. As adults, they reported spending more than half their time fantasizing. They would relive experiences or imagine scenes so vividly that occasionally they later had trouble differentiating remembered fantasies from their memories of actual events. Most of the women with fantasy-prone personalities were able to experience orgasm solely through sexual fantasy.

Are the many hours we spend in fantasy merely a way of escaping reality, or can this daydreaming serve another purpose? Studies of children have shown that daydreaming in the form of imaginative play has been shown to play an important role in social and cognitive development. Playful fantasies also enhance the creativity of scientists, writers, and artists. Albert Einstein felt this way about fantasy: *When I examined myself, and my methods of thought, I came to the conclusion that the gift of fantasy has meant more to me than my talent for absorbing positive knowledge.*

For many of us, fantasy is adaptive and useful. Daydreams can help us prepare for future events by keeping us aware of unfinished business. This unique kind of mind process can help us rehearse upcoming events, observe potential problems in our behavior, and resolve them before the event is experienced. Behavior therapy makes use of mental rehearsal to help us safely experience frightening thoughts or ideas.

Therapists use imagery, a kind of fantasy, to strip encounters that are intimidating or anxiety-producing of their fearful aspects. One woman dreaded appearing in court because she was intimidated by the authority of lawyers and judges. She was able to overcome this fear by imagining these authorities in tennis shorts and polo shirts with funny sayings on them. The use of imagery has been successful with people who suffer from test or performance anxiety by helping them to see themselves as feeling confident and accomplished when taking tests.

Can fantasy also substitute for impulsive and aggressive behavior? Dr. Singer has suggested that people who are prone to delinquency and violence, or who seek the artificial highs of dangerous drugs, have fewer vivid fantasies than average. Psychologist Seymour Feshbach from the University of California tested the theory that fantasy works to reduce subsequent aggression. He set up his experiment with students who were insulted by their instructor. Half of the students were given the opportunity to write imaginative stories about aggression, while the other half were not given the opportunity. There was also a control group of students who were not insulted. Feshbach's results showed that people who had been given the opportunity to write stories about aggression were less aggressive than those who were not given the opportunity. Both groups of insulted students were more aggressive than the control group of students who were not insulted at all.

A fantasy can be a map or a nagivational path that steers us safely between the reefs and shoals of anger, guilt, frustration, anxiety, and inhibition; it can help prepare us for future events; and it can add spice and excitement to an otherwise dull existence.

The Stability of Personality: Observations and Evaluations

Robert R. McCrae and
Paul T. Costa, Jr.

Robert R. McCrae *is Research Psychologist and* **Paul T. Costa, Jr.,** *is Chief, Laboratory of Personality and Cognition, both at the Gerontology Research Center, National Institute on Aging, National Institutes of Health. Address correspondence to Robert R. McCrae, Personality, Stress and Coping Section, Gerontology Research Center, 4940 Eastern Ave., Baltimore, MD 21224.*

"There is an optical illusion about every person we meet," Ralph Waldo Emerson wrote in his essay on "Experience":

> In truth, they are all creatures of given temperament, which will appear in a given character, whose boundaries they will never pass: but we look at them, they seem alive, and we presume there is impulse in them. In the moment it seems impulse; in the year, in the lifetime, it turns out to be a certain uniform tune which the revolving barrel of the music-box must play.[1]

In this brief passage, Emerson anticipated modern findings about the stability of personality and pointed out an illusion to which both laypersons and psychologists are prone. He was also perhaps the first to decry personality stability as the enemy of freedom, creativity, and growth, objecting that "temperament puts all divinity to rout." In this article, we summarize evidence in support of Emerson's observations but offer arguments against his evaluation of them.[2]

EVIDENCE FOR THE STABILITY OF ADULT PERSONALITY

Emerson used the term *temperament* to refer to the basic tendencies of the individual, dispositions that we call *personality traits*. It is these traits, measured by such instruments as the Minnesota Multiphasic Personality Inventory and the NEO Personality Inventory, that have been investigated in a score of longitudinal studies over the past 20 years. Despite a wide variety of samples, instruments, and designs, the results of these studies have been remarkably consistent, and they are easily summarized.

1. The mean levels of personality traits change with development, but reach final adult levels at about age 30. Between 20 and 30, both men and women become somewhat less emotional and thrill-seeking and somewhat more cooperative and self-disciplined—changes we might interpret as evidence of increased maturity. After age 30, there are few and subtle changes, of which the most consistent is a small decline in activity level with advancing age. Except among individuals with dementia, stereotypes that depict older people as being withdrawn, depressed, or rigid are unfounded.
2. Individual differences in personality traits, which show at least some continuity from early childhood on, are also essentially fixed by age 30. Stability coefficients (test-retest correlations over substantial time intervals) are typically in the range of .60 to .80, even over intervals of as long as 30 years, although there is some decline in magnitude with increasing retest interval. Given that most personality scales have short-term retest reliabilities in the range from .70 to .90, it is clear that by far the greatest part of the reliable variance (i.e., variance not due to measurement error) in personality traits is stable.
3. Stability appears to characterize all five of the major domains of personality—neuroticism, extraversion, openness to experience, agreeableness, and conscientiousness. This finding suggests that an adult's personality profile as a whole will change little over time, and studies of the stability of configural measures of personality support that view.
4. Generalizations about stability apply to virtually everyone. Men and women, healthy and sick people, blacks and whites all show the same pattern. When asked, most adults will say that their personality has not changed much in adulthood, but even those who claim to have had major changes show little objective evidence of change on repeated administrations of personality questionnaires. Important exceptions to this generalization include people suffering from dementia and certain

categories of psychiatric patients who respond to therapy, but no moderators of stability among healthy adults have yet been identified.[3]

When researchers first began to publish these conclusions, they were greeted with considerable skepticism—"I distrust the facts and the inferences" Emerson had written—and many studies were designed to test alternative hypotheses. For example, some researchers contended that consistent responses to personality questionnaires were due to memory of past responses, but retrospective studies showed that people could not accurately recall how they had previously responded even when instructed to do so. Other researchers argued that temporal consistency in self-reports merely meant that individuals had a fixed idea of themselves, a crystallized self-concept that failed to keep pace with real changes in personality. But studies using spouse and peer raters showed equally high levels of stability.[4]

The general conclusion that personality traits are stable is now widely accepted. Some researchers continue to look for change in special circumstances and populations; some attempt to account for stability by examining genetic and environmental influences on personality. Finally, others take the view that there is much more to personality than traits, and seek to trace the adult developmental course of personality perceptions or identity formation or life narratives.

These latter studies are worthwhile, because people undoubtedly do change across the life span. Marriages end in divorce, professional careers are started in mid-life, fashions and attitudes change with the times. Yet often the same traits can be seen in new guises. Intellectual curiosity merely shifts from one field to another, avid gardening replaces avid tennis, one abusive relationship is followed by another. Many of these changes are best regarded as variations on the "uniform tune" played by individuals' enduring dispositions.

ILLUSORY ATTRIBUTIONS IN TEMPORAL PERSPECTIVE

Social and personality psychologists have debated for some time the accuracy of attributions of the causes of behavior to persons or situations. The "optical illusion" in person perception that Emerson pointed to was somewhat different. He felt that people attribute behavior to the live and spontaneous person who freely creates responses to the situation, when in fact behavior reveals only the mechanical operation of lifeless and static temperament. We may (and we will!) take exception to this disparaging, if common, view of traits, but we must first concur with the basic observation that personality processes often appear different when viewed in longitudinal perspective: "The years teach much which the days never know."

Consider happiness. If one asks individuals why they are happy or unhappy, they are almost certain to point to environmental circumstances of the moment: a rewarding job, a difficult relationship, a threat to health, a new car. It would seem that levels of happiness ought to mirror quality of life, and that changes in circumstances would result in changes in subjective well-being. It would be easy to demonstrate this pattern in a controlled laboratory experiment: Give subjects $1,000 each and ask how they feel!

But survey researchers who have measured the objective quality of life by such indicators as wealth, education, and health find precious little association with subjective well-being, and longitudinal researchers have found surprising stability in individual differences in happiness, even among people whose life circumstances have changed markedly. The explanation is simple: People adapt to their circumstances rapidly, getting used to the bad and taking for granted the good. In the long run, happiness is largely a matter of enduring personality traits.[5] "Temper prevails over everything of time, place, and condition, and ... fix[es] the measure of activity and of enjoyment."

A few years ago, William Swann and Craig Hill provided an ingenious demonstration of the errors to which too narrow a temporal perspective can lead. A number of experiments had shown that it was relatively easy to induce changes in the self-concept by providing self-discrepant feedback. Introverts told that they were really extraverts rated themselves higher in extraversion than they had before. Such studies supported the view that the self-concept is highly malleable, a mirror of the evaluation of the immediate environment.

Swann and Hill replicated this finding, but extended it by inviting subjects back a few days later. By that time, the effects of the manipulation had disappeared, and subjects had returned to their initial self-concepts. The implication is that any one-shot experiment may give a seriously misleading view of personality processes.[6]

The relations between coping and adaptation provide a final example. Cross-sectional studies show that individuals who use such coping mechanisms as self-blame, wishful thinking, and hostile reactions toward other people score lower on measures of well-being than people who do not use these mechanisms. It would be easy to infer that these coping mechanisms detract from adaptation, and in fact the very people who use them admit that they are ineffective. But the correlations vanish when the effects of prior neuroticism scores are removed; an alternative interpretation of the data is thus that individuals who score high on this personality factor use poor coping strategies and also have low well-being: The association between coping and well-being may be entirely attributable to this third variable.[7]

Psychologists have long been aware of the problems of inferring causes from correlational data, but they have not recognized the pervasiveness of the bias that Emerson warned about. People tend to understand behavior and experience as the result of the immediate context, whether intrapsychic or environmental. Only by looking over time can one see the persistent effects of personality traits.

THE EVALUATION OF STABILITY

If few findings in psychology are more robust than the stability of personality, even fewer are more unpopular. Gerontologists often see stability as an affront to their commitment to continuing adult development; psychotherapists sometimes view it as an alarming challenge to their ability to help patients;[8] humanistic psychologists and transcendental philosophers think it degrades human nature. A popular account in *The Idaho Statesman* ran under the disheartening headline "Your Personality—You're Stuck With It."

In our view, these evaluations are based on misunderstandings: At worst, stability is a mixed blessing. Those individuals who are anxious, quarrelsome, and lazy might be understandably distressed to think that they are likely to stay that way, but surely those who are imaginative, affectionate, and carefree at age 30 should be glad to hear that they will probably be imaginative, affectionate, and carefree at age 90.

Because personality is stable, life is to some extent predictable. People can make vocational and retirement choices with some confidence that their current interests and enthusiasms will not desert them. They can choose friends and mates with whom they are likely to remain compatible. They can vote on the basis of candidates' records, with some assurance that future policies will resemble past ones. They can learn which coworkers they can depend on, and which they cannot. The personal and social utility of personality stability is enormous.

But it is precisely this predictability that so offends many critics. ("I had fancied that the value of life lay in its inscrutable possibilities," Emerson complained.) These critics view traits as mechanical and static habits and believe that the stability of personality traits dooms human beings to lifeless monotony as puppets controlled by inexorable forces. This is a misunderstanding on several levels.

First, personality traits are not repetitive habits, but inherently dynamic dispositions that interact with the opportunities and challenges of the moment.[9] Antagonistic people do not yell at everyone; some people they flatter, some they scorn, some they threaten. Just as the same intelligence is applied to a lifetime of changing problems, so the same personality traits can be expressed in an infinite variety of ways, each suited to the situation.

Second, there are such things as spontaneity and impulse in human life, but they are stable traits. Individuals who are open to experience actively seek out new places to go, provocative ideas to ponder, and exotic sights, sounds, and tastes to experience. Extraverts show a different kind of spontaneity, making friends, seeking thrills, and jumping at every chance to have a good time. People who are introverted and closed to experience have more measured and monotonous lives, but this is the kind of life they choose.

Finally, personality traits are not inexorable forces that control our fate, nor are they, in psychodynamic language, ego alien. Our traits characterize us; they are our very selves;[10] we act most freely when we express our enduring dispositions. Individuals sometimes fight against their own tendencies, trying perhaps to overcome shyness or curb a bad temper. But most people acknowledge even these failings as their own, and it is well that they do. A person's recognition of the inevitability of his or her one and only personality is a large part of what Erik Erikson called ego *integrity*, the culminating wisdom of a lifetime.

Notes

1. All quotations are from "Experience," in *Essays: First and Second Series*, R. W. Emerson (Vintage, New York, 1990) (original work published 1844).
2. For recent and sometimes divergent treatments of this topic, see R. R. McCrae and P. T. Costa, Jr., *Personality in Adulthood* (Guilford, New York, 1990); D. C. Funder, R. D. Parke, C. Tomlinson-Keasey, and K. Widaman, Eds., *Studying Lives Through Time: Personality and Development* (American Psychological Association, Washington, DC, 1993); T. Heatherton and J. Weinberger, *Can Personality Change?* (American Psychological Association, Washington, DC, 1994).
3. I. C. Siegler, K. A. Welsh, D. V. Dawson, G. G. Fillenbaum, N. L. Earl, E. B. Kaplan, and C. M. Clark, Ratings of personality change in patients being evaluated for memory disorders, *Alzheimers Disease and Associated Disorders, 5,* 240–250 (1991); R. M. A. Hirschfeld, G. L. Klerman, P. Clayton, M. B. Keller, P. McDonald-Scott, and B. Larkin, Assessing personality: Effects of depressive state on trait measurement, *American Journal of Psychiatry, 140,* 695–699 (1983); R. R. McCrae, Moderated analyses of longitudinal personality stability, *Journal of Personality and Social Psychology, 65,* 577–585 (1993).
4. D. Woodruff, The role of memory in personality continuity: A 25 year follow-up, *Experimental Aging Research, 9,* 31–34 (1983); P. T. Costa, Jr., and R. R. McCrae, Trait psychology comes of age, in *Nebraska Symposium on Motivation: Psychology and Aging,* T. B. Sonderegger, Ed. (University of Nebraska Press, Lincoln, 1992).
5. P. T. Costa, Jr., and R. R. McCrae, Influence of extraversion and neuroticism on subjective well-being: Happy and unhappy people, *Journal of Personality and Social Psychology, 38,* 668–678 (1980).
6. The study is summarized in W. B. Swann, Jr., and C. A. Hill, When our identities are mistaken: Reaffirming self-conceptions through social interactions, *Journal of Personality and Social Psychology, 43,* 59–66 (1982). Dangers of single-occasion research are also discussed in J. R. Council, Context effects in personality research, *Current Directions in Psychological Science, 2,* 31–34 (1993).
7. R. R. McCrae and P. T. Costa, Jr., Personality, coping, and coping effectiveness in an adult sample, *Journal of Personality, 54,* 385–405 (1986).
8. Observations in nonpatient samples show what happens over time under typical life circumstances; they do not rule out the possibility that psychotherapeutic interventions can change personality. Whether or not such change is possible, in practice much of psychotherapy consists of helping people learn to live with their limitations, and this may be a more realistic goal than "cure" for many patients. See P. T. Costa, Jr., and R. R. McCrae, Personality stability and its implications for clinical psychology, *Clinical Psychology Review, 6,* 407–423 (1986).
9. A. Tellegen, Personality traits: Issues of definition, evidence and assessment, in *Thinking Clearly About Psychology: Essays in Honor of Paul E. Meehl,* Vol. 2, W. Grove and D. Cicchetti, Eds. (University of Minnesota Press, Minneapolis, 1991).
10. R. R. McCrae and P. T. Costa, Jr., Age, personality, and the spontaneous self-concept, *Journals of Gerontology: Social Sciences, 43,* S177–S185 (1988).

Determinants of Behavior: Motivation, Environment, and Physiology

On the front pages of every newspaper, in practically every televised newscast, and on many magazine covers the problems of substance abuse in America haunt us. Innocent children are killed when caught in the crossfire of the guns of drug lords. Prostitutes selling their bodies for drug money spread the deadly AIDS virus. The white-collar middle manager loses his job because he embezzled company money to support his cocaine habit.

Why do people turn to drugs? Why doesn't all of the publicity about the ruining of human lives diminish the drug problem? Why can some people consume two cocktails and stop, while others feel helpless against the inebriating seduction of alcohol? Why do some people crave heroin as their drug of choice, while others choose marijuana?

The causes of individual behavior such as drug and alcohol abuse are the focus of this section. If physiology, either biochemistry or genes, is the determinant of our behavior, then solutions to such puzzles as alcoholism lie in the field of *psychobiology* (the study of behavior in relation to biological processes). However, if experience as a function of our environment and learning histories creates personality and coping ability and thus causes subsequent behavior, normal or not, then researchers must take a different tack and explore features of the environment responsible for certain behaviors. A third explanation is that ability to adjust to change is produced by some complex interaction or interplay between experience and biology. If this interaction accounts for individual differences in personality and ability to cope, scientists then have a very complicated task ahead of them.

Conducting research designed to unravel the determinants of behavior is difficult. Scientists must call upon their best design skills to develop studies that will yield useful and replicable findings. A researcher hoping to examine the role of experience in personal growth and behavior needs to be able to isolate one or two stimuli or environmental features that seem to control a particular behavior. Imagine trying to delimit the complexity of the world sufficiently so that only one or two events stand out as the cause of an individual's alcoholism. Likewise, researchers interested in psychobiology also need refined, technical knowledge. Suppose a scientist hopes to show that a particular form of mental illness is inherited. She cannot merely examine family genetic histories, because family members can also learn maladaptive behaviors from one another. The researcher's ingenuity will be challenged; she must use intricate techniques such as comparing children to their adoptive as well as to their biological parents. Volunteer subjects may be difficult to find, and, even then, the data may be hard to interpret.

The first unit article, by Marc Peyser and Anne Underwood, explores the joint contributions of nature and nurture. The article discusses the contributions of genes as well as the relative influence of the environment. The authors clearly but succinctly provide a general overview of the nature/nurture controversy.

The next article discusses why the nature/nurture issue is so controversial. Suppose criminality is indeed genetically determined. What does this mean for the treatment and prevention of criminal behavior? In the "Politics of Biology," Wray Herbert discusses why this issue is so controversial and what the debate means for such social problems as mental illness, alcoholism, and crime.

The next two articles pertain to heredity, one aspect of psychobiology. In "Nature's Clones" Jim Neimark discusses the nature of twins and twin studies designed to study genetics. Studies of identical twins who are raised apart often give scientists a good handle on whether a characteristic, psychological or not, is inherited. The companion piece on happiness, by Daniel Goleman, suggests that there is a personality trait that is genetically determined. The trait is happiness, and Goleman claims there is a set point, a predetermined level, of happiness that differentiates individuals from one another.

The nervous system is also an important component of the biological determinants of our personalities and behaviors. The next three articles reveal information about the brain, which is the focal point of the nervous system. In the first article on the brain, Kathleen Cahill Allison discusses how special and new techniques in molecular biology are helping us better understand brain disorders such as Alzheimer's disease and depression.

The next two articles discuss the influence of the brain on the expression of various behaviors. In "Violence and the Brain," Norbert Myslinski describes a rare but interesting disorder that causes fits of violence. Fortunately, this disorder is treatable, and understanding it helps us to understand the activity of the brain. A related article by Gina Kolata discusses the brain's role in dictating dif-

UNIT 2

ferences between men and women. This essay also reveals some of the miraculous techniques that assist us in studying the brain.

This section would be incomplete, though, if it did not offer a counterpoint to all of this information about psychobiology. The environment also is a powerful influence on us. In "Studies Show Talking with Infants Shapes Basis of Ability to Think," Sandra Blakeslee provides evidence that talking to infants is the basis for their later ability to reason and problem-solve. Learning from the environment, then, is the other side of the nature/nurture equation.

In the final article in this unit, we stray far from laboratory and scientific research. In "Faith and Healing," Claudia Wallis discloses that people are turning more and more to forms of healing other than medical treatment. Some individuals turn to religion; others look inward and examine their feelings and attitudes. In any event, astonishing new research is demonstrating that there is indeed a mind-body connection, and it is finding that those who turn to religion, for example, are healthier than those who do not.

In summary, this unit covers factors that determine our behavior, whether the factors are internal, such as genetics, physiology, and the nervous system, or external, such as our environment and those around us, or some combination of the two.

Looking Ahead: Challenge Questions

Based on your experience observing children, what would you say most contributes to their personal growth: physiological or environmental factors? Explain why you think different aspects of our behaviors and personalities are accounted for by physiology, experience, or some combination of the two.

Why is it important to study genetics? How is genetic research conducted on twins, and why is it important? If we knew that a certain form of cancer was inherited, what could we do about it? Would your answer be the same if asked what we should do about a certain kind of inherited mental illness? If we discover that a certain psychological characteristic, especially a negative one such as criminality, is indeed inherited, why would this be controversial or political?

What is a set point? Do you believe that there is only a limited amount of happiness for each of us? Are there individual differences in levels of happiness? What can we do for individuals who seem perpetually unhappy?

How can we map the brain? What are the various parts of the brain? Explain whether or not you can ascribe certain behaviors to certain parts of the brain. What brain disorders are being studied with modern scientific techniques? Why are we studying these already disordered brains; why not concentrate on normal brains?

Name some bona fide brain differences between the sexes that have been discovered by neuroscientists. What perceived differences are due to stereotypes and therefore untrue? Where do these differences originate? Do you think the sexes are more similar than they are different? Why or why not?

Besides sex differences, can you think of other psychological phenomena that would be interesting or worth examining to determine what factors contribute to them or to detect individual differences? Name some. What utility or practical application does searching for causes of individual differences in behaviors have?

What evidence do we have that biology does not provide the only influence on our psychological being? Can merely talking to infants influence the course of their development? How much of a role do you think the environment plays compared to biology? Do you think the environment's influence grows the further we proceed through life? Defend your answer.

How can our minds affect our physical health? Offer data to support your position. If the mind does affect the body, what can we do to keep ourselves mentally and physically well?

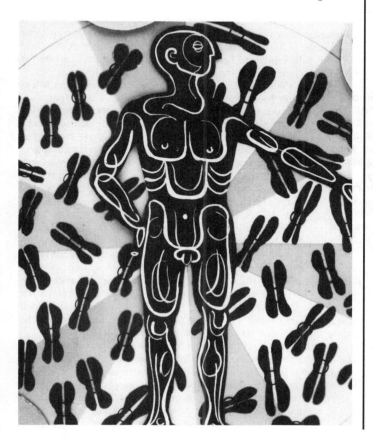

Article 5

The wizards of genetics keep closing in on the biological roots of personality. It's not your imagination that one baby seems born cheerful and another morose. But that's not the complete picture. DNA is not destiny; experience plays a powerful role, too.

Shyness, Sadness, Curiosity, Joy. Is It Nature or Nurture?

By Marc Peyser and Anne Underwood

IF ANY CHILD SEEMED DESTINED TO GROW UP AFRAID OF her shadow and just about anything else that moved, it was 2-year-old Marjorie. She was so painfully shy that she wouldn't talk to or look at a stranger. She was even afraid of friendly cats and dogs. When Jerome Kagan, a Harvard professor who discovered that shyness has a strong genetic component, sent a clown to play with Marjorie, she ran to her mother. "It was as if a cobra entered that room," Kagan says. His diagnosis: Marjorie showed every sign of inherited shyness, a condition in which the brain somehow sends out messages to avoid new experiences. But as Kagan continued to examine her over the years, Marjorie's temperament changed. When she started school, she gained confidence from ballet classes and her good grades, and she began to make friends. Her parents even coaxed her into taking horseback-riding lessons. Marjorie may have been born shy, but she has grown into a bubbly second grader.

For Marjorie, then, biology—more specifically, her genetic inheritance—was not her destiny. And therein lies our tale. In the last few years scientists have identified genes that appear to predict all sorts of emotional behavior, from happiness to aggressiveness to risk-taking. The age-old question of whether nature or nurture determines temperament seems finally to have been decided in favor of Mother Nature and her ever-deepening gene pool. But the answer may not be so simple after all. Scientists are beginning to discover that genetics and environment work together to determine personality as intricately as Astaire and Rogers danced. "If either Fred or Ginger moves too fast, they both stumble," says Stanley Greenspan, a pediatric psychiatrist at George Washington University and the author of "The Growth of the Mind." "Nature affects nurture affects nature and back and forth. Each step influences the next." Many scientists now believe that some experiences can actually alter the structure of the brain. An aggressive toddler, under the right circumstances, can essentially be rewired to channel his energy more constructively. Marjorie can overcome her shyness—forever. No child need be held captive to her genetic blueprint. The implications for child rearing—and social policy—are profound.

While Gregor Mendel's pea plants did wonders to explain how humans inherit blue eyes or a bald spot, they turn out to be an inferior model for analyzing something as complex as the brain. The human body contains about 100,000 genes, of which 50,000 to 70,000 are involved in brain function. Genes control the brain's neurotransmitters and receptors, which deliver and accept mental messages like so many cars headed for their assigned parking spaces. But there are billions of roads to each parking lot, and those paths are highly susceptible to environmental factors. In his book "The New View of Self," Dr. Larry Siever, a psychiatry professor at Mount Sinai Medical Center, writes about how the trauma of the Holocaust caused such intense genetic scrambling in some survivors that their children inherited the same stress-related abnormalities. "Perhaps the sense of danger and uncertainty associated with living through such a time is passed on in the family milieu and primes the biological systems of the children as well," says Siever. He added that that might explain why pianist David Helfgott, the subject of the movie "Shine," had his mental breakdown.

A gene is only a probability for a given trait, not a guarantee. For that trait to be expressed, a gene often must be "turned on" by an outside force before it does its job. High levels of stress apparently activate a variety of genes, including those suspected of being involved in fear, shyness and some mental illnesses. Children conceived during a three-month famine in the Netherlands during a Nazi blockade in 1945 were later found to have twice the rate of schizophrenia

> **61% of all parents believe that differences in behavior between girls and boys are not inborn but a result of the way they're raised**

5. Is It Nature or Nurture?

Scientists estimate that genes determine only about 50 percent of a child's personality

as did Dutch children born to parents who were spared the trauma of famine. "Twenty years ago, you couldn't get your research funded if you were looking for a genetic basis for schizophrenia, because everyone knew it was what your mother did to you in the first few years of life, as Freud said," says Robert Plomin, a geneticist at London's Institute of Psychiatry. "Now you can't get funded *unless* you're looking for a genetic basis. Neither extreme is right, and the data show why. There's only a 50 percent concordance between genetics and the development of schizophrenia."

SCIENTISTS HAVE BEEN DEvoting enormous energy to determining what part of a given character trait is "heritable" and what part is the result of socialization. Frank Sulloway's book "Born to Rebel," which analyzes the influence of birth order on personality, opened a huge window on a universal—and largely overlooked—environmental factor. But that's a broad brushstroke. Most studies focus on remarkably precise slivers of human emotions. One study at Allegheny University in Pennsylvania found that the tendency for a person to throw dishes or slam doors when he's angry is 40 percent heritable, while the likelihood a person will yell in anger is only 28 percent heritable. The most common method for determining these statistics is studying twins. If identical twins are more alike in some way than are fraternal twins, that trait is believed to have a higher likelihood of being inherited. But the nature-nurture knot is far from being untied.

The trick, then, is to isolate a given gene and study the different ways environment interacts with it. For instance, scientists believe that people with the longer variety of a dopamine-4 receptor gene are biologically predisposed to be thrill seekers. Because the gene appears to make them less sensitive to pain and physical sensation, the children are more likely to, say, crash their tricycles into a wall, just to see what it feels like. "These are the daredevils," says Greenspan. But they need not be. Given strict boundaries, Greenspan says, thrill-seeking kids can be taught to modulate and channel their overactive curiosity. A risk-taking child who likes to pound his fist into hard objects can be taught games that involve hitting softly as well. "If you give them constructive ways to meet their needs," says Greenspan, "they can become charismatic, action-oriented leaders."

Shyness has been studied perhaps more than any other personality trait. Kagan, who has monitored 500 children for more than 17 years at Harvard, can detect telltale signs of shyness in babies even before they're born. He's found that the hearts of shy children in the womb consistently beat faster than 140 times a minute, which is much faster than the heartbeats of other babies. The shy fetus is already highly reactive, wired to overmonitor his environment. But he can also outgrow this predisposition if his parents gently but firmly desensitize him to the situations that cause anxiety, such as encouraging him to play with other children or, as in Marjorie's fear of animals, taking her to the stables and teaching her to ride a horse. Kagan has found that by the age of 4, no more than 20 percent of the previously shy children remain that way.

78% of those polled who are in two-parent families say that they share equally when it comes to setting rules for their young child

Will the reprogramming last into adulthood? Because evidence of the role of genes has been discovered only recently, it's still too early to tell. But studies of animals give some indication. Stephen Suomi at the National Institute of Child Health and Human Development works with rhesus monkeys that possess the same genetic predisposition to shyness that affects humans. He's shown that by giving a shy monkey to a foster mother who is an expert caregiver, the baby will outgrow the shyness. Even more surprising, the once shy monkey will become a leader among her peers and an unusually competent parent, just like the foster mom. Though she will likely pass along her shyness genes to her own child, she will teach it how to overcome her predisposition, just as she was taught. And the cycle continues—generations of genetically shy monkeys become not just normal, but superior, adults and parents. The lesson, says Suomi: "You can't prejudge anyone at birth. No matter what your genetic background, a negative characteristic you're born with may even turn out to be an advantage."

But parents aren't scientists, and it's not always easy to see how experience can influence a child's character. A baby who smiles a lot and makes eye contact is, in part, determining her own environment, which in turn affects her temperament. As her parents coo and smile and wrinkle their noses in delighted response, they are reinforcing their baby's sunny disposition. But what about children who are born with low muscle tone, who at 4 months can barely hold up their own heads, let alone smile? Greenspan has discovered that mothers of these kids smile at the baby for a while, but when the affection isn't returned, they give up. And so does the baby, who over time fails to develop the ability to socialize normally. "If you move in the wrong patterns, the problem is exacerbated," Greenspan says. He has found that if parents respond to nonsmiling babies by being superanimated—like Bob Barker hosting a game show—they can engage their child's interest in the world.

The ramifications of these findings clearly have the potential to revolutionize child-rearing theory and practice. But to an uncertain end. "Our society has a strong belief that what happens in childhood determines your fate. If you have a happy childhood, everything will be all right. That's silly," says Michael Lewis, director of the Institute for the Study of Child Development in New Jersey and the author of "Altering Fate." Lewis estimates that experience ultimately rewrites 90 percent of a child's personality traits, leaving an adult with only one tenth of his inborn temperament. "The idea that early childhood is such a powerful moment to see individual differences in biology or environment is not valid," he says. "We are too open to and modifiable by experience." Some scientists warn that attempting to reprogram even a narrow sliver of childhood emotions can prove to be a daunting task, despite research's fascinating new insights. "Children are not a 24-hour controlled experiment," says C. Robert Cloninger, a professor of psychiatry and genetics at the Washington University School of Medicine in St. Louis. "If you put a child in a Skinner box, *then* maybe you could have substantial influence." So, mindful of the blinding insights of geneticists and grateful for the lingering influences of environment, parents must get on with the business of raising their child, an inexact science if ever there was one.

POLITICS OF BIOLOGY

How the nature vs. nurture debate shapes public policy—and our view of ourselves

BY WRAY HERBERT

Laurie Flynn uses the technology of neuroscience to light up the brains of Washington lawmakers. As executive director of the National Alliance for the Mentally Ill, she marshals everything from cost analysis to moral pleading to make the case for laws banning discrimination against people with mental illness. But her most powerful advocacy tool by far is the PET scan. She takes a collection of these colorful brain images up to Capitol Hill to put on a show, giving lawmakers a window on a "broken" brain in action. "When they see that it's not some imaginary, fuzzy problem, but a real physical condition, then they get it: 'Oh, it's in the brain'."

The view of mental illness as a brain disease has been crucial to the effort to destigmatize illnesses such as schizophrenia and depression. But it's just one example of a much broader biologizing of American culture that's been going on for more than a decade. For both political and scientific reasons—and it's often impossible to disentangle the two—everything from criminality to addictive disorders to sexual orientation is seen today less as a matter of choice than of genetic destiny. Even basic personality is looking more and more like a genetic legacy. Nearly every week there is a report of a new gene for one trait or another. Novelty seeking, religiosity, shyness, the tendency to divorce, and even happiness (or the lack of it) are among the traits that may result in part from a gene, according to new research.

This cultural shift has political and personal implications. On the personal level, a belief in the power of genes necessarily diminishes the potency of such personal qualities as will, capacity to choose, and sense of responsibility for those choices—if it's in your genes, you're not accountable. It allows the alcoholic, for example, to treat himself as a helpless victim of his biology rather than as a willful agent with control of his own behavior. Genetic determinism can free victims and their families of guilt—or lock them in their suffering.

On the political level, biological determinism now colors all sorts of public-policy debates on issues such as gay rights, health care, juvenile justice, and welfare reform. The effort to dismantle social programs is fueled by the belief that government interventions (the nurturing side in the nature-nurture debate) don't work very well—and the corollary idea that society can't make up for every unfortunate citizen's bad luck. It's probably no coincidence that the biologizing of culture has accompanied the country's shift to the political right, since conservatives traditionally are more dubious about human perfectability than are liberals. As Northeastern University psychologist Leon Kamin notes, the simplest way to discover someone's political leanings is to ask his or her view on genetics.

Even so, genetic determinism can have paradoxical consequences at times, leading to disdain rather than sympathy for the disadvantaged, and marginalization rather than inclusion. Cultural critics are beginning to sort out the unpredictable politics of biology, focusing on four traits: violence, mental illness, alcoholism, and sexual orientation.

The nature of violence. To get a sense of just how thorough—and how politicized—the biologizing of culture has been, just look at the issue of urban gang violence as it is framed today. A few years ago, Frederick Goodwin, then director of the government's top mental health agency, was orchestrating the so-called Federal Violence Initiative to identify inner-city kids at biological risk for criminal violence, with the goal of intervening with drug treatments for what are presumed to be nervous-system aberrations. Goodwin got himself fired for comparing aggressive young males with primates in the jungle, and the violence initiative died in the resulting furor. But even to be proposing such a biomedical approach to criminal justice shows how far the intellectual pendulum has swung toward biology.

The eugenics movement of the 1930s was fueled at least in part by a desire to get rid of habitual criminals, and many attempts have been made over the years to identify genetic roots for aggression, violence, and criminality. A

As with many psychopathologies, criminal aggression is difficult to define precisely for research. Indeed, crime and alcohol abuse are so entangled that it's often difficult to know whether genetic markers are associated with drinking, criminality—or something else entirely, like a personality trait. A 1993 National Research Council study, for example, reported strong evidence of genetic influence on antisocial personality disorder, but it also noted that many genes are probably involved. Getting from those unknown genes to an actual act of vandalism or assault—or a life of barbaric violence—requires at this point a monstrous leap of faith.

Yet it's a leap that many are willing to make. When geneticist Xandra Breakefield reported a possible genetic link to violent crime a few years ago, she immediately started receiving phone inquiries from attorneys representing clients in prison; they were hoping that such genetic findings might absolve their clients of culpability for their acts.

Mutations and emotions. Just two decades ago, the National Institute of Mental Health was funding studies of economic recession, unemployment, and urban ills as possible contributors to serious emotional disturbance. A whole branch of psychiatry known as "social psychiatry" was dedicated to helping the mentally ill by rooting out such pathogens as poverty and racism. There is no

tating emotional and mental disorder was caused by cold and distant mothering, itself the result of the mother's unconscious wish that her child had never been born. A nationwide lobbying effort was launched to combat such unfounded mother blaming, and 20 years later that artifact of the Freudian era is entirely discredited. It's widely accepted today that psychotic disorders are brain disorders, probably with genetic roots.

But this neurogenetic victory may be double edged. For example, family and consumer groups have argued convincingly that schizophrenia is a brain disease like epilepsy, one piece of evidence being that it is treatable with powerful antipsychotic drugs. Managed-care companies, however, have seized upon the disease model, and now will rarely authorize anything but drug treatment; it's efficient, and justified by the arguments of biological psychiatry. The American Psychiatric Association just this month issued elaborate guidelines for treating schizophrenia, including not only drugs but an array of psychosocial services—services the insurance industry is highly unlikely to pay for.

The search for genes for severe mental disorders has been inconclusive. Years of studies of families, adoptees, and twins separated at birth suggest that both schizophrenia and manic-depressive illness run in families. But if that family pattern is the result of genes, it's

VIOLENCE. How can an act of vandalism or a bank robbery be rooted in DNA? There are a lot of choices involved in living a life of crime.

1965 study, for instance, found that imprisoned criminals were more likely than other people to have an extra Y chromosome (and therefore more male genes). The evidence linking this chromosomal aberration to crime was skimpy and tenuous, but politics often runs ahead of the evidence: Soon after, a Boston hospital actually started screening babies for the defect, the idea being to intervene early with counseling should personality problems become apparent. The screening was halted when further study showed that XYY men, while slightly less intelligent, were not unusually aggressive.

longer much evidence of these sensibilities at work today. NIMH now focuses its studies almost exclusively on brain research and on the genetic underpinnings of emotional illnesses.

The decision to reorder the federal research portfolio was both scientific and political. Major advances in neuroscience methods opened up research that wasn't possible a generation ago, and that research has paid off in drugs that very effectively treat some disorders. But there was also a concerted political campaign to reinterpret mental illness. A generation ago, the leading theory about schizophrenia was that this devas-

clearly very complicated, because most of the siblings of schizophrenics (including half of identical twins, who have the same genes) don't develop the disorder. Behavioral geneticists suspect that several genes may underlie the illness, and that some environmental stress—perhaps a virus or birth complications—also might be required to trigger the disorder.

On several occasions in the past, researchers have reported "linkages" between serious mental illness and a particular stretch of DNA. A well-known study of the Amish, for example, claimed a link between manic-depression and an aberration on chromosome 11. But none of these findings has held up when other researchers attempted to replicate them.

Even if one accepts that there are genetic roots for serious delusional illnesses, critics are concerned about the biologizing of the rest of psychiatric illness. Therapists report that patients come in asking for drugs, claiming to be victims of unfortunate biology. In one case, a patient claimed he could "feel his neurons misfiring"; it's an impossibility, but the anecdote speaks to the thorough saturation of the culture with biology.

Some psychiatrists are pulling back from the strict biological model of mental illness. Psychiatrist Keith Russell Ablow has reintroduced the idea of "character" into his practice, telling depressed patients that they have the responsibility and capacity to pull themselves out of their illness. Weakness of character, as Ablow sees it, allows mental illness to grow. Such sentiment is highly controversial within psychiatry, where to suggest that patients might be responsible for some of their own suffering is taboo.

Besotted genes. The best that can be said about research on the genetics of alcoholism is that it's inconclusive, but that hasn't stopped people from using genetic arguments for political purposes. The disease model for alcoholism is practically a secular religion in this country, embraced by psychiatry, most treatment clinics, and (perhaps most important) by Alcoholics Anonymous. What this means is that those seeking help for excessive drinking are told they have a disease (though the exact nature of the disease is unknown), that it's probably a genetic condition, and that the only treatment is abstinence.

But the evidence is not strong enough to support these claims. There are several theories of how genes might lead to excessive drinking. A genetic insensitivity to alcohol, for example, might cause certain people to drink more; or alcoholics might metabolize alcohol differently; or they may have inherited a certain personality type that's prone to risk-taking or stimulus-seeking. While studies of family pedigrees and adoptees have on occasion indicated a familial pattern for a particular form of alcoholism (early-onset disorder in men, for example), just as often they reveal no pattern. This shouldn't be all that surprising, given the difficulty of defining alcoholism. Some researchers identify alcoholics by their drunk-driving record, while others focus on withdrawal symptoms or daily consumption. This is what geneticists call a "dirty phenotype"; people drink too much in so many different ways that the trait itself is hard to define, so family patterns are all over the place, and often contradictory.

Given these methodological problems, researchers have been trying to locate an actual gene (or genes) that might be involved in alcoholism. A 1990 study reported that a severe form of the disorder (most of the subjects in the study had cirrhosis of the liver) was linked to a gene that codes for a chemical receptor for the neurotransmitter dopamine. The researchers even developed and patented a test for the genetic mutation, but subsequent attempts to confirm the dopamine connection have failed.

The issues of choice and responsibility come up again and again in discussions of alcoholism and other addictive disorders. Even if scientists were to identify a gene (or genes) that create a susceptibility to alcoholism, it's hard to know what this genetic "loading" would mean. It certainly wouldn't lead to alcoholism in a culture that didn't condone drinking—among the Amish, for example—so it's not deterministic in a strict sense. Even in a culture where drinking is common, there are clearly a lot of complicated choices involved in living an alcoholic life; it's difficult to make the leap from DNA to those choices. While few would want to return to the time when heavy drinking was condemned as strictly a moral failing or character flaw, many are concerned that the widely accepted disease model of alcoholism actually provides people with an excuse for their destructive behavior. As psychologist Stanton Peele argues: "Indoctrinating young people with the view that they are likely to become alcoholics may take them there more quickly than any inherited reaction to alcohol would have."

Synapses of desire. It would be a mistake to focus only on biological explanations of psychopathology; the cultural shift is much broader than that. A generation ago, the gay community was at war with organized psychiatry, arguing (successfully) that sexual orientation was a lifestyle choice and ought to be deleted from the manual of disorders. Recently the same community was celebrating new evidence that homosexuality is a biological (and perhaps genetic) trait, not a choice at all.

Three lines of evidence support the idea of a genetic basis for homosexuality, none of them conclusive. A study of twins and adopted siblings found that about half of identical twins of homosexual men were themselves gay, compared with 22 percent of fraternal twins and 11 percent of adoptees; a similar pattern was found among women. While such a pattern is consistent with some kind of genetic loading for sexual orientation, critics contend it also could be explained by the very similar experiences many twins share. And, of course, half the identical twins did not become gay—which by definition means something other than genes must be involved.

A well-publicized 1991 study reported a distinctive anatomical feature in gay men. Simon LeVay autopsied the brains of homosexual men and heterosexual men and women and found that a certain nucleus in the hypothalamus was more than twice as large in heterosexual men as in gay men or heterosexual women. Although LeVay couldn't explain how this neurological difference might translate into homosexuality, he speculates that the nucleus is somehow

MENTAL ILLNESS. Are psychiatric disorders diseases? The answer influences everything from insurance coverage to new research funding.

related to sexual orientation. The hypothalamus is known to be involved in sexual response.

The only study so far to report an actual genetic connection to homosexuality is a 1993 study by Dean Hamer, a National Institutes of Health biologist who identified a genetic marker on the X chromosome in 75 percent of gay brothers. The functional significance of this piece of DNA is unknown, and subsequent research has not succeeded in duplicating Hamer's results.

Homosexuality represents a bit of a paradox when it comes to the intertwined issues of choice and determinism. When Hamer reported his genetic findings, many in the gay community celebrated, believing that society would be more tolerant of behavior rooted in biology and DNA rather than choice. LeVay, himself openly gay, says he undertook his research with the explicit agenda of furthering the gay cause. And Hamer testified as an expert witness in an important gay-rights case in Colorado where, in a strange twist, liberals found themselves arguing the deterministic position, while conservatives insisted that homosexuality is a choice. The argument of gay-rights advocates was that biological status conveyed legal status—and protection under the law.

History's warning. But history suggests otherwise, according to biologist and historian Garland Allen. During the eugenics movement of the 1920s and 1930s, both in the United States and Europe, society became less, not more, tolerant of human variation and misfortune. Based on racial theories that held Eastern Europeans to be genetically inferior to Anglo-Saxon stock, Congress passed (and Calvin Coolidge signed) a 1924 law to restrict immigration, and by 1940 more than 30 states had laws permitting forced sterilization of people suffering from such conditions as "feeblemindedness," pauperism, and mental illness. The ultimate outcome of the eugenics craze in Europe is well known; homosexuals were not given extra sympathy or protection in the Third Reich's passion to purify genetic stock.

Allen is concerned about the possibility of a "new eugenics" movement, though he notes that it wouldn't be called that or take the same form. It would more likely take the form of rationing health care for the unfortunate. The economic and social conditions today resemble conditions that provided fertile ground for eugenics between the wars, he argues; moreover, in Allen's view, California's Proposition 187 recalls the keen competition for limited resources (and the resulting animosity toward immigrants) of the '20s. Further, Allen is quick to remind us that eugenics was not a marginal, bigoted movement in either Europe or the United States; it was a Progressive program, designed to harness science in the service of reducing suffering and misfortune and to help make society more efficient.

These concerns are probably justified, but there are also some signs that we may be on the crest of another important cultural shift. More and more experts, including dedicated biologists, sense that the power of genetics has been oversold and that a correction is needed. What's more, there's a glimmer of evidence that the typical American may not be buying it entirely. According to a recent US. News/Bozell poll, less than 1 American in 5 believes that genes play a major role in controlling behavior; three quarters cite environment and society as the more powerful shapers of our lives. Whether the behavior under question is a disorder like addiction, mental illness, or violence, or a trait like homosexuality, most believe that heredity plays some role, but not a primary one. Indeed, 40 percent think genes play no role whatsoever in homosexuality, and a similar percentage think heredity is irrelevant to drug addiction and criminality. Across the board, most believe that people's lives are shaped by the choices they make.

These numbers can be interpreted in different ways. It may be that neurogenetic determinism has become the "religion of the intellectual class," as one critic argues, but that it never really caught the imagination of the typical American. Or we may be witnessing a kind of cultural self-correction, in which after a period of infatuation with neuroscience and genetics the public is becoming disenchanted, or perhaps even anxious about the kinds of social control that critics describe.

Whatever's going on, it's clear that this new mistrust of genetic power is consonant with what science is now beginning to show. Indeed, the very expression "gene for" is misleading, according to philosopher Philip Kitcher, author of *The Lives to Come*. Kitcher critiques what he calls "gene talk," a simplistic shorthand for talking about genetic advances that has led to the widespread misunderstanding of DNA's real powers. He suggests that public discourse may need to include more scientific jargon—not a lot, but some—so as not to oversimplify the complexity of the gene-environment interaction. For example, when geneticists say they've found a gene for a particular trait, what they mean is that people carrying a certain "allele"—a variation in a stretch of DNA that normally codes for a certain protein—will develop the given trait in a standard environment. The last few words—"in a standard environment"—are very important, because what scientists are *not saying* is that a given allele will necessarily lead to that trait in every environment. Indeed, there is mounting evidence that a particular allele will not

ALCOHOLISM. Heredity might be involved in some kinds of alcoholism. But no gene can make you buy a bottle of Scotch, pour a glass, and toss it down.

U.S. News/Bozell poll of 1,000 adults conducted by KRC Research Feb. 6–9, 1997. Margin of error: plus or minus 3.1 percent.

2. ❖ DETERMINANTS OF BEHAVIOR: MOTIVATION, ENVIRONMENT, AND PHYSIOLOGY

produce the same result if the environment changes significantly; that is to say, the environment has a strong influence on whether and how a gene gets "expressed."

It's hard to emphasize too much what a radical rethinking of the nature-nurture debate this represents. When most people think about heredity, they still think in terms of classical Mendelian genetics: one gene, one trait. But for most complex human behaviors, this is far from the reality that recent research is revealing. A more accurate view very likely involves many different genes, some of which control other genes, and many of which are controlled by signals from the environment. To complicate matters further, the environment is very complicated in itself, ranging from the things we typically lump under nurture (parenting, family dynamics, schooling, safe housing) to biological encounters like viruses and birth complications, even biochemical events within cells.

The relative contributions of genes and the environment are not additive, as in such-and-such a percentage of nature, such-and-such a percentage of experience; that's the old view, no longer credited. Nor is it true that full genetic expression happens once, around birth, after which we take our genetic legacy into the world to see how far it gets us. Genes produce proteins throughout the lifespan, in many different environ-loading that gives some people a susceptibility—for schizophrenia, for instance, or for aggression. But the development of the behavior or pathology requires more, what National Institute of Mental Health Director Stephen Hyman calls an environmental "second hit." This second hit operates, counterintuitively, through the genes themselves to "sculpt" the brain. So with depression, for example, it appears as though a bad experience in the world—for example, a devastating loss—can actually create chemical changes in the body that affect certain genes, which in turn affect certain brain proteins that make a person more susceptible to depression in the future. Nature or nurture? Similarly, Hyman's own work has shown that exposure to addictive substances can lead to biochemical changes at the genetic and molecular levels that commandeer brain circuits involving volition—and thus undermine the very motivation needed to take charge of one's destructive behavior. So the choice to experiment with drugs or alcohol may, in certain people, create the biological substrate of the addictive disorder. The distinction between biology and experience begins to lose its edge.

Nurturing potentials. Just as bad experiences can turn on certain vulnerability genes, rich and challenging experiences have the power to enhance life, again acting through the genes. chologist Urie Bronfenbrenner. Everything from lively conversation to games to the reading of stories can potentially get a gene to turn on and create a protein that may become a neuronal receptor or messenger chemical involved in thinking or mood. "No genetic potential can become reality," says Bronfenbrenner, "unless the relationship between the organism and its environment is such that it is *permitted* to be expressed." Unfortunately, as he details in his new book, *The State of Americans,* the circumstances in which many American children are living are becoming more impoverished year by year.

If there's a refrain among geneticists working today, it's this: The harder we work to demonstrate the power of heredity, the harder it is to escape the potency of experience. It's a bit paradoxical, because in a sense we end up once again with the old pre-1950s paradigm, but arrived at with infinitely more-sophisticated tools: Yes, the way to intervene in human lives and improve them, to ameliorate mental illness, addictions, and criminal behavior, is to enrich impoverished environments, to improve conditions in the family and society. What's changed is that the argument is coming not from left-leaning sociologists, but from those most intimate with the workings of the human genome. The goal of psychosocial interventions is optimal gene expression.

HOMOSEXUALITY. Gay-rights advocates once argued that homosexuality was a matter of lifestyle choice. Now they stress genes and destiny.

ments, or they don't produce those proteins, depending on how rich or harsh or impoverished those environments are. The interaction is so thoroughly dynamic and enduring that, as psychologist William Greenough says, "To ask what's more important, nature or nurture, is like asking what's more important to a rectangle, its length or its width."

The emerging view of nature-nurture is that many complicated behaviors probably have some measure of genetic Greenough has shown in rat studies that by providing cages full of toys and complex structures that are continually rearranged—"the animal equivalent of Head Start"—he can increase the number of synapses in the rats brains by 25 percent and blood flow by 85 percent. Talent and intelligence appear extraordinarily malleable.

Child-development experts refer to the life circumstances that enhance (or undermine) gene expression as "proximal processes" a term coined by psy- So assume for a minute that there is a cluster of genes somehow associated with youthful violence. The kid who carries those genes might inhabit a world of loving parents, regular nutritious meals, lots of books, safe schools. Or his world might be a world of peeling paint and gunshots around the corner. In which environment would those genes be likely to manufacture the biochemical underpinnings of criminality? Or for that matter, the proteins and synapses of happiness?

Nature's Clones

Can genes explain our passions and prejudices, the mates we choose, that mystery we call the self? New research on twins upsets some of our most cherished notions about how we become who we are—and gives nature and nurture a whole new meaning. By JILL NEIMARK

Last April I went down to West 27th Street in Manhattan to sit in the audience of the *Maury Povich* show, and meet four sets of identical twins who had been separated at birth and adopted into different families. I wanted to see if the same soul stared out of those matched pairs of eyes, to contemplate the near miracle of DNA—double helix twisting around itself like twin umbilical cords—ticking out a perfect code for two copies of a human. One pair, a Polish nun and a Michigan housewife, had been filmed at the airport by CNN the week before, reunited for the first time in 51 years and weeping in each other's arms, marveling at their instinctive rapport. Yet how alike were they really, if one spent her days on rescue missions to places like Rwanda, while the other cleaned houses to supplement her husband's income?

Twins are nature's handmade clones, doppelgangers moving in synchrony through circumstances that are often eerily similar, as if they were unwitting dancers choreographed by genes or fate or God, thinking each other's thoughts, wearing each other's clothes, exhibiting the same quirks and odd habits. They leave us to wonder about our own uniqueness and loneliness, and whether it's possible to inhabit another person's being. Twins provoke questions about the moment our passions first ignite—for they have been seen on sonogram in the womb, kissing, punching, stroking each other. They are living fault lines in the ever shifting geography of the nature/nurture debate, and their peculiar puzzle ultimately impacts politics, crime and its punishment, education, and social policy. It isn't such a short leap from studies of behavioral genetics to books like the infamous *The Bell Curve* (by Richard Herrnstein and Charles Murray) and a kind of sotto-voce eugenics. And so everything from homosexuality to IQ, religious affiliation, alcoholism, temperament, mania, depression, height, weight, mortality, and schizophrenia has been studied in identical and fraternal twins and their relatives.

Yet the answers—which these days seem to confirm biology's power—raise unsettling questions. Twin research is flawed, provocative, and fascinating, and it topples some of our most cherished notions—the legacies of Freud and Skinner included—such as our beliefs that parenting style makes an irrevocable difference, that we can mold our children, that we are free agents piecing together our destinies.

Today, we've gone twin-mad. Ninety thousand people gather yearly at the International Twins Day Festival in Twinsburg, Ohio. We're facing a near epidemic of twins. One in 50 babies born this year will have a fraternal or identical double; the number of such births rose 33 percent in 1994 alone, peaking at over 97,000—largely due to women delaying childbirth (which skewers the odds in favor of twins) and to the fertility industry, which relies on drugs that superovulate would-be mothers. Recently, a stunning scientific feat enabled an ordinary sheep to give up a few cells and produce a delayed identical twin—a clone named Dolly, who was born with her donor's 6-year-old nucleus in every cell of her body. The international furor this Scottish lamb engendered has at its heart some of the same wonder and fear that every twin birth evokes. Twins are a break, a rift in the customary order, and they call into question our own sense of self. Just how special and unique are we?

The history of twins is rich with stories that seem to reveal them as two halves of the same self—twins adopted into different families falling down stairs at the same age, marrying and miscarrying in the same year, identical twins inventing secret languages, "telepathic" twins seemingly connected across thousands of miles, "evil" twins committing arson or murder together, conjoined twins sharing a single body, so that when one coughs the other reflexively raises a hand to cover the first one's mouth. And yet the lives of twins are full of just as many instances of discordance, differences, disaffection. Consider the 22-year-old Korean twins, Sunny and Jeen Young Han of San Diego County; Jeen hired two teenagers to murder her sister, hoping to assume her identity.

So what is truly *other*, what is *self*? As the living embodiment of that question, twins are not just the mirrors of each other, they are a mirror for us all.

MY TWIN MARRIAGE

A few years ago, I was playing the messages back on my answering machine just as my husband, Jeff, was coming into the apartment. He heard a familiar voice and ran for the answering machine.

"It's Phil!" he yelled, shrugging out of his coat. "Pick up the phone. Phil's calling."

Only it wasn't Phil. It was Phil's identical twin brother, Jeff.

"Oh, it's me," my husband said sheepishly. Sheepish in the sense of Dolly, the cloned sheep.

When I was first dating Jeff, the prospect of marrying an identical twin seemed magical. Jeff spoke of his brother as if he were talking about himself, almost as if he could bi-locate and live two contrasting yet mutually enriching lives. Jeff worked at a literary agency in Manhattan and loved boy fiction, thrillers, and horror novels, while Phil was overtly spiritual, editing a journal dedicated to the study of myth and tradition. When they were together they seemed to merge into one complex yet cohesive personality. They talked like hyper-bright little boys, each of them bringing equal heat and erudition to Stephen King and esoteric teachings, baseball, and the possibility of spiritual transformation. They argued—and still argue—like Trotsky and Lenin, desperate to define themselves as individuals, yet they define themselves against each other. Jeff and Phil love their wives and children, but they obey the orders they get from the mothership of their identical DNA.

My husband and his twin brother live by E. M. Forster's admonition, "Only connect." The pair e-mail each other at their respective offices two, four, even more times a day. A few weeks ago, Phil wrote Jeff that he was trying to decide his favorite 10 films of all time. He listed *Journey to the Center of the Earth*, *Star Wars*, seven other boy classics, and asked for Jeff's help thinking up a 10th.

"Phil and I decided that *Jurassic Park* is our favorite movie of all time," announced Jeff the other evening at dinner. In the course of dozens of soothing little dispatches Phil's movie list and Jeff's movie list had become one.

My marriage to Jeff has locked me into a triangle. The bond between these twins amazes and amuses me, yet it fills me with an unappeasable longing. After all, unlike Phil's wife, Carol, who is an only child, I was conditioned even before I was born to be with a twin. I am a fraternal twin, a girl born 10 minutes after a boy.

"What do you get out of being a twin?" I asked my husband the first day we had lunch. "What insight does it give you that's harder for single people to understand?"

"Trust," said my husband. "That pure physical trust that comes when you know someone loves and accepts you completely because they are just like you are."

I knew the primordial closeness he was talking about. As tiny premature babies, my brother Steve and I used to cuddle in the same crib holding hands. My earliest memory is of being lifted up high and feeling incredible joy as I gazed into my mother's vast, radiant face. I was put back down on a big bed. I remember sensing another baby lying next to me, my twin. His presence felt deeply familiar, and I know I had sensed him before we were born. For me, in the beginning there was the light but there was also the son. In addition to the vertical relationship I had with Mommy, I also had a lateral relationship, a constant pre-verbal reassurance that I had a peer. I was in it with somebody else. This feeling of extending in two directions, horizontal and vertical, made up the cross of my emotional life.

Separated at Birth But Joined at the Hip

The woman seated alone onstage at the opening of the *Maury Povich* show was already famous in the twin literature: Barbara Herbert, a plump 58-year-old with a broad, pretty face and short, silver hair, found her lost twin, Daphne Goodship, 18 years ago. Both had been adopted as babies into separate British families after their Finnish single mother killed herself.

The concordances in their lives send a shiver up the spine: both women grew up in towns outside of London, left school at 14, fell down stairs at 15 and weakened their ankles, went to work in local government, met their future husbands at age 16 at the Town Hall dance, miscarried in the same month, then gave birth to two boys and a girl. Both tinted their hair auburn when young, were squeamish about blood and heights, and drank their coffee cold. When they met, both were wearing cream-colored dresses and brown velvet jackets. Both had the same crooked little fingers, a habit of pushing up their nose with the palm of their hand—which both had nicknamed "squidging"—and a way of bursting into laughter that soon had people referring to them as the Giggle Twins. The two have been studied for years now at the University of Minnesota's Center for Twin and Adoption Research, founded by Thomas J. Bouchard, Ph.D. It is the largest, ongoing study of separated twins in the world, with nearly 100 pairs registered, and they are poked, probed, and prodded by psychologists, psychiatrists, cardiologists, dentists, ophthalmologists, pathologists, and geneticists, testing everything from blood pressure to dental caries.

At the center, it was discovered that the two women had the same heart murmurs, thyroid problems, and allergies, as well as IQ's a point apart. The two showed remarkably similar personalities on psychological tests. So do the other sets of twins in the study—in fact, the genetic influence is pervasive across most domains tested. Another set of twins had been reunited in a hotel room when they were young adults, and as they unpacked found that they used the same brand of shaving lotion (Canoe), hair tonic (Vitalis), and toothpaste (Vademecum). They both smoked Lucky Strikes, and after they met they returned to their separate cities and mailed each other identical birthday presents. Other pairs have discovered they like to read magazines from back to front, store rubber bands on their wrists, or enter the ocean backwards and only up to their knees. Candid photos of every pair of twins in the study show virtually all the identicals posed the same way; while fraternal twins positioned hands and arms differently.

Bouchard—a big, balding, dynamic Midwesterner who can't help but convey his irrepressible passion about this research—recalls the time he reunited a pair of twins in their mid-30s at the Minneapolis airport. "I was following them down the ramp to baggage claim and they started talking to each other. One would stop and a nanosecond later the other would start, and when she stopped a nanosecond later the other would start. They never once interrupted each other. I said to myself, 'This is incredible, I can't carry on a conversation like that with my wife and we've been married for 36 years. No psychologist would believe this is happening.' When we finally got to baggage claim they turned around and said, 'It's like we've known each other all our lives.'"

Just Puppets Dancing To Music of the Genes?

I asked Bouchard if the results of his research puncture our myth that we consciously shape who we are.

"You're not a believer in free will, are you?" he laughed, a little too heartily. "What's free will, some magical process in the brain?"

Yet I am a believer (a mystical bent and fierce independence actually run in my family, as if my genes have remote controlled a beguiling but misbegotten sense of freedom and transcendence). I was mesmerized and disturbed by the specificity of the twins' concordances. David Teplica, M.D., a Chicago plastic surgeon who for the last 10 years has been photographing more than 100 pairs of twins, has found the same number of crow's feet at the corners of twins' eyes, the same skin cancer developing behind twins' ears in the same year. Says Teplica, "It's almost beyond comprehension that one egg and one sperm could predict that."

I could imagine, I told Bouchard, that since genes regulate hormones and neurochemicals, and thus impact sexual attraction and behavior, DNA might influence the shaving lotion twins liked or the hue they tinted their hair. But the same esoteric brand of toothpaste? Walking into the sea backwards? This implies an influence so far-reaching it's unnerving.

"Nobody has the vaguest idea how that happens," he admitted, unfazed. "We're studying a set of triplets now, two identical females and a brother, and all three have Tourette's syndrome. How can the genes get so specific? I was talking yesterday in Houston to a bunch of neuroscientists and I said, 'This is the kind of thing you guys have to figure out.' There is tons of stuff to work on here, it's all open territory."

He paused to marvel over the tremendous shift in our understanding of human behavior. "When we began studying twins at the university in 1979, there was great debate on the power of genetics. I remember arguing in one graduate school class that the major psychoses were largely genetic in origin. Everyone in the classroom just clobbered me. It was the era of the domination of behaviorism, and although there's nothing wrong with Skinner's work, it had been generalized to explain everything under the sun. Nothing explains everything. Even genetics influences us, on the average, about 50 percent."

Yet that 50 percent seems omnipresent. It impacts everything from extroversion to IQ to religious and so-

At the age of 3, I remember standing in the grass on a hot, bright day in El Paso, Texas, aware as never before that my brother was different from me, not just because he was smaller then and a boy, but because he was different inside. I loved him and felt protective towards him, as I would throughout my childhood, but I also felt the first stirrings of rebellion, of wanting to go vertical in my identity, to make it clear to my parents and everybody else that I was not the same as Steve.

I began to relish the idea of not being completely knowable. I developed a serious underground life. At 8, I twinned myself with an invisible black panther I called Striker. At 10, I became a spy. I made cryptic notes in a notebook. I had sinister passport photos taken. I had a plastic revolver I carried in a plastic attaché case. You may call me one of the twins, I thought to myself, but I come from a foreign country that has malevolent designs on your own.

No one ever calls me and Steve "the twins" anymore, except as an artifact of childhood. I tend to think of my birth twin, who is now a Porsche mechanic and a big, outdoorsy guy who lives with his wife and two kids in a small town outside of Boston, as the brother who was with me when I was born, who shared space with me in the womb. I feel close to him not because we are exactly the same, but because I still have bedrock sensation and empathy for his life.

Jeff claimed that his knowledge of trust from being an identical let him know that I was the person he wanted to marry. He felt twinship towards me right from the start he said, and I wasn't surprised. Accustomed to being twins, my husband and I fell right into acting like twins. We co-authored a book and both edit at *Publisher's Weekly*, yet we sometimes argue over who gets to use the little study in our apartment as if our identities were at stake. Lately, I've noticed that when I feel dominated by Jeff I tend to yearn for a "real" twin, a twin who mirrors me so lovingly and acceptingly that I can let go and be myself without fear or explanation. A single person might escape by daydreaming about a perfect lover, but my fantasies of romantic enmeshment have always incorporated the twin.

Years ago in Manhattan I was invited to attend a ceremony for the Santeria religion's god of thunder, Shango, because Shango loves twins. On the way, a revered old Cuban santera told me that twins were sacred in Santeria and in the African mother religion of Yoruba because they reflect the intersection of spirit and matter. Girl and boy twins were especially fascinating, according to the santera. Most girls were killed by the boy energy, they believed. A girl had to be very strong to survive.

The moment I heard that I realized that being a twin has heightened the drama of my life. Human beings are born double, pulled between the desire to merge with another yet emerge as an authentic self. Twins fascinate, I believe, because we are an externalized representation of an internal struggle everybody lives with all their lives. We cast the illusion of solving the unsolvable, though we're no closer than anyone else.—*Tracy Cochran*

cial attitudes—and drops only in the influence on homosexuality and death. Though some researchers have criticized Minnesota's twin sample for being too small and perhaps self-selected (how many separated twins out there don't participate or don't even know they're twins?), it generally confirms the results of larger studies

2. ❖ DETERMINANTS OF BEHAVIOR: MOTIVATION, ENVIRONMENT, AND PHYSIOLOGY

BEYOND NATURE AND NURTURE: TWINS AND QUANTUM PHYSICS

I've been interested in identical twins ever since I was old enough to realize I am one. When my brother and I were young we were close but nonetheless epitomized the struggle of twins to achieve individual identities. Now in our 50s, we have both noticed a real convergence of our intellectual, spiritual and philosophical views.

Are the strikingly similar thoughts and behaviors of twins, even those reared apart, due to nature or nurture—or to a third factor? What if what I call the "nonlocal" nature of the mind is involved?

Nonlocal mind is a term I introduced in 1989 to account for some of the ways consciousness manifests, ways suggesting that it is not completely confined or localized to specific points in space or time. Nobel physicist Erwin Schrödinger believed that mind by its very nature is singular and one, that consciousness is not confined to separate, individual brains, that it is ultimately a unified field. David Chalmers, a mathematician and cognitive scientist from the University of California at Santa Cruz, has suggested that consciousness is fundamental in the universe, perhaps on a par with matter and energy, and that it is not derived from, nor reducible to, anything else. Nobel physicist Brian Josephson, of Cambridge University's Cavendish Laboratory, has proposed that nonlocal events at the subatomic level for example, the fact that there are correlations between the spin of subatomic particles, even after they are separated—can be amplified and may emerge in our everyday experience.

In other words, the macrocosm reflects the microcosm. Systems theorist Erwin Laszio has suggested that nonlocal mind may mediate events such as intercessory prayer, telepathy, precognition, and clairvoyance.

If consciousness is unbounded and unitary, strikingly similar thoughts and behaviors of identical twins, even separated twins, would not be surprising. Genes do determine how individual brains function, how we each process information, and nonlocal mind could be easier to access if two brains were almost identical in their functioning. Indeed, some people see analogies between the behavior of separated, identical twins and separated, identical subatomic particles.

According to the late Irish physicist John S. Bell, if two subatomic particles once in contact are separated to some arbitrary distance, a change in one is correlated with a change in the other—instantly and to the same degree. There is no travel time for any known form of energy to flow between them. Yet experiments have shown these changes do occur, instantaneously. Neither can these nonlocal effects be blocked or shielded—one of the hallmarks of nonlocality. Perhaps distant twins are mysteriously linked, like distant particles—or, to quote Ecclesiastes, "All things go in pairs, one the counterpart of the other."
—*Larry Dossey, M.D.*

of twins reared together—studies that have taken place around the world.

Twin studies allow us to double blind our nature/nurture research in a unique way. Identical twins share 100 percent of their genes, while fraternals share 50 percent. But usually they grow up together, sharing a similar environment in the womb and the world. When separated, they give us a clue about the strength of genetic influence in the face of sometimes radically different environments. Soon Bouchard and his colleagues will study siblings in families that have adopted a twin, thus testing environmental influences when no genes are shared. Like a prism yielding different bands of light, twin studies are rich and multifaceted. Here are some of the major findings on nature and nurture thus far:

• **Political and social attitudes**, ranging from divorce to the death penalty, were found to have a strong genetic influence in one Australian study. A Swedish study found genes significantly influenced two of the so-called "big five" personality traits—"openness to experience" and "conscientiousness"—while environment had little impact. In contrast, environment influenced "agreeableness" more than genes did. (The two other traits are "neuroticism" and "extroversion.") Another study, at the University of Texas at Austin, found that personality in identicals correlated 50 percent, in fraternals about 25 percent.

• **Body fat is under genetic influence.** Identical twins reared together will have the same amount of body fat 75 percent of the time; for those reared apart it's 61 percent, showing a heavy genetic and mild environmental influence, according to a 1991 study.

• **Both optimism and pessimism** are heavily influenced by genes, but shared environment influences only optimism, not pessimism, according to a study of 522 pairs of middle-aged identical and fraternal twins. Thus family life and genes can be equal contributors to an optimistic outlook, which influences both mental and physical health. But pessimism seems largely controlled by genes.

• **Religiosity is influenced by genes.** Identical and fraternal twins, raised together and apart, demonstrate that 50 percent of religiosity (demonstrated by religious conviction and church attendance) can be attributed to genes.

• **Sexual orientation** is under genetic influence, though not solely, according to studies by Michael Bailey, Ph.D., associate professor of psychology at Northwestern University. In one study he found that if one identical twin is gay, the other is also gay 50 percent of the time. However, when Bailey analyzed a sample of 5,000 twins from the Australian twin registry, the genetic impact was less. In identical male twins, if one was gay the likelihood of his twin being gay was 20 percent; in fraternal twins the likelihood was almost zero. In women, there was little evidence of heritability for homosexuality.

• **When substance abuse** was studied in 295 identical and fraternal twin pairs, year of birth was the most powerful predictor of drug use. Younger twins were most likely to have abused drugs, reflecting widespread drug use in the culture at large. Alcoholism, however, has a significant genetic component, according to Andrew Heath, Ph.D., at the Virginia Institute for Psychiatric and

Behavioral Genetics at Virginia Commonwealth University School of Medicine.

- **Attention deficit disorder** may be influenced by genes 70 percent of the time, according to Lindon Eaves, M.D., director of the Virginia Institute for Psychiatric and Behavioral Genetics. Eaves and colleagues studied 1,400 families of twins and found genetic influence on "all the juvenile behavior disorders," usually in the range of 30 to 50 percent.
- **Twins tend to start dating**, to marry, and to start having children at about the same time. David Lykken, Ph.D., and Matthew McGue, Ph.D., at the University of Minnesota, found that if an identical twin had divorced, there was a 45 percent chance the other had also. For fraternals, the chance was 30 percent. The researchers think this is due to inherited personality traits.
- **Schizophrenia** occurs more often in identical twins, and if one twin suffers from the disorder, the children of the healthy identical sibling are also at greater risk, according to psychiatrist Irving Gottesman, M.D., of the University of Virginia. The risk is about twice as high for the children of a twin whose identical counterpart is ill, as it is for the children of a twin whose fraternal counterpart is ill.

Hidden Differences Between Twins

A few fascinating kinks in the biology of twin research have recently turned up, weaving an even more complex pattern for us to study and learn from. It turns out that not all identical twins are truly identical, or share all their genetic traits. In one tragic instance, one twin was healthy and a gymnast, while the other suffered from severe muscular dystrophy, a genetic disorder, and was dead by age 16. Yet the twins were identical.

One way twins can differ is in the sex chromosomes that turn them into a male or female, and which contain other genes as well, such as those that code for muscular dystrophy or color blindness. All girls inherit two X chromosomes, one from each parent, while boys inherit an X and a Y. Girls automatically shut off one X in every cell—sometimes some of the mother's and some of the father's, in other cases all the mother's or all the father's. A girl may not shut off her extra set of X chromosomes in the same pattern as her identical twin does.

Identical twins may not be exposed to the same world in the womb, either. It depends on the time their mother's fertilized egg splits—and that timing may explain why some identical twins seem more eerily alike than others. At Lutheran University, researchers have looked at the placentas of some 10,000 twin births. They've found that an egg that separates in the first four days of pregnancy develops not only into separate twins, but results in separate placentas, chorionic casings, and amniotic sacs. These twins are like two singletons in the womb and have the best chance of survival. Twins who separate between the fifth and eighth days share a single placenta and chorion, but still have the benefit of two amniotic sacs. Here, one twin can have a distinct advantage over the other. The umbilical cord may be positioned centrally on one sac, while the other is on the margin, receiving fewer nutrients. Studies of these twins show that with a nurturing environment, the weaker twin will catch up in the first few years of life. However, it's possible that viruses may penetrate separate sacs at

> Some twins are bonded by a lifelong passion for each other that the rest of us experience only in the almost unbearably intense first flush of romantic love. England's notorious Gibbons twins were one such pair.

different rates or in different ways—perhaps increasing the risk for schizophrenia or other illnesses later in life.

Twins who split between the eighth and 12th days share their amniotic sac, and often their cords get entangled. One cord may be squeezed until no blood flows through it, and that twin dies. Finally, twins who split after the 12th day become conjoined—and even though they share organs and limbs, anecdotal evidence suggests that they often have distinctly different temperaments, habits, and food cravings.

In one hotly debated hypothesis, pediatrician and geneticist Judith Hall, of the University of British Columbia in Vancouver, speculates that twinning occurs because of genetic differences within in an embryo. Perhaps mutations occur at a very early stage in some cells, which then are sensed as different, and expelled from the embryo. Those cells may survive and grow into a twin. Hall suggests this could account for the higher incidence of birth defects among twins.

While identical twins can be more distinct than we imagine, fraternal twins might come from the same egg, according to behavioral geneticist Charles Boklage, M.D., of the East Carolina University School of Medicine. Boklage proposes that occasionally an older egg may actually split before it is fertilized by two of the father's sperm. With advances in gene mapping and blood testing, he says, we may find that one-egg fraternal twins occur as often as do two-egg fraternals. We may be mistaking some same sex fraternal twins for identical twins.

Twins Who Vanish, Twins Who Merge

Whatever the cause of twinning, once it beings, mysterious and unsettling events can occur. Some twins disappear or even merge together into one person. Ultrasound equipment has revealed twin pregnancies that later turn into singletons. One of the twins is absorbed into the body, absorbed by the other twin, or shed and noticed by the mother only as some extra vaginal bleeding.

"Only one in 80 twin conceptions makes it to term as two living people," notes Boklage. "For every one that results in a twin birth, about 12 make it to term as a sole survivor. And those people never know they were twins." Because twins tend to be left-handed more often than singletons, Boklage speculates that many left-handers could be the survivors of a twin pregnancy. And a few of those twin pregnancies may lead to what Boklage terms a "chimera," based on the Greek monster with a tail of a serpent, body of a goat, and head of lion—a mosaic of separate beings. "We find people entirely by accident who have two different blood types or several different versions of a single gene. Those people look perfectly normal, but I believe they come from two different cell lines."

It's as if fantastical, primitive acts of love, death, merging, and emerging occur from the very moment life ignites, even as the first strands of DNA knit themselves into the human beings we will later become—carrying on those same acts in the world at large, acts that define us, and that we still are not certain we can call our own.

When Twins Die, Kill, Hate, and Burn

Though it doesn't happen often, occasionally in history a set of mythic twins seem to burst into our awareness, more wedded and bonded than any couple, even darkly so. Some twins live with a passion the rest of us experience only in the almost unbearably intense first flush of romantic love. England's Gibbons twins are one such pair.

Jennifer and June Gibbons were born 35 years ago, the youngest children of Aubrey Gibbons, a West Indian technician for the British Royal Air Force. The girls communicated with each other in a self-made dialect and were elective mutes with the rest of the world. By the time they were 11, they refused to sit in the same room with their parents or siblings. Their mother delivered their meals on a tray and slipped mail under the door. They taught themselves to read, and eventually locked themselves in their bedroom, writing literally millions of words in diaries.

Later they lost their virginity to the same boy within a week of each other, triggering jealous rage. Jennifer tried to strangle June with a cord, and June tried to drown Jennifer in a river. When publishers rejected their work, they went on a spree of arson and theft, and were committed to Broadmoor, England's most notorious institution for the criminally insane.

"Nobody suffers the way I do," June wrote in her diary. "This sister of mine, a dark shadow robbing me of sunlight, is my one and only torment." In another passage, Jennifer described June lying in the bunk bed above her: "Her perception was sharper than steel, it sliced through to my own perception... I read her mind, I knew all about her mood... My perception. Her perception... clashing, knowing, cunning, sly."

After more than a decade of confinement, they were set free. That same afternoon, Jennifer was rushed to the hospital with viral myocarditis, an inflammation of the heart, and that night she died. The pathologist who saw her heart seemed to be speaking poetically of their lethal passion when he described Jennifer's illness as "a fulminating, roaring inflammation with the heart muscle completely destroyed." June, the survivor, has said that she was "born in captivity, trapped in twinship." Eventually, June claims, they began to accept that one must die so the other could be free. Today, June lives in Wales.

Another set of twins, 22-year-old Jeen Young Han (nicknamed Gina) and her sister Sunny, have been dubbed the "evil" and "good" twins by the media, after one tried to murder the other. Although the twins were both valedictorians at their small country high school in San Diego County and got along well, after they graduated they began to battle one another. Both sisters were involved in petty crime, but when Gina stole Sunny's BMW and credit cards, Sunny had her jailed. She escaped, but in November 1996 Sunny and her roommate were attacked and Gina was arrested for conspiracy to commit murder. She'd planned to have Sunny killed at her Irvine condominium, and then assume her identity.

For twin researcher and obstetrician Louis Keith, M.D., of Northwestern University Medical School, the idea of killing a twin is practically unthinkable. "I'm an identical twin, and yesterday I attended the funeral of another identical twin. I kept trying to imagine what my life would be like without my twin. My brother and I have had telepathic experiences. I was in East Germany, being driven on a secluded highway with evening snow falling, and suddenly felt intense heat over the entire front of my body and knew it could only mean one thing, that my brother was sending intense signals to me to call him. When one of the Communist telephone operators agreed to put the call through, I found out that my aunt had died and my twin wanted me to come to the funeral. The twin bond is greater than the spousal bond, absolutely."

Raymond Brandt, publisher of *Twins World* magazine, agrees. "I'm 67, and my identical twin died when we were 20. I love my wife and sons in a very special way, but my twin was one half of me, he was my first love. Living without my twin for 47 years has been a hell of an existence."

These remarkable stories seem to indicate an extra dimension to the twin bond, as if they truly shared a common, noncorporeal soul. What little study has been done on paranormal phenomena and twins, however, indicates that—once again—genes may be responsible. A study by British parapsychologist Susan Blackmore found that when twins were separated in different rooms and asked to draw whatever came into their minds, they often drew the same things. When one was asked to draw an object and transmit that to the other twin, who then was asked to draw what she telepathically received, the results were disappointing. Blackmore concluded that when twins seem to be clairvoyant, it's simply because their thought patterns are so similar.

Is There No Nurture?

Over a century ago, in 1875, British anthropologist Francis Galton first compared a small group of identical and fraternal twins and concluded that "nature prevails enormously over nurture." Time and research seem to have proved him right. "It's no accident that we are what we are," contends Nancy Segal, Ph.D., professor of developmental psychology at California State University at Fullerton and director of the Twin Studies Center there. "We are born with biological propensities that steer us in one direction or another."

Yet critics of twin studies scoff. Richard Rose, Ph.D., professor of psychology and medical genetics at Indiana University in Bloomington, has studied personality in more than 7,000 pairs of identical twins and concluded that environment, both shared and unshared, has nearly twice the influence of genes.

However, both the nature and nurture camps may be looking at the same data and interpreting it differently. According to Lindon Eaves, unshared environment may actually be "chosen" by the genes, selected because of biological preferences. Scientists dub this the "nature of nurture." Genetically influenced personality traits in a child may cause parents to respond in specific ways. So how can we ever tease out the truth? Nature and nurture interact in a never-ending Mobius strip that can't be traced back to a single starting point.

Yet if genes are a powerful and a-priori given, they nonetheless have a range of activity that is calibrated in the womb by nutrition and later in life by the world. "Remember," says Eaves, "only 50 percent of who you are is influenced by genes. The other 50 percent includes the slings and arrows of outrageous fortune, accidents of development, sheer chaos, small and cumulative changes both within and without."

Environment, it turns out, may be most powerful when it limits—through trauma, deprivation, malnutrition. Studies by Sandra Scarr, Ph.D., professor of psychology at the University of Virginia, show that IQ scores for white twins at the bottom of the socioeconomic ladder, and for all black twins, are heavily influenced by environment. Social and economic deprivation keep scores artificially lower than twins' genetic potential.

Otherwise, Scarr postulates, genes bias you in a certain direction, causing you to select what you are already genetically programmed to enjoy. Children may be tiny gene powerhouses, shaping their parents' behavior as much as parents shape their children.

"Where does this leave us?" concludes Bouchard. "Your job as a parent is really to maximize the environment so that you and your children can manifest your full genetic potential." Under the best of environmental circumstances, our genes might be free to play the entire symphony of self.

And yet what of Irina, the Michigan housewife, and her twin, Yanina, the Polish nun? I sat with them over lunch, newly united twins who couldn't stop smiling at each other, clasping each other's hands. Their luminous hazel eyes were virtual replicas, but the two women couldn't have appeared more different otherwise: Irina bejeweled and blonde, Yanina in a combat-green nun's habit, a few tufts of brown hair peeping out, skin weathered. She described rescuing bloodied children from the arms of mothers who'd been shot to death and rising at dawn in the convent to pray silently for hours; her American counterpart portrayed a life filled with errands, cleaning homes, and caring for family.

"Rushing, rushing, rushing to get everything done" was Irina's summary of her life. "Teaching love, the kind of love that will make you happy," was her sister's. Listening to them speak, one in slow, gentle Midwestern cadences, the other in the rolled drumbeat of a Slavic tongue enriched by laughter and hand gestures, it was hard to believe they carried the same genetic imprint.

To me, their differences are so striking they seem to defy the last 20 years of twin research. "Right now we understand a little bit about human behavior and its biological and cultural roots," says Eaves. "But our lived understanding is far richer than any of that. People are yielding the ground too easily to genetics."

As I mused over the intricate turnings of twin research, I could only conclude the findings were as complex as the self we hope to illuminate with these studies. Fascinating, tantalizing, yes, but twin research, like any great scientific endeavor, ultimately points us toward the ineffable, inexplicable.

As Charles Boklage notes: "The development of the self is chaotic, nonlinear, and dynamic. Very small variations in conditions can lead to huge changes. Different twin studies give different answers. And whenever the mind tries to understand something, it has to be bigger than the subject it compasses. You cannot bite your own teeth."

"In the end," says Eaves, "I don't give a damn whether you call it God or natural selection, we're trying to find words that instill reverence for the mysterious stuff from which we are made."

God, fate, genes, luck, a random event like a move to America or Poland, or perhaps something stubbornly individual and free about us all, something that can never be quantified but can only be lived... The play of self goes on, and whatever hand or eye has orchestrated us, who in the end, twin or not, can know the dancer from the dance?

Forget Money; Nothing Can Buy Happiness, Some Researchers Say

By DANIEL GOLEMAN

WHEN it comes to that quintessential American passion, the pursuit of happiness, the news from science is mixed. The good news is that the sting of life's slings and arrows is surprisingly short. The bad news is for vacationers: the mellow glow from a week or two away will fade just as surely.

Happiness, many psychologists are concluding, seems to be largely determined by the genes, not by outside reality. However tragic or comic life's ups and downs, people appear to return inexorably to whatever happiness level is pre-set in their constitution.

The idea is similar to the set-point concept in weight control, a theory that says the brain seems to be wired to turn the body's metabolism up or down to maintain a pre-set weight. There is also, these scientists contend, a set point for happiness, a genetically determined mood level that the vagaries of life may nudge upward or downward, but only for a while. With time, the grouchy tend to become as cranky as before, and the lighthearted cheery again.

Interviews with a range of psychologists show that the idea of a biological set point for a sense of well-being has wide support in the field, though there are quibbles on details. "It's a brilliant idea—it's well worth pursuing," said Dr. Jerome Kagan, a developmental psychologist at Harvard University who has studied temperament in children. "It's clear that T. S. Eliot was by nature dour, and Jay Leno is congenitally upbeat. But we're far from filling in the biological blanks."

The set-point idea seems to make sense of longstanding data on happiness that have puzzled researchers. Some of the studies simply take people's word for how happy they are, while others use less direct measures—like observing how exuberant they are. Studies of happiness in several countries have found that money makes little difference to perceptions of happiness, except among the very poor. Nor do education, marriage and a family, or any of the many other variables that researchers have sought to correlate with contentment. Each factor may make a person a little happier, but it has a minor impact, compared with the individual's characteristic sense of well-being.

"We find that for events like being promoted or losing a lover, most of the effect on people's mood is gone by three months, and there's not a trace by six months," said Dr. Edward Diener, a psychologist at the University of Illinois at Urbana. Dr. Diener, with his wife, Dr. Carol Diener, also a psychologist there, proposed the notion of a happiness set point in the May issue of the journal Psychological Science.

Forget those if-only-I-could-win-the-lottery-I'd-find-happiness-forever fantasies; Dr. Edward Diener cites data showing that lottery winners are no happier a year after their good fortune than they were before. And several studies show that even people with spinal-cord injuries tend to rebound in spirits.

The brain may be wired to a preset level of well-being.

The set-point concept has been seized by some genetics researchers, who say new data on twins give the strongest support to date for that idea.

"About half of your sense of well-being is determined by your set point, which is from the genetic lottery, and the other half from the sorrows and pleasures of the last hours, days or weeks," said Dr. David T. Lykken, a behavioral geneticist at the University of Minnesota who published results from a study of 1,500 pairs of twins in the May issue

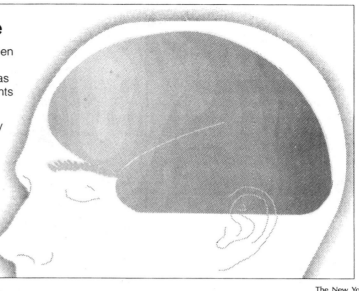

Pattern for Zest for Life

Researchers have found a correlation between relatively greater electrical activity in the left prefrontal region of the brain (the lighter areas at right) and strong agreement with statements like the following:

"When good things happen to me, it strongly affects me."

"I will often do things for no other reason than that they might be fun."

"When I get something I want, I feel excited and energized."

"When I'm doing well at something, I love to keep at it."

Source: Dr. Richard J. Davidson/University of Wisconsin

of Psychological Science. His estimates are based on comparing how members of pairs of fraternal and identical twins rate their sense of well-being.

A common way to estimate how much of a trait is based on genetics is to look at the similarities that show up in identical twins, who share their genes 100 percent, compared with fraternal twins, who are no more similar genetically than any other siblings.

"There is little difference in well-being among identical twins raised together, compared with those raised apart," said Dr. Auke Tellegen of the University of Minnesota, a co-author of the study with Dr. Lykken.

Life circumstances, like salary, education or marital status, predicted only 2 percent of the variation within each pair of twins, Dr. Lykken said. "Those in prestigious positions or professions were not happier than those who went to work in overalls, nor were those who finished their Ph.D.'s happier than those who never completed eighth grade. You can predict happiness levels vastly better just by knowing the other identical twin's score."

Still, doubts remain about the set-point idea. Dr. Howard Weiss, a psychologist at Purdue University, takes issue with Dr. Lykken's estimate that about 50 percent of a person's sense of well-being is due to an inherited set point. "A heritability estimate based on a single study has to be viewed with caution," Dr. Weiss said. "Though no one is disputing a part of your satisfaction in life is due to genetic factors, we don't really know yet if it's 25 percent, 50 percent or 75 percent."

The idea that a person's typical mood persists over time has been borne out by data from several large studies that followed people over many years. One is the National Health and Nutrition Examination, which monitored reports of well-being from close to 6,000 men and women over 10 years. "We find that the people who are relatively happiest now will be the happiest 10 years from now, despite the day-to-day fluctuations," said Dr. Robert R. McCrae, a research psychologist at the National Institute on Aging, who analyzed the data with a colleague, Dr. Paul T. Costa.

Supporters of the set-point idea agree that people can have deep mood changes for the worse after a serious trauma or loss. But researchers say that if such shifts persist for years, they mark clinical problems like depression that are overriding the set point for well-being, or they are being caused by serious disturbances that continue to prime the bad mood.

"For most of the widowed, or those who lose a job or get divorced," Dr. Edward Diener said, "the impact on daily mood disappears after a year or so. But when there is a more lasting effect on mood, it's because in some sense the bad event continues to happen—there are reminders every day." Even major setbacks in life, like being bereaved or divorced, "didn't change the stability of people's well-being in the long term," Dr. McCrae said.

"Years afterward, you see people return to whatever their basic level of well-being had been 10 years before," he added. "Those who were still depressed tended to be those who had been relatively depressed 10 years earlier."

Along with a set point for well-being, people also have typical ranges of ups and downs, researchers say. "There's a range of oscillation around a given person's stable set point," Dr. Tellegen said. "This latitude means that you can be an emotional Pavarotti, with extreme ups and downs, and it will still average out, tending to return to the same basic level."

Scientists who study changes within the brain say they may have even located an important area where happiness is registered and where the set-point mechanism may operate.

In studies with colleagues over the last decade, Dr. Richard Davidson, a psychologist at the University of Wisconsin, has found a strong relationship between the ratio of neural activity levels on the left and right sides of the prefrontal lobes and people's typical moods. "Those with relatively more activity in the left prefrontal area report more positive emotions," Dr. Davidson said. "They say they get more pleasure from life's ordinary activities, rate themselves as more enthusiastic, energetic and alert" in general than do those who have more activity on the right side. By contrast, those with relatively more right prefrontal activity report being more agitated, nervous, distressed and worried.

The people with the most right prefrontal activity, compared with the activity on the left, are those with clinical depression who say they have lost all sense of pleasure in life, Dr. Davidson found after studying brain changes in 25 patients with the imaging technique known as positron emission tomography scans.

Dr. Davidson, though not guided by the set-point theory, has found that in infants as young as 10 months, those with more active left prefrontal lobes are less likely to cry when separated briefly from their mother. The brain-activity patterns tend to remain stable when tracked over several years. For instance, Dr. Davidson found that children's brainwave patterns—as shown in electroencephalographs, or EEG's—at age 3 predict their exuberance at age 7.

When 7-year-olds in Dr. Davidson's study were asked to jump to pop bubbles blown over their heads, those with relatively more right-side prefrontal activity "were very restrained, just going up a bit on their tippy toes," Dr. Davidson said. But those with more activity on the left "were hopping all over, laughing and going bonkers."

Dr. Davidson says his findings seem to be related to receptors for the neurotransmitter dopamine. Animal studies suggest that a dopamine-mediated pathway from the left prefrontal areas to the emotional centers in the limbic area of the brain regulates positive emotions and that the left medial area of the prefrontal cortex is the site for inhibiting the signals for emotional distress. A 1995 study by Dr. Richard Depue, a psychologist at Cornell University, found that the higher people's levels of dopamine, the more positive their feelings.

A possible genetic basis for such differences in people's typical dopamine levels may have been found in research reported in January in the journal Nature by an Israeli group. Those researchers found that people differed in an allele for a portion of the D4 dopamine receptor that regulates how much dopamine binds there and that the differences were related to the moods people reported. The discovery, Dr. Davidson said, "is very exciting because it's the first time there's been a specific connection between a molecular genetic finding and people's levels of happiness."

Some psychologists dispute the choice of happiness itself as an index of the good life. "Satisfaction is a byproduct of a life that involves more than the mere pursuit of happiness," said Dr. Carol Ryff, a developmental psychologist at the University of Wisconsin. "I would argue that it's worse to wake up in the morning without having a larger purpose in life than to wake up unhappy. Just feeling good is a poor measure of the quality of a person's life."

Dr. Lykken sees in his data a recipe for living that calls for nudging one's level of happiness into the higher registers of one's range. Dr. Lykken's advice: "Be an experiential epicure. A steady diet of simple pleasures will keep you above your set point. Find the small things that you know give you a little high—a good meal, working in the garden, time with friends—and sprinkle your life with them. In the long run, that will leave you happier than some grand achievement that gives you a big lift for a while."

Revealing the Brain's Secrets

Is space truly the final frontier? Not according to scientists who are probing what they call the most complex and challenging structure ever studied: the human brain. "It is the great unexplored frontier of the medical sciences," said neurobiologist John E. Dowling, professor of natural science at Harvard University. Just as space exploration dominated science in the 1960s and 1970s, the human brain is taking center stage in the 1990s.

It may seem odd to compare an organ that weighs only about three pounds to the immensity of the universe. Yet the human brain is as awe-inspiring as the night sky. Its complex array of interconnecting nerve cells chatter incessantly among themselves in languages both chemical and electrical. None of the organ's magical mysteries has been easy to unravel. Until recently, the brain was regarded as a black box whose secrets were frustratingly secure from reach.

Now, an explosion of discoveries in genetics and molecular biology, combined with dramatic new imaging technologies, have pried open the lid and allowed scientists to peek inside. The result is a growing understanding of what can go wrong in the brain, which raises new possibilities for identifying, treating, and perhaps ultimately preventing devastating conditions such as Alzheimer's disease or stroke.

"The laboratory bench is closer to the hospital bed than it has ever been," said neurobiologist Gerald Fischbach, chairman of neurobiology at Harvard Medical School, where the brain and its molecular makeup are a primary focus of research.

One important challenge is to understand the healthy brain. By studying brain cells and the genetic material inside them, scientists are discovering how groups of specialized cells interact to produce memory, language, sensory perception, emotion, and other complex phenomena. Figuring out how the healthy brain goes about its business is an essential platform that researchers need in order to comprehend what goes wrong when a neurological disease strikes.

There have also been great strides toward elucidating some of the common brain disorders that rob people of memory, mobility, and the ability to enjoy life. The most promising of these fall into several broad categories.

- The discovery of disease-producing genetic mutations has made it possible not only to diagnose inherited disorders, but in cases such as Huntington's disease, to predict who will develop them. These findings have also pointed the way toward new therapies.
- Insights into the programmed death of nerve cells may lead to drugs that can halt the progression of degenerative diseases or contain stroke damage.
- Naturally occurring chemicals that protect nerve cells from environmental assaults may hold clues about preventing disease or reversing neurologic injury.
- Information about brain chemistry's role in mood and mental health has already helped people burdened by depression, for example, and is expected to benefit others as well.

Genetics opens a new door

Discovering a gene associated with a disease is like unlocking a storehouse of knowledge. Once researchers have such a gene, they may be able to insert it into experimental systems such as cell cultures or laboratory animals. This makes it easier to discern the basic mechanisms of the disorder, which in turn helps scientists figure out what diagnostic tests or therapies might be best. When a new treatment is proposed, genetically engineered models of human diseases make testing quicker and more efficient.

In recent years, scientists have found abnormal genes associated with Huntington's disease (HD), Alzheimer's disease (AD), amyotrophic lateral sclerosis (ALS or Lou Gehrig's disease), one form of epilepsy, Tay-Sachs disease, two types of muscular dystrophy, and several lesser-known neurological conditions.

A decade-long search for the HD gene ended in 1993, when Harvard researchers Marcy MacDonald and James Gusella, working with scientists at other institutions, identified a sequence of DNA that produces symptoms of the disease if it is repeated enough times. Huntington's is a progressive and ultimately fatal hereditary disorder that affects about 25,000 people in the United States. It typically strikes at midlife, and the researchers discovered that the more copies of the sequence a person inherited, the earlier symptoms show up.

Scientists quickly developed a highly reliable assay that enables people with a family history of HD to find out if they or their unborn fetus harbors the dangerous mutation. But because no cure for the disease exists, few people have rushed to have themselves tested.

Demand might increase, however, if scientists can use the HD gene to design effective treatments. Genes contain the assembly instructions for proteins, the molecules that carry out the day-to-day operations of the body. Scientists strive to identify the protein made by a disease-producing gene and to figure out what it does, which in turn helps them understand the event that initiates the disease process.

The HD gene codes for a protein that appears to contribute to the premature death of certain neurons. It is the loss of these cells that results in the involuntary movements and mental deterioration typical of Huntington's. When researchers know more about this protein, they may be able to develop drugs or other therapies that could slow the onset of symptoms or even block them entirely.

A downward spiral

The gradual extinction of certain brain cells is also the underlying cause of Alzheimer's disease. In this case, the impact is progressive loss of memory, changes in personality, loss of impulse control, and deterioration in reasoning power. Under the microscope, the brains of people who died with AD are studded with abnormalities called amyloid plaques and neurofibrillary tangles. About 20% of all AD cases are inherited, and these people develop symptoms earlier in life than those with the more common form, which typically appears well after age 65.

In recent years, scientists have discovered several different genetic mutations that can cause the unusual, inherited form of AD. One of these abnormal genes has successfully been introduced into mice by researchers at several pharmaceutical companies, and experts believe that this animal model will help them understand how all forms of the disease progress at the cellular and molecular level.

So far, it looks as though some of the animals' brains develop amyloid plaques like the ones that build up in humans. Long-standing doubt about whether plaques cause symptoms may be resolved by future observations of whether these genetically engineered mice show signs of memory loss. If there is a strong correlation between amyloid accumulation and symptom severity, these mice will be used to test drugs that might keep plaques from forming.

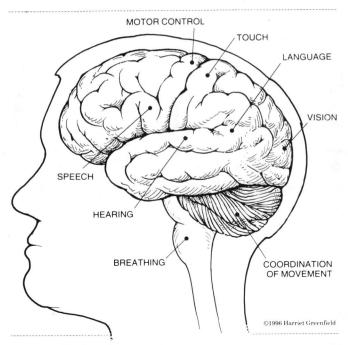

The cell death story

Unlike other types of cells, nerve cells (neurons) are meant to last a lifetime because they can't reproduce themselves. Struck by the realization that abnormal cell death is the key factor in neurologic problems ranging from Alzheimer's to stroke, scientists have embarked on a crusade aimed at understanding why nerve cells die and how this might be prevented.

It's normal to lose some brain cells gradually. Trouble arises when a large population of cells dies all of a sudden, as in a stroke, or when too many of a certain type die over time, such as in Alzheimer's or Parkinson's (PD) disease. While some scientists remain skeptical that inquiries into cell death will ever lead to effective means for preventing or treating neurodegenerative diseases, many others are enthusiastically pursuing this line of research.

Some scientists are racing to develop *neuroprotective* drugs that could guard brain cells against damage and death or even help them regenerate. There are many different ideas about how to do this.

For example, although Harvard scientists have identified the gene for HD and the protein it makes, they don't understand the mechanisms that lead to symptoms. One theory is that a phenomenon called *excitotoxicity* is responsible, and that Huntington's is only one of many diseases in which this process plays a role.

The idea behind excitotoxicity is that too much of a good thing is bad for cells. Glutamate, for example, is an ordinarily benign chemical messenger that stimulates certain routine cellular activities. Under extraordinary circumstances, however, "cells can be so excited by glutamate that they wear themselves out and die," said John

Penney Jr., a neurologist at Massachusetts General Hospital and a Harvard professor of neurology.

Sending a signal

One of the many types of doorways built into the walls of nerve cells is a structure called an NMDA receptor. One of its functions is to allow small amounts of calcium (a substance usually shut out of the cell) to enter it. This happens when the NMDA receptor is stimulated by glutamate. If excess glutamate is present, too much calcium rushes in—an influx that is lethal to the cell.

Someday it may be possible to halt the advance of Huntington's by injecting drugs which block the NMDA receptor so that calcium can't get in. In animal experiments, scientists have demonstrated that such receptor-blocking agents can keep brain cells from dying. Harvard researchers are seeking approval for a clinical trial that will test such neuroprotective drugs in patients with symptomatic disease. If participants obtain any relief from this treatment, the next step will be to determine whether this approach can prevent symptoms in patients who have the gene but do not have symptoms.

Scientists also hope that neuroprotection can be used to limit brain damage due to stroke. When a stroke shuts down the supply of blood to part of the brain, neurons in the immediate area die within minutes. Over the next several hours, more distant cells in the region are killed as excitotoxic signals spread. In an effort to limit the extent of brain damage, researchers are currently treating small numbers of patients with intravenous doses of experimental agents such as NMDA receptor blockers and free radical scavengers. Other neuroprotective agents under development, include protease inhibitors, nitric oxide inhibitors, and nerve growth factors.

"Our dream is a safe and effective neuroprotectant that can be given to the stroke patient in the ambulance or shortly after arrival in the emergency room," said neurologist Seth Finklestein, an associate professor at Harvard Medical School who conducts basic research at Massachusetts General Hospital. "That's the holy grail of neuroprotective treatment."

Applications for Alzheimer's

Neuroprotection is also making waves in Alzheimer's research, as scientists strive to inhibit the type of cell death that typifies this disease. One group of investigators has identified several *peptides* (small protein molecules) that block the formation of amyloid plaque in the test tube, said neurobiologist Huntington Potter, an associate professor at Harvard Medical School. The researchers hope to test these peptides in humans.

Brain cells manufacture several neuroprotective chemicals on their own, which scientists call *neurotrophic* or nerve growth factors. These small proteins may hold the key to keeping cells alive even in the face of stroke, degenerative diseases, or even spinal cord injury.

For example, several different neurotrophic factors are being tested in the laboratory to determine if they could protect the dopamine-producing cells that die prematurely in people with Parkinson's disease. Other uses are being studied as well, and some researchers anticipate that these chemicals will be tested in humans before the decade draws to a close.

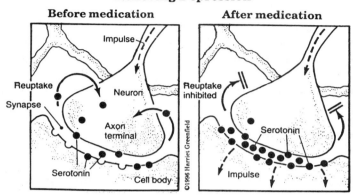

Relieving Depression

People who are depressed have less of the neurotransmitter serotonin than those who aren't. In the picture on the left, the axon terminal of one nerve cell releases serotonin, which travels across the synapse and activates the cell body (receiving cell). Serotonin is then reabsorbed by the sending cell. On the right, a selective serotonin reuptake inhibitor (SSRI), such as the antidepressant Prozac, slows the reabsorption of serotonin, keeping it in the synapse longer and boosting its effect on the receiving cell.

Mood, mind, and brain chemistry

Scientists have discovered that a surprising number of mental disorders, from depression to schizophrenia, are the result of brain chemistry gone awry. And this understanding has led them to design new medications for treating specific mental disorders and behavior problems.

The best known of this new breed of drugs is fluoxetine (Prozac), one of several selective serotonin reuptake inhibitors (SSRIs). It was possible to design these agents, which are widely prescribed to alleviate depression and related disorders, only after scientists came to understand how nerve cells communicate at the molecular level.

Each nerve cell has an *axon*, a long branch that reaches out and touches other nerve cells. A tiny space called a *synapse* separates the axon terminal (which sends a message) and the cell body (that receives it), and this is where the action is. The sending cell releases *neurotransmitters* (chemical messengers) into the synapse which either excite or inhibit a receiving cell that is equipped with the proper receptors. Messages pass from cell to cell in this manner, eventually leading to a physiologic action. In each synapse, the cell that sent the message sops up leftover neurotransmitters and stores them for future use. People who are depressed have less serotonin than those who aren't, and the SSRIs block the reuptake of this chemical, thereby boosting the effect of a small amount on the receiving cell. (*See illustration* "Relieving Depression.")

But Prozac and its relatives are only the tip of the iceberg. As researchers work to understand the roles of different chemical messengers and the highly specific receptors that bind them, a whole new approach to the treatment of mental disorders is evolving. The identification of highly specialized receptors is already paving the way for ever more specific drugs to treat these conditions.

Schizophrenia therapy is a case in point. As devastating as this form of mental illness is, treatments have sometimes appeared worse than the disease. Until very recently, the only drugs that relieved symptoms could also lead to spasmodic, uncontrollable movements known as *tardive dyskinesia*. This is because these agents block all types of receptors for dopamine, a neurotransmitter that is a key player in normal movement as well as in this mental disorder. Now there is a new drug for schizophrenia, clozapine, that blocks only a small subclass of dopamine receptors. It relieves symptoms of the illness in some people without leading to abnormal movements. Still, it can have other serious side effects.

Tailored to fit

The bottom line for the treatment of behavior and emotional disorders may be that drugs will become ever more specialized. Just as computers now help salespeople fit blue jeans to the individual purchasers, it is not inconceivable that psychopharmacologists may someday tailor drugs to the needs of each patient.

What does the future of brain research hold? Dr. Dowling anticipates that medications that can slow the process of degenerative disease, correct the chemical imbalances that cause mental disorders, prevent stroke damage, and repair spinal cord injuries may all be on the horizon. "We have learned so much about the cellular and molecular aspects of the brain," Dr. Dowling said. "We stand at a time of great opportunity, when we can take tremendous advantage of these things and turn them into practical clinical therapies."

—*KATHLEEN CAHILL ALLISON*

Violence and the Brain

Highly impulsive aggressive behavior may result from neurologic abnormalities related to injury, illness, chemical imbalance, or genetic defects.

Norbert Myslinski

Tell me, ye judges of our moral sins, where madness ends, and sanity begins?*

It began again, as it had hundreds of times before. Another uncontrollable rage. She started kicking and scratching and hitting anything and anyone in sight. Her foster parents had to hold her down for an hour until she was somewhat calmed. "This is the last time," they said. They had had enough. They finally decided to give up Rachel, as had other foster parents before them.

Rachel was nine years old, with a history of spontaneous, impulsive violence. Her psychiatrist labeled her as "attention deficit/hyperactive," a general term used to cover a wide range of abnormal behavior. Rachel was eventually hospitalized, but nothing helped to curb her violent behavior. Talk therapy, behavioral therapy, drug therapy—nothing worked, until she was given a drug that increased the levels of a chemical called *serotonin* in her brain.

Neuroscientists have long known that violent behavior can be correlated with neuroanatomy (brain structure) and neurochemistry (brain chemistry). Brain dysfunction, either genetic or acquired, can result in a decreased ability to control one's violent tendencies. This fact, however, has been dwarfed in the public's mind by the cultural and societal causes of violence. In 1979, Gelles and Strauss listed 15 theories of violence. None of them included the brain. It is important that we not ignore the brain.

Can scientific research into the brain help us understand and prevent violence? Most neuroscientists who study violent behavior believe that their work offers no cure, no "magic pill," for most of the violence that plagues society. Some chronically violent people, however, may suffer from structural or chemical imbalance in their brains. Restoring the normal balance may reverse a lifelong pattern of violence.

The type of violence we will focus on here is called *episodic dyscontrol*—that is, impulsive, physical aggression with the intent to harm. We will not be concerned with collective violence, opportunistic or premeditated violence, or violence that results from psychotic illusions, delusions, or hallucinations.

Episodic dyscontrol refers to individuals whose attacks of rage appeared for the first time after a brain insult, or in whom it has been present since childhood or adolescence in association with other developmental defects. individuals who possess this biological short fuse tend to act without fully considering the consequences.

Episodic dyscontrol is important because it is one of the causes of such acts as unpremeditated homicide, suicide, child abuse, spousal abuse, animal abuse, and property destruction. Sometimes it manifests itself as simply obscene and profane language, or excessively aggressive driving. The attacks can be triggered by the most trivial and impersonal of events. They are exacerbated by alcohol, usually followed by remorse.

Relation to brain structure

The ability to control our violent tendencies comes from our cerebral cortex, which is more complex than any other in the animal kingdom. It is the seat of our intelligence, creativity, and

---

* Excerpt from "Monomania," a poem published in 1843 in response to the verdict of "not guilty by reason of insanity" in the trial of accused murderer Daniel McNaughton.

2. ❖ DETERMINANTS OF BEHAVIOR: MOTIVATION, ENVIRONMENT, AND PHYSIOLOGY

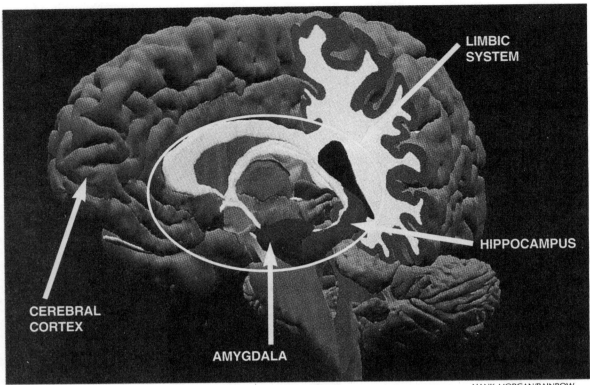

HANK MORGAN/RAINBOW

■ When a person controls his violent tendencies, his cerebral cortex inhibits the limbic system. The amygdala, which is part of the limbic system, is one type of structure found to play a role in aggressive behavior.

personal responsibility. Our brain also has an emotional center, called the limbic system. It is responsible for not only joy and affection but also fear and anger, which are the bases of most violent behavior. The control of our violent tendencies comes from inhibition of the limbic system by the cerebral cortex. While this control is active and healthy in most of us, it is lacking in many who commit violent crimes.

Just as damage to the brain can result in paralysis, chronic pain, mental retardation, or dementia, it may also result in loss of emotional control. Any form of brain damage, if it occurs in precisely the correct part of the brain, can lead to recurrent violent behavior in previously peaceful individuals. Possible causes of brain damage include trauma, tumors, stroke, brain infections such as encephalitis, or diseases that attack selective parts of the brain, such as multiple sclerosis or Alzheimer's disease. Among the best childhood predictors of violent behavior are neurological abnormalities. They include low IQ, attention deficit and hyperactivity, learning disabilities, head injuries, and prenatal and perinatal complications.

As far back as 1892, Dr. F.L. Goltz changed gentle dogs into vicious ones by removing part of their cerebral cortex. Since then, scientists have been able to turn an animal's rage on and off by stimulating certain parts of the brain. One of these parts is the *amygdala,* which is located in each temporal lobe.

Julie was a patient with epilepsy resulting from damage to her brain's temporal lobes. Besides seizures, she experienced sudden outbursts of anger. She once stabbed a woman who accidentally bumped into her. When Julie's physician inserted electrodes into the amygdala on both sides of her brain, he recorded abnormal activity from the right amygdala. To cure her, therefore, he destroyed her right amygdala by sending radio-frequency current through the electrode. Fifteen years later, she is still free of seizure activity and has no problem controlling her violent tendencies.

Attacks of aggressiveness are not uncommon in temporal lobe epileptics. Up to 50 percent of them exhibit impulsive violence between seizures. Vincent van Gogh suffered from the same condition, which led him to cut off part of his earlobe with a razor.

Numerous studies have shown that there is a higher prevalence of neurologic abnormalities in recurrently violent individuals than in nonviolent control subjects or the population at large. In one such study of 286 patients with episodic dyscontrol, 94 percent had neurological effects detectable by tests such as EEG or CAT scans. Most of the remaining 6 percent had one or more family members who exhibited explosive behavior, sometimes extending back two or three generations. One hundred and two patients exhibited initial violent episodes shortly after specific brain damage from head trauma, brain tumors, encephalitis, or stroke. All of the others had had violent episodes since childhood, and many of them had birth injuries. Although most of the patients had neurological defects, two-thirds of them were psychiatrically normal. Between violent attacks, they were indistinguishable from the normal population.

Just as brain damage can unleash violent behavior, in rare instances, damage can also subdue violent behavior. A 60-year-old man, who suffered from episodic dyscontrol since adolescence, experienced an abrupt personality change after a stroke. His uncontrollable rages stopped, and he became a gentler man. Another example is a woman with a brain tumor who reported as a first symptom the

10. Violence and the Brain

Any form of brain damage, in the correct part of the brain, can lead to recurrent violent behavior in previously peaceful individuals.

loss of a lifelong tendency to explosive behavior. The most dramatic example of controlling aggressiveness of an animal occurred in a bullfight. Scientists were able to stop a charging bull in its tracks by remotely activating a stimulating electrode that was implanted in the bull's brain.

The above examples demonstrate neuroanatomical correlates of aggression. In other words, just as a specific part of the brain is responsible for the movement of a toe or the storage of a memory, a particular part of the brain is correlated with impulsive physical violence. There are also neurochemical correlates of aggression in the brain: Certain chemicals are correlated with violent behavior and others, with inhibiting it.

Relation to brain chemistry

Like normal body temperature, normal aggression has a set point, maintained by a delicate balance of brain chemicals. Changing that balance can either increase or decrease aggressiveness. A number of studies point to the involvement of a naturally occurring substance called serotonin. It is one of a number of neurotransmitters that relay messages between nerve cells and along pathways connecting different parts of the brain.

Serotonin is involved in pathways that help regulate some of our most basic mental drives—including sleep, pain, perception, sex, and, it now appears, our violent tendencies. Serotonin is an intricate part of the brain's impulse control system. If we lose it, we lose control. In both humans and animals, there is an inverse relationship between serotonin and violence: Low serotonin levels are associated with increased violence; high serotonin levels, with decreased violence. Research has demonstrated this relationship in people incarcerated for violent crimes, marines discharged for excessive violence, and people who have attempted violent suicide. Serotonin levels are low in abused children. They are generally lower in males than in females. They tend to increase with age, which may be one reason why aggressive youths tend to mellow as they get older. Alcohol initially raises serotonin, but continued use reduces its levels. In one study of 29 children and adolescents with disruptive behavior disorders, low serotonin levels in the brain were the single most accurate predictor of which ones would go on to commit more violent crimes or suicide.

The cell bodies of serotonin producing neurons are located in the midbrain, from where they extend their fibers to the cerebral cortex, making about half a million connections with higher centers that deal with emotions and decision making. These fibers interact with at least 16 different types of receptors in the higher centers. Most evidence suggests that the receptor for serotonin known as 5-HT-1B is most important in modulating violent behavior. More recent evidence indicates that the 5-HT-1A receptor may also be involved. Just as the therapies for illnesses such as Parkinson's disease, Huntington's disease, Alzheimer's disease, schizophrenia, and depression have improved by manipulating the levels of certain brain chemicals, the treatment of episodic dyscontrol may be improved by manipulating serotonin levels or pharmacologically stimulating the 5-HT-1B receptors.

Norepinephrine (noradrenaline) is another neurotransmitter involved in violent behavior. This chemical seems to be out of balance in certain individuals, but its role is different from that of serotonin. It helps turn on the autonomic responses that accompany high emotions, such as increases in heart rate, respiration, perspiration, and so forth. When the brain perceives a threat, norepinephrine turns up the body's engines to prepare it to cope with the impending crises.

Norepinephrine levels are high in certain violence-prone individuals. A gene responsible for monoamine oxidase A, an enzyme that breaks down norepinephrine, seems to be defective in a single Dutch family line in which norepinephrine levels are high. The disorder, which affects only men, manifests itself as mild retardation and sudden outbursts of violence, including rape, arson, and attempted murder. Drugs that decrease norepinephrine levels tend to decrease aggressive behavior without dulling one's intellect or consciousness. Norepinephrine and serotonin may work in concert to regulate aggressive behavior.

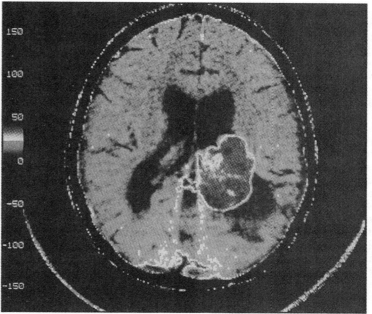

DAN MCCOY/RAINBOW

■ A tumor in the brain (as seen in this CAT scan) is one condition that may trigger violent outbursts. On rare occasions, however, it can reverse a lifelong pattern of uncontrolled aggressiveness.

2. ❖ DETERMINANTS OF BEHAVIOR: MOTIVATION, ENVIRONMENT, AND PHYSIOLOGY

COURTESY OF AMERICAN ENTERPRISE INSTITUTE

■ Not only does the brain influence behavior, but behavior can alter the brain, especially during the early years of life. *Above:* The hurt felt by an abused child, as depicted in a self-portrait, can adversely affect the development of his brain.

Genetic and other factors

While others have searched for the causes of violence in TV programming, some neuroscientists have focused on the genetic programming of rodents. Researchers have developed several genetically engineered violent mice that have either low levels of serotonin or fewer serotonin receptor sites. French neuroscientist René Hen developed one such mouse, the "outlaw mouse," whose gene for the 5-HT-1B receptor was deleted. It attacks intruders with remarkable ferocity.

One study of violent Finnish criminals demonstrated an association between altered serotonin levels and a possible flaw in a gene for tryptophan hydroxylase, an enzyme important for the synthesis of serotonin.

People can inherit defective genes that make them more likely to have a low level of serotonin, but early life experiences also have a role in determining how that gene will be expressed. It appears that stressful or traumatic childhood experiences can lead to the full expression of these genes. Violence, poverty, neglect, harsh discipline, or sensory deprivation may influence the brain's serotonin production, making children with defective genes more prone to violent behavior. A healthy stimulating environment seems to minimize the expression of these defective genes and the resultant violent behavior.

Episodic dyscontrol is more common in men than in women, but in the case of women, violence is often related to the premenstrual syndrome. Over 60 percent of violent crimes committed by women occur in the premenstrual week. The anomaly in which a male may have one X and two Y chromosomes has also been credited with predisposing him toward violent behavior.

Alcohol and certain drugs can also block the ability of our cerebral cortex to inhibit the violent tendencies of our lower brains. They produce a temporary condition rather than a chronic one. Not only is this effect of alcohol greater in people who have low serotonin levels, but alcohol itself tends to lower serotonin levels. individuals who have taken certain street drugs, such as PCP (phencyclidine) often exhibit explosive behavior.

Controlling aggressiveness

Recent research raises the hope that impulsive violent behavior in certain individuals can eventually be controlled by chemical or genetic manipulation. Tests are already available to measure serotonin levels in man. Several drugs, such as fluoxetine (Prozac®), are available to increase brain levels of serotonin. Regulating brain serotonin levels to control aggression, however, raises several ethical issues.

Responsibility for one's own actions is of basic importance in our society. Most of us believe that, except for the insane, retarded, and very young, we all have a free will and should take responsibility for our actions. Does this new information remove personal responsibility for one's own aggressive behavior? Normally, no, but in the cases of Rachel and Julie, their violence was related to their brain abnormalities. They had very little ability to control this behavior by free will.

It is disconcerting to think that our ability to control our behavior is dependent on brain chemicals or the genes that control them, or that a small lesion or electrical impulse at a precise site in our brain can produce impulsive violent behavior in a normally gentle person. Are we slaves to our genes? Do genes make certain behaviors inevitable, or just more likely? This apprehension was demonstrated in 1995, when Maryland hosted a national conference entitled "Research on Genetics and Criminal Behavior." The meeting was delayed for three years because of opposition, and when it was held it included 30 protesters who tried to shut it down because of what they called the racist implications of linking violence with genetics. Because of such sentiments and other reasons, the government and the pharmaceutical industry have shied away from developing new genetic or pharmacological treatments to manage violent behavior.

Most do not find the new knowledge threatening, however. It is more likely that knowledge of brain chemistry will be used to help people, rather than to stigmatize them as aggressive or violent. It places episodic dyscontrol in the same category as schizophrenia, depression, and other neurological disorders. Before the advent of psycho-pharmacology, schizophrenics and manic-depressives were considered evil. After science confirmed the biological basis for these disorders and psychoactive drugs arrived in the 1950s, the number of patients in mental hospitals declined drastically.

The type of violent behavior being discussed here is impulsive. But what

> *Does this new information remove personal responsibility for one's own aggressive behavior?*

of violent behavior that is not impulsive? Violent behavior that is cold-blooded rather than hot-blooded?

Like Ted Bundy and John Gacy, Donald Harvey was a serial killer. He premeditated his murders and carried them out in a casual, deliberate manner, with no sense of emotion. There was no sign that his behavior was impulsive or driven in any way. There was no sign of delusions, hallucinations, or mental illness, except for the reasoning that no sane man could commit such acts.

Was Harvey's behavior based on a neurological malfunction or a free-will decision? Just as we can perform feats of extreme courage and honor, can we not also perform acts of great evil? Will future neuroscientists be able to determine what went wrong in Harvey's brain, or should the explanation be left up to experts in ethics and morality?

As mentioned earlier, violence can also be traced to cultural and sociological causes. There is no substitute for a stable, loving environment for bringing up our children. Communities and nations that have maintained their cultural, legal, and social constraints have enjoyed relative immunity from violence. When this "cultural corset" is weakened, human behavior tends to regress.

One of the most important characteristics of our brains is that they change and adapt to changing environments. Not only can the brain create behavior, but behavior can create (alter) the brain. We can literally change the structure and chemistry of the brain, for better or worse, by exposing it to different experiences. This is especially true at certain critical times of development, such as the first few years of life, when the brain is extremely malleable by environmental and emotional stimuli [see "Nature, Nurture, Brains, and Behavior," THE WORLD & I, July 1996, p. 194].

We now know that the brain can malfunction because of conditions over which a person has no control, and that this malfunction can lead to impulsive violent behavior. This close relationship between neurologic dysfunction and violent behavior calls for more participation by neurologists in the assessment and treatment of these patients. Most people engage in violent behavior because of the situation they are in. Some do it because they are sick, and those are the people who require clinical help.

Norbert Myslinski is associate professor of neuroscience at the University of Maryland in Baltimore and past president of the Baltimore chapter of the Society for Neuroscience.

Man's World, Woman's World? Brain Studies Point to Differences

Gina Kolata

Dr. Ronald Munson, a philosopher of science at the University of Missouri, was elated when Good Housekeeping magazine considered publishing an excerpt from the latest of the novels he writes on the side. The magazine eventually decided not to publish the piece, but Dr. Munson was much consoled by a letter from an editor telling him that she liked the book, which is written from a woman's point of view, and could hardly believe a man had written it.

It is a popular notion: that men and women are so intrinsically different that they literally live in different worlds, unable to understand each other's perspectives fully. There is a male brain and a female brain, a male way of thinking and a female way. But only now are scientists in a position to address whether the notion is true.

The question of brain differences between the sexes is a sensitive and controversial field of inquiry. It has been smirched by unjustifiable interpretations of data, including claims that women are less intelligent because their brains are smaller than those of men. It has been sullied by overinterpretations of data, like the claims that women are genetically less able to do everyday mathematics because men, on average, are slightly better at mentally rotating three dimensional objects in space.

But over the years, with a large body of animal studies and studies of humans that include psychological tests, anatomical studies, and increasingly, brain scans, researchers are consistently finding that the brains of the two sexes are subtly but significantly different.

Now researchers have a new noninvasive method, functional magnetic resonance imaging, for studying the live human brain at work. With it, one group recently detected certain

New scanner finds more evidence of how the sexes differ in brain functions.

apparent differences in the way men's and women's brains function while they are thinking. While stressing extreme caution in drawing conclusions from the data, scientists say nonetheless that the groundwork was being laid for determining what the differences really mean.

"What it means is that we finally have the tools at hand to begin answering these questions," said Dr. Sally Shaywitz, a behavioral scientist at the Yale University School of Medicine. But she cautioned: "We have to be very very careful. It behooves us to understand that we've just begun."

The most striking evidence that the brains of men and women function differently came from a recent study by Dr. Shaywitz and her husband, Dr. Bennett A. Shaywitz, a neurologist, who is also at the Yale medical school. The Shaywitzes and their colleagues used functional magnetic resonance imaging to watch brains in action as 19 men and 19 women read nonsense words and determined whether they rhymed.

In a paper, published in the Feb. 16 issue of Nature, the Shaywitzes reported that the subjects did equally well at the task, but the men and women used different areas of their brains. The men used just a small area on the left side of the brain, next to Broca's area, which is near the temple. Broca's area has

Men have larger brains; women have more neurons.

long been thought to be associated with speech. The women used this area as well as an area on the right side of the brain. This was the first clear evidence that men and women can use their brains differently while they are thinking.

Another recent study by Dr. Ruben C. Gur, the director of the brain behavior laboratory at the University of Pennsylvania School of Medicine, and his colleagues, used magnetic resonance imaging to look at the metabolic activity of the brains of 37 young men and 24 young women when they were at rest, not consciously thinking of anything.

In the study published in the Jan. 27 issue of the journal Science, the investigators found that for the most part, the brains of men and women at rest were indistinguishable from each other. But there was one difference, found in a brain structure called the limbic system that regulates emotions. Men, on average, had higher brain activity in the more ancient and primitive regions of the limbic system, the parts that are more involved with action. Women, on average, had more activity in the newer and more complex parts of the limbic system, which are involved in symbolic actions.

Dr. Gur explained the distinction: "If a dog is angry and jumps and bites, that's an action. If he is angry and bares his fangs and growls, that's more symbolic."

Dr. Sandra Witelson, a neuroscientist at McMaster University in Hamilton, Ontario, has focused on brain anatomy, studying people with terminal cancers that do not involve the brain. The patients have agreed to participate in neurological and psychological tests and then to allow Dr. Witelson and her colleagues to examine their brains after they die, to look for relationships between brain structures and functions. So far she has studied 90 brains.

Several years ago, Dr. Witelson reported that women have a larger corpus callosum, the tangle of fibers that run down the center of the brain and enable the two hemispheres to communicate. In addition, she said, she found that a region in the right side of the brain that corresponds to the region women used in the reading study by the Shaywitzes was larger in women than in men.

Most recently Dr. Witelson discovered, by painstakingly counting brain cells, that although men have larger brains than women, women have about 11 percent more neurons. These extra nerve cells are densely packed in two of the six layers of the cerebral cortex, the outer shell of the brain, in areas at the level of the temple, behind the eye. These are regions used for understanding language and for recognizing melodies and the tones in speech. Although the sample was small, five men and four women, "the results are very very clear," Dr. Witelson said.

Going along with the studies of brain anatomy and activity are a large body of psychological studies showing that men and women have different mental abilities. Psychologists have consistently shown that men, on average, are slightly better than women at spatial tasks, like visualizing figures rotated in three dimensions, and women, on average, are slightly better at verbal tasks.

Dr. Gur and his colleagues recently looked at how well men and women can distinguish emotions on someone else's face. Both men and women were equally adept at noticing when someone else was happy, Dr. Gur found. And women had no trouble telling if a man or a woman was sad. But men were different. They were as sensitive as women in deciding if a man's face was sad—giving correct responses 90 percent of the time. But they were correct about 70 percent of the time in deciding if women were sad; the women were correct 90 percent of the time.

"A woman's face had to be really sad for men to see it," Dr. Gur said. "The subtle expressions went right by them."

Studies in laboratory animals also find differences between male and female brains. In rats, for example, male brains are three to seven times larger than female brains in a specific area, the preoptic nucleus, and this difference is controlled by sex hormones that bathe rats when they are fetuses.

"The potential existence of structural sex differences in human brains is almost predicted from the work in other animals," said Dr.

Approaches to Understanding Male-Female Brain Differences

Studies of differences in perception or behavior can suggest how male and female thinking may diverge; studies of structural or metabolic differences can suggest why. But only now are differences in brain organization being studied.

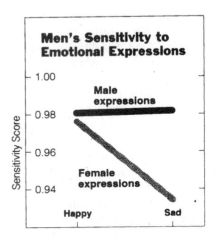 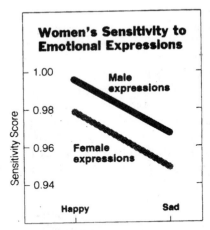

A study compared how well men and women recognized emotions in photos of actors portraying happiness and sadness. Men were equally sensitive to a range of happy and sad faces in men but far less sensitive to sadness in women's faces.

The women in the study were generally more sensitive to happy faces than to sad ones. They were also better able to recognize sadness in a man's face. For both sexes, sensitivity scores reflected the percent of the time the emotion was correctly identified.

Roger Gorski, a professor of anatomy and cell biology at the University of California in Los Angeles. "I think it's a really fundamental concept and I'm sure, without proof, that it applies to our brains."

But the question is, if there are these differences, what do they mean?

Dr. Gorski and others are wary about drawing conclusions. "What happens is that people overinterpret these things," Dr. Gorski said. "The brain is very complicated, and even in animals that we've studied for many years, we don't really know the function of many brain areas."

This is exemplified, Dr. Gorski said, in his own work on differences in rat brains. Fifteen years ago, he and his colleagues discovered that males have a comparatively huge preoptic nucleus and that the area in females is tiny. But Dr. Gorski added: "We've been studying this nucleus for 15 years, and we still don't know what it does. The most likely explanation is that it has to do with sexual behavior, but it is very very difficult to study. These regions are very small and they are interconnected with other things." Moreover, he said, "nothing like it has been shown in humans."

And, with the exception of the work by the Shaywitzes, all other findings of differences in the brains or mental abilities of men and women have also found that there is an amazing degree of overlap. "There is so much overlap that if you take any individual man and woman, they might show differences in the opposite direction" from the statistical findings, Dr. Gorski said.

Dr. Munson, the philosopher of science, said that with the findings so far, "we still can't tell whether the experiences are different" when men and women think. "All we can tell is that the brain processes are different," he said, adding that "there is no Archimedean point on which you can stand, outside of experience, and say the two are the same. It reminds me of the people who show what the world looks like through a multiplicity of lenses and say 'This is what the fly sees.'" "But, Dr. Munson added, "We don't know what the fly sees." All we know he explained, is what we see looking through those lenses.

Some researchers, however, say that the science is at least showing the way to answering the ancient mind-body problem, as applied to the cognitive worlds of men and women.

Dr. Norman Krasnegor, who directs the human learning and behavior branch at the National Institute of Child Health and Human Development, said the difference that science made was that when philosophers talked about mind, they "always were saying, 'We've got this black box.'" But now he said, "we don't have a black box; now we are beginning to get to its operations."

Dr. Gur said science was the best hope for discovering whether men and women inhabited different worlds. It is not possible to answer that question simply by asking people to describe what they perceive, Dr. Gur said, because "when you talk and ask questions, you are talking to the very small portion of the brain that is capable of talking." If investigators ask people to tell them what they are thinking, "that may or may not be closely related to what was taking place" in the brain, Dr. Gur said.

On the other hand, he said, scientists have discovered that what primates perceived depends on how their brains function. Some neurons fire only in response to lines that are oriented at particular angles, while others seem to recognize faces. The world may well be what the philosopher Descartes said it was, an embodiment of the workings of the human mind, Dr. Gur said. "Descartes said that we are creating our world," he said. "But there is a world out there that we can't know."

Dr. Gur said that at this point he would hesitate to boldly proclaim that men and women inhabit different worlds. "I'd say that science might be leading us in that direction," he said, but before he commits himself he would like to see more definite differences in the way men's and women's brains function and to know more about what the differences mean.

Dr. Witelson cautioned that "at this point, it is a very big leap to go from any of the structural or organizational differences that were demonstrated to the cognitive differences that were demonstrated." She explained that "all you have is two sets of differences, and whether one is the basis of the other has not been shown." But she added, "One can speculate."

Dr. Witelson emphasized that in speculating she was "making a very big leap," but she noted that "we all live in our different worlds and our worlds depend on our brains.

"And," she said, "if these sex differences in the brain, with 'if' in big capital letters, do have cognitive consequences, and it would be hard to believe there would be none, then it is possible that there is a genuine difference in the kinds of things that men and women perceive and how these things are integrated. To that extent it may be possible that in some respects there is less of an easy cognitive or emotional communication between the sexes as a group because our brains may be wired differently."

The Shaywitzes said they were reluctant even to speculate from the data at hand. But, they said, they think that the deep philosophical questions about the perceptual worlds of men and women can eventually be resolved by science.

"It is a truism that men and women are different," Dr. Bennett Shaywitz said. "What I think we can do now is to take what is essentially folklore and place it in the context of science. There is a real scientific method available to answer some of these questions."

Dr. Sally Shaywitz added: "I think we've taken a qualitative leap forward in our ability to ask questions." But, she said, "the field is simply too young to have provided more than a very intriguing appetizer."

Studies Show Talking With Infants Shapes Basis of Ability to Think

By SANDRA BLAKESLEE

When a White House conference on early child development convenes today, one of the findings Hillary Rodham Clinton will hear from scientists is that the neurological foundations for rational thinking, problem solving and general reasoning appear to be largely established by age 1—long before babies show any signs of knowing an abstraction from a pacifier.

Furthermore, new studies are showing that spoken language has an astonishing impact on an infant's brain development. In fact, some researchers say the number of words an infant hears each day is the single most important predictor of later intelligence, school success and social competence. There is one catch—the words have to come from an attentive, engaged human being. As far as anyone has been able to determine, radio and television do not work.

"We now know that neural connections are formed very early in life and that the infant's brain is literally waiting for experiences to determine how connections are made," said Dr. Patricia Kuhl, a neuroscientist at the University of Washington in Seattle and a key speaker at today's conference. "We didn't realize until very recently how early this process begins," she said in a telephone interview. "For example, infants have learned the sounds of their native language by the age of six months."

This relatively new view of infant brain development, supported by many scientists, has obvious political and social implications. It suggests that infants and babies develop most rapidly with caretakers who are not only loving, but also talkative and articulate, and that a more verbal family will increase an infant's chances for success. It challenges some deeply held beliefs—that infants will thrive intellectually if they are simply given lots of love and that purposeful efforts to influence babies' cognitive development are harmful.

If the period from birth to 3 is crucial, parents may assume a more crucial role in a child's intellectual development than teachers, an idea sure to provoke new debates about parental responsibility, said Dr. Irving Lazar, a professor of special education and resident scholar at the Center for Research in Human Development at Vanderbilt University in Nashville. And it offers yet another reason to provide stimulating, high quality day care for infants whose primary caretakers work, which is unavoidably expensive.

Environmental factors seem to take over for genetic influence.

The idea that early experience shapes human potential is not new, said Dr. Harry Chugani, a pediatric neurologist at Wayne State University in Detroit and one of the scientists whose research has shed light on critical periods in child brain development. What is new is the extent of the research in the field known as cognitive neuroscience and the resulting synthesis of findings on the influence of both nature and nurture. Before birth, it appears that genes predominantly direct how the brain establishes basic wir-

12. Talking with Infants

TIMETABLE
The Growing Brain: What Might Help Your Infant

Dr. William Staso, an expert in neurological development, suggests that different kinds of stimulation should be emphasized at different ages. At all stages, parental interaction and a conversational dialogue with the child are important. Here are some examples:

FIRST MONTH: A low level of stimulation reduces stress and increases the infant's wakefulness and alertness. The brain essentially shuts down the system when there is overstimulation from competing sources. When talking to an infant, for example, filter out distracting noises, like a radio.

MONTHS 1 TO 3 Light/dark contours, like high-contrast pictures or objects, foster development in neural networks that encode vision. The brain also starts to discriminate among acoustic patterns of language, like intonation, lilt and pitch. Speaking to the infant, especially in an animated voice, aids this process.

MONTHS 3 TO 5 The infant relies primarily on vision to acquire information about the world. Make available increasingly complex designs that correspond to real objects in the baby's environment; motion also attracts attention. A large-scale picture of a fork, moved across the field of vision, would offer more stimulation than just an actual fork.

MONTHS 6 TO 7 The infant becomes alert to relationships like cause and effect, the location of objects and the functions of objects. Demonstrate and talk about situations like how the turning of a doorknob leads to the opening of a door.

MONTHS 7 TO 8 The brain is oriented to make associations between sounds and some meaningful activity or object. For example, parents can deliberately emphasize in conversation that the sound of water running in the bathroom signals an impending bath, or that a doorbell means a visitor.

MONTHS 9 TO 12 Learning adds up to a new level of awareness of the environment and increased interest in exploration; sensory and motor skills coordinate in a more mature fashion. This is the time to let the child turn on a faucet or a light switch, under supervision.

MONTHS 13 TO 18 The brain establishes accelerated and more complex associations, especially if the toddler experiments directly with objects. A rich environment will help the toddler make such associations, understand sequences, differentiate between objects and reason about them.

---

ing patterns. Neurons grow and travel into distinct neighborhoods, awaiting further instructions.

After birth, it seems that environmental factors predominate. A recent study found that mice exposed to an enriched environment have more brain cells than mice raised in less intellectually stimulating conditions. In humans, the inflowing stream of sights, sounds, noises, smells, touches—and most importantly, language and eye contact—literally makes the brain take shape. It is a radical and shocking concept.

Experience in the first year of life lays the basis for networks of neurons that enable us to be smart, creative and adaptable in all the years that follow, said Dr. Esther Thelen, a neurobiologist at Indiana University in Bloomington.

The brain is a self-organizing system, Dr. Thelen said, whose many parts co-operate to produce coherent behavior. There is no master program pulling it together but rather the parts self-organize. "What we know about these systems is that they are very sensitive to initial conditions," Dr. Thelen said. "Where you are now depends on where you've been."

The implication for infant development is clear. Given the explosive growth and self-organizing capacity of the brain in the first year of life, the experiences an infant has during this period are the conditions that set the stage for everything that follows.

In later life, what makes us smart and creative and adaptable are networks of neurons which support our ability to use abstractions from one memory to help form new ideas and solve problems, said Dr. Charles Stevens, a neurobiologist at the Salk Institute in San Diego. Smarter people may have a greater number of neural networks that are more intricately woven together, a process that starts in the first year.

The complexity of the synaptic web laid down early may very well be the physical basis of what we call general intelligence, said Dr. Lazar at Vanderbilt. The more complex that set of interconnections, the brighter the child is likely to be since there are more ways to sort, file and access experiences.

Of course, brain development "happens" in stimulating and dull environments. Virtually all babies learn to sit up, crawl, walk, talk, eat independently and make transactions with others, said Dr. Steven Petersen, a neurologist at Washington University School of Medicine in St. Louis. Such skills are not at risk except in rare circumstances of sensory and social deprivation, like being locked in a closet for the first few years of life. Subject to tremendous variability within the normal range of environments are the abilities to perceive, conceptualize, understand, reason, associate and judge. The ability to function in a technologically complex society like ours does not simply "happen."

One implication of the new knowledge about infant brain development is that intervention programs like Head Start may be too little, too late, Dr. Lazar said. If educators hope to make a big difference, he said, they will need to develop programs for children from birth to 3.

Dr. Bettye Caldwell, a professor of pediatrics and an expert in child development at the University of Arkansas in Little Rock, who supports the importance of early stimulation, said that in early childhood education there is a strong bias against planned intellectual stimulation. Teachers of very young children are taught to follow "developmentally appropriate practices," she said, which means that the child chooses what he or she wants to do. The teacher is a responder and not a stimulator.

Asked about the bias Dr. Caldwell described, Matthew Melmed, executive director of Zero to Three, a research and training organization for early childhood development in Washington, D.C., said that knowing how much stimulation is too much or too little, especially for infants, is "a really tricky question. It's a dilemma parents and educators face every day," he said.

In a poll released today, Zero to Three found that 87 percent of parents think that the more stimulation a baby receives the better off the baby is, Mr. Melmed said. "Many parents have the concept that a baby is something you fill up with information and that's not good," he said.

"We are concerned that many parents are going to take this new information about brain research and rush to do more things with their babies, more activities, forgetting that it's not the activities that are important. The most important thing is connecting with the baby and creating an emotional bond," Mr. Melmed said.

There is some danger of overstimulating an infant, said Dr. William Staso, a school psychologist from Orcutt, Calif., who has written a book called "What Stimulation Your Baby Needs to Become Smart." Some people think that any interaction with very young children that involves their intelligence must also involve pushing them to excel, he said. But the "curriculum" that most benefits young babies is simply common sense, Dr. Staso said. It does not involve teaching several languages or numerical concepts but rather carrying out an ongoing dialogue with adult speech. Vocabulary words are a magnet for a child's thinking and reasoning skills.

This constant patter may be the single most important factor in early brain development, said Dr. Betty Hart, a professor emeritus of human development at the University of Kansas in Lawrence. With her colleague, Dr. Todd Ridley of the University of Alaska, Dr. Hart recently co-authored a book—"Meaningful Differences in the Everyday Experience of Young American Children."

Challenging the deep belief that lots of love is enough.

The researchers studied 42 children born to professional, working class or welfare parents. During the first two and a half years of the children's lives, the scientists spent an hour a month recording every spoken word and every parent-child interaction in every home. For all the families, the data include 1,300 hours of everyday interactions, Dr. Hart said, involving millions of ordinary utterances.

At age 3, the children were given standard tests. The children of professional parents scored highest. Spoken language was the key variable, Dr. Hart said.

A child with professional parents heard, on average, 2,100 words an hour. Children of working-class parents heard 1,200 words and those with parents on welfare heard only 600 words an hour. Professional parents talked three times as much to their infants, Dr. Hart said. Moreover, children with professional parents got positive feedback 30 times an hour—twice as often as working-class parents and five times as often as welfare parents.

The tone of voice made a difference, Dr. Hart said. Affirmative feedback is very important. A child who hears, "What did we do yesterday? What did we see?" will listen more to a parent than will a child who always hears "Stop that," or "Come here!"

By age 2, all parents started talking more to their children, Dr. Hart said. But by age two, the differences among children were so great that those left behind could never catch up. The differences in academic achievement remained in each group through primary school.

Every child learned to use language and could say complex sentences but the deprived children did not deal with words in a conceptual manner, she said.

A recent study of day care found the same thing. Children who were talked to at very young ages were better at problem solving later on.

For an infant, Dr. Hart said, all words are novel and worth learning. The key to brain development seems to be the rate of early learning—not so much what is wired but how much of the brain gets interconnected in those first months and years.

FAITH & HEALING

Can prayer, faith and spirituality really improve your physical health? A growing and surprising body of scientific evidence says they can.

Claudia Wallis

Draped in embroidered cloth, laden with candles, redolent with roses and incense, the altar at the Santa Fe, New Mexico, home of Eetla Soracco seems an unlikely site for cutting-edge medical research. Yet every day for 10 weeks, ending last October, Soracco spent an hour or more there as part of a controlled study in the treatment of AIDS. Her assignment: to pray for five seriously ill patients in San Francisco.

Soracco, an Estonian-born "healer" who draws on Christian, Buddhist and Native American traditions, did not know the people for whom she was praying. All she had were their photographs, first names and, in some cases, T-cell counts. Picturing a patient in her mind, she would ask for "permission to heal" and then start to explore his body in her mind: "I looked at all the organs as though it is an anatomy book. I could see where things were distressed. These areas are usually dark and murky. I go in there like a white shower and wash it all out." Soracco was instructed to spend one hour a day in prayer, but the sessions often lasted twice as long. "For that time," she says, "It's as if I know the person."

Soracco is one of 20 faith healers recruited for the study by Dr. Elisabeth Targ, clinical director of psychosocial oncology research at California Pacific Medical Center in San Francisco. In the experiment, 20 severely ill AIDS patients were randomly selected; half were prayed for, half were not. None were told to which group they had been assigned. Though Targ has not yet published her results, she describes them as sufficiently "encouraging" to warrant a larger, follow-up study with 100 AIDS patients.

Twenty years ago, no self-respecting M.D. would have dared to propose a double-blind, controlled study of something as intangible as prayer. Western medicine has spent the past 100 years trying to rid itself of remnants of mysticism. Targ's own field, psychiatry, couldn't be more hostile to spirituality: Sigmund Freud dismissed religious mysticism as "infantile helplessness" and "regression to primary narcissism." Today, while Targ's experiment is not exactly mainstream, it does exemplify a shift among doctors toward the view that there may be more to health than blood-cell counts and EKGS and more to healing than pills and scalpels.

"People, a growing number of them, want to examine the connection between healing and spirituality," says Jeffrey Levin, a gerontologist and epidemiologist at Eastern Virginia Medical School in Norfolk. To do such research, he adds, "is no longer professional death." Indeed, more and more medical schools are adding courses on holistic and alternative medicine with titles like Caring for the Soul. "The majority, 10 to 1, present the material uncritically," reports Dr. Wallace Sampson of Stanford University, who recently surveyed the offerings of every U.S. medical school.

This change in doctors' attitudes reflects a broader yearning among their patients for a more personal, more spiritual approach to health and healing. As the 20th century draws to an end, there is growing disenchantment with one of its greatest achievements: modern, high-tech medicine. Western medicine is at its best in a crisis—battling acute infection, repairing the wounds of war, replacing a broken-down kidney or heart. But increasingly, what ails America and other prosperous societies are chronic illnesses, such as high blood pressure, backaches, cardiovascular disease, arthritis, depression and acute illnesses that become chronic, such as cancer and AIDS. In most of these, stress and life-style play a part.

"Anywhere from 60% to 90% of visits to doctors are in the mind-body, stress-related realm," asserts Dr. Herbert Benson, president of the Mind/Body Medical Institute of Boston's Deaconess Hospital and Harvard Medical School. It is a triumph of medicine that so many of us live long enough to develop these chronic woes, but, notes Benson, "traditional modes of therapy—pharmaceutical and surgical—don't work well against them."

Not only do patients with chronic health problems fail to find relief in a doctor's office, but the endless high-tech scans and tests of modern medicine also often leave them feeling alienated and uncared for. Many seek solace in the offices of alternative therapists and faith healers—to the tune of $30 billion a year, by some estimates. Millions more is spent on best-selling books and tapes by New Age doctors such as Deepak Chopra, Andrew Weil and Larry Dossey, who offer an appealing blend of medicine and Eastern-flavored spirituality.

Some scientists are beginning to look seriously at just what benefits patients may derive from spirituality. To their surprise, they are finding plenty of relevant data buried in the medical literature. More than 200 studies that touch directly or indirectly on the role of religion have been ferreted out by Levin of Eastern Virginia and Dr. David Larson, a research psychiatrist formerly at the National Institutes of Health and now at the privately funded National Institute for Healthcare Research. Most of these studies offer evidence that religion is good for one's health. Some highlights:

• A 1995 study at Dartmouth-Hitchcock Medical Center found that one of the best predictors of survival among 232 heart-surgery patients

was the degree to which the patients said they drew comfort and strength from religious faith. Those who did not had more than three times the death rate of those who did.
• A survey of 30 years of research on blood pressure showed that churchgoers have lower blood pressure than nonchurchgoers—5 mm lower, according to Larson, even when adjusted to account for smoking and other risk factors.
• Other studies have shown that men and women who attend church regularly have half the risk of dying from coronary-artery disease as those who rarely go to church. Again, smoking and socioeconomic factors were taken into account.
• A 1996 National Institute on Aging study of 4,000 elderly living at home in North Carolina found that those who attend religious services are less depressed and physically healthier than those who don't attend or who worship at home.
• In a study of 30 female patients recovering from hip fractures, those who regarded God as a source of strength and comfort and who attended religious services were able to walk farther upon discharge and had lower rates of depression than those who had little faith.
• Numerous studies have found lower rates of depression and anxiety-related illness among the religiously committed. Nonchurchgoers have been found to have a suicide rate four times higher than church regulars.

There are many possible explanations for such findings. Since churchgoers are more apt than nonattendees to respect religious injunctions against drinking, drug abuse, smoking and other excesses, it's possible that their better health merely reflects these healthier habits.

Some of the studies, however, took pains to correct for this possibility by making statistical adjustments for life-style differences. Larson likes to point out that in his own study the benefits of religion hold up strongly, even for those who indulge in cigarette smoking. Smokers who rated religion as being very important to them were one-seventh as likely to have an abnormal blood-pressure reading as smokers who did not value religion.

Churchgoing also offers social support—which numerous studies have shown to have a salutary effect on well-being. (Even owning a pet has been shown to improve the health of the lonesome.) The Dartmouth heart-surgery study is one of the few that attempts to tease apart the effects of social support and religious conviction. Patients were asked separate sets of questions about their participation in social groups and the comfort they drew from faith. The two factors appeared to have distinct benefits that made for a powerful combination. Those who were *both* religious and socially involved had a 14-fold advantage over those who were isolated or lacked faith.

Could it be that religious faith has some direct influence on physiology and health? Harvard's Herbert Benson is probably the most persuasive proponent of this view. Benson won international fame in 1975 with his best-selling book, *The Relaxation Response*. In it he showed that patients can successfully battle a number of stress-related ills by practicing a simple form of meditation. The act of focusing the mind on a single sound or image brings about a set of physiological changes that are the opposite of the "fight-or-flight response." With meditation, heart rate, respiration and brain waves slow down, muscles relax and the effects of epinephrine and other stress-related hormones diminish. Studies have shown that by routinely eliciting this "relaxation response," 75% of insomniacs begin to sleep normally, 35% of infertile women become pregnant and 34% of chronic-pain sufferers reduce their use of painkilling drugs.

In his latest book, *Timeless Healing* (Scribner; $24), Benson moves beyond the purely pragmatic use of meditation into the realm of spirituality. He ventures to say humans are actually engineered for religious faith. Benson bases this contention on his work with a subgroup of patients who report that they sense a closeness to God while meditating. In a five-year study of patients using meditation to battle chronic illnesses, Benson found that those who claim to feel the intimate presence of a higher power had better health and more rapid recoveries.

"Our genetic blueprint has made believing in an Infinite Absolute part of our nature," writes Benson. Evolution has so equipped us, he believes, in order to offset our uniquely human ability to ponder our own mortality: "To counter this fundamental angst, humans are also wired for God."

In Benson's view, prayer operates along the same biochemical pathways as the relaxation response. In other words, praying affects epinephrine and other corticosteroid messengers or "stress hormones," leading to lower blood pressure, more relaxed heart rate and respiration and other benefits.

Recent research demonstrates that these stress hormones also have a direct impact on the body's immunological defenses against disease. "Anything involved with meditation and controlling the state of mind that alters hormone activity has the potential to have an impact on the immune system," says David Felten, chairman of the Department of Neurobiology at the University of Rochester.

It is probably no coincidence that the relaxation response and religious experience share headquarters in the brain. Studies show that the relaxation response is controlled by the amygdala, a small, almond-shaped structure in the brain that together with the hippocampus and hypothalamus makes up the limbic system. The limbic system, which is found in all primates, plays a key role in emotions, sexual pleasure, deep-felt memories and, it seems, spirituality. When either the amygdala or the hippocampus is electrically stimulated during surgery, some patients have visions of angels and devils. Patients whose limbic systems are chronically stimulated by drug abuse or a tumor often become religious fanatics. "The ability to have religious experiences has a neuroanatomical basis," concludes Rhawn Joseph, a neuroscientist at the Palo Alto VA Medical Center in California.

Many researchers believe these same neuronal and hormonal pathways are the basis for the renowned and powerful "placebo effect." Decades of research show that if a patient truly believes a therapy is useful—even if it is a sugar pill or snake oil—that belief has the power to heal. In one classic 1950 study, for instance, pregnant women suffering from severe morning sickness were given syrup of ipecac, which induces vomiting, and told it was a powerful new cure for nausea. Amazingly, the women ceased vomiting. "Most of the history of medicine is the history of the placebo effect," observes Benson in *Timeless Healing*.

Though Benson devotes much of his book to documenting the power of the placebo effect—which he prefers to call "remembered wellness"—he has come to believe the benefits of religious faith are even greater. "Faith in the medical treatment," he writes, "[is] wonderfully therapeutic, successful in treating 60% to 90% of the most common medical problems. But if you so believe, faith in an invincible and infallible force carries even more healing power ... It is a supremely potent belief."

Do the faithful actually have God on their side? Are their prayers answered? Benson doesn't say. But a true scientist, insists Jeffrey Levin, cannot dismiss this possibility: "I can't directly study that, but as an honest scholar, I can't rule it out."

A handful of scientists have attempted to study the possibility that praying works through some supernatural factor. One of the most cited examples is a 1988 study by cardiologist Randolph Byrd at San Francisco General Hospital. Byrd took 393 patients in the coronary-care unit and randomly assigned half to be prayed for by born-again Christians. To eliminate the placebo effect, the patients were not told of the experiment. Remarkably, Byrd found that the control group was five times as likely to need antibiotics and three times as likely to develop complications as those who were prayed for.

Byrd's experiment has never been replicated and has come under some criticism for design flaws. A more recent study of intercessory prayer with alcoholics found no benefit, while Elisabeth Targ's study of AIDS patients is still too small to produce significant results.

Science may never be able to pin down the benefits of spirituality. Attempts by Benson and others to do so are like "trying to nail Jell-O to the wall," complains William Jarvis, a public-health professor at California's Loma Linda University and the president of the National Council Against Health Fraud. But it may not be necessary to understand how prayer works to put it to use for patients. "We often know something works before we know why," observes Santa Fe internist Larry Dossey, the author of the 1993 best seller *Healing Words*.

A TIME/CNN poll of 1,004 Americans conducted last week by Yankelovich Partners found that 82% believed in the healing power of prayer and 64% thought doctors should pray with those patients who request it. Yet even today few doctors are comfortable with that role. "We physicians are culturally insensitive about the role of religion," says David Larson, noting that fewer than two-thirds of doctors say they believe in God. "It is very important to many of our patients and not important to lots of doctors."

Larson would like physicians to be trained to ask a few simple questions of their seriously or chronically ill patients: Is religion important to you? Is it important in how you cope with your illness? If the answers are yes, doctors might ask whether the patient would like to discuss his or her faith with the hospital chaplain or another member of the clergy. "You can be an atheist and say this," Larson insists. Not doing so, he argues, is a disservice to the patient.

Even skeptics such as Jarvis believe meditation and prayer are part of "good patient management." But he worries, as do many doctors, that patients may become "so convinced of the power of mind over body that they may decide to rely on that, instead of doing the hard things, like chemotherapy."

In the long run, it may be that most secular of forces—economics—that pushes doctors to become more sensitive to the spiritual needs of their patients. Increasingly, American medicine is a business, run by large HMOs and managed-care groups with a keen eye on the bottom line. Medical businessmen are more likely than are scientifically trained doctors to view prayer and spirituality as low-cost treatments that clients say they want. "The combination of these forces—consumer demand and the economic collapse of medicine—are very powerful influences that are making medicine suddenly open to this direction," observes Andrew Weil, a Harvard-trained doctor and author of *Spontaneous Healing*.

Cynics point out that there is an even more practical reason for doctors to embrace spirituality even if they don't believe. The high cost of malpractice insurance gives physicians an incentive to attend to their patients' spiritual needs—and, if necessary, get on their knees and pray with them. Not only might it help restore their image as infallible caregivers, but if something does go wrong, patients who associate their doctors with a higher power might be less likely to sue.

—Reported by Jeanne McDowell/Los Angeles, Alice Park/New York and Lisa H. Towle/Raleigh

Problems Influencing Personal Growth

At each stage of development from infancy to old age, humans are faced with new challenges. The infant has the rudimentary sensory apparati for seeing, hearing, and touching but needs to begin coordinating stimuli into meaningful information. For example, early in life the baby begins to recognize familiar and unfamiliar people and usually becomes attached to the primary caregivers. In toddlerhood, the same child must master the difficult skills of walking, talking, and toilet training. This energetic, mobile, and sociable child also needs to learn the boundaries set on his or her behavior by others. As the child matures, not only do physical changes continue to take place, but the family composition may change when siblings are added, parents divorce, or mother and father work outside the home. Playmates become more influential, and others in the community, such as day-care workers and teachers, have an increasing influence on the child. The child eventually may spend more time at school than at home. The demands in this new environment require that the child sit still, pay attention, learn, and cooperate with others for long periods of time—behaviors perhaps never before extensively demanded of him or her.

In adolescence the body changes noticeably. Peers may pressure the individual to indulge in new behaviors such as using illegal drugs or engaging in premarital sex. Some older teenagers are said to be faced with an identity crisis when they must choose among career, education, and marriage. The pressures of work and family life exact a toll on less mature youths, while others are satisfied with the workplace and home.

Adulthood and middle age may bring contentment or turmoil as individuals face career peaks, empty nests, advancing age, and perhaps the death of loved ones, such as parents. Again, some individuals cope more effectively with these events than do others.

At any step in the developmental sequence, unexpected stressors challenge individuals. These stressors include major illnesses, accidents, natural disasters, economic recessions, and family or personal crises. It is important to remember, however, that an event need not be negative to be stressful. Any major life change may cause stress. As welcome as weddings, new babies, and job promotions may be, they, too, can be stressful because of the changes in daily life that they require. Each challenge and each change must be met and adjusted to if the individual is going to move successfully to the next stage of development. Some individuals continue along their paths unscathed; others do not fare so well.

This unit of the book examines major problems in various stages of life from childhood to old age. The first unit article commences our chronological look at problems of development. In "Clipped Wings," the results of a report on the deleterious effects of drugs, alcohol, and other substances on the fetus are shared with the reader. As the article suggests, even before birth, problems for our development exist.

There are children who, despite early traumas, remain unscathed, unaffected by early ordeals. In "Invincible Kids," these types of children are examined. Who are they? What qualities do they possess that enable them to overcome early childhood trauma?

We move next to school-aged children and look at the schools. Many readers know that today's schools have been plagued with violence and unruliness. Lyric Wallwork Winik, writing in the *American Educator,* suggests that students are tired of disruptive classmates and that they want control back in their schools. What schools are doing and what students are saying are reviewed in this article.

Lance Morrow, in "Kids & Pot," writes about why marijuana use is rising among teens in America. Interestingly, many of these adolescents' parents tried marijuana in their youth but now prefer that their own children not smoke it. In the second part of this article, an Illinois high school is highlighted. The report "High Times at New Trier High," by James Graff, identifies levels of drug usage by students and reveals how this school is handling its teen drug problem.

In a scientific article, Martha McClintock and Gilbert Herdt rethink puberty. Puberty, they say, is but one stage in adolescence. Others exist, among them the stage formed during our first inkling of sexual attraction to another individual. Why we must reconsider our notion of this singular stage of adolescence is the focus of this article.

We move next to adulthood. Robert Bly, one of the leading critics of American adult life, says that we are really only half adults. In other words, we often behave like adolescents when we should be able to move beyond this stage. Bly blames society, for example, television, for this phenomenon. Why we behave this way and what we can do to promote maturity are the main points of this article. Bly warns that unless adults behave like adults, adolescents will follow our lead and never mature either.

Old age is the central issue in "Older, Longer." People perpetually seem to seek the fountain of youth, but how long can we live: what factors induce people to live to older ages? Jill Smolowe looks at research that is examin-

UNIT 3

ing ways to prevent aging, after first discussing what affects the aging process, nature or nurture.

The ultimate developmental stage is death. Death is a topic that both fascinates and frightens most of us. There are some individuals, however, who choose to die. In "The Mystery of Suicide," David Gelman grapples with the serious topic of suicide while our society currently struggles with right-to-die and euthanasia issues.

Finally, Brenda Koerner, in "Is There Life after Death?" examines the psychology and physiology behind near-death experiences.

Looking Ahead: Challenge Questions

Individuals face challenges at every phase of development. What challenges are typical of each stage, as mentioned in this unit? What are other challenges that have not been mentioned? What stage do you believe is most demanding? Why?

If drugs and other addictive substances have detrimental effects on the fetus, should we hold addicted parents responsible for the care and treatment of their addicted and deformed infants? Why or why not? If you answered "yes," what should we do? For example, should we imprison them for neglect? What other factors besides drugs and alcohol influence prenatal life?

How can we enhance children's early development? Even if a child suffers a trauma, does that mean this child is doomed? Who are the resilient children? What contributes to their resiliency? What can we do for children who experience trauma and who are negatively affected by it?

There is little discussion in these articles of children from other cultures. Some cultures rear their children quite differently from the way Americans do. What lessons can we learn from these cultures that we might incorporate into our child-rearing methods? What strategies and techniques could we teach others?

Are today's schools dangerous? What else occurs in schools besides learning? How do students feel about what is happening in American schools? What can we do to make schools safer and promote learning? Are the students the only ones responsible for what is happening in schools today?

Are teens using pot more than their parents did? If yes, from where is this trend originating? How are parents responding to this? Does marijuana use lead to use of other illicit drugs? Do you think marijuana use is one way to mark the transformation of an adolescent from childhood to adulthood? What other markers are there for adolescence? What do you think is the more important stage in adolescence: puberty or sexual attraction?

Are adults behaving more like adolescents than adults? Why? Is this a new trend? What must adults do to mature into reasonable adults? Why must adults behave like adults rather than adolescents, according to Robert Bly? Should we keep a bit of childishness in adulthood? To what avail?

Is adulthood as important to growth as childhood? How many stages do adults pass through? Discuss whether or not American adults face more crises today than did earlier generations. What could we do to change society so that adulthood provides continual positive growth experiences?

What myths do we hold about middle and old age? What truth is there to these myths? How can social scientists and older adults change our attitudes and correct any misinformation?

Can we live longer? Why do people want to live longer? Should we live longer? What must we do to live longer, healthier lives?

What is suicide? Explain why you agree or disagree that people should be able to end their lives by suicide when quality of life declines. Why do you think most people commit suicide? How and when should we intervene with an individual if she or he threatens to commit suicide?

CLIPPED WINGS

The Fullest Look Yet at How Prenatal Exposure to Drugs, Alcohol, and Nicotine Hobbles Children's Learning

LUCILE F. NEWMAN AND STEPHEN L. BUKA

Lucile F. Newman is a professor of community health and anthropology at Brown University and the director of the Preventable Causes of Learning Impairment Project. Stephen L. Buka is an epidemiologist and instructor at the Harvard Medical School and School of Public Health.

SOME FORTY thousand children a year are born with learning impairments related to their mother's alcohol use. Drug abuse during pregnancy affects 11 percent of newborns each year—more than 425,000 infants in 1988. Some 260,000 children each year are born at below normal weights—often because they were prenatally exposed to nicotine, alcohol, or illegal drugs.

What learning problems are being visited upon these children? The existing evidence has heretofore been scattered in many different fields of research—in pediatric medicine, epidemiology, public health, child development, and drug and alcohol abuse. Neither educators, health professionals, nor policy makers could go to one single place to receive a full picture of how widespread or severe were these preventable causes of learning impairment.

In our report for the Education Commission of the States, excerpts of which follow, we combed these various fields to collect and synthesize the major studies that relate prenatal exposure to nicotine, alcohol, and illegal drugs* with various indexes of students' school performance.

The state of current research in this area is not always as full and satisfying as we would wish. Most of what exists is statistical and epidemiological data, which document the frequency of certain high-risk behaviors and correlate those behaviors to student performance. Such data are very interesting and useful, as they allow teachers and policy makers to calculate the probability that a student with a certain family history will experience school failure. But such data often cannot control for the effects of other risk factors, many of which tend to cluster in similar populations. In other words, the same mother who drinks during her pregnancy may also use drugs, suffer from malnutrition, be uneducated, a teenager, or poor—all factors that might ultimately affect her child's school performance. An epidemiological study generally can't tell you how much of a child's poor school performance is due exclusively to a single risk factor.

Moreover, the cumulative damage wrought by several different postnatal exposures may be greater than the damage caused by a single one operating in isolation. And many of the learning problems that are caused by prenatal exposure to drugs can be compounded by such social factors as poverty and parental disinterest and, conversely, overcome if the child lives in a high-quality postnatal environment.

All of these facts make it difficult to isolate and interpret the level and character of the damage that is caused by a single factor. Further, until recently, there was little interest among researchers in the effects of prenatal alcohol exposure because there was little awareness that it was affecting a substantial number of children. The large cohort of children affected by crack is just now entering the schools, so research on their school performance hasn't been extensive.

What does clearly emerge from the collected data is that our classrooms now include many students whose ability to pay attention, sit still, or fully develop their visual, auditory, and language skills was impaired even before they walked through our schoolhouse doors. On the brighter side, the evidence that many of these impairments can be overcome by improved environmental

---

*The full report for the ECS also addressed the effect on children's learning of fetal malnutrition, pre- and postnatal exposure to lead, and child abuse and neglect.

conditions suggests that postnatal treatment is possible; promising experiments in treatment are, in fact, under way and are outlined at the end of this article.

1. Low Birthweight

The collection of graphs begins with a set on low birthweight, which is strongly associated with lowered

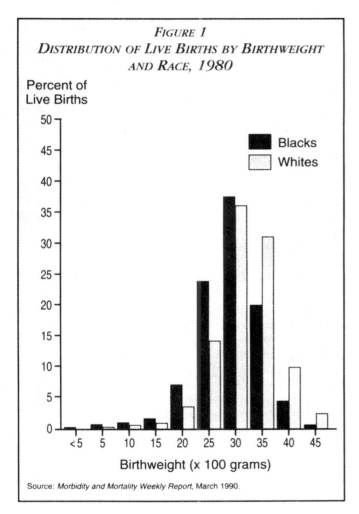

FIGURE 1
DISTRIBUTION OF LIVE BIRTHS BY BIRTHWEIGHT AND RACE, 1980

Source: *Morbidity and Mortality Weekly Report*, March 1990.

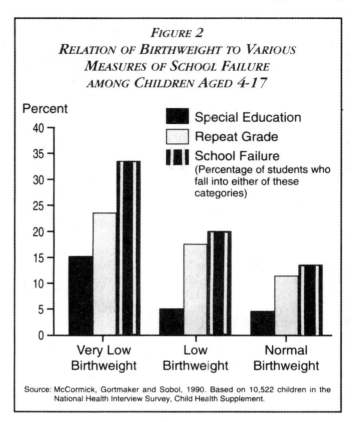

FIGURE 2
RELATION OF BIRTHWEIGHT TO VARIOUS MEASURES OF SCHOOL FAILURE AMONG CHILDREN AGED 4-17

Source: McCormick, Gortmaker and Sobol, 1990. Based on 10,522 children in the National Health Interview Survey, Child Health Supplement.

I.Q. and poor school performance. While low birthweight can be brought on by other factors, including maternal malnutrition and teenage pregnancy, significant causes are maternal smoking, drinking, and drug use.

Around 6.9 percent of babies born in the United States weigh less than 5.5 pounds (2,500 grams) at birth and are considered "low-birthweight" babies. In 1987, this accounted for some 269,100 infants. Low birthweight may result when babies are born prematurely (born too early) or from intrauterine growth retardation (born too small) as a result of maternal malnutrition or actions that restrict blood flow to the fetus, such as smoking or drug use.

In 1987, about 48,750 babies were born at very low birthweights (under 3.25 lbs. or 1,500 grams). Research estimates that 6 to 8 percent of these babies experience major handicaps such as severe mental retardation or cerebral palsy (Eilers et al., 1986; Hack and Breslau, 1986). Another 25 to 26 percent have borderline I.Q. scores, problems in understanding and expressing language, or other deficits (Hack and Breslau, 1986; Lefebvre et al., 1988; Nickel et al., 1982; Vohr et al., 1988). Although these children may enter the public school system, many of them show intellectual disabilities and require special educational assistance. Reading, spelling, handwriting, arts, crafts, and mathematics are difficult school subjects for them. Many are late in developing their speech and language. Children born at very low birthweights are more likely than those born at normal weights to be inattentive, hyperactive, depressed, socially withdrawn, or aggressive (Breslau et al., 1988).

New technologies and the spread of neonatal intensive care over the past decade have improved survival rates of babies born at weights ranging from 3.25 pounds to 5.5 pounds. But, as Figures 2 and 3 show, those born at low birthweight still are at increased risk of school failure. The increased risk, however, is very much tied to the child's postnatal environment. When the data on which Figure 2 is based are controlled to account for socioeconomic circumstances, very low-birthweight babies are approximately twice, not three times, as likely to repeat a grade.

Indeed, follow-up studies of low-birthweight infants at school age have concluded that "the influence of the environment far outweighs most effects of nonoptimal prenatal or perinatal factors on outcome" (Aylward et

3. ❖ PROBLEMS INFLUENCING PERSONAL GROWTH

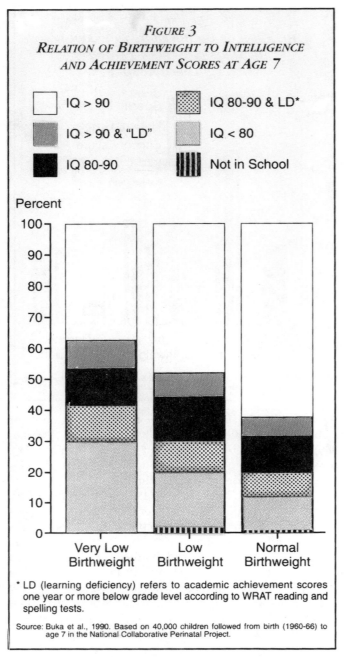

FIGURE 3
RELATION OF BIRTHWEIGHT TO INTELLIGENCE AND ACHIEVEMENT SCORES AT AGE 7

* LD (learning deficiency) refers to academic achievement scores one year or more below grade level according to WRAT reading and spelling tests.

Source: Buka et al., 1990. Based on 40,000 children followed from birth (1960-66) to age 7 in the National Collaborative Perinatal Project.

nitive development and educational achievement. These children are particularly subject to hyperactivity and inattention (Rush and Callahan, 1989).

Data from the National Collaborative Perinatal Project on births from 1960 to 1966 measured, among other things, the amount pregnant women smoked at each prenatal visit and how their children functioned in school at age seven. Compared to offspring of nonsmokers, children of heavy smokers (more than two packs per day) were nearly twice as likely to experience school failure by age seven (see Figure 4). The impact of heavy smoking is apparently greater the earlier it occurs during pregnancy. Children of women who smoked heavily during the first trimester of pregnancy were more than twice as likely to fail than children whose mothers did not smoke during the first trimester. During the second and third trimesters, these risks decreased. In all of these analyses, it is difficult to differentiate the effects of exposure to smoking before birth and from either parent after birth; to distinguish between learning problems caused by low birthweight and those caused by other damaging effects of smoking; or, to disentangle the effects of smoke from the socioeconomic setting of the smoker. But it is worth noting that Figure 4 is based on children born in the early sixties, an era when smoking mothers were fairly well distributed across socioeconomic groups.

One study that attempted to divorce the effects of smoking from those of poverty examined middle-class children whose mothers smoked during pregnancy (Fried and Watkinson, 1990) and found that the infants showed differences in responsiveness beginning at one week of age. Later tests at 1, 2, 3, and 4 years of age showed that on verbal tests "the children of the heavy smokers had mean test scores that were lower than those born to lighter smokers, who in turn did not perform as well as those born to nonsmokers." The study also indicated that the effects of smoke exposure, whether in the womb or after birth, may not be identifiable until later ages when a child needs to perform complex cognitive functions, such as problem solving or reading and interpretation.

al., 1989). This finding suggests that early assistance can improve the intellectual functioning of children at risk for learning delay or impairment (Richmond, 1990).

2. Maternal Smoking

Maternal smoking during pregnancy has long been known to be related to low birthweight (Abel, 1980), an increased risk for cancer in the offspring (Stjernfeldt et al., 1986), and early and persistent asthma, which leads to, among other problems, frequent hospitalization and school absence (Streissguth, 1986). A growing number of new studies has shown that children of smokers are smaller in stature and lag behind other children in cog-

3. Prenatal Alcohol Exposure

Around forty thousand babies per year are born with fetal alcohol effect resulting from alcohol abuse during pregnancy (Fitzgerald, 1988). In 1984, an estimated 7,024 of these infants were diagnosed with fetal alcohol syndrome (FAS), an incidence of 2.2 per 1,000 births (Abel and Sokol, 1987). The three main features of FAS in its extreme form are facial malformation, intrauterine growth retardation, and dysfunctions of the central nervous system, including mental retardation.

There are, in addition, about 33,000 children each year who suffer from less-severe effects of maternal alcohol use. The more prominent among these learning impairments are problems in attention (attention-deficit disor-

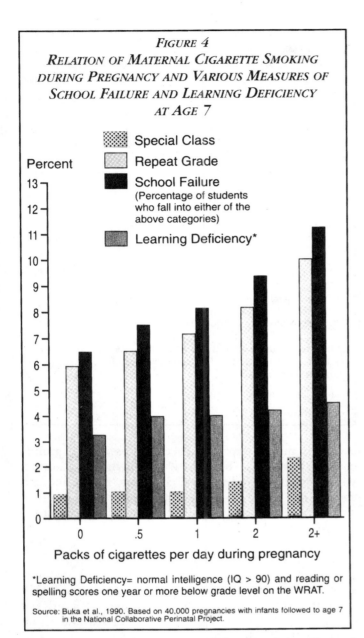

FIGURE 4
RELATION OF MATERNAL CIGARETTE SMOKING DURING PREGNANCY AND VARIOUS MEASURES OF SCHOOL FAILURE AND LEARNING DEFICIENCY AT AGE 7

*Learning Deficiency= normal intelligence (IQ > 90) and reading or spelling scores one year or more below grade level on the WRAT.

Source: Buka et al., 1990. Based on 40,000 pregnancies with infants followed to age 7 in the National Collaborative Perinatal Project.

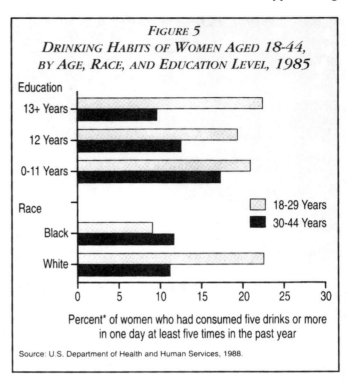

FIGURE 5
DRINKING HABITS OF WOMEN AGED 18-44, BY AGE, RACE, AND EDUCATION LEVEL, 1985

Percent* of women who had consumed five drinks or more in one day at least five times in the past year

Source: U.S. Department of Health and Human Services, 1988.

ders), speech and language, and hyperactivity. General school failure also is connected to a history of fetal alcohol exposure (Abel and Sokol, 1987; Ernhart et al., 1985). Figure 5 shows the drinking habits of women of childbearing age by race and education.

When consumed in pregnancy, alcohol easily crosses the placenta, but exactly how it affects the fetus is not well known. The effects of alcohol vary according to how far along in the pregnancy the drinking occurs. The first trimester of pregnancy is a period of brain growth and organ and limb formation. The embryo is most susceptible to alcohol from week two to week eight of development, a point at which a woman may not even know she is pregnant (Hoyseth and Jones, 1989). Researchers have yet to determine how much alcohol it takes to cause problems in development and how alcohol affects each critical gestational period. It appears that the more alcohol consumed during pregnancy, the worse the effect. And many of the effects do not appear until ages four to seven, when children enter school.

Nearly one in four (23 percent) white women, eighteen to twenty-nine, reported "binge" drinking (five drinks or more a day at least five times in the past year). This was nearly three times the rate for black women of that age (about 8 percent). Fewer women (around 3 percent for both black and white) reported steady alcohol use (two drinks or more per day in the past two weeks).

4. Fetal Drug Exposure

The abuse of drugs of all kinds—marijuana, cocaine, crack, heroin, or amphetamines—by pregnant women affected about 11 percent of newborns in 1988—about 425,000 babies (Weston et al., 1989).

Cocaine and crack use during pregnancy are consistently associated with lower birthweight, premature birth, and smaller head circumference in comparison with babies whose mothers were free of these drugs (Chasnoff et al., 1989; Cherukuri et al., 1988; Doberczak et al., 1987; Keith et al., 1989; Zuckerman et al., 1989). In a study of 1,226 women attending a prenatal clinic, 27 percent tested positive for marijuana and 18 percent for cocaine. Infants of those who had used marijuana weighed an average of 2.8 ounces (79 grams) less at birth and were half a centimeter shorter in length. Infants of mothers who had used cocaine averaged 3.3 ounces (93 grams) less in weight and .7 of a centimeter less in length and also had a smaller head circumference than babies of nonusers (Zuckerman et al., 1989). The study con-

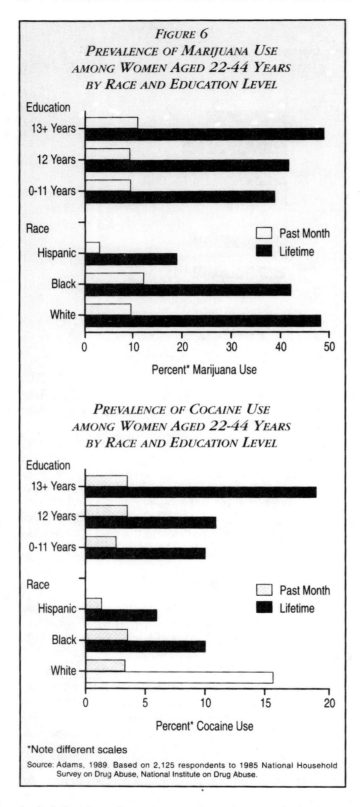

FIGURE 6
PREVALENCE OF MARIJUANA USE AMONG WOMEN AGED 22-44 YEARS BY RACE AND EDUCATION LEVEL

PREVALENCE OF COCAINE USE AMONG WOMEN AGED 22-44 YEARS BY RACE AND EDUCATION LEVEL

*Note different scales
Source: Adams, 1989. Based on 2,125 respondents to 1985 National Household Survey on Drug Abuse, National Institute on Drug Abuse.

cluded that "marijuana use and cocaine use during pregnancy are each independently associated with impaired fetal growth" (Zuckerman et al., 1989).

In addition, women who use these substances are likely to smoke and to gain less weight during pregnancy, two factors associated with low birthweight. The cumulative effect of these risk factors is demonstrated by the finding that infants born to women who gained little weight, who had smoked one pack of cigarettes a day, and who tested positive for marijuana and cocaine

TABLE 1

INFANT WEIGHT DIFFERENCES ASSOCIATED WITH SUBSTANCE ABUSE

Substance Use During Pregnancy at One Prenatal Clinic:

N = 1,226
Marijuana (n = 330) (27%)
Cocaine (n = 221) (18%)

	Birthweight difference:
Marijuana users only vs. non-users	– 2.8 oz.
Cocaine users only vs. non-users	– 3.3 oz.
Combination users (marijuana, cocaine, one pack of cigarettes a day, low maternal weight gain) vs. non-users	–14.6 oz.

Source: Zuckerman et al., 1989.

averaged nearly a pound (14.6 ounces or 416 grams) smaller than those born to women who had normal weight gain and did not use cigarettes, marijuana, and cocaine (see Table 1). The effect of these substances on size is more than the sum of the risk factors combined.

Like alcohol use, drug use has different effects at different points in fetal development. Use in very early pregnancy is more likely to cause birth defects affecting organ formation and the central nervous systems. Later use may result in low birthweight due to either preterm birth or intrauterine growth retardation (Kaye et al., 1989; MacGregor et al., 1987; Petitti and Coleman, 1990). While some symptoms may be immediately visible, others may not be apparent until later childhood (Weston et al., 1989; Gray and Yaffe, 1986; Frank et al., 1988).

In infancy, damaged babies can experience problems in such taken-for-granted functions as sleeping and waking, resulting in exhaustion and poor development. In childhood, problems are found in vision, motor control, and in social interaction (Weston et al., 1989). Such problems may be caused not only by fetal drug exposure but also by insufficient prenatal care for the mother or by an unstimulating or difficult home environment for the infant (Lifschitz et al., 1985).

WHAT CAN be done to ameliorate the condition of children born with such damage? Quite a bit, based on the success of supportive prenatal care and the results of model projects that have provided intensive assistance to both baby and mother from the time of birth. These projects have successfully raised the I.Q. of low- and very-low birthweight babies an average of ten points or more—an increase that may lift a child with below-average intelligence into a higher I.Q. category (i.e., from retarded to low average or from low average to average). Generally known as either educational day care or infant day care, these programs provide a developmentally stimulating environment to high-risk babies and/or intensive parent support to prepare the parent to help her child.

In one such program based at the University of California/Los Angeles, weekly meetings were held among staff, parents, and infants over a period of four years. By the project's end, the low-birthweight babies had caught up in mental function to the control group of normal birthweight children (Rauh et al., 1988). The Infant Health and Development Project, which was conducted in eight cities and provided low-birthweight babies with pediatric follow-up and an educational curriculum with family support, on average increased their I.Q. scores by thirteen points and the scores of very-low birthweight children by more than six points. Another project targeted poor single teenage mothers whose infants were at high risk for intellectual impairment (Martin, Ramey and Ramey, 1990). One group of children was enrolled in educational day care from six and one-half weeks of age to four and one-half years for five days a week, fifty weeks a year. By four and one-half years, the children's I.Q. scores were in the normal range and ten points higher than a control group. In addition, by the time their children were four and one-half, mothers in the experimental group were more likely to have graduated from high school and be self-supporting than were mothers in the control group.

These studies indicate that some disadvantages of poverty and low birthweight can be mitigated and intellectual impairment avoided. The key is attention to the cognitive development of young children, in conjunction with social support of their families.

Article 15

CULTURE & IDEAS

INVINCIBLE KIDS

Why do some children survive traumatic childhoods unscathed? The answers can help every child

Child psychologist Emmy Werner went looking for trouble in paradise. In Hawaii nearly 40 years ago, the researchers began studying the offspring of chronically poor, alcoholic, abusive and even psychotic parents to understand how failure was passed from one generation to the next. But to her surprise, one third of the kids she studied looked nothing like children headed for disaster. Werner switched her focus to these "resilient kids," who somehow beat the odds, growing into emotionally healthy, competent adults. They even appeared to defy the laws of nature: When Hurricane Iniki flattened Kauai in 1992, leaving nearly 1 in 6 residents homeless, the storm's 160-mpg gusts seemed to spare the houses of Werner's success stories.

Werner's "resilient kids," in their late 30s when Iniki hit, helped create their own luck. They heeded storm warnings and boarded up their properties. And even if the squall blew away their roofs or tore down their walls, they were more likely to have the financial savings and insurance to avoid foreclosure—the fate of many of Iniki's victims. "There's not a thing you can do personally about being in the middle of a hurricane," says the University of California–Davis's Werner, "but [resilient kids] are planners and problem solvers and picker-uppers."

For many of America's children, these are difficult times. One in five lives in poverty. More than half will spend some of their childhood living apart from one parent—the result of divorce, death or out-of-wedlock birth. Child abuse, teen drug use and teen crime are surging. Living in an affluent suburb is no protection: Suburban kids are almost as likely as those in violent neighborhoods to report what sociologists call "parental absence"—the lack of a mother and father who are approachable and attentive, and who set rules and enforce consequences.

In the face of these trends, many social scientists now are suggesting a new way of looking at kids and their problems: Focus on survivors, not casualties. Don't abandon kids who fail, but learn from those who succeed.

Such children, researchers find, are not simply born that way. Though genes play a role, the presence of a variety of positive influences in a child's environment is even more crucial; indeed, it can make the difference between a child who founders and one who thrives.

The implications of such research are profound. The findings mean that parents, schools, volunteers, government and others can create a pathway to resiliency, rather than leaving success to fate or to hard-wired character traits. Perhaps most important, the research indicates that the lessons learned from these nearly invincible kids can teach us how to help *all* kids—regardless of their circumstances—handle the inevitable risks and turning points of life. The Search Institute, a Minneapolis-based children's research group, identified 30 resiliency-building factors. The more of these "assets" present in a child's environment, the more likely the child was to avoid school problems, alcohol use, early sexual experimentation, depression and violent behavior.

Like the factors that contribute to lifelong physical health, those that create resilience may seem common-sensical, but they have tremendous impact. Locate a resilient kid and you will also find a caring adult—or several—who has guided him. Watchful parents, welcoming schools, good peers and extracurricular activities matter, too, as does teaching kids to care for others and to help out in their communities.

From thug to Scout. The psychologists who pioneered resiliency theory focused on inborn character traits that fostered success. An average or higher IQ was a good predictor. So was innate temperament—a sunny disposition may attract advocates who can lift a child from risk. But the idea that resiliency can be molded is relatively re-

ROBERT DOLE. He came of age during the tough years of the Great Depression. Later, he overcame a nearly fatal war injury.

"Why me, I demanded? ... Maybe it was all part of a plan, a test of endurance and strength and, above all, of faith."

cent. It means that an attentive adult can turn a mean and sullen teenage thug—a kid who would smash in someone's face on a whim—into an upstanding Boy Scout.

That's the story of Eagle Scout Rudy Gonzalez. Growing up in Houston's East End barrio, Gonzalez seemed on a fast track to prison. By the time he was 13, he'd already had encounters with the city's juvenile justice system—once for banging a classmate's head on the pavement until blood flowed, once for slugging a teacher. He slept through classes and fought more often than he studied. With his drug-using crew, he broke into warehouses and looted a grocery store. His brushes with the law only hardened his bad-boy swagger. "I thought I was macho," says Gonzalez. "With people I didn't like, [it was], 'Don't look at me or I'll beat you up.' "

Many of Gonzalez's friends later joined real gangs. Several met grisly deaths; others landed in prison for drug dealing and murder. More than a few became fathers and dropped out of school. Gonzalez joined urban scouting, a new, small program established by Boy Scouts of America to provide role models for "at risk" youth. At first glance, Gonzalez's path could hardly seem more different than that of his peers. But both gangs and Boy Scouts offer similar attractions: community and a sense of purpose, a hierarchical system of discipline and a chance to prove loyalty to a group. Gonzalez chose merit badges and service over gang colors and drive-by shootings.

Now 20, Gonzalez wears crisply pressed khakis and button-down shirts and, in his sophomore year at Texas A&M, seems well on his way to his goal of working for a major accounting firm. Why did he succeed when his friends stuck to crime? Gonzalez's own answer is that his new life is "a miracle." "Probably, God chose me to do this," he says.

There were identifiable turning points. Scoutmaster John Trevino, a city policeman, filled Gonzalez's need for a caring adult who believed in him and could show him a different way to be a man. Gonzalez's own father was shot and killed in a barroom fight when Rudy was just 6. Fate played a role, too. At 14, using survival skills he'd learned in scouting, Gonzalez saved the life of a younger boy stuck up to his chin in mud in a nearby bayou. The neighborhood hero was lauded in the newspaper and got to meet President Bush at the White House. Slowly, he began to feel the importance of serving his community—another building block of resiliency. For a Scout project he cleaned up a barrio cemetery.

Something special. Once his life started to turn around, Gonzalez felt comfortable enough to reveal his winning personality and transcendent smile—qualities that contributed further to his success. "When I met him, I wanted to adopt him," says his high school counselor, Betty Porter. "There's something about him." She remembers Gonzalez as a likable and prodigious networker who made daily visits to her office to tell her about college scholarships—some she didn't even know about.

> **BILL CLINTON.** He lost his father in an auto wreck before he was born. Later, he coped with an alcoholic, occasionally violent stepfather.
>
> "My mother taught me about sacrifice. She held steady through tragedy after tragedy and, always, she taught me to fight."

A little bit of help—whether an urban scouting program or some other chance to excel—can go a long way in creating resiliency. And it goes furthest in the most stressed neighborhoods, says the University of Colorado's Richard Jessor, who directs a multimillion-dollar resiliency project for the John D. and Catherine T. MacArthur Foundation. Looking back, Gonzalez agrees. "We were just guys in the barrio without anything better to do," he says. "We didn't have the YMCA or Little League, so we hung out, played sports, broke into warehouses and the school." Adds Harvard University's Katherine Newman: "The good news is that kids are motivated. They want to make it. The bad news is that there are too few opportunities."

Resiliency theory brightens the outlook for kids. Mental health experts traditionally have put the spotlight on children who emerge from bad childhoods damaged and scarred. But statistics show that many—if not most—children born into unpromising circumstances thrive, or at least hold their own. Most children of teen mothers, for example, avoid becoming teen parents themselves. And though the majority of child abusers were themselves abused as children, most abused children do not become abusers. Similarly, children of schizophrenics and children who grew up in refugee camps also tend to defy the odds. And many Iowa youths whose families lost their farms during the 1980s farm crisis became high achievers in school.

Living well. A person who has faced childhood adversity and bounced back may even fare *better* later in life than someone whose childhood was relatively easy—or so Werner's recently completed follow-up of the Kauai kids at age 40 suggests. Resilient children in her study reported stronger marriages and better health than those who enjoyed less stressful origins. Further, none had been on welfare, and none had been in trouble with the law. Many children of traumatic, abusive or neglectful childhoods suffer severe consequences, including shifts in behavior, thinking and physiology that dog them into adulthood. But though Werner's resilient kids turned adults tended to marry later, there was little sign of emotional turmoil. At midlife, these resilient subjects were more likely to say they were happy and only one third as likely to report mental health problems.

Can any child become resilient? That remains a matter of debate. Some kids, researchers say, simply may face too many risks. And the research can be twisted to suggest that there are easy answers. "Resiliency theory assumes that it's all or nothing, that you have it or you don't," complains Geoffrey Canada, who runs neighborhood centers for New York's poorest youth. "But for some people it takes 10,000 gallons of water, and for some kids it's just a couple of little drops."

In fact, as Canada notes, most resilient kids do not follow a straight line to success. An example is Raymond Marte, whom Canada mentored, teaching the youth karate at one of his Rheedlen Centers for Children and Families. Today, Marte, 21, is a freshman at New York's Bard College. But only a few years ago, he was just another high school dropout and teenage father, hanging out with gang friends and roaming the streets with a handgun in his pocket. "This is choice time," Canada told

3. ❖ PROBLEMS INFLUENCING PERSONAL GROWTH

> **DR. RUTH WESTHEIMER.** The sex therapist fled the Nazis at 10; her parents died in the Holocaust, and she grew up in a Swiss orphanage.

> "The values my family [instilled] left me with the sense I must make something out of my life to justify my survival."

Marte after five of the boy's friends were killed in three months. Marte re-enrolled in school, became an AmeriCorps volunteer and won a college scholarship. Today, when he walks the streets of his family's gritty Manhattan neighborhood, he is greeted as a hero, accepting high-fives from friends congratulating the guy who made it out.

Good parenting can trump bad neighborhoods. That parents are the first line in creating resilient children is no surprise. But University of Pennsylvania sociologist Frank Furstenberg *was* surprised to find that adolescents in the city's most violence prone, drug-ridden housing projects showed the same resilience as middle-class adolescents. The expectation was that the worst neighborhoods would overwhelm families. Inner-city housing projects do present more risk and fewer opportunities. But good parenting existed in roughly equal proportions in every neighborhood.

Sherenia Gibbs is the type of dynamo parent who almost single-handedly can instill resiliency in her children. The single mother moved her three children from a small town in Illinois to Minneapolis in search of better education and recreation. Still, the new neighborhood was dangerous, so Gibbs volunteered at the park where her youngest son, T. J. Williams, played. Today, six years later, Gibbs runs a city park, where she has started several innovative mentoring programs. At home, Gibbs sets aside time to spend with T. J., now 14, requires him to call her at work when he gets home from school or goes out with friends and follows his schoolwork closely. Indeed, how often teens have dinner with their family and whether they have a curfew are two of the best predictors of teen drug use, according to the National Center on Addiction and Substance Abuse at Columbia University. How often a family attends church—where kids are exposed to both values and adult mentors—also makes a difference. Says Gibbs: "The streets will grab your kids and eat them up."

Some resiliency programs study the success of moms like Gibbs and try to teach such "authoritative parenting" skills to others. When a kid has an early brush with the law, the Oregon Social Learning Center brings the youth's whole family together to teach parenting skills. Not only is the training effective with the offending youth, but younger brothers and sisters are less likely to get in trouble as well.

Despite the crucial role of parents, few—rich or poor—are as involved in their children's lives as Gibbs. And a shocking number of parents—25 percent—ignore or pay little attention to how their children fare in school, according to Temple University psychology professor Laurence Steinberg. Nearly one third of students across economic classes say their parents have no idea how they are doing in school. Further, half the parents Steinberg surveyed did not know their children's friends, what their kids did after school or where they went at night. Some schools are testing strategies for what educator Margaret Wang, also at Temple, calls "educational resilience."

One solution: teaching teams, which follow a student for a few years so the child always has a teacher who knows him well. In Philadelphia, some inner-city schools have set up "parents' lounges," with free coffee, to encourage moms and dads to be regular school visitors.

Given the importance of good parenting, kids are at heightened risk when parents themselves are troubled. But it is a trait of resilient kids that in such circumstances, they seek out substitute adults. And sometimes they become substitute adults themselves, playing a parental role for younger siblings. That was true of Tyrone Weeks. He spent about half his life without his mother as she went in and out of drug rehabilitation. Sober now for three years, Delores Weeks maintains a close relationship with her son. But Tyrone was often on his own, living with his grandmother and, when she died, with his basketball coach, Tennis Young. Young and Dave Hagan, a neighborhood priest in north Philadelphia, kept Weeks fed and clothed. But Weeks also became a substitute parent for his younger brother, Robert, while encouraging his mother in her struggle with cocaine. Says Weeks, "There were times when I was lost and didn't want to live anymore."

Like many resilient kids, Weeks possessed another protective factor: a talent. Basketball, he says, gave him a self-confidence that carried him through the lost days. Today, Weeks rebounds and blocks shots for the University of Massachusetts. Obviously, not all kids have Weeks's exceptional ability. But what seems key is not the level of talent but finding an activity from which they derive pride and sense of purpose.

Mon Ye credits an outdoor leadership program with "keeping me out of gang life." Born in a Cambodian refugee camp, Ye has lived with an older brother in a crime-ridden Tacoma, Wash., housing project since his mother's death a few years ago. Outdoor adventure never interested him. But then parks worker LeAnna Waite invited him to join a program at a nearby recreation center (whose heavy doors are dented with bullet marks from gang fights). Last year, Ye led a youth climb up Mount Rainier and now plans to go to college to become a recreation and park supervisor.

It helps to help. Giving kids significant personal responsibility is another way to build resiliency, whether it's Weeks pulling his family together or Ye supervising preteens. Some of the best youth programs value both service to others and the ability to plan and make choices, according to Stanford University's Shirley Brice Heath. The Food Project—in which kids raise 40,000 pounds of vegetables for Boston food kitchens—is directed by the young par-

> **KWEISI MFUME.** The NAACP chief's stepdad was abusive. After his mom died, he ran with gangs and had five sons out of wedlock.

> "We're all inbred with a certain amount of resiliency. It's not until it's tested... that we recognize inner strength."

ticipants, giving them the chance to both learn and then pass on their knowledge. Older teens often find such responsibility through military service.

Any program that multiplies contacts between kids and adults who can offer advice and support is valuable. A recent study of Big Brothers and Big Sisters found that the nationwide youth-mentoring program cuts drug use and school absenteeism by half. Most youth interventions are set up to target a specific problem like violence or teen sex—and often have little impact. Big Brothers and Big Sisters instead succeeds with classic resiliency promotion: It first creates supportive adult attention for kids, then expects risky behavior to drop as a consequence.

The 42,490 residents of St. Louis Park, Minn., know all about such holistic approaches to creating resiliency. They've made it a citywide cause in the ethnically diverse suburb of Minneapolis. Children First is the city's call for residents to think about the ways, big and small, they can help all kids succeed, from those living in the city's Meadowbrook housing project to residents of parkside ranch houses. The suburb's largest employer, HealthSystem Minnesota, runs a free kids' health clinic. (Doctors and staff donate their time.) And one of the smallest businesses, Steve McCulloch's flower shop,

DIANNE FEINSTEIN. The California senator was raised in privilege, but her mother was mentally ill and at times violent.

"I've never believed adversity is a harbinger of failure. On the contrary, [it] can provide a wellspring of strength."

gives away carnations to kids in the nearby housing project on Mother's Day. Kids even help each other. Two high school girls started a Tuesday night baby-sitting service at the Reformation Lutheran Church. Parents can drop off their kids for three hours. The cost: $1.

The goal is to make sure kids know that they are valued and that several adults outside their own family know and care about them. Those adults might include a police officer-volunteering to serve lunch in the school cafeteria line. Or Jill Terry, one of scores of volunteers who stand at school bus stops on frigid mornings. Terry breaks up fights, provides forgotten lunch money or reassures a sad-faced boy about his parents' fighting. The adopt-a-bus-stop program was started by members of a senior citizens' group concerned about an attempted abduction of a child on her way to school.

Another volunteer, Kyla Dreier, works in a downtown law firm and mentors Angie Larson. The 14-year-old has long, open talks with her mother but sometimes feels more comfortable discussing things with another adult, like Dreier.

Spreading out. St. Louis Park is the biggest success story of over 100 communities nationwide where the Search Institute is trying to develop support for childhood resiliency. In a small surburb, it was relatively easy to rally community leaders. Now Search is trying to take such asset building to larger cities like Minneapolis and Albuquerque, N.M.

In St. Louis Park, resiliency is built on a shoestring budget. About $60,000 a year—all raised from donations—covers the part-time staff director and office expenses. But that's the point, says Children First Coordinator Karen Atkinson. Fostering resiliency is neither complicated nor costly. It's basic common sense—even if practiced too rarely in America. And it pays dividends for all kids.

BY JOSEPH P. SHAPIRO WITH DORIAN FRIEDMAN IN NEW YORK, MICHELE MEYER IN HOUSTON AND MARGARET LOFTUS

STUDENTS WANT MORE DISCIPLINE, DISRUPTIVE CLASSMATES OUT

BY LYRIC WALLWORK WINIK

IT IS SEPTEMBER 3, 1996, the first day of the new school year. But for twenty-one high school students in the greater metropolitan area of a major American city, the first school night isn't spent hitting the books or even in front of the television. It's spent inside a windowless, nondescript room, seated around a wooden veneer table.

For four hours, two groups of young people, eleven from the city schools and another ten from the surrounding suburbs, talked about their education, their schools, their future. Dressed for the first day back in shorts, jeans, and assorted T-shirts, these students, ranging in grade from ninth to twelfth, may or may not be representative of American youth as a whole. But while the two focus groups were not designed for scientific accuracy, what these students had to say, in between fidgeting with pencils and doodling on notepads, should give pause to educators across the country.

According to these students, what their schools most lack—and what students most want—are discipline and order.

Violence, often coupled with drugs, disorder in the classroom, and the weak enforcement of school rules were of paramount concern. Overwhelmingly, the students' message was clear: Standards of behavior matter, both for everyday safety and for academic success.

School violence consumed much of the attention of both focus groups, whether it was sporadic, as at some of the suburban schools, or a more constant threat, as at several of the urban ones. When asked to grade personal behavior at their schools, most students gave their peers, and even their teachers and administrators, C's and D's. Both groups reported fights breaking out and the presence of weapons. Several suburban students spoke of the state police monitoring certain schools for drug problems and thefts, while many urban students told of schools where they were constantly on edge, despite metal detectors, private guards (also called "rent-a-cops"), and new security procedures.

"You think being in school, you be safe," said Jackie,* a sophomore at a city high school, "but you're in school and you're still not safe." "There's a lot of fighting," added Takera, a junior, "... Sometimes I be scared to walk down the hall because somebody will turn off the lights and the boys be hiding in the lockers. So when you walk down the hallway, you don't know what's going to jump out from behind you or in front of you." The trip to and from school may also be a time of danger. "Sometimes I be scared to go on that bus out there," said Lynn, a senior, "so sometimes I walk.... You know how boys will get, like drunk or something at school, so when they get on the bus they don't know how to act and they'll start fighting or something."

Several city students also complained of the easy access outsiders and strangers seem to have to their schools, explaining that almost anyone can enter the building and start a fight. "I mean they let you get in with a temporary ID, instead of enforcing the rules like they're supposed to," Takera explained. "They just let you in with a temporary ID and they don't do anything about it.... I'm saying, if you don't have an ID, you

---

Lyric Wallwork Winik, a Washington, D.C.-area writer, is a frequent contributor to Parade *magazine, where she often covers educational issues. She has also written for* Washingtonian *magazine,* The New York Times, *and other publications.*

*EDITOR'S NOTE: For the purposes of this article, all student names have been changed.

16. Students Want More Discipline

ILLUSTRATED BY ROBERT BARKIN

shouldn't be able to get inside, because everybody's sister, mother, and cousin could be in [my school]."

While episodes of violence seemed to be more common in the city schools, suburban students reported that they were far from exempt. Dave, a suburban sophomore, described the problems in his school as serious: "There's a lot of drugs, but they don't do anything about it. People pull guns on each other and they don't do anything...." Jared, a senior whose school has been plagued by fires, including one where the women's bathroom was doused in magnesium and set ablaze, explained, "People don't respect our school."

This apparent lack of respect carries over from the buses and the bathrooms to the classroom—from how students behave toward each other to how they behave toward teachers. If violence was seen as problematic, classroom disruptions were described as epidemic. Several students—mostly, but not exclusively, urban—indicated that disruptions had become so common that they were almost a regular part of each class period. And they resent having to pay an academic price for their classmates' misbehavior. "It makes you upset, especially like around exam time when you really need to know what's happening," explained Aisha, a city sophomore. "The teacher's telling you what you need to study, and they're disrupting the class and making it hard for you to learn."

While many students feel that their peers bear much of the responsibility for classroom disruptions—"you should already know how to act," explained one urban student—they also fault those teachers who fail to exert their authority in the classroom. "Some teachers just don't have control, and their students take over," said Aisha, "but I can have the same classmates in a different class and they don't say anything." James, a city junior, placed half the blame for disruptions on students and half on teachers, explaining, "... I think the teachers, they need to set precedents. Like on the first day of school, you know, show to the students that they have control. Because, like, if you don't and if they see that they can walk over him, they are going to take that opportunity. And also you've just got a few ignorant students out there who just want to get in detention or whatever else."

Several teens also placed the blame for class disruptions and school tensions directly on the students' shoulders. "I definitely think it's the students' fault, at least in my school," said Marc, a suburban junior. "There's just a lot of ignorant people in my school. They're just disrespectful.... They don't respect people except for themselves or their group."

Many students expressed sympathy for teachers in their struggle to manage and discipline large, unruly classes. Jackie, the urban sophomore, even raised the issue of teachers' personal safety. "Because it's like some people, if they can hit their mother, they can hit a teacher. ... You can't hit a student, but then a student can hit you, really. That's how it is." Added Kim, a freshman, many teachers "are scared of the students."

Many students also expressed frustration with the ineffectiveness of schools' disciplinary procedures, a source of repeated complaints from both sets of students, although with several variations. "The problem lies in the students," said Doug, a suburban senior, "but the fault lies in the administration. The school is there to do something, and [even] if the students are the ones with the problem, they're not going to change on their own. If the administration's not going to do anything—which they won't—nothing's ever going to change. I put the fault in the administration."

Some students thought that their school's disciplinary code needed to be made tougher; some thought that the rules were adequate but said that lack of enforcement was the problem. Others said that there were far too many rules, but the serious problems remained unaddressed. "We've got plenty of rules that's like in binders this thick," said Dave. "They expect you to know every rule. They've got everything from if your pants are too big around your waist, you've got to wear a belt. Your boxers can only show this far. [But] they only do anything about the stupid stuff, like talking in class. The

3. ❖ PROBLEMS INFLUENCING PERSONAL GROWTH

people that bring drugs into the schools and guns, a month after they get expelled, they're back in school. [For] the most serious acts, students need to get kicked out of school—for good—and need to go to an alternative school. And then them schools have to have stronger rules too."

In fact, urban and suburban students, alike, felt themselves plagued by violent and disruptive peers—students who may have been removed from class or even expelled from the school—only to return in a week, a month, or just a day, as if nothing had happened. "...[T]hey're going to know they can do whatever they want and just come back. I think there needs to be a certain point, you know, just kick them out," explained an urban junior, who attends one of the city's more prestigious magnet schools. Lynn, a city senior, agreed. "Just kick them out of class. If you don't show that you're serious about it, then the students aren't going to take you seriously. Like if you just let them get away with things, then students are going to keep doing them."

The support for permanently removing unruly classmates was just as strong among suburban students: "If a student is being disruptive, then just kick him out. Get him out of the class.... I mean, if they don't want to learn, you gave them the chance," said Alan, a senior with an interest in law and graphic design. He went on to add, in obvious frustration, that disruptive students should be told, "This is your high school education, and if you don't want it, we're not going to give it to you. ... If a person is constantly disruptive, then they obviously don't care. If they're throwing paper and whatnot, get them out of class. I mean, sure, everybody may do something to a substitute teacher, everybody may do something once in a while, but there are people who are constantly, absolutely disruptive who just shouldn't be there, who aren't learning but yet they're still there."

Indeed, students' desire for orderly classrooms clearly overlaps with their concern over academics. And here again, the wish is for identifiable standards. In fact, the same preference among many students for enforceable standards for classroom conduct extends, in varying forms, to their views on academic achievement.

"I don't think I'll be prepared for college," said Dave, the suburban sophomore, "because there are just too many students in the school that are just like [not serious].... There are just too many disruptions." For some, large class sizes—several suburban students spoke of classes of forty-five or more—seem to guarantee a certain level of anonymity in which standards of behavior and academic achievement are both allowed to slide.

Several urban students also complained that, in some instances, good behavior is allowed to substitute for academic achievement. "I think they just grade you on the way you act," said Aisha, "If you was quiet, you get a 90." Added Takera, "They give you what they think you deserve...."

One suburban student explained that there was very little difference in the actual work between standard and honors classes. The real difference was to be found in students' behavior: "... the kids in there actually want to learn, that's why they're signed up for honors, they actually want to be there."

Indeed, most of these high schoolers have come to *expect* other students to behave badly. Alan, the suburban senior, summarized students' frustrations this way, "I think it's the whole setting. The teachers don't care, the kids don't care, the administration doesn't care, when it comes down to it, after three years, you don't care."

For Guy Molyneux at Peter D. Hart Research Associates, observations like Alan's lead to some larger and troubling conclusions. "Most students accept their current school conditions," he says. "And although they voice specific complaints, they do not have a sense that their schools may have been or could become better." Perhaps most disturbing is the researcher's comment that, "Most of these high schoolers have a hard time imagining a school in which students and teachers are respectful of one another and in which learning and hard work are valued."

For anyone concerned with the state of education, such observations and conclusions raise an important question well beyond the scope of these two focus groups: These students clearly expressed a desire for higher standards, for themselves and their peers, in the areas of both discipline and academics. At the same time, it appears that the students' standards for and expectations of their schools are declining. The question now is: How does the nation and its public school system raise students' expectations—and fulfill them?

KIDS & POT

Marijuana use among teens is up, but baby-boomer parents (who know something about the subject) aren't sure what to do

By LANCE MORROW

IN A DRUG-AND-ALCOHOL REHAB, THE WOUNDED sit grimly on folding chairs, acknowledging the folly of their old life—their misadventures with alcohol, cocaine or other poisons. Then comes the afternoon that is set aside for atonement on the subject of marijuana. Now the chastened air gives way to argument. The house divides along generational lines. The oldest of the sinners (mostly age 50 or older) nod agreement with the official message: Yes, indeed—devil weed. The baby boomers, however, with their rich pharmaceutical histories, begin to snigger and squirm. "Give me a break!" rings out in the hall. The youngest members of the congregation (some in their teens) sit in bewilderment, trying to decide whether to support the geezers or the boomers.

There it is again: the Marijuana Exception... the Reefer Loophole. All the idiots who drank Canadian Club and Heineken for breakfast, or wrecked themselves on smack or meth—they know they done wrong. But "merely" smoking pot? Well...

The question of whether marijuana is a dangerous menace or something less than that—even, perhaps, a kind of benign and unfairly persecuted folk medicine—suddenly dominates discussions of the great American drug habit. Last month voters in Arizona and California passed ballot propositions that legalize the use of marijuana for medicinal purposes, a kind of backdoor quasi-legitimation alarming to the pot hawks, who fear that high-minded tolerance (pot as pain reliever, glaucoma salve, general angel of mercy) may become infectious and spread to the other states.

In August the U.S. Department of Health and Human Services released a study that surveyed almost 18,000 Americans and concluded that marijuana use among youths (ages 12 to 17) has roughly doubled in the past few years. Use of pot by young people rose 105% from 1992 to 1994, and gained 37% between 1994 and 1995. At the Phoenix House Foundation 10 years ago, 13% of adolescents sought treatment for marijuana; today that figure has jumped to 40%.

It is possible that the increased popularity of marijuana is merely cyclical, part of the usual flux and reflux that have also seen harder drugs like cocaine and heroin rise in their allure for a time, and then decline when the consequences became more luridly obvious—only to rise again when a generational forgetfulness sets in and a drug's glamour could assert itself afresh. Indeed, today some experts are worried that an obsessive concern about marijuana may confuse overall perspectives. Says Mark Kleiman, a UCLA professor who specializes in national drug policy: "It's destructive to focus the country on one small part of drug use. Focusing on marijuana ignores the rising use of methamphetamine and the fact that heroin appears to be coming back, and ignores the No. 1 drug of abuse among high school kids—alcohol."

But after all that is said, the marijuana question remains—and is in some ways a more complicated dilemma than, say, heroin, because the problem is morally, culturally and politically subtler. The young indulging in pot these days are mostly the children of the baby boomers, who, once upon a time in the '60s, took to reefer as their recrea-

---

By the time teens reach 17:

68%
can buy marijuana within a day

62%
have friends who use marijuana

58%
have been solicited to buy marijuana

3. ❖ PROBLEMS INFLUENCING PERSONAL GROWTH

tional sacrament, their generation's almost universal drug of defiance. Now the boomers, who were raised on episodes of *Ozzie and Harriet* (and, if anything, identified with David and Ricky), find, to their astonishment, that they themselves have become Ozzie and Harriet: middle-aged! Parents! Conventional! It is a discomfiting transition, as if former members of a Dionysus cult were asked to take up duties as parole officers. The boomers raised hell with authority in the '60s; now some have mixed feelings about exerting that authority themselves—as if it would somehow turn them into their own enemies.

What should the boomers tell their children about marijuana? Should the parents be candid about their own pot use when young? On what authority can the parents persuade their children to avoid pot when the parents have made it to full adulthood more or less seemingly intact, none the worse for their youthful indulgences?

During the '70s, when a certain amount of marijuana burnout from the '60s became evident, pot fell into relative disfavor. But in the past decade, media stories registering disapproval of marijuana have tapered off. It has hardly discredited the substance that Head Boomer Bill Clinton, after stating four years ago that he hadn't inhaled, told an MTV audience that he wishes he could have done so. The President's sneaking snickering line (a kid still putting one over on his parents) suggested the boomers' ambivalence about pot and a kind of time-warping refusal to see it or themselves honestly. A haze of self-cherishing nostalgia confuses them. They want to be their child's friend; they do not wish to be uncool. They may still smoke sometimes and hide it from their kids, as they once hid it from their parents—an amazingly demeaning drama of arrested development.

> **49%**
> of boomer parents tried marijuana in their youth
>
> **32%**
> of kids think their parents used or tried marijuana
>
> **92%**
> of parents said they would tell their teens about their own marijuana use
>
> From a 1996 survey of 1,200 teens and 1,166 parents for the National Center on Addiction and Substance Abuse at Columbia University

The case against marijuana remains relatively undramatic. It is true that the new generation of weed is stronger than what the boomers remember; that potency means it takes fewer puffs to get high, thus cutting down on damage to the respiratory system, for example. On the other hand, stronger pot and higher kids lead to more reckless driving and car accidents. It is true that smoking pot is less harmful than heavy drinking and does not threaten one's life, as do addictions to harder drugs. Proselytical pot smokers love to point out that a fatal overdose would require, say, 40 lbs. of grass smoked over a period of, say, 25 min.

Apologies and rationales for marijuana are often ingenious, sometimes fervent, and in their essence, when applied to marijuana use by adolescents, dangerously wrong. The stage of development through which a child passes from ages 12 to 18 is critical. Adolescence is the labor that gives birth to the adult. It is a painful, indispensable process. Adolescence quite precisely requires the pain and difficulty of learning in order to come out well. Among the lessons, of course, are how to love and support others and how to be responsible.

When people are stoned on marijuana, they tend to focus on one thing at a time: the food, the music, the dog. Conversation deteriorates. More important, says Steve Sussman, a drug-abuse researcher and associate professor at U.S.C., "you don't learn how to cope with real life. You don't learn how to experience life in real terms, to feel bad *normally*. Let's say you smoked marijuana heavily from age 16 to 26, then stopped. The way you process life events emotionally after that may be more like a 16-year-old." Could it be that the famous reluctance of the baby boomer to imagine himself as an adult has something to do with the weed he smoked when young?

It is in the realm of emotional development that marijuana does its damage. In any case, it seems there has been a mistake. Pot is not the drug of youth but rather of old age, the threshold of death—a little buzz before Kevorkian. It is a dulling drug, certainly useful as a palliative for the elderly. The young don't need to have their pain dulled. They need to learn from it. Perhaps baby-boomer parents, as they grow old, should reserve the world's marijuana supply for themselves and for what will no doubt be the gaudy and self-important theatrics of their dying, and encourage their children to be satisfied with becoming better adults than some boomers have managed to be. —*Reported by James L. Graff/Chicago, Elaine Rivera/New York, Ann M. Simmons/Washington and James Willwerth/Los Angeles*

HIGH TIMES AT NEW TRIER HIGH

A model school struggles with a vexing national issue: kids on pot

By JAMES L. GRAFF

WINNETKA

EVEN WITH HIS LEATHER JACKET, WRAP-around shades and permanent slouch, Matt can't quite pull off the menacing air people attach to drug dealers. Maybe it's the fact that he operates under the stately trees of Chicago's wealthy North Shore, or that he is only 17 and wears braces. He parks his late-model Lincoln in the student lot and saunters through the after-school crowd loitering on "Smokers' Corner," a short block from New Trier Township High School. Matt talks the language of business, not crime. "The way to make a large sum of money is with repeat customers," he explains. "With me, these kids can walk out of school and get good quality at good prices—$35 for an eighth [of an ounce of marijuana]. I'm not a pusher, which is disgusting; I'm a dealer—people who want it can get it from me."

Marijuana is Matt's top seller, but today he is hawking some psilocybin mushrooms to two ninth-graders, Russell and Jared. As a bonus, Matt drives his young clients to a Chicago head shop, where they spend $50 on an elaborate porcelain hookah shaped like a mushroom. Afterward they stop at Matt's place, where everyone repairs to the garage for a few bongfuls of "excellent bud" before heading home for dinner.

It is a classic afternoon's adventure for young suburbanites, with a touch—but no more—of peril. In Wilmette, Winnetka, Glencoe and Kenilworth, the posh white suburbs served by New Trier, drug use isn't associated with gang violence, crack houses, addiction or dead-end despair. Getting high has become almost boringly conventional. Drew (names and some other identifying features have been changed), a regular at the Corner, has even kicked around the notion of buying "New Trier Smoking Club" jackets with his friends and awarding mock varsity letters.

Most New Trier kids who smoke pot—by all accounts more than three-fifths of the student body—wouldn't be caught dead in a jacket like that. Only a fraction of New Trier's pot smokers—the denizens of the Corner among them—view getting high as the main part of their identity. For most, marijuana is an ancillary pleasure of growing up comfortably in the '90s, not the least bit incompatible with varsity athletics, the spring musical or advanced-placement chemistry. After all, most of the kids at New Trier will go on to succeed, just as their parents did. The fact that they have tried pot won't cancel out the perks of good breeding and unbounded opportunity.

Situated in Winnetka, where last year the median sale price for a house was $515,000, New Trier regularly sends 95% of its graduates to four-year colleges, many of them the same élite institutions that produced the lawyers, doctors and corporate executives who live here in large part because of the excellent school system. New Trier offers its students—85% white, 12% Asian, 2% Hispanic and 1% African American—everything from international relations and classical Greek to operatic choir and gourmet food. At New Trier, there's nothing called gym class or phys ed; it's kinetic wellness.

"Everybody here overplays marijuana, like it's some horrible thing," says Melinda, a senior who wants to attend an East Coast college. "It's not just something that 'bad' people do. My dad went to an Ivy League school, and he and my mom both tried it in high school." Her parents' concern, she says, is that she'll buy pot laced with speed or crack. But Melinda, who seems representative of the average user at New Trier, smokes only occasionally and seems able to take it or leave it. "The people with problems are the ones who want being high to be reality," she says. "That's not me."

Once a badge of hipness, marijuana today welcomes everyone at New Trier—jocks and literati, nerds and debutantes. "These days it's everywhere," says Dottie, 17. "Cheerleaders puff. Sixth-graders puff." The very ordinariness of drug use leads some to conclude that it is without risk. But there are plenty of kids on the Corner at New Trier who started out as recreational users and now admit they can't stop. One prematurely wise senior voices disdain for "gumpy sophomores who think it's harmless." Some end up in rehab programs, which far more often than not fail initially with adolescents. The sad fact is that many will have a substance-abuse habit all their lives.

If teenage drug use were the kind of problem a school could solve, New Trier would probably ace it. It was among the first high schools in Illinois to face up to the last teenage drug explosion, in 1981. "We made a decision then to go public and say we have a problem," says Jon White, assistant principal for student services. When school officials decided in 1985 to go outside to hire a full-time person to deal with substance abuse, they opted not for an enforcer or an educator but for Mary Dailey, a social worker from an adolescent treatment center.

Dailey, now in her 12th year as the self-styled "drug czarina" of New Trier, heads the oldest and one of the best-funded student-assistance programs in the state. In 1988 she received an award, signed by William Bennett and presented by Nancy Reagan, honoring New Trier's "excellence in drug-prevention education." "I've devoted a career to this," says Dailey, "but I know that drug use is more prevalent in the freshman class than ever before." Despite all the societal angst generated over drug use during the 1980s, she feels that attitudes since then have softened. "In the late '70s and early '80s there was plenty of denial but also the idea that drugs aren't good," says Dailey. "Honestly, today a lot of parents don't feel that way. They hark back to the days when they used. And they don't realize what's happened to drug content or what the implications are of using at such young ages."

New Trier has always prided itself on its enlightened policy toward drug infractions. Some schools, such as nearby Glenbrook High, will permanently expel a student for merely having a roach clip. At New Trier, a student found for the first time under the influence of drugs or alcohol is suspended for five days, but four of those days are placed "in abeyance" if the student and his or her parents agree to go through a substance-abuse program together.

If a law is broken—possession of marijuana, for instance—charges are filed by Scott Harty, a Winnetka police officer per-manently assigned to the school. For amounts less than 10 grams, that can mean a minor fine under a village ordinance; for more or for dealing, kids land in county court. "I don't give warnings," Harty says. The friend-to-friend commerce is hard to infiltrate, he says, so a bust "really puts blood in the water" as kids try to figure out whether someone was "narked" on. But Harty has been around long enough to know that many kids can't be scared straight by the law. "I've arrested kids who just love to see the squad car pull up," he says. "Some of them see a rap sheet as a badge of honor."

The school does what it can to insulate its students. Two years ago, New Trier, formerly an open campus, started keeping its 3,000 students on school grounds all day, except for about 300 juniors and seniors whose parents give permission for them to leave. But even a wealthy, concerned alma mater like New Trier can't fill the shoes of parents who either don't care that their kids are smoking or fail at the task of stopping them. "How could a school eradicate it?" asks New Trier's superintendent, Henry S. Bangser. "Schools have a responsibility to address the problem, but students didn't learn to do drugs here, and mostly they don't do it here."

There are many cooler places for them to do it. Most evenings a party evolves at Dottie's apartment. She moved there after her parents forbade her to smoke marijuana at home. The scene is right out of the '70s: a black light, a beanbag chair and an African drum in the corner. Pink Floyd is cranked up loud. There seems to be a curious lack of sexual tension among the 15 or so adolescent boys and girls, most of them from New Trier, sitting in a rough circle on the floor in the eerie light. No one necks in the corner; attention is focused on the bong slowly circling the assemblage. Everyone who has pot shares it. "The ethics here is if you're 'holding,' you contribute," explains a kid as he fills the bong one more time.

Among kids who admit they can't control their pot smoking, trouble at home often lurks in the background. Even in Chicago's relatively tranquil North Shore, dysfunction blooms in a thousand ways. Drew, for instance, a thoughtful 16-year-old junior who began getting high in the eighth grade, has had trouble handling marijuana from the start. He claims that his absent father once had a substance-abuse problem. By the ninth grade, he says, "my priorities were totally screwed up. I didn't even buy the books I needed. I was selling pot in the boys' room."

Drew ended up in outpatient rehab. "They tell you you're a drug addict, and if you say you're not, you're in denial," he says. "If you say you only use it occasionally, they say you're rationalizing." Still, things improved. Some therapy sessions included Drew's mother. "There was complete honesty," he recalls. "It was the best our relationship has even been."

3. ❖ PROBLEMS INFLUENCING PERSONAL GROWTH

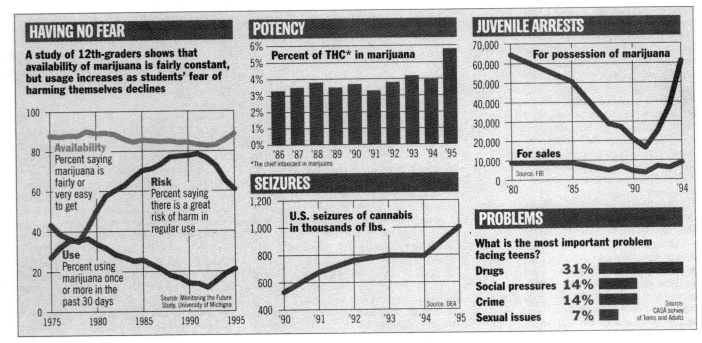

Last school year Drew not only stayed clean, he even talked to younger kids about the perils of drug use. But doubts were gnawing at him. "I didn't think my use justified a whole life in a 12-step program," he remembers. He started to think, as he still does, that recovery was "a blue-collar thing." He says, "It's fine for people who are going to take their dads' places on road crews, but as a creative person, it holds you back. Just look at groups like Aerosmith or the Red Hot Chili Peppers—they got sober, and they started to suck."

When school was out, Drew gave his demons free rein: he rented a cheap cottage in Wisconsin with some friends and laid into a quarter-pound of pot and lots of booze. "We got sick all over everything—it was definitely my failure self. I was like a dog that had been tied up in front of a steak and then finally let loose." Late last summer, a grandparent interceded to put him in a residential treatment center out of state. A week after his return, he says, he was using again.

Drew knows he has an addictive personality. "Even as a kid, I was the one who had to have every baseball card, every comic book," he says. And while he thinks about quitting every day, he doesn't believe he can just stop. So he converts his vice into a twisted virtue. Bolstered by a smattering of existentialism, Beat poetry and rock 'n' roll, Drew and plenty of teenagers like him justify what they do as a glorification of immediate pleasure over conventional restraint, a familiar theme from the '60s. For Drew, smoking copious quantities of pot confers membership in the select club of "the failures," people who were dealt a good hand of money,

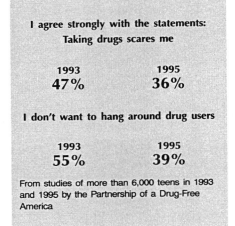

talent and support but who opt for a path of all-but-deliberate self-destruction.

While some New Trier parents are disengaged, as Drew claims his were, others are more hands-on—and angry. But the results of greater parental discipline are not necessarily much better. Michael, a preternaturally bright 16-year-old sophomore, is a case in point. Last year he was smoking up to five times a day, and his grades were suffering. But it wasn't until his scoutmaster caught him getting high on a Boy Scout outing that his parents found out. Their reaction was to ground him for the summer. The punishment gave him a chance to read Dante's *Divine Comedy* and some Shakespeare but did nothing to change his attitude; his friends came over to his place to get high.

At the end of the summer, Michael says, "I realized this wasn't good for me," and he stopped smoking. In what he now describes as a cry for help, he came clean with his parents and told them about the pot, the acid, the mushrooms, everything. "I thought they'd help me, but they were furious," he says. Michael has shelved further attempts to bridge the gap. "It's one thing to punish me and another to alienate me," he says. "Now there's no way I'm going to talk straight with them again. I do, and I'm heading right for a military academy." Michael seems neither disposed nor able to quit entirely. "I've been cutting down a lot, and really only do it on the weekends," he says. "But I can't go cold turkey."

Many parents seem similarly unable to turn their outrage about drug use into a clear and compelling message. When Marta, a willowy junior who sports a nose ring, was caught smoking pot on the street last spring, her mother arrived at the police station in a fury. "She just kept slapping me in the face, left and right," the 17-year-old remembers. But the anger only went so far. "My mom and I didn't tell my dad," Marta says. "He would have gone ballistic, and I would never get my car." Marta figures her mother thinks getting busted has scared her straight, but it has not. And she still expects her promised new car.

The cops on Chicago's North Shore see that kind of enabling behavior all the time. "Parents tell me they never go into their kids' rooms—then they wonder why they have a problem," says Officer Harty. No student has been convicted of a drug felony at New Trier in recent memory. When a kid does get caught in the prosperous communities of the North Shore, police and prosecutors frequently come up against formidable legal talent. "The first reaction of any parent is protection," says John Fay, juvenile officer for the Glencoe police department. "They hire the best because they can afford it. And let's face it, we've got judges who live in this area. They'll explore every avenue before sending a suburban kid to [Cook County Jail at] 26th and California."

THE SCHOOL AND THE POLICE CAN'T do much about pot use without the support and concern of parents, many of whom can't seem to decide whether to be the good cop or the bad cop with their kids. Emily, 48, turned into an enforcer when she found a pipe as she was redecorating her 16-year-old son's room. "I told him I didn't approve, that I didn't think it was necessary," she says. Emily's reaction wasn't as cool when another parent called to tell her that her 14-year-old daughter was smoking pot too. "That really shocked me," says Emily. "I didn't try it until I was 20, and she's all of 14—that's a big difference. What I worry about is the acceleration of gratification: if she's doing marijuana now, what'll she do as a senior?"

Before she caught her kids, Emily attended several meetings of Parent Alliance for Drug and Alcohol Awareness, which is linked to the New Trier school district. "I remember thinking these parents seemed so radical about marijuana," she says. Now she wonders whether random searches of lockers and mandatory drug testing ought to be introduced at school, two options Superintendent Bangser regards as unnecessary. But while she still considers the tone of PADAA too apocalyptic, she finds other parents too lackadaisical. "There's a definite head-in-the-sand attitude here," she says. "People figure our kids' SAT scores are so high they can't be doing it." PADAA sponsors public forums and blankets the community with literature to combat precisely those attitudes, but it's an uphill battle. "It used to be that the parents who got involved were the ones who had problems," sighs PADAA activist Sandra Plowden. "Now it seems like it's the ones without them."

The dilemma for Emily and many other parents of her generation is that she wants to enjoy her children, to be liked by them, so she feels constrained not to crack down too hard. "When we were growing up, there was a big black line between us and our parents," she says. Now she wears sandals, socks and jeans, just like her kids. In the car with her husband and two children, they can all agree on music by Santana, the Beatles and the Doors. "In a way, that makes things easier," says Emily, "but on the other hand, when we tell them something, they just say, 'Whatever.'" Emily even bought a T shirt emblazoned with that word for her son, who refuses to wear it.

So Emily and her husband, a doctor, are left in a parental limbo familiar to her peers: she is on to her kids about smoking marijuana, but she knows that won't be enough to stop them. Next time she catches them, she swears, "I'll lock them in every afternoon"—but she looks doubtful even as she says it. Ultimately, she hopes, the striving for success they've grown up with will check the urge to rebel. "I want to be like Holden Caulfield in The Catcher in the Rye and stop these kids from going off the cliff," she says. "But then I look at the breadth of the problem and think I can't do it."

Rethinking Puberty: The Development of Sexual Attraction

Martha K. McClintock and Gilbert Herdt[1]

Department of Psychology, The University of Chicago, Chicago, Illinois

A youth remembers a time when he was sitting in the family room with his parents watching the original "Star Trek" television series. He reports that he was 10 years old and had not yet developed any of the obvious signs of puberty. When "Captain Kirk" suddenly peeled off his shirt, the boy was titillated. At 10 years of age, this was his first experience of sexual attraction, and he knew intuitively that, according to the norms of his parents and society, he should not be feeling this same-gender attraction. The youth relating this memory is a self-identified gay 18-year-old in Chicago. He also reports that at age 5 he had an absence of sexual attractions of any kind, and that even by age 8 he had not experienced overt awareness of sexual attraction. By age 10, however, a profound transformation had begun, and it was already completed by the time he entered puberty; sexual attraction to the same gender was so familiar to him (Herdt & Boxer, 1993) that it defined his selfhood.

Recent findings from three distinct and significant studies have pointed to the age of 10 as the mean age of first sexual attraction—well before puberty, which is typically defined as the age when the capacity to procreate is attained (Timiras, 1972). These findings are at odds with previous developmental and social science models of behavioral sexual development in Western countries, which suggested that *gonadarche* (final maturation of the testes or ovaries) is the biological basis for the child's budding interest in sexual matters. Earlier studies postulated that the profound maturational changes during puberty instigate the transition from preadolescent to adult forms of sexuality that involve sexual attraction, fantasy, and behavior (Money & Ehrhardt, 1972). Thus, adult forms of sexuality were thought to develop only after gonadarche, typically around ages 12 for girls and 14 for boys, with early and late bloomers being regarded as "off time" in development (Boxer, Levinson, & Petersen, 1989). But the new findings, which locate the development of sexual attraction before these ages, are forcing researchers to rethink the role of gonadarche in the development of sexual attraction as well as the conceptualization of puberty as simply the product of complete gonadal maturation.

Many researchers have conflated puberty and gonadarche, thinking that the two are synonymous in development. The new research on sexual orientation has provided data that invalidate the old model of gonadarche as the sole biological cause of adult forms of sexuality. To the extent that sexual attraction is affected by hormones, the new data indicate that there should be another significant hormonal event around age 10. Indeed, there is: the maturation of the adrenal glands during middle childhood, termed *adrenarche*. (The adrenal glands[2] are the biggest nongonadal source of sex steroids.) This biological process, distinctively different from gonadarche, may underlie the development not only of sexual attraction, but of cognition, emotions, motivations, and social behavior as well. This observation, in turn, leads to a redefinition of prepubertal and pubertal development.

GONADARCHE IS NOT A SUFFICIENT EXPLANATION

Previous biopsychological models of sexual development have attributed changes in adolescent behavior to changes in hormone levels accompanied by gonadarche (Boxer et al., 1989), presumably because of a focus on the most dramatic features of gonadal development in each gender: menarche in girls and spermarche in boys. If gonadarche were responsible for first sexual attractions, then the mean age of the development of sexual attractions should be around the age of gonadarche. Moreover, one would expect a sex difference in the age of first attraction, corresponding to the sex difference in age of gonadarche: 12 for girls and 14 for boys. Neither of these predictions, however, has been borne out by recent data.

In three studies attempting to illuminate the sources of sexual orientation, adolescents have been asked to recall their earliest sexual thoughts; their answers are surprising. One study (Herdt & Boxer, 1993) investigated the development of sexual identity and social relations in a group of self-identified gay and lesbian teenagers (ages 14–20, with a mean age of 18) from Chicago. The mean age for first same-sex attraction was around age 10 for both males and females. Moreover, sexual attraction marked the first event in a developmental sequence: same-sex attraction, same-sex fantasy, and finally same-sex behavior (see Table 1).

This evidence provides a key for understanding sexuality as a process of development, rather than thinking of it as a discrete event, which emerges suddenly at a single moment in time. Virtually all models of adolescent sexual development, from Anna Freud and Erik Erikson up to the present, have been based on the gonadarche model (Boxer et al., 1989). It conceptualizes the development of sexuality as a precipitous, singular, psychological event, fueled by intrinsic changes in hormone levels. Gonadarche is seen as a "switch," turning on desire and attraction, and hence triggering the developmental sequelae of adult sexuality.

Instead, the new data suggest a longer series of intertwined erotic and gender formations that differentiate beginning in middle childhood. Indeed, the psychological sequence of attraction, fantasy, and behavior may parallel the well-known Tanner stages, which are routinely used by clinicians to quantify the process of physical development during puberty (Timiras, 1972). For example, in girls, onset of sexual attraction may co-occur with Tanner Stage II (development of breast buds); sexual fantasy may co-occur with Tanner Stage III (enlargement of mammary glands); and sexual behavior may co-occur with Tanner Stage IV (full breast development), with each psychosexual stage reflecting a different stage of hormonal development. If so, then we may begin to look for a biological mechanism for psychosexual development in the physiological basis for these early Tanner stages that occur prior to the final gonadal maturation that enables procreation.

The generality of these psychological findings is substantiated by two other recent studies that also reported the age of first sexual attraction to be around 10 (see Fig. 1). Pattatucci and Hamer (1995) and Hamer, Hu, Magnuson, Hu, and Pattatucci (1993) asked similar retrospective questions of two distinctive samples of gay- and lesbian-identified adults in the United States. Unlike the Chicago study (Herdt & Boxer, 1993), these studies gathered information from subjects throughout the United States and interviewed adults who were mostly in their mid-30s (range from 18 to 55). They also used different surveys and interview methodologies. Nevertheless, all three studies pinpointed 10 to 10.5 as the mean age of first sexual attraction. Admittedly, none of the studies was ideal for assessing early development of sexuality; the age of first recalled sexual attraction may not be the actual age. Nonetheless, this work is an essential part of the systematic investigation of same-gender attractions in children.

The question then arises whether there is a similar developmental pattern among heterosexuals. We know of no reason to assume that heterosexuals and homosexuals would have different mechanisms for the activation of sexual attraction and desire. Fortunately, we could test this hypothesis because both Pattatucci's and Hamer's samples had comparison groups of heterosexuals. Indeed, the reported age of first attraction was the same for heterosexually as for homosexually identified adults (only the attraction was toward the opposite sex). Thus, regardless of sexual orientation or gender, the age of initial sexual attraction hovered just over age 10. In sum, the switch mechanism responsible for "turning on" sexual attraction seems to be operating at the same time both for boys and for girls, and regardless of whether their sexual orientation is toward the same or opposite gender.

Thus, we surmise that the maturation of the gonads cannot explain the data found independently by these three studies in different samples and geographic areas. There is no known mechanism that would enable the gonads to supply sufficient levels of hormones at that age to cause sexual attraction, because they are not fully developed. The mean age of sexual attraction is the same in both genders and in both structural forms of sexual orientation; therefore, the biological counterpart in both genders and in both structural forms of sexual orientation of sexual attraction is probably the same. These constraints effectively eliminate gonadarche as a candidate to explain the observed findings.

ADRENARCHE IN MIDDLE CHILDHOOD

In the pediatric literature, it is well recognized that children between the ages of 6 and 11 are experiencing a rise in sex steroids. These hormones come from the maturing adrenal glands. Adrenarche is clinically recognized primarily by the onset of pubic hair, but it also includes a growth spurt, increased oil on the skin, changes in the external genitalia, and the development of body odor (New, Levine, & Pang, 1981; Parker, 1991). Nonetheless, both the psychological literature and the institutions of our culture regard this period of middle childhood as hormonally quiescent. Freud's (1905/1965) classic notion of a "latency" period between ages 4 to 6 and puberty perhaps best distills the cultural prejudices. In contrast, we have hypothesized that the rise in adrenal steroid production is critical for understanding interpersonal and intrapsychic development in middle childhood.

Both male and female infants have adult levels of sex steroids during the first days of life, and their adrenal androgens also approach the adult range (see Fig. 2). After a few months, the sex hormone levels begin to fall to a very low level and then remain low until the maturation of the adrenal glands and gonads. When children are between 6 and 8 years of age, their adrenal glands begin to mature. Specifically, the adrenal cortex begins to secrete low levels of androgens, primarily dehydroepiandrosterone (DHEA; see Fig. 2) (Parker, 1991). The metabolism of DHEA leads to both testosterone and estradiol, the primary sex steroids in men and women.

It is noteworthy that both girls and boys experience a rise in androgens, although androgens are typically misidentified as male hormones. Moreover, there is no sex difference in the age at which these androgens begin to rise or the rate at which they do so. After adrenarche, an individual's level of androgens plateaus until around 12 years of age in girls and 14 years of age in boys, whereupon gonadarche triggers a second hormonal rise into the adult range (Parker, 1991).

In adults, the androgens that are produced by the adrenal cortex and their metabolites are known to have psychological effects in a variety of developmental areas relating to aggression,

Table 1. *Ages (years) at which males and females recall having their first same-sex attraction, fantasy, and activity (from Herdt & Boxer, 1993)*

	Males			Females		
Developmental event	M	SD	n	M	SD	n
First same-sex attraction	9.6	3.6	146	10.1	3.7	55
First same-sex fantasy	11.2	3.5	144	11.9	2.9	54
First same-sex activity	13.1	4.3	136	15.2	3.1	49

3. ❖ PROBLEMS INFLUENCING PERSONAL GROWTH

cognition, perception, attention, emotions, and sexuality. Although adult levels of DHEA are not reached until after gonadarche, levels of this hormone do increase significantly around age 10 (see Fig. 2; De Peretti & Forest, 1976), when they become 10 times the levels experienced by children between 1 and 4 years or age. It is plausible that this marked increase in androgen levels alters the brain, and thus behavior, either by modifying neural function or by permanently altering cellular structure.

WHAT IS SPECIAL ABOUT THE FOURTH GRADE?

We considered the hypothesis that the age of first sexual attraction is similar for boys and girls, both homosexual and heterosexual, because there is some marked change in environmental stimuli, socialization, or cognitive abilities around the age of 10. If so, then the 10-fold rise in DHEA would be only correlated with the emergence of sexuality and should not be considered its direct cause.

A major weakness of the idea that environmental stimuli lead to the emergence of sexual attraction at age 10 is the fact that, in the United States, there is no marked cultural prompt for sexuality in a 10-year-old. Children this age are typically in fourth grade. To our knowledge, there is no overt change in social expectations between Grades 3 and 4, or between Grades 4 and 5, that might account for the developmental emergence of sexual attraction at age 10. In U.S. culture, the typical ages for the so-called rites of passage are 12 to 13, when the adolescent becomes a "teenager," or around 15 to 16, when the driver's license is issued. Perhaps between Grades 5 and 6 (or, depending on the school system, between Grades 6 and 7), we might identify a critical change during the transition from elementary to middle school. Yet all of these culturally more prominent transitions occur later than age 10. Other subtle changes, such as girls wearing ornate earrings or boys forming preteenage groups, may occur around age 10, but these social factors seem too weak to adequately explain the sudden emergence of sexual attraction before anatomical changes are noteworthy in the child.

We also considered the possibility that although the social environment does not change at age 10, sexual attraction arises at this age because of an increase in the child's cognitive capability to perceive and understand the sexual and social environment. When the child becomes cognitively capable of understanding sexual interactions among adults, the child is capable also of imitating and putting into action the behaviors he or she has observed. This may be a plausible explanation for development of an awareness of sexual attraction in heterosexuals, and no doubt plays a role in the development of sexuality (after all, people typically do not develop sexuality in a vacuum). But does the explanation hold for children who are sexually attracted to the same gender?

The simple social-learning hypothesis predicts that as soon as children become aware of a strong cultural taboo on the expression of homosexual feelings, they should inhibit or even extinguish these desires in subsequent sexual development. We would therefore expect to find that homosexuals would reveal same-sex attraction significantly later than the age when heterosexuals reveal opposite-sex attraction. But this is not the case.

If 10-year-old children are simply mimicking the sexual behavior most commonly seen in adults (and the biological ability to actually carry out the behavior will arise only with gonadarche), then, given the predominant culture, all 10-year-old boys should demonstrate sexual attraction toward females, and all 10-year-old girls should show sexual attraction toward males. However, this also is not the case.

Other criticisms of simple learning-theory hypotheses regarding sexual development are well known and need not be repeated here (Abramson & Pinkerton, 1995). However, the Sambia of Papua New Guinea (Herdt, 1981) provide particularly compelling counterevidence to a simple learning theory model. The Sambia provide powerful reinforcement for same-gender relations by institutionalizing the practice of men inseminating boys over a period of many years beginning at age 7 to 10. The goal of the men is to masculinize and "grow" the youths into competent reproductive adult men. This intensive training and reinforcement of sexual relationships between males does not result in exclusive homosexuality in adulthood. Instead, adult Sambia men reveal marked bifurcation of their sexual interest; they generality stop all same-gender relations after marriage and enjoy sexual relations with women.

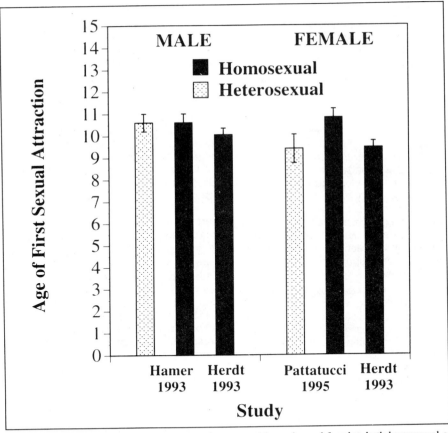

Fig. 1. Mean age (±*SEM*) of first sexual attraction reported by males and females, both homosexual and heterosexual. The data are reported in three studies: Herdt and Boxer (1993), Pattatucci and Hamer (1995), and Hamer, Hu, Magnuson, Hu, and Pattatucci (1993).

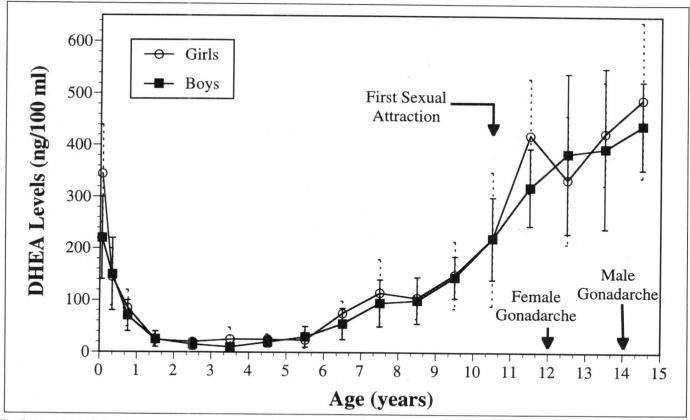

Fig. 2. Mean levels (±*SEM*) of the primary adrenal androgen dehydroepiandrosterone (DHEA) from birth through gonadarche in boys (solid error bars) and girls (dashed error bars). (Data redrawn from De Peretti & Forest, 1976.)

THE RELATIONSHIP BETWEEN ADRENARCHE AND SEXUALITY: CAUSE OR CORRELATION?

Does the inability of the hypotheses of gonadarche and social learning to explain the data imply that adrenarche is the key to the emergence of sexual attraction at age 10? That question cannot yet be answered conclusively. It is entirely possible that the sequential changes in attraction, fantasy, and behavior result from major structural changes in the brain that have their etiology in sources other than sex steroids. However, there has been no documented evidence for such neural structures as of yet. Moreover, if structural changes in the brain do prove to be the cause of the emergence of sexual attraction, modification of all current sexual developmental models and theories will still be needed because they assume that adult desires and behaviors develop from gonadarche.

A change in the nervous system that results from hormones released at adrenarche does look like the most likely developmental mechanism for several reasons. First, girls and boys experience their first sexual attraction, but not gonadarche, at the same age. Second, DHEA, the primary androgen released by the adrenal, is intimately linked with testosterone and estradiol, the major adult sex hormones. Their dynamic relationship is based on the fact that they share many of the fundamental features of steroid function: metabolic pathways that produce the steroids, binding proteins in the blood that carry them to their target tissue, and receptors that enable the cells in the target tissue, including the brain, to change their function in response to the hormonal information. Third, these androgens are known to affect the sexual fantasies and behavior of adolescents and adults, and it is plausible that the same hormones would have similar effects at an earlier age.

RETHINKING PUBERTY: IMPLICATIONS FOR MANY DOMAINS

Given the strong possibility that the currently popular model of puberty is limited, if not incorrect, researchers need to rethink puberty and test the new models in a wide range of psychological disciplines. Adrenarche clearly raises androgens to significant levels, and if these hormones are responsible for the effects seen in sexual attraction, then they are likely to affect a wide range of other behaviors: aggression, cognition, perception, attention, arousal, emotions, and, of course, sexual identity, fantasy, and behavior.

Even if it turns out that hormones released from the adrenal glands are not responsible for the onset of sexual attraction, the behavioral data themselves demonstrate that the concept of puberty must be greatly elaborated and its various stages unpacked. Indeed, Freud's idea of a latency period is seriously flawed. The current behavioral work reinforces the well-established clinical understanding that puberty is composed of at least two separate maturational processes: adrenarche and gonadarche. Any psychosocial research that uses puberty as a stage in development needs to break down the relevant developmental and social behaviors into these two different stages. Researchers need to take into account the hormonal fact that the start of puberty in normal individuals is around ages 6 to 8 and the end of puberty is not until around ages 15 to 17.

The idea of sexuality developing in stages is nothing new to social scientists. But the idea that sexuality is a continuous process that begins from the inside, well before gonadarche, and extends into adulthood is a conceptual advance. These new data from sexual orientation research force a reevaluation of the social and health models of sexual development. No longer can the brain at puberty be treated as a black box, which is suddenly able to process sexual stimuli *de novo* at the time of gonadal change.

Although adrenarche may not be the answer to all the riddles of sexual development, the new data from the developmental and social study of sexual identity have triggered a major conceptual advance in the understanding of both puberty and sexual development as psychobiological phenomena.

Acknowledgements—We extend our profound thanks to Colin Davis, who coordinated the data and helped substantially with manuscript preparation; to Ruvance Pietrz, who edited text and figures; and to Amanda Woodward for her insightful and constructive comments. This work was supported by National Institute of Mental Health MERIT Award R37 MH41788 to Martha K. McClintock.

Notes

1. Address correspondence to Martha K. McClintock, 5730 Woodlawn Ave., Chicago, IL 60637; e-mail: mkml@midway.uchicago.edu.
2. The adrenal glands are small, pyramidal glands located above the kidneys. They produce hormones that affect metabolism, salt regulation, response to stress, and reproductive function, in part by binding in the brain and altering neural function.

References

Abramson, P., & Pinkerton, S. (Eds.). (1995). *Sexual nature, sexual culture.* Chicago: University of Chicago Press.

Boxer, A., Levinson, R. A., & Petersen, A. C. (1989). Adolescent sexuality. In J. Worell & F. Danner (Eds.), *The adolescent as decision-maker* (pp. 209–244). San Diego: Academic Press.

De Peretti, E., & Forest, M. G. (1976). Unconjugated dehydroepiandrosterone plasma levels in normal subjects from birth to adolescence in humans: The use of a sensitive radioimmunoassay. *Journal of Clinical Endocrinology and Metabolism, 43,* 982–991.

Freud, S. (1965). *Three essays on the theory of sexuality.* New York: Basic Books. (Original work published 1905)

Hamer, D. H., Hu, S., Magnuson, V. L., Hu, N., Pattatucci, A. M. L. (1993). A linkage between DNA markers on the X chromosome and male sexual orientation. *Science, 261,* 321–327.

Herdt, G. (1981). *Guardians of the flutes.* New York: McGraw-Hill.

Herdt, G., & Boxer, A. (1993). *Children of horizons.* New York: Beacon Press.

Money, J., & Ehrhardt, A. (1972). *Man, woman, boy, girl.* Baltimore: Johns Hopkins University Press.

New, M. I., Levine, L. S., & Pang, S. (1981). Adrenal androgens and growth. In M. Ritzen (Ed.), *The biology of normal human growth: Transactions of the First Karolinska Institute Nobel Conference* (pp. 285–295). New York: Raven Press.

Parker, L. N. (1991). Adrenarche. *Endocrinology and Metabolism Clinics of North America, 20(1),* 71–83.

Pattatucci, A. M. L., & Hamer, D. H. (1995). Development and familiality of sexual orientation in females. *Behavior Genetics, 25,* 407–420.

Timiras, P. S. (1972). *Developmental physiology and aging.* New York: Macmillan.

Recommended Reading

Becker, J. B., Breedlove, S. M., & Crews, D. (Ed.). (1992). *Behavioral endocrinology.* London: MIT Press.

Boxer, A., & Cohler, B. (1989). The life-course of gay and lesbian youth: An immodest proposal for the study of lives. In G. Herdt (Ed.), *Gay and lesbian youth* (pp. 315–335). New York: Harrington Park Press.

Korth-Schütz, S. S. (1989). Precocious adrenarche. In F. G. Maguelone (Ed.), *Pediatric and adolescent endocrinology* (pp. 226–235). New York: Karger.

Rosenfield, R. L. (1994). Normal and almost normal precocious variations in pubertal development: Premature pubarche and premature thelarche revisited. *Hormone Research, 41,* (Suppl. 2), 7–13.

A World of Half-Adults

Feel younger than your age? Resisting the ravages of time? Your extended adolescence may be leading to the decline and fall of everything you hold dear

AN EXCLUSIVE EXCERPT FROM *THE SIBLING SOCIETY*

Robert Bly

It's the worst of times; it's the best of times. That's how we feel as we navigate from a paternal society, now discredited, to a society in which impulse is given its way. People don't bother to grow up, and we are all fish swimming in a tank of half-adults. The rule is: Where repression was before, fantasy will now be; we human beings limp along, running after our own fantasy. We can never catch up, and so we defeat ourselves by the simplest possible means: speed. Everywhere we go there's a crowd, and the people all look alike.

We begin to live a lateral life, catch glimpses out of the corners of our eyes, keep the TV set at eye level, watch the scores move horizontally across the screen.

We see what's coming out the sideview mirror. It seems like intimacy; maybe not intimacy as much as proximity; maybe not proximity as much as sameness. Americans who are 20 years old see others who look like them in Bosnia, Greece, China, France, Brazil, Germany, and Russia, wearing the same jeans, listening to the same music, speaking a universal language that computer literacy demands. Sometimes they feel more vitally connected to siblings elsewhere than to family members in the next room.

When we see the millions like ourselves all over the world, our eyes meet uniformity, resemblance, likeness, rather than distinction and differences. Hope rises immediately for the long-desired possibility of community. And yet it would be foolish to overlook the serious implications of this glance to the side, this tilt of the head. "Mass society, with its demand for work without responsibility, creates a gigantic army of rival siblings," in German psychoanalyst Alexander Mitscherlich's words.

Commercial pressures push us backward, toward adolescence, toward childhood. With no effective rituals of initiation, and no real way to know when our slow progress toward adulthood has reached its goal, young men and women in our culture go around in circles. Those who should be adults find it difficult or impossible to offer help to those behind. That pressure seems even more intense than it was in the 1960s, when the cry "Turn on, tune in, drop out" was so popular. Observers describe many contemporaries as "children with children of their own."

> **What the young need—stability, presence, attention, advice, good psychic food, unpolluted stories—is exactly what the sibling society won't give them.**

"People look younger all the time." Photographs of men and women a hundred years ago—immigrants, for example—show a certain set of the mouth and jaws that says, "We're adults. There's nothing we can do about it."

By contrast, the face of Marilyn Monroe, of Kevin Costner, or of the ordinary person we see on the street says, "I'm a child. There's nothing I can do about it."

People watching Ken Burns' *History of Baseball* remarked that faces of fans even in the 1920s looked more mature than

3. ❖ PROBLEMS INFLUENCING PERSONAL GROWTH

faces of fans now. Looking at those old photos, one sees men and women who knew how to have fun, but they had one foot in Necessity. Walk down a European street these days and you will see that American faces stand out for their youthful and naive look. Some who are 50 look 30. Part of this phenomenon is good nutrition and exercise, but part of it is that we are losing our ability to mature.

Perhaps one-third of our society has developed these new sibling qualities. The rest of us are walking in that direction. When we all arrive, there may be no public schools at all, nor past paradigms, because only people one's own age will be worth listening to.

We know that the paternal society had an elaborate and internally consistent form with authoritative father reflected upward to the strong community leader and beyond him to the father god up among the stars, which were also arranged in hierarchical levels, called "the seven heavens." Children imitated adults and were often far too respectful for their own good to authorities of all kinds. However, they learned in school the adult ways of talking, writing, and thinking. For some, the home was safe, and the two-parent balance gave them maximum possibility for growth; for others, the home was a horror of beatings, humiliation, and sexual abuse, and school was the only safe place. The teaching at home and in school encouraged religion, memorization, ethics, and discipline, but resolutely kept hidden the historical brutalities of the system.

Our succeeding sibling society, in a relatively brief time, has taught itself to be internally consistent in a fairly thorough way. The teaching is that no one is superior to anyone else; high culture is to be destroyed, and business leaders look sideways to the other business leaders. The sibling society prizes a state of half-adulthood in which repression, discipline, and the Indo-European, Islamic, Hebraic impulse-control system are jettisoned. The parents regress to become more like children, and the children, through abandonment, are forced to become adults too soon, and never quite make it. There's an impulse to set children adrift on their own. The old (in the form of crones, elders, ancestors, grandmothers and grandfathers) are thrown away, and the young (in the form of street children in South America, or latchkey children in the suburbs of this country, or poor children in the inner city) are thrown away.

When I first began to write about this subject, I found it hard to understand why a society run by adolescents should show so much disregard for children, who are, in the mass, worse off under Bill Clinton than they were under Theodore Roosevelt or Warren Harding. And yet, in an actual family, adolescents do not pay much attention to the little ones or to the very old. Newt Gingrich's Contract with America is adolescent.

The deepening rage of the unparented is becoming a mark of the sibling society. Of course, some children in our society feel well parented, and there is much adequate parenting; but there is also a new rage. A man said to me, "Having made it to the one-parent family, we are now on our way toward the zero-parent family."

The actual wages of working-class and middle-class parents have fallen significantly since 1972, so that often both parents work, one parent the day shift, another at night; family meals, talks, reading together no longer take place.

What the young need—stability, presence, attention, advice, good psychic food, unpolluted stories—is exactly what the sibling society won't give them. As we look at the crumbling schools, the failure to protect students from guns, the cutting of funds for Head Start and breakfasts for poor children, cutting of music and art lessons, the enormous increase in numbers of children living in poverty, the poor prenatal care for some, we have to wonder whether there might not be a genuine anger against children in the sibling society.

If we think of catching these changes in story form, "Jack and the Beanstalk" immediately comes to mind. There a fatherless boy, Jack, living alone with his mother, climbs the stalk and finds himself in danger of being eaten by a cruel and enormous giant. Jack, from his hiding place in the kitchen, "was astonished to see how much the giant devoured, and thought he would never have done eating and drinking." That's the way the rest of the world thinks of the United States.

> **American movies in the late 1950s vividly brought forward an old theme of adolescence: the impulse not to defend common projects, common stories, common values.**

> **That most adolescents these days reject the common stories is no surprise. More often than not, they reject them without having read or heard them.**

More specifically, the boy, as helpless and vulnerable as the young ones are today, finds himself faced with an enemy much stronger than he is. We could say that the giant represents the current emphasis on greed, violent movies, and pornographic advertising. The giant is television. It eats up more and more of childhood each year. In the original story Jack learns to steal back some of his family treasures—the gold and silver coins, the divine hen, the golden harp—from the giant. But we have not gotten to that part of the story in our time. We have no idea how to steal back "gold" from the giant. Rather than keeping the children hidden, the adults in the sibling society call the giant over to the cabinet where the children are hidden, open the door, and say, "Here they are!" In the sibling society Jack gets eaten alive.

Television is the thalidomide of the 1990s. In 1995 American children spent about one-third of their waking hours out of school watching television. The National Assessment of Educational Progress reported that only 5 percent of high school graduates could make their way through college-level literature. A recent 1,200-subject study, supported by the National Institute of Mental Health and guided by Mihaly Csikszentmihalyi and Robert Kuby, found that more skill and concentration were needed to eat a meal than to watch television, and the watching left people passive, yet tense, and it left them unable to concentrate.

Television provides a garbage dump of obsessive sexual material inappropriate to the child's age, minute descriptions of brutalities, wars, and tortures all over the world: an avalanche of specialized information that stuns the brain. Even lyrics of songs come too fast for the brain to hear.

Grade school teachers report that in recent years they have had to repeat instructions over and over, or look each child in the face and give instructions separately, which interrupts class work. We know that the sort of music children hear much of—characterized by a heavy beat—is processed mainly by the right brain, which hears the tune as a whole and doesn't see its parts or question it. The brain goes into an alpha state, which rules out active thinking or learning.

American movies in the late 1950s vividly brought forward an old theme of adolescence: the impulse not to defend common projects, common stories, common values. James Dean and Marlon Brando played the roles of young men who demonstrated this rebellion, and the theme began to have an edge on it. "What are you rebelling against?" a Brando character is asked. "What do you have?" is the witty reply.

Human beings often struggle to preserve a given cultural group through the stories it holds in common, its remembered history or fragments of it, and certain agreed-on values and courtesies. A gathering of novels, plays, poems, and songs—these days wrongly called "the canon," more properly "the common stories"—held middle-aged people, elders, and the very young together.

That most adolescents these days reject the common stories is no surprise. More often than not, they reject them without having read or heard them. When adolescence lasted only three or four years, the youths' refusal to support the commonly agreed on novels and poems did not affect the long-range commitment of the group to this reservoir; but now, as American adolescence stretches from age 15 or so all the way to 35, those 20 years of sullen silence or active rejection of any commonality, in literature or otherwise, can have devastating results. One can say that colleges and universities are precisely where the gifts of the past are meant to be studied and ab-

If adults do not turn and help pull the adolescents over the line to adulthood, the adolescents will stay exactly where they are for another 20 or 30 years.

sorbed, yet those very places are where the current damage to the common reservoir is taking place. Men and women in their 20s take teaching jobs, and if they are still adolescent in their 30s, their hostility to the group's literature and to the group itself becomes palpable.

We know it is essential to open the cabinet of common stories to include literature from other cultures besides the European, and to include much more women's literature than the old reservoir held. That is long overdue. But inclusion, one could say, is a job for adults. When the adolescent gets hold of it, a deeply-lying impulse comes into play, and it says, "I'm taking care of people my age, and that's it! My needs are important, and if the group doesn't survive, it doesn't deserve to."

What is asked of adults now is that they stop going *forward*, to retirement, to Costa Rica, to fortune, and turn to face the young siblings and the adolescents—the thousands of young siblings we see around us. Many of these siblings are remarkable and seem to have a kind of emotional knowledge that is far older than they are. Some have sharper intuitions into human motives and people's relationships with each other than any of us had at that age. Some who expect to die early—as many do—see with a brilliant clarity into the dramas taking place all around them.

One can imagine a field with the adolescents on one side of a line drawn on the earth and adults on the other side looking into their eyes. The adult in our time is asked to reach his or her hand across the line and pull the youth into adulthood. That means of course that the adults will have to decide what genuine adulthood is. If the adults do not turn and walk up to this line and help pull the adolescents over, the adolescents will stay exactly where they are for another 20 or 30 years. If we don't turn to face the young ones, their detachment machines, which are louder and more persistent than ours, will say, "I am not a part of this family," and they will kill any relationship with their parents. The parents have to know that.

3. ❖ PROBLEMS INFLUENCING PERSONAL GROWTH

During the paternal society, there were "representatives" of the adult community: highly respected grade school and high school teachers, strong personalities of novels and epics, admired presidents and senators, Eleanor Roosevelts and Madame Curies, priests untouched by scandal, older men and women in each community, both visible and capable of renunciation, who drew young people over the line by their very example. But envy and the habit of ingratitude have ended all that.

The hope lies in the longing we have to be adults. If we take an interest in younger ones by helping them find a mentor, by bringing them along to adult activities, by giving attention to young ones who aren't in our family at all, then our own feeling of being adult will be augmented, and adulthood might again appear to be a desirable state for many young ones.

In the sibling society, as a result of the enormous power of the leveling process, few adults remain publicly visible as models. Because they are invisible, the very idea of the adult has fallen into confusion. As ordinary adults, we have to ask ourselves, in a way that people 200 years ago did not, what an adult is. I have to ask myself what I have found out in my intermittent, poem-ridden attempts to become an adult. Someone who has succeeded better than I could name more qualities of the adult than I will, but I will list a few.

I would say that an adult is a person not governed by what we have called pre-Oedipal wishes, the demands for immediate pleasure, comfort, and excitement. The adult quality that has been hardest to understand for me, as a greedy person, is renunciation. Moreover, an adult is able to organize the random emotions and events of his or her life into a memory, a rough meaning, a story.

It is an adult perception to understand that the world belongs primarily to the dead, and we only rent it from them for a little while. The idea that each of us has the right to change everything is a deep insult to them.

The true adult is the one who has been able to preserve his or her intensities, including those intensities proper to his or her generation and creativity, so that he or she has something with which to meet the intensities of the adolescent. We could say that an adult becomes an elder when he not only preserves his intensities but adds more. In the words of the Persian poet Ansari, an adult is a person who goes out into the world and "gathers jewels of feeling for others."

The hope lies in our longing to be adults, and the longing for the young ones, if they knew what an honorable adulthood is, to become adults as well. It's as if all this has to be newly invented, and the adults then have to imagine as well what an elder is, what the elder's responsibilities are, what it takes for an adult to become a genuine elder.

I will end with a Norwegian story. A man walking through the forest and in danger of dying from cold sees at last a house with smoke rising from the chimney. He sees a 30-year-old man chopping wood and says to him, "Pardon me, but I am a traveler who has been walking all day. Would it be possible for me to stay overnight in your house?" The man says, "It's all right with me, but I am not the father of the house. You'll have to ask my father." He sees a 70-year-old man standing just inside the door, and the man says, "Pardon me, but I am a traveler and have been walking all day. Would it be possible to stay overnight in your house?" The old man says, "It's all right with me, but I am not the father of this house. You'll have to ask my father, who is sitting at the table." He says to this man, who looks about a hundred years old, "Pardon me, but I am a traveler who has been walking all day. Would it be possible for me to stay overnight in your house?" The hundred-year-old says, "It's all right with me, but I am not the father of this house. You'll have to ask my father." And he gestures toward the fireplace. He sees a very old man sitting in a chair near the fire. He goes up to him and says, "I am a traveler, and I have been walking all day. Would it be possible for me to stay overnight in your house?" In a hoarse voice this old old man says, "It's all right with me, but I am not the father of the house. You'll have to ask my father." The traveler glances at the boxed-in bed, and he sees a very, very old man who seems no more than four feet tall lying in the bed. He raises his voice and says to him, "Pardon me, I am a traveler, and I have been walking all day. Would it be possible for me to stay overnight in your house?" The little man in the bed says in a weak voice. "It's all right with me, but I am not the father of this house. You'll have to ask my father." Suddenly the traveler sees a cradle standing at the foot of the bed. In it, there is a very, very little man, hardly the size of a baby, lying curled in the cradle. The man says, "Pardon me, but I am a traveler. I have been walking all day. Would it be possible for me to stay at your house tonight?" In a voice so faint it can hardly be heard, the man in the cradle says, "It's all right with me, but I am not the father of this house. You'll have to ask my father." As the traveler lifts his eyes, he sees an old hunting horn hanging on the wall, made from a sheep's horn, curved like the new moon. He stands and walks over to it, and there he sees a tiny old man no more than six inches long with his head on a tiny pillow and a tiny wisp of white hair. The traveler says, "Pardon me, I am a traveler, and I have been walking all day. Would it be possible for me to stay overnight in your house?" He puts his ear down close to the hunting horn, and the oldest man says, "Yes."

We know there is a Seventh Mother of the House, who is also very small. Perhaps she is far inside the womb, or sitting in the innermost cell of our body, and she gives us permission to live, to be born, to have joy. Her contribution is life. The contribution of the Seventh Father is a house. Together they grant permission from the universe for civilization.

AGING

Older, Longer

Researchers are finding more ways to keep senility at bay, but how long should we aim to live?

By JILL SMOLOWE

WHEN LEMUEL Gulliver encountered the Struldbruggs in the course of his exotic travels, he was enchanted by their immortality—until his hosts set him straight. By age 80, most of the Struldbruggs were "melancholy and dejected," so cut off from pleasure that they were "dead to natural affection." By 90, they were so senile that they could neither sustain a conversation nor read a book. Left alone to combat their assorted physical ailments, Struldbruggs could at best look forward to an eternity of "envy and impotent desires." They were, Gulliver concluded, "the most mortifying sight I ever beheld."

More than two centuries later, Jonathan Swift's grim portrait of senescence delivers a double-edged message. On the one hand, it describes the classic image of old age that still predominates: a period of inevitable and distressing physical and mental decline. On the other, it starkly illustrates the folly of life lived too long—a dilemma that is at the heart of today's debate about the consequences of increased longevity.

It is, however, a problem with a kind of golden lining. Science now believes that much of the physical deterioration brought on by age is far from inevitable. Fast-paced advances in physiological and biomedical research currently under way give hope that old age may finally cast off its pall and become a healthier and more active time of life for millions of people. Just how the elderly will adjust to those extra, active years is a worthy subject for philosophers and accountants alike.

Old age is, in fact, fast becoming the quintessential American experience. Medical breakthroughs and saner life-styles have increased life expectancy by a year or two in each recent decade. Today average life expectancy in the U.S. is 75.5 years, up from 47 at the turn of the century. In the past half-decade alone, the 65-and-older crowd has increased 7%—almost twice the growth rate of those under 65—to reach 34 million, or 13% of the U.S. population. Demographers project that after the first baby boomers hit retirement in 2011, the numbers will explode, with people 65 and older numbering 1 in 5 by the middle of the next century.

That is only part of the story. The 3.8 million seniors who have celebrated their 85th birthday already constitute the fastest-growing segment of the population. The U.S. Census Bureau projects that by 2030, this group, inelegantly dubbed the old-old, will number 9 million, then will swell to 19 million in the following two decades. (Other demographers predict as many as 48 million.) Moreover, while most experts cap average life expectancy at around 85, a research team in Denmark maintains that America's current crop of newborns will live on average to 100. "It will be 80 years before they are 80," says Danish researcher James Vaupel. "In those years there will be a lot of health and biomedical progress."

3. ❖ PROBLEMS INFLUENCING PERSONAL GROWTH

Medical advances are already having a pronounced effect on the seniors' quality of life. A yearly federal survey of 20,000 people 65 and older showed a steady decrease through the 1980s in chronic disabilities of all kinds—with the most dramatic reductions in the 85-plus segment. "It is evolutionary, not revolutionary," says Kenneth Manton, a demographer at Duke University in North Carolina. Nonetheless, it is a welcome relief for the aging. "Life is a lot better now for older people than it was just 20 years ago," says Dr. Harold Karpman, a Beverly Hills, California, cardiologist.

To ensure that those added years continue to be a blessing rather than a painful and expensive curse, gerontologists are pursuing two different strategies to retard the aging process. The preventive approach accepts biological aging as nature's given but believes attendant disease, disability and decline can be delayed or staved off through exercise, diet and medical advances. The more radical strategy challenges nature to a duel by aiming to halt or reverse degeneration in the body's cells.

The medical breakthroughs that have already had the deepest impact are those that enhance sight and mobility. Nationwide, more than a million cataract procedures are performed each year to correct clouding in the lens of the eye. Until 20 years ago, the main treatment was the removal of the patient's lens and its replacement with a thick pair of cataract glasses to correct his vision. Now ophthalmologists are able to implant a new, artificial lens behind the iris, a procedure that has become so routine that it is usually done on an outpatient basis.

Surgery to replace the body's injured or worn-out joints has also risen dramatically. Between 1983 and 1993, the number of hip replacements swelled from 49,000 to 83,000, and knee replacements almost quadrupled, to 131,000. Typically following fractures, the surgery restored patients to the level of mobility they enjoyed before the bone break. That has meant liberation from a walker or wheelchair—and from a housebound existence.

Such surgery, of course, carries the risk of precipitating a stroke or heart attack. In addition, rehabilitation can be long and painful. And though artificial joints are generally durable for 10 years or more, they sometimes fail far earlier—resulting in more surgery, rehabilitation and pain.

The real battle, then, is to prevent such fractures in the first place, and that involves slowing the onset of osteoporosis, a disease that makes bones brittle. Among menopausal women, estrogen-replacement therapy has gained wide usage, despite its risks of depression and endometrial cancer. A newer treatment that received federal approval just last year involves the use of aminobisphosphonates, a class of drugs that inhibit the cells that govern bone loss.

Among men, who tend not to suffer from severe osteoporosis until their mid-80s, researchers are just beginning to explore the benefits and risks of testosterone-replacement therapy. At the University of Pennsylvania Medical School, where a groundbreaking three-year study is at the midway point, some of the 100 test subjects already boast of significantly improved health. But researchers are wary of drawing any conclusions before discovering whether the potential benefits outweigh the risks of heightened cholesterol levels and cardiovascular disease. Whatever the results, insists Dr. Diane Meier, associate professor of geriatrics at Mount Sinai Medical Center in New York City, "the view that nothing can be done is inappropriate. There is no place for therapeutic nihilism."

That sort of spirit also guides the efforts researchers are making to identify the types of degeneration that can be forestalled through preventive—and often remarkably simple—measures. Since 1993, physiologist Ethan Nadel and epidemiologist Loretta DiPietro, both of Yale University, have been pioneering a five-year study on the effects of exercise. The question at the heart of the effort is whether exercise can slow the effects of aging—and if so, which ones. "It is no secret that exercise is beneficial, but people age differently," says DiPietro. "The question we are asking is whether we can truly separate the decline that is a function of biological aging from the decline that is due simply to disuse."

The project's self-volunteered guinea pigs don high-tech gear that monitors their circulatory, respiratory and nervous systems. With their face masks and unique watches that measure and record heart and pulse rates, they look like astronauts in training—an apt resemblance as it turns out. "If you go up in space for three weeks, stay in bed for three weeks or age 30 years," says Nadel, "the wasting that goes on in the muscles, bones and water volume is remarkably similar." The seniors in the program are so pleased by the immediate benefits of the assorted aerobic and muscle-stretching exercises that they seem undaunted by any discomfort. "I was an exercise agnostic. Now I'm a believer," says Alexander Garfinkel, 75. Nancy Gilbert, 81, exults, "It's absolutely fantastic how much better I feel."

The question is: Why do the exercisers feel better? To find answers, the researchers are looking, for instance, at the effects of stretching on the taste buds. If, as they suspect, such exercise enhances the sense of taste, that could be a great boon for the elderly. A common problem of aging is a lessening sense of taste, which makes eating less attractive and can lead to unwanted weight loss. More dangerously, the thirst sensation also appears to slacken. When seniors forget to drink, dehydration can set in without their being aware of it, inducing a drop in blood volume that causes a greater sensitivity to heat changes. The result can be as dramatic as the unexpected deaths among the aged that attended Chicago's heat wave last summer.

Nadel and DiPietro have also noted a related degeneration in the seniors' sense of smell that has equally dangerous consequences. Many seniors, for example, are unable to smell the artificial odorant used in natural gas to signal a leak. As a result, an older person is far more likely to set off an explosion in an unlit stove. The researchers hope their test results will prompt the government either to order an increase in the amount of odorant commonly mixed in with natural gas or to issue an advisory encouraging seniors to install gas detectors in their kitchens.

The research may also prove invaluable in heading off some serious diseases, particularly late-onset diabetes (more accurately called noninsulin-dependent diabetes), which affects 10% of the elderly population. "It is well known that some proteins combine with insulin to allow glucose to move from the blood to the muscle itself," says Nadel—a transfer that would benefit diabetics. "The question is: Do these older people have an increased number of such transporter proteins once they start [exercising]? What has changed? How is the genetic mechanism responding to the training stimuli to produce more transport proteins?" Understanding how the muscle changes in its capability to transport glucose could be a tremendous boost to those suffering from this type of diabetes.

The study's findings may also lead to changes at retirement communities like Heritage Village, the 4,500-person settlement outside Southbury, Connecticut, from which DiPietro and Nadel draw their volunteers. For example, Heritage carefully designed its condominiums and environs to ensure that members never have to use stairs, thus unwittingly promoting the sort of inactivity that researchers suspect fuels degeneration in the aged. Heritage also provides a 24-hour maintenance crew that takes care of gardening services, depriving seniors of a mild form of exercise that gerontologists believe could be a key to helping them maintain good health.

Such activity, in turn, could substantially pare the medical bills of the elderly, which total $50 billion annually and account for 30% of the nation's hefty health-care tab. Fully one-fifth of those dollars are applied to the costs that accumulate after a senior takes a fall. The average bill for emergency treatment resulting from a tumble is $11,000. Dr. Mary Tinetti, a professor of medicine at Yale, who has been researching falls, estimates that the average cost to equip a senior with the hardware that could prevent falls—bathtub grips, stairway railings, bright lights—is just $900. "Although all these things are common sense and doable," she says, "none of them is paid for under Medicare."

In addition to environmental factors, Tinetti's ongoing research has turned up three other main reasons for spills. Foremost is the disorienting side effects of medications, which often cause the drop in blood pressure that brings on dizziness. "Every time you add a medication," she says, "the likelihood of an accident increases exponentially." Seniors also suffer from postural hypertension, a fancy term for the sharp drop in blood to the brain that can result if they stand up too quickly. Also common is a deteriorating sense of balance, the result of erosion in several systems, including visual perception and sensory information from the inner ear and the neurological network.

To address these problems, Tinetti consults with physicians, making sure they monitor the effects of medications on blood pressure. "It's a question of fine-tuning the medication, not eliminating it," she says. To help seniors maintain steadier blood pressure, she instructs them in minor adjustments in routine: sit for a minute or two before getting out of bed; clench and release the fists and wiggle the ankles throughout the day; and stay away from shoes with sticky rubber bottoms, which are as treacherous as slippery soles. She also advises them in the strategic placement of rudimentary safety equipment. This is pretty simple stuff—but highly effective. Within Tinetti's sample population of seniors, the number of falls has declined 40%.

It may be years before the wizards of biomedical science will know if they can match these impressive results. The science of aging, though progressing rapidly, is still in its infancy, and scientists need to know a lot more about how the body's mechanisms work. For many years the biggest debate was whether the aging of cells, or senescence, is driven by hostile elements in the environment or is dictated by genes. Nowadays there is little doubt that both elements are at play. "You have genetics overlaid by environmental factors," says Dr. James Smith, co-chairman of the Huffington Center on Aging at Houston's Baylor College of Medicine. "There's something going on inside the human body to determine a maximum possible life-span of 115 to 120 years. There's a limit—but we have no idea what defines it."

Although gerontologists acknowledge the interplay of heredity and environment, they tend to fall into camps in explaining how aging works. Wear-and-tear theorists hold that living itself is fundamentally dangerous. The same breath that gives and sustains human life produces oxygen radicals, unstable compounds that when combined with just about anything, have toxic effects on cells. Add to that the weakening over time of the immune system, which leads to the body's fight against disease, and decline is inevitable. Biologists are now experimenting on rats and rhesus monkeys to see if restricting the intake of calories (while maintaining healthy nutrient levels) will slow the metabolic rate, producing a lower body temperature that in turn will decrease oxygen consumption. A lower rate of metabolism equals fewer radicals equals longer life.

Or so the theory goes. Experiments involving restricted diets on primates have produced lower bone mass, a dangerous condition for older people. Moreover, because lab animals do not have the life-span of humans, all this remains highly speculative. Dr. Anna McCormick, chief of the biology section at the National Institute on Aging, cautions that cutting calories may never be an effective method of retarding age in humans. But, she says, "there may be a way to find a hormone or a drug that would have the same effect."

Toward that end, research is also under way to see if low doses of hormones or high doses of vitamins can reduce the effects of oxygen radicals. The NIA is supporting limited research into the risks and benefits of boosting the levels of three hormones that decrease as people age: melatonin, which affects sleep cycles; dehydroepiandrosterone, a product of the adrenal glands that converts to estrogen and testosterone; and human-growth hormone, which affects bone and organ development, as well as metabolic rate. Limited lab tests on animals suggest to some investigators that melatonin may serve as an antioxidant, wiping out the free radicals that can harm the body's cells. But scientists are cautious because results have not been repeated in additional animal studies—and the different metabolism of animals may preclude replication of such results in humans.

Many scientists are skeptical of the hype surrounding fountain-of-youth hormones. "If it was all due to wear and tear, I'd buy the theory that you could live 500 years," says Dr. Richard Sprott, associate director of the NIA's biology of aging program. "But there is some basic genetic programming, and the only way to significantly increase the life-span is to alter genetics."

Gerontologists and gene theorists generally embark from the premise that cell division holds the key to unlocking the mystery of aging. Laboratory experiments have shown that over the course of a human lifetime, healthy cells complete a specific number of divisions. When that process is disrupted, as commonly happens in old cells, problems like osteoporosis and immunological failure set in. Conversely, so-called immortal cells that continue to divide past their allotted count turn cancerous and can proliferate indefinitely. "We'd be in worse shape if cells didn't undergo senescence," says Smith, who studies the aging of cells. "In that case, we might have cancers earlier and more frequently."

On the other hand, scientists hypothesize, aging takes place at the cellular level, and if cells did not grow old, biological aging might be slowed. But what drives the process? Why do some cells accumulate dysfunction with time? And can that dysfunction be prevented or slowed? Before those questions can be answered, cautions Baylor professor Olivia Pereira-Smith, who researches the genetics of aging, "we have to find the genes first."

One popular theory posits the existence of clock-type genes that in essence predetermine a human's life-span. Human cells appear to have some sort of counting mechanism and "remember" where they are in the sequence of divisions they must go through. Certain "longevity assurance" genes then make sure that the cell population keeps dividing until the clock winds down. A newer theory champions the role of stress-response genes, which regulate the body's maintenance and repair functions. As yet, researchers are unsure whether these genes merely affect susceptibility to disease or actually control the aging processes.

Scientists are also trying to understand the role of telomerase, an enzyme that regulates growth at the ends of chromosomes. At the tip of every chromosome is a chunk of DNA that experts long assumed to be superfluous, since it gets lost in replication. Now they think that piece of DNA may be critical in aging, and some speculate that the key to preserving it may lie in preventing the shrinkage of the telomeres that protect chromosome tips from deteriorating.

As esoteric and complicated as some of this may be at this stage of exploration, the end goal is abundantly clear: intervening sufficiently in the aging process to improve the quality of the later years and perhaps even extend them. "Ultimately," says Smith, "we'd like to be able to design drugs that have an effect on disabling processes."

That day, however, is still a distant sci-fi dream—or nightmare, if one cares to dwell on the social and economic impact of such a development. In the meantime, little can be done for those who refuse to do for themselves. Dr. Lewis Lipsitz, chief of geriatrics at Boston's Hebrew Rehabilitation Center for the Aged, pointedly warns, "Geriatric medicine starts in the 40s." And the NIA's Sprott cautions that "the difference comes in life-style changes, not in the pills you take." Health and biomedical researchers all agree that for now, the best offense against the ravages of time is a level-headed defense: watch your weight, knock off the booze, quash the cigarettes, get plenty of sleep and exercise, keep tabs on your blood pressure and, for good measure, fasten your seat belt.

—Reported by Sam Allis/Boston, Ann Blackman and Hannah Bloch/Washington and William Dowell/Southbury

The Mystery of Suicide

The road to self-destruction starts with depression and ends in the grave. But who chooses to die and why? Is it stress? Brain chemistry? A despair rotting the soul? The answers are as varied as the weapons.

David Gelman

They inhabit a strange pantheon of the suicidal, prowled by brilliant, troubled ghosts. Some came to grief in the nightfall of acclaimed careers, some in the withering, high-noon glare of public adulation. There are Hemingway and Plath, Monroe and Garland, dead by premeditation or by cumulative acts of self-destruction. There are Presley, Morrison, Hendrix and Joplin, all of them fatally overdosed on drugs and fame. Some are noted almost as much for the manner of their deaths as for the impact of their lives. Last summer a depression-prone White House counsel named Vincent Foster burst into unwelcome national prominence with his final act, a self-inflicted gunshot wound to the head. And last week police in Seattle found the bloodied body of Kurt Cobain, leader of the hugely popular group Nirvana, sprawled in his home. He had apparently killed himself at least a day earlier, the police said, with the shotgun they found resting against him.

Once again, the rock world was shaken by the death of one of its gifted young artists, a tragedy that seems endemic to the pop-music scene. To many it was all too predictable. "The whole thing reeks of cliché: 'Pop icon commits suicide'," said Chris Dorr, a 23-year-old Seattle college student. "It makes you wonder if our icons are genetically programmed to self-destruct in their late 20s."

But Cobain's death hit hardest in Seattle. Thousands of grieving callers bombarded local radio stations, prompting the stations to broadcast crisis-hot-line numbers and organize a candlelight vigil for Sunday. Meanwhile, dozens of mourners gathered outside his house, leaving flowers and carting off mementos.

Suicides always take their own portion of mystery with them, as President Bill Clinton suggested after Foster, his close friend and aide, killed himself. For all the recent advances in the study of behavior, there's still much that doctors don't understand about the persistent phenomenon of people taking their own lives. "We can't talk with the person who committed suicide, so we can only piece together the data," says psychiatrist George Murphy, of Washington University in St. Louis. But researchers are making a determined effort to chart the process, and what they're finding, especially on the cutting edge of brain science, may help bring down the annual toll of suicide deaths.

That toll, of course, takes its full measure on those left behind. Suicides don't simply give up on life: they leave a smear of nullity behind them. Their private act of negation attacks our own often tenuous sense of a meaning in existence. It's a kind of desertion, making everyone feel a little less defended against nothingness. "The suicide does not play the game, does not observe the rules," wrote the novelist Joyce Carol Oates in a 1978 meditation on the subject. "He leaves the party too soon, and leaves the other guests painfully uncomfortable."

In life, Cobain was often in pain. Until his death, he was scarcely known outside the youth culture. But his band, most of whose bitter-edged lyrics he wrote and sang, had become the authentic voice of the 20-plus generation. In the few years since its formation, Nirvana helped establish grunge rock as the sound and style of '90s disillusionment. Its 1991 album, "Nevermind," sold nearly 10 million copies, and one of its songs, "Smells Like Teen Spirit," has become a virtual anthem for the rebellious young.

Besieged: Cobain's life began unraveling not long after his band hit the charts, bringing him attention he couldn't seem to handle. He felt besieged by fans and critics. Between bouts of heroin abuse, he was subject to episodes of depression. Yet friends described him as gentle and caring, not really prone to the violence that surrounds much of the rock culture. Small and almost frail-looking, he wrote music that was oddly melodic despite the abrasiveness of its lyrics. But in the end, by some process still unknown, the sadness of life led him to put a shotgun to his head.

In most instances, suicide seems an enormously selfish act. One of the strongest arguments against it is the harm it can do to others, especially the shattering legacy of guilt and grief it bequeaths to the family of the deceased. Many people reacting to Cobain's death expressed concern about what it might do to his 19-month-old daughter, Frances Bean, the only issue of his troubled marriage to singer Courtney Love.

On the other hand, libertarians and others posit a "right" to suicide, especially for the elderly and the ill. Some argue that such suicides, while tragic, may be "rational"— a proposition that Michigan's Dr. Jack Kevorkian is testing in the courts. "There's an honest debate going on, especially on the front of physician-assisted suicides," says clinical psychologist David Jobes, of Catholic University in Washington, D.C. "Should we continue to uphold the principle that suicide is never acceptable? That's the hottest evolving area in the field."

Whatever the ethics of suicide, researchers are digging closer to its roots. The 19th-century French founder of sociology, Emile Durkheim, thought the source lay in the ups and downs of society itself. Modern researchers put more emphasis on genes and neurotransmitters. Nor do all agree with assertions that the primary cause is "life stress." Says Dr. David Clark, director of the Center for Suicide Research and Prevention at Chicago's Rush-Presbyterian-St. Luke's Medical Center: "That's the lay public assumption and that's what drives a lot of suicide-prevention work. And it simply doesn't hold water."

Researchers know, says Clark, that there's as much suicide among the rich as there is among the poor and the middle class. They cite a wide range of potential suicide triggers, from loss of employment or loved ones to aging and physical impairment. But, in almost all cases, they agree there is an underlying psychiatric illness—primarily depression, followed by alcoholism and substance abuse. Clinically depressed people are at a 50 percent greater risk of killing themselves. But the doctors can't agree on whether suicidal depression itself is a state of mind or a result of chemical deficiency.

The good news, if there can be any about suicide, is that it's a relatively rare event: 99.9 percent of Americans don't kill themselves; for better or worse, they stick to the rules—the unspoken "covenant" we all have with each other to affirm life even, perhaps, when there's little left to affirm. The figures tend to climb and fall in waves, but they've remained stable in this country since the end of World War II: at the latest count, around 30,000 people took their own lives in 1991. Gender differences have remained fairly steady as well. Females, by around 3 to 1, attempt suicide more often than males, but males, partly because they employ more violent means, are four times more likely to die. It's estimated there are 20 persons who try suicide for every person who tries successfully.

Violence and despair: The rate for teenagers, after climbing steeply for two decades, began leveling off in the mid-1970s—although it's still not dropping as experts had hoped. The only groups going against the grain are black males and the elderly, especially white men over 65—many of them perhaps victims of the loss of status and income incurred with retirement. The increase among blacks, some demographers guess, might be because suicide is part of the continuum of violence and despair that surrounds many of them. The old are getting older and healthier; their suicide rate dropped through much of the century after 1933. Yet since about 1980, the rate has begun climbing to higher levels. Yeates Conwell, a geriatric psychiatrist at the University of Rochester, conjectures that as they live longer, people are also growing frailer, more isolated, and harder to find and rescue. The suicide rate for the elderly is higher all over the world than it is for teenagers and young adults, says Conwell. "But it is in the U.S. that we find more elderly men committing suicide."

No profile of likely suicides has emerged. However, there are some typical signs to watch for. According to Clark, for instance, in about two thirds of cases there is usually some form of suicidal communication before the actual attempt. Edwin Shneidman, emeritus professor of thanatology at UCLA, who founded the American Association of Suicidology, was also the leading developer of the "psychological autopsy," aimed, among other things, at finding such patterns. Reviewing several years' worth of postmortems, Shneidman and his colleagues at UCLA found that around 90 percent of the suicides left clear behavioral and verbal clues, such as giving away possessions.

Shneidman, although one of the pioneers in the field, has also become one of its mavericks. He objects, for instance, to the emphasis that mainstream suicide researchers place on psychiatric illness, preferring, he says, the Oxford English Dictionary to psychiatry's diagnostic manual. No one dies of depression, he says. "It's not a tenable entry on the death certificate."

Suicide Weapon

% OF TOTAL NUMBER OF SUICIDES IN U.S. IN 1990

Firearms	61.0
Hanging & Strangulation	14.5
Gas Poisoning	7.5
Other Poisoning	10.0
Other	7.0

SOURCE: BUREAU OF THE CENSUS

As with much of psychiatry these days, the real cutting edge of suicide research is in biochemistry. In the past few years there have been some exciting advances in studies of serotonin, the ubiquitous neurotransmitter that modulates the action of other brain chemicals. A variety of violent, impulsive behaviors have been associated with low levels of serotonin. And Dr. Frederick Goodwin, head of the National Institute of Mental Health, reports that 22 of 22 autopsy studies of brains and body fluid have also connected low levels of the chemical with suicide. Since the newer antidepressant medications, like Prozac and Zoloft, are aimed specifically at boosting serotonin, Goodwin says, doctors may eventually have a selective way to treat depressions associated with suicidal behavior.

Greater risk: Lately, researchers studying particular types of serotonin-related suicide have discovered they tend to be the more serious attempts—those characterized by careful planning and greater medical damage. According to psychiatrist J. John Mann, head of the NIMH research center at the University of Pittsburgh School of Medicine, studies in Sweden of hospitalized depressives with low serotonin levels found that about 20 percent committed suicide within the year. In another group with normal levels, between 1 and 2 percent killed themselves. "That's a tenfold greater risk," says Mann. It remains unclear why some people have low serotonin levels. Mann believes the reasons could be genetic, developmental or environmental. Not surprisingly, he notes, men tend to have lower levels than women.

Suicide by Race

RATES PER 100,000 IN 1970

White Male	18.0
Black Male	8.0
White Female	7.1
Black Female	2.6

DEATH RATES IN 1980

White Male	19.9
Black Male	10.3
White Female	5.9
Black Female	2.2

DEATH RATES IN 1990

White Male	22.0
Black Male	12.0
White Female	5.3
Black Female	2.3

SOURCE: BUREAU OF THE CENSUS

That may be one of the reasons why two or three men complete suicides compared with women. We don't know if it has any relationship to [unsuccessful] attempts."

What researchers do know, says Mann, is that a person's serotonin level reveals "some sort of vulnerability" to suicide. "This is the biggest leap we've made in terms of identifying people at high risk, as well as offering meaningful intervention." The serotonin connection points the way not only to a potential screening technique, but to treatment. By raising serotonin levels, as the newer antidepressants do, researchers believe they can raise the threshold for acting on suicidal impulses. "It's similar to the way we're treating epilepsy today, by raising the threshold at which seizures occur, says Mann. "In the short term, our hypothesis is that antidepressants may reduce your chances of acting on suicidal thoughts. We believe the antisuicidal effects occur before the antidepressant effects kick in."

But some treatment may actually increase the risk of suicide. "When a person is profoundly depressed," says Goodwin, "what protects them is, they can't figure out how to kill themselves. Suicide requires energy, and they don't have it." With treatment, the first thing that comes back is energy and functional capacity. "When they become activated and are still depressed, that is a very dangerous period," he says, "so drugs have to be carefully monitored."

While science tries to piece together the suicide puzzle, other forces seem determined to muddle it. Goodwin is irked by such opportunistic books as the best-selling "Final Exit," a kind of how-to manual for would-be suicides, although the way the book was snatched up suggests many people saw no reason to shun such advice. He thinks, also, that the attention given to Kevorkian's suicide machine "trivializes" suicide and ignores the fact that in Western culture it is not looked on as a normal practice. Rather, he says, "people go to enormous lengths to stay alive, even under the worst possible conditions."

On the whole, we *are* life-affirming, but it's an affirmation that often needs boostering. "Every one ... is bound to preserve himself," wrote the 17th-century English philosopher John Locke, "and not to quit his station willfully." Locke was talking about an obligation to the Creator, but it's also a duty we owe to ourselves, our families and the society we live in.

With MARY HAGER *and* PAT WINGERT *in Washington,* VICKI QUADE *in Chicago,* TESSA NAMUTH *in New York and* JEANNE GORDON *in Los Angeles*

CULTURE & IDEAS

Is there life after death?

Near-death experiences may be physiological. Or they may be peepholes into a world beyond

BY BRENDAN I. KOERNER

On the talk-show circuit and the bestseller list, the tales are legion. After being struck by lightning, a man meets a "Being of Light" who grants forgiveness for a lifetime of violence. In full cardiac arrest on the operating table, a grade-school teacher travels down a long tunnel to "a place filled up with love, and a beautiful bright white light." And Elvis Presley takes her gently by the hand.

As sophisticated medical technology has permitted more and more people to journey back from the brink of death, such seemingly mystical reports have become almost commonplace. Of the nearly 18 percent of Americans who claimed in a recent *U.S. News* poll to have been on the verge of dying, many researchers estimate that a third have had unusual experiences while straddling the line between life and death—perhaps as many as 15 million Americans. A small percentage recall vivid images of an afterlife—including tunnels of light, peaceful meadows, and angelic figures clad in white.

No matter what the nature of the experience, it alters some lives. Alcoholics find themselves unable to imbibe. Hardened criminals opt for a life of helping others. Atheists embrace the existence of a deity, while dogmatic members of a particular religion report "feeling welcome in any church or temple or mosque."

> "Most near-death survivors say they don't think there is a God. **They Know.**"
>
> **NANCY EVANS BUSH,** *president emeritus of the International Association for Near-Death Studies*

Such dramatic changes have piqued the imagination of those searching for evidence of the mystical. Bruce Greyson, 50, is a psychiatrist at the University of Virginia Medical School who has spent much of his professional life investigating these events as possible "peepholes" into a world beyond. Greyson says that those who have such experiences "become enamored with the spiritual part of life, and less so with possessions, power, and prestige." Nancy Evans Bush, president emeritus of the International Association for Near-Death Studies, says the experience is revelatory. "Most near-death survivors say they don't *think* there is a God," she says. "They *know*."

Stories about strange events in the borderland between life and death are hardly new. Over two millenniums ago, in the *Republic,* Plato recounted a gravely wounded soldier's journey toward "a straight light like a pillar, most nearly resembling a rainbow, but brighter and purer." Near-death experiences aren't fresh to popular literature, either. Thirteenth-century monks wrote of a farmer who returned from the edge with tales of "corridors of fire" and "icy" paths to the afterlife.

Heavenly cars. And tales from the realm between life and death aren't limited to the West. In Micronesia, "experiencers" have reported that heaven resembles a bustling American city with skyscrapers and plenty of automobiles. In India, the afterlife has frequently been described as a giant bureaucracy, in which survivors are sent back to life because of "clerical error." "There's a lot of cultural overlay," says Greyson,

3. ❖ PROBLEMS INFLUENCING PERSONAL GROWTH

who also edits the *Journal of Near-Death Studies*. It publishes articles on topics ranging from the scholarly ("Near-death Experiences: A Neurophysiological Explanatory Model") to the suspect ("Death and Renewal in *The Velveteen Rabbit*"). "Many people describe it as an ineffable experience, so it's no surprise that they come up with models based on their background," Greyson recounts. Almost all reports from around the world bear similarities to familiar daytime TV fare—the out-of-body feeling, the life review, the presence of deceased relatives on "the other side."

Until recently, however, these anecdotes were usually dismissed as hallucinations or after-the-fact inventions, lumped in with alien abductions. Many who were convinced they had glimpsed an afterlife were afraid to describe their experiences for fear of being labeled crazy. The medical community's perception of these reports began to change in 1975 when Raymond Moody published *Life After Life,* a book that coined the term near-death experience (NDE) to describe this hard-to-define phenomenon. Moody interviewed 150 near-death patients who reported vivid experiences (flashing back to childhood, coming face to face with Christ). He found that those who had undergone NDEs became more altruistic, less materialistic, and more loving.

"NDEs offer a transient reduction in pain and suffering."

DANIEL ALKON, *neuroscientist*

Scores of psychiatrists and neuroscientists have since sought to uncover the roots of these powerful experiences. But serious research into the phenomenon has been difficult. "It's very much like trying to conduct research on humor," says John Sappington, a psychologist at Augusta College. "You can't just get people into the lab and say, 'Now, be funny!'" The task is complicated by the personal nature of the experience; researchers must rely on hearsay that, by definition, cannot be corroborated.

Seeking the greater certainty of controlled observations in the laboratory, a number of researchers are taking a physiological approach to uncovering the causes behind NDEs. Michael A. Persinger, a neuroscientist at Laurentian University in Sudbury, Ontario, has induced many of the characteristics of an NDE—the sensation of moving through a tunnel, the brilliant white light. He has done so by stimulating the brain's right temporal lobe, the area above the right ear responsible for perception, with mild electromagnetic fields. In England, Karl Jansen has zeroed in on the brain's reaction to shifting levels of ketamine, a powerful neurotransmitter. Often ingested as a recreational drug—its street name is Special K—ketamine frequently causes the out-of-body sensation common to NDEs. The U.S. Navy has managed to replicate many of the sensations of an NDE by subjecting test pilots to massive centrifugal force—a physical stress that can include the presence of a patriarchal figure interpreted by some as God. "There's nothing magical about the NDE," Persinger asserts.

Physiological findings have led many researchers to view NDEs not as glimpses into a world beyond but as insights into the world within the human mind. "I think it is an evolutionary adaptation," says Sherwin Nuland, the National Book Award-winning author of *How We Die.* He ascribes NDEs to the actions of opiate-like compounds known as endorphins, which are released by the brain at times of great physical stress to deaden pain and alleviate fear. He scoffs at those who view NDEs as a temporary bridge to an afterlife. "I think that the mind is just trying to save itself from the horror of unbelievable trauma," he says.

Daniel Alkon, chief of the Neural Systems Laboratory at the National Institutes of Health, says anoxia (oxygen deprivation in the brain) lies at the root of all NDEs. When death appears certain, he argues, the body will often shut down and "play dead" as a last course of action. His skepticism is significant because many years ago, as a result of a hemorrhage, he had a near-death experience himself.

Despite the strides in explaining NDEs through clinical investigation, some researchers believe that the physiological approach is insufficient. "These are just armchair speculations. Finding a chemical change in the brain does not necessarily prove that it causes NDEs," argues Greyson. For Greyson and others who view NDEs as mystical experiences, the skeptics in the lab are only solving a small part of the puzzle.

"I came away convinced that these are real spiritual experiences."

DIANE KOMP, *pediatric oncologist*

Watching heart patients. A block from the University of Virginia's Charlottesville campus, in an old house labeled Division of Personality Studies, Greyson and Ian Stevenson, 79, are in the middle of a three-year, $250,000 study they hope will answer many of the questions that, in their view, the physiological approach doesn't address. The pair, whose funding comes from a German psychiatric institute rather than the university, have been monitoring cardiac arrest patients. They are searching for insight into notable changes that often accompany the experience, such as heightened zest for life and unconditional love for all humans.

The two are annoyed by those who have made near-death experiences a pop culture fad more likely to be featured in a tabloid alongside a scoop about an 800-pound human baby than in a medical journal. "It makes people take us less seriously," says Greyson. For many scholars, Greyson and Stevenson's work has never threatened to enter the realm of serious inquiry. Nuland debunks near-death research as pseudoscience investigating nothing more than "pleasant illusions." Moody insists "there is no imaginable empirical evidence to prove that there is an afterlife."

Despite the unmuffled snickering of some colleagues, Greyson and Stevenson insist that their research is intellectually rigorous. "Most scientists shy away from the area of the paranormal," says Greyson. "I think the research we're doing here is breaking down some of those prejudices."

Greyson and Stevenson have been instrumental in gathering evidence indicating that religious backgrounds do not affect who is most likely to have an NDE. They have mapped out the conversion-

22. Is There Life after Death?

like effects of NDEs that can sometimes lead to hardship. ("They can see the good in all people," Greyson says of people who have experienced the phenomenon: "They act fairly naive, and they often allow themselves to be opened up to con men who abuse their trust.") They have gathered reports of high divorce rates and problems in the workplace following near-death experiences. "The values you get from an NDE are not the ones you need to function in everyday life," says Greyson. Having stared eternity in the face, he observes, those who return often lose their taste for ego-boosting achievement.

Greyson and Stevenson's interest is not limited to the psychological realm, however. They are intrigued by reports of the chronically ill regaining their vigor, and even "miraculous" cures from cancer or HIV infection—claims most of the scientific community put in the same category as snake oil and faith healing. The Virginia researchers are undiscouraged by this scorn. They believe that they may be pushing the boundaries of human knowledge. "NDEs demonstrate how little we know, and how far we have to go to understand our role in the universe," says Greyson. Stevenson, now in the 35th year of a study of children who claim to recall past lives, concurs. "The evidence for survival after death comes from a wide variety of sources, including NDEs," he says. "Certain communications through mediums deserve attention, too." Operating in terrain disdained by many scientists as a twilight zone, Greyson and Stevenson hope to peer through a portal into an afterlife.

Not even the diehard skeptics doubt the powerful personal effects of NDEs. "This is a profound emotional experience," explains Nuland. "People are convinced that they've seen heaven." Persinger adds: "The fact that we're studying a neural basis for it doesn't demean its significance." Diane Komp, a pediatric oncologist at Yale, was transformed by witnessing children's NDEs—an 8-year-old with cancer envisioning a school bus driven by Jesus, a 7-year-old leukemia patient hearing a chorus of angels before passing away. "I was an atheist, and it changed my view of spiritual matters," recalls Komp. "Call it a conversion. I came away convinced that these are real spiritual experiences."

For the many Americans who believe they have been privy to a glimpse of life after death, no amount of clinical explanation will shake their faith.

With Joshua Rich

> "**Most say that** words cannot describe the experience."
>
> **BRUCE GREYSON,** *psychiatrist, with his colleague, Ian Stevenson.*

Relating to Others

People in groups can be seen everywhere: couples in love, parents with their children, teachers and students, gatherings of friends, church groups, theatergoers. People have much influence on one another when they congregate in groups.

Groups spend a great deal of time communicating with members and nonmembers. The communication can be intentional and forceful, such as when protesters demonstrate against a totalitarian regime in a far-off land. Or communication can be more subtle, for example, when fraternity brothers reject a prospective brother who refuses to wear the symbols of pledging.

In some groups, the reason a leader emerges is clear—perhaps the most skilled individual in the group is elected leader by the group members. In other groups, for example, during a spontaneous nightclub fire, the qualities of the rapidly emerging, perhaps self-appointed, leader are less apparent. Nonetheless, the followers flee unquestioningly in the leader's direction. Even in dating couples, one person may seem to lead or be dominant over the other.

Some groups, such as corporations, issue formal rules in writing; discipline for rule breaking is also formalized. Other groups, families or trios of friends, for example, possess fewer, less formal rules and disciplinary codes, but their rules are still quickly learned by and are important to all unit members.

Some groups are large but seek more members, such as nationalized labor unions. Other groups seek to keep their groups small and somewhat exclusive, such as teenage cliques. Groups exist that are almost completely adversarial with other groups. Conflict between youth gangs is receiving much media attention today. Other groups pride themselves on their ability to remain cooperative, such as neighbors who band together in a community crime watch.

Psychologists are so convinced that interpersonal relationships are important to the human experience that they have intensively studied them. There is ample evidence that contact with other people is a necessary part of human existence. Research has shown that most individuals do not like being isolated from other people. In fact, in laboratory experiments in which subjects experience total isolation for extended periods, they begin to hallucinate the presence of others. In prisons, solitary confinement is often used as a form of punishment because of its aversive effect. Other research has shown that people who must wait under stressful circumstances prefer to wait with others, even if the others are total strangers, rather than wait alone. This unit examines intimate groups, groups of friends, dating partners, and married couples. The next unit examines the effects of larger groups, specifically, of society at large.

The first unit essay examines a new and hot issue: emotional intelligence, or EQ. Daniel Goleman's pioneering book on this topic suggests that emotional intelligence is more important to our success in life than any other aspect of our being. In her article on EQ, Nancy Gibbs discusses the concept and its utility. She also reveals some scientific research on this topic. After this general introduction, we move to a special type of relationship, friendship.

The next article in this unit pertains to friendships. In "The Enduring Power of Friendship," Susan Davis probes adult friendships, which are far less studied than childhood friendships. She also queries why adult friendships end. Interestingly, they do not end catastrophically, as do some adult intimate relationships. Most adult friendships fizzle out when life circumstances change.

An idea relevant to interacting with others is morality. Should we take advantage of our friends? Should we steal from them? Morality is that which prevents us from doing malicious things to others, even when they are not present. In "Born to Be Good?" Celia Kitzinger ponders the origins and purposes of moral behavior. She suggests that the available psychological theories do not encompass enough of the diversity of society and ought to be revised.

Of course, if we take advantage of or mistreat our friends, they will no longer be our friends. If we are shy, however, it is hard for us to make friends in the first place. "Are You Shy?" not only discusses why some people suffer from shyness but how shy people are perceived by others.

Another reason friendships end or people do not become friends in the first place is that some individuals are hotheads. That is, they are often hostile to others around them. In fact, Edward Dolnick suggests that chronic hostility toward others is actually detrimental to our health in that it causes heart attacks.

Should we find ourselves in a position where we have blemished our friendship, the next selection explores how and when to apologize. A well-placed apology can go a long way toward mending broken friendships. This is the topic of "Go Ahead, Say You're Sorry."

Friendship is not the only type of close relationship we have. Loving or romantic relationships are just as or more important. First, Geoffrey Cowley writes about the biology of beauty. He ponders why we are attracted to one person but not another. Interestingly, he explores the universality of what determines whether an individual is considered beautiful. The answers might surprise you.

UNIT 4

A companion article discusses the future of love. Americans tend to idealize and glamorize love, according to Barbara Graham. She suggests that, given this tendency, it is difficult for us to maintain any intimate relationship. We simply expect too much of it. Taking the pressure off intimacy and romance is the focus of this article.

It is not surprising that some romantic relationships result in sex, marriage, and/or pregnancy. In the next surprising article, adult premarital sex and out-of-wedlock pregnancies in adulthood are described. Why we do not hear about these pregnancies as much as about teen pregnancies and what they mean for society are explored here.

Looking Ahead: Challenge Questions

What is emotional intelligence? How does it develop? How can we tell if we possess it? How are people with EQ different from people without it? Do you have EQ? If not, can you do anything to cultivate it?

What are friends for? Why do friendships last? Are special types of friendships, say between homosexuals, better or different from typical friendships? What methods are there for saving a failing friendship? How can a wounded friendship be mended? When would a friendship not be worth salvaging?

What is morality? Why is it such a valuable commodity? From where does a sense of morality originate? What are some of the theories of development or conscience? Are these theories as inclusive as they should be?

How can you tell if you are shy? What are the causes of shyness? How do others perceive shy individuals? What can a shy person do to overcome shyness?

Why is hostility toward others so destructive? Is it destructive only to the opponent? Describe the hostile personality. How can hostility kill us? How can we overcome hostility and cynicism against others?

What is an apology? What are the elements of a sincere apology (one that would have the effect of reestablishing trust and friendship)?

Why is attractiveness so important? Why would psychologists study it? What determines whether a person is attractive or not? Are the dimensions of attraction the same in every culture?

What is love? What is romance? Do the two go together? Do you think Americans overidealize love? Why? How? Why might idealization of what love ought to be become destructive to our most intimate relationships? What can we do about this?

Discuss whether or not love is found only in our society. How do individuals in other societies express love to each other? Discuss why you agree or disagree that our society is obsessed with intimacy and love.

Are there more unwed pregnant teens or unwed pregnant adults? Why does this trend exist? Should we do anything about it? What can we do?

The unit examines close relationships including friends and lovers. For each, which factors make the relationship better, and which make it worse? Explain whether or not the same social processes are operative in all close relationships. What interpersonal relationships and processes besides the ones discussed in this anthology would be important to study?

The EQ Factor

New brain research suggests that emotions, not IQ, may be the true measure of human intelligence

NANCY GIBBS

IT TURNS OUT THAT A SCIENTIST CAN SEE THE future by watching four-year-olds interact with a marshmallow. The researcher invites the children, one by one, into a plain room and begins the gentle torment. You can have this marshmallow right now, he says. But if you wait while I run an errand, you can have two marshmallows when I get back. And then he leaves.

Some children grab for the treat the minute he's out the door. Some last a few minutes before they give in. But others are determined to wait. They cover their eyes; they put their heads down; they sing to themselves; they try to play games or even fall asleep. When the researcher returns he gives the children their hard-earned marshmallows. And then, science waits for them to grow up.

By the time the children reach high school, something remarkable has happened. A survey of the children's parents and teachers found that those who as four-year-olds had the fortitude to hold out for the second marshmallow generally grew up to be better adjusted, more popular, adventurous, confident and dependable teenagers. The children who gave in to temptation early on were more likely to be lonely, easily frustrated and stubborn. They buckled under stress and shied away from challenges. And when some of the students in the two groups took the Scholastic Aptitude Test, the kids who held out longer scored an average of 210 points higher.

When we think of brilliance we see Einstein, deep-eyed, woolly haired, a thinking machine with skin and mismatched socks. High achievers, we imagine, were wired for greatness from birth. But then you have to wonder why, over time, natural talent seems to ignite in some people and dim in others. This is where the marshmallows come in. It seems that the ability to delay gratification is a master skill, a triumph of the reasoning brain over the impulsive one. It is a sign, in short, of emotional intelligence. And it doesn't show up on an IQ test.

For most of this century, scientists have worshiped the hardware of the brain and the software of the mind; the messy powers of the heart were left to the poets. But cognitive theory could simply not explain the questions we wonder about most: why some people just seem to have a gift for living well; why the smartest kid in the class will probably not end up the richest; why we like some people virtually on sight and distrust others; why some people remain buoyant in the face of troubles that would sink a less resilient soul. What qualities of the mind or spirit, in short, determine who succeeds?

The phrase "emotional intelligence" was coined by Yale psychologist Peter Salovey and the University of New Hampshire's John Mayer five years ago to describe qualities like understanding one's own feelings, empathy for the feelings of others and "the regulation of emotion in a way that enhances living." Their notion is about to bound into the national conversation, handily shortened to EQ, thanks to a new book, *Emotional Intelligence* (Bantam; $23.95) by Daniel Goleman. Goleman, a Harvard psychology Ph.D. and a *New York Times* science writer with a gift for making even the chewiest scientific theories digestible to lay readers, has brought together a decade's worth of behavioral research into how the mind processes feelings. His goal, he announces on the cover, is to redefine what it means to be smart. His thesis: when it comes to predicting people's success, brainpower as measured by IQ and standardized achievement tests may actually matter less than the qualities of mind once thought of as "character" before the word began to sound quaint.

At first glance, there would seem to be little that's new here to any close reader of fortune cookies. There may be no less original idea than the notion that our hearts hold dominion over our heads. "I was so angry," we say, "I couldn't think straight." Neither is it surprising that "people skills" are useful, which amounts to saying, it's good to be nice. "It's so true it's trivial," says Dr. Paul McHugh, director of psychiatry at Johns Hopkins University School of Medicine. But if it were that simple, the book would not be quite so interesting or its implications so controversial.

This is no abstract investigation. Goleman is looking for antidotes to restore "civility to our streets and caring to our communal life." He sees practical applications everywhere for how companies should decide whom to hire, how couples can increase the odds that their marriages will last, how parents should raise their children and how schools should teach them. When street gangs substitute for families and schoolyard insults end in stabbings, when more than half of marriages end in divorce, when the majority of the children murdered in this country are killed by parents and stepparents, many of whom say they were trying to discipline the child for behavior like blocking the TV or crying too much, it suggests a demand for remedial emotional education. While children are still young, Goleman argues, there is a "neurological window of opportunity" since the brain's prefrontal circuitry, which regulates how we act on what we feel, probably does not mature until mid-adolescence.

And it is here the arguments will break out. Goleman's highly popularized conclusions, says McHugh, "will chill any veteran scholar of psychotherapy and any neuroscientist who worries about how his research may come to be applied." While many researchers in this relatively new field are glad to see emotional issues finally taken seriously, they fear that a notion as handy as EQ invites misuse. Goleman admits the danger of suggesting that you can assign a numerical yardstick to a person's character as well as his intellect; Goleman never even uses the phrase EQ in his book. But he (begrudgingly) approved an "unscientific" EQ test in *USA Today* with choices like "I am aware of even subtle feelings as I have them," and "I can sense the pulse of a group or relationship and state unspoken feelings."

"You don't want to take an average of your emotional skill," argues Harvard psychology professor Jerome Kagan, a pioneer in child-development research. "That's what's wrong with the concept of intelligence for mental skills too. Some people handle anger well but can't handle fear. Some people can't take joy. So each emotion has to be viewed differently."

EQ is not the opposite of IQ. Some people are blessed with a lot of both, some with little of either. What researchers have been trying to understand is how they complement each other; how one's ability to handle stress, for instance, affects the ability to concentrate and put intelligence to use. Among the ingredients for success, researchers now generally agree that IQ counts for about 20%; the rest depends on everything from class to luck to the neural pathways that have developed in the brain over millions of years of human evolution.

It is actually the neuroscientists and evolutionists who do the best job of explaining the reasons behind the most unreasonable behavior. In the past decade or so, scientists have learned enough about the brain to make judgments about where emotion comes from and why we need it. Primitive emotional responses held the keys to survival: fear drives the blood into the large muscles, making it easier to run; surprise triggers the eyebrows to rise, allowing the eyes to widen their view and gather more information about an unexpected event. Disgust wrinkles up the face and closes the nostrils to keep out foul smells.

Emotional life grows out of an area of the brain called the limbic system, specifically the amygdala, whence come delight and disgust and fear and anger. Millions of years ago, the neocortex was added on, enabling humans to plan, learn and remember. Lust grows from the limbic system; love, from the neocortex. Animals like reptiles that have no neocortex cannot experience anything like maternal love; this is why baby snakes have to hide to avoid being eaten by their parents. Humans, with their capacity for love, will protect their offspring, allowing the brains of the young time to develop. The more connections between limbic system and the neocortex, the more emotional responses are possible.

It was scientists like Joseph LeDoux of New York University who uncovered these cerebral pathways. LeDoux's parents owned a meat market. As a boy in Louisiana, he first learned about his future specialty by cutting up cows' brains for sweetbreads. "I found them the most interesting part of the cow's anatomy," he recalls. "They were visually pleasing—lots of folds, convolutions and patterns. The cerebellum was more interesting to look at than steak." The butchers' son became a neuroscientist, and it was he who discovered the short circuit in the brain that lets emotions drive action before the intellect gets a chance to intervene.

A hiker on a mountain path, for example, sees a long, curved shape in the grass out of the corner of his eye. He leaps out of the way before he realizes it is only a stick that looks like a snake. Then he calms down; his cortex gets the message a few milliseconds after his amygdala and "regulates" its primitive response.

Without these emotional reflexes, rarely conscious but often terribly powerful, we would scarcely be able to function. "Most decisions we make have a vast number of possible outcomes, and any attempt to analyze all of them would never end," says University of Iowa neurologist Antonio Damasio, author of *Descartes' Error: Emotion, Reason and the Human Brain*. "I'd ask you to lunch tomorrow, and when the appointed time arrived, you'd still be thinking about whether you should come." What tips the balance, Damasio contends, is our unconscious assigning of emotional values to some of those choices. Whether we experience a somatic response—a gut feeling of dread or a giddy sense of elation—emotions are helping to limit the field in any choice we have to make. If the prospect of lunch with a neurologist is unnerving or distasteful, Damasio suggests, the invitee will conveniently remember a previous engagement.

When Damasio worked with patients in whom the connection between emotional brain and neocortex had been severed because of damage to the brain, he discovered how central that hidden pathway is to how we live our lives. People who had lost that linkage were just as smart and quick to reason, but their lives often fell apart nonetheless. They could not make decisions because they didn't know how they felt about their choices. They couldn't react to warnings or anger in other people. If they made a mistake, like a bad investment, they felt no regret or shame and so were bound to repeat it.

If there is a cornerstone to emotional intelligence on which most other emotional skills depend, it is a sense of self-awareness, of being smart about what we feel. A person whose day starts badly at home may be grouchy all day at work without quite knowing why. Once an emotional response comes into awareness—or, physiologically, is processed through the neocortex—the chances of handling it appropriately improve. Scientists refer to "metamood," the ability to pull back and recognize that "what I'm feeling is anger," or sorrow, or shame.

Metamood is a difficult skill because emotions so often appear in disguise. A person in mourning may know he is sad, but he may not recognize that he is also angry at the person for dying—because this seems somehow inappropriate. A parent who yells at the child who ran into the street is expressing anger at disobedience, but the degree of anger may owe more to the fear the parent feels at what could have happened.

In Goleman's analysis, self-awareness is perhaps the most crucial ability because it allows us to exercise some self-control. The idea is not to repress feeling (the reaction that has made psychoanalysts rich) but rather to do what Aristotle considered the hard work of the will. "Anyone can become angry—that is easy," he wrote in the *Nicomachean Ethics*. "But to be angry with the right person, to the right degree, at the right time, for the right purpose, and in the right way—that is not easy."

Some impulses seem to be easier to control than others. Anger, not surprisingly, is one of the hardest, perhaps because of its evolutionary value in priming people to action. Researchers believe anger usually arises out of a sense of being trespassed against—the belief that one is being robbed of what is rightfully his. The body's first response is a surge of energy, the release of a cascade of neurotransmitters called catecholamines. If a person is already aroused or under stress, the threshold for release is lower, which helps explain why people's tempers shorten during a hard day.

Scientists are not only discovering where anger comes from; they are also exposing myths about how best to handle it. Popular wisdom argues for "letting it all hang out" and having a good cathartic rant. But Goleman cites studies showing that dwelling on anger actually increases its power; the body needs a chance to process the adrenaline through exercise, relaxation techniques, a well-timed intervention or even the old admonition to count to 10.

Anxiety serves a similar useful purpose, so long as it doesn't spin out of control. Worrying is a rehearsal for danger; the act of fretting focuses the mind on a problem so it can search efficiently for solutions. The danger comes when worrying blocks thinking, becoming an end in itself or a path to resignation instead of perseverance. Over-wor-

4. ❖ RELATING TO OTHERS

rying about failing increases the likelihood of failure; a salesman so concerned about his falling sales that he can't bring himself to pick up the phone guarantees that his sales will fall even further.

But why are some people better able to "snap out of it" and get on with the task at hand? Again, given sufficient self-awareness, people develop coping mechanisms. Sadness and discouragement, for instance, are "low arousal" states, and the dispirited salesman who goes out for a run is triggering a high arousal state that is incompatible with staying blue. Relaxation works better for high energy moods like anger or anxiety. Either way, the idea is to shift to a state of arousal that breaks the destructive cycle of the dominant mood.

The idea of being able to predict which salesmen are most likely to prosper was not an abstraction for Metropolitan Life, which in the mid-'80s was hiring 5,000 salespeople a year and training them at a cost of more than $30,000 each. Half quit the first year, and four out of five within four years. The reason: selling life insurance involves having the door slammed in your face over and over again. Was it possible to identify which people would be better at handling frustration and take each refusal as a challenge rather than a setback?

The head of the company approached psychologist Martin Seligman at the University of Pennsylvania and invited him to test some of his theories about the importance of optimism in people's success. When optimists fail, he has found, they attribute the failure to something they can change, not some innate weakness that they are helpless to overcome. And that confidence in their power to effect change is self-reinforcing. Seligman tracked 15,000 new workers who had taken two tests. One was the company's regular screening exam, the other Seligman's test measuring their levels of optimism. Among the new hires was a group who flunked the screening test but scored as "superoptimists" on Seligman's exam. And sure enough, they did the best of all; they outsold the pessimists in the regular group by 21% in the first year and 57% in the second. For years after that, passing Seligman's test was one way to get hired as a MetLife salesperson.

Perhaps the most visible emotional skills, the ones we recognize most readily, are the "people skills" like empathy, graciousness, the ability to read a social situation. Researchers believe that about 90% of emotional communication is nonverbal. Harvard psychologist Robert Rosenthal developed the PONS test (Profile of Nonverbal Sensitivity) to measure people's ability to read emotional

---

One Way to Test Your EQ

UNLIKE IQ, WHICH IS GAUGED BY THE FAMOUS STANFORD-Binet tests, EQ does not lend itself to any single numerical measure. Nor should it, say experts. Emotional intelligence is by definition a complex, multifaceted quality representing such intangibles as self-awareness, empathy, persistence and social deftness.

Some aspects of emotional intelligence, however, can be quantified. Optimism, for example, is a handy measure of a person's self-worth. According to Martin Seligman, a University of Pennsylvania psychologist, how people respond to setbacks—optimistically or pessimistically—is a fairly accurate indicator of how well they will succeed in school, in sports and in certain kinds of work. To test his theory, Seligman devised a questionnaire to screen insurance salesmen at MetLife.

In Seligman's test, job applicants were asked to imagine a hypothetical event and then choose the response (A or B) that most closely resembled their own. Some samples from his questionnaire:

You forget your spouse's (boyfriend's/girlfriend's) birthday.
A. I'm not good at remembering birthdays.
B. I was preoccupied with other things.

You owe the library $10 for an overdue book.
A. When I am really involved in what I am reading, I often forget when its due.
B. I was so involved in writing the report, I forgot to return the book.

You lose your temper with a friend.
A. He or she is always nagging me.
B. He or she was in a hostile mood.

You are penalized for returning your income-tax forms late.
A. I always put off doing my taxes.
B. I was lazy about getting my taxes done this year.

You've been feeling run-down.
A. I never get a chance to relax.
B. I was exceptionally busy this week.

A friend says something that hurts your feelings.
A. She always blurts things out without thinking of others.
B. My friend was in a bad mood and took it out on me.

You fall down a great deal while skiing.
A. Skiing is difficult.
B. The trails were icy.

You gain weight over the holidays, and you can't lose it.
A. Diets don't work in the long run.
B. The diet I tried didn't work.

Seligman found that those insurance salesman who answered with more B's than A's were better able to overcome bad sales days, recovered more easily from rejection and were less likely to quit. People with an optimistic view of life tend to treat obstacles and setbacks as temporary (and therefore surmountable). Pessimists take them personally; what others see as fleeting, localized impediments, they view as pervasive and permanent.

The most dramatic proof of his theory, says Seligman, came at the 1988 Olympic Games in Seoul, South Korea, after U.S. swimmer Matt Biondi turned in two disappointing performances in this first two races. Before the Games, Biondi had been favored to win seven golds—as Mark Spitz had done 16 years earlier. After those first two races, most commentators thought Biondi would be unable to recover from his setback. Not Seligman. He had given some members of the U.S. swim team a version of his optimism test before the races; it showed that Biondi possessed an extraordinarily upbeat attitude. Rather than losing heart after turning in a bad time, as others might, Biondi tended to respond by swimming even faster. Sure enough, Biondi bounced right back, winning five gold medals in the next five races.

—*By Alice Park*

cues. He shows subjects a film of a young woman expressing feelings—anger, love, jealousy, gratitude, seduction—edited so that one or another nonverbal cue is blanked out. In some instances the face is visible but not the body, or the woman's eyes are hidden, so that viewers have to judge the feeling by subtle cues. Once again, people with higher PONS scores tend to be more successful in their work and relationships; children who score well are more popular and successful in school, even [though] their IQs are quite average.

Like other emotional skills, empathy is an innate quality that can be shaped by experience. Infants as young as three months old exhibit empathy when they get upset at the sound of another baby crying. Even very young children learn by imitation; by watching how others act when they see someone in distress, these children acquire a repertoire of sensitive responses. If, on the other hand, the feelings they begin to express are not recognized and reinforced by the adults around them, they not only cease to express those feelings but they also become less able to recognize them in themselves or others.

Empathy too can be seen as a survival skill. Bert Cohler, a University of Chicago psychologist, and Fran Stott, dean of the Erikson Institute for Advanced Study in Child Development in Chicago, have found that children from psychically damaged families frequently become hypervigilant, developing an intense attunement to their parents' moods. One child they studied, Nicholas, had a horrible habit of approaching other kids in his nursery-school class as if he were going to kiss them, then would bite them instead. The scientists went back to study videos of Nicholas at 20 months interacting with his psychotic mother and found that she had responded to his every expression of anger or independence with compulsive kisses. The researchers dubbed them "kisses of death," and their true significance was obvious to Nicholas, who arched his back in horror at her approaching lips—and passed his own rage on to his classmates years later.

Empathy also acts as a buffer to cruelty, and it is a quality conspicuously lacking in child molesters and psychopaths. Goleman cites some chilling research into brutality by Robert Hare, a psychologist at the University of British Columbia. Hare found that psychopaths, when hooked up to electrodes and told they are going to receive a shock, show none of the visceral responses that fear of pain typically triggers: rapid heartbeat, sweating and so on. How could the threat of punishment deter such people from committing crimes?

It is easy to draw the obvious lesson from these test results. How much happier would we be, how much more successful as individuals and civil as a society, if we were more alert to the importance of emotional intelligence and more adept at teaching it? From kindergartens to business schools to corporations across the country, people are taking seriously the idea that a little more time spent on the "touchy-feely" skills so often derided may in fact pay rich dividends.

In the corporate world, according to personnel executives, IQ gets you hired, but EQ gets you promoted. Goleman likes to tell of a manager at AT&T's Bell Labs, a think tank for brilliant engineers in New Jersey, who was asked to rank his top performers. They weren't the ones with the highest IQs; they were the ones whose E-mail got answered. Those workers who were good collaborators and networkers and popular with colleagues were more likely to get the cooperation they needed to reach

Square Pegs in the Oval Office?

IF A HIGH DEGREE OF EMOTIONAL INTELLIGENCE IS A PREREQUISITE FOR OUTSTANDing achievement, there ought to be no better place to find it than in the White House. It turns out, however, that not every man who reached the pinnacle of American leadership was a gleaming example of self-awareness, empathy, impulse control and all the other qualities that mark an elevated EQ.

Oliver Wendall Holmes, who knew intelligence when he saw it, judged Franklin Roosevelt "a second-class intellect, but a first-class temperament." Born and educated as an aristocrat, F.D.R. had polio and needed a wheelchair for most of his adult life. Yet, far from becoming a self-pitying wretch, he developed an unbridled optimism that served him and the country well during the Depression and World War II—this despite, or because of, what Princeton professor Fred Greenstein calls Roosevelt's "tendency toward deviousness and duplicity."

Even a first-class temperament, however, is not a sure predictor of a successful presidency. According to Duke University political scientist James David Barber, the most perfect blend of intellect and warmth of personality in a Chief Executive was the brilliant Thomas Jefferson, who "knew the importance of communication and empathy. He never lost the common touch." Richard Ellis, a professor of politics at Oregon's Willamette University who is skeptical of the whole EQ theory, cites two 19th century Presidents who did not fit the mold. "Martin Van Buren was well adjusted, balanced, empathetic and persuasive, but he was not very successful," says Ellis. "Andrew Jackson was less well adjusted, less balanced, less empathetic and was terrible at controlling his own impulses, but he transformed the presidency."

Lyndon Johnson as Senate majority leader was a brilliant practitioner of the art of political persuasion, yet failed utterly to transfer that gift to the White House. In fact, says Princeton's Greenstein, L.B.J. and Richard Nixon would be labeled "worst cases" on any EQ scale of Presidents. Each was touched with political genius, yet each met with disaster. "To some extent," says Greenstein, "this is a function of the extreme aspects of their psyches; they are the political versions of Van Gogh, who does unbelievable paintings and then cuts off his ear."

History professor William Leuchtenburg of the University of North Carolina at Chapel Hill suggests that the 20th century Presidents with perhaps the highest IQs—Wilson, Hoover and Carter—also had the most trouble connecting with their constituents. Woodrow Wilson, he says, "was very high strung [and] arrogant; he was not willing to strike any middle ground. Herbert Hoover was so locked into certain ideas that you could never convince him otherwise. Jimmy Carter is probably the most puzzling of the three. He didn't have a deficiency of temperament; in fact, he was too temperate. There was an excessive rationalization about Carter's approach."

That was never a problem for John Kennedy and Ronald Reagan. Nobody ever accused them of intellectual genius, yet both radiated qualities of leadership with an infectious confidence and openheartedness that endeared them to the nation. Whether President Clinton will be so endeared remains a puzzle. That he is a Rhodes scholar makes him certifiably brainy, but his emotional intelligence is shaky. He obviously has the knack for establishing rapport with people, but he often appears to eager to please that he looks weak. "As for controlling his impulses," says Willamette's Ellis, "Clinton is terrible." —*By Jesse Birnbaum. Reported by James Carney/Washington and Lisa H. Towle/Raleigh*

4. ❖ RELATING TO OTHERS

their goals than the socially awkward, lone-wolf geniuses.

When David Campbell and others at the Center for Creative Leadership studied "derailed executives," the rising stars who flamed out, the researchers found that these executives failed most often because of "an interpersonal flaw" rather than a technical inability. Interviews with top executives in the U.S. and Europe turned up nine so-called fatal flaws, many of them classic emotional failings, such as "poor working relations," being "authoritarian" or "too ambitious" and having "conflict with upper management."

At the center's executive-leadership seminars across the country, managers come to get emotionally retooled. "This isn't sensitivity training or Sunday-supplement stuff," says Campbell. "One thing they know when they get through is what other people think of them." And the executives have an incentive to listen. Says Karen Boylston, director of the center's team-leadership group: "Customers are telling businesses, 'I don't care if every member of your staff graduated with honors from Harvard, Stanford and Wharton. I will take my business and go where I am understood and treated with respect.'"

Nowhere is the discussion of emotional intelligence more pressing than in schools, where both the stakes and the opportunities seem greatest. Instead of constant crisis intervention, or declarations of war on drug abuse or teen pregnancy or violence, it is time, Goleman argues, for preventive medicine. "Five years ago, teachers didn't want to think about this," says principal Roberta Kirshbaum of P.S. 75 in New York City. "But when kids are getting killed in high school, we have to deal with it." Five years ago, Kirshbaum's school adopted an emotional literacy program, designed to help children learn to manage anger, frustration, loneliness. Since then, fights at lunchtime have decreased from two or three a day to almost none.

Educators can point to all sorts of data to support this new direction. Students who are depressed or angry literally cannot learn. Children who have trouble being accepted by their classmates are 2 to 8 times as likely to drop out. An inability to distinguish distressing feelings or handle frustration has been linked to eating disorders in girls.

Many school administrators are completely rethinking the weight they have been giving to traditional lessons and standardized tests. Peter Relic, president of the National Association of Independent Schools, would like to junk the SAT completely. "Yes, it may cost a heck of a lot more money to assess someone's EQ rather than using a machine-scored test to measure IQ," he says. "But if we don't, then we're saying that a test score is more important to us than who a child is as a human being. That means an immense loss in terms of human potential because we've defined success too narrowly."

This warm embrace by educators has left some scientists in a bind. On one hand, says Yale psychologist Salovey, "I love the idea that we want to teach people a richer understanding of their emotional life, to help them achieve their goals." But, he adds, "what I would oppose is training conformity to social expectations." The danger is that any campaign to hone emotional skills in children will end up teaching that there is a "right" emotional response for any given situation—laugh at parades, cry at funerals, sit still at church. "You can teach self-control," says Dr. Alvin Poussaint, professor of psychiatry at Harvard Medical School. "You can teach that it's better to talk out your anger and not use violence. But is it good emotional intelligence not to challenge authority?"

S OME PSYCHOLOGISTS GO further and challenge the very idea that emotional skills can or should be taught in any kind of formal, classroom way. Goleman's premise that children can be trained to analyze their feelings strikes Johns Hopkins' McHugh as an effort to reinvent the encounter group: "I consider that an abominable idea, an idea we have seen with adults. That failed, and now he wants to try it with children? Good grief!" He cites the description in Goleman's book of an experimental program at the Nueva Learning Center in San Francisco. In one scene, two fifth-grade boys start to argue over the rules of an exercise, and the teacher breaks in to ask them to talk about what they're feeling. "I appreciate the way you're being assertive in talking with Tucker," she says to one student. "You're not attacking." This strikes McHugh as pure folly. "The author is presuming that someone has the key to the right emotions to be taught to children. We don't even know the right emotions to be taught to adults. Do you really think a child of eight or nine really understands the difference between aggressiveness and assertiveness?"

The problem may be that there is an ingredient missing. Emotional skills, like intellectual ones, are morally neutral. Just as a genius could use his intellect either to cure cancer or engineer a deadly virus, someone with great empathic insight could use it to inspire colleagues or exploit them. Without a moral compass to guide people in how to employ their gifts, emotional intelligence can be used for good or evil. Columbia University psychologist Walter Mischel, who invented the marshmallow test and others like it, observes that the knack for delaying gratification that makes a child one marshmallow richer can help him become a better citizen or—just as easily—an even more brilliant criminal.

Given the passionate arguments that are raging over the state of moral instruction in this country, it is no wonder Goleman chose to focus more on neutral emotional skills than on the values that should govern their use. That's another book—and another debate. —**Reported by Sharon E. Epperson and Lawrence Mondi/New York, James L. Graff/Chicago and Lisa H. Towle/Raleigh**

The Enduring Power of Friendship

Susan Davis

Susan Davis is a writer in San Francisco.

A few years ago one of my best friends suddenly stopped returning my calls. There had been some tension between us for about a year. We'd all but stopped seeing each other. Given our long history, I figured we would pick up again soon. But for her, it was time to end the friendship.

It was a hard pill for me to swallow. In the 12 years we'd known each other, Kelly and I had gone through a lot together. We shared a house in Boston, traveled cross-country and talked endlessly of our rural roots, our families and our dreams of the future. We wept when I moved to California for graduate school, but we stayed close through letters, phone calls and visits. "We're best friends forever," Kelly used to say. "We'll grow old together on a porch somewhere."

I always agreed. But when Kelly came to California to start a new life several years after I had, something was out of kilter. I had begun a career and met the man I wanted to marry; she wanted neither a "real" job nor a husband. I wanted to talk about my new feelings. She acted as if I'd betrayed her by even having them.

When Kelly finally stopped speaking to me, I was devastated. We had shared everything. Now my confidante was gone. Worse, she no longer even liked me. I felt unsure and exposed, as if we were schoolgirls on a playground and she were telling stories about me.

Does everyone go through what I went through? As it turns out, many of us do. For years sociologists and psychologists have focused primarily on friendships in childhood and adolescence, because it's during these rich periods that we learn to approach and interact with others. Now they're realizing that the long decades of adulthood are equally vital. With job demands and "downsizing" increasing our mobility, and divorce rates still sky high, family ties are strained to their limits. That means adult friendships are perhaps more important than ever. We learn to make friends in our early years, researchers say, but as adults we learn to depend on these essential links.

It isn't always easy. We like to think friendships are warm, casual, fairly simple affairs. In reality they're more complicated. "Friendships involve a good deal of ambiguity and ambivalence," says Dr. William Rawlins, an interpersonal communications expert at Purdue University in West Lafayette, Ind., and author of *Friendship Matters*. Every friendship entails subtle, usually silent negotiations over such fundamental questions as whether we're "just" friends, "good" friends or "best" friends and how generous we'll be with our time. Friction occurs when one friend wants more, gives more or even reveals more than the other.

Unfortunately, guidance on nurturing friendships is sparse. Dr. Diane Prusank, a specialist in interpersonal communications at the University of Hartford (Conn.), looked at scores of articles in eight magazines for women and teenage girls published between 1974 and 1990. She found 125 stories on romantic relationships and families and only nine on friendship. "Our culture is obsessed with romance," says Prusank. "Friendship is secondary; no one thinks it has to be talked about."

It should be. Friendships provide varying degrees of indispensable support, from the agreeable neighbor who lends you his hedge clipper to the former college roommate you can call at any hour of the night for advice or commiseration. But since friendships are voluntary, unbound by obligations of law or

4. ❖ RELATING TO OTHERS

Most adults tend to make new friends. Many people are comfortable casually meeting others, while some feel the need to join some structured club or other social group.

kinship, they're especially susceptible to life's ups and downs, particularly when one friend's life changes in a way that the other's does not. Whether it's marriage, divorce or a career switch, these "developmental transitions" make us see ourselves—and our friends—in a new light.

"Sometimes it's something major, like having children," says study author Dr. Donald Pannen, a psychologist at the University of Puget Sound in Tacoma, Wash. "Other times it's just a little thing like a disagreement about a political candidate. But these changes can create barriers and awkward feelings. They can make it more difficult to maintain the friendship." In fact, according to one study of 17- to 64-year-olds who had recently ended friendships, 77% said life changes precipitated the rift.

People have always gone through developmental transitions, but these days two people rarely hit the same transition at the same time. It's quite conceivable, for instance, for a 35-year-old woman to be a stay-at-home mom with two children while her close friend of the same age works 60-hour weeks and goes out on dates.

Certain developmental transitions are more disruptive than others. Career success—and the envy it provokes—can turn even the closest friendship sour. Some friendships may falter simply because two people no longer share the same values, say, about money or politics. Marriage poses one of the biggest threats to friendship, especially for women. Spousal intimacy may weaken a woman's need for a best friend, says Prusank. This seeming abandonment can be hard on the single friends who are left behind.

The hectic pace of modern life also makes keeping up with friends difficult. The new friendships we make on the job are often tenuous, because of the unstable nature of corporate life today. Not only do we leave jobs more often, but we also compete more with our coworkers to hang on to the jobs we have. Add children, hobbies and volunteer or religious activities to the mix, and our social contacts get spread pretty thin. "It used to be that everyone lived and worked and socialized in the same town," says Pannen. "But it takes much more effort to keep friends in today's fragmented society."

It's rare too for an adult to have a single best friend. Most of us have several "very good" friends in different circles. "The bond between adult best friends just isn't the same as in childhood," says Prusank. "The tight connection is diluted by many activities and obligations."

Trouble is, few of us actually acknowledge these pressures, much less discuss them with our friends. "Most people are afraid to burden a friendship with too much talk," says Dr. Julia T. Wood, an expert in communication at the University of North

Carolina at Chapel Hill. "If you speak up about what's bothering you, there's a risk that the other person will shy away."

That reticence often continues to the bitter end. Unlike romantic relationships, which tend to break apart with a bang, friendships typically dissolve with barely a whimper. In the Puget Sound study, only 13% of subjects said their friendships ended abruptly, and just 15% managed to have an open discussion of the relationship's problems. "We have no language for describing friendship difficulties," says Prusank. "We don't have 'breakup' conversations, and we don't give back the objects we exchanged. Without these symbolic displays of finality—for example, returning gifts or photographs—it can be difficult to move on."

Both men and women take the loss of a pal hard: Six months after their friendships ended, 70% of the Puget Sound subjects said they felt ambivalent about their conflicts, 50% admitted to still feeling sad and 14% felt angry; only 17% said they were happy to have the friend out of their life.

And once we lose a few friends, whether it's due to work changes, moving, having children or death, it gets harder to approach new people. "Go through a lot of these transitions and you become wary," says Wood. "Older people often withdraw because they have endured so many losses."

Still, most adults tend to make new friends, though often they have to take active measures to do so. "Many people join groups, like local political clubs, or even move to a new neighborhood or city specifically to meet people," says Dr. Rosemary Blieszner, a gerontologist at Virginia Polytechnic Institute and State University in Blacksburg, Va., and coauthor of *Adult Friendships*. If you're shy, try giving yourself "homework assignments," such as approaching two new people a week or reapproaching someone you've met recently and asking them to join you for a cup of coffee.

Of course, low self-esteem or lack of trust in others can make even these minor social interactions difficult. Simply deciding to embark on a friend-making campaign won't make these impediments go away, though a professional counselor can often help.

Much has happened since Kelly and I parted. I've switched jobs, married the man I fell in love with and become closer to my family. I'm sorry that Kelly hasn't been able to share these developments with me. But to endure, adult friendships need to be flexible. And that, say researchers, may be a rare quality.

"Part of what makes a friendship resilient is a mutual ability to weather changes and tolerate shifting demands on your friend's life," says Wood. If your best friend suddenly meets the man of her dreams, for instance, the wisest course of action might be to let her go for a while. To maintain a friendship, you need to be willing to come back and rejuvenate it after a period of less contact. "If you always think the silence stems from a lack of affection or care," says Wood, "the bond becomes less stable."

Then again, part of being a good friend is knowing when to let go. One instance, Purdue's Rawlins says, is when an unforgivable betrayal occurs, for example if a friend sleeps with your spouse or damages your reputation. Another is when a friend makes you feel bad about yourself. "There's a value to being able to let go as we take on new roles," says Wood. "This ability to adapt and change is healthy."

I'm not ready to say the breakup of my own friendship was healthy. I still miss Kelly too much. But perhaps my mother, listening to me moan yet again about the loss of my friend, put it best: "You met when you were girls," she said. "You laughed and cried together as girls. Now you're not girls anymore."

Born to be good?

What motivates us to be good, bad or indifferent towards others?
Celia Kitzinger examines the psychology of morality.

Celia Kitzinger teaches psychology at the University of Loughborough, England.

MANY of us, much of the time, act to benefit others. There are small kindnesses of everyday life—like holding open a door, sharing food or expressing compassion for someone in distress. Things so ordinary that we simply take them for granted.

We are pleased, but not particularly surprised that people commonly care for sick relatives, give money to help famine victims, donate blood to hospitals, or volunteer to assist at hospices. At times what people do for others is truly spectacular. In the US, Lenny Skutnik risked his life diving into the icy waters of the Potomac River to save an airline crash victim; in Nazi Europe many people risked their lives in offering protection to Jews. In both mundane and exceptional ways people often act to help others—which is why psychologists describe human beings not just as 'social' but also as 'pro-social' animals.

But why do people spend so much time and money and effort on others, when we could keep it all for ourselves? One argument is that self-interest lies at the root of all superficially 'moral' behaviour. According to sociobiologists, we are biologically driven towards those forms of altruism—caring for our families, for example—which improve the survival of our genes.[1] Moral actions are simply automatic and instinctive, of no greater or lesser significance than the behaviour of a mother bird putting her own life at risk leading a predator away from her chicks. Helping people who are not genetically related to us can also be in the best interest of our genes if it sets up the expectation that we—or those who share our genes—will be helped in turn.

There are many subtle ways in which helping others can offer rewards which serve our self-interest. These include the praise of onlookers; gratitude from the person being helped; the warm glow of knowing we have done a good deed; and the benefit of avoiding guilt, shame or punishment. Most people agree that some good behaviour can be attributed to self-interest. But is that all there is?

In an ingenious set of experiments, a group of psychologists set out to test the idea that empathy—the ability to imagine ourselves in the place of another and to feel their emotions—can result in genuine altruism.[2] Subjects were encouraged to be empathetic while watching a 'worker' who they believed was reacting badly to a series of uncomfortable electric shocks. They were then given a chance to help the worker by receiving the shocks themselves. If helping were only self-serving egoism, then people who felt empathy for the victim would simply want to escape from the upsetting experience. But researchers found that those with strong empathetic feelings volunteered to take the worker's place, even when told they that they could leave immediately if they refused. The researchers also found that high-empathy people, who were deprived of the opportunity to help, felt just as good when someone else helped instead. This suggests that the offer to help reflected a genuine wish to relieve the victim's suffering, rather than a desire for praise from other people. So it looks as if the cynical view that even good actions have selfish motives may well be wrong. Empathy is common in very small children who often respond to another's distress with crying and sadness, and may attempt to comfort them with a hug or a cuddly toy. Some psychologists believe that behaviour like this signals the start of moral development.[3]

Although empathy may be an important component of moral behaviour, morality cannot rely on empathy alone because this emotion is too circumscribed and partial. It can also lead us to make unfair decisions—taking sides in a dispute, for example. Another explanation for why people behave well is that they are motivated not by emotions but by reasoned moral principles. This is what Lawrence Kohlberg proposes in his 'cognitive-development model' theory.[4] Children, he says, begin at a 'preconventional' level in which they see morality in relation to obedience and punishments from adults. At the second, 'conventional' level, reached in late childhood or early adolescence, they are oriented first to pleasing and helping others and later to maintaining the existing social order. At the third and highest stage of moral development—reached by only a small proportion of adults—people begin to define moral values and principles such as human dignity, justice, universal human rights. According to this theory, morality is a matter of cognitive (not emotional) development: it matters not one whit whether we care about or empathize with other people so long as we respect their rights as human beings.

Some critics, notably feminist psychologist Carol Gilligan, have challenged the theory as sexist: men may favour abstract theoretical notions of rights and justice, but women, she says, are more likely to construct morality rooted in their sense of connection with other people, a morality of care and empathy.[5] Others criticize the ethnocentrism of the model, pointing out that Kohlberg has elevated to the highest stage of moral development precisely those views most likely to be held by white, middle-class, educated North Americans.[6]

It's more likely that moral behaviour comes about in a variety of ways: sometimes we may act well in the hope of rewards; other times good behaviour may be motivated by empathy; sometimes it is the outcome of reasoned moral arguments. Crucially, though, neither strong feelings of empathy nor high moral principles guarantee that people will behave well. There is often a gap between moral beliefs and moral action—between how people think and hope they would behave in a situation and how they actually do behave. Some of the classic studies of psychology were prompted by situations in which people failed to act in accordance with their moral values.

In the 1960s a young woman named Kitty Genovese was murdered by a man who raped and stabbed her repeatedly for half an hour in front of 38 residents of a respectable New York City neighbourhood. Nobody went to help her. Only one person finally called the police, after she was dead. This incident prompted a flood of research into what became known as the 'bystander effect' which examined why people don't intervene when others are in pain or in danger.[7] Sometimes people fail to intervene out of callousness or indifference. But more often they fail to act in spite of what they feel they should do, and then feel ashamed afterwards. Why is this?

A common finding is that people are uncertain how to behave because, unsure about what they are seeing, they conform with the behaviour of others, who are equally unsure. Emergencies are rare events which happen suddenly and unexpectedly. How can we know that an emergency is real and is not a prank, a game, or a film being produced? The safest thing is to sit tight and wait to see how others react. If nobody else does anything, then people worry about making fools of themselves. A large group can stand by and do nothing, each lulled into thinking that there is no need to act, each waiting for someone else to make the first move. What looks like callous indifference is actually fear of what other people will think if they make an inappropriate response in an ambiguous situation.

Someone in Kitty Genovese's situation is less likely to be helped if many people are watching than if only one person witnesses the attack. For example, subjects asked to wait in a room before being interviewed heard a woman in the next room apparently fall, hurt herself, and cry out in distress. Of those waiting alone, 70 per cent went to help her, compared with only 7 per cent of those waiting with a stranger who did nothing. Today's altruist may be tomorrow's passive bystander; it all depends on the social situation because people tend to behave in accordance with socially prescribed roles rather than as individuals.

In a well-known study by Stanley Milgram, subjects were recruited through newspaper advertisements for what was described as 'an experiment in learning'. They were seated in front of a shock machine that could administer up 450 volts to the 'learner', a man strapped into a chair.[8] Each time the 'learner' made a mistake the subject had to pull a lever to give him an electric shock, increasing the voltage each time. (In fact, the lever was a dummy, and the 'learner' was acting out his response). At 150 volts the learner started shouting. At 180 volts, he cried out in pain and pleaded to be released. At 300 volts he screamed with pain and yelled about his heart condition. Later still there was only deathly silence. If subjects wanted to stop giving shocks, the experimenter said only 'the experiment requires that you continue'. No threats, no incentives to go on, just the order. Under these conditions—and contrary to the predictions of psychiatrists who had guessed that virtually no-one would obey to the end—nearly two-thirds of subjects delivered the full range of shocks, proceeding beyond the levers marked 'Danger: Severe Shock' to the ones marked 'XXX'.

These people were not sadists or psychopaths. They were ordinary people who believed that you shouldn't hurt others, who often showed empathy for the learner, and who disliked what they were ordered to do. Virtually all of them complained to the experimenter and asked for permission to stop giving shocks. But when ordered to continue the majority did as they were told. As Milgram says: 'With numbing regularity, good people were seen to knuckle under the demands of authority and perform actions that were callous and severe.' Women were as likely as men to deliver shocks up to maximum intensity.

What all these studies illustrate is the extent to which moral behaviour is a social, not an individual issue. In thinking about why people fail to offer help, why they behave punitively, or why they inflict pain on others, we often resort to explanations which depend on individual characteristics—their personal religious beliefs, their capacity for empathy, their understanding of moral principles, or the kind of upbringing they had. But these explanations overlook the key role of social context. The frightening truth uncovered by these classic psychological studies is that it is not too difficult to set up situations in which most of us behave worse than we could have thought possible, out of conformity, fear of what others might think, loss of individual identity or obedience to authority.

The traditional view of moral behaviour is that people are intrinsically selfish beings whose natural anti-social impulses have been curbed by social structures designed to promote obedience to authority, law and order. An alternative possibility is that people are fundamentally pro-social beings, whose ability to act on altruistic impulses and moral principles is sometimes inhibited by precisely these social pressures. At the very least it is obvious that this is sometimes true, and that we need to develop ways of recognizing and challenging those social pressures which result in apathetic or cruel behaviour in our everyday lives.

Notes

1. Richard Dawkins, *The Selfish Gene,* OUP 1976.
2. CD Batson, *The Altruism Question,* Erlbaum Associates 1991.
3. C Zahn-Waxler & M Radke-Yarrow, 'The Development of Altruism' in N Eisenberg-Berg (ed.) *The Development of Prosocial Behaviour,* Academic Press 1986.
4. L Kohlberg, *The Philosophy of Moral Development,* Harper and Row 1981.
5. C Gilligan, *In a Different Voice,* Harvard University Press 1982.
6. EEL Simpson, 'Moral Development Research: A Case Study of Scientific Cultural Bias', *Human Development 17,* 1974.
7. B Latané & JM Draley, *The Unresponsive Bystander. Why doesn't he help?* Appleton-Century-Croft 1970.
8. S Milgram, 'Some Conditions of Obedience and Disobedience to Authority', *Human Relations 18,* 1965.

ARE YOU SHY?

You have lots of company. Nearly one of two Americans claims to be shy. What's more, the incidence is rising, and technology may be turning ours into a culture of shyness.

Bernardo J. Carducci, Ph.D., with Philip G. Zimbardo, Ph.D.

In sharp contrast to the flamboyant lifestyle getting under way at dance clubs across the country, another, quieter, picture of Americans was emerging from psychological research. Its focus: those on the sidelines of the dance floor. In 1975 *Psychology Today* published a ground-breaking article by Stanford University psychologist Philip Zimbardo, Ph.D., entitled "The Social Disease Called Shyness." The article revealed what Zimbardo had found in a survey conducted at several American colleges: An astonishing 40 percent of the 800 questioned currently considered themselves to be shy.

In addition to documenting the pervasiveness of shyness, the article presented a surprising portrait of those with the condition. Their mild-mannered exterior conceals roiling turmoil inside. The shy disclosed that they are excessively self-conscious, constantly sizing themselves up negatively, and overwhelmingly preoccupied with what others think of them. While everyone else is meeting and greeting, they are developing plans to manage their public impression (*If I stand at the far end of the room and pretend to be examining the painting on the wall, I'll look like I'm interested in art but won't have to talk to anybody*). They are consumed by the misery of the social setting (*I'm having a horrible time at this party because I don't know what to say and everyone seems to be staring at me*). All the while their hearts are pounding, their pulses are speeding, and butterflies are swarming in their stomach—physiological symptoms of genuine distress.

The article catalogued the painful consequences of shyness. There are social problems, such as difficulty meeting people and making new friends, which may leave the shy woefully isolated and subject to loneliness and depression. There are cognitive problems; unable to think clearly in the presence of others, the shy tend to freeze up in conversation, confusing others who are trying to respond to them. They can appear snobbish or disinterested in others, when they are in fact just plain nervous. Excessively egocentric, they are relentlessly preoccupied with every aspect of their own appearance and behavior. They live trapped between two fears: being invisible and insignificant to others, and being visible but worthless.

The response to the article was overwhelming. A record number of letters to the editor screamed HELP ME!, surprising considering that then, as now, PT readers were generally well-educated, self-aware, and open-minded—not a recipe for shyness.

The article launched a whole new field of study. In the past 20 years, a variety of researchers and clinicians, including myself, have been scrutinizing shyness. To celebrate the 20th anniversary of PTs epochal report, we decided to spotlight recent advances in understanding this social disease:

• Research in my laboratory and elsewhere suggests that, courtesy of changing cultural conditions, the incidence of shyness in the U.S. may now be as high as 48 per-cent—and rising.

• Most shyness is hidden. Only a small percentage of the shy appear to be obviously ill at ease. But all suffer internally.

• Some people are born with a temperamental tilt to shyness. But even that inheritance doesn't doom one to a life of averting others' eyes. A lot depends on parenting.

• Most shyness is acquired through life experiences.

• There is a neurobiology of shyness. At least three brain centers that mediate fear and anxiety orchestrate the whole-body response we recognize as shyness. Think of it as an over-generalized fear response.

• The incidence of shyness varies among countries. Israelis seem to be the least shy inhabitants of the world. A major contributing factor: cultural styles of assigning praise and blame to kids.

• Shyness has huge costs to individuals at all ages, especially in Western cultures.

• Shyness does have survival value.

• Despite the biological hold of shyness, there are now specific and well-documented ways to overcome its crippling effects.

Shy on the Sly

How is it possible that 40 to 50 percent of Americans—some of your friends, no doubt—are shy? Because while some people are obviously, publicly shy, a much larger percentage are privately shy. Their shyness, and its pain, is invisible to everyone but themselves.

Only 15 to 20 percent of shy people actually fit the stereotype of the ill-at-ease person. They use every excuse in the book to avoid social events. If they are unlucky enough to find themselves in casual conversation, they can't quite manage to make eye contact, to reply to questions without stumbling over their words, or to keep up their end of the conversation; they seldom smile. They are easy to pick out of a crowd because their shyness is expressed behaviorally.

The other 80 to 85 percent are privately shy, according to University of Pittsburgh psychologist Paul Pilkonis, Ph.D. Though their shyness leaves no behavioral traces—it's felt subjectively—it wreaks personal havoc. They feel their shyness in a pounding heart and pouring sweat. While they may seem at ease and confident in conversation, they are actually engaging in a self-deprecating inner dialogue, chiding themselves for being inept and questioning whether the person they are talking to really likes them. "Even though these people do fairly well socially, they have a lot of negative self-thought going on in their heads," explains Pilkonis. Their shyness has emotional components as well. When the conversation is over, they feel upset or defeated.

"There are a lot of people who have private aspects of shyness who are willing to say they are shy but don't quite jibe with the people we can see trembling or blushing," notes Pilkonis.

The Natural History of Shyness

Shyness has not always been a source of pain. Being shy or inhibited serves a very protective function: it breeds caution. No doubt shyness has pulled *H. sapiens* out of some pretty tight spots over the eons.

Originally, shyness served as protective armor around the physical self. After all, only after an animal has fully acquainted itself with a new environment is it safe to behave in a more natural, relaxed manner and explore around. The process of habituation is one of the most fundamental characteristics of all organisms.

As conscious awareness has increased, the primary threat is now to the psychological self—embarrassment. Most people show some degree of social inhibition; they think about what they are going to say or do before hand, as well as the consequences of saying or doing it. It keeps us from making fools of ourselves or hurting the feelings of others.

According to Wellesley psychologist Jonathan Cheek, Ph.D., situational shyness "can help to facilitate cooperative living; it inhibits behaviors that are socially unacceptable." So, a little bit of shyness

Shyness can lurk in unlikely hosts—even those of the talk show variety. Take David Letterman, king of late-night TV. Although his performance in front of a live studio audience and countless viewers seems relaxed and spontaneous, Letterman is known to be relentless in the planning and orchestration of each nightly performance down to the last detail. Like Johnny Carson, he spends little time socializing outside a very small circle of friends and rarely attends social functions.

Letterman is the perfect example of what Zimbardo calls the shy extrovert: the cool, calm, and collected type whose insides are in fact churning. A subset of the privately shy, shy extroverts may be politicians, entertainers, and teachers. They have learned to act outgoing—as long as they are in a controlled environment. A politician who can speak from a prepared script at a mass political rally really may get tongue-tied during a question-and-answer period. A professor may be comfortable as long as she is talking about her area of expertise; put in a social gathering where she may have to make small talk, she clams up.

Zimbardo's short list of notable shy extroverts: funny lady Carol Burnett, singer Johnny Mathis, television reporter Barbara Walters, and international opera star Joan Sutherland. These stars are not introverts, a term often confused with shyness. Introverts have the conversational skills and self esteem necessary for interacting successfully with others but prefer to be alone. Shy people want very much to be with others but lack the social skills and self-esteem.

What unites the shy of any type is acute self-consciousness. The shy are even self-conscious about their self-consciousness. Theirs is a twisted egocentricity. They spend so much time focusing on themselves and their weaknesses, they have little time or inclination to look outward.

Wired for Shyness?

According to developmental psychologist Jerome Kagan, Ph.D., and colleagues at Harvard University, up to a third of shy adults were born with a temperament that inclined them to it. The team has been able to identify shyness in young infants before environmental conditions make an impact.

In his longitudinal studies, 400 four-month-old infants were brought into the lab and subjected to such stimuli as moving mobiles, a whiff of a Q-Tip dipped in alcohol, and a tape recording of the human voice. Then they were brought back at a later age for further study. From countless hours of observation, rerun on videotapes, Kagan, along with Harvard psychologists Nancy Snidman, Ph.D, and Doreen Arcus, Ph.D., have nailed down the behavioral manifestations of shyness in infants.

About 20 percent of infants display a pattern of extreme nervous-system reactivity to such common stimuli. These infants grow distressed when faced with unfamiliar people, objects, and events. They momentarily extend their arms and legs spastically, they vigorously wave their arms and kick their legs, and, on occasion, arch their backs. They also show signs of distress in the form of excessive fretting and crying, usually at a high pitch and sustained tension that communicates urgency. Later on, they cling to their parents in a new play situation.

In contrast, 40 percent of all infants exposed to the same stimuli occasionally move an arm or leg but do not show the motor outbursts or fretting and crying typical of their highly reactive brethren. When the low-reactive infants do muster up a crying spell, it is nothing out of the ordinary.

Lab studies indicate that highly reactive infants have an easily excitable sympathetic nervous system. This neural network regulates not only many vital organs, including the heart, but the brain response of fear. With their high-strung, hair-trigger temperament, even the suggestion of danger—a stranger, a new environment—launches the psychological and physiologic arousal of fear and anxiety.

One of the first components of this reaction is an increased heart rate. Remarkably, studies show that high-reactive infants have a higher-than-normal heart rate—and it can be detected even before birth, while the infant is still *in utero*. At 14 months, such infants have over-large heart rate acceleration in response to a neutral stimulus such as a sour taste.

Four years later, the same kids show another sign of sympathetic arousal—a cooler temperature reading in their right ring finger than in their left ring finger while watching emotionally evocative film clips. Too, as children they show more brain wave activity in the right frontal lobe; by contrast, normally reactive children display more brain wave activity in the left frontal area. From other studies it is known that the right side of the brain is more involved in the expression of anxiety and distress.

The infant patterns point to an inborn variation in the response threshold of the amygdala, an almond-shaped brain structure linked to the expression of fear and anxiety (see "The Shy Brain"). This neural hypersensitivity eventually inclines such children to avoid situations that give rise to anxiety and fear—meeting new people or being thrown into new environments. In such circumstances they are behaviorally inhibited.

Though it might sound strange, there may even be a season for shyness—specifically early fall. Kagan and Harvard sociologist Stephen Gortmaker, Ph.D., have found that women who conceive in August or

4. ❖ RELATING TO OTHERS

September are particularly likely to bear shy children. During these months, light is waning and the body is producing increasing amounts of melatonin, a hormone known to be neurally active; for example, it helps set our biological clocks. As it passes through the placenta to the developing fetal brain, Kagan surmises, the melatonin may act on cells to create the hyperaroused, easily agitated temperament of the shy.

Further evidence of a biological contribution to shyness is a pattern of inheritance suggesting direct genetic transmission from one generation to the next. Parents and grandparents of inhibited infants are more likely to report being shy as children than the relatives of uninhibited children, Snidman found in one study. Kagan and company are looking for stronger proof—such as, say, an elevated incidence of panic disorder (acute episodes of severe anxiety) and depression in the parents of inhibited children. So far he has found that among preschool children whose parents were diagnosed with panic attack or depression, one-third showed inhibited behavior. By contrast, among children whose parents experience neither panic disorder nor depression, only about five percent displayed the inhibited reactive profile.

Are inhibited infants preordained to become shy adults? Not necessarily, Doreen Arcus finds. A lot has to do with how such children are handled by their parents. Those who are overprotected, she found from in-home interviews she conducted, never get a chance to find some comfortable level of accommodation to the world; they grow up anxious and shy. Those whose parents do not shield them from stressful situations overcome their inhibition.

Snidman, along with Harvard psychiatrist Carl Schwartz, M.D., examined the staying power of shyness into adolescence. They observed 13- and 14-year-olds who were identified as inhibited at two or three years of age. During the laboratory interview, the adolescents with a history of inhibition tended to smile less, made fewer spontaneous comments, and reported being more shy than those who were identified as uninhibited infants.

Taken over a lifetime, gender doesn't figure much into shyness. Girls are more apt to be shy from infancy through adolescence, perhaps because parents are more protective of them than boys, who are encouraged to be more explorative. Yet in adolescence, boys report that shyness is more painful than do girls. This discomfort is likely related to sex-role expectations that boys must be bold and outgoing, especially with girls, to gear up for their role as head of family and breadwinner. But once into adulthood, gender differences in shyness disappear.

Bringing Biology Home

If only 15 to 20 percent of infants are born shy and nearly 50 percent of us are shy in adulthood, where do all the shy adults come from? The only logical answer is that shyness is acquired along the way.

One powerful source is the nature of the emotional bond parents forge with their children in the earliest years of life. According to Paul Pilkonis, children whose parenting was such that it gave rise to an insecure attachment are more likely to end up shy. Children form attachments to their caregivers from the routine experiences of care, feeding, and caressing. When caretaking is inconsistent and unreliable, parents fail to satisfy the child's need for security, affection, and comfort, resulting in insecure bonds. As the first relationship, attachment becomes the blueprint for all later relationships. Although there are no longitudinal studies spotlighting the development of shyness from toddlerhood to adulthood, there is research showing that insecure early attachment can predict shyness later on.

"The most damnable part of it is that this insecure attachment seems to become self-fulfilling," observes Pilkonis. Because of a difficult relationship to their parents, children internalize a sense of themselves as having problems with all relationships. They generalize the experience—and come to expect that teachers, coaches, and peers won't like them very much.

These are the narcissistically vulnerable—the wound to the self is early and deep, and easily evoked. They are quick to become disappointed in relationships, quick to feel rejection, shame, ridicule. They are relentlessly self-defeating, interpreting even success as failure. "They have negative perceptions of themselves and of themselves in relation to others that they hold onto at all costs," says Pilkonis. The narcissistically vulnerable are among the privately shy—they are seemingly at ease socially but torture themselves beneath the surface. Theirs is a shyness that is difficult to ameliorate, even with psychotherapy.

Shyness can also be acquired later on, instigated at times of developmental transition when children face new challenges in their relationships with their peers. For instance, entering the academic and social whirl of elementary school may leave them feeling awkward or inept with their peers. Teachers label them as shy and it sticks; they begin to see themselves that way—and act it.

Adolescence is another hurdle that can kick off shyness. Not only are adolescents' bodies changing but their social and emotional playing fields are redefining them. Their challenge is to integrate sexuality and intimacy into a world of relationships that used to be defined only by friendship and relatives. A complicated task!

Nor are adults immune. Shyness may result from tail-spinning life upheavals. Divorce at mid-life might be one. "A whole new set of problems kick in with a failure of a relationship, especially if you are interested in establishing new relationships," says Pilkonis. For highly successful, career-defined people, being fired from a long-held job can be similarly debilitating, especially in the interviewing process.

Count in the Culture

Biology and relationship history are not the sole creators of shyness. Culture counts, too. Shyness exists universally, although it is not experienced or defined the same way from culture to culture. Even Zimbardo's earliest surveys hinted at cultural differences in shyness: Japanese and Taiwanese students consistently expressed the highest level of shyness, Jewish stu-

---

Helping Others Beat Shyness

You may not be shy, but one out of two people are. Be sensitive to the fact that others may not be as outgoing and confident. It's your job to make others comfortable around you. Be a host to humanity.

• Make sure no one person at a social gathering—including yourself—is the focus of attention. That makes it possible for everyone to have some of the attention some of the time.

• Like the host of any party, make it your job to bring out the best in others, in any situation. At school, teachers should make it a point to call on kids who are reluctant to speak up. At work, bosses should seek out employees who don't comment in meetings; encouragement to express ideas and creativity will improve any company. At parties, break the ice by approaching someone who is standing alone.

• Help others put their best foot forward. Socially competent people feel comfortable because they tend to steer conversation to their own interests. Find out what the shy person next to you is interested in; introduce the topic.

• Help others keep the conversation going. Shy people often don't speak up in ongoing conversations. Ask a shy person his or

dents the lowest. With these clues, Zimbardo took himself to Japan, Israel, and Taiwan to study college students. The cross-cultural studies turned up even greater cultural differences than the American survey. In Israel, only 30 percent of college-age students report being shy—versus 60 percent in Japan and Taiwan.

From conversations with foreign colleagues and parents, Zimbardo acquired unprecedented insights into how culture shapes behavior in general, and more specifically the cultural roots of shyness. The key is in the way parents attribute blame or praise in the performance of their children. When a child tries and fails at a task, who gets the blame? And when a child tries and succeeds, who gets the credit?

In Japan, if a child tries and succeeds, the parents get the credit. So do the grandparents, teachers, coaches, even Buddha. If there's any left over, only then is it given to the child. But if the child tries and fails, the child is fully culpable and cannot blame anyone else. An "I can't win" belief takes hold, so that children of the culture never take a chance or do anything that will make them stand out. As the Japanese proverb states, "the nail that stands out is pounded down." The upshot is a low-key interpersonal style. Kids are likely to be modest and quiet; they do little to call attention to themselves. In fact, in studies of American college students' individuation tendencies—the endorsement of behaviors that will make a person stand out, unique, or noticed—Asian students tend to score the lowest. They are much less likely to speak or act up in a social gathering for fear of calling attention to themselves.

In Israel, the attributional style is just the opposite. A child who tries gets rewarded, regardless of the outcome. Consider the Yiddish expression *kvell*, which means to engage in an outsize display of pride. If a child tries to make a kite, people *kvell* by pointing out what a great kite it is. And if it doesn't fly, parents blame it on the wind. If a child tries and fails in a competitive setting, parents and others might reproach the coach for not giving the child enough training. In such a supportive environment, a child senses that failure does not have a high price—and so is willing to take a risk. With such a belief system, a person is highly likely to develop *chutzpah*, a type of audacity whereby one always take a chance or risk—with or without the talent. Children of such a value system are more apt to speak up or ask someone to dance at a party without overwhelming self-consciousness.

Shyness, then, is a relative, culture-bound label. It's a safe bet that a shy Israeli would not be considered shy in Japan. Nancy Snidman brings the point home. In studying four-month-olds in Ireland and the U.S., she found no differences in degree

We Shall Overcome

1. Overcoming the Anxiety: To tame your racing heart and churning stomach, learn how to relax. Use simple breathing exercises that involve inhaling and exhaling deeply and slowly.

You can ride out the acute discomfort by staying around for a while. If you give into your distress and flee a party after only five minutes, you guarantee yourself a bad time. Stick around.

2. Getting Your Feet Wet: Nothing breeds success like success. Set up a nonthreatening social interaction that has a high probability of success and build from there. Call a radio show with a prepared comment or question. Call some sort of information line.

3. Face to Face: Then tackle the art of very, very small talk face-to-face. Start a casual, quick exchange with the person next to you, or the cashier, in the supermarket checkout line. Most people in such situations would be very responsive to passing the time in light conversation. Since half the battle is having something to say, prepare. Scan the newspaper for conversation topics, and practice what you are going to say a few times.

5. Smile and Make Eye Contact: When you smile you project a benign social force around you; people will be more likely to notice you and smile back. If you frown or look at your feet, you don't exist for people, or worse, you project a negative presence. Once you have smiled and made eye contact, you have opened up a window for the casual "This elevator is so slow"–type comment. Always maintain eye contact in conversation; it signals that you are listening and interested.

6. Compliment: The shortest route to social success is via a compliment. It's a way to make other people feel good about themselves and about talking to you. Compliment someone every day.

7. Know How to Receive Compliments: Thank the person right away. Then return the compliment: "That's great coming from you, I've always admired the way you dress." Use this as a jumping-off point for a real conversation. Elaborate, ask him where he gets his ties or shops for suits.

8. Stop Assuming the Worst: In expecting the worst of every situation, shy people undermine themselves—they get nervous, start to stutter, and forget what they wanted to say. Chances are that once you actually throw yourself into that dreaded interaction it will be much easier than you thought. Only then will you realize how ridiculous your doomsday predictions are. Ask your workmate if he likes his job. Just do it.

9. Stop Whipping Yourself: Thoughts about how stupid you sound or how nobody really likes you run through your head in every conversation. No one would judge your performance as harshly as you do. Search for evidence to refute your beliefs about yourself. Don't get upset that you didn't ask someone to dance; focus on the fact that you talked to a woman you wanted to meet.

Don't overgeneralize your social mishaps. Say you start to stutter in conversation with someone at a party. Don't punish yourself by assuming that every other interaction that night or in your life will go the same way.

10. Lose the Perfectionism: Your jokes have to be hilarious, your remarks insightful and ironic. Truth is, you set standards so impossible they spawn performance anxiety and doom you to failure. Set more realistic standards.

11. Learn to Take Rejection: Rejection is one of the risks *everyone* takes in social interaction. Try not to take it personally; it may have nothing to do with you.

12. Find Your Comfort Zone: Not all social situations are for everybody. Go where your interests are. You might be happier at an art gallery, book club, or on a volleyball team than at a bar.

13. Comfort Is Not Enough: The goal in overcoming shyness is to break through your self-centeredness. In an interaction, focus on the other person. Make other people's comfort and happiness your main priority. If people think to themselves, "I really enjoyed being with her," when they leave you, then you have transformed your shyness into social competence. Congratulations.

of nervous system reactivity. But at age five, the Irish kids did not talk as much nor were they as loud as the American kids. The difference lies in the cultural expectations expressed in child-rearing. Using American norms of social behavior as the standard of comparison, the normal Irish child would be labeled shy. But, in their own culture, with their own norms of behavior, they are not. By the same token, American kids may be perceived as boorish by the Irish.

The Scarlet S

Shyness is un-American. We are, after all, the land of the free and the home of the brave. From the first settlers and explorers who came to the New World 500 years ago to our leadership in space exploration, America has always been associated with courageous and adventurous people ready to boldly go where others fear to tread. Our culture still values rugged individualism and the conquering of new environments, whether in outer space or in overseas markets. Personal attributes held high in our social esteem are leadership, assertiveness, dominance, independence, and risk-taking. Hence a stigma surrounding shyness.

The people given the most attention in our society are expressive, active, and sociable. We single out as heroes actors, athletes, politicians, television personalities, and rock stars—people expert at calling attention to themselves: Madonna, Rosanne, Howard Stern. People who are most likely to be successful are those who are able to obtain attention and feel comfortable with it.

What shy people don't want, above all else, is to be the focus of attention. Thus, in elementary school, the shy child may not even ask the teacher for help. In college, the shy student is reluctant to ask a question in class. In adulthood, the shy employee is too embarrassed to make a formal presentation to those who grant promotions. In every case, shyness undermines the ability to access the attention of others who would increase the likelihood of success. In a culture where everybody loves a winner, shyness is like entering a foot race with lead insoles.

Consider the findings of Stanford Business School professor Thomas Harrell. To figure out the best predictors of success in business, he gathered the records of Stanford B-School graduates, including their transcripts and letters of recommendation. Ten years out of school, the graduates were ranked from most to least successful based on the quality of their jobs. The only consistent and significant variable that could predict success (among students who were admittedly bright to start with) was verbal fluency—exactly what the typically tongue-

The Shy Brain

We all take time to get used to (or habituate to) a new stimulus (a job interview, a party) before we begin to explore the unfamiliar. After all, a novel stimulus may serve as a signal for something dangerous or important. But shy individuals sense danger where it does not exist. Their nervous system does not accommodate easily to the new. Animal studies by Michael Davis, Ph.D., of Yale University, indicate that the nerve pathways of shyness involve parts of the brain involved in the learning and expression of fear and anxiety.

Both fear and anxiety trigger similar physiologic reactions: muscle tension, increased heart rate, and blood pressure, all very handy in the event an animal has to fight or flee sudden danger. But there are important differences. Fear is an emotional reaction to a specific stimulus; it's quick to appear, and just as quick to dissipate when the stimulus passes. Anxiety is a more generalized response that takes much longer to dissipate.

Studies of cue conditioning implicate the **amygdala** as a central switchboard in both the association of a specific stimulus with the emotion of fear and the expression of that fear. Sitting atop the brain stem, the amygdala is crucial for relaying nerve signals related to emotions and stress. When faced with certain stimuli—notably strangers, authority figures, members of the opposite sex—the shy associate them with fearful reactions.

In contrast to such "explicit" conditioning is a process of "contextual" conditioning. It appears more slowly, lasts much longer. It is often set off by the context in which fear takes place. Exposure to that environment then produces anxiety-like feelings of general apprehension. Through contextual conditioning, shy people come to associate general environments—parties, group discussions where they will be expected to interact socially—with unpleasant feelings, even before the specific feared stimulus is present.

Contextual conditioning is a joint venture between the amygdala and the **hippocampus**, the sea horse–shaped cell cluster near the amygdala, which is essential to memory and spatial learning. Contextual conditioning can be seen as a kind of learning about unpleasant places.

But a crucial third party participates in contextual conditioning. It's the **bed nucleus of the stria terminalis (BNST)**. The long arms of its cells reach to many other areas of the brain, notably the **hypothalamus** and the brain stem, both of which spread the word of fear and anxiety to other parts of the body. The BNST is principally involved in the generalized emotional-behavioral arousal characteristic of anxiety. The BNST may be set off by the neurotransmitter corticotropin releasing factor (CRF).

Once alerted, the hypothalamus triggers the sympathetic nervous system, culminating in the symptoms of inner turmoil experienced by the shy—from rapid heartbeat to sweaty paleness. Another pathway of information, from the amygdala to the brain stem, freezes movement of the mouth.

The shy brain is not different in structure from yours and mine; it's just that certain parts are more sensitive. Everyone has a "shyness thermostat," set by genes and other factors. The pinpointing of brain structures and neurochemicals involved in shyness holds out the promise that specific treatment may eventually be developed to curb its most debilitating forms.

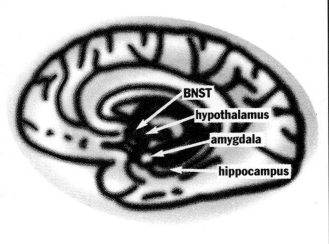

tied shy person can't muster. The verbally fluent are able to sell themselves, their services, and their companies—all critical skills for running a corporation; think of Lee Iacocca. Shy people are probably those behind the scenes designing the cars, programs, and computers—impressive feats, but they don't pay as much as CEO.

The costs of shyness cut deeper than material success, and they take on different forms over a lifetime.

• A shy childhood may be a series of lost opportunities. Think of the child who wants so much to wear a soccer uniform and play just like all the other kids but can't muster the wherewithal to become part of a group. And if the parents do not find a way to help a child overcome feelings of nervousness and apprehension around others, the child may slip into more solitary activities, even though he really wants to be social. The self-selection into solitary activities further reduces the likelihood of the child developing social skills and self-confidence.

• Shy kids also have to endure teasing and peer rejection. Because of their general disposition for high reactivity, shy children make prime targets for bullies. Who better to tease and taunt than someone who gets scared easily and cries?

• Whether inherited or acquired, shyness predisposes to loneliness. It is the natural consequence of decades spent shunning others due to the angst of socializing. Reams of research show that loneliness and isolation can lead to mental and physical decline, even a hastened death.

• Without a circle of close friends or relatives, people are more vulnerable to risk. Lacking the opportunity to share feelings and fears with others, isolated people allow them to fester or escalate. What's more, they are prone to paranoia; there's no one around to correct their faulty thinking, no checks and balances on their beliefs. We all need someone to tell us when our thinking is ridiculous, that there is no Mafia in suburban Ohio, that no one is out to get you, that you've just hit a spate of bad luck.

• Shyness brings with it a potential for abusing alcohol and drugs as social lubricants. In Zimbardo's studies, shy adolescents report feeling greater peer pressure to drink or use drugs than do less shy adolescents. They also confide that they use drugs and alcohol to feel less self-conscious and to achieve a greater sense of acceptance.

• Call it the Hugh Grant Effect. Shyness is linked to sexual, uh, difficulties. Shy people have a hard time expressing themselves to begin with; communicating sexual needs and desires is especially difficult. Shy men may turn to prostitutes just to avoid the awkwardness of intimate negotiations. When Zimbardo asked them to describe their typical client, 20 San Francisco prostitutes said that the men who frequented them were shy and couldn't communicate their sexual desires to wives or girlfriends. And the shy guys made distinctive customers. They circled a block over and over again in their car before getting the nerve to stop and talk to the prostitute. To shy men, the allure of a prostitute is simple—she asks what you want, slaps on a price, and performs. No humiliation, no awkwardness.

Performance anxiety may also make the prospect of sex overwhelming. And be-

---

Helping Shy Kids

Infants with a touchy temperament are not necessarily doomed to become shy adults. Much depends on the parenting they receive.

Do not overprotect or overindulge: Although it may sound counterintuitive, you can help your child cope more effectively with shyness by allowing him or her to experience moderate amounts of anxiety in response to challenges. Rather than rush to your child's aid to soothe away every sign of distress, provide indirect support. Gradually expose your child to new objects, people, and places so that the child will learn to cope with his own unique level of sensitivity to novelty. Nudge, don't push, your child to continue to explore new things.

Show respect and understanding: Your children have private emotional lives separate from yours. It is important to show your shy child that you can understand and sympathize with her shyness, by talking with the child about her feelings of nervousness and being afraid. Then talk with her about what might be gained by trying new experiences *in spite of* being afraid. Revealing related experiences from your own childhood is a natural way to start the ball rolling. Overcoming fears and anxieties is not an easy process; the feelings may remain even after specific shy behaviors have been overcome. Key ingredients are sympathy, patience, and persistence.

Ease the tease: Shy children are especially sensitive to embarrassment. Compared to other children, they need extra attention, comfort, and reassurance after being teased and more encouragement to develop positive self-regard.

Help build friendships: Invite one or two playmates over to let the child gain experience in playing with different kids in the security of familiar surroundings. But allow them as much freedom as possible in structuring play routines. Shy kids sometimes do better when playing with slightly younger children.

Talk to teachers: Teachers often overlook a shy child or mistake quietness and passivity for disinterest or a lack of intelligence. Discuss what measure[s] might be taken in the classroom or playground.

Prepare the child for new experiences: You can help to reduce fears and anxieties by helping your child get familiar with upcoming novel experiences. Take the child to a new school before classes actually start. Help rehearse activities likely to be performed in new situations, such as practicing for show-and-tell. Also role play with the child any anticipated anxiety-provoking situations, such as how to ask someone to dance at a party (if they'll let you) or speak up in a group at summer camp.

Find appropriate activities: Encourage your child to get involved in after-school activities as a means of developing a network of friends and social skills.

Provide indirect support: Ask the child the degree to which he wants you to be involved in his activities. For some kids, a parent cheering in the bleachers is humiliating. Better is indirect support—discussing the child's interests with him and letting him know of your pleasure and pride in him for participating.

Fit not fight: It's not as important to overcome shyness as to find a comfort zone consistent with your child's shyness. Rather than try to make your daughter outgoing, help her find a level of interaction that is comfortable and consistent with her temperament.

Own your temperament: Think how your own personality or interaction style operates in conjunction with your child's. If you aren't shy, understand that your child may need more time to feel comfortable before entering a novel situation or joining a social group. If you are shy, you may need to address your own shyness as a bridge to helping your child with hers.

Bottom Line: Talk, listen, support, and love shy children for who they are, not how outgoing you would like them to be.

cause shy people avoid seeking help, any problems created by embarrassment or self-doubt will likely go untreated.

- Another cost—time. Shy people waste time deliberating and hesitating in social situations that others can pull off in an instant. Part of their problem is that they don't live in the present, observes Zimbardo, who is currently focusing on the psychology of time perspective. "Shy people live too much in their heads," obsessed with the past, the future, or both. A shy person in conversation is not apt to think about what is being said at the moment, but about how past conversations have initially gone well and then deteriorated—just as the current one threatens to. Says Zimbardo: "These are people who cannot enjoy that moment because everything is packaged in worries from the past—a Smithsonian archive of all the bad—that restructure the present."

Or shy people may focus all their thoughts and feelings on future consequences: If I say this, will he laugh at me? If I ask him something simple like where he is from, he'll be bored and think I'm a lousy conversationalist, so why bother anyway? The internal decision trees are vast and twisted. "Concern for consequences always makes you feel somewhat anxious. And that anxiety will impair the shy person's performance," says Zimbardo.

Factoring in past and future is wise, but obsession with either is undermining. Shy people need to focus on the now—the person you are talking to or dancing with—to appreciate any experience. "Dancing is a good example of being completely of the moment," comments Zimbardo. "It is not something you plan, or that you remember, you are just doing it." And enjoying it.

If the costs of shyness are paid by shy people, the benefits of shyness are reaped by others—parents, teachers, friends, and society as a whole.

Yet shy people are often gifted listeners. If they can get over their self-induced pressures for witty repartee, shy people can be great at conversation because they may actually be paying attention. (The hard part comes when a response is expected.) According to Harvard's Doreen Arcus, shy kids are apt to be especially empathic. Parents of the children she studies tell her that "even in infancy, the shy child seemed to be sensitive, empathic, and a good listener. They seem to make really good friends and their friends are very loyal to them and value them quite a bit." Even among children, friendships need someone who will talk and someone who will listen.

For any society to function well, a variety of roles need to be played. There is a place for the quiet, more reflective shy individual who does not jump in where angels fear to tread or attempt to steal the limelight from others. Yet as a culture we have devalued these in favor of boldness and expressiveness as a means of measuring worth.

The Future of Shyness

To put it bluntly, the future of shyness is bleak. My studies have documented that since 1975 its prevalence has risen from 40 percent to 48 percent. There are many reasons to expect the numbers to climb in the decades ahead.

Most significantly, technology is continually redefining how we communicate. We are engaging in a diminishing number of face-to-face interactions on a daily basis. When was the last time you talked to a bank teller? Or a gas station attendant? How often do you call friends or colleagues when you know they aren't in just so you can leave a message on their machine? Voice mail, faxes, and E-mail give us the illusion of being "in touch" but what's to touch but the keyboard? This is not a Luddite view of technology but a sane look at its deepest costs.

The electronic age was supposed to give us more time, but ironically it has stolen it from us. Technology has made us time-efficient—and redefined our sense of time and its value. It is not to be wasted, but to be used quickly and with a purpose.

Office encounters have become barren of social interaction. They are information-driven, problem-oriented, solution-based. No pleasantries. No backs slapped. We cut to the chase: I need this from you. Says Zimbardo, "You have to have an agenda." Some people don't even bother to show at the office at all; they telecommute.

The dwindling opportunities for face-to-face interaction put shy people at an increasing disadvantage. They no longer get to practice social skills within the comfort of daily routine. Dropping by a colleague's office to chat becomes increasingly awkward as you do it less and less. Social life has shrunk so much it can now be entirely encapsulated in a single, near-pejorative phrase: "face time," denoting the time employees may engage in eyeball-to-eyeball conversation. It's commonly relegated to morning meetings and after 4:00 P.M.

Electronic hand-held video games played solo now crowd out the time-honored social games of childhood. Even electronically simulated social interactions can't substitute—they do not permit people to learn the necessary give and take that is at the heart of all interpersonal relationships.

Technology is not the only culprit. The rise of organized sports for kids and the fall of informal sidewalk games robs kids of the chance to learn to work out their own relationship problems. Instead, the coach and the referee do it.

If technology is ushering in a culture of shyness, it is also the perfect medium for the shy. The Internet and World Wide Web are conduits for the shy to interact with others; electronic communication removes many of the barriers that inhibit the shy. You prepare what you want to say. Nobody knows what you look like. The danger, however, is that technology will become a hiding place for those who dread social interaction.

The first generation to go from cradle to grave with in-home computers, faxes, and the Internet is a long way from adulthood. We will have to wait at least another 20 years to accurately assess shyness in the wake of the new electronic age. But to do so, we must find a group of infants—shy and nonshy—and follow them through their life, rather than observe different people, from different generations, in different periods of their lives. Only then will we see the course of shyness over a lifetime. Stay tuned for PT's next shyness article, in 2015.

hotheads
and heart attacks

Blowing your stack—or even seething silently—can put your heart at risk. So what are you supposed to do about it? Take a deep breath and read on

Edward Dolnick

Jaw clenched, voice rising, short, sturdy finger jabbing furiously as if to impale her victim, Mary Brown pauses momentarily to catch her breath. "She's my grandmother, for God's sake!" she yells at the nursing home supervisor. "We're paying all this money, and nobody even checks on her? Don't you tell me you can't do it. You went into this business to take care of people. If you can't do it, get out of the business!"

The anger is real, but little else in the scene is genuine. Brown, though she seems to have forgotten it, is a volunteer in a study designed to gauge the impact of anger on the heart. Hooked up to a blood pressure cuff and heart monitors in a physiology lab at Baltimore's V.A. hospital, is simply acting a role, though it helps that her own grandmother was once neglected by the staff at a nearby nursing home.

Brown has focused all her attention on the young man playing the role of the nursing supervisor. She has ignored the true source of her torment, a small figure standing quietly at the edge of the room. He is Aron Siegman, a softspoken 66-year-old psychologist with a slight paunch and a fringe of white hair.

His mild appearance to the contrary Siegman spends his days stirring up trouble—coaxing a college student to recall a spouse's adulterous affair, for example, or repeatedly interrupting a volunteer's answer to a question he has posed about her aging father. A connoisseur of anger, he is as caught up in the nuances of his favorite subject as any wine collector. The reason is simple: A host of studies seem to show that we have become a nation of Rumplestiltskins, so much more likely to lose our cool than we were even a few decades ago that we have pushed our bodies to the breaking point.

It's not a pretty picture. Too many of us overreact to the countless provocations of everyday life—traffic jams and surly clerks and brutish bosses—by boiling over. Heart pounding, blood pressure skyrocketing, adrenaline surging, we are doing ourselves in prematurely, the experts say, by pushing our bodies beyond what they can take. One of the leading proponents of this new theory summarizes it with a succinctness more common on bumper stickers than in science. Current wisdom, declares Duke University stress researcher Redford Williams, is that "anger kills."

Fortunately, a simple remedy may be at hand. Siegman is now testing a theory that anger in itself isn't bad for your heart; the unhealthy consequences only kick in, he says, if you act out that anger. If he is right, the cry from the sixties to "let it all hang out" had it exactly backwards. It's perfectly okay, says the University of Maryland psychologist, to think that the nitwit who just turned left from the right lane shouldn't be let outdoors without a keeper; what's not okay is to scream at him and pound the steering wheel.

The Mary Brown experiment, for example, has two halves. First, Siegman wants to show that expressing anger sets the heart racing and blood pressure soaring. The lab's recording devices make that clear. Her blood pressure alone, normally 176/75, has skyrocketed to 213/98 since her tirade began. The experiment's second half involves coaxing Brown to replay the same infuriating scene, but this time without any outward displays of anger.

> **A study that** looked at 118 lawyers found that of those who scored in the top quarter for hostility, one in five was dead by age 50.

What physiological changes do the various monitors reveal when a person feels angry but chooses not to express it? "Virtually nothing," says Siegman. "We don't get anything."

Here no news truly is good news. Heart disease is the nation's leading killer, and anger is emerging as a risk factor as important as smoking or high cholesterol or any of the other well-known villains. If Siegman is right that anger can be tamed, and tamed fairly simply, he's on to something big.

THE KIND OF HOSTILE personality that may put people at especially high risk for heart disease does not yet have a name. For the moment, let's call it Type H, for hostility, and to acknowledge its link to the famous Type A personality.

Type A behavior is a mix of impatience, aggressiveness, anger, and competitiveness. Mix Donald Trump with Margaret Thatcher, stir in Murphy Brown, and you have a Type A. For decades, everyone living this high-strung, fast-paced life was seen as a heart attack waiting (impatiently) to happen.

By 1981, the Type A theory had earned an official stamp of approval. An all-star panel appointed by the National Heart, Lung, and Blood Institute to evaluate the evidence had come back with a hearty endorsement.

This was major news. Medicine had long paid lip service to the idea that the mind affects the body—no one who has ever blushed could deny it—but this was more. After years in the shadows, psychology had suddenly leapt onstage. In predicting heart disease, a psychological trait seemed as important as any biological measure.

But no sooner had the experts committed their enthusiasm for Type A to print than a slew of new and authoritative studies appeared. Their message: Type A's faced no higher risk of heart disease than anyone else. Two studies that looked at patients who already had heart disease came to an even more unwelcome conclusion. Type A's, it seemed, fared *better* than their laid-back counterparts.

Oops!

The Type H theory salvages something important from that wreckage. Indeed, it seems Type A theorists weren't entirely off the mark, after all. Type A was a package, and though most of its ingredients were irrelevant to heart disease, one component—hostility—may truly be toxic. Impatience and competitiveness, on the other hand, seem to have been innocents who got a bad reputation by hanging out with the wrong crowd.

Type H theory rests on some compelling findings. In one study, for example, 255 doctors who had taken a standard personality test while attending the University of North Carolina's medical school were tracked down 25 years later. Those whose hostility scores had been in the top half were four to five times as likely to have developed heart disease in the intervening decades as were those whose hostility scores had been in the lower half.

A similar study that looked at 118 lawyers found equally striking results. Of those lawyers who had scored in the top quarter for hostility, nearly one in five was dead by age 50. Of those in the lowest quarter, only one in 25 had died.

What's more, say the Type H proponents, such findings have a straightforward biological explanation. Evolution, they note, has designed the human body to respond to acutely stressful situations with a cascade of changes. In crises, your heart pumps faster and harder, arteries that carry blood to your muscles dilate so that blood flow increases still more, your platelets become stickier so that you are less likely to bleed to death if an attacker takes a bite out of you.

It's a fine system if you're running from a lion. If you start the whole process up every time the elevator is late, though, everyday life will soon lay you low. As blood surges through your arteries and stress hormones pour from your adrenal glands, once-smooth artery walls begin to scar and pit. Then fatty cells clump on that pocked surface, like mineral deposits in an old water pipe. Arteries narrow, blood flow decreases, and your body is starved of oxygen. The downward spiral eventually ends in chest pain or strokes or heart attacks.

The mechanism behind Type A, in contrast, was a good deal harder to picture. Exactly how would competitiveness, say, put the body at risk? Even in its heyday, Type A had other problems, as well. For one, it seemed to call for a personality transplant. To teach his frazzled patients mellowness, for example, one Type-A pioneer had them wait in the longest line at the bank and drive all day in the right-hand lane. It sounds brutal, the brainstorm of a malicious researcher who had grown bored with harassing rats and was looking for bigger game.

"With the original Type A," says David Krantz, a psychologist at Uniformed Services University of the Health Sciences, in Bethesda, Maryland, "people would say 'You're telling me I can't be competitive? I shouldn't meet deadlines? How am I going to explain that to my boss?' Now the message is more manageable: 'Ambition is not the problem. Aggressiveness is not the problem. *Hostility* is the problem.'

"What your boss wants is for you to get a hell of a lot of work done," Krantz adds. "He doesn't necessarily want you to act like a son of a bitch."

The Type H theory differs from its forebear in one other important way—it specifically includes women. In theory, Type A did, too, but in practice it focused heavily on males. In part, the reason was a matter of convenience for the researchers: Most men have their heart attacks ten years earlier than women; in larger part, the reason was that when scientists thought Type A, the stereotype that came to mind was a male executive.

They might have thought of Mary Brown instead. She is a delightful woman, lively and down-to-earth and a good storyteller. It's just that, as the Pompeians said about Vesuvius, there is this one, tiny quirk. Brown is in her sixties now and works hard to keep her temper in bounds, but for as long as she can remember she has erupted at the slightest provocation. "I'm real proud if I can go two days without getting upset," she says. "I blow up. I know it's terrible, but I just do."

If someone cuts ahead of her in the supermarket line, Brown tells them off. "I'd like to see someone try to butt in front of me," she boasts. If they venture into the express line with a dozen items rather than the legal ten, Brown dresses them down and makes sure the cashier knows of their sin, too. On the freeway, preparing to exit, she sticks close to

Men, Women, and Anger

Is a fiery display of temper as common in a woman as it is in a man? Lately psychologists have begun to fill in the hostility picture.

WE ALL GET ANGRY

According to a number of studies, women and men tend to get angry equally often (about six or seven times a week), equally intensely, and for more or less the same reasons. Tests designed to reveal aggressive feelings, hidden anger, or hostility turned inward haven't discovered any sex differences at all.

MEN EXPLODE, WOMEN MOSTLY SEETHE

Some angry women do shout and pound their fists, of course—just as some men do. But in general, studies show, women and men have very different styles when it comes to getting angry. Women are more likely to express anger by crying, for example, or to keep their anger under wraps. "Women have cornered the market on the seething, unspoken fury that is always threatening to explode," says Anne Campbell, a psychologist at England's Durham University. Women are also more likely to express their anger in private. They might get angry at a boss or coworker, but chances are they'll wait until they're alone or with a spouse or close friend to show their anger.

IN WOMEN, AN ANGRY OUTBURST, THEN REGRET

Surveys show that anger itself means different things to men than it does to women. Men's anger tends to be uncomplicated by restraint and guilt, says Campbell. It is straightforwardly about winning and losing. Women are more likely to feel embarrassed when they show anger, equating it with a loss of control, she says. Women are also more likely than men to believe their anger is out of proportion to the events that caused it. "After an outburst," she says, "women tell themselves, 'Whoa! Get a grip.' Men say, 'That ought to show him.'" According to one study, the more furious a woman gets, the longer it takes her to get over the episode. That's not true for men—at least not to the same degree.

The way women and men view crying is different, too. According to Campbell and other researchers, men often see women's crying as a sign of remorse or contrition—or as a tactic used to win a fight. Women are more likely to view crying as a sign of frustration or rage—a way to release tension. According to one study, 78 percent of women who cried during fights did so out of frustration.

So what does all this mean for women's risk of heart disease? Researchers say that whether anger is expressed through clenched teeth or raised voices, in public or in private, it appears to wreak the same havoc on the heart.—*E.D.*

> **Give in to your anger,** Siegman says, and you become all the more angry. Resist it, and the anger seeps away.

the car in front of her so that no one else can cut in. "I'm not going to let you in," she snarls at anyone trying it. "You should have moved in way back there."

Mary Brown is no tyrant. She's funny, and, once the storm has passed, she can laugh at her tirades. She has been married to the same man for 50 years. "It's incredible, some of what he's had to put up with," she says with a rueful smile. And she is close to her son and daughter.

Outsiders are more at risk. Brown cannot abide injustice, and she sees it in every driver who runs a yellow light, in every shopper with an extra can of soup. "To me," she says, "silence is acceptance. If I don't say anything, I'm agreeing with something that's wrong, and"—she hammers out the last words, like a general exhorting the troops to defend their homeland—"that cannot happen."

THE MEDICAL ESTABLISHMENT tends to wrinkle its nose in distaste at this whole subject. Many cardiologists concede that a diseased heart can be undone by such sudden stresses as winning the lottery or getting robbed at gun point; in ways that are not well understood, stress somehow sets the heart's ventricles to chaotic quivering. But they question whether chronic stress in general, or hostility in particular, can undo a healthy heart.

Look again, for example, at the study that showed a high number of deaths among hostile lawyers. It's tempting, critics say, to conclude that hostility gradually undermined their healthy hearts. But maybe not. Maybe heart disease strikes randomly at the hostile and the pleasant alike, and hostility serves only to speed up the dying process in those who are already vulnerable. In large measure, this is simply "show me" skepticism. Where, doubters ask, is clear-cut proof?

Part of the problem is that a theory based on hostility is harder to pin down than one based on something as easy to measure as blood pressure. Even Siegman concedes that the case for Type H is far from airtight. "Look," he says, "it's a complicated story. It was the same with cholesterol. That started out, Cholesterol is bad. Then somebody found out cholesterol levels alone didn't predict so well, and then there was HDL and LDL, and then the ratio between them. It's an ongoing story."

But even if Siegman and his colleagues are right that hostility is bad for the heart, is there anything we can do about it?

To begin with, everyone agrees that we cannot banish anger. Even if we wanted to, we could no more stop getting angry than we could stop getting hungry. But who would want to? Anger has its place. There is injustice in the world, after all, and righteous indignation is an honorable emotion.

In a rare lyric moment, psychologists have dubbed the real problem free-floating hostility. An occasional flash of temper is fine, they say; a permanent snarl is not. Hostile people are perpetually suspicious, wary, and snappish, forever tense and on edge. They see every sales clerk as determined to linger on the phone for hours, every compliment as a dig in disguise, every colleague as a rival in waiting.

That's bad for two reasons, says Timothy Smith, a psychologist at the University of Utah in Salt Lake City. First, hostility is harmful for all the Type H reasons. Second, hostility feeds on itself, typically leaving its "victims" precariously alone. That's worrisome because a variety of studies have shown that people with friends and families, or even pets, fare better than those without such support.

So what is a hostile person to do? The advice from the experts is surprisingly straightforward: Relax, take a deep breath, decide whether this latest injustice really merits a battle. Give in to your anger, they say, and you become all the more angry. Resist it, by keeping your voice down or your teeth ungritted, and the anger seeps away.

"Anger is not just emotion, it's physiology, too," Siegman says. "Your blood pressure goes up, your voice gets loud, you clench your jaws"—he has worked himself into a mini-tirade, bellowing at the top of his voice, windmilling his arms, thrusting his chin out belligerently—"but then, if you lower your voice, speak more slowly, relax your muscles"—he has followed his own instructions and collapsed weakly into his seat, like a balloon with a slow leak—"if you do that, if you eliminate any part of the cycle, then you weaken the whole performance, and you can't sustain the feelings of anger."

Siegman's experiments seem to support this theory. In its own way Hollywood has tested the same idea. Audiences watching an actor in a supposed rage see and hear all the familiar signs of anger—we recognize *bad* acting precisely because there is a dissonance between spoken words and body language—and actors, by their own report, feel the emotions they simulate. Similarly, studies on laughter and smiling have shown that simulated merriment offers the same benefits—increased blood flow, reduced levels of hormones that create stress, reduced pain perception—as the genuine article.

But even among those who believe that Type H's are putting themselves at risk, Siegman's strategy for taming anger is controversial. "What if your anger is unresolved?" asks Lynda Powell, a psychologist at Chicago's Rush-Presbyterian-Saint Luke's Medical Center. "What if it's inside and you haven't dealt with it? Sometimes when you express it, you get it out and get beyond it. If you've just stuffed it inside, then the question is, Could that do just as much damage to your heart?"

Siegman is impatient with such objections, which he sees as smacking of an outdated Freudianism. "The psychoanalysts thought that anger was like physical energy," he complains. "They thought it couldn't be dissipated—the only choice was to express it or repress it. But anger is not like physical energy," he says. "An angry person who chooses to divert his attention will no longer be angry. We have a lot of evidence to show that."

Siegman tries to head off the doubters by making a distinction between suppressing the outward expressions of anger, which he favors, and repressing anger itself, which he warns against. The difference, he says, is that people who repress their anger don't merely stifle it; they hide it so well that they themselves are unaware of it. The person who follows Siegman's advice walks a middle road; she neither denies her rage nor gives in to it. Instead she simply decides that the matter isn't worth the theatrical fireworks—whether expressed in pounded fists and shouting or in

Are You Too Angry for Your Own Good?

THE TEST

Gauging your hostility quotient isn't as simple as measuring blood pressure or cholesterol. But the following 12 questions—supplied by Redford Williams, director of behavioral research at Duke University and the author of *Anger Kills*—could indicate whether a hostile temperament is getting the best of you.

1. Have you ever been so angry at someone that you've thrown things or slammed a door?
2. Do you tend to remember irritating incidents and get mad all over again?
3. Do little annoyances have a way of adding up during the day, leaving you frustrated and impatient?
4. Stuck in a long line at the express checkout in the grocery store, do you often count to see if anyone ahead of you has more than ten items?
5. If the person who cuts your hair trims off more than you wanted, do you fume about it for days afterward?
6. When someone cuts you off in traffic, do you flash your lights or honk your horn?
7. Over the past few years, have you dropped any close friends because they just didn't live up to your expectations?
8. Do you find yourself getting annoyed at little things your spouse does that get under your skin?
9. Do you feel your pulse climb when you get into an argument?
10. Are you often irritated by other people's incompetence?
11. If a cashier gives you the wrong change, do you assume he's probably trying to cheat you?
12. If someone doesn't show up on time, do you find yourself planning the angry words you're going to say?

To gauge your level of hostility, add up your yes responses. If you scored three or less, consider yourself one cool cucumber. A score of four to eight is a warning sign that anger may be raising your risk of heart disease. A score of nine or more puts you squarely in the hot zone for hostility, significantly increasing your risk of dying prematurely.

THE CURE

A few simple strategies can cool down even the hottest temper. First, when you feel yourself getting angry, stop long enough to ask yourself three questions: Is this really serious enough to get worked up over? Am I justified in getting angry? And is getting angry going to make any difference? If the answer to all three is yes, experts say, go ahead and get mad—it just might make you feel better. If not—if the answer to any of the questions is no—cool out. Often, just asking reasonable questions is enough to take the edge off anger. But if you're still simmering, distract yourself by picking up a magazine, turning on music, taking a walk. Or simply close your eyes and concentrate on your breathing.

—*Peter Jaret*

the seething language of gritted teeth—and calmly talks it out or lets it go. The result is that the anger neither festers nor explodes, but gradually loses its hold.

DESPITE SKEPTICS' OBJECTIONS, the hostility-heart disease connection is undeniably tantalizing. For one thing, it seems suspicious that so many studies of heart disease in the past few years have fingered hostility as a culprit. Where there's smoke, there's ire.

So if we are a long way from proof beyond a reasonable doubt, we may still have enough evidence to justify a small bet.

What seems called for, in fact, is a mundane version of Pascal's wager. The French philosopher opted to believe in God, on the grounds that he had everything to gain if he was right and nothing to lose by being wrong.

When it comes to hostility, there doesn't seem to be much downside in taking the experts' advice to ease up a bit. This is unusual. With most medical advice—quit eating chocolate cake, say—the risks are considerable. Giving up cake cuts out part of life's pleasure, first of all, and the loss could be even worse. In five years, researchers might come back and say, "It turns out we had it wrong. It's really, The more cake the better. Sorry about that."

Here, the experts' advice amounts to every grandmother's list of maxims: Take a deep breath and count to ten, look on the bright side, don't say anything if you can't say anything nice, and so on. What's the risk? At best, you'll live longer and better. At worst, you'll be better company.

Go Ahead, Say You're Sorry

We tend to view apologies as a sign of weak character. But in fact, they require great strength. And we better learn how to get them right, because it's increasingly hard to live in the global village without them

Aaron Lazare, M.D.

Aaron Lazare, M.D., is chancellor/dean of the University of Massachusetts Medical Center in Worcester. He has authored 66 articles and written or edited six books.

A genuine apology offered and accepted is one of the most profound interactions of civilized people. It has the power to restore damaged relationships, be they on a small scale, between two people, such as intimates, or on a grand scale, between groups of people, even nations. If done correctly, an apology can heal humiliation and generate forgiveness.

Yet, even though it's such a powerful social skill, we give precious little thought to teaching our children how to apologize. Most of us never learned very well ourselves.

Despite its importance, apologizing is antithetical to the ever-pervasive values of winning, success, and perfection. The successful apology requires empathy and the security and strength to admit fault, failure, and weakness. But we are so busy winning that we can't concede our own mistakes.

The botched apology—the apology intended but not delivered, or delivered but not accepted—has serious social consequences. Failed apologies can strain relationships beyond repair or, worse, create life-long grudges and bitter vengeance.

As a psychiatrist who has studied shame and humiliation for eight years, I became interested in apology for its healing nature. I am perpetually amazed by how many of my friends and patients—regardless of ethnicity or social class—have long-standing grudges that have cut a destructive swath through their own lives and the lives of family and friends. So many of their grudges could have been avoided altogether or been reconciled with a genuine apology.

In my search to learn more about apologies, I have found surprisingly little in the professional literature. The scant research I've unearthed is mostly in linguistics and sociology, but little or nothing touches on the expectations or need for apologies, their meaning to the offender and offended, and the implications of their failure.

Religious writings, however, in both Christian and Jewish traditions, are a rich source of wisdom on the subject, under such headings as absolution, atonement, forgiveness, penance, and repentance. The *Talmud*, in fact, declares that God created repentance before he created the universe. He wisely knew humans would make a lot of mistakes and have a lot of apologizing to do along the way.

What makes apologies work is an exchange of shame and power between offender and offended.

No doubt the most compelling and common reason to apologize is over a personal offense. Whether we've ignored, belittled, betrayed, or publicly humiliated someone, the common denominator of any personal offense is that we've diminished or injured a person's self-concept. The self-concept is our story about ourselves. It's our thoughts and feelings about who we are, how we would like to be, and how we would like to be perceived by others.

If you think of yourself first and foremost as a competent, highly valued professional and are asked tomorrow by your boss to move into a cramped windowless office, you would likely be personally offended. You might be insulted and feel hurt or humiliated. No matter whether the interpersonal wound is delivered in a professional, family, or social setting, its depth is determined by the meaning the event carries to the offended party, the relationship between offender and offended, and the vulnerability of the offended to take things personally.

No-shows at family funerals, disputes over wills, betrayals of trust—whether in love or friendship—are situations ripe for wounds to the self-concept. Events of that magnitude put our self-worth on the line, more so for the thin-skinned. Other events people experience as personal offenses include being ignored, treated unfairly, embarrassed by someone else's behavior, publicly humiliated, and having one's cherished beliefs denigrated.

So the personal offense has been made, the blow to the self-concept landed, and an apology is demanded or expected. Why bother? I count four basic motives for apologizing:

- **The first is to salvage or restore the relationship.** Whether you've hurt someone you love, enjoy, or just plain need as your ally in an office situation, an apology may well rekindle the troubled relationship.
- **You may have purely empathic reasons for apologizing.** You regret that you have caused someone to suffer and you apologize to diminish or end their pain.

The last two motives are not so lofty:

- **Some people apologize simply to escape punishment,** such as the criminal who apologizes to his victim in exchange for a lesser plea.
- **Others apologize simply to relieve themselves of a guilty conscience.** They feel so ashamed of what they did that, even though it may not have bothered you that much, they apolo-

4. ❖ RELATING TO OTHERS

gize profusely. A long letter explaining why the offender was a half hour late to dinner would be such an occasion. And in so doing, they are trying to maintain some self-respect, because they are nurturing an image of themselves in which the offense, lack of promptness, violates some basic self-concept.

Whatever the motive, what makes an apology work is the exchange of shame and power between the offender and the offended. By apologizing, you take the shame of your offense and redirect it to yourself. You admit to hurting or diminishing someone and, in effect, say that you are really the one who is diminished—I'm the one who was wrong, mistaken, insensitive, or stupid. In acknowledging your shame you give the offended the power to forgive. The exchange is at the heart of the healing process.

ANATOMY OF AN APOLOGY

But in practice, it's not as easy as it sounds. There's a right way and a wrong way to apologize. There are several integral elements of any apology and unless they are accounted for, an apology is likely to fail.

First, you have to acknowledge that a moral norm or an understanding of a relationship was violated, and you have to accept responsibility for it. You must name the offense—no glossing over in generalities like, "I'm sorry for what I have done." To be a success, the apology has to be specific—"I betrayed you by talking behind your back" or "I missed your daughter's wedding."

You also have to show you understand the nature of your wrongdoing and the impact it had on the person—"I know I hurt you and I am so very sorry."

This is one of the most uniting elements of the apology. By acknowledging that a moral norm was violated, both parties affirm a similar set of values. The apology reestablishes a common moral ground.

The second ingredient to a successful apology is an explanation for why you committed the offense in the first place. An effective explanation makes the point that what you did isn't representative of who you are. You may offer that you were tired, sick, drunk, distracted, or in love—and that it will not happen again. Such an explanation protects your self-concept.

A recent incident widely reported in the news provides an excellent, if painful, illustration of the role of an apology in protecting the offender's self-concept. An American sailor apologized at his court-martial for brutally beating to death a homosexual shipmate: "I can't apologize enough for my actions. I am not trying to make any excuses for what happened that night. It was horrible, but I am not a horrible person."

A successful apology also has to make you suffer. You must express soul-searching regret.

Another vital part of the explanation is to communicate that your behavior wasn't intended as a personal affront. This lets the offended person know that he should feel safe with you now and in the future.

A good apology also has to make you suffer. You have to express genuine, soul-searching regret for your apology to be taken as sincere. Unless you communicate guilt, anxiety, and shame, people are going to question the depth of your remorse. The anxiety and sadness demonstrate that the potential loss of the relationship matters to you. Guilt tells the offended person that you're distressed over hurting him. And shame communicates your disappointment with yourself over the incident.

YOU OWE ME AN APOLOGY

When there's the matter of settling debt. The apology is a reparation of emotional, physical, or financial debt. The admission of guilt, explanation, and regret are meant, in part, to repair the damage you did to the person's self-concept. A well-executed apology may even the score, but sometimes words are just not enough. An open offer of, "Please let me know if there is anything I can do?" might be necessary. Some sort of financial compensation, such as replacing an object you broke, or reimbursing a friend for a show you couldn't make it to, could be vital to restoring the relationship. Or, in long-term close relationships, an unsolicited gift or favor may completely supplant the verbal apology—every other dimension of the apology may be implicit.

Reparations are largely symbolic. They are a way of saying, "I know who you are, what you value, and am thoughtful about your needs. I owe you." But they don't always have to be genuine to be meaningful. Say your boss wrongfully accused you in front of the whole office. A fair reparation would require an apology—in front of the whole office. His questionable sincerity might be of secondary importance.

Ultimately, the success of an apology rests on the dynamics between the two parties, not on a pat recipe. The apology is an interactive negotiation process in which a deal has to be struck that is emotionally satisfactory to both involved parties.

Nor is the need for an apology confined to intimates. Used strategically, it has great social value within the public domain. The apology is, after all, a social contract of sorts. It secures a common moral ground, whether between two people or within a nation. Present in all societies, the apology is a statement that the harmony of the group is more important than the victory of the individual. Take a look at what will certainly go down in history as one of the world's greatest apologies, F.W. de Klerk's apology to all South Africans for his party's imposition of apartheid.

On April 29, 1993, during a press conference, de Klerk *acknowledged* that apartheid led to forced removals of people from their homes, restrictions on their freedom and jobs, and attacks on their dignity.

He *explained* that the former leaders of the party were *not vicious people* and, at the time, it seemed that the policy of separate nations was better than the colonial policies. "It was not our intention to deprive people of their rights and to cause misery, but eventually apartheid led to just that. Insofar as that occurred, we deeply regret it."

"*Deep regret*," de Klerk continued, "goes further than just saying you are sorry. Deep regret says that if I could turn the clock back, and if I could do anything about it, I would have liked to have avoided it."

In going on to describe a new National Party logo, he said: "It is a statement that we have broken with that which was wrong in the past and are not afraid to say we are deeply sorry that our past policies were wrong." He promised that the National Party had scrapped apartheid and opened its doors to all South Africans.

De Klerk expressed all the same ingredients and sentiments essential in interpersonal apologies. He enumerated his offenses and explained why they were made. He assured himself and others that the party members are not vicious people. Then he expressed deep regret and offered symbolic reparations in the form of his public apology itself and the new party logo.

In fact, as the world becomes a global village, apologies are growing increasingly important on both national and international levels. Communications, the media, and travel have drawn the world ever closer together. Ultimately we all share the same air, oceans, and world economy. We are all upwind, downstream, over the mountains, or through the woods from one another. We can't help but be concerned with Russia's failing economy, Eastern Bloc toxic waste, Middle Eastern conflicts, and the rain forest, whether it be for reasons of peace, fuel, or just plain oxygen.

In this international community, apologies will be vital to peaceful resolution of

28. Go Ahead, Say You're Sorry

conflicts. Within the last several years alone Nelson Mandela apologized for atrocities committed by the African National Congress in fighting against apartheid; Exxon for the *Valdez* spill; Pope John Paul II "for abuses committed by Christian colonizers against Indian peoples"; former Japanese Prime Minister Morihiro Hosokawa for Japanese aggression during World War II; and Russian President Boris Yeltsin apologized for the massacre of 15,000 Polish army officers by Soviet forces during World War II. And that's only the start of it.

But apologies are useful only if done right. There are in the public arena ample examples of what not to do—stunning portraits of failed apologies. They typically take the form of what I call "the pseudo-apology"—the offender fails to admit or take responsibility for what he has done. Recent history furnishes two classics of the genre.

Reel back to August 8, 1974—President Richard Nixon's resignation speech. "I regret deeply any injuries that may have been done in the course of events that have led to this decision. I would say only that if some of my judgments were wrong, and some were wrong, they were made in what I believed at the time to be in the best interest of the nation." Unlike de Klerk, Nixon never acknowledges or specifies his actual offense, nor does he describe its impact. By glossing over his wrongdoing he never takes responsibility for it.

Consider, too, the words of Senator Bob Packwood, who was accused of sexually harassing at least a dozen women during his tenure in Congress. His 1994 apology outfails even Nixon's: "I'm apologizing for the conduct that it was alleged that I did." No acceptance of responsibility or accounting for his alleged offense to be found. An *alleged* apology, not even named.

The most common cause of failure in an apology—or an apology altogether avoided—is the offender's pride. It's a fear of shame. To apologize, you have to acknowledge that you made a mistake. You have to admit that you failed to live up to values like sensitivity, thoughtfulness, faithfulness, fairness, and honesty. This is an admission that our own self-concept, our story about ourself, is flawed. To honestly admit what you did and show regret may stir a profound experience of shame, a public exposure of weakness. Such an admission is especially difficult to bear when there was some degree of intention behind the wrongdoing.

'The apology is a show of strength. It's an act of generosity, because it restores the self-concept of those we offended.'

Egocentricity also factors into failed or avoided apologies. The egocentric is unable to appreciate the suffering of another person; his regret is that he is no longer liked by the person he offended, not that he inflicted harm. That sort of apology takes the form of "I am sorry that you are upset with me" rather than "I am sorry I hurt you." This offender simply says he is bereft—not guilty, ashamed, or empathic.

Another reason for failure is that the apology may trivialize the damage incurred by the wrongdoing—in which case the apology itself seems offensive. A Japanese-American who was interned during World War II was offended by the U.S. government's reparation of $20,000. He said that the government stole four years of his childhood and now has set the price at $5,000 per year.

Timing can also doom an apology. For a minor offense such as interrupting someone during a presentation or accidentally spilling a drink all over a friend's suit, if you don't apologize right away, the offense becomes personal and grows in magnitude. For a serious offense, such as a betrayal of trust or public humiliation, an immediate apology misses the mark. It demeans the event. Hours, days, weeks, or even months may go by before both parties can integrate the meaning of the event and its impact on the relationship. The care and thought that goes into such apologies dignifies the exchange.

For offenses whose impact is calamitous to individuals, groups, or nations, the apology may be delayed by decades and offered by another generation. Case in point: The apologies now being offered and accepted for apartheid and for events that happened in WWII, such as the Japanese Imperial Army's apology for kidnapping Asian women and forcing them into a network of brothels.

Far and away the biggest stumbling block to apologizing is our belief that apologizing is a sign of weakness and an admission of guilt. We have the misguided notion we are better off ignoring or denying our offenses and hope that no one notices.

In fact the apology is a show of strength. It is an act of honesty because we admit we did wrong; an act of generosity, because it restores the self-concept of those we offended. It offers hope for a renewed relationship and, who knows, possibly even a strengthened one. The apology is an act of commitment because it consigns us to working at the relationship and at our self-development. Finally, the apology is an act of courage because it subjects us to the emotional distress of shame and the risk of humiliation, rejection, and retaliation at the hands of the person we offended.

All dimensions of the apology require strength of character, including the conviction that, while we expose vulnerable parts of ourselves, we are still good people.

THE BIOLOGY OF BEAUTY

By Geoffrey Cowley

Looking good is a universal human obsession. How do we perceive physical beauty, and why do we place so much stock in it? Scientists are now taking those questions seriously, and gaining surprising insights.

WHEN IT COMES TO CHOOSING a mate, a female penguin knows better than to fall for the first creep who pulls up and honks. She holds out for the fittest suitor available—which in Antarctica means one chubby enough to spend several weeks sitting on newly hatched eggs without starving to death. The Asian jungle bird *Gallus gallus* is just as choosy. Males in that species sport gaily colored head combs and feathers, which lose their luster if the bird is invaded by parasites. By favoring males with bright ornaments, a hen improves her odds of securing a mate (and bearing offspring) with strong resistance to disease. For female scorpion flies, beauty is less about size or color than about symmetry. Females favor suitors who have well-matched wings—and with good reason. Studies show they're the most adept at killing prey and at defending their catch from competitors. There's no reason to think that any of these creatures understands its motivations, but there's a clear pattern to their preferences. "Throughout the animal world," says University of New Mexico ecologist Randy Thornhill, "attractiveness certifies biological quality."

Is our corner of the animal world different? That looks count in human affairs is beyond dispute. Studies have shown that people considered attractive fare better with parents and teachers, make more friends and more money, and have better sex with more (and more beautiful) partners. Every year, 400,000 Americans, including 48,000 men, flock to cosmetic surgeons. In other lands, people bedeck themselves with scars, lip plugs or bright feathers. "Every culture is a 'beauty culture'," says Nancy Etcoff, a neuroscientist who is studying human attraction at the MIT Media Lab and writing a book on the subject. "I defy anyone to point to a society, any time in history or any place in the world, that wasn't preoccupied with

29. Biology of Beauty

Beauty isn't all that matters in life; most of us manage to attract mates and bear offspring despite our physical imperfections. And the qualities we find alluring say nothing about people's moral worth. Our weakness for 'biological quality' is the cause of endless pain and injustice.

beauty." The high-minded may dismiss our preening and ogling as distractions from things that matter, but the stakes can be enormous. "Judging beauty involves looking at another person," says University of Texas psychologist Devendra Singh, "and figuring out whether you want your children to carry that person's genes."

It's widely assumed that ideals of beauty vary from era to era and from culture to culture. But a harvest of new research is confounding that idea. Studies have established that people everywhere—regardless of race, class or age—share a sense of what's attractive. And though no one knows just how our minds translate the sight of a face or a body into rapture, new studies suggest that we judge each other by rules we're not even aware of. We may consciously admire Kate Moss's legs or Arnold's biceps, but we're also viscerally attuned to small variations in the size and symmetry of facial bones and the placement of weight on the body.

This isn't to say that our preferences are purely innate—or that beauty is all that matters in life. Most of us manage to find jobs, attract mates and bear offspring despite our physical imperfections. Nor should anyone assume that the new beauty research justifies the biases it illuminates. Our beautylust is often better suited to the Stone Age than to the Information Age; the qualities we find alluring may be powerful emblems of health, fertility and resistance to disease, but they say nothing about people's moral worth. The human weakness for what Thornhill calls "biological quality" causes no end of pain and injustice. Unfortunately, that doesn't make it any less real.

NO ONE SUGGESTS THAT points of attraction never vary. Rolls of fat can signal high status in a poor society or low status in a rich one, and lip plugs go over better in the Kalahari than they do in Kansas. But local fashions seem to rest on a bedrock of shared preferences. You don't have to be Italian to find Michelangelo's David better looking than, say, Alfonse D'Amato. When British researchers asked women from England, China and India to rate pictures of Greek men, the women responded as if working from the same crib sheet. And when researchers at the University of Louisville showed a diverse collection of faces to whites, Asians and Latinos from 13 countries, the subjects' ethnic background scarcely affected their preferences.

To a skeptic, those findings suggest only that Western movies and magazines have overrun the world. But scientists have found at least one group that hasn't been exposed to this bias. In a series of groundbreaking experiments, psychologist Judith Langlois of the University of Texas, Austin, has shown that even infants share a sense of what's attractive. In the late '80s, Langlois started placing 3- and 6-month-old babies in front of a screen and showing them pairs of facial photographs. Each pair included one considered attractive by adult judges and one considered unattractive. In the first study, she found that the infants gazed significantly longer at "attractive" white female faces than at "unattractive" ones. Since then, she has repeated the drill using white male faces, black female faces, even the faces of other babies, and the same pattern always emerges. "These kids don't read Vogue or watch TV," Langlois says. "They haven't been touched by the media. Yet they make the same judgments as adults."

What, then, is beauty made of? What are the innate rules we follow in sizing each other up? We're obviously wired to find robust health a prettier sight than infirmity. "All animals are attracted to other animals that are healthy, that are clean by their standards and that show signs of competence," says Rutgers University anthropologist Helen Fisher. As far as anyone knows, there isn't a village on earth where skin lesions, head lice and rotting teeth count as beauty aids. But the rules get subtler than that. Like scorpion flies, we love symmetry. And though we generally favor average features over unusual ones, the people we find extremely beautiful share certain exceptional qualities.

WHEN RANDY THORNHILL started measuring the wings of Japanese scorpion flies six years ago, he wasn't much concerned with the orgasms and infidelities of college students. But sometimes one thing leads to another. Biologists have long used bilateral symmetry—the extent to which a creature's right and left sides match—to gauge what's known as developmental stability. Given ideal growing conditions, paired features such as wings, ears, eyes and feet would come out matching perfectly. But pollution, disease and other hazards can disrupt development. As a result, the least resilient individuals tend to be the most lopsided. In chronicling the scorpion flies' daily struggles, Thornhill found that the bugs with the most symmetrical wings fared best in the competition for food and mates. To his amazement, females preferred symmetrical males even when they were hidden from view; evidently, their smells are more attractive. And when researchers started noting similar trends in other species, Thornhill turned his attention to our own.

Working with psychologist Steven Gangestad, he set about measuring the body symmetry of hundreds of college-age men and women. By adding up right-left disparities in seven measurements—the breadth of the feet, ankles, hands, wrists, and elbows, as well as the breadth and length of the ears—the researchers scored each subject's overall body asymmetry. Then they had the person fill out a confidential questionnaire covering everything from temperament to sexual behavior, and set about looking for connections. They weren't disappointed. In a 1994 study, they found that the most symmetrical males had started having sex three to four years earlier than their most lopsided brethren. For both men and women, greater symmetry predicted a larger number of past sex partners.

That was just the beginning. From what they knew about other species, Thornhill and Gangestad predicted that women would be more sexually responsive to symmetrical men, and that men would exploit that advantage. To date, their findings support both suspicions. Last year they surveyed 86 couples and found that women with highly symmetrical partners were more than twice as likely to climax during intercourse (an event that may foster conception by ushering sperm into the uterus) than those with low-symmetry partners. And in separate surveys, Gangestad and Thornhill have found that, compared with regular Joes, extremely symmetrical men are less attentive to their partners and more likely to cheat on them. Women showed no such tendency.

It's hard to imagine that we even notice the differences between people's elbows, let alone stake our love lives on them. No one carries calipers into a singles bar. So why do these measurements predict so much? Because, says Thornhill, people with symmetrical elbows tend to have "a whole suite of attractive features." His findings suggest that besides having attractive (and symmetrical) faces, men with symmetrical bodies are typically larger, more muscular and more athletic than their peers, and more dominant in personality. In a forthcoming study, researchers at the University of Michigan find evidence that facial symmetry is also associated with health. In analyzing diaries kept by 100 students over a two-month period, they found that the least symmetrical had the most physical complaints, from insomnia to nasal congestion, and reported more anger, jealousy and withdrawal. In light of all Thornhill and Gangestad's findings, you can hardly blame them.

IF WE DID GO COURTING WITH calipers, symmetry isn't all we would measure. As we study each other in the street, the office or the gym, our beauty radars pick up a range of signals. Oddly enough, one of the qualities shared by attractive people is their averageness. Researchers discovered more than a century ago that if they superimposed photographs of several faces, the resulting composite was usually better looking than any of the images that went into it. Scientists can now average faces digitally, and it's still one of the surest ways to make them more attractive. From an evolutionary perspective, a preference for extreme normality makes sense. As Langlois has written, "Individuals with average population characteristics should be less likely to carry harmful genetic mutations."

So far, so good. But here's the catch: while we may find average faces attractive, the faces we find most beautiful are not average. As New Mexico State University psychologist Victor Johnston has shown, they're extreme. To track people's preferences, Johnston uses a computer program called FacePrints. Turn it on, and it generates 30 facial images, all male or all female, which you rate on a 1–9 beauty scale. The program then "breeds" the top-rated face with one of the others to create two digital offspring, which replace the lowest-rated faces in the pool. By rating round after round of new faces, you create an ever more beautiful population. The game ends when you award some visage a perfect 10. (If you have access to the World Wide Web, you can take part in a collective face-breeding experiment by visiting http://www-psych.nmsu.edu/~vic/faceprints/.)

For Johnston, the real fun starts after the judging is finished. By collecting people's ideal faces and comparing them to average faces, he can measure the distance between fantasy and reality. As a rule, he finds that an ideal female has a higher forehead than an average one, as well as fuller lips, a shorter jaw and a smaller chin and nose. Indeed, the ideal 25-year-old

BODY LANGUAGE

When men are asked to rank figures with various weights and waist-hip ratios (0.7 to 1.0), they favor a pronounced hourglass shape. The highest-ranked figures are N7, N8 and U7 (in that order). The lowest ranked is O10.

Underweight

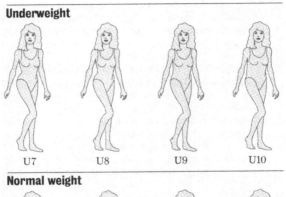

U7   U8   U9   U10

Normal weight

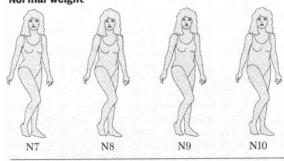

N7   N8   N9   N10

Overweight

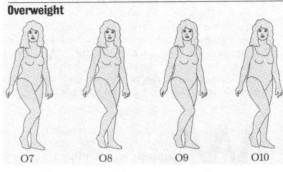

O7   O8   O9   O10

THE ORDER CHOSEN: (1) N7, (2) N8, (3) U7, (4) U8, (5) N9, (6) N10, (7) O7, (8), U9, (9) O8, (10) U10, (11) O9, (12) O10 SOURCE: DEVENDRA SINGH, UNIVERSITY OF TEXAS AT AUSTIN

woman, as configured by participants in a 1993 study, had a 14-year-old's abundant lips and an 11-year-old's delicate jaw. Because her lower face was so small, she also had relatively prominent eyes and cheekbones.

The participants in that study were all college kids from New Mexico, but researchers have since shown that British and Japanese students express the same bias. And if there are lingering doubts about the depth of that bias, Johnston's latest findings should dispel them. In a forthcoming study, he reports that male volunteers not only consciously prefer women with small lower faces but show marked rises in brain activity when looking at pictures of them. And though Johnston has yet to publish specs on the ideal male, his unpublished findings suggest that a big jaw, a strong chin and an imposing brow are as prized in a man's face as their opposites are in a woman's.

Few of us ever develop the heart-melting proportions of a FacePrints fantasy. And if it's any consolation, beauty is not an all-or-nothing proposition. Madonna became a sex symbol despite her strong nose, and Melanie Griffith's strong jaw hasn't kept her out of the movies. Still, special things have a way of happening to people who approximate the ideal. We pay them huge fees to stand on windblown bluffs and stare into the distance. And past studies have found that square-jawed males not only start having sex earlier than their peers but attain higher rank in the military.

None of this surprises evolutionary psychologists. They note that the facial features we obsess over are precisely the ones that diverge in males and females during puberty, as floods of sex hormones wash us into adulthood. And they reason that hormonal abundance would have been a good clue to mate value in the hunter-gatherer world where our preferences evolved. The tiny jaw that men favor in women is essentially a monument to estrogen—and, obliquely, to fertility. No one claims that jaws reveal a woman's odds of getting pregnant. But like breasts, they imply that she could.

Likewise, the heavy lower face that women favor in men is a visible record of the surge in androgens (testosterone and other male sex hormones) that turns small boys into 200-pound spear-throwers. An oversized jaw is biologically expensive, for the androgens required to produce it tend to compromise the immune system. But from a female's perspective, that should make jaw size all the more revealing. Evolutionists think of androgen-based features as "honest advertisements" of disease resistance. If a male can afford them without falling sick, the thinking goes, he must have a superior immune system in the first place.

No one has tracked the immune responses of men with different jawlines to see if these predictions bear out (Thornhill has proposed a study that would involve comparing volunteers' responses to a vaccine). Nor is it clear whether penis size figures into these equations. Despite what everyone thinks he knows on the subject, scientists haven't determined that women have consistent preferences one way or the other.

OUR FACES ARE SIGNAtures, but when it comes to raw sex appeal, a nice chin is no match for a perfectly sculpted torso—especially from a man's perspective. Studies from around the world have found that while both sexes value appearance, men place more stock in it than women. And if there are social reasons for that imbalance, there are also biological ones. Just about any male over 14 can produce sperm, but a woman's ability to bear children depends on her age and hormone levels. Female fertility declines by two thirds between the ages of 20 and 44, and it's spent by 54. So while the both sexes may eyeball potential partners, says Donald Symons, an anthropologist at the University of California in Santa Barbara, "a larger proportion of a woman's mate value can be detected from visual cues." Mounting evidence suggests there is no better cue than the relative contours of her waist and hips.

FACIAL FANTASIES

As a rule, average faces are more attractive than unusual ones. But when people are asked to develop ideal faces on a computer, they tend to exaggerate certain qualities.

 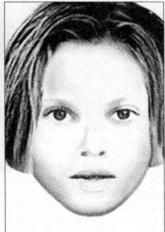

Average proportions
This computer-generated face has the dimensions typical of Caucasian 20-year-olds.

Ideal proportions
Most visions of the perfect female face have small jaws and abnormally lush lips.

SOURCE: VICTOR JOHNSTON, NEW MEXICO STATE UNIVERSITY

and thighs. Those pounds contain roughly the 80,000 calories needed to sustain a pregnancy, and the curves they create provide a gauge of reproductive potential. "You have to get very close to see the details of a woman's face," says Devendra Singh, the University of Texas psychologist. "But you can see the shape of her body from 500 feet, and it says more about mate value."

Almost anything that interferes with fertility—obesity, malnutrition, pregnancy, menopause—changes a woman's shape.

this range are healthy and capable of having children, of course. But as researchers in the Netherlands discovered in a 1993 study, even a slight increase in waist size relative to hip size can signal reproductive problems. Among 500 women who were attempting in vitro fertilization, the odds of conceiving during any given cycle declined by 30 percent with every 10 percent increase in WHR. In other words, a woman with a WHR of .9 was nearly a third less likely to get pregnant than one with a WHR of .8, regardless of her age or weight. From an evolutionary perspective, it's hard to imagine men not responding to such a revealing signal. And as Singh has shown repeatedly, they do.

Defining a universal standard of body beauty once seemed a fool's dream; common sense said that if spindly Twiggy and Rubens's girthy Three Graces could all excite admiration, then nearly anyone could. But if our ideals of size change from one time and place to the next, our taste in shapes is amazingly stable. A low waist-hip ratio is one of the few features that a long, lean Barbie doll shares with a plump, primitive fertility icon. And Singh's findings suggest the fashion won't change any time soon. In one study, he compiled the measurements of Playboy centerfolds and Miss America winners from 1923 to 1990. Their bodies got measurably leaner over the decades, yet their waist-hip ratios stayed within the narrow range of .68 to .72. (Even Twiggy was no tube; at the peak of her fame in the 1960s, the British model had a WHR of .73.)

The same pattern holds when Singh generates line drawings of different female fig-

---

Even infants spend more time gazing at pictures of 'attractive' faces than at 'unattractive' ones. 'These kids don't read Vogue or watch TV, yet they make the same judgments as adults,' says psychologist Judith Langlois.

Before puberty and after menopause, females have essentially the same waistlines as males. But during puberty, while boys are amassing the bone and muscle of paleolithic hunters, a typical girl gains nearly 35 pounds of so-called reproductive fat around the hips

Healthy, fertile women typically have waist-hip ratios of .6 to .8, meaning their waists are 60 to 80 percent the size of their hips, whatever their actual weight. To take one familiar example, a 36-25-36 figure would have a WHR of .7. Many women outside

ures and asks male volunteers to rank them for attractiveness, sexiness, health and fertility. He has surveyed men of various backgrounds, nationalities and ages. And whether the judges are 8-year-olds or 85-year-olds, their runaway favorite is a figure of average

4. ❖ RELATING TO OTHERS

weight with a .7 WHR. Small wonder that when women were liberated from corsets and bustles, they took up girdles, wide belts and other waist-reducing contraptions. Last year alone, American women's outlays for shape-enhancing garments topped a half-billion dollars.

To SOME CRITICS, THE search for a biology of beauty looks like a thinly veiled political program. "It's the fantasy life of American men being translated into genetics," says poet and social critic Katha Pollitt. "You can look at any feature of modern life and make up a story about why it's genetic." In truth, says Northwestern University anthropologist Micaela di Leonardo, attraction is a complicated social phenomenon, not just a hard-wired response. If attraction were governed by the dictates of baby-making, she says, the men of ancient Greece wouldn't have found young boys so alluring, and gay couples wouldn't crowd modern sidewalks. "People make decisions about sexual and marital partners inside complex networks of friends and relatives," she says. "Human beings cannot be reduced to DNA packets."

Homosexuality is hard to explain as a biological adaptation. So is stamp collecting. But no one claims that human beings are mindless automatons, blindly striving to replicate our genes. We pursue countless passions that have no direct bearing on survival. If we're sometimes attracted to people who can't help us reproduce, that doesn't mean human preferences lack any coherent design. A radio used as a doorstop is still a radio. The beauty mavens' mission—and that of evolutionary psychology in general—is not to explain everything people do but to unmask our biases and make sense of them. "Our minds have evolved to generate pleasurable experiences in response to some things while ignoring other things," says Johnston. "That's why sugar tastes sweet, and that's why we find some people more attractive than others."

The new beauty research does have troubling implications. First, it suggests that we're designed to care about looks, even though looks aren't earned and reveal nothing about character. As writer Ken Siman observes in his new book, "The Beauty Trip," "the kind [of beauty] that inspires awe, lust, and increased jeans sales cannot be evenly distributed. In a society where everything is supposed to be within reach, this is painful to face." From acne to birth defects, we wear our imperfections as thorns, for we know the world sees them and takes note.

A second implication is that sexual stereotypes are not strictly artificial. At some level, it seems, women are designed to favor dominant males over meek ones, and men are designed to value women for youthful qualities that time quickly steals. Given the slow pace of evolutionary change, our innate preferences aren't likely to fade in the foreseeable future. And if they exist for what were once good biological reasons, that doesn't make them any less nettlesome. "Men often forgo their health, their safety, their spare time and their family life in order to get rank," says Helen Fisher, the Rutgers anthropologist, "because unconsciously, they know that rank wins women." And all too often, those who can trade cynically on their rank do.

But do we have to indulge every appetite that natural selection has preserved in us? Of course not. "I don't know any scientist who seriously thinks you can look to nature for moral guidance," says Thornhill. Even the fashion magazines would provide a better compass.

With KAREN SPRINGEN

The Future of Love

In search of a new vision of intimacy

By Barbara Graham

In a snapshot taken at my first "wedding," I look deliriously happy. I am a picture-book bride, dressed all in white—except for my tennis shoes—with one of my mother's silky half slips draped over my head like a veil. My groom is wearing short pants and has one hand on his hip; the other hand rests in mine. We are 6 years old. The setting is a pier on the bay in Miami Beach, with the inky water in the background. We're looking squarely at the camera, but my beloved is angling his body away from me and, in contrast to my blissed-out grin, has a look on his face that suggests he'd rather be swallowing worms. I don't seem to notice. Neither did my mother, who wrote "The Boyfriend!" on the border of the photograph before preserving it in the family album.

We pin our hopes for happiness on romantic love so early. In elementary school, before my faux nuptials in Miami Beach, I desperately wanted to marry Danny Harris, a fellow kindergartner. Later, when I was 12 and *Exodus* had just been released, I believed with all my heart that if Paul Newman laid eyes on me, I would be his forever. So I did what I had to do: I found out where he lived in New York City and spent the better part of my weekends camped out on the sidewalk in front of his apartment building, until the temperature dropped below freezing and I was forced to tether my dreams of true love—and my soul's liberation—to another hero.

Freud and his psychoanalytic descendants are no doubt correct in their assessment that the search for ideal love—for that one perfect soulmate—is the futile wish of not-fully developed selves. But it also seems true that the longing for a profound, all-consuming erotic connection (and the heightened state of awareness that goes with it) is in our very wiring. The yearning for fulfillment through love seems to be to our psychic structure what food and water are to our cells.

Just consider the stories and myths that have shaped our consciousness: Beauty and the Beast, Snow White and her handsome prince, Cinderella and Prince Charming, Fred and Ginger; Barbie and Ken. (Note that, with the exception of the last two couples, all of these lovers are said to have lived happily ever after—even though we never get details of their lives after the weddings, after children and gravity and loss have exacted their price.) Still, it's not just these lucky fairy tale characters who have captured our collective imagination. The tragic twosomes we cut our teeth on—Romeo and Juliet, Tristan and Iseult, Launcelot and Guinevere, Heathcliff and Cathy, Rhett and Scarlett—are even more compelling role models. Their love is simply too powerful and anarchic, too shattering and exquisite, to be bound by anything so conventional as marriage or a long-term domestic arrangement.

If recent divorce and remarriage statistics are any indication, we're not as astute as the doomed lovers. Instead of drinking poison and putting an end to our love affairs while the heat is still turned up full blast, we expect our marriages and relationships to be long-running fairy tales. When they're not, instead of examining our expectations, we switch partners and reinvent the fantasy, hoping that this time we'll get it right. It's easy to see why: Despite all the talk of family values, we're constantly bombarded by visions of perfect romance. All you have to do is turn on the radio or TV or open any magazine and check out the perfume and lingerie ads. "Our culture is deeply regressed," says Florence Falk, a New York City psychotherapist. "Everywhere we turn, we're faced with glamorized, idealized versions of love. It's as if the culture wants us to stay trapped in the fantasy and does everything possible to encourage and expand that fantasy." Trying to forge an authentic relationship amidst all the romantic hype, she adds, makes what is already a tough proposition even harder.

What's unique about our culture is our feverish devotion to the belief that romantic love and marriage should be synonymous. Starting with George and Martha, continuing through Ozzie and Harriet right up to the present day, we have tirelessly tried to formalize, rationalize, legalize, legitimize, politicize, and sanitize rapture. This may have something to do with our puritanical roots, as well as our tendency toward oversimplification. In any event, this attempt to satisfy all of our contradictory desires under the marital umbrella must be put in historical context in order to be properly understood.

"Personal intimacy is actually quite a new idea in human history and was never part of the marriage ideal before the 20th century," says John Welwood, a California-

4. ❖ RELATING TO OTHERS

based psychologist and author, most recently, of *Love and Awakening*. "Most couples throughout history managed to live together their whole lives without ever having a conversation about what was going on within or between them. As long as family and society prescribed the rules of marriage, individuals never had to develop any consciousness in this area."

In short, marriage was designed to serve the economic and social needs of families, communities, and religious institutions, and had little or nothing to do with love. Nor was it expected to satisfy lust. In *Myths To Live By*, Joseph Campbell explains how the sages of ancient India viewed the relationship between marriage and passion. They concluded that there are five degrees of love, he writes, "through which a worshiper is increased in the service and knowledge of his God." The highest form is passionate, illicit love. "In marriage, it is declared, one is still possessed of reason," Campbell writes. "The seizure of passionate love can be, in such a context, only illicit, breaking in upon the order of one's dutiful life in virtue as a devastating storm."

No wonder we're having problems. The pressures we place on our tender unions are unprecedented. Even our biochemistry seems to militate against long-term sexual relationships. Dr. Helen Fisher, an anthropologist at Rutgers University and author of *Anatomy of Love*, believes that human pair-bonds originally evolved according to "the ancient blueprint of serial monogamy and clandestine adultery" and were originally meant to last around four years—just long enough to raise a single dependent child through toddlerhood. The so-called seven-year-itch may be the remains of a four-year reproductive cycle, Fisher suggests.

Increasingly, Fisher and other researchers are coming to view what we call love as a series of complex biochemical events governed by hormones and enzymes. "People cling to the idea that romantic love is a mystery, but it's also a chemical experience," Fisher says, explaining that there are three distinct mating emotions and each is supported in the brain by the release of different chemicals. Lust, an emotion triggered by changing levels of testosterone in men and women, is associated with our basic sexual drive. Infatuation depends on the changing levels of dopamine, norepinephrine, and phenylethylamine (PEA) also called the "chemicals of love." They are natural—addictive—amphetaminelike chemicals that stimulate euphoria and make us want to stay up all night sharing our secrets. After infatuation and the dizzying highs associated with it have peaked—usually within a year or two—a new chemical system made up of oxytocin, vasopressin, and the endorphins kicks in and supports a steadier, quieter, more nurturing intimacy. In the end, regardless of whether biochemistry accounts for cause or effect in love, it may help to explain why some people—those most responsive to the release of the attachment chemicals—are able to sustain a long-term partnership, while thrillseekers who feel depressed without regular hits of dopamine and PEA, are likely to jump from one liaison to the next in order to maintain a buzz.

But even if our biochemistry suggests that there should be term limits on love, the heart is a stubborn muscle and, for better or worse, most of us continue to yearn for a relationship that will endure. As a group, Generation Xers—many of whom are children of divorce—are more determined than any other demographic group to have a different kind of marriage than their parents and to avoid divorce, says

The author and her "groom" tie the knot in Miami Beach.

Howard Markman, author of *Fighting For Your Marriage*. What's more, lesbians and gay men, who once opposed marriage and all of its heterosexual, patriarchal implications, now seek to reframe marriage as a more flexible, less repressive arrangement. And, according to the U.S. National Center for Health Statistics, in one out of an estimated seven weddings, either the bride or the groom—or both—are tying the knot for at least the third time—nearly twice as many as in 1970. There are many reasons for this, from the surge in the divorce rate that began in the '70s to our ever-increasing life span. Even so, the fact that we're still trying to get love right—knowing all we know about the ephemeral nature of passion, in a time when the stigmas once associated with being divorced or single have all but disappeared—says something about our powerful need to connect.

And, judging from the army of psychologists, therapists, clergy, and other experts who can be found dispensing guidance on the subject, the effort to save—or reinvent, depending on who's doing the talking—love and marriage has become a multimillion dollar industry. The advice spans the spectrum. There's everything from *Rules,* a popular new book by Ellen Fein and Sherrie Schneider that gives '90s women '50s-style tips on how to catch and keep their man, to Harville Hendrix's *Getting The Love You Want,* and other guides to "conscious love." But regardless of perspective, this much is clear: Never before have our most intimate thoughts and actions been so thoroughly dissected, analyzed, scrutinized, and medicalized. Now, people who fall madly in love over and over are called romance addicts. Their disease, modeled on alcoholism and other chemical dependencies, is considered "progressive and fatal."

Not everyone believes the attempt to deconstruct love is a good thing. The late philosopher Christopher Lasch wrote in his final (and newly released) book, *Women And The Common Life:* "The exposure of sexual life to scientific scrutiny contributed to the rationalization, not the liberation, of emotional life." His daughter, Elisabeth Lasch-Quinn, a historian at Syracuse University and the editor of the book, agrees. She contends that the progressive demystification of passionate life since Freud has promoted an asexual, dispassionate and utilitarian form of love. Moreover, like her father, she believes that the national malaise about romance can be attributed to insidious therapeutic modes of social control, a series of mechanisms that have reduced the citizen to a consumer of expertise. "We have fragmented life in such a way," she says, "as to take passion out of our experience."

Admittedly, it's a stretch to picture a lovesick 12th century French troubadour in a 12-step program for romance addicts. Still, we can't overlook the fact that our society's past efforts to fuse those historically odd bedfellows—passionate love and marriage—have failed miserably. And though it's impossible to know whether all the attention currently being showered on relationships is the last gasp of a dying social order—marriage—or the first glimmer of a new paradigin for relating to one another; it's obvious that something radically different is needed.

For one thing, many of us raised in the stultifying, claustrophobic nuclear families that were glorified in '50s and '60s sitcoms

Love Line

Prehistory

The wedding ring as we know it stems from the ancient German practice of offering a ring to a bride on the tip of a sword—a pledge of union.

5th Century BC

Socrates writes, "By all means marry; if you get a good wife, you'll become happy, if you get a bad one, you'll become a philosopher."

323 BC

The Egyptian wife has plenty of power over her husband: He must pay a fine to his first wife, for example, if he wishes to marry a second one.

1st Century AD

With the emergence of Christianity, Roman marriage changes from a procreative duty into a choice. Marriage requires female consent, and the role of "wife" takes on as much dignity as that of "friend." But "love" isn't necessary for marriage. In Greece, Plutarch calls love a "frenzy" and says that "those who are in love must be forgiven as though ill." Meanwhile, virginity is glorified, sexual connection is deemed foul and homosexuality is punishable by death.

c. 270

St. Valentine is martyred on Feb. 14. The association of this chaste, holy man with the ancient pagan fertility festival of the Lupercalia, an ancestor of Valentine's Day, is believed to be pure accident.

2nd–3rd Centuries

Christians stress morality in love. Intercourse is to be passionless and, as Clement of Alexandria stresses, should occur only after supper so that daylight hours can be devoted to studies or prayer. "He who too ardently loves his own wife," he writes, "is an adulterer."

but were, in fact, less than glorious have tried it all: Bob and Carol; Bob and Carol and Ted and Alice; Bob and Ted, Carol and Alice; and just plain Bob. Or Alice. And still we're searching.

In his latest work, *A Little Book On Love*, philosopher and San Francisco State University professor Jacob Needleman writes, "The social and sexual revolutions of the 20th century have shown us that relaxing marriage laws and customs, in the end, simply replaced one sort of suffering with another. If we love who and when we want and then break the bond whenever the impulse to do so is strong, we see that it brings no happiness to our lives. Nor, of course, did it bring happiness tensely to maintain the old rules, the old customs. So the meaning of living together in love cannot lie in either direction."

Although the experimentation of the '60s and '70s unquestionably wreaked havoc, it was a vital and creative havoc, without which we might have remained trapped in old, unsatisfying patterns of relating. "Two important developments in the '60s laid the ground for a more adult stage of couple consciousness, which we seem to be entering now," says Welwood. "The women's movement cast off old stereotypes and made relationships more egalitarian. And the dissemination of psychological ideas into the culture started to give people a new language and a new set of concepts to talk about what actually goes on in a relationship." Moreover, adds Needleman, the '60s were also the beginning of an awakening, the time when people began to realize there is such a thing as transcendence.

The key to the emerging vision of love seems to be intention. Welwood, Needleman and others speak of conscious relationship, conscious marriage. Today, these theorists—in their own ways—are redefining relationship as a vehicle for awakening and self-discovery. In their view genuine, enduring love is possible only when couples let go of adolescent smoke-and-mirrors fantasies of each other and the relationship and dedicate themselves to the search for truth. As Stephen Levine, author—with his wife, Ondrea—of *Embracing The Beloved*, puts it, "When your priority becomes consciousness, even more than relationship, then conscious relationship is possible."

According to Harville Hendrix, founder and president of the Orlando-based Institute for Imago Relationship Therapy, a primary function of marriage is for couples to help one another identify and heal unconscious childhood wounds and unmet needs. "Romantic love is a selection process based on your childhood," he explains, adding that, in spite of any conscious intent to find a partner who does not resemble your parents, most people are attracted to mates who have both their parents' posi-

3rd–4th Centuries

In India, Brahmin priest Vatsyayana, believed to be a lifelong celibate and ascetic, writes the erotic classic, the *Kama Sutra*. In Europe, Jovian, a maverick monk, is excommunicated in 385 A.D. on the grounds of heresy and blasphemy for calling marriage superior to celibacy.

5th Century

Religion governs marriage. Almost all weddings in the Roman Empire now include an ecclesiastical benediction, and marriage is considered a sacrament. In the centuries to come, Emperor Justinian will make adultery a capital offense and divorce nearly impossible.

6th Century

Buddhists and Hindus in India begin to practice Tantrism in an attempt to transform the human body into a mystical one. Through maithuna (ceremonial sex), human union becomes a sacred act.

939

In one of the first known attempts to suppress the ancient Japanese practice of phallic worship, a large phallic image that had been displayed and worshipped in Kyoto is moved to a less prominent place.

11th Century

Chinese philosophers begin to interpret the ancient yin and yang symbols as interdependent—like man and woman. The undivided circle becomes known as t'ai chi t'u: "the supreme ultimate." Around the same time, a few wags in southern France concoct a little game of flattery called "cortezia, courtesie." Soon their little amusement blossoms into the social philosophy of courtly love.

1244

Sufi teacher and poet Rumi meets Shams of Tabriz and abandons himself to divine and earthly love.

4. ❖ RELATING TO OTHERS

tive and negative traits. And, typically, he says, "the negative traits carry a higher charge." Moreover, if we stay locked in unawareness, once the initial rush of romance wanes, we become either mired in frustration or move on and reenact the drama with someone else. But, if we stretch ourselves to help each other grow, says Hendrix, childhood vulnerabilities eventually diminish—freeing up enormous reserves of creative energy.

The new vision of love, however, is not confined to achieving psychological wholeness. Awakening, transcendence, connection to the divine—call it what you will—are also central to the vision. In this context, intimate relationship becomes a spiritual practice, a sacred, mystical union of two people connected to a larger reality.

Though the idea of relationship as a vehicle for embodying the sacred is hardly new—especially in the tantric practices of India and Tibet, as well as in other Eastern traditions—never before has intimacy been so closely aligned with spirituality. "Now we have the opportunity to bring the sacred fully into our relationships, in a much more personal way," says Welwood—and not just for our own individual pleasure. "This is where we can start to regenerate our world. It has to begin between one person and another. How can we hope to create a better world when we can't even relate to our partner when we come home at night?"

On the one hand, it sounds extraordinary—marvelous—this blending of body, mind, and spirit into relationship. On the other hand, it sounds like madness: We've had enough trouble bringing together body and mind, and now we want to toss spirituality into the fire, too? As Needleman points out, "The whole of human nature is an obstacle to conscious love—our unawareness and our lack of clear, deep un-

> "When your priority becomes consciousness, even more than relationship, then conscious relationship is possible."
> —Stephen Levine

derstanding that the other person is in the same boat we're in."

Then there's the matter of the body. "My body is playing catch-up with my mind and spirit," admits Mark Matousek, the author of *Sex Death Enlightenment* who has always espoused the ideal of being sexually faithful, but until he entered a relationship three years ago with his partner, Louis, never believed it was possible. "Monogamy pushes every major button I have," says Matousek. "It brings out the best and, frequently, the worst in me. But I had to learn how to live as a sexual person on a spiritual path. Celibacy didn't work for me and neither did promiscuity. Monogamy is part of the whole search for soul."

Despite all the obstacles, maybe the sacred is the glue, the binding and holy energy that got lost—first while we tried desperately to merge marriage and passion in airtight nuclear families that valued acquiring over being and, later, as we turned our attention to rediscovering pleasure, as well as redefining our roles, sexual and gender identities, and traditional family structures.

But what about longing? Desire? The very human craving for delirious romance? Even when we know better, even when we've learned the hard way that no other person can possibly make us whole and we've entered into a conscious relationship, where does the longing go?

"Longing is a wonderful, very vital energy," says Florence Falk. "It's not the longing that's the problem, it's what you do with it." As we begin to reclaim our selves and find our core strength, she says, not only is it possible to develop a real, loving relationship, but the longing can be redirected to something greater than ourselves, something transcendent.

And, says Stephen Levine: "If another person is the most important thing in your life, then you're in trouble and they're in trouble because they become responsible for your suffering. But if consciousness is the most important thing in our lives and relationship is a means toward that end . . . Ah! then we are approaching paradise. We are approaching the possibility of actually becoming a human being before we die."

Barbara Graham is a regular contributor to Utne Reader *and the author of* Women Who Run with the Poodles *(Avon, 1994).*

Editorial assistant Rebecca Scheib provided additional reporting for this article.

Adult premarital sex is the 'sin' Americans wink at. But if you think casual sex is a problem only for teenagers, take a look at the numbers for grown-ups

Was it good for us?

BY DAVID WHITMAN

Teen pregnancy, Bill Clinton says, is the nation's "most serious social problem," and he has vowed to do something about it. The issue is a frequent "talking point" in his speeches, and earlier this month, in an elegant White House ceremony designed to underscore the administration's commitment, the first lady honored a dozen organizations for their work in tackling the problem.

For Clinton, as for politicians of every partisan stripe, lamenting the scourge of "babies having babies" is a no-lose proposition. Who could object? In preaching the virtues of abstinence during adolescence, however, the president and the first lady are not likely to mention one startling statistic: Many more 20-something adults than teenagers give birth to kids out of wedlock. In fact, most of the current social ills tied to sexual behavior—not only children born to unwed parents but sexually transmitted diseases, abortions, and the like—stem chiefly from adults who have sex before they marry, not from sexually active teens.

In an "enlightened" 1990s America, where a person old enough to vote and serve in the armed forces is also deemed old enough to make mature sexual decisions, the elaboration of these statistics is sobering. In 1994, just 22 percent of children born out of wedlock had mothers age 18 or under; more than half had mothers ages 20 to 29. Over half the women who obtain abortions each year, most unmarried, are in their 20s, while just a fifth are under 20. And the same age disparity is evident among those who contract sexually transmitted diseases, including AIDS. Although a disproportionate number of teens contract STDs, only 1 in 3 reported cases of gonorrhea and syphilis in 1995 involved people under 20. Teen pregnancy is an urgent problem, hard on mothers and even harder on their kids. But teenagers account for a smaller proportion of unwed births today than 20 years ago. (As late as 1975, teen girls bore the majority of all out-of-wedlock children in the United States.)

Yet when it comes to the negative social consequences of premarital sex between *adults,* there is silence in the White House—and in every other political institution. Conservatives, quick to decry sex between unwed teens and outspoken on many other sexual issues, turn suddenly shy when asked about adult premarital liaisons. Among those who declined to be interviewed for this article were William Bennett, editor of the anthology *The Book of Virtues;* Gary Bauer, head of the Family Research Council and a former aide to Ronald Reagan; John Podhoretz, a onetime speechwriter for George Bush and deputy editor of the *Weekly Standard* ("he's really not comfortable talking about the subject," said Podhoretz's assistant); and Laura Ingraham, a CBS News analyst who was featured in a 1995 *New York Times Magazine* cover story on young conservatives.

Mum's the word. The clergy, once loquacious on the topic of premarital "sin," are equally subdued. "Have you ever heard a sermon on 'living together'?" asks religious columnist Michael McManus in his 1995 book, *Marriage Savers.* Condemnation of adult premarital sex has virtually vanished from religious preaching, even in the homilies of Catholic priests. "In the pulpits there has been a backing away from moralizing about sex before marriage," says Bishop James McHugh, the bishop of Camden, N.J.

Why such reticence? The answer may seem obvious. Americans, at least tacitly, have all but given up on the notion that the appropriate premarital state is one of chastity. The Bible may have warned that like the denizens of Sodom and Gomorrah, those who give "themselves over to fornication" will suffer "the vengeance of eternal fire." Yet for most Americans, adult premarital sex has become the "sin" they not only wink at but quietly endorse. On television, adult virgins are as rare as caribou in Manhattan. Several studies have found that prime-time network shows implicitly condone premarital sex, and air as many as 8 depictions of it for every 1 of sex between married couples. And a

4. ❖ RELATING TO OTHERS

U.S. News poll shows that while most Americans—74 percent—have serious qualms about teens having sex before marriage, more than half believe it is not at all wrong, or wrong only sometimes, for *adults* to have premarital sex.

Yet this surface consensus reflects a rather rapid—and surprisingly complex—transformation in American attitudes. The notion that sex ought to be reserved for marriage may now seem antiquated, but it wasn't very long ago that a large majority of Americans held just that belief. As late as 1968, for example, millions of Americans found it newsworthy that two unwed 20-year-old college students would publicly admit to living together. Newspapers and newsmagazines replayed the tale of Linda LeClair, a sophomore at Barnard College, and Peter Behr, a Columbia University undergraduate, who conceded they had violated Barnard College's housing regulations by "shacking up" together in an off-campus apartment.

Love and let love. When Barnard students held protest rallies on LeClair's behalf, a beleaguered faculty-student committee relented and decided not to recommend her expulsion from the college. *Time* warned darkly of LeClair's "moment of immoral victory." And William F. Buckley likened LeClair in his syndicated column to an "unemployed concubine." Even the tabloids purported to be shocked by the couple's open cohabitation, penning stories with headlines such as "Suffragette of Love and let-love" and "Nine-to-sex coed!"

Between that dimly remembered past and today's indulgence of sexual experimentation before marriage stand the arrival of the pill and the various skirmishes of the sexual revolution. As it turns out, if converting Americans to free love and loose sexual mores was the goal, the revolution was pretty much a dud. Despite the stereotype of the promiscuous American, most men and women are still sexually conservative in belief and practice. Just over 70 percent of Americans say they have had only one sexual partner in the past year, and more than 80 percent report they have never had an extramarital affair. For the past 25 years, there has been almost no change in how Americans view adultery, homosexuality, or teenage sex—a substantial majority think all three are always, or almost always, wrong.

In the aftermath of that turbulent era, however, there was one definite casualty: Americans' long-held conviction

---

THE UNWED 30-SOMETHING

Jennifer Grossman, *30, is single and an MSNBC-TV contributor. She's a self-described libertarian but questions today's sexual freedom.*

I used to complain to my mother, who is

a liberal, about how boyfriends seemed commitment shy. And she would say, "Well, why buy the cow if the milk is free?" We're in the sexual promised land now, the milk is free, people are surfeited with sex—and yet we're starved for love. In locker rooms, in coffeehouses, women are getting together with their girlfriends the next morning after their dates and asking in hushed tones: "I hope you didn't sleep with him?"

Some of the men I've dated have been married before. The safe-sex jingle—"You're sleeping with everyone your lover has ever slept with"—has added resonance now: You're sharing emotional space with those ex-wives and girlfriends. You begin to play tricks on yourself—this one wasn't important, this one wasn't meaningful. The acceptance, even encouragement of premarital sex makes it very difficult to sustain the fantasy that we are loved alone.

I didn't kiss the man I'm dating now until the seventh date. I didn't have sex with him until the seventh month. He respects and values me a lot more than the men I dated in college, when I just was a lot more casual with my body. Women have spoiled men.

---

that virginity should be relinquished only in the marriage bed. To be sure, America has never been sexually pristine. Since the first settlers arrived, lots of unwed teens and young adults took a roll or two in the hay. And there was always a perceived double standard for men, who were expected to "sow their oats," and women, who were expected to save themselves for their husbands. Yet there are fundamental differences between the premarital sex of the 1960s and earlier eras, and that of the 1990s. In the mid-1960s, many more women were virgins at marriage than is now the case, and men and women who did engage in premarital sex often did so with their betrothed. Cohabitation was comparatively rare, and "shotgun weddings" for pregnant brides were common.

Almost certainly, television has had a central role in eroding the stigma of premarital sex. The sexual content of prime time has changed slowly, so viewers often fail to realize just how differently adult premarital sex is treated today from even a decade ago. Once, adolescents watched *Mork and Mindy,* the *Cosby Show, Little House on the Prairie,* and the like. Today, more than 6 million children under the age of 11 watch "family hour" shows that include *Beverly Hills 90210, Friends,* and *Roseanne.*

Sex, more sex. TV's characterization of out-of-wedlock sex has also done a flip-flop. Sen. Daniel Patrick Moynihan might say that television's treatment of premarital sex is a classic example of "defining deviancy down"—what was once considered deviant or abnormal now is treated as the norm. In his book, *Prime Time,* Robert Lichter and his colleagues at the Center for Media and Public Affairs found that prime-time television now by implication endorses unmarried adults' intentions to have sex in about 3 out or 4 cases and raises concerns only about 5 percent of the time. "On shows like *Three's Company* the characters hinted around a lot about premarital sex," says Lichter. "But the shows back then did not specifically seek to justify unmarried sex."

Producers and screenwriters appear largely inured to this permissiveness, though viewers seem troubled. In a *U.S. News* poll last year, just 38 percent of the Hollywood elite were concerned about how TV depicted premarital sex, compared with 83 percent of the public. "Hollywood has glorified adult premarital sex," argues Sen. Joseph Lieberman. "And that is unhelpful if your goal is to reduce teen pregnancy and out-of-wedlock births."

In this climate, the suggestion that abstinence is preferable to sex for unwed adults seems hopelessly retrograde, about as timely as recommending that hansom cabs replace automobiles. It is virginity now that makes news. When a *TV Guide* columnist learned recently that college senior Donna Martin, the character played by Tori Spelling on

> **THE ATHLETE**
>
> **A. C. Green,** *a basketball star with the Dallas Mavericks, is 33 and has never married. He promotes the cause of abstinence through the Phoenix-based A. C. Green Programs for Youth.*
>
> I am still a virgin. Abstaining from extramarital sex is one of the most unpopular things a person can do, much less talk about. From a sheer numbers standpoint, it can be a lonely cause—but that doesn't mean it's not right.
>
> I abstain as an adult for the same reasons I did as a teen—the principle doesn't change, or the feeling of self-respect I get. My fellow ballplayers do not tell me, "You are crazy"—it's more that they think I'm being unrealistic. It's ironic, but the guys who are parents—and especially the guys who have daughters—tend to look at sex before marriage a lot more carefully now.

Beverly Hills 90210, was scheduled to lose her virginity in the season's finale, the magazine issued a press release to detail this "scoop."

It is possible to argue that, on balance, the removal of premarital sex from the roster of moral or religious transgressions is a good thing. Certainly, most young singles believe they won't personally be hurt by premarital sex because they feel they use contraception responsibly. They minimize their own risk, on the assumption that unintended pregnancies, STDs, and abortions are problems that mostly afflict the careless.

In fact, the *U.S. News* poll shows that a majority of respondents under the age of 45 think that adult premarital sex generally benefits people quite apart from the issue of expanding their sexual pleasure. Unlike their elders, younger adults widely endorsed the sowing-one's-oats rationale for premarital sex, so long as the sowing is not done promiscuously. Less than half of those under 45 thought it was a good idea for adults to remain virgins until they marry. And a majority of respondents agreed that having had a few sexual partners makes it easier for a person to pick a compatible spouse.

America's acceptance of premarital sex also makes it easier to avoid rushing into marriage. By delaying family formation until after college, young couples escape being saddled with large loans and child-rearing duties while they are still trying to earn their degrees. And couples who wed for the first time after they turn 25 are less likely to be divorced a decade later than couples who wed while still in their teens. For all the nostalgia about the '50s, few Americans want to turn back the clock to that era, when about half the nation's women wed before their 20th birthday. Less than 8 percent of those surveyed by *U.S. News* thought it ideal for a woman to marry before she turns 20, and fewer than 5 percent though it ideal for a man to marry before his 20s. The best age for a woman to marry, in most Americans' minds, is 24. For men, the ideal age is 25.

Yet such "benefits" may be more wishful thinking than fact. Cohabitation may seem a good "trial run" for a solid marriage. But in practice, cohabiting couples who marry—many of whom already have children—are about 33 percent more likely to divorce than couples who don't live together before their nuptials. Virgin brides, on the other hand, are *less* likely to divorce than women who lost their virginity prior to marriage.

But we didn't inhale. Cohabitation is associated with other risks for young couples. Live-in boyfriends are far more likely to beat their partners than are spouses. And young adults who move in together, without being engaged to be married, are more likely to use cocaine and cigarettes after they start cohabiting than beforehand. All in all, muses Harvard sociologist Christopher Jencks, adult premarital sex "may ultimately prove to be a little like smoking dope in the 1960s. In retrospect, maybe it isn't so good for you after all."

In a broader sense, the public willingness to tolerate and even condone premarital sex makes it much harder for teachers, clerics, and law enforcement officials to curb other types of extramarital sex that are more controversial. Public acceptance of premarital sex has undermined the efforts of government officials to encourage abstinence among teens and to prosecute men who have out-of-wedlock sex with minors, and it has even colored the efforts of the clergy to keep gays and lesbians from being ordained. The Presbyterian Church (U.S.A.) recently enacted an amendment barring anyone currently engaged in extramarital sex—heterosexual or otherwise—from serving as an officer of the church. Put another way, sex before marriage has proved to be the runaway horse of traditional values. Once it took off, all the other old-time mores became more difficult to keep in their place.

An old joke among sex educators is that a conservative is a progressive with a teenage daughter. Few voters, with or without children, question that teens are generally less prepared to shoulder the consequences of sex than adults, or that there is an especially forceful case to be made for having teens—particularly younger adolescents—abstain from sex. Yet it is hard for parents to, say, convince a 17-year-old that she should abstain from sex now but that when she turns 18 or 21 it will be OK for her to start sleeping with her boyfriends. "I find it easy to distinguish between an adult with some emotional maturity and a 15-year-old having

---

The facts about premarital sex

- **Sexual initiation.** In the 1960s, 25 percent of young men and 45 percent of young women were virgins at age 19; by the 1980s, fewer than 20 percent of males and females were.
- **Sexual history.** About 30 percent of Americans say they have had one or no sex partners since turning 18; 30 percent say two to four partners; 22 percent say five to 10 partners; 20 percent say 10 partners or more.
- **Cohabitation.** In the 1950s, roughly 9 in 10 young women got married without living with their partner, compared with 1 in 3 in the early 1990s.
- **Virgin brides.** Percentage of white women married from 1960–65 who were virgins: 43; from 1980–85: 14.

Source: *Sex in America; The Social Organization of Sexuality; Journal of Marriage and the Family*

4. ❖ RELATING TO OTHERS

sex," says former Clinton White House aide William Galston, now a board member of the National Campaign to Prevent Teen Pregnancy. "Whether the 15-year-old will find it easy to make that distinction is another matter altogether. They may very well view it as hypocritical for a 45-year-old to say, 'Do as we say and not as we do.'"

Drawing a line between teen sex and adult sex is further complicated by the fact that many teenage women sleep with males age 20 and over, not with teen boys. Teen pregnancy is chiefly a result of these older men fathering out-of-wedlock babies with 18- and 19-year-old women, who are responsible for about 3 out of 5 teen births. Only a quarter of the men who impregnate women under the age of 18 are also under 18. As Mike Males put it in *The Scapegoat Generation:* "If the president really wanted to prevent junior high sex, he would lecture grown-ups."

Tough love. One renascent reform for curbing adult-teen sex is enforcement of statutory rape laws, which generally prohibit sex between girls who have not reached the age of consent (typically between ages 14 and 18) and older adult males. In the *U.S. News* poll, 64 percent of Americans said it was always wrong for a man over the age of 20 to have sex with a teenage girl. Both President Clinton and Bob Dole urged states last year to start reapplying the laws, and a handful have done so. But no state is seriously considering enforcing existing antifornication laws—which essentially prohibit consensual sex between unmarried adults.

Some of the reticence might be written off to the fear of seeming hypocritical, especially among younger conservative lawmakers: We had sex before marriage, so we can't suggest that others shouldn't—at least, not with a straight face. But the trepidation of those on the right has more complex roots, too. Conservatives with libertarian leanings believe that consensual sex between adults is a private matter, one the state shouldn't meddle in. About half those surveyed by *U.S. News* said unmarried couples who live together are "doing their own thing and not affecting anyone else." And at least some on the political right have come to accept the popular belief, echoed in the *U.S. News* poll, that premarital sex between consenting adults generally serves a positive purpose. As Richard Posner, a prominent conservative jurist and intellectual, puts it in his book *Sex and Reason:* "There is no good reason to deter premarital sex, a generally harmless source of pleasure and for some people an important stage of marital search."

Just what, if anything, can be done about the negative consequences of premarital sex is far from clear. Twenty years ago, Jimmy Carter told employees at the Department of Housing and Urban Development: "Those of you who are living in sin—I hope you'll get married." Carter's suggestion, Galston recalls, provoked "a massive horse laugh, particularly from the press corps." More recently, state officials have begun to ponder how to reduce adult premarital sex in a formal way, owing largely to the new welfare law. During the Reagan and Bush years, Congress authorized several small "abstinence only" programs to teach high school students the benefits of abstinence, without offering information on birth control. The new welfare law sets aside $50 million for each of the next five years for states to fund abstinence-only programs. In toto, the U.S. government will spend about nine times as much on abstinence education in 1997-98 as in previous years. The vast bulk of the spending will surely be aimed at teens. But the programs funded in the welfare law need not be limited to them.

THE CONVERT

Lisa Schiffren, *37, wrote Dan Quayle's famous 1992 Murphy Brown speech in which Quayle criticized the TV character for bearing a child out of wedlock. Schiffren married in 1993 and has a daughter.*

I did not abstain from premarital sex. I
was raised in a secular, Upper East Side Manhattan-liberal home and now I'm a quasi-religious conservative. I wish I could say that premarital sex was morally wrong. Sometimes, I think it's OK. It's very hard to send young women to college and tell them they're going to be investment bankers and lawyers, and yet they can't have sex. Plus, we don't really want people getting married too, too early. I did a lot of things in my 20s I couldn't have done if I were married, like spend a lot of time overseas.

More often than not, though, premarital sex is a bad idea. Nobody I knew at the women's college I went to would have had the guts to say that premarital sex was especially bad. Yet nobody liked a social system where sex was expected in any given relationship. The experience of my generation suggests people very rarely get what they are looking for from premarital sex, unless what they're looking for is purely sexual. When it's too available, sex itself loses its meaning.

Among the elite there is more public posturing about not smoking, or not being fat, than about not having promiscuous sexual relationships. People are afraid to sound like prigs. I myself have overcome this and am happy to be a prig. But I no longer have to date.

THE CLERGYMAN

James McHugh *is the bishop of Camden, N.J., and one of the Catholic Church's spokesmen on family issues.*

All sexual activity outside of marriage
is wrong and has no moral justification. Sex before marriage diminishes respect for sexuality itself. Many young adults who have engaged in sex before marriage aren't so sure they want their younger brothers and sisters to live through the same experience. But they feel restrained from honestly saying what they think to upcoming generations, either from guilt, ineptitude, or fear that they will be rejected or ridiculed. If everybody's doing it, and everybody accepts that everybody is doing it, then the young man or woman who has a more ennobling vision of human sexuality ends up looking like the oddball.

31. Was It Good for Us?

THE POLICY MAKER

William Galston, *a former White House aide, helped design President Clinton's teen pregnancy strategy.*

As a religious and moral matter, I per-
sonally cannot look at a long-standing relationship outside the bonds of matrimony and say, no, that's totally wrong, that's morally forbidden. I have no problems telling my 12-year-old son he should abstain from sex in high school. I would have a hard time, based on my own experience, telling my son, "Well, after you get to college, I want you to follow the same course of conduct I asked you to follow while you were in high school and lived at home." I don't know that I would want my son to wait until he was 27 or 28 to get married. I got married at 22.

There is a sense in which we believe what we believe about premarital sex because it is convenient for us to do so. It would be extremely inconvenient to conclude that all this premarital sex we tolerate isn't such a good thing, after all.

Deterrence. A second part of the new law deals more directly with the social ills that can attend premarital sex. It provides up to $100 million a year in bonuses for the five states that can show the largest reductions in out-of-wedlock births without corresponding increases in abortions. Since most out-of-wedlock births are to adults, state officials will, somehow, have to address premarital sex. Yet even conservatives aren't pretending they want the government to discourage most adult premarital sex. Their chief concern is out-of-wedlock births among welfare mothers, more than 90 percent of whom are currently 20 or older. "If the parents can support the child, fine; if they can't, then they ought to be discouraged from having it," says Posner.

THE CHRISTIAN SOLDIER

Ralph Reed *is the executive director of the Christian Coalition. U.S. News asked him if he was a virgin when he married.*

I wouldn't say that. I would say when
my wife and I married, we had both been faithful to each other up until that time. We did not engage in premarital sex and abstaining was important to us.... Yes, I think it is morally wrong to have sex before marriage. But I'm not going to condemn someone who is engaged in conduct that I don't agree with. I will encourage my children to abstain until they are married, even if they are adults.

It's hard for me to deliver lectures about finishing college before you get married, since my wife was 19 when I married her. I would prefer to have my daughter finish college before she marries, because career and livelihood issues are much more easily resolved now if you have a college degree. But I don't think you want to set up a situation where you've been so Pharisaic about not approving marriage until after college that you end up having children elope.

Even though we had to struggle financially, my wife and I were infinitely better off having gone ahead and gotten married. If we'd had to wait, it would have been harder to remain consistent with what we believed was morally right. It shouldn't be the overwhelming reason, but the truth is, the sexual drive is one of the things that brings you to your mate.

The truth, for now, is that nobody has proven ideas about how to reduce adult premarital sex, nor has anyone shown much inclination to do so. The prospects for an en masse return to premarital chastity are almost nil, though some young singles may become more sexually conservative. Earlier this month, the U.S. government announced that the proportion of teens who reported having sexual intercourse went down for the first time since similar surveys began in the 1970s.

The budding discomfort with casual sex is evident, too, in the enormous popularity of *The Rules,* the retro-guide that advises women how to coyly lure Mr. Right to the altar. Its authors don't counsel chastity. But they do advise "*Rules* girls" not to kiss a man on the first date and to put off sleeping with him for a few weeks or months. Jennifer Grossman, an MSNBC-TV contributor who is single, 30, and writes often on women's issues, argues that the appeal of *The Rules* among college-educated women reflects their search for a middle ground between casual sex and premarital chastity. "This all-you-can-eat sexual buffet is leaving a lot of men and women feeling very empty," she says. "I see a pattern among my girlfriends—when they sleep with men, they cry. Sleeping with a man you've known for a week is such an 'almost.' It's almost what you want—but a chasm away from what you really need."

In theory, more responsible use of contraception might provide another avenue for eliminating the worst complications of sex before marriage. In practice, though, the increased availability of contraception has not halted the rise in out-of-wedlock births or put an end to abortions and STDs. Adult premarital sex, the little-noticed heart of the sexual revolution, is here to stay. There may be little to do about this silent "epidemic"—except to acknowledge that sex before marriage may not always be the simple pleasure that many Americans assume it to be.

With Paul Glastris and Brendan I. Koerner

Dynamics of Personal Adjustment: The Individual and Society

The passing of each decade brings changes to society. Some historians have suggested that changes are occurring more rapidly now than in the past. In other words, history appears to take less time to occur. How has American society changed historically? The inventory is long. Technological advances can be found everywhere. A decade ago, few people knew what "user-friendly" or "16MB RAM" signified. Today these terms are readily identified with the quickly expanding computer industry. Fifteen years ago, Americans felt fortunate to own a 13-inch television that received three local stations. Now people feel deprived if they cannot select from 100 different worldwide channels on their big, rear-screen sets. Today we can fax a message to the other side of the world faster than we can propel a missile to the same place.

In the Middle Ages, Londoners worried about the bubonic plague. Before vaccines were available, people feared polio and other diseases. Today much concern is focused on the transmission and cure of AIDS, the discovery of more carcinogenic substances, and the greenhouse effect. In terms of mental health, psychologists see few hysterics, the type of patient seen by Sigmund Freud in the 1800s. Psychosomatic ulcers and alcohol and drug addiction are more common today. In other words, lifestyle, more than disease, is killing Americans. Similarly, issues concerning the changing American family continue to grab headlines.

Nearly every popular magazine carries a story or two bemoaning the passing of the traditional, nuclear family and the decline in "family values." And as if these spontaneous or unplanned changes are not enough to cope with, some individuals are intentionally trying to change the world. Witness the continuing dramatic changes in Eastern Europe and the Middle East, for example.

This list of societal transformations, while not exhaustive, reflects society's continual demand for adaptation by each of its members. However, it is not just society at large that places stress on us. Smaller units within society, such as our work group, demand constant adaptation by individuals. Work groups expand and contract with every economic fluctuation. Even when group size remains stable, new members come and go as turnover takes place; hence, changes in the dynamics of the group occur in response to the new personalities. Each of these changes, welcome or not, probably places less strain on society as a whole and more stress on the individual, who then needs to adjust or cope with the change.

This unit addresses the interplay between the individual and society in producing the problems each creates for the other.

The first few essays feature ideas about societal problems such as violence and racism. In the unit's first article, crime and society are discussed by David Lykken. He posits several theories about what causes crime in America and dismisses arguments suggesting that the tendency to commit crime is inherited. Instead he lays the blame squarely on parents.

In "Mixed Blood," racism is discussed by Jefferson Fish, who believes that our use of the word "race" and our categories for race in the United States are contrived and are unlike any others found in the rest of the world. If Fish is correct, our research into race differences (for example, differences in intelligence), is misguided.

Ray Surette, in the third unit article, blames the media for encouraging our violent behavior. He examines research into media violence. These writers seem to tell us that violence and racism are rising in American society, and that the causes might be multiple. Approaches to decreasing them, then, might also have to be multipronged.

While on the topic of the media, it might also serve us well to investigate the effects of other media on us. In "The Evolution of Despair," Robert Wright suggests that modern technology has a major disadvantage. According to Wright, evolution places us on the branch of creatures that are social, yet modern technology (for example, the hours that we spend on computers) tends to isolate us.

The last article of this unit offers a sensible and scientific approach to a topic that has been in the media of late: cults. Perhaps you recall the 1997 suicide of the Heaven's Gate members. Most people find cults abhorrent, but others gladly join. Why they join and the kinds of influences that cults have on their members are investigated in this essay.

Looking Ahead: Challenge Questions

What do you think causes the high crime rates in American society? Do you think individuals can inherit a propensity for criminality? What should we do if the an-

UNIT 5

swer is "yes"? Are parents responsible for what their children do? If you think that parents are responsible, should we also hold them culpable when their children commit heinous crimes?

What is the definition of race in American society? Do other cultures use this same definition? If not, why not? What is it about our society that perpetuates the "isms" (racism, sexism, and other prejudices)? How can we eliminate or overcome racism, sexism, and sexual harassment?

What do you think has caused the epidemic of violence on American streets? Discuss whether or not televised violence has encouraged this epidemic. Is the decline of the family an important ingredient? If so, what can we do to reduce violence? If not, what else has caused violence to increase over the last decade? To what positive uses can television be put? For what negative uses has television been developed? Should we censor or restrict certain types of television? Why and for whom? Do you agree that networks should voluntarily make programming changes or that such changes should be legislated? Why or why not? If families are important, how can true family values be revived?

Besides television, what other modern technologies are available to us? How do these technologies enhance the human experience? How might they detract from it?

What is a cult? Why do people join cults? Would you ever join a cult? What are the advantages to members of cults? What recruiting techniques do cults use? What tragedies seem to follow cults?

Symposium: Licensing Parents

Psychopathy, Sociopathy, and Crime

David T. Lykken

Since the beginnings of psychiatry in the early nineteenth century, it has been recognized that there are persons whose persisting antisocial behavior cannot be understood in terms of mental disorder or neurotic motivations. Psychiatric befuddlement is evident in the diagnostic labels used to classify these people. The father of French psychiatry, Phillipe Pinel, noted in 1801 that they seemed to behave crazily without actually being crazy, and he coined the term "*manie sans delire.*" Benjamin Rush, the first American psychiatrist, in 1812 described patients with "innate preternatural moral depravity." An English psychiatrist, Pritchard, employed a similar label, "moral insanity," in 1835. The German systematists, like Robert Koch, first used the term "psychopathic" in 1891 for a heterogeneous collection of what we would now call personality disorders, and Emil Kraepelin, in the seventh edition (1915) of his influential textbook, first used "psychopathic personality" specifically to describe the amoral or immoral criminal type. In 1930, an American psychiatrist named Partridge pointed out that these people had in common a disposition to violate social norms of behavior and introduced the term "sociopath." I shall use this term to refer specifically to antisocial personalities whose behavior is a consequence of social or familial dysfunction. I use "psychopath" to refer to those people whose antisocial behavior appears to result from a defect or aberration within themselves rather than in their rearing.

The Psychopath

While not deeply vicious, he carries disaster lightly in each hand.

—Hervey Cleckley, 1982

More than a hundred years after Pinel and Pritchard, an American expert on criminal psychiatry, Benjamin Karpman, concluded: "When all of the cases which I group under symptomatic psychopathy are removed and accounted for, there would still remain a small group which may be designated as primary or idiopathic psychopathy." There seem to be several "species" of psychopath, several different innate peculiarities of temperament or endowment that conduce toward a complete or partial failure of socialization or toward intermittent lapses of socialization and to antisocial behavior. Many of these innate vagaries—choleric temperament or hypersexuality, for example—can be easily identified, but the etiology of what Karpman called "primary psychopathy" is more mysterious and has been the subject of extensive research and debate.

In his classic monograph *The Mask of Sanity*, psychiatrist Hervey Cleckley illustrated the problem of understanding the primary psychopath by means of a collection of vividly drawn case histories from his own practice. Here were people of good families, intelligent and rational, sound of mind and body, who lied without compunction, cheated, stole, casually violated any and all norms of social conduct whenever it suited their whim. Moreover, they seemed surprisingly unaffected by the bad consequences of their actions, whether visited upon themselves or on their families or friends.

Cleckley also cited several examples from literature of the kind of individual he had in mind, including Shakespeare's Iago and Falstaff, Henrik Ibsen's Peer Gynt, and Ferenc Molnár's character Liliom, the prototype of Billy Bigelow in the Rodgers and Hammerstein musical *Carousel*. Unaccountably, however, Cleckley neglected the Shakespearean character who best epitomizes the primary psychopath: Richard III, who, in the first speech of scene 1, declares himself bored, looking for action: "Now is the winter of our discontent / ... / Why, I, in this weak piping time of peace, / Have no delight to pass away the time."

In the next scene, the Lady Anne enters with bearers carrying the corpse of her husband, Henry VI. It was Richard who had killed Henry, and Anne fears and despises him, yet he commands the bearers to set the coffin down while he proceeds to make love to the grieving widow! Richard talks her around in just three pages—surely one of the greatest tours de force ever essayed by a dramatist or by an actor—and then he gloats: "Was ever woman in this humour woo'd? / Was ever woman in this humour won? / I'll have her; but I will not keep her long. / What, I, that kill'd her husband and his father, / To take her in her heart's extremest hate, / With curses in her mouth, tears in her eyes, / The bleeding witness of my hatred by; / Having God, her conscience, and these bars against me, / And I no friends to back my suit withal / But the plain deveil and dissembling looks. / And yet to win her, all the world to nothing!"

Some female psychopaths in literature include Mildred in Somerset Maugham's *Of Human Bondage*; Sally Bowles, the heroine in *Cabaret*; Ibsen's Hedda Gabler (Hedda is a nice example of a "secondary" psychopath); and Bizet's Carmen. We can see primary psychopathy in the characters played by the actor Jack Nicholson in numerous movies, including *Five Easy Pieces, Chinatown, The Last Detail*, and, especially, *One Flew over the Cuckoo's Nest*. Harry Lyme as portrayed by Orson Welles in the film *The Thin Man* conveys the eerie combination of charm and menace found in some of these individuals. The character played by child actress Patty McCormack in the film *The Bad Seed* and the eponymous hero in Thomas Mann's *The Confessions of Felix Krull, Confidence Man* are contrasting portraits of the psychopath as mendacious manipulator. The brother in Graham Greene's novel *The Shipwrecked* is a good example of the feckless, self- and other-deluding, poseur type of psychopath, as is the protagonist's father in John le Carré's *The Perfect Spy*, a character said to be based on the author's own father. The psychopath in youth can be found as the hero of E. L. Docterow's book *Billy Bathgate*, which also provides a more dangerous version in the character of the gangster Dutch Schultz.

As used by the media, "psychopath" conveys an impression of danger and implacable evil. This is mistaken, however, as Cleckley made very clear. Like the unsocialized sociopath, the psychopath is characterized by a lack of the restraining effect of conscience and of empathic concern for other people. Unlike the ordinary sociopath, the primary psychopath has failed to develop conscience and empathic feelings, not because of a lack of socializing experience but, rather, because of some inherent psychological peculiarity that makes him especially difficult to socialize. An additional consequence of this innate peculiarity is that the psychopath behaves in a way that suggests that he is relatively indifferent to the probability of punishment for his actions. This essential peculiarity of the psychopath is not in itself evil or vicious, but combined with perverse appetites or with an unusually hostile and aggressive temperament, the lack of these normal constraints can result in an explosive and dangerous package. Examples of such combinations include the serial killer Ted Bundy, Gary Gilmore, Diane Downs, and the sex-murdering Royal Air Force officer Neville Heath. *Without Conscience: The Disturbing World of the Psychopaths among Us*, a recent and highly readable book by R. D. Hare, the leading researcher in this area, provides numerous sketches of real-life criminal psychopaths.

In marked contrast to these dangerous characters, and illustrative of why psychologists find such fascination in the psychopath, is the case of Oscar Schindler, the savior of hundreds of Krakow Jews, the protagonist of Steven Spielberg's *Schindler's List*. Opportunist, bon vivant, ladies' man, manipulator, unsuccessful in legitimate business by his own admission but wildly successful in the moral chaos of wartime, Schindler's rescue of those Jews can be best understood as a thirty-five-year-old con man's response to a kind of ultimate challenge: Schindler against the Third Reich. Any swine could kill people under the conditions of that time and place; the real challenge—in the words that his biographer may have put in his mouth, the "real power"—lay in rescuing people, especially in rescuing Jews. Some parts of Spielberg's film do not fit with my diagnosis of Schindler as a primary psychopath, in particular, the scene near the end in which Schindler breaks down in tears while addressing his Jewish workers. British filmmaker Jon Blair, whose earlier documentary film *Schindler* was truer to history than Spielberg's feature film, noted this same discrepancy. "It was slightly out of character, and, of course, it never actually happened," Blair said.

Some other biographies of colorful primary psychopaths include N. von Hoffman's *Citizen Cohn*, Neil Sheehan's *A Bright Shining Lie: John Paul Vann and America in Vietnam*, and Daniel Akst's *Wonderboy: Barry Minkow, the Kid Who Swindled Wall Street*. Some historical figures who, I believe, had the talent for psychopathy but who achieved great worldly success include Lyndon Johnson,

Winston Churchill, the explorer Sir Richard Burton, and Chuck Yeager, the first man to break the sound barrier.

The fact that many of these illustrative characters were not adjudicated criminals reminds us that we are talking here about a class of actors rather than a pattern of actions. Psychopaths are at high risk for engaging in criminal behavior, but not all of them succumb to that risk. Even the identical twins of criminal psychopaths, with whom they share all their genes and many of their formative experiences, do not necessarily become criminal themselves. To mention Churchill, Johnson, Burton, and Yeager in this context may seem especially surprising, but all four set out as daring, adventurous, unconventional youngsters who began playing by their own rules early in life. Talent, opportunity, and plain luck enabled them to achieve success and self-esteem through (mainly) licit rather than illicit means. Johnson and Burton were borderline psychopaths, if we can believe their biographers, while Churchill and Yeager seem merely to have shared what I call the "talent for psychopathy." What I believe to be the nature of this talent will be explicated later in this article.

Theories of Psychopathy

Cleckley concluded that the psychopath lacks the normal emotional accompaniments of experience, that the raw feel of his emotional experience is attenuated much as is the color experience of people who are color-blind. Whereas Pritchard and Rush believed that there was an innate lack of moral sensibility, Cleckley took the more modern view that moral feelings and compunctions are not God-given but must be learned and that this learning process is guided and enforced by the power of emotional feelings. When these normal feelings are attenuated, the development of morality—the very mechanism of socialization—is compromised. Thus we can see that Cleckley regarded the primary psychopath as someone for whom the normal socializing experiences are ineffective because of an innate defect, which he thought to be as profound and debilitating as psychosis. As we acknowledged at the outset, some children are harder to socialize than others, and a child whose capacity for emotional experience is innately very weak would presumably be especially difficult.

There is no real evidence, however, that the primary psychopath *is* incapable of genuine emotion. He seems clearly able to feel anger, satisfaction, delight, self-esteem—indeed, if he did not have such feelings, it seems improbable that he would do many of the things, proper and improper, that he does do. As Gilbert and Sullivan pointed out: "When the felon's not engaged in his employment, / Or maturing his felonious little plans, / His capacity for innocent enjoyment, / Is just as great as any honest man's." Other investigators have tried to identify more focal defects to explain the Cleckley type of psychopath. Several of these conjectured species of this genus are described below.

1. *Lykken's "low fear quotient" theory*. One of the first alternative proposals was my own suggestion in 1957 that the primary psychopath has an attenuated experience not of all emotional states but specifically of anxiety or fear. We are all endowed with the innate tendency to fear certain stimuli—loss of support, snake-like or spider-like objects, strangers, fire—and to associate, or *condition*, fear to stimuli and situations that have been

---

> A child with a low fear quotient, whose parents nonetheless succeed in instilling the essentials of good citizenship, would grow up to be the kind of person one would like to have on hand when stress and danger threaten.

---

previously experienced together with pain or punishment. Like all biological variables, fearfulness, or what I have called the innate "fear quotient," varies from person to person. Some individuals have a very high fear quotient and are victimized from childhood on by fearful inhibitions. It is noteworthy that such individuals are especially *unlikely* to become juvenile delinquents or adult sociopaths.

My theory of primary psychopathy is that people at the low end of this same distribution of innate fearfulness are at risk to develop primary psychopathy. The basic idea is that because much of the normal socialization process depends upon punishment of antisocial behavior and because punishment works, when it works, by the fearful inhibition of those impulses toward antisocial behavior the next time that temptation knocks, then someone who is relatively fearless will be relatively harder to socialize in this way. "Harder to socialize" does not mean "impossible to socialize," and it is interesting to note that being less fearful than the average person is not necessarily a disadvantage. A child with a low fear quotient, whose parents nonetheless succeed in instilling the essentials of good citizenship, would grow up to be the kind of person one would like to have on hand when stress and danger threaten. I believe, in short, that the hero and the psychopath may be twigs on the same genetic branch.

An example of a relatively fearless child at risk for developing an antisocial lifestyle is provided in the following excerpt from a letter I received from a single mother in August 1982 after an article of mine on fearlessness appeared in a popular magazine:

> Your article on fearlessness was very informative. I was able to identify with many of the traits. However, being thirty-six and a single parent of three children, I have managed to backpack on the "edge" without breaking my neck. I have a 14-year-old daughter who seems to be almost fearless to anything in her environment. She jumps out second-story windows. When she was in first grade, I came home from work one afternoon and found her hanging by her fingers from our upstairs window. I "calmly" asked her what she was doing. She replied that she was "getting refreshed." Later, she stated that she did things like that when she needed a lift—that she was bored and it made her feel better. Nancy is bright, witty, attractive, charismatic, and meets people easily. She tends to choose friends who are offbeat, antisocial, and into dope, alcohol, etc. During her month's visit here with me, she stole money from my purse, my bank card, etc., etc.

Another letter prompted by my article on fearlessness came from an inmate of a Florida prison, a surfer. He might qualify as a primary psychopath (although better socialized than most, in spite of his being in prison), and it seems clear that his basic attribute is relative fearlessness:

> I am an inmate at Lake Butler Reception and Medical Center, serving a ten year sentence for drug trafficking. Prior to my arrest and conviction, I taught in the public school system, sold real estate, and owned a construction company. In retrospect, I believe that one of the main reasons that I left teaching was the lack of risk. As you know, there is a great deal of risk associated in real estate, running a business, and there certainly is a great deal of risk in drug trafficking and smuggling. I knew a long time ago that the thrill of facing the fear of failure and succeeding were far more important to me that the financial rewards. One group of people that I am familiar with that you might find interesting is surfers. I have surfed for the past 15 years in many parts of the world, meeting surfers from all parts of the globe, and many countries. The one common thread that I find in the group is the total disregard for fear, in fact, it is as if all of us seek it for the adrenaline "rush" you can get, how close to losing your life, and still escape. Witness surfers that ride ten foot waves that break in three feet of water over an urchin-infested coral reef. There certainly is no financial reward, it all must come from the thrill. Needless to say, not all surfers are as fearless as others, but the common thread is there. For years, when smuggling "kingpins" have wanted fearless men to do the actual smuggling, they often have chosen their men from the ranks of the surfing population. It is no accident that many "kingpins" are surfers or ex-surfers themselves.

Another illustrative case is that of Kody Scott, also known as Sanyka Shakur, who was a member of the Eight-Tray Gangster Crips in South Central Los Angeles, where he was known as "Monster"; he is currently serving a seven-year sentence in solitary confinement in a northern California prison. His autobiography required little editing because Monster is intelligent and remarkably articulate, especially considering his negligible education. Kody was initiated into the Eight-Trays when he was twelve and shot his first victim that same night. The name "Monster" resulted from an incident in Kody's early teens, in which a victim Kody was mugging attempted to fight back: Kody stomped him to a bloody pulp.

Kody's mother, Birdie, at twenty-one was a single mother of two, living in Houston, when she met a thirty-three-year-old visitor from Los Angeles; she later moved there to marry him. The marriage was unstable and violent, but Birdie produced four more children before it broke up. One of these four, Kody, was fathered by a professional football player with the L.A. Rams with whom Kody's mother had a brief affair. Kody never knew his biological father, and his mother's husband had gone for good by the time Kody was six.

Kody's mother was a hard worker, mostly at bartending jobs, and the family's circumstances were lower middle class, with the mother, six children, and miscellaneous animals living in a two-bedroom house. There were gangs in the vicinity, and an older brother was briefly involved while in seventh grade; he was caught stealing a leather jacket and spent a night in a juvenile detention center; that one experience stayed with him and he never joined a gang. Kody was different; as M. Horowitz reported in the December 1993 issue of *Atlantic Monthly*:

> Kody was always the daredevil. "He was like a demolition derby," his sister Kendis says, "reckless, wild, and intriguing." "He had no fear," says his older brother Kerwin. Kody built wooden ramps on the street and raced his bike at top speeds, jumping crates like a junior Evil Knieval. "No one else would do it," Kerwin says, "but he would."

A bright, muscular, adventurous boy with no fear and no father, a boy who might have become a professional athlete if his real father had been there to guide and inspire him, or a boxer or policeman or soldier, perhaps even an astronaut—but he became "Monster" instead, a classic example of primary psychopathy in its second-most dangerous form. (The most dangerous form is exemplified by Ted Bundy, the handsome, ingratiating serial killer whose psychopathy was compounded with a perverse sexualized blood lust.) Although they were reared without a father in the same gang-infested neighborhood as was Kody Scott, his siblings were apparently adequately socialized; this is why I would classify him as a psychopath rather than a sociopath, although he exemplifies the frequent overlap between the two groups.

5. ❖ DYNAMICS OF PERSONAL ADJUSTMENT: THE INDIVIDUAL AND SOCIETY

Suppose that Kody Scott's football-player father had started teaching his daredevil son the rudiments of that game when Kody was very small. Suppose his father had enrolled him in a Little League team and shared his triumphs and disappointments with him. What committed Kody to a life of crime early on was his discovery that he was good at it, that he could dominate other boys, beat people up, become feared and respected by his peers. What if he had learned instead that he could dominate and be respected on the football field? I think he might have learned in that context that it is more gratifying to win within the rules than by flouting them. Punishment is an inefficient means of socializing the potential psychopath, whereas pride is an incentive that works as well with him as with anyone.

2. *The Neurobehavioral Theories of Fowles and Gray.* The English psychologist Jeffrey Gray has identified in the brain what he calls the "Behavioral Inhibition System" (BIS), which is activated by cues associated with fear or with "frustrative nonreward" (not getting the expected reward) and which produces the experience of anxiety and the inhibition of ongoing behavior. The BIS organizes passive avoidance by inhibiting previously punished responses, inhibiting the child's impulse to hit someone or take something not his own or to otherwise break the rules.

Another mechanism, the Behavioral Activation System (BAS), a term introduced by the American psychologist Don Fowles, is activated by stimuli associated with reward or with escape from fear or pain. The BAS organizes approach behavior and also active avoidance, that is, behavior to escape from threat. Where freezing in place would be passive avoidance, attacking the threat or running away from it are two examples of active avoidance. Both Gray and Fowles noted that there are individual differences in the strength or reactivity of the BIS and that persons with a relatively weak BIS might show poor passive avoidance, low general anxiety, and the other characteristics of the primary psychopath. This formulation will be seen to be quite similar to my low-fear hypothesis.

Fowles and Gray have also noted that persons with an unusually strong or overreactive BAS might also manifest poor passive avoidance; that is, their normal inhibitions may often be overcome by their abnormally strong desires for the forbidden object or activity. This *secondary psychopath* appears to behave impulsively due to this failure of passive avoidance, and he is likely to get into trouble as a result. Unlike the primary psychopath, however, he is anxious during or after the commission of his crimes (assuming that he has a normal BIS) and is likely to make a poor adjustment to the stresses of prison life.

Also unlike the primary type, the secondary psychopath is likely to show anxiety, irritability, and tension because the lure of temptation leads him to select a stressful and disquieting lifestyle. Whether he would tend to be as free of guilt and empathic feeling as the primary type will depend on the extent to which his difficult behavior as a child disrupted his parents' attempts to socialize him.

3. *Inhibitory Defect or Underendowment.* As I have already suggested, some psychopathic individuals appear to act impulsively, "without thinking," without giving themselves time to assess the situation, to appreciate the dangers, to foresee the consequences, or even to anticipate how they will feel about their action themselves when they have time to consider it. Although many young children tend to act impulsively, watchful parents

---

Even those with strong nervous systems can find themselves temporarily vulnerable when their protective inhibition has been exhausted by an extended period of overuse.

---

will reward more deliberate behavior and, if necessary, interrupt and punish heedless, thoughtless actions because teaching self-control is a part of the socialization process. Once again, however, self-control training is much harder with some children than with others.

Lesions in certain brain areas can cause a decrease in inhibitory control in animals and also in humans; the case of Phineas Gage is one example. Gage was the foreman of a nineteenth-century railway track crew until a construction accident drove a steel rod through his head, destroying much of his frontal lobes. A conscientious worker prior to the accident, Gage subsequently became "fitful, irreverent, indulging at times in the grossest profanity (which had not previously been his custom), manifesting but little deference for his fellows, impatient of restraint or advice when it conflicts with his desires, . . . capricious."

Neurologist A. R. Damasio and colleagues recently described a thirty-five-year-old professional man, "EVR," who was successful and happily married and "who led an impeccable social life, and was a role model to younger siblings." EVR developed a brain tumor that required surgical excision of the frontal orbital (behind the eyes) brain cortex on both sides. After recovery his IQ and memory test scores were uniformly in the superior range, and his performance on several other tests designed to detect frontal lobe damage was entirely normal. EVR's social conduct, however, "was profoundly affected by his brain injury. Over a brief period of time, he entered disastrous business ventures (one of which led to predictable bankruptcy), and was divorced twice (the second marriage, which was to a prostitute, only lasted 6 months). He has been unable to hold any paying job since the time of surgery, and his plans for future activity are defective." Previously a model citizen, EVR now meets criteria for primary psychopathy.

These findings do not, of course, demonstrate that all—or even many—primary psychopaths have lesions or qualitative defects in their frontal cortex areas; they demonstrate merely that frontal lesions can produce a syndrome very similar to primary psychopathy.

4. *The Hysterical Psychopath.* Individuals with a special talent for Freudian repression may be able to avoid fearful apprehension or escape the pangs of guilt simply by repressing awareness of distressing stimuli, including memories or ideas that elicit these unpleasant feelings. Repression involves an inhibition not of overt responding but of the processes of perception, recall, and cognitive processing. All of us have this ability to shut out or attenuate painful or distracting stimuli, whether from internal or external sources, but as is true of all abilities, this one is distributed in varying degrees among different people. Those who are underendowed with this inhibitory capacity, who have what Ivan Pavlov called "weak nervous systems" (or defective "shields," in the idiom of *Star Trek*), are especially vulnerable to the slings and arrows of outrageous fortune and seek sheltered and protective environments.

Even those with strong nervous systems can find themselves temporarily vulnerable (shields down) when their protective inhibition has been exhausted by an extended period of overuse. Most people would agree that they are more irritable, more distractable, more sensitive to pain, and the like, at the end of a tiring day than when they are well rested. One of my colleagues for many years conducted studies of the effect of noise on human hearing and hired healthy undergraduates to sit in a large room filled with loudspeakers that intermittently produced extended blasts of 120-decibel white noise. The subjects could read or try to relax during their six-hour session except while undergoing periodic hearing tests. Subjects willing to tolerate these conditions were presumably self-selected for having strong nervous systems; they were healthy and resilient young people who felt relatively invulnerable to strong stimulation. However, a common report of these subjects was that, after completing a day's stint in this simulated boiler factory, they felt irritable, nervous, unable to relax, and overresponsive to noises; they had difficulty sleeping that first night.

A child unusually well-endowed with such inhibitory capacity might grow up to look very like a fearless, guilt-free psychopath, not because of a lack of these emotional reactions but, rather, because of the ability to shut out or block these feelings—as long as the shields were up. One such person was Donna, whom I met in 1953 when I was a graduate student in the Psychiatry Department of the Minneapolis General Hospital. At that time the hospital boasted one full-time psychologist, a part-time psychiatrist (the Chief, who came around three mornings a week to do rounds and to push the button on the electroconvulsive shock machine), and lots of very crazy patients. In the summer of 1953, the psychologist went off for a three-month tour of Europe while I took her place, trying not to look too foolish to the veteran psychiatric nurses who really ran the place. Donna was a tall, thin nineteen-year-old made by the same firm that created the actress Audrey Hepburn. It was hard to believe that Donna was in the psychiatric ward on referral from the county jail; she had been picked up with a man trying to burglarize a pharmacy for drugs. It was almost impossible to believe that Donna was a heroin addict who had spent the previous three months in Chicago, working as a prostitute to support her pimp and her habit.

You must picture a shy, tremulous, soft-spoken young woman, demure and vulnerable, who could hardly bring herself to speak of these experiences, just as I could hardly imagine her enacting them. The court agreed to put Donna on probation contingent on my taking her as a patient, and the head of psychiatry at the University Hospital agreed to have her transferred there when the summer was over. I saw her daily for the six weeks that she remained an inpatient, then once a week for several months, then intermittently over the next fifteen years.

During those years Donna completed a kind of rake's progress in reverse, from prostitute and heroin addict to becoming the star turn at a local lesbian bar to a serious relationship with a black Army lieutenant and finally to a reasonably stable marriage with a young musician. There was much backsliding along the way, binges of wild self-indulgence, impromptu romances, unplanned trips with new acquaintances. I would not hear from her for months at a time, and then I would hear a faint, frightened voice on the phone: "Dr. Lykken? Can I see you?" I would pry out of her a summary of what she had been up to this time, and always the protagonist of those wild adventures seemed unconnected to the farouche and vulnerable girl who was reluctantly recounting them. It was hard to believe that the person I had come to know was capable of doing the things that other Donna did; my Donna could barely talk about them, much less do them. I saw the other Donna just once, when she dropped in for an unscheduled social visit; it was the only time I saw her laugh or heard her swear. Having burned thus fitfully but at both ends, Donna's candle guttered out; she died of uterine cancer when she was thirty-six.

It is noteworthy that alleged examples of multiple personality, such as the patient described in Cleckley and Thigpen's *The Three Faces of Eve*, often include at least one personality, like Eve Black, one of Eve's three "faces," who appears to be a psychopath. (I doubt that Donna was a true multiple since in her timid state she seemed fully aware of what had happened in her bold state, and

5. ❖ DYNAMICS OF PERSONAL ADJUSTMENT: THE INDIVIDUAL AND SOCIETY

vice versa.) It may also be relevant that hysterical personality disorder may have a familial linkage to psychopathy, occurring in higher-than-normal frequency among the relatives of psychopaths. It is also thought that hysterics often are the sex or marriage partners of psychopaths, due to the former's tendency to repress awareness of the dangers of such liaisons, but this assortative-mating hypothesis has not been systematically investigated.

Sociopathy and Crime

> Thus, when it comes to the homicidal violence of the contemporary inner city, we are dealing with very bad boys from very bad homes, kids who in most cases have suffered or witnessed violent crimes in the past. These juveniles are not criminally depraved because they are economically deprived; they are totally depraved because they are completely unsocialized.
>
> —J. J. DiIulio, Jr., 1995

Is crime increasing? The U.S. Department of Justice manages two statistical programs for measuring crime, and they paint very different pictures, one reassuring and the other, perhaps, more realistic. The National Crime Victimization Survey (NCVS), begun in 1973, interviews all persons aged twelve or over in a stratified sample of U.S. households, asking who had been victims of various specified crimes. In 1992, for example, most teenagers and adults in 52,000 households nationwide were interviewed, in person or by phone, some 108,000 people altogether. The victimization data suggest that the rate of aggravated assaults (the most common of violent crimes) increased by only 6 percent from 1973 to 1992. Victimization by theft actually decreased by some 35 percent. Although most Americans believe that their homes and streets are more at risk with each passing year, the truth is otherwise—if we can believe the Bureau of Justice Statistics.

The other federal crime-counting program, the FBI's Uniform Crime Report (UCR), provides data on crimes actually reported to the police and then, by local and state police agencies, reported to the FBI. According to the FBI data, the rate of aggravated assaults has increased substantially, more than doubling over the same twenty-year period. Most citizens are inclined to believe, with the FBI, that crime rates have gone up sharply since the 1970s. This is presumably why the U.S. Congress is appropriating still more tens of billions of dollars to combat crime. Citizens, of course, as well as politicians, can be wrong in the impressions gleaned from news reports. I think, however, that they are right in this case, that the FBI statistics tell the truest story in this important instance.

Part of the explanation for the discrepancy between the victimization and FBI trendlines was pointed out in a recent study of violence in the United States by the National Research Council (NRC). The problem with victim surveys is that they undersample those people in the population who are most vulnerable to violent crime. Victims who are currently in jail or in the hospital, and also those who are transients or homeless, do not turn up in household surveys, but if they have been victims of serious crimes, that event is likely to be known to the police. More important, in our inner cities, where crime and violence is most rampant, there are housing projects and, indeed, whole neighborhoods where the survey interviewers are unlikely to venture. Most of the serious crimes tabulated by the FBI occur in urban ghettos, and this is where crime rates have been going up. These same areas are undersampled by NCVS interviewers, and this explains much of the difference between the UCR and NCVS trend lines. The NCVS data tell us about crime in the vast middle-class community where crime rates have been relatively level, while the NRC data—and the nightly television news reports—give us the whole picture, middle-class and also ghetto crime. In 1995, Minneapolis set a new record for number of homicides, but more than two-thirds of those victims (and of their killers) were young, black males, members of the underclass.

The rates of violent crime among the middle class *should have* decreased substantially over the past twenty years for two reasons: (1) The proportion of the population who are elderly has increased, while (2) the proportion of young males, the group that furnishes most criminal predators, has sharply decreased due to the aging of the baby boomers. The people at highest risk to be victims of violent crime are the young; in the United States, those aged fifteen to twenty-four, for example, are ten to fifteen times more likely to be assaulted, robbed, or murdered than are persons aged sixty-five or older. From 1973 to 1992, the proportion of relatively protected seniors in the population increased more than 20 percent, while the proportion of young males aged fifteen to twenty-four—the potential perpetrators—decreased nearly 30 percent.

If we divided the total number of joggers by the total population each year from 1973, it is likely that the jogging-rate trend might also be surprisingly flat because there are proportionately fewer young people now than in 1973 and most of the growing proportion of seniors are at low risk for jogging. But who can doubt that there are relatively more young and middle-aged joggers out there now than twenty-odd years ago? And there are relatively more—many more—violent criminals out there now as well.

The U.S. murder rate is an especially reliable statistic since nearly all murders are reported to the police, who report them in turn to the FBI. The trend since 1973 in murders coincides nicely with the victimization data for other violent crimes; the murder rate has increased only slightly over the past two decades. But in 1973, the murder rate was double what it had been in 1960 (in New

York City, the increase was 400 percent), largely because the proportion of the U.S. population who were males in the most violent age group increased by a third from 1960 to 1973 as the post–World War II baby boomers passed through the ages of highest risk. In 1960, most murders were family affairs, spouse killing spouse and the like. Since then, as the relative numbers of unsocialized young males increased, the number of "stranger murders" has increased apace until now, in our cities, for every victim murdered by a family member there are four persons murdered by strangers.

Beginning about 1980, as the fraction of the population in the high-risk age group started to return to 1960 levels and below, the murder rate should have decreased again—but it did not; the murder rate has actually increased somewhat during the past ten years. Although the proportion of the total population who are young males has decreased substantially in this period, the rate at which those in this murderous age group have been arrested for homicide increased 55 percent from 1973 to 1992. Meanwhile, the proportion of seniors, who are relatively protected from violent crime, has increased by 20 percent. The next male you encounter on the street will be about 30 percent less likely to be aged fifteen to twenty-four than in 1973, but if he is in that age group, he will be 55 percent more likely to be—or to become—a murderer.

The juvenile crime rate, violent crimes committed by offenders under age eighteen, also has increased in recent years. The number of juveniles arrested for aggravated assault in the United States per 100,000 juveniles in the surveyed population increased more than 130 percent from 1973 to 1992 according to FBI age-specific arrest-rate figures. Could this frightening trend be a statistical artifact? Perhaps, but only if we assume that the police for some reason failed to locate and arrest more than half of the juvenile perpetrators in 1973 but not in recent years. More than 200,000 boys between twelve and seventeen years old were arrested in 1992 in the U.S. for murder, forcible rape, aggravated assault, or robbery. By now, most of them are back on the streets with long careers of active predation still ahead of them.

Reared without Fathers

The most urgent domestic challenge facing the United States at the close of the twentieth century is the re-creation of fatherhood as a vital social role for men. At stake is nothing less than the success of the American experiment. For unless we reverse the trend of fatherlessness, no other set of accomplishments—not economic growth or prison construction or welfare reform or better schools—will succeed in arresting the decline of child well-being and the spread of male violence. To tolerate the trend of fatherlessness is to accept the inevitability of continued societal recession.

—David Blankenhorn, 1995

The majority of these young criminals are not psychopaths, however. Psychopaths are relatively rare; they can be dangerous, although many are not violent, and I believe that some of them could have been transmuted from a major liability into a useful asset to society by truly skillful parenting. Most recidivistic criminals are *sociopaths*, and sociopaths are just as dangerous and, because of their numbers, an even greater social liability than psychopaths. They are why we lock our doors, stay off the streets at night, carry Mace, and invest in guns and guard dogs and electronic surveillance systems. We are currently producing sociopaths with factory-like efficiency in the United States. Although we do not know how to cure sociopathy, I think we can figure out what needs to be done to prevent it.

Our species was designed by natural selection to live relatively amicably in extended-family groups. Just as we evolved an innate readiness for learning language, so we evolved a proclivity for learning and obeying basic social rules, for nurturing our children and helping our neighbors, and for pulling our own weight in the group effort for survival. But like the ability to acquire language, our innate readiness to become socialized in these ways must be elicited, developed, and practiced during childhood, otherwise we would remain permanently mute and also, perhaps, permanently unsocialized.

In her novel *Breathing Lessons*, Anne Tyler imagines the thoughts of a new mother:

> Wait. Are they going to let me just walk off with him? I don't know beans about babies! I don't have a license to do this.... I mean you're given all these lessons for the unimportant things—piano-playing, typing. You're given years and years of lessons in how to balance equations, which Lord knows you will never have to do in normal life. But what about parenthood? ... Before you can drive a car you need a state-approved course of instruction, but driving a car is nothing, nothing, compared to... raising up a new human being.

In ancestral times, as in traditional societies that still exist today, parents had help from the extended family. With all those uncles and aunts and older children keeping an eye on them, it was hard for the youngsters to get away with much. Moreover, in those societies, this sharing of parental responsibilities provided training in parenting for children as they grew up. In what we call the developed societies of today, although parenting is widely regarded as one of the most difficult as well as the most important of adult responsibilities, it is a task we expect most young people to assume with no training whatever. If we were truly "developed," every high school would include a required course emphasizing the rigors and responsibilities of parenthood and every community college would offer practicum courses for new parents or parents-to-be.

Traditional societies in which children are socialized communally, in the manner to which our species is evolutionarily adapted, have little intramural crime, and any persistent offender is likely to be someone whose innate temperament made him unusually difficult to socialize. These are the people I call psychopaths. Our modern society now entrusts this basic responsibility of socializing children either to the two biological parents collaborating as a team or, with increasing frequency, to single parents, usually single mothers, often single mothers who are immature or unsocialized themselves.

The feral products of indifferent, incompetent, or overburdened parents—the sociopaths—are growing rapidly in number because the proportion of this nation's children who are being reared by (or, rather, domiciled with) such parents is increasing rapidly. Males aged fifteen to twenty-five are responsible for 60 percent of all violent crime in the United States. The proportion of those in this age group who were born out-of-wedlock increased from 4 percent in 1973 to 12 percent in 1992; the proportion whose parents divorced prior to the boy's fifth birthday also tripled over the same period. Most of the first group and many of the second were raised without significant participation of their biological fathers. We know that about 70 percent of the adults and juveniles currently incarcerated were reared without their biological fathers, and we can compute from this that fatherless young males are about *seven times* more likely to become first delinquent and then criminal than are boys reared by both biological parents. The proportion of the high-risk age group whose fathers planted their seed and then moved on has been growing exponentially since the early 1970s.

This is, incidentally, an added reason for believing the crime trends reported by the UCR; if boys reared without fathers are therefore seven times more likely to become criminal, and if the proportion of young males reared without fathers has trebled in the last twenty years, then surely the crime rate has increased, as the UCR indicates, rather than stayed level, as certain ostrich-like commentators would have us believe.

Is There a Solution?

> The idea that every woman has an inherent right to have a child, regardless of other considerations, recurs in every upsurge of feminism. I do not consider this a viable option.
>
> —Margaret Mead, 1979

Causing the existence of a human being is one of the most responsible actions in the range of human life. To undertake this responsibility—to bestow a life which may be either a curse or a blessing—unless the being on whom it is to be bestowed will have at least the ordinary chances of a desirable existence, is a crime against that being.

—John Stuart Mill, 1859

Because there is no cure for adult sociopathy, the only useful option is prevention. Gerald Patterson, at the Oregon Social Learning Center, has shown that at least some high-risk parents can be trained to competently socialize their children, but the process is laborious and only a few of those who need such training can be expected to participate. A system of professionalized foster care will be required to salvage most of these children, but no such system currently exists on the scale required. In many states, statutes prevent transracial adoption or foster care and child-protection workers are encouraged to return abused or neglected children to their biological mother or, if the mother is in prison or hopelessly addicted, to the grandparent who failed to socialize that mother in the first place.

Providing healthy and successful rearing environments for the millions of American children now being incompetently reared will be very expensive, but not providing them will be more expensive still. In his important new book, *Licensing Parents,* child psychiatrist Jack Westman estimates that each typical sociopath will cost society about $3 million over the course of his lifetime. That means that each million potential sociopaths now out there on the production line of our American crime factory will end up costing us $3 trillion by the middle of the next century.

The only long-term solution, I believe, is Westman's proposal that we require prospective parents to meet the same minimum requirements that we now expect of couples hoping to adopt a baby: a mature man and woman, sufficiently committed to parenthood to be married to each other, who are self-supporting and neither criminal nor actively psychotic. Such a licensure requirement would offend those who believe that people have an inalienable right to produce as many babies as they wish, no matter how incompetent, immature, abusive, or depraved they may be. Because I am more concerned about the rights of those helpless babies than I am about the alleged procreative rights of their feckless parents—and about the lives of crime, violence, and social dependency that most of these babies are doomed to lead when they grow up—I shall testify in support of a parental licensure bill to be introduced at the next session of the Minnesota State Legislature. The only sanction proposed in this bill for unlicensed parents who produce a child is periodic visits by child-protection caseworkers who will do an annual audit of each child's physical, social, and educational progress. By the time my own grandchildren have grown up, I believe that the incidence of delinquency, school dropout, teenage pregnancy, substance abuse, and other social pathology will be so much greater among these at-risk children than among the children of licensed parents that Minnesotans and their legislative representatives will recognize the need to take one further step. That step, I suggest, should be to take custody of babies born to unlicensed mothers, before bonding occurs, and to place them for adoption or permanent care by professionally trained and supervised foster parents. The result should be a society in which all children are reared by an adult couple, self-supporting and socialized themselves, and thus—unlike millions of American babies today—with a real chance to achieve the American birthright of life, liberty, and the pursuit of happiness.

SUGGESTED FURTHER READING

D. Blankenhorn. *Fatherless America: Confronting Our Most Urgent Social Problem.* New York: Basic Books, 1995.

H. Cleckley. *The Mask of Sanity.* Rev. ed. St. Louis, Mo.: C. V. Mosby, 1982.

R. D. Hare. *Without Conscience: The Disturbing World of the Psychopaths among Us.* New York: Pocket Books, 1993.

D. T. Lykken. *The Antisocial Personalities.* Mahwah, N.J.: Erlbaum, 1995.

G. R. Patterson, J. B. Reid, and T. J. Dishion. *Antisocial Boys.* Eugene, Oreg.: Castalia, 1992.

S. Shakur (AKA Monster Kody Scott). *Monster: The Autobiography of an L.A. Gang Member.* New York: Atlantic Monthly Press, 1993.

J. C. Westman. *Licensing Parents: Can We Prevent Child Abuse and Neglect?* New York: Plenum Press, 1994.

J. Q. Wilson and R. J. Herrnstein. *Crime and Human Nature.* New York: Simon & Schuster, 1985.

Portions of this article were taken, with permission, from my book *The Antisocial Personalities* (Mahwah, N.J.: Erlbaum Associates, 1995).

David T. Lykken is a professor of psychology at the University of Minnesota, where he is director of the Minnesota Twin Registry. He is a past president of the Society for Psychophysiological Research, and in 1990 he received the American Psychological Association's Award for Distinguished Contribution to Psychology in the Public Interest. Dr. Lykken is the author of A Tremor in the Blood: Uses and Abuses of the Lie Detector *(1981) and of* The Antisocial Personalities *(1995).*

Mixed Blood

Race is an immutable biological given, right? So how come the author's daughter can change her race just by getting on a plane? Because race is a social classification, not a biological one. We might just have categorized people according to body type rather than skin color. As for all those behavioral differences attributed to race, like I.Q.—don't even ask.

Jefferson M. Fish, Ph.D.

Jefferson M. Fish, Ph.D., is a professor of psychology at St. John's University, in New York.

Last year my daughter, who had been living in Rio de Janeiro, and her Brazilian boyfriend paid a visit to my cross-cultural psychology class. They had agreed to be interviewed about Brazilian culture. At one point in the interview I asked her, "Are you black?" She said, "Yes." I then asked him the question, and he said "No."

"How can that be?" I asked. "He's darker than she is."

Psychologists have begun talking about race again. They think that it may be useful in explaining the biological bases of behavior. For example, following publication of *The Bell Curve,* there has been renewed debate about whether black-white group differences in scores on IQ tests reflect racial differences in intelligence. (Because this article is about race it will mainly use racial terms, like black and white, rather than cultural terms, like African-American and European-American.)

The problem with debates like the on[e] over race and IQ is that psychologists on both sides of the controversy make a totally unwarranted assumption: that there is a biological entity called "race." If there were such an entity, then it would at least be possible that differences in behavior between "races" might be biologically based.

Before considering the controversy, however, it is reasonable to step back and ask ourselves "What is race?" If, as happens to be the case, race is not a biologically meaningful concept, then looking for biologically based racial differences in behavior is simply a waste of time.

The question "What is race?" can be divided into two more limited ones. The answers to both questions have long been known by anthropologists, but seem not to have reached other social or behavioral scientists, let alone the public at large. And both answers differ strikingly from what we Americans think of as race.

The first question is "How can we understand the variation in physical appearance among human beings?" It is interesting to discover that Americans (including researchers, who should know better) view only a part of the variation as "racial," while other equally evident variability is not so viewed.

The second question is "How can we understand the kinds of racial classifications applied to differences in physical appearance among human beings?" Surprisingly, different cultures label these physical differences in different ways. Far from describing biological entities, American racial categories are merely one of numerous, very culture-specific schemes for reducing uncertainty about how people should respond to other people. The fact that Americans believe that Asians, blacks, Hispanics, and whites constitute biological entities called races is a matter of cultural interest rather than scientific substance. It tells us something about American culture—but nothing at all about the human species.

The short answer to the question "What is race?" is: There is no such thing. Race is a myth. And our racial classification scheme is loaded with pure fantasy.

Let's start with human physical variation. Human beings are a species, which means that people from anywhere on the planet can mate with others from anywhere else and produce fertile offspring. (Horses and donkeys are two different species because, even though they can mate with each other, their offspring—mules—are sterile.)

The American concept of race does not correspond to the ways physical appearance varies.

Our species evolved in Africa from earlier forms and eventually spread out around the planet. Over time, human populations that were geographically separated from one another came to differ in physical appearance. They came by these differences through three major pathways: mutation, natural selection, and genetic drift. Since genetic mutations occur randomly, different mutations occur and accumulate over time in geographically separated populations. Also, as we have known since Darwin, different geographical environments select for different physical traits that confer a survival advantage. But the largest proportion of variability among populations may well result from purely random factors; this random change in the frequencies of already existing genes is known as genetic drift.

If an earthquake or disease kills off a large segment of a population, those who survive to reproduce are likely to differ from the original population in many ways. Similarly, if a group divides and a subgroup moves away, the two groups will, by chance, differ in the frequency of various genes. Even the mere fact of physical separation will, over time, lead two equivalent populations to differ in the frequency of genes. These randomly acquired population differences will accumulate over successive generations along with any others due to mutation or natural selection.

A number of the differences in physical appearance among populations around the globe appear to have adaptive value. For example, people in the tropics of Africa and South America came to have dark skins, presumably, through natural selection, as protection against the sun. In cold areas, like northern Europe or northern North America, which are dark for long periods of time, and where people covered their bodies for warmth, people came to have light skins—light skins make maximum use of sunlight to produce vitamin D.

The indigenous peoples of the New World arrived about 15,000 years ago, during the last ice age, following game across the Bering Strait. (The sea level was low enough to create a land bridge because so much water was in the form of ice.) Thus, the dark-skinned Indians of the South American tropics are descended from light-skinned ancestors, similar in appearance to the Eskimo. In other words, even though skin color is the most salient feature thought by Americans to be an indicator of race—and race is assumed to have great time depth—it is subject to relatively rapid evolutionary change.

Meanwhile, the extra ("epicanthic") fold of eyelid skin, which Americans also view as racial, and which evolved in Asian populations to protect the eye against the cold, continues to exist among South American native peoples because its presence (unlike a light skin) offers no reproductive disadvantage. Hence, skin color and eyelid form, which Americans think of as traits of different races, occur together or separately in different populations.

Like skin color, there are other physical differences that also appear to have evolved through natural selection—but which Americans do not think of as racial. Take, for example, body shape. Some populations in very cold climates, like the Eskimo, developed rounded bodies. This is because the more spherical an object is, the less surface area it has to radiate heat. In contrast, some populations in very hot climates, like the Masai, developed lanky bodies. Like the tubular pipes of an old-fashioned radiator, the high ratio of surface area to volume allows people to radiate a lot of heat.

In terms of Americans' way of thinking about race, lanky people and rounded people are simply two kinds of whites or blacks. But it is equally reasonable to view light-skinned people and dark-skinned people as two kinds of "lankys" or "roundeds." In other words, our categories for the racial classification of people arbitrarily include certain dimensions (light versus dark skin) and exclude others (rounded versus elongated bodies).

There is no biological basis for classifying race according to skin color instead of body form or according to any other variable, for that matter. All that exists is variability in what people look like—and the arbitrary and culturally specific ways different societies classify that variability. There is nothing left over that can be called race. This is why race is a myth.

Skin color and body form do not vary together: Not all dark-skinned people are lanky; similarly, light-skinned people may be lanky or rounded. The same can be said of the facial features Americans think of as racial—eye color, nose width (actually, the ratio of width to length), lip thickness ("evertedness"), hair form, and hair color. They do not vary together either. If they did, then a "totally white" person would have very light skin color, straight blond hair, blue eyes, a narrow nose, and thin lips; a "totally black" person would have very dark skin color, black tight curly hair, dark brown eyes, a broad nose, and thick lips; those in between would have—to a correlated degree—wavy light brown hair, light brown eyes, and intermediate nose and lip forms.

Race is just one culture-specific scheme for reducing uncertainty about how people should respond.

While people of mixed European and African ancestry who look like this do exist, they are the exception rather than the rule. Anyone who wants to can make up a chart of facial features (choose a location with a diverse population, say, the New York City subway) and verify that there are people with all possible admixtures of facial features. One might see someone with tight curly blond hair, light skin, blue eyes, broad nose, and thick lips—whose features are half "black" and half "white." That is, each of the person's facial features occupies one end or the other of a supposedly racial continuum, with no intermediary forms

33. Mixed Blood

(like wavy light brown hair). Such people are living proof that supposedly racial features do not vary together.

Since the human species has spent most of its existence in Africa, different populations in Africa have been separated from each other longer than East Asians or Northern Europeans have been separated from each other or from Africans. As a result, there is remarkable physical variation among the peoples of Africa, which goes unrecognized by Americans who view them all as belonging to the same race.

In contrast to the very tall Masai, the diminutive stature of the very short Pygmies may have evolved as an advantage in moving rapidly through tangled forest vegetation. The Bushmen of the Kalahari desert have very large ("steatopygous") buttocks, presumably to store body fat in one place for times of food scarcity, while leaving the rest of the body uninsulated to radiate heat. They also have "peppercorn" hair. Hair in separated tufts, like tight curly hair, leaves space to radiate the heat that rises through the body to the scalp; straight hair lies flat and holds in body heat, like a cap. By viewing Africans as constituting a single race, Americans ignore their greater physical variability, while assigning racial significance to lesser differences between them.

Although it is true that most inhabitants of northern Europe, east Asia, and central Africa look like Americans' conceptions of one or another of the three purported races, most inhabitants of south Asia, southwest Asia, north Africa, and the Pacific islands do not. Thus, the 19th century view of the human species as comprised of Caucasoid, Mongoloid, and Negroid races, still held by many Americans, is based on a partial and unrepresentative view of human variability. In other words, what is now known about human physical variation does not correspond to what Americans think of as race.

In contrast to the question of the actual physical variation among human beings, there is the question of how people classify that variation. Scientists classify things in scientific taxonomies—chemists' periodic table of the elements, biologists' classification of life forms into kingdoms, phyla, and so forth.

In every culture, people also classify things along culture-specific dimensions of meaning. For example, paper clips and staples are understood by Americans as paper fasteners, and nails are not, even though, in terms of their physical properties, all three consist of differently shaped pieces of metal wire. The physical variation in pieces of metal wire can be seen as analogous to human physical variation; and the categories of cultural meaning, like paper fasteners vs. wood fasteners, can be

153

seen as analogous to races. Anthropologists refer to these kinds of classifications as folk taxonomies.

Consider the avocado—is it a fruit or a vegetable? Americans insist it is a vegetable. We eat it in salads with oil and vinegar. Brazilians, on the other hand, would say it is a fruit. They eat it for dessert with lemon juice and sugar.

How can we explain this difference in classification?

The avocado is an edible plant, and the American and Brazilian folk taxonomies, while containing cognate terms, classify some edible plants differently. The avocado does not change. It is the same biological entity; but its folk classification changes, depending on who's doing the classifying.

Human beings are also biological entities. Just as we can ask if an avocado is a fruit or a vegetable, we can ask if a person is white or black. And when we ask race questions, the answers we get come from folk taxonomies, not scientific ones. Terms like "white" or "black" applied to people—or "vegetable" or "fruit" applied to avoca-

Americans believe in 'blood,' a folk term for the quality presumed carried by members of 'races.'

dos—do not give us biological information about people or avocados. Rather, they exemplify how cultural groups (Brazilians or Americans) classify people and avocados.

Americans believe in "blood," a folk term for the quality presumed to be carried by members of so-called races. And the way offspring—regardless of their physical appearance—always inherit the less prestigious racial category of mixed parentage is called "hypo-descent" by anthropologists. A sentence thoroughly intelligible to most Americans might be, "Since Mary's father is white and her mother is black, Mary is black because she has black 'blood.'" American researchers who think they are studying racial differences in behavior would, like other Americans, classify Mary as black—although she has just as much white "blood."

According to hypo-descent, the various purported racial categories are arranged in a hierarchy along a single dimension, from the most prestigious ("white"), through intermediary forms ("Asian"), to the least prestigious ("black"). And when a couple come from two different categories, all their children (the "descent" in "hypo-descent") are classified as belonging to the less prestigious category (thus, the "hypo"). Hence, all the offspring of one "white" parent and one "black" parent—regardless of the children's physical appearance—are called "black" in the United States.

The American folk concept of "blood" does not behave like genes. Genes are units which cannot be subdivided. When several genes jointly determine a trait, chance decides which ones come from each parent. For example, if eight genes determine a trait, a child gets four from each parent. If a mother and a father each have the hypothetical genes BBBBWWWW, then a child could be born with any combination of B and W genes, from BBBBBBBB to WWWWWWWW. In contrast, the folk concept "blood" behaves like a uniform and continuous entity. It can be divided in two indefinitely—for example, quadroons and octoroons are said to be people who have one-quarter and one-eighth black "blood," respectively. Oddly, because of hypo-descent, Americans consider people with one-eighth black "blood" to be black rather than white, despite their having seven-eighths white "blood."

Hypo-descent, or "blood," is not informative about the physical appearance of people. For example, when two parents called black in the United States have a number of children, the children are likely to vary in physical appearance. In the case of skin color, they might vary from lighter than the lighter parent to darker than the darker parent. However, they would all receive the same racial classification—black—regardless of their skin color.

All that hypo-descent tells you is that, when someone is classified as something other than white (e.g., Asian), at least one of his or her parents is classified in the same way, and that neither parent has a less prestigious classification (e.g., black). That is, hypo-descent is informative about ancestry—specifically, parental classification—rather than physical appearance.

There are many strange consequences of our folk taxonomy. For example, someone who inherited no genes that produce "African"-appearing physical features would still be considered black if he or she has a parent classified as black. The category "passing for white" includes many such people. Americans have the curious belief that people who look white but have a parent classified as black are "really" black in some biological sense, and are being deceptive if they present themselves as white. Such examples make it clear that race is a social rather than a physical classification.

From infancy, human beings learn
to recognize very subtle differences in the faces of those around them. Black babies see a wider variety of black faces than white faces, and white babies see a wider variety of white faces than black faces. Because they are exposed only to a limited range of human variation, adult members of each "race" come to see their own group as containing much wider variation than others. Thus, because of this perceptual learning, blacks see greater physical variation among themselves than among whites, while whites see the opposite. In this case, however, there is a clear answer to the question of which group contains greater physical variability. Blacks are correct.

Why is this the case?

Take a moment. Think of yourself as an amateur anthropologist and try to step out of American culture, however briefly.

It is often difficult to get white people to accept what at first appears to contradict the evidence they can see clearly with their own eyes—but which is really the result of a history of perceptual learning. However, the reason that blacks view themselves as more varied is not that their vision is more accurate. Rather, it is that blacks too have a long—but different—history of perceptual learning from that of whites (and also that they have been observers of a larger range of human variation).

The fact of greater physical variation among blacks than whites in America goes back to the principle of hypo-descent, which classifies all people with one black parent and one white parent as black. If they were all considered white, then there would be more physical variation among whites. Someone with one-eighth white "blood" and seven-eighths black "blood" would be considered white; anyone with any white ancestry would be considered white. In other words, what appears to be a difference in biological variability is really a difference in cultural classification.

Perhaps the clearest way to
understand that the American folk taxonomy of race is merely one of many—arbitrary and unscientific like all the others—is to contrast it with a very different one, that of Brazil. The Portuguese word that in the Brazilian folk taxonomy corresponds to the American "race" is "tipo." Tipo, a cognate of the English word "type," is a descriptive term that serves as a kind of shorthand for a series of physical features. Because people's physical features vary separately from one another, there are an awful lot of tipos in Brazil.

Since tipos are descriptive terms, they vary regionally in Brazil—in part reflecting regional differences in the development of colloquial Portuguese, but in part because the physical variation they describe is different in different regions. The Brazilian situation is so complex I will limit my delineation of tipos to some of the main ones used in the city of Salvador, Bahia, to describe people whose physical appearance is understood to be made up of African and European features. (I will use the female terms throughout; in nearly all cases the male term simply changes the last letter from "a" to "o.")

Proceeding along a dimension from the "whitest" to the "blackest" tipos, a *loura* is whiter-than-white, with straight blond hair, blue or green eyes, light skin color, narrow nose, and thin lips. Brazilians who come to the United States think that a *loura* means a "blond," and are surprised to find that the American term refers to hair color only. A *branca* has light skin color, eyes of any color, hair of any color or form except tight curly, a nose that is not broad, and lips that are not thick. *Branca* translates as "white," though Brazilians of this tipo who come to the United States—especially those from elite families—are often dismayed to find that they are not considered white here, and, even worse, are viewed as Hispanic despite the fact that they speak Portuguese.

A *morena* has brown or black hair that is wavy or curly but not tight curly, tan skin, a nose that is not narrow, and lips that are not thin. Brazilians who come to the United States think that a *morena* is a "brunette," and are surprised to find that brunettes are considered white but *morenas* are not. Americans have difficulty classifying *morenas*, many of whom are of Latin American origin: Are they black or Hispanic? (One might also observe that *morenas* have trouble with Americans, for not

they would draw the line between *morenas* and *mulatas*; whereas Americans, if offered only visual information, would draw the line between *brancas* and *morenas*.

The proliferation of tipos, and the difference in the white-black dividing line, do not, however, exhaust the differences between Brazilian and American folk taxonomies. There are tipos in the Afro-European domain that are considered to be neither black nor white—an idea that is difficult for Americans visiting Brazil to comprehend. A person with tight curly blond (or red) hair, light skin, blue (or green) eyes, broad nose, and thick lips, is a *sarará*. The opposite features—straight black hair, dark skin, brown eyes, narrow nose, and thin lips—are those of a *cabo verde*. *Sarará* and *cabo verde* are both tipos that are considered by Brazilians in Salvador, Bahia, to be neither black nor white.

When I interviewed my American daughter and her Brazilian boyfriend, she said she was black because her mother is black (even though I am white). That is, from her American perspective, she has "black blood"—though she is a *morena* in Brazil. Her boyfriend said that he was not black because, viewing himself in terms of Brazilian tipos, he is a *mulato* (not a *preto*).

There are many differences between the Brazilian and American folk taxonomies of race. The American system tells you about how people's parents are classified but not what they look like. The Brazilian system tells you what they look like but not about their parents. When two parents of intermediate appearance have many children in

pearance, and even includes the amazing term (for foreigners of African appearance) un blanc noir—literally, "a black white." In the classic study Patterns of Race in the Americas, anthropologist Marvin Harris gives a good introduction to the ways in which the conquests by differing European powers of differing New World peoples and ecologies combined with differing patterns of slavery to produce a variety of folk taxonomies. Folk taxonomies of race can be found in many—though by no means all—cultures in other parts of the world as well.

The American concept of race does not correspond to the ways in which human physical appearance varies. Further, the American view of race ("hypodescent") is just one among many folk taxonomies, none of which correspond to the facts of human physical variation. This is why race is a myth and why races as conceived by Americans (and others) do not exist. It is also why differences in behavior between "races" cannot be explained by biological differences between them.

When examining the origins of IQ scores (or other behavior), psychologists sometimes use the term "heritability"—a statistical concept that is not based on observations of genes or chromosomes. It is important to understand that questions about the heritability of IQ have nothing to do with racial differences in IQ. "Heritability" refers only to the relative ranking of individuals *within* a population, under given environmental conditions, and not to differences *between* populations. Thus, among the population of American whites, it may be that those with high IQs tend to have higher–IQ children than do those with low IQs. Similarly, among American blacks, it may be that those with high IQs also tend to have higher–IQ children.

In both cases, it is possible that the link betweeen the IQs of parents and children may exist for reasons that are not entirely environmental. This heritability of IQ *within* the two populations, even if it exists, would in no way contradict the average social advantages of American whites as a group compared to the average social disadvantages of American blacks as a group. Such differences in social environments can easily account for any differences in the average test scores *between* the two groups. Thus, the heritability of IQ *within* each group is irrelevant to understanding the differences *between* the groups.

Beyond this, though, studies of differences in behavior between "populations" of whites and blacks, which seek to find biological causes rather than only social ones, make a serious logical error. They assume

'When researchers study racial differences in behavior in search of biological causes, they are wasting their time.'

just accepting their appearance as a given, but asking instead "Where do you come from?" "What language did you speak at home?" "What was your maiden name?" or even, more crudely, "What *are* you?")

A *mulata* looks like a *morena*, except with tight curly hair and a slightly darker range of hair colors and skin colors. A *preta* looks like a *mulata*, except with dark brown skin, broad nose, and thick lips. To Americans, *mulatas* and *pretas* are both black, and if forced to distinguish between them would refer to them as light-skinned blacks and dark-skinned blacks, respectively.

If Brazilians were forced to divide the range of tipos, from *loura* to *preta,* into "kinds of whites" and "kinds of blacks" (a distinction they do not ordinarily make),

the United States, the children are all of one race; in Brazil they are of many tipos.

Americans believe that race is an immutable biological given, but people (like my daughter and her boyfriend) can change their race by getting on a plane and going from the United States to Brazil—just as, if they take an avocado with them, it changes from a vegetable into a fruit. In both cases, what changes is not the physical appearance of the person or avocado, but the way they are classified.

I have focused on the Brazilian system to make clear how profoundly folk taxonomies of race vary from one place to another. But the Brazilian system is just one of many. Haiti's folk taxonomy, for example, includes elements of both ancestry and physical ap-

that blacks and whites are populations in some biological sense, as sub-units of the human species. (Most likely, the researchers make this assumption because they are American and approach race in terms of the American folk taxonomy.)

In fact, though, the groups are sorted by a purely social rule for statistical purposes. This can easily be demonstrated by asking researchers how they know that the white subjects are really white and the black subjects are really black. There is no biological answer to this question, because race as a biological category does not exist. All that researchers can say is, "The tester classified them based on their physical appearance," or "Their school records listed their race," or otherwise give a social rather than biological answer.

So when American researchers study racial differences in behavior, in search of biological rather than social causes for differences between socially defined groups, they are wasting their time. Computers are wonderful machines, but we have learned about "garbage in/garbage out." Applying complex computations to bad data yields worthless results. In the same way, the most elegant experimental designs and statistical analyses, applied flawlessly to biologically meaningless racial categories, can only produce a very expensive waste of time.

As immigrants of varied physical appearance come to the United States from countries with racial folk taxonomies different from our own, they are often perplexed and dismayed to find that the ways they classify themselves and others are irrelevant to the American reality. Brazilians, Haitians, and others may find themselves labeled by strange, apparently inappropriate, even pejorative terms, and grouped together with people who are different from and unreceptive to them. This can cause psychological complications (a Brazilian immigrant—who views himself as white—being treated by an American therapist who assumes that he is not).

Immigration has increased, especially from geographical regions whose people do not resemble American images of blacks, whites, or Asians. Intermarriage is also increasing, as the stigma associated with it diminishes. These two trends are augmenting the physical diversity among those who marry each other—and, as a result, among their children. The American folk taxonomy of race (purportedly comprised of stable biological entities) is beginning to change to accommodate this new reality. After all, what race is someone whose four grandparents are black, white, Asian, and Hispanic?

Currently, the most rapidly growing census category is "Other," as increasing numbers of people fail to fit available options. Changes in the census categories every 10 years reflect the government's attempts to grapple with the changing self-identifications of Americans—even as statisticians try to maintain the same categories over time in order to make demographic comparisons. Perhaps they will invent one or more "multiracial" categories, to accommodate the wide range of people whose existence defies current classification. Perhaps they will drop the term "race" altogether. Already some institutions are including an option to "check as many as apply" when asking individuals to classify themselves on a list of racial and ethnic terms.

Thinking in terms of physical appearance and folk taxonomies helps to clarify the emotionally charged but confused topic of race. Understanding that different cultures have different folk taxonomies suggests that we respond to the question "What race is that person?" not by "Black" or "White," but by "Where?" and "When?"

MEDIA, VIOLENCE, YOUTH, AND SOCIETY

Ray Surette

Ray Surette is professor of criminal justice in the School of Public Affairs and Services, Florida International University, North Miami, and author of Media, Crime and Criminal Justice: Images and Realities.

> It is guns, it is poverty, it is overcrowding, and it is the uniquely American problem of a culture that is infatuated with violence. We love it, we glamorize it, we teach it to our children.[1]

The above testimony by Dr. Deborah Prothrow-Stith on gangs and youth violence presented before the U.S. Senate contains two important points concerning the mass media and youth violence. First, it does not mention the media as a factor in violence, lending support to the view that the media are not crucial agents in youth violence. Second, it does cite an American culture that is infatuated with violence, and the glamorization and teaching of violence to our children, as problems. Culture, glamorization, and instruction, however, are areas where the media have been shown to play important social roles. The above statement simultaneously provides support for the position that the media are indeed important players in the production of youth violence and yet paradoxically also supports the position that they are not contributors. The relative validity of these two dichotomous positions, the media as unimportant and the media as central in fostering youth violence, has dominated the public discussion, resulting in much confusion about this issue and public posturing by various groups and individuals. The actual relationship of the media to youth violence lies somewhere between these two extremes.

Research interest in the relationship of the mass media to social violence has been elevated for most of this century. Over the twentieth century, the issue of the media as a source of violence has moved into and out of

> *If a consensus has emerged from the research and public interest, it is that the media's particular relationship to social violence is extremely complicated.*

the public consciousness in predictable ten-to-twenty-year cycles. If a consensus has emerged from the research and public interest, it is that the sources of violence are complex and tied to our most basic nature as well as the social world we have created and that the media's particular relationship to social violence is extremely complicated. (See the discussion in this author's *Media, Crime, and Criminal Justice* [1992] and in *Crime and Human Nature* [1985] by J. Wilson and R. Herrnstein.)

Therefore, when discussing the nature of the relationship between the media and violence, it is important not to be myopic. Social violence is embedded in historical, social forces and phenomena, while the media are components of a larger information system that creates and distributes knowledge about the world. The media and social violence must both be approached as parts of phenomena that have numerous interconnections and paths of influence between them. Too narrow a perspective on youth violence or the media's role in its generation oversimplifies both the problem and the solutions we pursue. Nowhere is this more apparent than in the current concern about media, youth, and violence.

STATISTICS ON YOUTH VIOLENCE

The source of this concern is revealed by a brief review of the statistics of youth violence.[2] Youth violence, and particularly violent crime committed by youth, has recently increased dramatically. Today about 5 out of every 20 robbery arrests and 3 of every 20 murder, rape, and aggravated assault arrests are of juveniles. In raw numbers, this translates into 3,000 murder, 6,000 forcible rape, 41,000 robbery, and 65,000 aggravated assault arrests of youths annually.

The surge in youth criminal violence is concentrated within the past five years. During the first part of the 1980s, there was a general decline in youth arrests for both violent and property crimes. In the latter half of the 1980s, however, youth arrests increased at a pace greater than that of adults for violent crimes. Youth arrests increased substantially between 1981 and 1990 for nonaggravated assault

(72 percent), murder and nonnegligent manslaughter (60 percent), aggravated assault (57 percent), weapons violations (41 percent), and forcible rape (28 percent). Looking over a generational time span from 1965 to 1989, the arrest rate for violent crimes by youths grew between the mid-1960s and the mid-1970s but then leveled off and remained relatively constant until the late 1980s. At that time, the rate again began to increase, reaching its highest recorded level in the most recent years.

Thus, while the proportion of youth in the general population has declined as the baby-boom generation has aged, the rate of violence from our youth has increased significantly. We have fewer youth proportionately, but they are more violent and account for increased proportions of our violent crime. Attempts to comprehend and explain this change have led invariably to the mass media as prime suspects, but deciphering the media's role has not been a simple or straightforward task.

This difficulty in deciphering the media's role is due to the fact that the relationship of media to violence is complex, and the media's influence can be both direct and indirect. Research on their relationship (reported, for example, in George Comstock's 1980 study *Television in America*) has revealed that media effects that appear when large groups are examined are not predictable at the individual subject level. The media are also related to social violence in ways not usually considered in the public debate, such as their effects on public policies and general social attitudes toward violence.

Adding to the complexity of the media's relationship, there are many other sources of violence that either interact with the media or work alone to produce violence. These sources range from individual biology to characteristics of our history and culture. The importance of nonmedia factors such as neighborhood and family conditions, individual psychological and genetic traits, and our social structure, race relations, and economic conditions for the generation of violence are commonly acknowledged and analyzed, as in Jeffrey Goldstein's 1986 study *Aggression and Crimes of Violence*. The role of the mass media is confounded with these other sources, and its significance is often either lost or exaggerated. One task of this essay is thus to dispel the two popular but polarizing notions that have dominated the public debate. The first is that the media are the primary cause of violence in society. The second is that the media have no, or a very limited, effect on social violence.

The former view of the media as the source of primary effects is often advanced along with draconian policy demands such as extensive government intervention or direct censorship of the media. The counterargument to this position is supported by a number of points. The most basic is that we were a violent nation before we had mass media, and there is no evidence that the removal of violent media would make us nonviolent.[3] Some research into copy-cat crime additionally provides no evidence of a criminalization effect from the media as a cause.[4] The media alone cannot turn a law-abiding individual into a criminal one nor a nonviolent youth into a violent one. In sum, individual and national violence cannot be blamed primarily on the media, and violence-reducing policies directed only at the media will have little effect.

The latter argument, that the media have limited to no effect on levels of social violence, is structured both in posture and approach to the tobacco industry's response to research linking smoking to lung cancer and it rings just as hollow. The argument's basic approach is to expound inherent weaknesses in the various methodologies of the media-violence research and to trumpet the lack of evidence of strong, direct effects, while ignoring the persistent pattern of positive findings. Proponents of the nil effect point out that laboratory experiments are biased toward finding an effect. To isolate the effect of a single factor, in this case the media, and observe a rare social behavior, namely violence, experiments must exaggerate the link between media and aggression and create a setting that will elicit violent behavior. They therefore argue that all laboratory research on the issue is irrelevant. They continue, however, to dismiss the nonlaboratory research because of a lack of strict variable controls and designs that leave open noncausal interpretations of the results. "No effects" proponents lastly argue that while society reinforces some behaviors shown in the media such as that found in commercials, it does not condone or reinforce violence and, therefore, a violence-enhancing effect should not be expected (a view discussed in "Smoking Out the Critics," a 1984 *Society* article [21:36–40] by A. Wurtzel and G. Lometti).

In reality, the research shows persistent behavioral effects from violent media under diverse situations for differing groups.[5] Regarding the strong behavioral effects apparent in fashion and fad, effects that Madison Avenue touts, the argument of a behavioral effect only on sanctioned behavior but not on unsanctioned violence is specious. The media industry claim of having only positive behavioral effects is as valid as the tobacco industry claiming that their ads do not encourage new smokers but only persuade brand switching among established smokers. First, violence is sometimes socially sanctioned, particularly within the U.S. youth and hypermasculine culture that is the target audience of the most prominently violent media. And although the media cannot criminalize someone not having criminal predispositions, media-generated, copy-cat crime is a significant criminal phenomenon with ample anecdotal and case evidence providing a form for criminality to take.[6] The recurring mimicking of dangerous film stunts belies the argument of the media having only positive behavioral effects. It is apparent that while the media alone cannot make someone a criminal, it can change the criminal behavior of a predisposed offender.

CONFLICTING CAUSAL CLAIMS

The two arguments of primary cause and negligible cause compete for public support. These models not only posit differing causal relations between the media and violence but imply vastly different public policies regarding the media as well. The primary-cause model (fig. 1) is that of a significant, direct linear relationship between violent media and violent be-

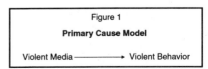

Figure 1
Primary Cause Model

Violent Media ⟶ Violent Behavior

havior. In this model, violent media, independent of other factors, directly cause violent behavior. If valid, it indicates that strong intervention is necessary in the content, distribution, and creation of violent media.

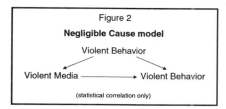

Figure 2
Negligible Cause model

The negligible-cause model (fig. 2) concedes a statistical association between the media and violent behavior but poses the connection as due not to a causal relationship but to persons predisposed to violence simultaneously seeking out violent media and more often behaving violently. As the relationship is associative and not causal in this model, policies targeted at the media will have no effects on violent behavior and the media can be safely ignored.

Both models inaccurately describe the media-violence relationship. The actual relationship between the factors is felt to be bidirectional and cyclical (fig. 3). In addition to violently predisposed people seeking out violent media and violent media causing violent behavior, violent media play a role in the generation of violently predisposed people through their effects on attitudes. And as the made-for-TV movie industry reflects, violent behavior sometimes results in the creation of more violent media. Finally, by providing live models of violence and creating community and home environments that are more inured to and tolerant of violence, violent behavior helps to create more violently predisposed youth in society. Therefore, while the direct effect of media on violence may not be initially large, its influence cycles through the model and accumulates.

An area of research that provides an example of the bidirectional model is the relationship of pornography to sexual violence; a recent (1993) overview of such research can be found in *Pornography*, by D. Linz and N. Malamuth. On one hand, the research establishes that depictions of sexual violence, specifically those that link sex with physical violence toward women, foster antisocial attitudes toward women and lenient perceptions of the crime of rape. Aberrant perceptions, such as increased belief in the "rape myth" (that women unconsciously want to be raped or somehow enjoy being raped), have been reported. Virtually none of the research, however, reveals strong direct effects from pornography, and even sexually violent media do not appear to negatively affect all male viewers. Many cultural and individual factors appear to mediate the effects and to foster the predisposition to sexually violent media and sexual violence. Researchers in this area have concluded that the media are one of many social forces that affect the development of intervening variables, such as thought patterns, sexual arousal patterns, motivations,

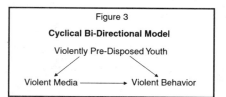

Figure 3
Cyclical Bi-Directional Model

and personality characteristics that are associated with tolerance for sexual violence and perhaps an increase in sexually violent behavior in society.[7] As in other areas of media-violence research, sexually violent media emerge as neither a primary engine nor an innocuous social factor.

THE KEY TO MEDIA EFFECTS

The key to media effects occurring in any particular instance, then, are the intermediate, interactive factors. In terms of the media, there are numerous interactive factors that have been identified as conducive to generating aggressive effects. Among the many delineated in the research, a sample includes: reward or lack of punishment for the perpetrator, portrayal of violence as justified, portrayal of the consequences of violence in a way that does not stir distaste, portrayal of violence without critical commentary, the presence of live peer models of violence, and the presence of sanctioning adults (all discussed in Comstock's *Television in America*). Only unambiguous linking of violent behavior with undesirable consequences or motives by the media appears capable of inhibiting subsequent aggression in groups of viewers.

A list of nonmedia factors deemed significant in the development of crime and the number of violently predisposed individuals can be culled from *Crime and Human Nature* by J. Wilson and R. Herrnstein. The authors list constitutional, developmental, and social-context factors including gender, age, intelligence, personality, psychopathology, broken and abusive families, schools, community, labor markets, alcohol and heroin, and finally history and culture. As can be seen, most aspects of modern life are implicated, and only tangential factors like diet and climate (which other researchers would have included) are left out. With such a large number of factors coming into play, the levels of interactions and complexity of relationships are obviously enormous.

The research on violence suggests that certain factors are basic to violent crime, as detailed by Wilson and Herrnstein. None of these factors dominates, but none are without significant effects.

Accordingly, the research (contained in this author's 1992 study *Media, Crime and Criminal Justice*) clearly signifies the media as only some of many factors in the generation of youth violence and that media depictions of violence do not affect all persons in the same way. The media contribute to violence in combination with other social and psychological factors. Whether or not a particular media depiction will cause a particular viewer to act more aggressively is not a straightforward issue. The emergence of an effect depends on the interaction between each individual viewer, the content of the portrayal, and the setting in which exposure to the media occurs. This gives the media significant aggregate effects but makes these effects difficult to predict for individuals. There is no doubt, however, that violent children, including those who come to have significant criminal records, spend more time exposed to violent media than do less violent children. The issue is not the existence of a media effect but the magnitude or importance of the effect.

Media violence correlates as strongly with and is as causally related to the magnitude of violent behavior as any other social behavioral variable that has been studied. This reflects both the media's impact and our lack of knowledge about the etiology of violence. Because of the many individual and social factors that come into play in producing any social behavior, one should not expect to find more than a modest direct relationship between the media and violence. Following their review of the research, Thomas Cook and his colleagues conclude:

> No effects emerge that are so large as to hit one between the eyes, but early measure of viewing violence adds to the predictability of later aggression over and above the predictability afforded by earlier measures of aggression. These lagged effects

A Brief History of Television and Youth Violence Research

The logic of science requires that in order to establish the causal effect of a variable, one must be able to examine a situation without the variable's effect. In terms of television and violence, this requirement means that a group of subjects (a control group) who have not been exposed to violent television is necessary for comparison with a violent television-exposed group. Television, however, is ubiquitous and an integral part of a modern matrix of influences on social behaviors. Therefore, when the interest is in the effects of television on mainstream citizens in Western industrialized and urbanized nations, finding nontelevision-exposed controls is essentially impossible. In response, artificial laboratory situations are created, or statistical controls and large data sets are employed. Thus, while social sciences abound with research reporting variables that are correlated with one another, research firmly establishing causal relationships is rare. Unlike the content of television, there are few smoking guns in social science. Rather than conclusively proven, cause is more often inferred in a trial-like decision from the predominance of evidence. Such is the case with television and violence.

In a traditional laboratory experiment, two sets of matched, usually randomly assigned, subjects are placed in identical situations except for a single factor of interest. Early research in the television-violence quest were in this vein, with the seminal ones conducted in the 1960s by researchers Bandura, Ross, and Ross.[1] These laboratory studies basically consisted of exposing groups of young children to either a short film containing violence (frequently an adult beating up an inflated Bobo doll) or a similar but nonviolent film. The two groups of children were then placed in playrooms and observed. Children who watched the film where a doll was attacked would significantly more often attack a similar doll if given the opportunity shortly after viewing their film than children who had observed a nonviolent film. These and other studies established the existence of an "observational imitation" effect from visual violence; in short, children will imitate violence they see in the media. It was concluded by many that television violence must therefore be a cause of youth violence.

However, critics of this conclusion argued that because laboratory situations are purposely artificial and contrived to isolate the influence of a single variable, the social processes producing aggression in the laboratory are not equal to those found in the real world. In summary, one cannot assume that behavior and variable relationships observed in the lab are occurring in the home or street.

In addition to the laboratory studies, at about the same time a number of survey studies were reporting positive correlations between youth aggression and viewing violent television.[2] Efforts to extend the laboratory findings and determine if the correlational studies reflected real-world causal relationships led to two types of research: natural field experiments[3] and longitudinal panel studies.

The better known and most discussed research efforts came from longitudinal panel studies conducted in the 1970s and early '80s. Expensive and time consuming, in panel studies a large number of subjects are selected and followed for a number of years. Three such studies are particularly important due to their renown, similarities in approach, and differences in conclusions.

The first study (called the Rip van Winkle study) by L. Rowell Huesmann, Leonard Eron, and their colleagues used a cross-lag panel design (that is, comparison over time and with different populations) in which television habits at grade three (approximately age eight) were correlated with aggression in grade three and with television viewing and aggression ten years later for a sample of 211 boys.[4] The researchers collected their data in rural New York State from students in the third, eighth, and "thirteenth" grades (one year after graduation). Favorite television programs were rated based on their violent content, and frequency of viewing

---

1. See, for example, A. Bandura, D. Ross, and S. A. Ross, "Transmission of Aggression through Imitation of Aggressive Models," *Journal of Abnormal and Social Psychology* 63 (1961), 575–82; and "Imitation of Film-Mediated Aggressive Models," *Journal of Abnormal and Social Psychology* 66 (1963), 3–11.

2. See G. Comstock, et al., *Television and Human Behavior* (New York: Columbia University Press, 1978) for a review.

3. Natural field experiments typically take advantage of a planned introduction of television to a previously unexposed population. This allows both a pretelevision and posttelevision comparison of the new television group and comparisons with similar but still unexposed other groups. Although rare because of the unique circumstances necessary and by definition confined to nonmainstream populations, these studies report significant increases in aggressive behavior for children who watched a lot of television in the new-television populations. See, for example, G. Granzberg, "The Introduction of Television into a Northern Manitoba Cree Community" in G. Granzberg and J. Steinberg, eds. *Television and the Canadian Indian* (Winnipeg, Manitoba; University of Winnipeg Press, 1980); and T. Williams, ed., *The Impact of Television: A Natural Experiment in Three Communities* (New York: Academic Press, 1985).

4. M. Lefkowitz, et al., "Television Violence and Child Aggression: A Follow-up Study" in G. A. Comstock and E. A. Rubinstein, eds. *Television and Social Behavior,* vol. 3, *Television and Adolescent Aggressiveness* (Washington, D.C.: U.S. Government Printing Office, 1971).

was obtained from the children's mothers in grade three and from the subjects in grades eight and thirteen. The measure of aggression was a peer-nominated rating obtained from responses to questions such as, "Who starts fights over nothing?" The most significant finding reported was a strong, positive association between violent television viewing at grade three and aggression at grade thirteen. However, this study was criticized for a number of reasons. For example, the measure of aggression used in grade thirteen was poorly worded and phrased in the past tense (i.e., "Who started fights over nothing?") and thus the answers were ambiguous in that the grade thirteen subjects may have been referring to general reputations rather than current behaviors. In addition, cross-lagged correlation analysis has a built-in bias toward finding relationships where none exist. Despite the study's weaknesses, Huesmann and Eron concluded that a causal relationship between television violence and aggression existed. This study had a strong public impact.

A second longitudinal panel study was conducted by Ronald Milavsky and his colleagues in the early 1970s that had an opposite conclusion. This study was based on surveys of about 2,400 elementary students age seven to twelve, and 403 male teenagers age twelve to sixteen in Minneapolis, Minnesota, and Fort Worth, Texas.[5] The subjects were surveyed five to six times over nineteen months. This study also used peer-nominated aggression measures for the younger group and four self-reported measures of aggression for the teenagers.[6] Unlike the "van Winkle" study, which used the children's mothers' selection of favorite programs, this study measured exposure to violent programming based on the subjects' own reports. Their analysis further controlled for earlier levels of aggression and exposure to television violence, in effect searching for evidence of significant incremental increases in youth aggression that could be attributed to past exposure to television violence after taking into account past levels of aggressive behavior.

Huesmann and Eron report meaningful lagged associations between later aggression and a number of prior conditions such as earlier aggression in a child's classroom, father's use of physical punishment, family conflict, and violent environments—but not for prior exposure to violent television. Although some significant positive relationships were found between exposure to television violence and later aggression, the overall pattern and number of findings regarding television were interpreted as inconsistent. These researchers conclude that chance, not cause, is the best explanation for their findings regarding television and aggression.

Partly in response to the Milavsky study and criticisms of their earlier methodology, Huesmann, Eron, and their colleagues conducted a third panel study (the Chicago Circle study) in the late 1970s using first and third graders in Chicago public and parochial schools as subjects.[7] Six hundred seventy-two students were initially sampled and tested for three consecutive years in two groups. One group was followed from first through third grades, the second from third through fifth grades. Aggression was measured once more by a peer-generated scale in which each child designated other children on fifteen descriptive statements, ten of which dealt with aggression. (An example is, "Who pushes and shoves other children?") Exposure to violent television was measured by asking each child to select the show most often watched and frequency of watching from eight different ten-program lists. Each list contained a mix of violent and nonviolent programs.

The study was simultaneously conducted in the United States, Australia, Finland, Israel, the Netherlands, and Poland. Their analysis of the U.S. data showed a significant general effect for television violence on girls but not for boys. However, the interaction of viewing violent television and identification with aggressive television characters was a significant predictor of male aggression. Huesmann and Eron conclude that the relationship between television violence and viewer aggression is causal and significant but bidirectional.

At this time, most reviewers of these studies and the subsequent research that followed conclude that a modest but genuine causal association does exist between media violence and aggression.[8] The fact is that, once introduced, the effect of television on a society or an individual can never be fully extricated from all the other forces that may contribute to violence. Television's influence is so intertwined with these parallel forces that searches for strong direct causal effects are not likely to be fruitful. But similar to smoking/lung cancer research, evidence of a real causal connection of some sort has been established beyond a reasonable doubt for most people.

—*R.S.*

---

5. J. Milavsky, et al., *Television and Aggression: A Panel Study* (New York: Academic Press, 1982).

6. Personal aggression toward others, aggression against a teacher (rudeness or unruliness), property aggression (theft and vandalism), and delinquency (serious or criminal behaviors).

7. See Rowell Huesmann and Leonard Eron, "Television Violence and Aggressive Behavior" in D. Pearl, L. Bouthilet, and J. Lazar, eds. *Television and Behavior: Ten Years of Scientific Progress and Implications for the 80's* (Washington, D.C., 1982); and "Factors Influencing the Effect of Television Violence on Children" in Michael Howe, ed., *Learning from Television: Psychological and Educational Research* (New York: Academic Press, 1983).

8. See, for example, L. Heath, L. Bresolin, and R. Rinaldi, "Effects of Media Violence on Children: A Review of the Literature," *Archives of General Psychiatry* 46 (1989), 376–79.

are consistently positive, but not large, and they are rarely statistically significant, although no reliable lagged negative effects have been reported.... But is the association causal? If we were forced to render a judgment, probably yes.... There is strong evidence of causation in the wrong setting (the lab) with the right population (normal children) and in the right setting (outside the lab) with the wrong population (abnormal adults).[8]

MEDIA AMONG MANY FACTORS

In summation, despite the fact that the media are among many factors, they should not be ignored, regardless of the level of their direct impact. Because social violence is a pressing problem, even those factors that only modestly contribute to it are important. Small effects of the media accumulate and appear to have significant long-term social effects.[9] The research strongly indicates that we are a more violent society because of our mass media. Exactly how and to what extent the media cause long-term changes in violent behavior remains unknown, but the fact that it plays an important, but not independent, role is generally conceded.

What public policies are suggested by the knowledge we now possess about media and violence? Not all of the factors discussed above are good candidates for public intervention strategies, but there are three sources of youth violence that government policy can influence. In order of importance, they are: extreme differences in economic conditions and the concentration of wealth in America; the American gun culture; and, exacerbating the problems created by the first two, the media's violence-enhancing messages. Family, neighborhood, and personality factors may be more important for generating violence in absolute magnitude, but they are not easily influenced by public actions.

The magnitude of economic disparity and the concentration of wealth in the United States is greater than in comparable (and, not surprisingly, less violent) societies. Our richest citizens not only earn vastly more than our poorest, but, more important, the wealth in the country is increasingly concentrated in fewer and fewer hands. The trend during this century, which accelerated during the 1980s, is for an ever-shrinking percentage of the richest Americans to control greater proportions of the country's wealth,

The fear and loathing we feel toward criminals—youthful, violent, or not—is tied to our media-generated image of criminality.

while the poorest have access to increasingly smaller proportions. The burden of these economic disenfranchisement, both psychologically and fiscally, falls heavily on the young, and especially on the young who are urban poor minorities, as is shown in Elliott Currie's 1985 study *Confronting Crime*. In a consumerism-saturated society like the United States, hopelessness, bitterness, and disregard for moral values and law are heightened by this growing economic disparity.

And as the economic polarization and violent crime have grown, we also became nationally fixated on heightening and extending our punishment capacities in an attempt to suppress violent behavior, evidenced by Diana Gordon's 1991 study *The Justice Juggernaut*. Since 1975, we have increased the rate of juvenile incarceration steadily. Today we hold in custody approximately one hundred thousand juveniles every year. Despite our strengthened capacity to punish, however, youth violence has not abated.

This result should have been expected because two social mechanisms are needed to reduce violence—punishing violent criminal behavior and rewarding law-abiding, nonviolent behavior. Societies that are more successful in balancing the two mechanisms are less violent, as shown in *Crime and Control in Comparative Perspective*, by H. Heiland and L. Shelley (1992). While punishment of violent behavior is certainly necessary and justified, its emphasis, coupled with the concentration of wealth in America, has resulted in the degrading of the equally important social capacity to reward law-abiding behavior. By emphasizing one, we have lamed and discredited the other. Nonmaterial rewards like social status, an esteemed reputation, and a clear conscience have been losing their legitimacy with the young, while material rewards for law-abiding life-styles such as careers, comfortable incomes and affordable goods are less generally available to our poorest and, not surprisingly, most crime-prone and violent citizens.

We have chosen to emphasize the mechanism, punishment, that is actually the weaker of the two in actually influencing behavior. As operant conditioning theory would predict, punishment, if severe enough, can suppress one type of violent crime. But the suppression of one behavior gives no push toward a desirable replacement activity, and a substitute violent crime will likely emerge. So "smash and grab" robberies give way to "bump and rob" holdups. Shaping behavior requires a credible reward system. In social terms, youth must see law-abiding behavior as credible and potentially rewarding as well as seeing violent behavior as potentially resulting in punishment.

The second area that government policy can immediately address is the gun culture in America. Our culture of violence, referred to in the opening quote, is made immeasurably more deadly by the enfolded gun culture. The availability of guns as cheap killing mechanisms is simply a national insanity. The mass production of these killing "toys" and the easy access to them must he addressed. The most recent statistics show that one out of every ten high school students report that they carry a handgun. Gun buyback programs should be supported, and production and availability must be reduced if a positive net effect is to he expected. Irrespective of the difficulty of controlling the sources of individual violent behavior, the implements of fatal violence should not be ignored.

The third area of policy concern, the mass media, exacerbates the gun culture by portraying guns as glamorous, effective, omnipotent devices. The mass media also heighten the negative effects of economic disparities through their consumer messages in advertising and entertainment. Although both of these effects that add to the problem of youth violence are sometimes discussed, the debate about the media remains tightly focused on measuring and reviewing violent media content. Within this focus, the emphasis has been on counting violent acts rather than on exploring the context of its portrayal. Deciphering the media's moral and value messages about violence has been mostly ignored.

EFFECTS ON CRIMINAL JUSTICE

A closer examination of the context of violence in the media would tell us that we should not try to purge the media of violence, for violent media can be good when programs teach that violence is bad. Our goal should be to reduce graphic, gratuitous, and glorified violence; to portray it not as a problem solver but as a reluctant, distasteful, last resort with tragic, unanticipated consequences. Violence shown consistently as a generator of pain and suffering, not as a personal or social panacea, would be positive media violence. Too often, violence in the media is shown

Youth violence will not be seriously reduced without violence in other aspects of our culture being addressed.

as an effective solution, and, too often, it is simply met by increased counterviolence. But, despite the recurring interest and current debate about media violence, there is little direction for the media industry regarding the context of violence and its effects. A goal should be to provide better information to the industry that details the various contexts and messages of violence and their effects.

Perhaps the most significant social effect of media violence is, however, not the direct generation of social violence but its impact on our criminal justice policy. The fear and loathing we feel toward criminals—youthful, violent, or not—is tied to our media-generated image of criminality. The media portray criminals as typically animalistic, vicious predators. This media image translates into a more violent society by influencing the way we react to all crime in America. We imprison at a much greater rate and make reentry into law-abiding society, even for our nonviolent offenders, more difficult than other advanced (and, not coincidentally, less violent) nations. The predator-criminal image results in policy based on the worst-case criminal and a constant ratcheting up of punishments for all offenders. In its cumulative effect, the media both provide violent models for our youth to emulate and justify a myopic, harshly punitive public reaction to all offenders.

Currently, the debate concerning both the media and youth violence has evolved into "circles of blame" in which one group ascribes blame for the problem to someone else in the circle. Thus, in the media circle, the public blames the networks and studios, which blame the producers and writers, who blame the advertisers, who blame the public. In the violence circle, the government blames the youth, who blame the community, which blames the schools, which blame the parents, who blame the government. A more sensible, productive process would be a shift to a "ring of responsibility" with the groups addressing their individual contributions to the problem and arriving at cooperative policies. We can't selectively reduce one aspect of violence in a violent society and expect real results. Youth violence will not be seriously reduced without violence in other aspects of our culture being addressed. In the same vein, modifying media violence alone will not have much effect but to ignore it will make efforts on other fronts less successful. Ironically, despite the fact that the media have limited independent effects on youth violence, we need to expand the focus on them. This should incorporate other social institutions, such as the media industry itself, and the social norms and values reflected in the media. We could then derive more general models of media effects and social violence.

Violence is a cultural product. The media are reflections of the culture and engines in the production process. Although they are not the only or even the most powerful causes, they are tied into the other violence-generating engines, and youth pay particular attention to them. The aggregate result of all of these forces in the United States is a national character that is individualistic, materialistic, and violence prone. If we wish to change our national character regarding violence, we cannot take on only some aspects of its genesis. We must address everything we can, such as economic inequities, the gun culture, and the glamorization of violence. And, by a slow, painful, generational process of moral leadership and example, we must work to modify the individual, family, and neighborhood factors that violently predispose youth.

In conclusion, our youth will be violent as long as our culture is violent. The local social conditions in which they are raised and the larger cultural and economic environments that they will enter generate great numbers of violently predisposed individuals. As we have experienced, violently predisposed youth, particularly among our poor, will fully develop their potential and come to prey upon us. Faced with frightful predators, we subsequently and justly punish them, but the use of punishment alone will not solve the problem. The role that the media play in the above scenario versus their potential role in deglorifying violence and showing our youth that armed aggression is not an American cultural right, will determine the media's ultimate relationship to youthful violence in society.

Notes

1. Dr. Deborah Prothrow-Stith testifying before the Senate Subcommittee on Juvenile Justice, November 26, 1991.
2. Sources of the statistics cited in this essay are drawn from "Arrests of Youth 1990," January 1992, *Office of Juvenile Justice and Delinquency Prevention Update on Statistics;* and *Sourcebook of Criminal Justice Statistics—1992,* Bureau of Justice Statistics, U.S. Department of Justice, 1993.
3. Hugh Davis Graham and Ted Robert Gurr, eds., *Violence in America* (Beverly Hills, CA: Sage, 1979).
4. See S. Milgram and R. Shotland, *Television and Antisocial Behavior: Field Experiments* (New York: Academic Press, 1973) and A. Schmid and J. de Graaf, *Violence as Communication* (Newbury Park, CA: Sage, 1982).
5. T. Cook, D. Kendzierski, and S. Thomas, "The Implicit Assumptions of Television Research," *Public Opinion Quarterly* 47: 161–201.
6. For a listing of examples see S. Pease and C. Love, "The Copy-Cat Crime Phenomenon," in *Justice and the Media* by R. Surette (Springfield, IL: Charles C. Thomas, 1984), 199–211; and A. Schmid and J. de Graaf, *Violence as Communication* (Newbury Park, CA: Sage, 1982).
7. N. Malamuth and J. Briere (1986), "Sexual Violence in the Media: Indirect Effects on Aggression against Women," *Journal of Social Issues* 42, 89.
8. T. Cook, D. Kendzierski, and S. Thomas (1993), "The Implicit Assumptions of Television Research," *Public Opinion Quarterly* 47: 191–92.
9. R. Rosenthal (1986), "Media Violence, Anti-Social Behavior, and the Social Consequences of Small Effects," *Journal of Social Issues* 42: 141–54.

ADDITIONAL READING

George Comstock, *Television in America,* Sage, Newbury Park, Calif., 1980.

Elliott Currie, *Confronting Crime,* Pantheon, New York, 1985.

Jeffrey Goldstein, *Aggression and Crimes of Violence,* Oxford University Press, New York, 1986.

Diana Gordon, *The Justice Juggernaut,* Rutgers University Press, New Brunswick, N.J., 1991.

Joshua Meyrowitz, *No Sense of Place,* Oxford University Press, New York, 1985.

Ray Surette, *Media, Crime, and Criminal Justice,* Brooks/Cole, Pacific Grove, Calif., 1992.

James Q. Wilson and Richard Herrnstein, *Crime and Human Nature,* Simon & Schuster, New York, 1985.

The Evolution of Despair

A new field of science examines the mismatch between our genetic makeup and the modern world, looking for the source of our pervasive sense of discontent

ROBERT WRIGHT

"[I] attribute the social and psychological problems of modern society to the fact that society requires people to live under conditions radically different from those under which the human race evolved..."
—THE UNABOMBER

THERE'S A LITTLE BIT OF THE UNAbomber in most of us. We may not share his approach to airing a grievance, but the grievance itself feels familiar. In the recently released excerpts of his still unpublished 35,000-word essay, the serial bomber complains that the modern world, for all its technological marvels, can be an uncomfortable, "unfulfilling" place to live. It makes us behave in ways "remote from the natural pattern of human behavior." Amen. VCRs and microwave ovens have their virtues, but in the everyday course of our highly efficient lives, there are times when something seems deeply amiss. Whether burdened by an overwhelming flurry of daily commitments or stifled by a sense of social isolation (or, oddly, both); whether mired for hours in a sense of life's pointlessness or beset for days by unresolved anxiety; whether deprived by long workweeks from quality time with offspring or drowning in quantity time with them—whatever the source of stress, we at times get the feeling that modern life isn't what we were designed for.

And it isn't. The human mind—our emotions, our wants, our needs—evolved in an environment lacking, for example, cellular phones. And, for that matter, regular phones, telegraphs and even hieroglyphs—and cars, railroads and chariots. This much is fairly obvious and, indeed, is a theme going back at least to Freud's *Civilization and Its Discontents*. But the analysis rarely gets past the obvious; when it does, it sometimes veers toward the dubious. Freud's ideas about the evolutionary history of our species are now considered—to put it charitably—dated. He hypothesized, for example, that our ancestors lived in a "primal horde" run by an autocratic male until one day a bunch of his sons rose up, murdered him and ate his flesh—a rebellion that not only miraculously inaugurated religion but somehow left a residue of guilt in all subsequent descendants, including us. Any questions?

A small but growing group of scholars—evolutionary psychologists—are trying to do better. With a method less fanciful than Freud's, they're beginning to sketch the contours of the human mind as designed by natural selection. Some of them even anticipate the coining of a field called "mismatch theory," which would study maladies resulting from contrasts between the modern environment and the "ancestral environment," the one we were designed for. There's no shortage of such maladies to study. Rates of depression have been doubling in some industrial countries roughly every 10 years. Suicide is the third most common cause of death among young adults in North America, after car wrecks and homicides. Fifteen percent of Americans have had a clinical anxiety disorder. And, pathological, even murderous alienation is a hallmark of our time. In that sense, the Unabomber is Exhibit A in his own argument.

The suburbs have been particularly hard on women.

Evolutionary psychology is a long way from explaining all this with precision, but it is already shedding enough light to challenge some conventional wisdom. It suggests, for example, that the conservative nostalgia for the nuclear family of the 1950s is in some ways misguided—that the household of Ozzie and Harriet is hardly a "natural" and healthful living arrangement, especially for wives. Moreover, the bygone American life-styles that do look fairly natural in light of evolutionary psychology appear to have been eroded largely by capitalism—another challenge to conservative orthodoxy. Perhaps the biggest surprise from evolutionary psychology is its depiction of the "animal" in us. Freud, and various thinkers since, saw "civilization" as an oppressive force that thwarts basic animal urges such as lust and aggression, transmuting them into psychopathology. But evolutionary psychology suggests that a larger threat to mental health may be the way civilization thwarts civility. There is a kinder, gentler side of human nature, and it seems increasingly to be a victim of repression.

THE EXACT SERIES OF SOCIAL CONtexts that shaped the human mind over the past couple of million years is, of course, lost in the mists of prehistory. In trying to reconstruct the "ancestral environment," evolutionary psychologists analyze the nearest approximations available—the sort of technologically primitive societies that the Unabomber extols. The most prized examples are the various hunter-gatherer societies that anthropologists have studied this century, such as the Ainu of Japan, the !Kung San of southern Africa and the Ache of South America. Also valuable are societies with primitive agriculture in the few cases where—as with some Yanomamo villages in Venezuela—they lack the contaminating contact with moderners that reduces the anthropological value of some hunter-gatherer societies.

None of these societies is Nirvana. Indeed, the anthropological record provides little support for Jean-Jacques Rousseau's notion of the "noble savage" and rather more for Thomas Hobbes' assertion that life for our distant ancestors was "nasty, brutish, and short." The anthropologist Napoleon Chagnon has written of his first encounter with the Yanomamo: "The excitement of meeting my first Indians was almost unbearable as I duck-waddled through the low passage into the village clearing." Then "I looked up and gasped when I saw a dozen burly, naked, filthy, hideous men staring at us down the shafts of their drawn arrows!" It turned out that Chagnon "had arrived just after a serious fight. Seven women had been abducted the day before by a neighboring group, and the local men and their guests has just that morning recovered five of them in a brutal club fight." The men were vigilantly awaiting retaliation when Chagnon popped in for a chat.

In addition to the unsettling threat of *mano-à-mano* violence, the ancestral environment featured periodic starvation, incurable disease and the prospect of being eaten by a beast. Such inconveniences of primitive life have recently been used to dismiss the Unabomber's agenda. The historian of science Daniel Kevles, writing in the *New Yorker*, observes how coarse the "preindustrial past" looks, Once "stripped of the gauzy romanticism of myth." Regarding the Unabomber's apparent aim of reversing technological history and some how transporting our species back toward a more primitive age, Kevles declares, "Most of us don't want to live in a society like that."

Quite so. Though evolutionary psychologists would love somehow to visit the ancestral environment, few would buy a one-way ticket. Still, to say we wouldn't want to live in our primitive past isn't to say we can't learn from it. It is, after all, the world in which our currently malfunctioning minds were designed to work like a Swiss watch. And to say we'll decline the Unabomber's invitation somehow to turn the tide of technological history isn't to say technology doesn't have its dark side. We don't have to slavishly emulate, say, the Old Order Amish, who use no cars, electricity or alcohol; but we can profitably ask why it is that they suffer depression at less than one-fifth the rate of people in nearby Baltimore.

The barbaric violence Chagnon documented is in some ways misleading. Though strife does pervade primitive societies, much of the striving is subtler than a club fight. Our ancestors, it seems, competed for mates with guile and hard work. They competed for social status with combative wordplay and social politicking. And this competition, however subtle, had Darwinian consequences. Anthropologists have shown, for example, that hunter-gatherer males successful in status competition have better luck in mating and thus getting genes into the next generation.

And getting genes into the next generation was, for better or worse, the criterion by which the human mind was designed. Mental traits conducive to genetic proliferation are the traits that survived. They are what constitute our minds today; they are us, we are designed to steer genes through a technologically primitive social structure. The good news is that doing this job entailed some quite pleasant feelings. Because social cooperation improves the chances of survival, natural selection imbued our minds with an infrastructure for friendship, including affection, gratitude and trust. (In technical terms, this is the machinery for "reciprocal altruism.") And the fact that offspring carry our genes into posterity accounts for the immense joy of parental love.

Still, there is always a flip side. People have enemies—social rivals—as well as friends, feel resentful as well as grateful, feel nervously suspicious as well as trusting. Their children, being genetic conduits, can make them inordinately proud but also inordinately disappointed, angry or anxious. People feel the thrill of victory but also the agony of defeat, not to mention pregame jitters. According to evolutionary psychology, such unpleasant feelings are with us today because they helped our ancestors get genes into the next generation. Anxiety goaded them into keeping their children out of harm's way or adding to food stocks even amid plenty. Sadness or dejection—after a high-profile social failure, say—led to soul-searching that might discourage repeating the behavior that led to the failure. ("Maybe flirting with the wives of men larger than me isn't a good idea.") The past usefulness of unpleasant feelings is the reason periodic unhappiness is a natural condition, found in every culture, impossible to escape.

What isn't natural is going crazy—for sadness to linger on into debilitating depression, for anxiety to grow chronic and paralyzing. These are largely diseases of modernity. When researchers examined rural villagers in Samoa, they discovered what were by Western standards extraordinarily low levels of cortisol, a biochemical by-product of anxiety. And when a Western anthropologist tried to study depression among the Kaluli of New Guinea, he couldn't find any.

One thing that helps turn the perfectly natural feeling of sadness or dejection into the pathology known as depression is social isolation. Today one-fourth of American households consist of a single person. That's up from 8% in 1940—and, apparently, from roughly zero percent in the ancestral environment. Hunter-gatherer societies, for all their diversity, typically feature intimacy and stability: people live in close contact with roughly the same array of several dozen friends and relatives for decades. They may move to another village, but usually either to join a new family network (as upon marriage) or to return to an old one (as upon separation). The evolutionary psychologists John Tooby and Leda Cosmides see in the mammoth popularity of the TV show *Cheers* during the 1980s a visceral yearning for the world of our ancestors—a place where life brought regular, random encounters with friends, and not just occasional, carefully scheduled lunches with them; where there were spats and rivalries, yes, but where grievances were usually heard in short order and tensions thus resolved.

As anyone who has lived in a small town can attest, social intimacy comes at the price of privacy: everybody knows your business. And that's true in spades when next-door neighbors live not in Norman Rockwell clapboard homes but in thatched huts.

Still, social transparency has its virtues. The anthropologist Phillip Walker has studied the bones of more than 5,000 children from hundreds of preindustrial cultures, dating back to 4,000 B.C. He has yet to find the scattered bone bruises that are the skeletal hallmark of "battered-child syndrome." In some modern societies, Walker estimates, such bruises would be found on more than 1 in 20 children who die between the ages of one and four. Walker accounts for this contrast with several factors, including a grim reminder of Hobbesian barbarism: unwanted children in primitive societies were often killed at birth, rather than resented and brutalized for years. But another factor, he believes, is the public nature of primitive child rearing, notably the watchful eye of a child's aunts, uncles, grandparents or friends. In the ancestral environment, there was little mystery about what went on behind closed doors, because there weren't any.

In that sense, Tooby and Cosmides have noted, nostalgia for the suburban nuclear family of the 1950s—which often accompanies current enthusiasm for "family values"—is ironic. The insular coziness of Ozzie and Harriet's home is less like our natural habitat than, say, the more diffuse social integration of Andy Griffith's Mayberry. Andy's son Opie is motherless, but he has a dutiful great-aunt to watch over him—and, anyway, can barely sit on the front porch without seeing a family friend.

The ultimate in isolating technologies is television.

---

5. ❖ DYNAMICS OF PERSONAL ADJUSTMENT: THE INDIVIDUAL AND SOCIETY

To be sure, keeping nuclear families intact has virtues that are underscored by evolutionary psychology, notably in keeping children away from stepfathers, who, as the evolutionary psychologists Martin Daly and Margo Wilson predicted and then documented, are much more prone to child abuse than biological fathers. But to worship the suburban household of the 1950s is to miss much of the trouble with contemporary life.

Though people talk about "urbanization" as the process that ushered in modern ills, many urban neighborhoods at mid-century were in fact fairly communal; it's hard to walk into a Brooklyn brownstone day after day without bumping into neighbors. It was suburbanization that brought the combination of transience and residential isolation that leaves many people feeling a bit alone in their own neighborhoods. (These days, thanks to electric garage-door openers, you can drive straight into your house, never risking contact with a neighbor.)

The suburbs have been particularly hard on women with young children. In the typical hunter-gatherer village, mothers can reconcile a homelife with a work life fairly gracefully, and in a richly social context. When they gather food, their children stay either with them or with aunts, uncles, grandparents, cousins or lifelong friends. When they're back at the village, child care is a mostly public task—extensively social, even communal. The anthropologist Marjorie Shostak wrote of life in an African hunter-gatherer village, "The isolated mother burdened with bored small children is not a scene that has parallels in !Kung daily life."

Evolutionary psychology thus helps explain why modern feminism got its start after the suburbanization of the 1950s. The landmark 1963 book *The Feminine Mystique* by Betty Friedan grew out of her 1959 conversation with a suburban mother who spoke with "quiet desperation" about the anger and despair that Friedan came to call "the problem with no name" and a doctor dubbed "the housewife's syndrome." It is only natural that modern mothers rearing children at home are more prone to depression than working mothers, and that they should rebel.

But even working mothers suffer depression more often than working men. And that shouldn't shock us either. To judge by hunter-gatherer societies, it is unnatural for a mother to get up each day, hand her child over to someone she barely knows and then head off for 10 hours of work—not as unnatural as staying home alone with a child, maybe, but still a likely source of guilt and anxiety. Finding a middle ground, enabling women to be workers and mothers, is one of the great social challenges of our day.

Much of this trouble, as the Unabomber argues, stems from technology. Suburbs are largely products of the automobile. (In the forthcoming book *The Lost City*, Alan Ehrenhalt notes the irony of Henry Ford, in his 60s, building a replica of his hometown—gravel roads, gas lamps—to recapture the "saner and sweeter idea of life" he had helped destroy.) And in a thousand little ways—from the telephone to the refrigerator to ready-made microwavable meals—technology has eroded the bonds of neighborly interdependence. Among the Aranda Aborigines of Australia, the anthropologist George Peter Murdock noted early this century, it was common for a woman to breastfeed her neighbor's child while the neighbor gathered food. Today in America it's no longer common for a neighbor to borrow a cup of sugar.

Of course, intensive interdependence also has its downside. The good news for our ancestors was that collectively fending off starvation or saber-toothed tigers forged bonds of a depth moderners can barely imagine. The bad news was that the tigers and the starvation sometimes won. Technology is not without its rewards.

Perhaps the ultimate in isolating technologies is television, especially when linked to a VCR and a coaxial cable. Harvard professor Robert Putnam, in a recent and much noted essay titled "Bowling Alone," takes the demise of bowling leagues as a metaphor for the larger trend of asocial entertainment. "Electronic technology enables individual tastes to be satisfied more fully," he concedes, but at the cost of the social gratification "associated with more primitive forms of entertainment." When you're watching TV 28 hours a week—as the average American does—that's a lot of bonding you're not out doing.

As the evolutionary psychiatrist Randolph Nesse has noted, television can also distort our self-perception. Being a socially competitive species, we naturally compare ourselves with people we see, which meant, in the ancestral environment, measuring ourselves against fellow villagers and usually finding at least one facet of life where we excel. But now we compare our lives with "the fantasy lives we see on television," Nesse writes in the recent book *Why We Get Sick: The New Science of Darwinian Medicine*, written with the eminent evolutionary biologist George Williams. "Our own wives and husbands, fathers and mothers, sons and daughters can seem profoundly inadequate by comparison. So we are dissatisfied with them and even more dissatisfied with ourselves." (And, apparently, with our standard of living. During the 1950s, various American cities saw theft rates jump in the particular years that broadcast television was introduced.)

Relief from TV's isolating and at times depressing effects may come from more communal technologies. The inchoate Internet is already famous for knitting congenial souls together. And as the capacity of phone lines expands, the Net may allow us to, say, play virtual racketball with a sibling or childhood friend in a distant city. But at least in its current form, the Net brings no visual (much less tactile) contact, and so doesn't fully gratify the social machinery in

> *The problem is that too little of our "social" contact is social in the natural, intimate sense of the word.*

our minds. More generally the Net adds to the information overload, whose psychological effects are still unknown but certainly aren't wholly benign.

This idea that modern society is dangerously asocial would surprise Freud. In *Civilization and Its Discontents,* he lamented the tension between crude animal impulses and the dictates of society. Society, he said, tells us to cooperate with one another, indeed, even to "love they neighbor as thyself"; yet by our nature, we are tempted to exploit our neighbor, "to humiliate him, to cause him pain, to torture and to kill him. *Homo homini lupus* [Man is a wolf to man]." The Unabomber, too, in his mode as armchair psychologist, celebrates our "WILD nature" and complains that in modern society "we are not supposed to hate anyone, yet almost everyone hates somebody at some time or other." This sort of cramping of our natural selves, he opines, creates "oversocialized" people. He seems to agree with Freud's claim that "primitive man was better off in knowing no restrictions of instinct."

Yet evolutionary psychology suggests that primitive man knew plenty of "restrictions of instinct." True, hatred is part of our innate social repertoire, and in other ways as well we are naturally crude. But the restraint of crude impulses is also part of our nature. Indeed, the "guilt" that Freud never satisfactorily explained is one built-in restrainer. By design, it discourages us from, say, neglecting kin through unbridled egoism, or imperiling friendships in the heat of anger—or, at the very least, it goads us to make amends after such imperiling, once we've cooled down. Certainly modern society may burden us unduly with guilt. After erupting in anger toward an acquaintance, we may not see him or her for weeks, whereas in the ancestral environment we might have reconciled in short order. Still, feeling guilty about spasms of malice is no invention of modern civilization.

This points to the most ironic of evolutionary psychology's implications: many of the impulses created by natural selection's ruthless imperative of genetic self-interest aren't selfish in any straightforward way. Love, pity, generosity, remorse, friendly affection and designing neighborhoods that foster affiliation—large common recreational spaces, extensive pedestrian thoroughfares and even, in some cases, parking spaces that make it

We are designed to seek trusting relationships.

enduring trust, for example, are part of our genetic heritage. And, oddly, some of these affiliative impulses are frustrated by the structure of modern society at least as much as the more obviously "animal" impulses. The problem with modern life, increasingly, is less that we're "oversocialized" than that we're undersocialized—or, that too little of our "social" contact is social in the natural, intimate sense of the word.

Various intellectual currents reflect this shortage of civility in modern civilization. The "communitarian" movement, lately championed by Democratic and Republican leaders alike, aims to restore a sense of social kinship, and thus of moral responsibility. And various scholars and politicians (including Putnam) are now bemoaning the shrinkage of civil society, that realm of community groups, from the Boy Scouts to the Rotary Club, that once not only kept America shipshape but met deep social needs.

The latest tribute to civil society comes in Francis Fukuyama's book *Trust,* whose title captures a primary missing ingredient in modern life. As of 1993, 37% of Americans felt they could trust most people, down from 58% in 1960. This hurts; according to evolutionary psychology, we are designed to seek trusting relationships and to feel uncomfortable in their absence. Yet the trend is hardly surprising in a modern, technology-intensive economy, where so much leisure time is spent electronically and so much "social" time is spent nurturing not friendships but professional contacts.

As scholars and public figures try to resurrect community, they might profitably draw on evolutionary psychology. Prominent communitarian Amitai Etzioni, in highlighting the shortcomings of most institutionalized child care, has duly stressed the virtues of parents' "co-oping," working part time at day-care centers. Still, the stark declaration in his book The *Spirit of Community* that "infants are better off at home" gives short shrift to the innately social nature of infants and mothers. That women naturally have a vocational calling as well as a maternal one suggests that workplace-based, cooperative day-care centers may deserve more attention.

Residential planners have begun to account implicitly for human nature. They're hard to hop from car to living room without traversing some turf in between. In effect: drive-in, hunter-gatherer villages.

Still, many nice features of the ancestral environment can't be revived with bricks and mortar. Building physically intimate towns won't bring back the extended kin networks that enmeshed our ancestors and, among other benefits, made child rearing a much simpler task than it is for many parents today. Besides, most adults, given a cozy community, will still spend much of the day miles away, at work. And even if telecommuting increasingly allows them to work at home, they won't be out bonding with neighbors in the course of their vocations, as our ancestors were.

One reason the sinews of community are so hard to restore is that they are at odds with free markets. Capitalism not only spews out cars, TVs and other antisocial technologies; it also sorts people into little vocational boxes and scatters the boxes far and wide. Economic opportunity is what drew farm boys into cities, and it has been fragmenting families ever since. There is thus a tension within conservative ideology between laissez-faire economics and family values, as various people have noted. (The Unabomber complains that conservatives "whine about the decay of traditional values," yet "enthusiastically support technological progress and economic growth.")

That much modern psychopathology grows out of the dynamics of economic freedom suggests a dearth of miracle cures; Utopian alternatives to capitalism have a history of not working out. Even the more modest reforms that are imaginable—reforms that somewhat blunt modernization's antisocial effects—will hardly be easy or cheap. Workplace-based day care costs money. Ample and inviting public parks cost money. And it costs money to create good public schools—which by diverting enrollment from private schools offer the large communal virtue of making a child's neighborhood peers and schoolyard friends one and the same. Yikes: taxes! Taxes, as Newt Gingrich and others have patiently explained, slow economic growth. True enough. But if economic growth places such a strain on community to begin with—a fact that Gingrich seems to grasp—what's so bad about a marginally subdued rate of growth?

Besides, how large is the psychological toll? Evolutionary psychology suggests that we're designed to compare our material well-being not so much with some absolute standard but with that of our neighbors. So if our neighbors don't get richer—and if the people on *Lifestyles of the Rich and Famous* don't get richer—then we shouldn't, in theory, get less happy than we already are. Between 1957 and 1990, per capita income in America more than doubled in real terms. Yet, as the psychologist David Myers notes in *The Pursuit of Happiness,* the number of Americans who reported being "very happy" remained constant, at one-third. Plainly, more gross domestic product isn't the answer to our deepest needs. (And that's especially true when growth only widens the gap between richest and poorest, as has done lately.)

There is a lesson here not just for policymakers but also for the rest of us. "It is human nature always to want a little more," writes the psychologist Timothy Miller in the recent book *How to Want What You Have,* perhaps the first self-help book based explicitly on evolutionary psychology. "People spend their lives honestly believing that they have almost enough of whatever they want. Just a little more will put them over the top; then they will be contented forever." This is a built-in illusion, Miller notes, engrained in our minds by natural selection.

The illusion was designed to keep us constantly striving, adding tiny increments to the chances that our genes would get into the next generation. Yet in a modern environment—which, unlike the ancestral environment, features contraception—our obsession with material gain rarely has that effect. Besides, why should any of us choose to pursue maximum genetic proliferation—or relentless material gain, or anything else—just because that is high on the agenda of the process that designed the human mind? Natural selection, for better or worse, is our creator, but it isn't God; the impulses it implanted into our minds aren't necessarily good, and they aren't wholly beyond resisting.

Part of Miller's point is that the instinctive but ultimately fruitless pursuit of More—the 60-hour workweeks, the hour a month spent perusing the Sharper Image catalog—keeps us from indulging what Darwin called "the social instincts." The pursuit of More can keep us from better knowing our neighbors, better loving our kin—in general, from cultivating the warm, affiliative side of human nature whose roots science is just now starting to fathom.

THE LURE OF THE CULT

Out where religion and junk culture meet, some weird new offspring are rising

By RICHARD LACAYO

ON SATURDAY, MARCH 22, AROUND the time that the disciples of Heaven's Gate were just beginning their quiet and meticulous self-extinction, a small cottage in the French Canadian village of St.-Casimir exploded into flames. Inside the burning house were five people, all disciples of the Order of the Solar Temple. Since 1994, 74 members of that group have gone to their death in Canada, Switzerland and France. In St.-Casimir the dead were Didier Quèze, 39, a baker, his wife Chantale Goupillot, 41, her mother and two others of the faithful. At the last minute the Quèze children, teenagers named Tom, Fanie and Julien opted out. After taking sedatives offered by the adults, they closeted themselves in a garden shed to await their parents' death. Police later found them, stunned but alive.

For two days and nights before the blast, the grownups had pursued a remarkable will to die. Over and over they fiddled with three tanks of propane that were hooked to an electric burner and a timing device. As many as four times, they swallowed sedatives, then arranged themselves in a cross around a queen-size bed, only to rise in bleary frustration when the detonator fizzled. Finally, they blew themselves to kingdom come. For them that would be the star Sirius, in the constellation Canis Major, nine light-years from Quebec. According to the doctrines of the Solar Temple, they will reign there forever, weightless and serene.

Quite a mess. But no longer perhaps a complete surprise. Eighteen years after Jonestown, suicide cults have entered the category of horrors that no longer qualify as shocks. Like plane crashes and terrorist attacks, they course roughly for a while along the nervous system, then settle into that part of the brain reserved for bad but familiar news. As the bodies are tagged and the families contacted, we know what the experts will say before they say it. That in times of upheaval and uncertainty, people seek out leaders with power and charisma. That the established churches are too fainthearted to satisfy the wilder kinds of spiritual hunger. That the self-denial and regimentation of cult life will soften up anyone for the kill.

The body count at Rancho Santa Fe is a reminder that this conventional wisdom falls short. These are the waning years of the 20th century, and out on the margins of spiritual life there's a strange phosphorescence. As predicted, the approach of the year 2000 is coaxing all the crazies out of the woodwork. They bring with them a twitchy hybrid of spirituality and pop obsession. Part Christian, part Asian mystic, part Gnostic, part *X-Files*, it mixes immemorial longings with the latest in trivial sentiments. When it all dissolves in overheated computer chat and harmless New Age vaporings, who cares? But sometimes it matters, for both the faithful and the people who care about them. Sometimes it makes death a consummation devoutly, all too devoutly, to be desired.

So the worst legacy of Heaven's Gate may yet be this: that 39 people sacrificed themselves to the new millennial kitsch. That's the cultural by-product in which spiritual yearnings are captured in New Age gibberish, then edged with the glamour of sci-fi and the consolations of a toddler's bedtime. In the Heaven's Gate cosmology, where talk about the end of the world alternates with tips for shrugging off your fleshly container, the cosmic and the lethal, the enraptured and the childish come together. Is it any surprise then that it led to an infantile apocalypse, one part applesauce, one part phenobarbital? Look at the Heaven's Gate Website. Even as it warns about the end of the world, you find a drawing of a space creature imagined through insipid pop dust-jacket conventions: aerodynamic cranium, big doe eyes, beatific smile. We have seen the Beast of the Apocalypse. It's Bambi in a tunic.

By now, psychologists have arrived at a wonderfully elastic profile of the people who attach themselves to these intellectual chain gangs: just about anybody. Applicants require only an unsatisfied spiritual longing, a condition apt to strike anyone at some point in life. Social status is no indicator of susceptibility and no defense against it. For instance, while many of the dead at Jonestown were poor, the Solar Temple favors the carriage trade. Its disciples have included the wife and son of the founder of the Vuarnet sunglass company. The Branch Davidians at Waco came from many walks of life. And at Rancho Santa Fe they were paragons of the entrepreneurial class, so well organized they died in shifts.

The U.S. was founded by religious dissenters. It remains to this day a nation where faith of whatever kind is a force to be reckoned with. But a free proliferation of raptures is upon us, with doctrines that mix the sacred and the tacky. The approach of the year 2000 has swelled the ranks of the fearful and credulous. On the Internet, cults multiply in service to Ashtar and Sananda, deities with names you could find at a perfume counter, or to extraterrestrials—the Zeta Reticuli, the Draconian Reptoids—who sound like softball teams at the *Star Wars* cantina. Carl Raschke, a cult specialist at the University of Denver, predicts "an explosion of bizarre and dangerous" cults. "Millennial fever will be on a lot of minds."

As so often in religious thinking, the sky figures importantly in the New Apocalypse. For centuries the stars have been where the meditations of religion, science and the occult all converged. Now enter Comet Hale-Bopp. In an otherwise orderly and predictable cosmos, where the movement of stars was charted confidently by Egyptians and Druids, the appearance of a comet, an astronomical oddity, has long been an opportunity for panic. When Halley's comet returned in 1910, an Oklahoma religious sect, the Select Followers, had to be stopped by the police from sacrificing a virgin. In the case of Hale-Bopp, for months the theory that it might be a shield for an approaching UFO has roiled the excitable on talk radio and in Internet chat rooms like—what else?—*alt.conspiracy.*

ASTRONOMICAL CHARTS MAY ALSO have helped determine the timing of the Heaven's Gate suicides. They apparently began on the weekend of March 22–23, around the time that Hale-Bopp got ready to make its closest approach to Earth. That weekend also witnessed a full moon and, in parts of the U.S., a lunar eclipse. For good measure it included Palm Sunday, the beginning of the Christian Holy Week. Shrouds placed on the corpses were purple, the color of Passiontide, or, for New Agers, the color of those who have passed to a higher plane.

The Heaven's Gate philosophy added its astronomical trappings to a core of weirdly adulterated Christianity. Then came a whiff of Gnosticism, the old heresy that regarded the body as a burden from which the fretful soul longs to be freed. From the time of St. Paul, some elements of Christianity have indulged an impulse to subjugate the body. But like Judaism and Islam, it ultimately teaches reverence for life and rejects suicide as a shortcut to heaven.

The modern era of cultism dates to the 1970s, when the free inquiry of the previous decade led quite a few exhausted seekers into intellectual surrender. Out from the rubble of

JONESTOWN, 1978
At the Peoples Temple, more than 900 cult members died because Jim Jones decided it was time

the countercultures came such groups as the Children of God and the Divine Light Mission, est and the Church of Scientology, the robotic political followers of Lyndon LaRouche and the Unification Church of the Rev. Sun Myung Moon. On Nov. 18, 1978, the cultism of the '70s arrived at its dark crescendo in Jonestown, Guyana, where more than 900 members of Jim Jones' Peoples Temple died at his order, most by suicide.

Since then two developments have fostered the spread of cultism. One is the end of communism. Whatever the disasters of Marxism, at least it provided an outlet for utopian longings. Now that universalist impulses have one less way to expend themselves, religious enthusiasms of whatever character take on a fresh appeal. And even Russia, with a rich tradition of fevered spirituality and the new upheavals of capitalism, is dealing with modern cults.

Imported sects like the Unification Church have seen an opening there. Homegrown groups have also sprung up. One surrounds a would-be messiah named Vissarion. With his flowing dark hair, wispy beard and a sing-song voice full of aphorisms, he has managed to attract about 5,000 followers to his City of the Sun. Naturally it's in Siberia, near the isolated town of Minusinsk. According to reports in the Russian press, Vissarion is a former traffic cop who was fired for drinking. In his public appearances, he speaks of "the coming end" and instructs believers that suicide is not a sin. Russian authorities are worried that he may urge his followers on a final binge. In the former Soviet lands, law enforcement has handled cults in the old Russian way, with truncheons and bars. Some have been banned. Last year a court in Kiev gave prison terms to leaders of the White Brotherhood, including its would-be messiah, Marina Tsvigun.

The second recent development in cultism is strictly free market and technological. For the quick recruitment of new congregations, the Internet is a magical opportunity. It's persuasive, far reaching and clandestine. And for better and worse, it frees the imagination from the everyday world. "I think that the online context can remove people from a proper understanding of reality and of the proper tests for truth," says Douglas Groothuis, a theologian and author of *The Soul in Cyberspace.* "How do you verify peoples' identity? How do you connect 'online' with real life?"

"The Internet allows different belief systems to meet and mate," adds Stephen O'Leary, author of *Arguing the Apocalypse,* which examines end-of-the-world religions. "What you get is this millennial stew, a mixture of many different belief systems." Which is the very way that the latest kinds of cultism have flourished. As it happens, that's also the way free thought develops generally. Real ideas sometimes rise from the muck, which is why free societies willingly put up with so much muck.

In Gustave Flaubert's story *A Simple Heart,* an old French woman pines for a beloved nephew, a sailor who has disappeared in Cuba. Later she acquires a parrot. Because it comes from the Americas, it reminds her of him. When the parrot dies, she has it stuffed and set in her room among her items of religious veneration. On her deathbed, she has a vision of heaven. The clouds part to reveal an enormous parrot.

The lessons there for Heaven's Gate? The religious impulse sometimes thrived on false sentiment, emotional need and cultural fluff. In its search for meaning, the mind is apt to go down some wrong paths and to mistake its own reflection for the face of God. Much of the time, those errors are nothing more than episodes of the human comedy. Occasionally they become something worse. This is what happened at Rancho Santa Fe, where foolish notions hardened into fatal certainties. In the arrival of Comet Hale-Bopp, the cult members saw a signal that their lives would end soon. There are many things about which they were badly mistaken. But on that one intuition, they made sure they were tragically correct. —**Reported by Andrew Meier/Moscow, Richard N. Ostling/New York and Andrew Purvis/Toronto**

Enhancing Human Adjustment: Learning to Cope Effectively

On each college and university campus a handful of students experience overwhelming stress and life-shattering crises. One student learns that her mother, living in a distant city, has terminal cancer and 2 months to live. Another receives the sad news that his parents are divorcing; he descends into a deep depression that lowers his grades. A sorority blackballs a young woman who was determined to become their sister; she commits suicide. The sorority sisters now experience the weighty sense of responsibility and guilt.

Fortunately, almost every campus houses a counseling center for students; some universities also offer assistance to employees. At the counseling service, trained professionals such as psychologists are available to offer aid and therapy to troubled members of the campus community.

On the other hand, many individuals are able to cope on their own. They are able to adapt to life's vagaries, even to life's disasters. Other individuals flounder. They simply do not know how to adjust to change and cope with negative and sometimes positive life events. These individuals sometimes seek temporary professional assistance from a therapist or counselor. For these professionals, the difficulty may be *how* to intervene as well as *when* to intervene. Very few individuals, fortunately, require long-term care or institutionalization in our society.

There are as many definitions of *maladjustment* as there are mental health professionals. Some practitioners define maladjustment or mental illness as "whatever society cannot tolerate." Others define maladjustment in terms of statistics: "If a majority do not behave that way, then the behavior signals maladjustment." Some professionals suggest that an inadequate self-concept is the cause of maladjustment. Others cite a lack of contact with reality as an indicator of mental illness. A few psychologists claim that mental disorder is a fiction: to call one individual ill suggests that the rest are healthy by contrast, when, in fact, there may be few real distinctions among people.

Because maladjustment is difficult to define, it is sometimes difficult to treat. For each definition, a theorist develops a different treatment strategy. Psychoanalysts press clients to recall their dreams, their childhoods, and their intrapsychic conflicts in order to empty and analyze the contents of the unconscious. Humanists encourage clients to explore all of the facets of their lives in order to become less defensive and more open to experience. Behaviorists are usually not concerned with the psyche but rather with observable and therefore treatable symptoms or behaviors. For behaviorists, no underlying causes, such as intrapsychic conflict, are postulated to be the roots of adjustment problems. Other therapists, namely psychiatrists who are physicians by training, may utilize these therapies and add somatotherapies, such as drugs and psychosurgery.

This brief list of interventions raises further questions. For instance, is one form of therapy more effective, less expensive, or longer lasting than another? Should a particular diagnosis be treated by one form of therapy while another diagnosis is more amenable to another treatment? Who should make the diagnosis? If two experts disagree on the diagnosis and treatment, which one is correct? Should psychologists be allowed to prescribe psychoactive drugs? These questions continue to be debated.

Some psychologists question whether professional intervention is necessary at all. In one well-publicized but highly criticized study, researcher Hans Eysenck was able to show that spontaneous remission rates were as high as therapeutic "cure" rates. You, yourself, may be wondering whether professional help is always necessary. Can people be their own healers? Is support from friends as productive as professional treatment?

The first readings offer general information to individuals who are having difficulty adjusting and coping. They pertain to the process of change as induced by treatments such as psychotherapy. In "What You Can Change and What You Cannot Change," noted psychologist Martin Seligman discusses what can be realistically managed in terms of self-improvement. He emphasizes diets and various psychological disorders. In "No More Bells and Whistles," several therapists/authors discuss psychotherapy and what makes it successful. Interestingly, there is now a wealth of research on whether or not psychotherapy works and what makes it helpful.

We next look at forms of treatment other than "talking cures." In "Targeting the Brain," Judith Hooper discusses modern knowledge about what forms of mental disorder may be caused by chemical imbalances. When disorders are more biological than psychological, there are a variety of psychopharmaceuticals that can be utilized to treat them. These disorders and treatments are showcased here.

Kerry Hannon, in "Upset? Try Cybertherapy," takes a brief look at computerized psychological consultation. Because this form of therapy is new, practice standards, including ethical standards, have lagged. Caution is therefore needed.

UNIT 6

We then look at various adjustment disorders. In "Defeating Depression," Nancy Wartik describes the complex relationship between heredity, personality, and life events that can trigger depression, a common disorder. Included are a self-assessment quiz and a discussion of various forms of treatment for depression.

Two other adjustment problems are discussed. One is addiction. Addictions to various substances have plagued humans for centuries. We are just now beginning to understand what causes addiction. J. Madeleine Nash discusses addiction and ponders the question of its origin in the body. She identifies the neurotransmitter dopamine as the likely culprit.

Stress is another modern American plague. It affects our physical and psychological being. Fortunately, there are good techniques for managing stress, one of which is detailed in the next article, "Don't Face Stress Alone." In this article, Benedict Carey suggests that the social support of friends is an effective stress management technique.

Next, a really baffling disorder, borderline personality, is detailed by Patrick Perry. Individuals with borderline personalities are difficult to manage and often sabotage their best relationships. What the symptomatology is, what these individuals are like, and how to help them are explained here. Profiles of several famous persons who may have had borderline personalities are also shared.

We end on a more positive note and examine optimism. Closing this anthology, Michael Scheier and Charles Carver discuss optimism, a likely companion to happiness. Optimism, as construed by these researchers, enhances psychological and physical well-being. It is related also to an important concept, self-efficacy, which is the feeling that we can master our environment. Mastery is what healthy adjustment is all about.

Looking Ahead: Challenge Questions

There are a myriad of definitions for maladjustment. List and discuss the pros and cons of each one. Discuss whether or not maladjustment is a fiction created by society to repress the few who are differently adjusted. In what way is mental health the absence of mental illness? How do idiosyncrasies and quirks differ from mental disorders? Explain whether or not there is a reason for psychic pain and for physical pain.

People often feel distressed at home or on the job, miss deadlines, feel moody, and gain weight. What are signs and symptoms of other everyday adjustments? How do most people cope with these situations? Explain whether or not these are the best ways to cope.

After reading "What You Can Change and What You Cannot Change," what does Martin Seligman suggest can be changed by self-determination? With professional assistance? Is one approach better than the other? Discuss what problems seem immune to change. Can most individuals successfully cope with everyday difficulties? When do you believe professional intervention is necessary? Can most of us effectively change on our own, so that professional help is not necessary? Explain your answers.

What types of psychotherapy are available? Does one form seem better than another? Which type of therapy might suit you best and why? What ingredients seem to make therapy effective? Do you think therapy is more art than science? Explain your answer.

What do you know about the physiology of mental disorder? Do you think chemical imbalances cause some of these disorders? If yes, how should these disorders be treated? What do you think about using medications to treat mental disorder? Should medications be our first line of defense? Should psychologists be given prescribing privileges? Why or why not?

What is cybertherapy? Would you ever try cybertherapy? Why or why not? How is this form of therapy different from traditional psychotherapy? What are its advantages and disadvantages?

For depression and addiction, what are the major symptoms and forms of treatment? What seems to cause or exacerbate each problem? What are other causes of maladjustment?

What is stress? Is it always deleterious? Explain. Why is stress at epidemic proportions in modern American society? How can people better cope with stress? Do you think friends can be as effective in assisting a distressed person as a therapist?

What is a borderline personality? Do you know anyone with this syndrome? Do you think women are more prone to this than men? Why? What can we do to help people with borderline personalities?

What is optimism? What is self-efficacy? How are optimists and pessimists different? How does a positive attitude affect physical health?

What You Can Change & What You Cannot Change

There are things we can change about ourselves and things we cannot. Concentrate your energy on what is possible—too much time has been wasted.

Martin E. P. Seligman, Ph.D.

This is the age of psychotherapy and the age of self-improvement. Millions are struggling to change: We diet, we jog, we meditate. We adopt new modes of thought to counteract our depressions. We practice relaxation to curtail stress. We exercise to expand our memory and to quadruple our reading speed. We adopt draconian regimens to give up smoking. We raise our little boys and girls to androgyny. We come out of the closet and we try to become heterosexual. We seek to lose our taste for alcohol. We seek more meaning in life. We try to extend our life span.

Sometimes it works. But distressingly often, self-improvement and psychotherapy fail. The cost is enormous. We think we are worthless. We feel guilty and ashamed. We believe we have no willpower and that we are failures. We give up trying to change.

On the other hand, this is not only the age of self-improvement and therapy, but also the age of biological psychiatry. The human genome will be nearly mapped before the millennium is over. The brain systems underlying sex, hearing, memory, left-handedness, and sadness are now known. Psychoactive drugs quiet our fears, relieve our blues, bring us bliss, dampen our mania, and dissolve our delusions more effectively than we can on our own.

Our very personality—our intelligence and musical talent, even our religiousness, our conscience (or its absence), our politics, and our exuberance—turns out to be more the product of our genes than almost anyone would have believed a decade ago. The underlying message of the age of biological psychiatry is that our biology frequently makes changing, in spite of all our efforts, impossible.

But the view that all is genetic and biochemical and therefore unchangeable is also very often wrong. Many people surpass their IQs, fail to "respond" to drugs, make sweeping changes in their lives, live on when their cancer is "terminal," or defy the hormones and brain circuitry that "dictate" lust, femininity, or memory loss.

The ideologies of biological psychiatry and self-improvement are obviously colliding. Nevertheless, a resolution is apparent. There are some things about ourselves that can be changed, others that cannot, and some that can be changed only with extreme difficulty.

What can we succeed in changing about ourselves? What can we not? When can we overcome our biology? And when is our biology our destiny?

I want to provide an understanding of what you can and what you can't change about yourself so that you can concentrate your limited time and energy on what is possible. So much time has been wasted. So much needless frustration has been endured. So much of therapy, so much of child rearing, so much of self-improving, and even some of the great social movements in our century have come to nothing because they tried to change the unchangeable. Too often we have wrongly thought we were weak-willed failures, when the changes we wanted to make in ourselves

37. What You Can Change

were just not possible. But all this effort was necessary: Because there have been so many failures, we are now able to see the boundaries of the unchangeable; this in turn allows us to see clearly for the first time the boundaries of what *is* changeable.

With this knowledge, we can use our precious time to make the many rewarding changes that are possible. We can live with less self-reproach and less remorse. We can live with greater confidence. This knowledge is a new understanding of who we are and where we are going.

CATASTROPHIC THINKING: PANIC

S. J. Rachman, one of the world's leading clinical researchers and one of the founders of behavior therapy, was on the phone. He was proposing that I be the "discussant" at a conference about panic disorder sponsored by the National Institute of Mental Health (NIMH).

"Why even bother, Jack?" I responded. "Everyone knows that panic is biological and that the only thing that works is drugs."

"Don't refuse so quickly, Marty. There is a breakthrough you haven't yet heard about."

Breakthrough was a word I had never heard Jack use before.

"What's the breakthrough?" I asked.

"If you come, you can find out."

So I went.

I had known about and seen panic patients for many years, and had read the literature with mounting excitement during the 1980s. I knew that panic disorder is a frightening condition that consists of recurrent attacks, each much worse than anything experienced before. Without prior warning, you feel as if you are going to die. Here is a typical case history:

The first time Celia had a panic attack, she was working at McDonald's. It was two days before her 20th birthday. As she was handing a customer a Big Mac, she had the worst experience of her life. The earth seemed to open up beneath her. Her heart began to pound, she felt she was smothering, and she was sure she was going to have a heart attack and die. After about 20 minutes of terror, the panic subsided. Trembling, she got in her car, raced home and barely left the house for the next three months.

Since then, Celia has had about three attacks a month. She does not know when they are coming. She always thinks she is going to die.

Panic attacks are not subtle, and you need no quiz to find out if you or someone you love has them. As many as five percent of American adults probably do. The defining feature of the disorder is simple: recurrent awful attacks of panic that come out of the blue, last for a few minutes, and then subside. The attacks consist of chest pains, sweating, nausea, dizziness, choking, smothering, or trembling. They are accompanied by feelings of overwhelming dread and thoughts that you are having a heart attack, that you are losing control, or that you are going crazy.

THE BIOLOGY OF PANIC

There are four questions that bear on whether a mental problem is primarily "biological" as opposed to "psychological":

- Can it be induced biologically?
- Is it genetically heritable?
- Are specific brain functions involved?
- Does a drug relieve it?

Inducing panic. Panic attacks can be created by a biological agent. For example, patients who have a history of panic attacks are hooked up to an intravenous line. Sodium lactate, a chemical that normally produces rapid, shallow breathing and heart palpitations, is slowly infused into their bloodstream. Within a few minutes, about 60 to 90 percent of these patients have a panic attack. Normal controls—subjects with no history of panic—rarely have attacks when infused with lactate.

Genetics of panic. There may be some heritability of panic. If one of two identical twins has panic attacks, 31 percent of the cotwins also have them. But if one of two fraternal twins has panic attacks, none of the cotwins are so afflicted.

Panic and the brain. The brains of people with panic disorders look somewhat unusual upon close scrutiny. Their neurochemistry shows abnormalities in the system that turns on, then dampens, fear. In addition, the PET scan (positron-emission tomography), a technique that looks at how much blood and oxygen different parts of the brain use, shows that patients who panic from the infusion of lactate have higher blood flow and oxygen use in relevant parts of their brain than patients who don't panic.

Drugs. Two kinds of drugs relieve panic: tricyclic antidepressants and the antianxiety drug Xanax, and both work better than placebos. Panic attacks are dampened, and sometimes even eliminated. General anxiety and depression also decrease.

Since these four questions had already been answered "yes" when Jack Rachman called, I thought the issue had already been settled. Panic disorder was simply a biological illness, a disease of the body that could be relieved only by drugs.

A few months later I was in Bethesda, Maryland, listening once again to the same four lines of biological evidence. An inconspicuous figure in a brown suit sat hunched over the table. At the first break,

What Can We Change?

When we survey all the problems, personality types, patterns of behavior, and the weak influence of childhood on adult life, we see a puzzling array of how much change occurs. From the things that are easiest to those that are the most difficult, this rough array emerges:

Panic	Curable
Specific Phobias	Almost Curable
Sexual Dysfunctions	Marked Relief
Social Phobia	Moderate Relief
Agoraphobia	Moderate Relief
Depression	Moderate Relief
Sex Role Change	Moderate
Obsessive-Compulsive Disorder	Moderate Mild Relief
Sexual Preferences	Moderate Mild Change
Anger	Mild Moderate Relief
Everyday Anxiety	Mild Moderate Relief
Alcoholism	Mild Relief
Overweight	Temporary Change
Posttraumatic Stress Disorder (PTSD)	Marginal Relief
Sexual Orientation	Probably Unchangeable
Sexual Identity	Unchangeable

Jack introduced me to him—David Clark, a young psychologist from Oxford. Soon after, Clark began his address.

"Consider, if you will, an alternative theory, a cognitive theory." He reminded all of us that almost all panickers believe that they are going to die during an attack. Most commonly, they believe that they are having heart attacks. Perhaps, Clark suggested, this is more than just a mere symptom. Perhaps it is the root cause. Panic may simply be the *catastrophic misinterpretation of bodily sensations.*

For example, when you panic, your heart starts to race. You notice this, and you see it as a possible heart attack. This makes you very anxious, which means that your heart pounds more. You now notice that your heart *is really* pounding. You are now *sure* it's a heart attack. This terrifies you, and you break into a sweat, feel nauseated, short of breath—all symptoms of

6. ❖ ENHANCING HUMAN ADJUSTMENT: LEARNING TO COPE EFFECTIVELY

terror, but for you, they're confirmation of a heart attack. A full-blown panic attack is under way, and at the root of it is your misinterpretation of the symptoms of anxiety as symptoms of impending death.

I was listening closely now as Clark argued that an obvious sign of a disorder, easily dismissed as a symptom, is the disorder itself. If he was right, this was a historic occasion. All Clark had done so far, however, was to show that the four lines of evidence for a biological view of panic could fit equally well with a misinterpretation view. But Clark soon told us about a series of experiments he and his colleague Paul Salkovskis had done at Oxford.

First, they compared panic patients with patients who had other anxiety disorders and with normals. All the subjects read the following sentences aloud, but the last word was presented blurred. For example:

dying
If I had palpitations, I could be
excited

choking
If I were breathless, I could be
unfit

When the sentences were about bodily sensations, the panic patients, but no one else, saw the catastrophic endings fastest. This showed that panic patients possess the habit of thinking Clark had postulated.

Next, Clark and his colleagues asked if activating this habit with words would induce panic. All the subjects read a series of word pairs aloud. When panic patients got to "breathlessness-suffocation" and "palpitations-dying," 75 percent suffered a full-blown panic attack right there in the laboratory. No normal people had panic attacks, no recovered panic patients (I'll tell you more in a moment about how they got better) had attacks, and only 17 percent of other anxious patients had attacks.

The final thing Clark told us was the "breakthrough" that Rachman had promised.

"We have developed and tested a rather novel therapy for panic," Clark continued in his understated, disarming way. He explained that if catastrophic misinterpretations of bodily sensation are the cause of a panic attack, then changing the tendency to misinterpret should cure the disorder. His new therapy was straightforward and brief.

Patients are told that panic results when they mistake normal symptoms of mounting anxiety for symptoms of heart attack, going crazy, or dying. Anxiety itself, they are informed, produces shortness of breath, chest pain, and sweating. Once they misinterpret these normal bodily sensations as an imminent heart attack, their symptoms become even more pronounced because the

---

Self-Analysis Questionnaire

Is your life dominated by anxiety? Read each statement and then mark the appropriate number to indicate how you generally feel. There are no right or wrong answers.

1. I am a steady person.

Almost never	Sometimes	Often	Almost always
4	3	2	1

2. I am satisfied with myself.

Almost never	Sometimes	Often	Almost always
4	3	2	1

3. I feel nervous and restless.

Almost never	Sometimes	Often	Almost always
1	2	3	4

4. I wish I could be as happy as others seem to be.

Almost never	Sometimes	Often	Almost always
1	2	3	4

5. I feel like a failure.

Almost never	Sometimes	Often	Almost always
1	2	3	4

6. I get in a state of tension and turmoil as I think over my recent concerns and interests.

Almost never	Sometimes	Often	Almost always
1	2	3	4

7. I feel secure.

Almost never	Sometimes	Often	Almost always
4	3	2	1

8. I have self-confidence.

Almost never	Sometimes	Often	Almost always
4	3	2	1

9. I feel inadequate.

Almost never	Sometimes	Often	Almost always
1	2	3	4

10. I worry too much over something that does not matter.

Almost never	Sometimes	Often	Almost always
1	2	3	4

To score, simply add up the numbers under your answers. Notice that some of the rows of numbers go up and others go down. The higher your total, the more the trait of anxiety dominates your life. If your score was:

10–11, you are in the lowest 10 percent of anxiety.

13–14, you are in the lowest quarter.

16–17, your anxiety level is about average.

19–20, your anxiety level is around the 75th percentile.

22–24 (and you are male) your anxiety level is around the 90th percentile.

24–26 (and you are female) your anxiety level is around the 90th percentile.

25 (and you are male) your anxiety level is at the 95th percentile.

27 (and you are female) your anxiety level is at the 95th percentile.

Should you try to change your anxiety level? Here are my rules of thumb:

- If your score is at the 90th percentile or above, you can probably improve the quality of your life by lowering your general anxiety level—regardless of paralysis and irrationality.
- If your score is at the 75th percentile or above, and you feel that anxiety is either paralyzing you or that it is unfounded, you should probably try to lower your general anxiety level.
- If your score is 18 or above, and you feel that anxiety is unfounded and paralyzing, you should probably try to lower your general anxiety level.

misinterpretation changes their anxiety into terror. A vicious circle culminates in a full-blown panic attack.

Patients are taught to reinterpret the symptoms realistically as mere anxiety symptoms. Then they are given practice right in the office, breathing rapidly into a paper bag. This causes a buildup of carbon dioxide and shortness of breath, mimicking the sensations that provoke a panic attack. The therapist points out that the symptoms the patient is experiencing—shortness of breath and heart racing—are harmless, simply the result of overbreathing, not a sign of a heart attack. The patient learns to interpret the symptoms correctly.

"This simple therapy appears to be a cure," Clark told us. "Ninety to 100 percent of the patients are panic free at the end of therapy. One year later, only one person had had another panic attack."

This, indeed, was a breakthrough: a simple, brief psychotherapy with no side effects showing a 90-percent cure rate of a disorder that a decade ago was thought to be incurable. In a controlled study of 64 patients comparing cognitive therapy to drugs to relaxation to no treatment, Clark and his colleagues found that cognitive therapy is markedly better than drugs or relaxation, both of which are better than nothing. Such a high cure rate is unprecedented.

How does cognitive therapy for panic compare with drugs? It is more effective and less dangerous. Both the antidepressants and Xanax produce marked reduction in panic in most patients, but drugs must be taken forever; once the drug is stopped, panic rebounds to where it was before therapy began for perhaps half the patients. The drugs also sometimes have severe side effects, including drowsiness, lethargy, pregnancy complications, and addictions.

After this bombshell, my own "discussion" was an anticlimax. I did make one point that Clark took to heart. "Creating a cognitive therapy that works, even one that works as well as this apparently does, is not enough to show that the *cause* of panic is cognitive." I was niggling. "The biological theory doesn't deny that some other therapy might work well on panic. It merely claims that panic is caused at the bottom by some biochemical problem."

Two years later, Clark carried out a crucial experiment that tested the biological theory against the cognitive theory. He gave the usual lactate infusion to 10 panic patients, and nine of them panicked. He did the same thing with another 10 patients, but added special instructions to allay the misinterpretation of the sensations. He simply told them: "Lactate is a natural bodily substance that produces sensations similar to exercise or alcohol. It is normal to experience intense sensations during infusion, but these do not indicate an adverse reaction." Only three out of the 10 panicked. This confirmed the theory crucially.

The therapy works very well, as it did for Celia, whose story has a happy ending. She first tried Xanax, which reduced the intensity and the frequency of her panic attacks. But she was too drowsy to work and she was still having about one attack every six weeks. She was then referred to Audrey, a cognitive therapist who explained that Celia was misinterpreting her heart racing and shortness of breath as symptoms of a heart attack, that they were actually just symptoms of mounting anxiety, nothing more harmful. Audrey taught Celia progressive relaxation, and then she demonstrated the harmlessness of Celia's symptoms of overbreathing. Celia then relaxed in the presence of the symptoms and found that they gradually subsided. After several more practice sessions, therapy terminated. Celia has gone two years without another panic attack.

Everyday Anxiety

Attend to your tongue—right now. What is it doing? Mine is swishing around near my lower right molars. It has just found a minute fragment of last night's popcorn (debris from *Terminator 2*). Like a dog at a bone, it is worrying the firmly wedged flake.

Attend to your hand—right now. What's it up to? My left hand is boring in on an itch it discovered under my earlobe.

Your tongue and your hands have, for the most part, a life of their own. You can bring them under voluntary control by consciously calling them out of their "default" mode to carry out your commands: "Pick up the phone" or "Stop picking that pimple." But most of the time they are on their own. They are seeking out small imperfections. They scan your entire mouth and skin surface, probing for anything going wrong. They are marvelous, nonstop grooming devices. They, not the more fashionable immune system, are your first line of defense against invaders.

Anxiety is your mental tongue. Its default mode is to search for what may be about to go wrong. It continually, and without your conscious consent, scans your life—yes, even when you are asleep, in dreams and nightmares. It reviews your work, your love, your play—until it finds an imperfection. When it finds one, it worries it. It tries to pull it out from its hiding place, where it is wedged inconspicuously under some rock. It will not let go. If the imperfection is threatening enough, anxiety calls your attention to it by making you uncomfortable. If you do not act, it yells more insistently—disturbing your sleep and your appetite.

37. What You Can Change

You can reduce daily, mild anxiety. You can numb it with alcohol, Valium, or marijuana. You can take the edge off with meditation or progressive relaxation. You can beat it down by becoming more conscious of the automatic thoughts of danger that trigger anxiety and then disputing them effectively.

But do not overlook what your anxiety is trying to do for you. In return for the pain it brings, it prevents larger ordeals by making you aware of their possibility and goading you into planning for and forestalling them. It may even help you avoid them altogether. Think of your anxiety as the "low oil" light flashing on the dashboard of your car. Disconnect it and you will be less distracted and more comfortable for a while. But this may cost you a burned-up engine. Our *dysphoria*, or bad feeling, should, some of the time, be tolerated, attended to, even cherished.

Guidelines For When To Try To Change Anxiety

Some of our everyday anxiety, depression, and anger go beyond their useful function. Most adaptive traits fall along a normal spectrum of distribution, and the capacity for internal bad weather for everyone some of the time means that some of us may have terrible weather all of the time. In general, when the hurt is pointless and recurrent—when, for example, anxiety insists we formulate a plan but no plan will work—it is time to take action to relieve the hurt. There are three hallmarks indicating that anxiety has become a burden that wants relieving:

First, is it *irrational*?

We must calibrate our bad weather inside against the real weather outside. Is what you are anxious about out of proportion to the reality of the danger? Here are some examples that may help you answer this question. All of the following are not irrational:

- A fire fighter trying to smother a raging oil well burning in Kuwait repeatedly wakes up at four in the morning because of flaming terror dreams.
- A mother of three smells perfume on her husband's shirts and, consumed by jealousy, broods about his infidelity, reviewing the list of possible women over and over.
- A student who had failed two of his midterm exams finds, as finals approach, that he can't get to sleep for worrying. He has diarrhea most of the time.

The only good thing that can be said about such fears is that they are well-founded.

In contrast, all of the following are irrational, out of proportion to the danger:

- An elderly man, having been in a fender bender, broods about travel and will no longer take cars, trains, or airplanes.
- An eight-year-old child, his parents having been through an ugly divorce, wets his bed at night. He is haunted with visions of his bedroom ceiling collapsing on him.
- A housewife who has an MBA and who accumulated a decade of experience as a financial vice president before her twins were born is sure her job search will be fruitless. She delays preparing her résumés for a month.

The second hallmark of anxiety out of control is *paralysis*. Anxiety intends action: Plan, rehearse, look into shadows for lurking dangers, change your life. When anxiety becomes strong, it is unproductive; no problem-solving occurs. And when anxiety is extreme, it paralyzes you. Has your anxiety crossed this line? Some examples:

- A woman finds herself housebound because she fears that if she goes out, she will be bitten by a cat.
- A salesman broods about the next customer hanging up on him and makes no more cold calls.
- A writer, afraid of the next rejection slip, stops writing.

The final hallmark is *intensity*. Is your life dominated by anxiety? Dr. Charles Spielberger, one of the world's foremost testers of emotion, has developed well-validated scales for calibrating how severe anxiety is. To find out how anxious *you* are, use the self-analysis questionnaire.

LOWERING YOUR EVERYDAY ANXIETY

Everyday anxiety level is not a category to which psychologists have devoted a great deal of attention. Enough research has been done, however, for me to recommend two techniques that quite reliably lower everyday anxiety levels. Both techniques are cumulative, rather than one-shot fixes. They require 20 to 40 minutes a day of your valuable time.

The first is *progressive relaxation*, done once or, better, twice a day for at least 10 minutes. In this technique, you tighten and then turn off each of the major muscle groups of your body until you are wholly flaccid. It is not easy to be highly anxious when your body feels like Jell-O. More formally, relaxation engages a response system that competes with anxious arousal.

The second technique is regular *meditation*. Transcendental meditation ™ is one useful, widely available version of this. You can ignore the cosmology in which it is packaged if you wish, and treat it simply as the beneficial technique it is. Twice a day for 20 minutes, in a quiet setting, you close your eyes and repeat a *mantra* (a syllable whose "sonic properties are known") to yourself. Meditation works by blocking thoughts that produce anxiety. It complements relaxation, which blocks the motor components of anxiety but leaves the anxious thoughts untouched.

Done regularly, meditation usually induces a peaceful state of mind. Anxiety at other times of the day wanes, and hyperarousal from bad events is dampened. Done religiously, TM probably works better than relaxation alone.

There's also a quick fix. The minor tranquilizers—Valium, Dalmane, Librium, and their cousins—relieve everyday anxiety. So does alcohol. The advantage of all these is that they work within minutes and require no discipline to use. Their disadvantages outweigh their advantages, however. The minor tranquilizers make you fuzzy and somewhat uncoordinated as they work (a not uncommon side effect is an automobile accident). Tranquilizers soon lose their effect when taken regularly, and they are habit-forming—probably addictive. Alcohol, in addition, produces gross cognitive and motor disability in lockstep with its anxiety relief. Taken regularly over long periods, deadly damage to liver and brain ensue.

If you crave quick and temporary relief from acute anxiety, either alcohol or minor tranquilizers, taken in small amounts and only occasionally, will do the job. They are, however, a distant second-best to progressive relaxation and meditation, which are each worth trying before you seek out psychotherapy or in conjunction with therapy. Unlike tranquilizers and alcohol, neither of these techniques is likely to do you any harm.

Weigh your everyday anxiety. If it is not intense, or if it is moderate and not irrational or paralyzing, act now to reduce it. In spite of its deep evolutionary roots, intense everyday anxiety is often changeable. Meditation and progressive relaxation practiced regularly can change it forever.

DIETING: A WAIST IS A TERRIBLE THING TO MIND

I have been watching my weight and restricting my intake—except for an occasional binge like this—since I was 20. I weighed about 175 pounds then, maybe 15 pounds over my official "ideal" weight. I weigh 199 pounds now, 30 years later, about 25 pounds over the ideal. I have tried about a dozen regimes—fasting, the Beverly Hills Diet, no carbohydrates, Metrecal for lunch, 1,200 calories a day, low fat, no lunch, no starches, skipping every other dinner. I lost 10 or 15 pounds on each in about a month. The pounds always came back, though, and I have gained a net of about a pound a year—inexorably.

This is the most consistent failure in my life. It's also a failure I can't just put out of mind. I have spent the last few years reading the scientific literature, not the parade of best-selling diet books or the flood of women's magazine articles on the latest way to slim down. The scientific findings look clear to me, but there is not yet a consensus. I am going to go out on a limb, because I see so many signs all pointing in one direction. What I have concluded will, I believe, soon be the consensus of the scientists. The conclusions surprise me. They will probably surprise you, too, and they may change your life.

Here is what the picture looks like to me:

- Dieting doesn't work.
- Dieting may make overweight worse, not better.
- Dieting may be bad for health.
- Dieting may cause eating disorders—including bulimia and anorexia.

ARE YOU OVERWEIGHT?

Are you above the ideal weight for your sex, height, and age? If so, you are "overweight." What does this really mean? Ideal weight is arrived at simply. Four million people, now dead, who were insured by the major American life-insurance companies, were once weighed and had their height measured. At what weight on average do people of a given height turn out to live longest? That weight is called ideal. Anything wrong with that?

You bet. The real use of a weight table, and the reason your doctor takes it seriously, is that an ideal weight implies that, on average, if you slim down to yours, you will live longer. This is the crucial claim. Lighter people indeed live longer, on average, than heavier people, but how much longer is hotly debated.

But the crucial claim is unsound because weight (at any given height) has a normal distribution, *normal* both in a statistical sense and in the biological sense. In the biological sense, couch potatoes who overeat and never exercise can legitimately be called overweight, but the buxom, "heavy-boned" slow people deemed overweight by the ideal table are at their natural and healthiest weight. If you are a 155-pound woman and 64 inches in height, for example, you are "overweight" by around 15 pounds. This means nothing more than that the average 140-pound, 64-inch-tall woman lives somewhat longer than the average 155-pound woman of your height. It does not follow that if you slim down to 125 pounds, *you* will stand any better chance of living longer.

In spite of the insouciance with which dieting advice is dispensed, no one has properly investigated the question of whether slimming down to "ideal" weight produces longer life. The proper study would compare the longevity of people who are at their ideal weight without dieting to people who achieve their ideal weight by dieting. Without this study the common medical advice to diet down to your ideal weight is simply unfounded.

This is not a quibble; there is evidence that dieting damages your health and that this damage may shorten your life.

MYTHS OF OVERWEIGHT

The advice to diet down to your ideal weight to live longer is one myth of overweight. Here are some others:

- *Overweight people overeat.* Wrong. Nineteen out of 20 studies show that obese people consume no more calories each day than nonobese people. Telling a fat person that if she would change her eating habits and eat "normally" she would lose weight is a lie. To lose weight and stay there, she will need to eat excruciatingly less than a normal person, probably for the rest of her life.
- *Overweight people have an overweight personality.* Wrong. Extensive research on personality and fatness has proved little. Obese people do not differ in any major personality style from nonobese people.
- *Physical inactivity is a major cause of obesity.* Probably not. Fat people are indeed less active than thin people, but the inactivity is probably caused more by the fatness than the other way around.
- *Overweight shows a lack of willpower.* This is the granddaddy of all the myths. Fatness is seen as shameful because we hold people responsible for their weight. Being overweight equates with being a weak-willed slob. We believe this primarily because we have seen people decide to lose weight and do so in a matter of weeks.

But almost everyone returns to the old weight after shedding pounds. Your body has a natural weight that it defends vigorously against dieting. The more diets tried, the harder the body works to defeat the next diet. Weight is in large part genetic. All this gives the lie to the "weak-willed" interpretations of overweight. More accurately, dieting is the conscious will of the individual against a more vigilant opponent: the species' biological defense against starvation. The body can't tell the difference between self-imposed starvation and actual famine, so it defends its weight by refusing to release fat, by lowering its metabolism, and by demanding food. The harder the creature tries not to eat, the more vigorous the defenses become.

BULIMIA AND NATURAL WEIGHT

A concept that makes sense of your body's vigorous defense against weight loss is *natural weight*. When your body screams "I'm hungry," makes you lethargic, stores fat, craves sweets and renders them more delicious than ever, and makes you obsessed with food, what it is defending is your natural weight. It is signaling that you have dropped into a range it will not accept. Natural weight prevents you from gaining too much weight or losing too much. When you eat too much for too long, the opposite defenses are activated and make long-term weight gain difficult.

There is also a strong genetic contribution to your natural weight. Identical twins reared apart weigh almost the same throughout their lives. When identical twins are overfed, they gain weight and add fat in lockstep and in the same places. The fatness or thinness of adopted children resembles their biological parents—particularly their mother—very closely but does not at all resemble their adoptive parents. This suggests that you have a genetically given natural weight that your body wants to maintain.

The idea of natural weight may help cure the new disorder that is sweeping young America. Hundreds of thousands of young women have contracted it. It consists of bouts of binge eating and purging alternating with days of undereating. These young women are usually normal in weight or a bit on the thin side, but they are terrified of becoming fat. So they diet. They exercise. They take laxatives by the cup. They gorge. Then they vomit and take more laxatives. This malady is called *bulimia nervosa* (bulimia, for short).

Therapists are puzzled by bulimia, its causes, and treatment. Debate rages about whether it is an equivalent of depression, or an expression of a thwarted desire for control, or a symbolic rejection of the feminine role. Almost every psychotherapy has been tried. Antidepressants and other drugs have been administered with some effect but little success has been reported.

I don't think that bulimia is mysterious, and I think that it will be curable. I believe that bulimia is caused by dieting. The bulimic goes on a diet, and her body attempts to defend its natural weight. With repeated dieting, this defense becomes more vigorous. Her body is in massive revolt—insistently demanding food, storing fat, craving sweets, and lowering metabolism. Periodically, these biological defenses will overcome her extraordinary willpower (and extraordinary it must be to even approach an ideal weight, say, 20 pounds lighter than her natural weight). She will then binge. Horrified by what this will do to her figure, she vomits and takes laxatives to purge calories. Thus, bulimia is a natural consequence of self-starvation to lose weight in the midst of abundant food.

The therapist's task is to get the patient to stop dieting and become comfortable with her natural weight. He should first convince the patient that her binge eating is caused by her body's reaction to her diet. Then he must confront her with a question: Which is more important, staying thin or getting rid of bulimia? By stopping the diet, he will tell her, she can get rid of the uncontrollable binge-purge cycle. Her body will now settle at her natural weight, and she need not worry that she will balloon beyond that point. For some patients, therapy will end there because they would rather be bulimic than "loathsomely fat." For these patients, the central issue—ideal weight versus natural weight—can now at least become the focus of therapy. For others, defying the social and sexual pressure to be thin will be possible, dieting will be abandoned, weight will be gained, and bulimia should end quickly.

These are the central moves of the cognitive-behavioral treatment of bulimia. There are more than a dozen outcome studies of this approach, and the results are good. There is about 60 percent reduction in binging and purging (about the same as with antidepressant drugs). But unlike drugs, there is little relapse after treatment. Attitudes toward weight and shape relax, and dieting withers.

Of course, the dieting theory cannot fully explain bulimia. Many people who diet don't become bulimic; some can avoid it because their natural weight is close to their ideal weight, and therefore the diet they adopt does not starve them. In addition, bulimics are often depressed, since binging-purging leads to self-loathing. Depression may worsen bulimia by making it easier to give in to temptation. Further, dieting may just be another symptom of bulimia, not a cause. Other factors aside, I can speculate that dieting below your natural weight is a necessary condition for bulimia, and that returning to your natural weight and accepting that weight will cure bulimia.

OVERWEIGHT VS. DIETING: THE HEALTH DAMAGE

Being heavy carries some health risk. There is no definite answer to how much, because there is a swamp of inconsistent findings. But even if you could just wish pounds away, never to return, it is not certain you should. Being somewhat above your "ideal" weight may actually be your healthiest natural condition, best for your particular constitution and your particular metabolism. Of course you can diet, but the odds are overwhelming that most of the weight will return, and that you will have to diet again and again. From a health and mortality perspective, should you? *There is, probably, a serious health risk from losing weight and regaining it.*

In one study, more than five thousand men and women from Framingham, Massachusetts, were observed for 32 years. People whose weight fluctuated over the years had 30 to 100 percent greater risk of death from heart disease than people whose weight was stable. When corrected for smoking, exercise, cholesterol level, and blood pressure, the findings became more convincing, suggesting that weight fluctuation (the primary cause of which is presumably dieting) may itself increase the risk of heart disease.

If this result is replicated, and if dieting is shown to be the primary cause of weight cycling, it will convince me that you should not diet to reduce your risk of heart disease.

DEPRESSION AND DIETING

Depression is yet another cost of dieting, because two root causes of depression are failure and helplessness. Dieting sets you up for failure. Because the goal of slimming down to your ideal weight pits your fallible willpower against untiring biological defenses, you will often fail. At first you will lose weight and feel pretty good about it. Any depression you had about your figure will disappear. Ultimately, however, you will probably not reach your goal; and then you will be dismayed as the pounds return. Every time you look in the mirror or vacillate over a white chocolate mousse, you will be reminded of your failure, which in turn brings depression.

On the other hand, if you are one of the fortunate few who can keep the weight from coming back, you will probably have to stay on an unsatisfying low-calorie diet for the rest of your life. A side effect of prolonged malnutrition is depression. Either way you are more vulnerable to it.

If you scan the list of cultures that have a thin ideal for women, you will be struck by something fascinating. All thin-ideal cultures also have eating disorders. They also have roughly twice as much depression in women as in men. (Women diet twice as much as men. The best estimate is that 13 percent of adult men and 25 percent of adult women are now on a diet.) The cultures without the thin ideal have no eating disorders, and the amount of depression in women and men in these cultures is the same. This suggests that around the world, the thin ideal and dieting not only cause eating disorders, but they may also cause women to be more depressed than men.

THE BOTTOM LINE

I have been dieting off and on for 30 years because I want to be more attractive, healthier, and more in control. How do these goals stack up against the facts?

Attractiveness. If your attractiveness is a high-enough priority to convince you to diet, keep three drawbacks in mind. First, the attractiveness you gain will be temporary. All the weight you lose and maybe more will likely come back in a few years. This will depress you. Then you will have to lose it again and it will be harder the second time. Or you will have to resign yourself to being less attractive. Second, when women choose the silhouette figure they want to achieve, it turns out to be thinner than the silhouette that men label most attractive. Third, you may well become bulimic particularly if your natural weight is substantially more than your ideal weight. On balance, if short-term attractiveness is your overriding goal, diet. But be prepared for the costs.

Health. No one has ever shown that losing weight will increase my longevity. On balance, the health goal does not warrant dieting.

Control. For many people, getting to an ideal weight and staying there is just as biologically impossible as going with much less sleep. This fact tells me not to diet, and defuses my feeling of shame. My bottom line is clear: I am not going to diet anymore.

DEPTH AND CHANGE: THE THEORY

Clearly, we have not yet developed drugs or psychotherapies that can change all the problems, personality types, and patterns of behavior in adult life. But I believe that success and failure stems from something other than inadequate treatment. Rather, it stems from the depth of the problem.

We all have experience of psychological states of different depths. For example, if you ask someone, out of the blue, to answer quickly, "Who are you?" they will usually tell you—roughly in this order—their name, their sex, their profession, whether they have children, and their religion or race. Underlying this is a continuum of depth from surface to soul—with all manner of psychic material in between.

I believe that issues of the soul can barely be changed by psychotherapy or by drugs. Problems and behavior patterns somewhere between soul and surface can be changed somewhat. Surface problems can be changed easily, even cured. What is changeable, by therapy or drugs, I speculate, varies with the depth of the problem.

My theory says that it does not matter *when* problems, habits, and personality are acquired; their depth derives only from their biology, their evidence, and their power. Some childhood traits, for example, are deep and unchangeable but not because they were learned early and therefore have a privileged place.

Rather, those traits that resist change do so either because they are evolutionarily prepared or because they acquire great power by virtue of becoming the framework around which later learning crystallizes. In this way, the theory of depth carries the optimistic message that we are not prisoners of our past.

When you have understood this message, you will never look at your life in the same way again. Right now there are a number of things that you do not like about yourself and that you want to change: your short fuse, your waistline, your shyness, your drinking, your glumness. You have decided to change, but you do not know what you should work on first. Formerly you would have probably selected the one that hurts the most. Now you will also ask yourself which attempt is most likely to repay your efforts and which is most likely to lead to further frustration. Now you know your shyness and your anger are much more likely to change than your drinking, which you now know is more likely to change than your waistline.

Some of what does change is under your control, and some is not. You can best prepare yourself to change by learning as much as you can about what you can change and how to make those changes. Like all true education, learning about change is not easy; harder yet is surrendering some of our hopes. It is certainly not my purpose to destroy your optimism about change. But it is also not my purpose to assure everybody they can change in every way. My purpose is to instill a new, warranted optimism about the parts of your life you can change and so help you focus your limited time, money, and effort on making actual what is truly within your reach.

Life is a long period of change. What you have been able to change and what has resisted your highest resolve might seem chaotic to you: for some of what you are never changes no matter how hard you try, and other aspects change readily. My hope is that this essay has been the beginning of wisdom about the difference.

THERAPY UNDER THE GLASS

NO MORE BELLS AND WHISTLES

Effective therapy doesn't have much to do with either theory or technique.

BY SCOTT MILLER, MARK HUBBLE AND BARRY DUNCAN

In one ancient Zen story, the master of four apprentice monks who are seeking enlightenment counsels them to observe strict silence. Upon hearing this, the first young monk responds impetuously, "Then I shall not say a word." The second monk then chastises the first, saying, "Ha, you have already spoken." "Both of you are stupid," the third monk remarks and then asks, "Why did you talk?" In a proud voice, the fourth monk concludes, "I am the only one who has not said anything!"

These four apprentice monks competing to show their unique grasp of the truth are not unlike the proponents of various treatment models in the field of therapy. All are eager to demonstrate their special insight into the mysteries of the treatment process and the superiority of their chosen method. Yet while the number of therapy models has proliferated, mushrooming from 60 to more than 400 since the mid-1960s, 30 years of clinical outcome research

This article first appeared in *Family Therapy Networker*, March/April 1995, pp. 53-63. © 1995 by The Family Therapy Network, Inc. Reprinted by permission.

6. ❖ ENHANCING HUMAN ADJUSTMENT: LEARNING TO COPE EFFECTIVELY

> **Given the clear demonstrations from research that there is little appreciable difference in outcome among the various therapy models, it is puzzling that they remain the centerpiece of so much graduate professional training. How can something that *makes so little difference* continue to dominate professional discussion?**

have not found any one theory, model, method or package of techniques to be reliably better than any other. In fact, virtually all of the available data indicate that the different therapy models, from psychodynamic and client-centered approaches to marriage and family therapies, work equally well. (1) This startling truth applies even to comparisons between talk therapies and the much-ballyhooed advances in biological psychiatry. Recent publicity aside, data comparing a variety of psychotropic medications with numerous psychological interventions indicate that they all achieve roughly equivalent results. Furthermore, findings that once appeared to show the superiority of cognitive and behavioral therapies turned out to be artifacts of the measures being used and the confirmatory bias of the investigators.

Given the clear demonstrations from research that there is little appreciable difference in outcome among the various therapy models, it is puzzling that they remain the centerpiece of so many graduate education programs, continuing education seminars and professional publications. How can something that makes so little difference continue to dominate professional discussion? The answer is simple: treatment models really do make a difference, just not to the client.

Consider the current popularity of brief therapy. Proponents of these approaches have gone to great lengths to point out the difference between brief and more traditional forms of treatment. The differences are so numerous that Steve deShazer, the developer of one brief treatment approach, devoted no less than five chapters to detailing them in his book, *Putting Difference to Work.* The proponents of brief therapy promise that these differences translate into more efficient and more effective forms of clinical practice. For example, in *Shifting Contexts: The Generation of Effective Therapy,* Bill O'Hanlon and James Wilk claim their brief therapy approach will enable clinicians to "achieve dramatic therapeutic successes more rapidly, more enduringly, more effortlessly, more pleasurably, and more reliably than any psychotherapeutic approach [and] most in a single session."

The only problem is that there is not a single shred of evidence to support such claims. In fact, there is not any evidence that brief therapy is actually briefer than existing therapeutic approaches. (2) Rather, the research clearly indicates that most therapy is of relatively short duration and always has been *regardless of the treatment model employed.* The average client of any therapy, for example, only attends five or six sessions! Similarly, there is no evidence that brief therapy results in more single-session cures. Once again, the research indicates that a single session is the modal number of sessions for all clients in therapy *regardless of the treatment model employed.* Finally, there is absolutely no evidence that brief therapy results in more effortless, reliable or even enduring change than "longer term" treatment. Indeed, available data suggest that brief therapy achieves roughly the same results as the traditional approaches they are supposed to replace. In short, whatever differences the experts may believe exist between brief and traditional therapy, there simply isn't a difference in terms of outcome.

Why then do the developers of treatment models spend so much time and effort highlighting the differences between their respective approaches when no empirical support exists for such differences? One possibility is that advocates for the various models are trying to influence and impress their primary consumers—not clients, but *other therapists.* After all, therapists are the ones most likely to be interested in one theory or another, to use the various models to conceptualize and organize their clinical work and to buy professional books and attend training workshops. From a marketing point of view, proponents of brief therapy should be considered especially skilled salespeople since they have successfully convinced large numbers of clinicians to buy a model that produces essentially the same results as other models presently in use. How could such a large segment of practicing clinicians be sold such a bill of goods?

To succeed in the "therapy model marketplace," the proponents of a particular brand of treatment must somehow manage to make their model stand out from the competition. Clearly, the more exclusive the product and the more distinguishable from rival brands, the better. One way to distinguish one treatment model from another in the absence of validating data is to develop a special way of talking about the techniques and theory that are exclusive to that model; having a special language imbues it with an aura of difference that seems to justify its claims of uniqueness. In fact, most psychotherapy models seem different because they *sound* different. As in the advertising business, making distinctions with words is tremendously important in the psychotherapy market-place precisely because words are practically all that separates one model from another.

However, as Abraham Lincoln was fond of saying, agreeing to call a dog's tail a foot does not mean that the dog really has five feet. At a time when therapists are more than ever before being held accountable for the service they provide to clients, equating differences in language with differences in effect may ultimately prove very costly to the practice of therapy. In order to survive in the new millennium, psychotherapy *as a whole* must be able to document that the methods employed by clinicians actually deliver what they promise. More and more, third-party payers want to know about the effectiveness of the services that professionals provide. They are increasingly insisting that, to be reimbursed, therapists must be able to deliver the goods.

In the late 1970s, the makers of Alka Seltzer surprised everybody by firing the advertising company that created the slogan, "I can't believe I ate the whole thing." The announcement came as a shock since the series of clever commercials had so quickly become part of the national vernacular and garnered much critical acclaim within the industry. Advertising companies all over the world had rushed to produce look-alike commercials. The makers of Alka Seltzer, however, had one fundamental problem with the commercials—they didn't sell more Alka Seltzer. Likewise, the time has come for therapists to "fire" treatment models and their ideological proponents for that same, simple reason—they do not work. They neither explain nor contribute to effective therapy.

Rejecting the hegemony of treatment models does not mean that therapy in general should be dismissed as ineffective. On the contrary, considerable evidence now exists demonstrating the superiority of therapy to both placebo and no-treatment control groups. Among other things, this research indicates that the average client receiving treatment is better off than 80 percent of people in a control group with a similar difficulty who received no treatment. Therapists, the research makes clear, are not tricksters, snake-oil peddlers or ineffectual do-gooders.

Neither does challenging the central role that models play in the field mean that "anything goes" in treatment or that no guidelines exist for helping therapists navigate the ambiguities of therapeutic work. In fact, we already have 30 years of research evidence that makes it clear that the *similarities* rather than the *differences* between models account for most of the change that clients experience across therapies. What emerges from examining these similarities is a group of common factors that cut across models and contrast sharply with the current emphasis on differences in theory and technique characterizing most professional discussion.

The whole idea of a set of common therapeutic factors is not new. Indeed, in 1961, in his groundbreaking book, *Persuasion and Healing*, Jerome Frank posited that a core group of factors was responsible for the relatively uniform outcomes of different treatment models. Later on, Stupp and Hadley added research support to Frank's observations in a classic study titled "Specific and nonspecific factors in psychotherapy," which appeared in *Archives of General Psychiatry*.

The greatest support for the common factors, however, comes from studies that originally set out to demonstrate the unique effects of one particular approach or another and instead found that all models work equally well. The body of this work indirectly but unequivocally demonstrates the importance of a set of core factors common to all methods that really account for therapy's positive outcome, regardless of what the model's theoreticians believe. Unfortunately, these factors do not, in themselves, have the ideological allure that initially draws many practitioners to a given model. They simply do not *sound* unique, special or intriguingly arcane. They have no charisma! Moreover, they lack the promise of complexity and seeming explanatory power that clinicians have come to expect of psychotherapy theories. Finally, they are not touted by persuasive advocates. As H.L. Mencken once observed, the problem with truth is that "it is mainly uncomfortable, and often dull. The human mind seeks something more amusing, and often caressing." Yet, despite these disadvantages, these factors do offer something no current model can provide—clear, empirically validated guidelines for clinical practice in this era of accountability.

Four common factors, each central to all forms of therapy despite theoretical orientation, mode (i.e., individual, group, marriage, family, etc.), or dosage (frequency and number of sessions), underlie the effectiveness of therapy: (5)

Therapeutic technique. In any given session, one may see a therapist asking questions, listening and reflecting, dispensing reassurance, confronting, providing information, offering explanations (reframes, interpretations), making suggestions, self-disclosing or assigning tasks to be done both within and outside the therapy session. The content of the talk or questions is different depending on the therapist's orientation and technique. Whatever model is employed, however, most therapeutic procedures prepare clients to take some action to help themselves. Across all models, therapists expect their clients to do something different—develop new understandings, feel emotions, face fears, take risks or alter old patterns of behavior.

In his widely cited review of psychotherapy outcome research, Brigham Young University researcher Michael Lambert estimates that the therapist's model and technique contribute only 15 percent to the impact of psychotherapy. (3) While this may be troubling to some schools of therapy that pride themselves on their unique conceptualization of therapeutic process or innovations in intervention methods (e.g., family sculpting, genograms, miracle questions, etc.), the data are clear: clients are largely unimpressed with their therapist's technique. As Lambert puts it: "Patients don't appreciate techniques and they don't regard them as necessary. They hardly ever mention a specific technical intervention the therapist made. I'd encourage therapists to realize that their phenomenological world regarding the experience of therapy is quite different from that of their patients. The nontechnical aspects are the ones patients mention. Also, when objective judges listen to tapes of therapy, the nontechnical aspects are the things that correlate with outcome more than any technical intervention."

Expectancy and placebo. As a factor in outcome, technique matters no more than the "placebo effect"—the increased hope and positive expectation for change that clients experience simply from making their way into treatment. As one might expect, the creation of such hope is greatly influenced by the therapist's attitude toward the client during the opening moments of therapy. Pessimistic attitudes conveyed to the client by an emphasis on psychopathology or the difficult, long-term nature of change are likely to minimize the effect of these factors. In contrast, an emphasis on possibilities and a belief that therapy can work will likely counteract demoralization, mobilize hope and advance improvement.

Therapeutic relationship. Lambert estimates that the therapeutic relationship contributes a hefty 30 percent to outcome in psychotherapy, making it a far more critical factor than either therapeutic technique or expectancy. Clients who are motivated, engaged and connected with the therapist in a common endeavor will benefit the most from therapy. Their participation is, of course, largely a result of the bond or alliance that clients form with the helping professional; studies show that the consumer's participation in therapy is the single most important determinant of outcome. What is more, several studies have found that clients' ratings of that bond or alliance, rather than the therapists' perceptions, are more highly correlated with outcome.

A positive bond or alliance results, at least in part, when the therapist is empathic, genuine and respectful—when he or she exhibits the relationship factors that humanistic psychotherapist Carl Rogers considered the "core conditions" of effective psychotherapy. In this regard, the latest thinking and research indicate that strong alliances are formed when *clients* perceive the therapist as warm, trustworthy, nonjudgmental and empathic. Therapists' own evaluations of their success in creating this kind of therapeutic environment for the client are not enough. The core conditions must actually be perceived by the client, and each client will experience the core conditions differently. The most helpful alliance will develop when the therapist establishes a therapeutic environment that matches the client's definition of empathy, genuineness and respect.

Client factors. In the clinical literature, clients have long been stereotyped as the message-bearers of family dysfunction, the manufacturers of resistance and, in the stra-

THE VIEW FROM THE OTHER CHAIR

BY ERIC E. McCOLLUM AND JIM BEER

It was a hot August morning when Jim Beer picked me up at the office and we began the hour-long drive through Midwestern cornfields. The back of Jim's car was packed with equipment—video camera, tripod, tape recorder, extra tapes—and I felt like a *National Geographic* explorer heading out into the unknown. There was only one difference: *National Geographic* explorers aim their cameras at other people, but today, I was to be the object of study—at least one of them.

Jim turned off the main road, wound through elm-shaded streets, and finally stopped the car in front of Jerry and Cathy's house. While he unpacked his equipment, I stood for a moment, looking around. Kids' voices from a basketball game drifted across the vacant lot next door. Somewhere down the block, a screen door slammed, accompanied by a shout of "I'm leaving, Mom." Neither the town nor the house were as I had imagined them from listening to Jerry and Cathy talk during our sessions. Their conflicts and concerns didn't seem to fit the neat corner house in this serene neighborhood. I'd imagined something less wholesome, I guess; a house that mirrored the struggles going on within it—an unkempt lawn perhaps, or peeling paint. What strange images of our clients' lives we build based on 50-minute sessions, once a week.

I gave Jim a hand with the camera and tripod as he led the way to the front porch. He'd been here before, but this was my first visit. Cathy met us at the door, dressed in shorts and a sleeveless blouse, her fair hair pulled back with a headband. Although casually dressed, she still had a stylish flair, and I could see how she'd made a success out of her home cosmetics business. She directed Jim to the front room while Jerry took me to the kitchen to show me the new drywall and window frames they'd put up—a remodeling job that had been a contentious issue between them in past sessions. Tall and with crew-cut hair, his hands showed the ravages of his job as a mechanic. After the tour, they offered us iced tea and cake and then, like teenagers on a first date, we sat for a moment wondering how to begin. Jim broke the ice.

"Shall we look at the tape?" he asked.

We all nodded, and Jim pushed the play button on the VCR. An image of our most recent therapy session flashed on the screen.

"I'm curious to know what you all think of the session as we go along," Jim said, fastforwarding the tape past the getting-settled stage, "and what questions you'd like to ask each other about the work you've been doing together."

We all took a deep breath at that point, wondering what we'd gotten ourselves into.

That morning with Jerry and Cathy was a unique opportunity in my nearly 20 years as a therapist. While I'd occasionally looked at tapes of sessions with clients before, the focus had always been on *them*—their problems, what they were doing that got them in trouble, what they might do to change. Never before had I sat down with my clients to view a tape of a session and talk about the process—what was helpful, what wasn't, how they felt about what we'd done, how I felt about it. Never before had I made such a direct effort to cross the border that separated my clients' world and mine.

This journey started when Jim approached me about helping him with his Ph.D. dissertation. I assumed he wanted me to be on his committee and assured him that I would be. But that wasn't what he wanted. He was looking for a therapist to study, someone to help him examine a single case of marital therapy in depth to see how clients and therapists learn to work together. I was his candidate. He wanted to find a willing couple for me to see, observe each of our sessions, talk to us separately afterward to hear what we thought about what had happened, and then go over the videotapes with us, asking us to comment on what was going on. Jim called it an ethnographic study, but I saw it as a chance to finally hear what my clients thought of being in therapy with me. Although I hadn't any idea what they would say, I was curious to know.

Jim observed the first 10 of my sessions with Jerry and Cathy before he left for an internship. After the 10th session, we all met together to look at the tape. When Jim was gone, Jerry, Cathy and I met 11 more times. We continued to tape our meetings and sent the videos on to Jim, sometimes recording an addendum of our thoughts about the session. "Research without the researchers," we called it. The whole project was, by turns, exhilarating and sobering, and it brought me face-to-face with fundamental questions about our field: What does it really mean to collaborate with clients? What can be learned from the study of just one couple working with one therapist? What do I really think is important in therapy? One of Jim's questions proved consistently hard to answer: "What do you think Jerry and Cathy would say about the session today?" he asked after each therapy meeting. "How do you think they saw what happened?"

Most days, I was damned if I knew.

In the history of our profession, the views of clients have had little influence on the development of what we do. Psy-

> I left feeling it had been a good session. I found out months later, when therapy was done and I read their reactions in Jim's dissertation, that the couple felt the session was a flop.

choanalysis interpreted clients' criticisms of therapy as an expression of what was wrong with the client. Analyzing this phenomenon—resistance was the heart of treatment—and accepting clients' suggestions or complaints about therapy at face value didn't make sense when the conventional wisdom said those dissatisfactions reflected the clients' inner conflicts, not

38. No More Bells and Whistles

the shortcomings of psychoanalysis. While we've come a long way from traditional psychoanalysis, I think some vestiges of that approach remain. Even now, when we pride ourselves on being client-focused, co-constructive and conversational, in important ways we're not. Therapists still set the rules and rarely consult clients about how to make therapy more helpful to them. Is it always good to steer away from "problem talk" and ask about solutions? Does interrupting a sequence always help? Are there times when compliments annoy clients? Had Freud asked his clients what they thought would help them or what they wanted from therapy, we might have a very different profession today.

JERRY AND CATHY CAME TO SEE ME after 14 years of marriage. They were struggling with a slow-growing marital malaise that had no specific focus. While they didn't like where they found themselves as a couple, they weren't sure where they wanted to be, either. And the stakes were high. Cathy was clear from the beginning that if therapy didn't help, divorce was the only other option. In our fourth session, I tried a technique I'd learned about from Australian therapist Michael White's work and externalized the disquiet they felt. If they joined forces to fight their dissatisfaction, I thought, maybe they could pull closer together.

"Are there ever times when you conquer this Pressure between the two of you?" I asked. "Are there times when you tell Pressure to back off and let you enjoy your marriage?"

When Jerry and Cathy could recount only a few recent good times, I suggested that they go home and try for a week to observe instances when they could keep Pressure from driving a wedge between them.

I left feeling it had been a good session, meeting many of my criteria for competent therapy—coherent, organized around a theme, using a theoretical model consistently. I found out months later, when therapy was done and I read their reactions in Jim's dissertation, that the couple felt the session was a flop. In a post-session interview with Jim, Cathy said the focus on exceptions was "corny" and was worried that I misunderstood her grave doubts about whether or not the marriage could survive. She felt it was fine to talk about good things, but not at the expense of discussing the "real problems." Jerry felt the session had had a "surface" feel to it.

I was chagrined when I read their comments. I'd been trying so hard to help them and had been so convinced of my success, that hearing their criticisms hurt. It helped to know that therapy was over and that Jerry and Cathy were satisfied with the outcome. My "Michael White session," as Jim and I came to call it, hadn't been a fatal flaw, but we'd seen things so differently! Jerry and Cathy clearly didn't share my standards for "good therapy," and wanted something very different. Cathy told Jim, "To me, the positive is not what we need to fix. It's the negative. What's the use of having wonderful bonding time if the night before was terrible? To me, Eric clearly didn't see the depth of the problem at that point."

"WHAT'S ERIC THINKING? WHAT does he think of us?" Cathy and Jerry asked Jim time after time in their post-session interviews. The issue came up again when we all met together.

"It kills me sometimes to not know what you're thinking," Cathy said to me in her living room. "I'd give anything to know." Jerry nodded his agreement.

Their wish to know what I thought challenged what I'd been taught early in my career—that we must protect our clients from what we think of them, doling out our opinions only in scrupulously constructed interventions. There's a reason for this injunction, of course. The therapists's power in the therapeutic relationship may give an offhand remark more impact than we would ever guess. We need to be careful, but how careful? Jerry and Cathy said they would sacrifice a little caution for a better sense of my reactions.

"I respect your opinion," Cathy told me. "You've talked to lots of people about problems and have a lot of experience that I don't have."

What about the fear that I would unduly influence them?

"I may not agree with you," Cathy continued. "I'll still make up my own mind."

Cathy told me how dismayed she had been in the first session when Jerry brought up their two earlier experiences in therapy. My reassurance that I would try not to repeat what they had found unhelpful before (the counselors told Cathy she needed to accept that Jerry wouldn't change and "quit whining about it"), was, in fact, not reassuring at all. When we all met together, Cathy told me, "I don't want you to be afraid to say 'You're doing *this* wrong,' or 'You're looking at *this* out of perspective.'" Unfortunately, there was some accuracy in what she feared. I had found myself being careful with her, knowing how she'd been treated in therapy before. When I saw her ambivalence about Jerry—asking him to change something but still being dissatisfied when he did—I was reluctant to point it out, fearing it would sound like what she'd been told before. I saw my restraint as helpful. Cathy didn't. My efforts to protect her without knowing what protection, if any, she felt she needed, had backfired. And without Jim's research, I'd never have known about it.

As important to Cathy and Jerry as knowing what I thought about them was being sure that I understood them. Both rated our third session a "10" on the 1 to 10 scale Jim used with all of us. "One" meant the session had not been helpful, while "10" meant it had been extremely helpful. What made the third session a "10"? Cathy explained it to Jim this way: "I really felt Eric knows where I am today . . . I don't think he ever heard me before as to where I really feel I am . . . until today." What had been so helpful to Cathy and Jerry that day wasn't some clever intervention. The difference was my ability to let them know I understood that their lives were on the line here, that their problems had tied them in knots they weren't sure could ever be untied. It wasn't so important that I help them do something about it just then, only that I grasp how serious it was.

To get away from the endless search for understanding that can stretch traditional therapy into a years-long venture, family therapists have taken the path of problem solving and action. We acknowledge the importance of empathy and the client-therapist relationship, but often relegate them to the murky land of "joining"—something to be gotten out of the way before real therapy can begin. For Cathy and Jerry, at least, this wasn't so. Feeling understood as they told their story was powerful. And healing.

"WERE YOU EMBARRASSED THE DAY we brought up our sex problems?" Jerry asked me that morning in August.

I thought for a moment, remembering the session several weeks before, trying to reconstruct what I'd been thinking.

"I wasn't embarrassed," I said, "but I felt pretty cautious, because I could tell it was a painful thing for both of you."

"I could see on your face that you were nervous," Jerry said.

Cathy chimed in, "I told Jerry in the car on the way home that I thought we'd embarrassed you. I could see you didn't know exactly what to say."

Her comment brought me up short. I *hadn't* known what to say, but should I tell them that? Talking about my indecision and uncertainty felt dangerous. Would

(continued)

it hurt them to know I sometimes didn't know what to do? Would it shake their confidence in our work together? And who would my silence protect—them or me? Despite the fear that I was breaking another therapy taboo, I struggled to match their candor with my own.

"I guess I really didn't know what to say. Would it have been better if I'd just told you that I felt like we were into something deep here, and that I needed your help in knowing exactly how far we could go?"

It might have," Jerry said. "I felt bad about it later. I wondered if we'd done something wrong."

Cathy had a different view.

"I like it better when you're in charge," she said to me, "especially when it comes to the hard things. We're the ones who made a mess of our marriage, after all."

It was the kind of talk I've often wanted to have with my clients, the chance to step out of character and ask, "What is it you want from me, *really*? I know you're scared. Sometimes, so am I. Now, how can I help?" Later, Jim asked Jerry and Cathy why they hadn't shared some of their ideas with me during our sessions.

"Eric's the professional," Jerry replied. "It just doesn't seem right. It's kind of like I wouldn't go to my doctor and tell him that I sure liked those X-rays he took of me. I don't know anything about X-rays, so it wasn't my place."

Hearing that comment, it dawned on me what different people Cathy and Jerry were in their own home as they responded to Jim's questions, offered their own views, and asked questions of me. In therapy, they were nothing like this. Many of our sessions had a tension and desperation you could feel. I'd picture them at home as a dispirited, humorless couple. Instead, I saw Cathy fondly needle Jim about his "famous 10-point scales,"

Jerry work to put his thoughts into words, and the two of them discuss easily and clearly their ongoing evaluation of therapy. The discrepancy left my head spinning. Had I been wrong about these two? Had I misjudged them and seen them as defective when clearly they weren't?

The answer is more complicated than a simple personal failing. Jerry's comment about "his place" offered a clue. I hadn't misjudged them. I'd only seen what the therapy room let me see and had missed the parts of Cathy and Jerry that weren't in "therapy character." That's not to say that there was something duplicitous about what they said or did in our sessions. Rather, it is a testament to how limiting the therapy room is, how what happens there is organized to allow only a slim and circumscribed part of both the client and the therapist to appear. Clients' troubles and therapists' expertise come through the door easily, while clients' strengths, successes and playfullness, and therapists' doubts, confusion and uncertainty are rarely seen. That reality doesn't diminish therapy or its usefulness. But we will always know only one small part of our clients. They are infinitely more complex than what emerges in therapy. For that matter, so are we.

THROUGHOUT THERAPY, MY EFFORTS TO compliment Jerry and Cathy on the progress they made often left Cathy feeling unsettled.

"It scares me when you say we're doing a good job," she told me in our 10th session, as I once again tried to highlight progress. "I don't trust it. We've been here before and then slid back."

After watching herself say that again on tape in her living room, Cathy stopped the VCR.

"Right there, I just pushed Eric all the way back." She laughed. "He tried to say something nice and I just went, 'Whaooa! Don't say that nice thing.' "

She got more serious and she turned to me.

"How did you feel, Eric, when I said that to you?"

It was a startling moment. Rarely had one of my clients asked me so straightforwardly how I felt about working with them. If they had, I'd turned the focus back to them, wondering if their curiosity indicated some insecurity about how they were coming across. Cathy's earnest question, however, and the openness of our conversation that morning nudged me out of the protective shell of "therapist" by inviting a more personal response. I told her that I hadn't felt put on, that I realized she was scared. I didn't want to push her, but I didn't want to ignore good things, either. I reminded her that we'd made a little joke of it in the session as I changed from saying they'd made progress to saying, "you two are talking about some tiny, little differences in how you get along."

"It felt nice that I could joke with you about it," I said, "because when I first met you, I don't think I could have done that. I don't think you'd have known me well enough to know that when I was joking, I wasn't making fun of you."

Cathy agreed. "I was in a different place emotionally back then," she said.

Then Jim offered another thought: "I wonder if Eric can joke with you now, Cathy, because you've had enough interaction with him to know he understands."

"I do now," she replied.

It was a sweet moment, full of understanding and a kind of connection I'd never felt with a client before. We'd

---

tegic tradition, the targets for the presumably all-important technical intervention. Rarely, however, have clients been identified as the chief agents of change. Nevertheless, the client is actually the single most potent factor, contributing an impressive 40 percent to outcome. The quality of a client's participation in treatment, his or her perceptions of the therapist and what the therapist is doing, determine whether *any* treatment will work. In fact, the total matrix of who they are—their strengths and resources, the duration of their complaints, their social supports, the environments in which they live, even fortuitous events that weave in and out of their lives—matters more heavily than anything therapists might do.

The importance of client factors was clearly demonstrated in a meta-analytic study statistically compiling results from many other studies reporting that in the treatment of anxiety and depression—the two most common mental health complaints—self-help approaches worked about as well as treatments conducted by therapists. While perhaps humbling, this research makes clear that the most influential contributor to change is the client—not the therapy, not the technique, not the therapist, but *the client*. The sheer impact of their contribution when compared to other factors serves as a powerful reminder that whatever the theory, model or nature of the therapeutic relationship, however famous the therapist or dazzling the procedure, no change is likely to occur without the client's involvement.

TO GENERATIONS OF THERAPISTS REARED on the proposition that ingenious and intellectually stimulating treatment models and their associated techniques make the real difference in therapy, the four common factors that really count may seem pallid and anti-climactic. Therapists have been taught that producing change is a complicated, technical and often dramatic business. Faced with the ardors of day-to-day clinical work, many therapists may feel that the four factors are simply too inert, offering little help in addressing the complex problems modern clients bring to the consulting room.

peeked through the scrim of "therapy" and caught a glimpse of each other as people.

IN THE THREE YEARS SINCE I LAST SAW Jerry and Cathy, I've taken them with me, in my mind at least, to several professional meetings and workshops and as I read professional journals and articles I've been sent for review. They've followed along as I supervised, taught and met with clients. Their presence has given me a new vantage point from which to assess the work I do. Much of what I've noticed has been disturbing.

Amid all the talk of collaboration, equalizing professional hierarchies and creating space for our clients' voices, I've yet to find an actual client participating in the debate. At conferences, presenters and panels opine about what clients need and want, but no client is there to speak for him- or herself. Our codes of ethics are formulated to protect clients. Have we ever asked them what kind of protection they need or want? As we move toward shorter, more focused therapy to "better serve our clients," why don't we ask if briefer approaches are helpful, or if they serve clients' needs? How many of our outcome studies include measures of client satisfaction with treatment? How many of our training programs use client input as part of students' evaluations? As we educate ourselves about gender, race and class differences, does it occur to us to ask our clients if they find our knowledge of these things helpful?

Hearing our clients voices doesn't mean we must blindly do anything they say. I honestly don't know, for example, if it's better for a couple to stay together or divorce, nor do I know who's right or who's wrong in most situations. When clients ask me to make such judgments, I have to decline. When I suggest that we listen to our clients' voices, what I have in mind is that we invite them into the larger conversations about therapy we are currently having as a field. We need such talk not to change *them* but to change *us*, to reshape our ideas of what therapy is, how it can help, what place it should occupy in society. And it's only fair, after all. Our clients hold a major stake in the outcome.

CATHY AND JERRY LEFT THERAPY AFTER 21 sessions. Like so many therapy experiences, we ended not with a bang but with a gradual realization that they didn't need to come back. The time between sessions lengthened. We sometimes found ourselves with little to talk about. They'd made many changes during the months of our work together and were more settled than they had been in a long time. Cathy had come out from behind her emotional wall and felt the marriage would be livable for her, now. Jerry had learned to turn the TV off and listen to his wife.

We said goodbye in the same waiting room where we'd met. I found myself lingering with them, wondering if I had the courage to ask the questions I hadn't asked. They were the hardest ones, the most personal—Did I really help you? Do you think I'm a good therapist? Do you like me as much as I've come to like you? Crossing the last barrier, however, and acknowledging some of my own needs as a therapist, was more than I could do that day. Instead, I tried to put some closure to all that we'd done.

"You two have really given me something special," I said. "Therapists and clients don't usually get together and talk about therapy the way we did. You've taught me a lot."

It sounded lame to me, pale against the excitement of our experiment. But it was the best I could do.

What Cathy and Jerry taught me has woven its way into my life as a therapist, lying quietly below the surface for weeks at a time before emerging when I need it. Just last week, I watched one of my students try to compliment a single mother on what a good job she was doing with her son.

"But you don't understand," the client said plaintively. "I don't feel like I'm doing a good job. I don't feel like I'm doing anything right."

As the student was about to try again, I called in and interrupted, remembering Cathy's admonition that problems had to be understood before strengths would seem relevant.

"Listen to her," I said to my student over the phone. "Slow down. Explore it a little more. She knows what she needs to be talking about."

Eric E. McCollum, Ph.D., is the clinical director of the Marriage and Family Therapy Program at Virginia Tech. Address: 2990 Telstar Court, Room 232, Falls Church, VA 22042. Jim Beer is executive director of the Santa Fe Mountain Center.

While this article is written from Eric's point of view, it grew out of many discussions he and Jim have had about the project and what it means and is therefore a joint creation. In addition, Jerry and Cathy's willingness to share their impressions of therapy with us formed the backbone of the entire endeavor and we are deeply thankful to them for their candor. At their request, pseudonyms have been used to protect their privacy.

The fact of the matter, however, is that while therapists' theories of problems and their experience of the therapeutic process may be complex, the factors that contribute to successful therapy are not. The data indicate that successful psychotherapy would be more correctly construed as a rather simple, straightforward business, distinguishable from other helpful experiences in life only by the explicit, socially sanctioned contract to be helpful that exists between a therapist and client. To be sure, the practice of psychotherapy is not always an easy one. Easy and *simple* are, however, two very different matters.

Clinical work may frequently be trying, but that does not mean that the factors contributing to successful psychotherapy are necessarily complicated. As evidence of this, consider a growing body of literature demonstrating that minimally trained and paraprofessional psychotherapists achieve largely the same results as highly trained, highly paid professionals. (6) While this may be alarming to some mental health providers, it says something profoundly optimistic about the possibilities for human change.

To establish a more empirically based practice, therapists can begin by simply examining their own practice. No guru, no complex theory of human behavior and no advanced psychotherapy workshop is needed. Like Dorothy in *The Wizard of Oz,* therapists have always had the means to get back to Kansas.

Start by setting aside your chosen theory and look for the proven factors that are currently operating in your own clinical work. How do you, for example, draw on the strengths, resources and worldview of your clients to help them achieve their goals? To what extent do you take into account and use the client's environment and existing support network? Do you expand on the spontaneous changes that clients experience outside of therapy?

In our own work, one of the ways we make use of client factors is simply by listening for and validating any and all evidence of their strengths and resourcefulness. Questions may also be used to highlight areas of competence, past successes or unrecognized resources. When clients make their first contact with us for therapy, we try to actively incorporate into the treatment process their natural tendency to experience improvement between the time they first make contact and their first session of therapy. For example, during that initial phone call, we might ask clients to be on the lookout for any improvement that occurs before the first meeting. In many cases, at the first session, they report improvement directly related to their reasons for seeking therapy, which can be incorporated into the treatment process. Asking about such change is not, however, an invariant technical procedure to be applied unthinkingly to everybody, nor is there anything magical about it. Most clients contact a treatment professional when they are feeling the greatest distress or discouragement; they have no place to go but up. As a result, simply making the first call to a therapist propels them in the direction of improvement.

Our awareness of the importance of client factors has led us to pay considerably more attention to any fortuitous events in the lives of clients that result in change or improvement and to actively make use of such events in treatment. In the process, we have been humbled by the recognition that some of our most successful cases resulted more from events outside than inside therapy. For example, one man came to therapy complaining of depression that he believed resulted from long-standing marital problems. Since an argument nearly two years earlier, the man and his wife had slept in separate bedrooms and spoken to each other only when they needed to take care of business. Although we worked with the man individually for several sessions, he continued to be depressed and his marital problems remain unchanged. Attempts to draw his wife into counseling were not successful and, increasingly, it looked as if we might not be helpful to the man, until relatives showed up unexpectedly one evening at the couple's home.

Not having seen each other for some time, the two couples talked, laughed and allowed the evening to slip by unnoticed. When they finally realized the time, it was too late for the visitors to drive home or find a hotel room, so they stayed the night. Since there were only two bedrooms in the house, our client and his wife were forced to sleep together in the same room, which set a chain of events in motion. For the first time in two years, the two spoke to each other about matters other than business. Before the night was over, they had even made love. The talk continued into the next day and they slept together again that night. Much to our surprise, the couple showed up together for the man's next appointment. They told us what had happened and how their relationship had been improving since that evening. We spent most of the session talking about the improvements. Time was also spent making sure that the changes dovetailed with what each of the partners wanted, and discussing their ideas for maintaining momentum. By the conclusion of therapy, the relationship had improved considerably and the man's depression had resolved. Therapy was clearly helpful to this couple, but not because it was comprised of some technically marvelous intervention. Basically, we did little more than encourage, or at least keep from interfering with, their own efforts to improve their lives.

In addition to being aware of client factors, therapists can examine how they use relationship factors in their clinical work. Given that the quality of the therapeutic relationship is the second largest contributor to psychotherapy outcome, consider how you establish a strong working alliance. What do you do, for example, to engage the client in treatment; and how do you engage those clients who seem uninterested or unmotivated? What special ways have you found for encouraging the client on the fringe of engagement to assume a more active role in treatment? Are the goals and the tasks for therapy defined largely by the model of therapy you practice or do they result from a collaborative effort between you and your client? Most important, what do you do to provide the core conditions of empathy, genuineness and respect, and how do you tailor them to the individual client? For example, in contrast to what most therapists learned in graduate school, the research indicates that the majority of clients do *not* experience empathy from the therapist as a nurturing, warm-and-fuzzy focus on their feelings, but rather as discerning and thoughtful appreciation of their situation. Therapists who want to maximize the core effective factors of therapy, therefore, will make a concerted effort to speak in the language and worldview of their clients rather than in the terminology of their own treatment model.

In our practice, we spend little time developing a diagnosis or a theory about the possible etiology of the presenting complaint and even less on what therapeutic approach or techniques will be most useful. The process of treatment is comprised of careful listening combined with questions aimed at defining and refining the client's goals for treatment. As may be obvious, the immediate emphasis on the client's goals and consequent de-emphasis of the client's history and psychopathology also make use of placebo and expectancy factors. From the outset, feelings of hope and expectancy are stimulated.

During therapy, we also devote considerable attention to working collaboratively with the client to develop the strategies, tasks and/or homework assignments that will help them reach their desired outcome. In doing so, we have gained new respect for the resourcefulness of our clients and confirmed our belief that many, if not most, of the clever therapeutic procedures attributed to master therapists may actually have come from their clients themselves. For example, 10-year-old Hannah was brought to treatment by her parents because of recurrent nightmares and an inability to sleep in her own room. Hannah and her family had already seen two other therapists. The first, we learned, had thoughtfully and carefully listened to and explored Hannah's feelings about the nightmares. Hannah liked the therapist, but the nightmares didn't go away, so the family went to a second therapist, who had been recommended by a friend. They stopped treatment, however, when they were told that they needed marital therapy because Hannah's problems were a symptom of the conflicts in their marriage.

From the beginning of the first session with the family, there was agreement about the goals for therapy. Everyone wanted the nightmares to stop and for Hannah to be able to sleep in her own room. We asked Hannah herself what she thought might help solve her dual problems. She had a number of ideas, including using extra pillows and her favorite stuffed animals to build a fortress for herself in bed that would keep out the nightmares. With some help from her parents to arrange the pillows and animals in just the right way, Hannah's idea worked. She resumed sleeping in her own room and experienced no further nightmares.

Of course, it would be a mistake to extract the strategy that Hannah used to overcome her nightmares and attempt to apply it in other clinical situations. The key was not that we found the *right* technique for all complaints of childhood nightmares, but rather that we depended on the client's input, participation and involvement to determine the goals and tasks for therapy. While Hannah's example is particularly striking, all cases ultimately require a similar dependence on the client. The more conscious, deliberate and focused the attempt to draw the client into treatment, the less significant formal explanatory models and clinical techniques come to seem.

SOME MAY ARGUE THAT PAYING ATTENTION to the factors common to all therapy is, itself, a type of model or orientation. In our clinical work, however, there are no fixed techniques, no certainties or invariant patterns that emerge from the therapeutic process, no generalizations that can or need be made about our clients. Of course, there are variations in our respective personal styles and ways of interacting with clients. Compared to the commonalities of our work, however, these differences seem insignificant—we all share the same outcome figures.

We are not proposing an eclectic approach to practice, with therapists sampling from a variety of models in an attempt to individualize treatment. Rather, we are suggesting that all treatment, to the extent that it reflects these four common factors, will be successful. Good therapy, whether it's done by cognitive, behavioral or psychodynamic therapists, looks roughly the same. The common factors, like notes of written music, may be arranged in different orders and patterns and played in a variety of styles, but they are still based on a common language—a language that allows for maximum flexibility and creativity, but that still serves to unify rather than separate the speakers, cutting across the theoretical divisions that have characterized psychotherapy from its inception.

In this era of accountability, professional dialogue can no longer afford to be the modern equivalent of the Tower of Babel. Recently, the field has become the subject of increasing scrutiny. Besides the growing demands of third-party payers for demonstrated effectiveness, therapists now face a cascade of critical mass-market books, articles and news stories accusing them of greed, fraud, incompetence, failed ethics and extreme susceptibility to every ephemeral fad touted in the popular culture. Serious questions have been raised about the right of therapists to practice any form of treatment that has not been empirically tested and its effectiveness validated. Indeed, legislation, ostensibly for the protection of mental health consumers, has already been proposed that would effectively ban third-party reimbursement for psychotherapy procedures that have not been documented as both safe and effective—and not by therapists, but by the scientific research community, which might or might not include practicing clinicians.

While these proposals evoke outrage in many in our field, to some extent we have only ourselves to blame. Too many exaggerated claims without experimental backing, fancy and exotic sounding techniques that come and go with the seasons and loudly publicized internecine quarrels about relative success have begun to give therapy a bad name, undercutting its very real and deeply helpful benefits.

It is possible for the field to survive into the new millennium. At the heart of the four factors that characterize all good therapy is the desire and the capacity to form helpful and healing bonds with troubled people who have, for the time being, lost their way and need some directional signals back to their own best selves. To recover the currently tarnished reputation of the field, we need to put treatment models in their place, stop speaking in the tongues of our pet theories, and learn a simpler, more accessible language. We can no longer afford to pretend that it is the treatment model and not our clients and the relationship with our clients that comprises the real substance of our clinical work. To do otherwise is to risk having the destiny of our field taken out of our own hands. But, most of all, we need to remember, as the words of one of the most cherished maxims of the field has it, that the map, however helpful, is not, never was and never will be the territory.

Scott Miller, Ph.D., is the director of Brief Therapy Training Consortium. Address: P. O. Box 578264, Chicago, IL 60657-8264. *Mark Hubble, Ph.D., is director of the Brief Therapy Clinic Counseling and Testing Center, University of Missouri, Kansas City, MO. Barry Duncan, Psy.D., is in private practice in Port St. Lucie, FL.*

The authors are currently at work on a book about the common factors in psychotherapy to be published by W. W. Norton in early 1996.

FOR FURTHER REFERENCE:

1. *For a review of the studies showing that all treatments achieve roughly equivalent results:*
   - Lambert, M.J., Shapiro, D.A. & Bergin, A.E. (1986). The effectiveness of psychotherapy. In Garfield, S. & Bergin, A.E. (eds.). *Handbook of Psychotherapy and Behavior Change* (3rd ed.). New York: John Wiley.
   - Shadish, W.R., et al. (1993). Effects of family and marital psychotherapies: A meta-analysis. *Journal of Consulting and Clinical Psychology, 61*, 992–1002.

2. *For a critical review of the claims and research about brief therapy:*
   - Koss, M.D. & Butcher. Research on brief therapy. In Garfield, S. & Bergin, A.E. (eds.). *Handbook of Psychotherapy and Behavior Change* (3rd ed.). New York: John Wiley.
   - Miller, S.D. (1994a). The solution conspiracy: A mystery in three installments. *Journal of Systemic Therapies, 13(1),* 18–37.

3. *For a discussion of the relative contribution of different factors to the outcome of psychotherapy:*
   - Lambert, M.J. (1992). Implications of outcome research for psychotherapy integration. In Norcross, J.C. & Goldfried, M.R (eds.), *Handbook of Psychotherapy Integration.* New York: Basic Books.

4. *For a review of the studies showing the general benefits of psychotherapy:*
   - Garfield, S.L. & Bergin, A.E. (eds.) (1971). *Handbook of Psychotherapy and Behavior Change: An Empirical Analysis.* New York: John Wiley.
   - Smith, M.L., Glass, G.V. & Miller, T.L. (1980). *The Benefits of Psychotherapy.* Baltimore: The Johns Hopkins University Press.

5. *For a review of the studies demonstrating support for the common factors:*
   - Duncan, B.L. & Moynihan, D.W. (1994). Applying outcome research: Intentional utilization of the client's frame of reference. *Psychotherapy, 31(2),* 294–302.
   - Duncan, B.L, Solovey, A.D. & Rusk, G.S. (1992). *Changing the Rules: A Client-Directed Approach to Therapy.* New York: Guilford.
   - Frank, J.D., Frank, J.B. (1991). *Persuasion and Healing: A Comparative Study of Psychotherapy* (3rd ed.). Baltimore: Johns Hopkins University Press.

6. *For information on the lack of correlation between therapist experience, level of training, professional licensure and outcome in psychotherapy:*
   - Dawes, R.M. (1994). *House of cards: Psychology and Psychotherapy Built on Myth.* New York: Free Press.
   - Lambert, M. & Bergin, A.E. (1994). The effectiveness of psychotherapy. In Bergin, A.E. & Garfield, S.L. (eds.). *Handbook of Psychotherapy and Behavior Change* (4th ed.). New York: John Wiley, pp. 143–189.
   - Stein, D.M. & Lambert, M.J (1984). On the relationship between therapist experience and psychotherapy outcome. *Clinical Psychology Review, 4,* 1–16.

MENTAL DISORDERS

Targeting the Brain

The 3-lb. organ that rules the body is finally giving up its secrets. Goodbye, Oedipus

By JUDITH HOOPER

THE DISEASE IS KNOWN TO DOCTORS as "irrational rationality" because it forces its victims to defy reason while seeming to embrace it. Characters as disparate as Howard Hughes, Lady Macbeth and Freud's sexually conflicted "Rat Man" are among its victims. Today, in every elementary school of 200 pupils or so, three or four youngsters are likely to suffer from it. Howard Hughes' symptoms included an insistence on having a germ-free environment and all his windows permanently sealed. The schoolchildren are more inclined to count cracks in the blacktop (for them, "Step on a crack, break your mother's back" is frighteningly literal) or meticulously arrange their crayons in neat rows, again and again, to avert some imagined catastrophe.

All of them are suffering or have suffered from a mental disease known as obsessive-compulsive disorder (OCD), which torments its victims with clouds of horrific anxieties and forces them, like primitive priests propitiating unknown gods, to indulge in senseless and repetitive rituals. Not long ago, this disease—along with most other so-called mental illnesses—was considered to be a chronic, untreatable condition, a psychological crippler whose roots lay hidden deep within the brain's mysterious recesses.

But the brain is finally giving up its secrets, and the biggest secret of all is that this 3-lb. maze of nerves and tissue is also a veritable laboratory of chemicals whose workings and interactions largely determine the state of our mental health, down to the latest mood swing. Many mental illnesses once thought to be purely psychological conditions—among them schizophrenia, panic disorder, post-traumatic stress disorder and OCD—turn out to be caused by specific chemical imbalances. Those who suffer from them are racked not by toilet-training traumas or the "unceasing terror and tension of the fetal night" (as an early psychoanalyst put it) but by something as simple—and complex—as an imperfectly mixed chemical cocktail. The Oedipus complex has been reduced to a matter of molecules.

The good news is that many if not most of these brain afflictions can now be remedied by increasingly precise psychoactive drugs. In the past few years, scientists have joined disciplines and come up with a whole new pharmacopoeia of compounds to deal with mental disorders. "Today the psychiatrists who treat patients are working hand in hand with the 'wet-brain guys'—the pharmacologists, chemists and molecular biologists," says Dr. Steven Hyman, director of the National Institute of Mental Health (NIMH) in Bethesda, Maryland. While the effects of earlier psychiatric drugs were discovered largely by trial and error, the latest compounds are aimed at exact targets in the brain. "When you wanted to develop a new drug, you used to copy an old one that worked, add a little twist to the molecule and test it out on patients," explains Dr. Kenneth Davis, chairman of psychiatry at Mount Sinai School of Medicine in New York City. "If you were lucky, you got a drug that worked as well as the old one but had fewer side effects. Now we can be very specific and say, 'Let's go after the D3 receptor or the D4 receptor.'"

Scientists consider receptors—which are specially tailored protein molecules—and the substances that bind to them to be the critical junction in the ongoing chemical processes that underlie thinking, feeling, dreaming and remembering. For an electrical signal to travel from neuron to neuron in the brain, it must cross a minuscule gap, the synapse, between them. A number of different chemical messengers known as neurotransmitters ferry the signal across the synapse and then lock on to receptors that lie on the membrane of the next nerve cell in line.

Some neurotransmitters induce other neurons to fire; others dampen neuron activity. In either case, once the chemical locks on to the receptor, it sets in motion a cascade of chemical events in the receiving cell. This ongoing dance of neurotransmitters and receptors is the intricate code that brain cells use to communicate with one another.

Many psychoactive drugs—including opiates, the Valium-type compounds and angel dust—mimic the action of neurotransmitters by binding to particular receptors and influencing the neuron's firing. Pharmacologists have acquired the tools to screen new drugs quickly, testing their affinity for particular receptors by cloning, or duplicating, the receptors and then designing molecules that bind to them. So refined are the new techniques that scientists now know of 14 different receptors for serotonin, the ubiquitous chemical messenger that plays a critical role in sleep, mood, depression and anxiety. They have also discerned five different receptor subtypes for dopamine, a neurotransmitter thought to be involved in schizophrenia. By formulating compounds that selectively bind to particular dopamine receptors, for example, drug designers can craft schizophrenia drugs that curb hallucinations without triggering disabling Parkinsonian symptoms.

The development of drugs for schizophrenia, one of the most perplexing and devastating of all mental illnesses, was an early success story. After several decades as a hopeless research backwater, the schizophrenia field was reborn in 1989, when the U.S. Food and Drug Administration approved a remarkable drug, clozapine (brand name: Clozaril). Made by the Swiss pharmaceutical firm Sandoz, Clozaril was aimed at patients who did not benefit from other drugs. While traditional antipsychotic drugs such as chlorpromazine (Thorazine) and haloperidol (Haldol) work by blocking dopamine receptors, Clozaril appears to bind to serotonin receptors as well. "It is what we call a dirty drug," says Mount Sinai's Davis. "It probably binds to a whole bunch of receptors. We used to think that was a bad thing. Now we think that's maybe a good thing." Perhaps because of its affinity for serotonin receptors, Clozaril is largely free of the Parkinsonian side effects (the "Thorazine shuffle" and so on) that plague the classic antipsychotic drugs. It was also the first drug to ameliorate symptoms of schizophrenia that are resistant to other drugs. But Clozaril has a major drawback: a life-threatening side effect called agranulocytosis, a drastic drop in white blood cells that requires patients to undergo expensive weekly blood monitoring.

Now scientists are exploring an entire spectrum of what Dr. Steven Paul, vice president for central-nervous-system research at Eli Lilly, calls "Clozaril wannabes" that they hope will work as well without triggering agranulocytosis. One of the wannabes, risperidone (Risperdal), made by Belgium-based Janssen Pharmaceutica, entered the market in 1993, and four others are nearing approval by the FDA, including Lilly's Zyprexa and Abbott Labs' Serlect. Meanwhile, further down the drug-development pipeline are a number of third-generation Clozaril cousins, some of which are specifically targeted at the little-known D3 and D4 receptors.

"We're not curing schizophrenia with these new antipsychotics," says Paul. "But we can treat it better. What would happen if we designed a drug that was 10 times better than Clozaril?" Mount Sinai's Davis, on the other hand, thinks future schizophrenia drugs might well be based on altogether different chemical-messenger systems. "There is evidence that schizophrenics have abnormalities in two very common neurotransmitters, GABA [gamma-aminobutyric acid] and glutamate," he says. "None of the current drugs do anything for the most incapacitating symptom of schizophrenia, the cognitive deficits. Maybe it's time to get off the dopamine merry-go-round we've been on for 40 years."

New drugs have also drastically altered the outlook for panic disorder, a chronic illness characterized by recurrent panic attacks and a lifetime of fear in between. The symptoms of an attack—among them palpitations, breathlessness, sweating, dizziness, tingling sensations, hot flashes or chills, as well as a sense of impending doom—seem so dire and life-threatening that patients frequently turn up in emergency rooms convinced they are having a heart attack or going insane. Thirty percent of the 2.4 million Americans with panic disorder go on to develop agoraphobia, the fear of leaving home lest they succumb to panic on the freeway, in a store or at a concert. Some 20% of patients attempt suicide.

Panic disorder probably results from a "combination of a genetic predisposition and some number of traumatic separations in childhood," according to Dr. Jack Gorman, a Columbia University psychiatrist. But whatever the cause, the brain of a person who suffers from it is different from that of someone who does not. Stimulation studies using the drug yohimbine have revealed an abnormal firing rate in an area of the brain stem called the locus ceruleus, which is rich in cells that release the neurotransmitter norepinephrine, the trigger for human fight-or-flight response. This primal alarm system has obvious survival value—useful for fleeing man-eating tigers and such. But in patients with panic disorder, it appears to kick in at too low a threshold.

A decade ago, many a panic-disorder patient ended up as a tragic, misunderstood recluse. But today panic disorder is one of the most treatable mental illnesses. Studies have shown that 70% of patients benefit from cognitive behavioral therapy, which includes breathing training, "cognitive restructuring" and "exposure therapy." Most patients can be helped by short-acting antianxiety drugs such as Xanax and long-acting antidepressants such as desipramine and imipramine.

The superstar of the hour, however, is the family of antidepressant drugs known as SSRIS (selective serotonin re-uptake inhibitors). There is evidence linking panic disorder to a serotonin deficiency, and these compounds appear to work by boosting serotonin levels. The best known of all this family is Prozac, Eli Lilly's $2.1 billion-a-year baby, which has become a societal catchword for relief from anxiety. But another family member, Paxil (manufactured by SmithKline Beecham), is the first to be approved by the FDA specifically for the treatment of panic disorder. While drug therapy by itself is successful in 70% of cases—the same rate as cognitive behavioral therapy alone—preliminary, unpublished research suggests that the success rate might climb as high as 90% when the treatments are combined. But Gorman cautions that this needs to be studied in more detail.

Nonetheless, says Dr. Una McCann, head of the unit on anxiety and affective disorders at the NIMH, "serotonin is obviously not the whole story. If it were, the SSRIS would not take two to four weeks to kick in." Recently, some researchers have begun to eye a naturally occurring chemical called cholecystokinin (CCK), an anxiety-causing compound that binds to receptors in the brain stem as well as the gut. This dual affinity may explain the butterflies-in-the-stomach sensations that often herald panic attacks. CCK-mimicking compounds trigger attacks in panic-disorder patients but not in normal volunteers, so a likely candidate for a new panic-disorder pill would be a drug that blocks CCK.

Other anxiety disorders appear to share a common fear circuitry in the brain and are treated by similar methods. Generalized anxiety disorder, for example, is different from panic disorder in that it does not strike suddenly but follows a predictable pattern of worries and fears. In social phobias, the trigger is an exaggerated dread of public embarrassment. "These people have panic attacks only in specific situations, such as writing a check in public, using public rest rooms or eating out," explains McCann.

The multifaceted SSRIS have also dramatically altered the treatment of depression, which remains the most common form of mental illness. Although no more efficacious than traditional anti-depressants, they do not produce many of the unpleasant side effects, such as sedation and weight gain, that have caused thousands of potential patients to shun treatment. "SSRIS have revolutionized, and continue to revolutionize, the comfort levels with which psychiatrists and family practitioners treat depression," says Dr. David Kupfer, chairman of psychiatry at the University of Pittsburgh School of Medicine. "Suddenly, physicians are more willing to prescribe these medications for people who truly need them, and people suffering from a depression are more willing to take them and stay on them."

Even patients who have been chronically depressed for five years or more respond well in 65% to 70% of the cases, Kupfer points out, and recent research underlines the importance of remaining on the medications long enough to prevent a relapse. "New studies show that the dosage that got you better will keep you better," he says. "Depression is a chronic, lifelong illness, and we're beginning to think of these drugs as being similar to insulin for diabetes."

Still, a new generation of medications—perhaps tailored to particular serotonin receptors—is urgently needed for the 20% of depressed patients who do not benefit from existing drugs. Researchers hope to come up with compounds that begin acting immediately rather than in a period of weeks. "The Holy Grail of new antidepressant treatment is rapid onset," asserts Dr. John Ascher, a research physician at Glaxo Wellcome in Research Triangle Park, North Carolina. "We're talking about medicine that takes effect in just a day or two."

Ultimately, scientists would like to figure out how genetic defects cause depression, and then to design drugs to correct whatever has gone awry. Gene mapping would be particularly helpful to people at risk for manic-depressive illness: although lithium and related drugs usually relieve the manic episodes, current antidepressants are often ineffective against the acute depressive ones. Says Ascher: "That's the real frontier."

Obsessive-compulsive disorder, which affects 1% to 3% of Americans, was until recently considered a chronic, untreatable condition. Victims more ordinary than Lady Macbeth and Howard Hughes are haunted by persistent, intrusive thoughts or worries (obsessions), and may spend countless hours performing repetitive rituals (compulsions) such as hand washing, counting, hoarding old clothes, arranging napkins in a meaningless symmetry or checking a hundred times to make sure the electric coffeemaker is turned off. Themes of dirt, contamination or germs rule their thoughts, and other common obsessions center on horrific or violent images, a need for symmetry or exactness, or an exaggerated sense of sin or morality.

A key breakthrough in OCD treatment came about in the late 1980s, when researchers discovered that a particular antidepressant, clomipramine hydrochloride (brand name: Anafranil), relieved obsessions and compulsions as no others did. The presumed secret of its success was its ability to inhibit the reabsorption of serotonin in the brain. A few years later, the advent of the SSRI family made it even more obvious that obsessive-compulsive disorder was at least in part a serotonin problem. Some 75% to 80% of OCD patients today get substantial relief—sometimes complete remission—from one or another member of the SSRIS.

Recently, positron-emission tomography (PET) scan studies at the UCLA School of Medicine have revealed that either Prozac or cognitive therapy can actually restore normal function in the obsessive-compulsive brain. The scans have documented that OCD patients have abnormal activity in the head of the caudate nucleus, a part of the brain's deep-dwelling basal ganglia, coupled with unusual activity in the orbital prefrontal cortex, just above the eye sockets. The caudate nucleus normally acts as a gatekeeper, determining which thoughts, feelings and behaviors take priority. When it malfunctions, the "worry inputs" generated in the orbital prefrontal region run unchecked, and irrational beliefs become rigid and intractable.

In any case, the worry circuits quieted down after the patients completed 10 weeks of either successful drug treatment or behavior therapy involving exposure and response prevention—demonstrating that either a molecule or a learning experience can materially alter the brain. "What we now know," says the NIMH's Hyman, "is that anything—whether a drug, a war experience or a talking therapy—changes the way nerve cells talk to each other. In the brain, hardware as well as software is always changing."

In post-traumatic stress disorder, the picture of a brain reshaped by experience is even more startling. Only recently, PTSD was deemed an exclusively psychological (not biological) phenomenon. Moreover, many clinicians regarded it as something of a scam, not a real mental illness like schizophrenia. But new medical discoveries, coupled with the wide publicity given to the experiences of Vietnam War veterans in particular, have changed that.

By definition, PTSD victims have suffered a trauma that involved death or serious injury and provoked feelings of intense fear, helplessness and horror that have long outlasted the event. They are hypervigilant, often sleeping with one eye open. "One Vietnam veteran will never stand in the center of the room when he comes here because he is afraid someone will stab him in the back," says Dr. Edna Foa, a psychiatrist at the Medical College of Pennsylvania. Victims are haunted by intrusive, disturbing memories—even entire flashbacks triggered by certain cues. "If I hear a helicopter, it ruins my whole day," said a Vietnam veteran. To avoid any such reminders, PTSD victims may retreat into virtual isolation, and commonly suffer from emotional numbing, fear of intimacy, memory deficits and depression.

One intriguing clue surfaced recently when magnetic-resonance-imaging scans of brains of combat veterans with PTSD were compared with those of civilians who did not have the disorder. Scans of the veterans' brains showed that the right hippocampus, a crescent-shaped structure that plays a key role in memory, was slightly smaller than normal. This may indicate that war, rape or torture actually harms the brain as well as the spirit.

PET scans tell another tale. When eight PTSD victims, civilian and military, volunteered for an experiment at Massachusetts General Hospital in Boston, a PET scan revealed that an area of their brains—the right amygdala, a small, almond-shaped structure—was abnormally active while they were reliving traumatic memories. "The amygdala is the key to the conditioned-fear response in animal studies," explains Dr. Roger Pitman, a psychiatrist at the VA Medical Center in Manchester, New Hampshire. "This study shows us that traumatic memories are activating this 'hot learning center.' It may be that stress hormones burn these memories into the brain, and that is why you have World War II vets still suffering from flashbacks of Iwo Jima."

Yet all this new knowledge has not led to a PTSD pill; unlike the other anxiety disorders, PTSD remains a hard problem to solve. Many medications relieve certain symptoms, such as insomnia, without remedying the underlying disorder. But scientists hope that current research—for example, studies indicating that PTSD patients' memories of disturbing images can be blunted by drugs that block one type of norepinephrine receptor—will produce a generation of medications to treat PTSD.

Is it possible that such studies will come up with a drug that could inoculate soldiers against war shock before they go into battle, or mute the horrifying images within hours, days or weeks? "The logistics would be difficult, but it could be done," says psychiatrist Dr. J. Douglas Bremner of the Veterans Affairs Medical Center in West Haven, Connecticut. "Soldiers suffering from acute-stress reactions on the battlefield are often treated with Valium and other drugs. We now think that acute-stress reaction is the prelude to PTSD. It would be nice to avert PTSD by interrupting the memory-consolidation process before those traumatic memories become pathological."

More secrets of the brain are emerging every day. There is evidence, for instance, that long-term use of antidepressants changes the intracellular environment permanently, even turning certain genes on or off. And new molecular techniques have revealed that individual receptors come in various genetic forms, or polymorphisms. This kind of knowledge opens the gateway to a whole panoply of fresh possibilities. The brain is a vast continent, and scientists have barely landed on its shores. —*With reporting by Hannah Bloch/Washington and Lisa H. Towle/Raleigh*

UPSET? TRY CYBERTHERAPY

An online visit to the psychologist may provide an answer, cheap

KERRY HANNON

Got the blues? Can't stop scarfing down bags of potato chips? Your spouse is always hostile, and you and the kids are, too? Therapy might help—at $125 a session. Or you could test a '90s solution: E-mail your way to mental health for a fraction of the cost.

> *The cybercouch is best at giving people who can clearly identify the dilemma a start toward a solution.*

In the past year, angst has become a thriving niche on the World Wide Web. Many psychologists who are setting up home pages see electronic consultation as a way to plump up incomes hit by managed care and to attract new patients to the office. For the most part, these cyberpractitioners are careful to warn potential patients that the medium doesn't allow for detailed probing. "I give advice like Ann Landers and Dear Abby do," explains Dorothy Litwin, a New York psychologist who specializes in substance abuse, women's issues and couples therapy.

Litwin is one of five women who joined forces about a year ago to form an electronic practice, Shrink-Link...[*http://www.westnet.com/shrink*]. Four are New York State-licensed psychologists; one is a psychiatrist. Each has her own regular practice and specializes in a particular area of psychotherapy. For $20—you pay upfront by typing in your credit card number—you can send off your 200-word (or less) question; it is then routed to the appropriate therapist. Within 72 hours (often within 24 hours), you get back two or three paragraphs of privately E-mailed advice.

The short answer. The cybercouch is most effective at giving people who can clearly identify the dilemma (my daughter is anorexic; I'm deep in debt and can't stop spending) a start toward a solution. A typical Shrink-Link question: "My 5-year-old was diagnosed with attention deficit disorder (ADD) in 1993 and has been on Ritalin ever since. She has been having trouble falling asleep for the past several months and has been moodier than usual of late. What do you think?"

The gist of the response: "Some trial and error is often required before the correct dosage and timing are found, and symptoms such as sleep disturbance and moodiness often occur in the interim. Moreover, since children's rates of metabolism change, dosages often need to be adjusted. Even if the dosage is correct, the behavior irregularities you describe could be caused by administering the drug too late in the afternoon or by a host of other factors, such as nighttime fears. These possibilities need to be ruled out one by one until the culprit is found."

The advice could well be to seek face-to-face counseling. E-mail exchanges are no basis for a diagnosis, for example, warns Marlene Maheu, a San Diego clinical psychologist who headed the American Psychological Association's subcommittee that recently looked into the ethics of cybertherapy. "It's impossible to get an anonymous patient's complete family history in a 200-word question," she says. And without such cues as voice tone, facial expressions and body language, how can a therapist be sure what the problems really are? "Smiley screen faces are a poor substitute for real communication," agrees Leonard Holmes, a therapist based in Newport News, Va., who says his online services are not therapy but "E-mail discussions." ("It's a bit more private than a call-in radio show," he notes.) Holmes charges $1.50 per minute and will spend as much time "with" a patient as the patient desires.

Maheu's subcommittee and other psychology professionals worry that a lack of standards makes people seeking online help vulnerable. "When you are answering questions by E-mail, it's tempting to stray beyond your area of expertise," says Maheu. "The APA's ethical principles prohibit that." Critics also worry that confidentiality is at risk. While patients remain anonymous, a hacker could conceivably identify them. And these Internet sessions aren't encrypted. "You have no way of knowing who is printing the E-mail message out or where it is stored," says Thomas Nagy, a psychologist and Stanford University School of Medicine psychiatry professor. Nagy also worries that people with really significant problems will stop with an online Band-Aid.

Troubling, too, is the fact that patients may know little about the therapist and his or her qualifications. Many sites don't disclose details about the counselors' experience and where they earned their credentials. Leonard Holmes, by contrast, provides a complete biography on his Web page that includes his educational background, what state he is licensed in, as well as areas of expertise. That way, interested patients can check out his professional background before a session.

Beyond the couch. Aside from the various psychologists' couches, other Net offerings can be a great resource for someone trying to research a particular mental illness. One of the richest sites is the American Psychological Association's PsychNET, where you can find a wealth of downloadable material on topics from eating disorders to panic disorders to childhood abuse to how to choose a psychologist. A list of state psychological and mental health organizations is provided, and you can link to related home pages of interest. Other sites that provide entree to a comprehensive list of psychology-related pages: the online *Self-Help & Psychology Magazine,* Psychology.Com's Cyber-Psych link and the Psych Central page. You might look up an article in the *American Journal of Psychology,* for example—or check out the services of the National Alliance for the Mentally Ill or take the Myers Briggs Personality Profile.

Much of the Internet action takes place on a portion of the Web dedicated to a collection of electronic bulletin boards, or newsgroups, where people can look to their peers for support and advice. Each such mental health forum is dedicated to a specific topic: depression *(news:alt.support.depression),* shyness *(news:alt.support.shyness),* loneliness *(news:alt.support.loneliness),* for example. "For consumers who want to compare notes, exchange information and have a virtual shoulder to cry on, these can offer some real solace," says Maheu. All three major online services—America Online, CompuServe and Prodigy—offer similar mental health forums, with lengthy lists of links to other sites. For many people, the knowledge and companionship to be tapped online will be worth much more than byte-size advice.

DEFEATING Depression

An array of new treatments combats the "common cold of mental illness"

Nancy Wartik

Nancy Wartik is a Contributing Editor at AMERICAN HEALTH.
For Charles Kennedy* of Princeton, N.J., the overwhelming sensation was a leaden slowness, as if a heavy weight were bearing down on him. Just beginning a competitive retraining program, the 51-year-old banker needed all his wits about him. Instead Kennedy found it harder and harder to function.

"Usually a challenge triggers my adrenaline," he says. "This time I found it difficult to respond. I couldn't understand the course assignments, much less complete them, which made me feel helpless and hopeless. Everything became very slow." At night Kennedy tossed and turned. He plodded through days in a pall of indifference. "The feeling was, 'Oh yeah, a bus is coming right at me. Should I move or not?' " he says. It was not until a therapist suggested he try an antidepressant drug that Kennedy found relief. "I could sleep better, proceed with initiative," he says. "My indifference disappeared. I became much more of a player again."

Everyone falls into the doldrums at times, or luxuriates in a bit of self-pity or melancholy. But depression is different. A mind-warping, energy-sapping malady, it unbalances the normal rhythms of the body and turns the psychic landscape bleak, robbing a person of vigor and hope. For someone afflicted with clinical (also called unipolar) depression, the sensations of sadness and loss, familiar to everyone on occasion, stretch into weeks or months. Nor does there seem to be an end in sight: Perhaps depression's worst torment is the conviction that things will never change. The depressed feel they will be mired in numbing despair forever.

The trappings of good fortune—wealth, talent or power—confer no immunity. "I am now the most miserable man living," wrote Abraham Lincoln. "If what I feel were equally distributed to the whole human family, there would not be one cheerful face on earth." Sir Winston Churchill, writer Sylvia Plath and actress Jean Seberg were similarly visited with bouts of despair. More recently, TV journalist Mike Wallace, author William Styron and talk show host Dick Cavett went public about their struggles with depression. Last summer, White House aide Vincent Foster committed suicide in the throes of depression apparently triggered by the Capitol Hill pressure cooker. Like Foster, 15% of those suffering from the more severe form of the disorder, which doctors call major depression, will ultimately take their own lives.

Not so long ago, the prevailing belief was that depressed people simply needed to pull themselves together and snap out of it. But an explosion of new research in recent decades has shown depression to be a real disorder that can be diagnosed and successfully treated. "Depression used to be viewed as some sort of moral weakness or personal failure," says Dr. Ewald Horwath, director of the intensive care unit at the New York State Psychiatric Institute in New York City. "Now there's more of a tendency to think of it as a disease, and that's a big improvement."

Most scientists think depression results from an interaction of biochemical, genetic and psychological factors, often, although not always, combined with a change in life circumstances—from the failure of a relationship to the loss of a job. In other words, depression is like many other diseases. "The factors that cause a physical illness such as coronary artery disease include diet, genetics and the way people who have a Type A personality put pressure on themselves," says Horwath. "Cultural factors influence who gets it, how frequent it is in each sex, and how prevalent it is in different epochs. It's the same kind of thing with depression."

Exercise can alleviate moderate cases.

Treatments for depression have expanded along with knowledge of its origins. There are now more than 20 anti-depressants on the market, many of them "cleaner" drugs with fewer side effects than their predecessors. The most popular is the

[*Real names are not used in this article.]

much-ballyhooed Prozac, already prescribed to more than 5 million Americans. Not that pills are the only antidote to depression: Cognitive psychotherapy, developed specifically to attack the disorder, teaches people how to correct the thought patterns that generate black moods. There's now evidence that regular exercise can alleviate more moderate cases of depression, perhaps because it increases levels of certain brain chemicals that mediate mood, and has arousing effects on body metabolism and energy. Victims of seasonal affective disorder, whose despondency comes and goes as the seasons change, often benefit from light therapy. And in some extreme cases of depression, electroconvulsive therapy, a much refined and milder form of the "shock therapy" first used here in the 1940s, can help when other treatments fail or would take too long—as when there is a likelihood of suicide. Through one or more of these treatments, the National Institute of Mental Health estimates that 80% to 90% of the depressed can find relief. As researchers sometimes say jokingly, today is the best time in history to feel miserable.

That's fortunate, because huge numbers of Americans do. More than 9 million people endure major depression yearly in this country, and about one in 20 will face the struggle at some point in his or her life. So ubiquitous is depression that researchers now refer to it as the "common cold of mental illness." And millions more are affected by other mood-related disorders. Victims of dysthymia, a recently identified form of chronic, milder depression, may battle gloom for years at a time (see "Long-Term Blues"). People with manic depression (also called bipolar disorder) veer dizzyingly between protracted emotional heights and depths, and cyclothymics go through less intense but more frequent ups and downs.

Many more women than men experience depression. Puberty is the dividing line: Before it, young boys and girls feel gloomy in almost equal numbers, but at adolescence, girls' depression rates begin to soar. At least twice as many women as men will fall prey to the disorder over the course of a lifetime, most studies have shown. Recent research by Johns Hopkins University psychiatrist Alan Romanoski paints an even more alarming picture: Although women and men have a similar risk of major depression, women suffer from more moderate depressions at *10 times* the rate men do. Researchers hotly debating the reason for this disparity have focused on three areas: physiological causes, such as genetic factors or hormonal imbalances; psychological factors, including differences in how men and women learn to deal with emotions; and social issues, from women's greater susceptibility to sexual abuse and battering to their lower economic status.

Sadly, the greatest obstacles to eliminating depression are ignorance and lack of understanding. For all its prevalence, and despite the many therapies available, two-thirds of those who have it don't get the help they need, often because they don't want to admit the problem or don't recognize its signs. "Many people who have major depression wouldn't even call themselves depressed," says psychiatrist A. John Rush of the University of Texas Southwestern Medical Center in Dallas. "If you ask them, 'Do you know you have clinical depression?'—depression serious enough to need treatment—they

DESPAIR BEYOND DESPAIR

William Styron

the pain is unrelenting, and what makes the condition intolerable is the foreknowledge that no remedy will come—not in a day, an hour, a month or a minute. If there is mild relief, one knows that it is only temporary; more pain will follow. It is hopelessness even more than pain that crushes the soul. So the decision-making of daily life involves not, as in normal affairs, shifting from one annoying situation to another less annoying—or from discomfort to relative comfort, or from boredom to activity—but moving from pain to pain. One does not abandon, even briefly, one's bed of nails, but is attached to it wherever one goes. And this results in a striking experience—one which I have called, borrowing military terminology, the situation of the walking wounded. For in virtually any other serious sickness, a patient who felt similar devastation would be lying flat in bed, possibly sedated and hooked up to the tubes and wires of life-support systems, but at the very least in a posture of repose and in an isolated setting. His invalidism would be necessary, unquestioned and honorably attained. The sufferer from depression has no option and therefore finds himself, like a walking casualty of war, thrust into the most intolerable social situations. There he must, despite the anguish devouring his brain, present a face approximating the one that is associated with ordinary events and companionship. He must try to utter small talk, and be responsive to questions, and knowingly nod and frown and, God help him, even smile. But it is a fierce trial attempting to speak a few simple words.

That December evening, for example, I could have remained in bed as usual during those worst hours, or agreed to the dinner party my wife had arranged downstairs. But the very idea of a decision was academic. Either course was torture, and I chose the dinner not out of any particular merit but through indifference to what I knew would be indistinguishable ordeals of fogbound horror. At dinner I was barely able to speak, but the quartet of guests, who were all good friends, were aware of my condition and politely ignored my catatonic muteness. Then, after dinner, sitting in the living room, I experienced a curious inner convulsion that I can describe only as despair beyond despair. It came out of the cold night; I did not think such anguish possible.

Excerpted from Darkness Visible: A Memoir of Madness, © *1990 by William Styron. Reprinted by permission of Random House.*

41. Defeating Depression

say, 'I don't know what that is.' " Trying to intervene in more cases, the Department of Health and Human Services (HHS) this year issued guidelines to alert general practitioners and other primary-care physicians to depression's warning signs.

As yet, there's no physical test to pinpoint the disease. Instead doctors look for a constellation of symptoms that persist for longer than two weeks. These include deep sadness or numbing apathy, a lack of interest in things that once brought pleasure—from sex to socializing—and at least four of seven other markers: appetite disturbances, sleep problems, fatigue, difficulty concentrating, undue restlessness or lethargy, feelings of worthlessness, or suicidal thoughts. (Someone mourning a death may have one or more of these symptoms for several months without necessarily being clinically depressed.) Many depressed people are also afflicted with vague physical symptoms or complaints.

"They come into the doctor's office with stomachaches or joint pain, or they feel blah," says Dr. Rush. "Many of these patients turn out to have major depression." Untreated, the disorder typically lasts for six months or longer.

Researchers now know several risk factors that raise a person's vulnerability to depression, including a family history of the disorder. Research with twins has provided evidence that depression's roots are at least partially inherited. A 1992 study of more than 1,000 pairs of female twins showed that if one identical twin (who shares all of her sister's genes) suffered major depression, the other's risk was 66% higher than that of someone from the general population. If a fraternal twin was depressed, however, her twin (who is no more genetically similar to her than any other sibling) had a risk only 27% higher. While such statistics suggest genetics play a significant role in depression, Medical College of Virginia psychiatrist Kenneth Kendler, who conducted the study, notes that "depression isn't something you inherit 100%, as you do eye color or height. It's probably about 40% influenced by your genes."

Inheritance may also influence certain personality traits that can make a person depression-prone. Some researchers now argue for the existence of a syndrome—at least partially innate—known as depressive personality disorder, which predisposes those who have it to depression problems. People with this disorder, explains psychiatrist Robert Hirschfeld of the University of Texas Medical Branch in Galveston, tend to be pessimistic and brooding, critical of themselves and others. The probability that such individuals will develop clinical depression is correspondingly higher than the average person's.

Genetics or personality structure may prime a person for depression, but life's travails often play a marked role in pushing someone over the brink. Although some people fall into depressions with no apparent cause, the experience of Angela Wolf* is more typical. A vice president at a Manhattan marketing firm, she plunged into paralyzing despair after she discovered that her husband of 16 years was cheating on her. She was unable to work efficiently or sleep soundly; she cried often and paced restlessly. Not until a friend referred her to a cognitive therapist did Wolf realize what was happening to her.

"It was a relief when he told me I was depressed," she says. "I could say, 'No wonder! So there's a reason I feel this way.' "

A growing body of research supports the idea that major depressions are often triggered by stressful events of the kind Wolf experienced. A study of 680 pairs of female twins, published this year in *The American Journal of Psychiatry,* ranked the importance of nine risk factors for serious depression, including recent upsetting events, genetics, lack of social support, traumas suffered over a lifetime (for example, rape or sexual abuse), and childhood loss of a parent. Of all the variables, recent stress—divorce, illness, legal troubles, bereavement—was the best predictor of a depressive episode. A family history of the disorder ranked second. Similarly, Dr. Romanoski's study, based on data gathered from 800 Baltimore residents, found that 86% of major depressions were precipitated by a real-life event or situation. This research contradicts a prevailing belief that depressions triggered by an identifiable event aren't really illnesses and don't need professional treatment. "Just because we can understand why a person is depressed doesn't mean we shouldn't treat the problem seriously," says psychiatrist Sidney Zisook of the University of California at San Diego. "Depression can develop a life of its own, and once it does, it needs to be addressed, because it's still associated with decreased functioning and suicide."

Painful experiences in early life can also sow the seeds of future gloom. A 1991 Stanford University study attributed up to 35% of the discrepancy between male and female depression rates to sexual abuse of women in childhood. Other research suggests that growing up in the wake of a divorce may also predispose a person to depression. Such trauma may literally be etched into a young brain, some scientists speculate. "Life experiences might create enduring changes in the central nervous system," says Horwath, "and that might alter neurochemistry and place the person at higher risk for depression. The environmental factor ultimately has a biological effect."

Studies have long linked alcoholism and depression, but it's not always clear which is cause and which is effect. Logic would suggest that people in pain drink to ease their sorrow. Yet many studies show that people who are already alcoholic—men in particular—go on to develop major depression, perhaps because high levels of prolonged intoxication eventually unbalance brain chemistry. For women, the cause-and-effect pattern tends to go the other way, although researchers aren't sure why as yet.

No matter what its origins are, the neurochemistry of despair is the same. Imbalances of certain mood-regulating neurotransmitters—chemical messengers that transmit electrochemical signals between brain cells—are thought to underlie depression at its most fundamental level. Among possible scenarios of what goes awry in the brain: Levels of the neurotransmitters that control mood may be abnormally low, or the neural receptors that normally intercept neurotransmitters as they pass from cell to cell may malfunction.

Scientists have so far identified about 100 of the brain's many neurotransmitters. Two of these, norepinephrine and serotonin, appear to be most closely tied to depression. Says psychiatrist Elliott Richelson, director of research at a branch of the Mayo Clinic in Jacksonville, Fla., "It could be that changes in norepinephrine or serotonin levels affect some other neurotransmitter more directly involved in depression. There are probably at least 100 neurotransmitters we haven't even identified yet, so it's highly possible we still have to find the one that's absolutely key in regulating depression."

Antidepressants, which correct brain chemistry imbalances, have been on the market for over 30 years. Some early ones—specifically the tricyclic drugs, such as imipramine—affect neurochemicals other than serotonin and norepinephrine, causing a wide range of potential side effects, including dry mouth, weight gain and drowsiness. Other early antidepressants, the so-called monoamine oxidase (MAO) inhibitors, are inconvenient to take: Patients must avoid cheese, wine and a long list of other foods containing a chemical that reacts with the drug and can send blood pressure soaring. More targeted medications that act solely on mood-regulating neurotransmitters are generally easier on patients' systems. For example, Prozac and another relatively new drug, Zoloft, act only on serotonin. Fewer side effects combined with tales of miracle cures have made these new drugs more popular than the previous generations of antidepressants, which may nonetheless work as well or better in some people.

About 75% can benefit from medication.

Researchers estimate that about 75% of those suffering from major depression can benefit from one of these medications. "In the last decade, there's been a shift toward using antidepressants, and I think that's good," says Brown University psychologist Tracie Shea. "They can be extremely helpful when depression has started to affect functioning. Pills don't solve life's problems, but they can put people in a better position to solve the problems themselves. They give people the energy to look at issues going on in their lives, and that gives them more choice and control."

This sort of talk alarms some mental health professionals, who worry that antidepressants are turning into the latest pharmaceutical fad, used in ever milder cases of the blues, rather than for the severe disorders they were developed to treat. "I'm not saying they should never be used," says Dr. Roger Greenberg, a psychologist at the State University of New York Health Science Center in Syracuse, "but I'm concerned at the promise being held out for drugs. I think people should be more cautious about taking them than they have been up to now. We want quick and easy solutions for complex and difficult problems—it's a fast-food kind of mentality. Drugs have a natural appeal, they help people say, 'I'm not responsible for my actions, it's my body chemistry.'"

Psychiatrist Peter Kramer, author of the best-selling book *Listening to Prozac,* views drug treatment differently. "There's an idea that there's a moral price to be paid if you're on medication, and that it's better to do things by other means. Is it more comfortable and easier to believe that disorders can be

Long-Term Blues

a milder form of depression known as dysthymia can dog a sufferer for years on end. "It's like a low-grade infection people just can't get rid of," says psychologist James McCullough, director of the Unipolar Mood Disorders Institute at Virginia Commonwealth University in Richmond. "They're not taken out of the work force or the home—they just feel bad most of the time. They don't know why, but they've felt that way for as long as they can remember."

An estimated 3% to 4% of Americans—two out of three of them women—experience dysthymia during their lifetime. Like victims of major depression, they may have sleep, appetite, energy and concentration problems. The disorder often strikes early in life: Dr. James Kocsis, a dysthymia expert at Cornell Medical Center in New York City, says his average patient has been despondent for 20 years, usually beginning in childhood or adolescence. Only about 10% to 15% of cases clear up on their own. Not surprisingly, dysthymics tend to have interpersonal problems, poor self-esteem and difficulty asserting themselves. They're also at significantly increased risk of major depression: Those who experience a severe slump are said to have "double depression."

Prior to 1980, when the disorder was first identified, dysthymics were typically dismissed as dark, gloomy people. Now mental health practitioners increasingly treat dysthymia like depression, with promising results. A 1988 study by Kocsis published in the *Archives of General Psychiatry* showed that six out of 10 dysthymics respond to antidepressants. "Patients say, 'This is the first time in my life I've ever felt normal,'" says Kocsis. "Their occupational underachievement and social problems tend to improve rapidly. One of the outcomes of treating dysthymia is that you start receiving wedding invitations. Patients get married and invite their psychiatrists to their weddings."

Unfortunately, even after a year of drug treatment, 60% to 70% of patients who discontinue medication will relapse. So far, there have been no controlled clinical trials of psychotherapy's effectiveness against the disorder. But Dr. McCullough, who has treated some 150 dysthymics with a combination of cognitive and behavioral therapy, says he's encouraged by the outcome. Of 20 therapy patients on whom he's kept systematic records, 70% were still depression-free after two years. "If their basic thought and behavior patterns don't change, dysthymics will stay depressed no matter what good things happen to them," notes McCullough. "These are issues that therapy can address."

treated through honesty and hard work? Yes. But if you have someone in front of you who's suffering, you have to be realistic about choosing the best way to alleviate their pain."

Patients who've benefited from antidepressants tend to agree with Dr. Kramer. Charlotte Goldberg,* 30, of New York City was plagued by depression after she separated from her husband and switched careers. Yet she had reservations about trying an antidepressant. "I was very hesitant," she recalls. "I was afraid I'd become falsely happy, that it wouldn't really be me. It bothered me to think of being chemically altered." But after she began taking Zoloft, Goldberg changed her mind: "I feel good but not in a stupid, high way," she says. "I can think more clearly, I'm calmer, not as anxious. Being less moody and having more energy has helped me to work through my problems better."

In sum, antidepressants can often restore emotional and physical equilibrium, but they don't make people euphoric or eliminate life stresses. After reviewing more than 400 clinical trials of antidepressants, a panel of distinguished researchers who developed the HHS depression treatment guidelines concluded that "no one antidepressant is clearly more effective than another. No single medication results in remission for all patients." Only 50% to 60% of patients respond to the first drug they try; the rest need to experiment until they find a drug that works for them. Moreover, for reasons researchers still don't understand, it usually takes four to six weeks before patients begin to feel the medication's full effects.

When the HHS guidelines were issued, the American Psychological Association, whose members specialize in talk therapy, issued a press release disassociating the organization from the guidelines on the grounds that they "do not encourage sufficient collaboration with mental health specialists and appear to be biased toward medication." In fact, says Rush of Texas Southwestern Medical Center, who chaired the government panel, 60% of antidepressants are now distributed by primary-care doctors, meaning that many people already take the drugs without accompanying psychotherapy. Some experts see no problem with that. "For the severely depressed patient, I don't think talk therapy is helpful," says the Mayo Clinic's Richelson. "The folks I see are really ill, and they're not going to be helped by the addition of a 50-minute hour."

Still, when the HHS panel compared the efficacy of talk therapy *and* medication with drug treatment alone, they found the combination treatment to be somewhat more effective. And a number of studies show that in less severe depressions psychotherapy by itself may work just as well as antidepressants. "My hunch is that whatever drugs are doing to brain chemistry, effective therapy can do also," notes Vanderbilt University clinical psychologist Steven Hollon, a specialist in cognitive therapy. "You're changing an attitude and that changes biology—just as biology changes attitude. I think the two are interactive processes."

A 1989 National Institute of Mental Health study of people with mild to moderate depressions found therapy to be as successful as medication in helping patients recover over a 16-week period. Overall, research suggests that some 50% of the depressed can alleviate the symptoms of depression with either cognitive therapy or other types.

Cognitive therapy was developed in the '60s by psychiatrist Aaron Beck, now at the University of Pennsylvania. Its premise is that thoughts create feelings: Change destructive ideas, Beck said, and unhappy emotions will change too. One such destructive pattern is a tendency to blame oneself exclusively when something goes wrong. Explains Dr. Hollon, "Someone who loses his job and says, 'I'm not good enough,' is more likely to get depressed than someone who says, 'It's a lousy economy and Bill Clinton is to blame.' "

The inclination to brood rather than act on difficulties is another pattern believed to be self-defeating and one that might help explain some of the male-female disparity in depression rates. When Stanford University psychologist Susan Nolen-Hoeksema reviewed the literature, she was struck by the fact that "women generally seem to stay with negative emotions, like depression or anxiety, more than men do. It's often talked of as a woman's strength to be able to acknowledge negative emotions, but I started looking at how it works against them."

Dr. Nolen-Hoeksema concluded that people who obsessively ponder a problem and its negative implications can find themselves sucked into a vicious circle of gloom. Those who distract themselves with sports or other enjoyable activities—as many men seem to do instinctively—emerge from unhappy moods faster and in a better state to tackle problems. Why do women tend to be brooders and men doers? "One of our guesses is that young boys aren't allowed to ruminate," says Nolen-Hoeksema. "They're taught to be active from an early age. Research on preschoolers seems to show that one thing parents will not tolerate is emotionality in boys. It's also possible that the things girls worry about actually are harder to deal with than the things boys worry about. Girls think a lot more about interpersonal relationships than boys do, and those are hard to control."

The logic behind cognitive therapy may sound simplistic, but it boasts many enthusiastic converts. Angela Wolf, the woman whose depression was triggered by her husband's infidelities, says cognitive therapy saved her life. "I was assaulted by automatic negative thoughts and my therapist would have me try to prove them to myself, the way you would to a jury. I'd think, 'If I leave this marriage, no man will ever be attracted to me.' Then I'd have to write down why I thought that statement was true, and also why I thought it wasn't. Inevitably, I'd wind up proving it *wasn't* true." Now divorced, Wolf says, "I'm infinitely happier today."

One particularly controversial issue among scientists who debate the merits of psychological vs. drug treatments is recurrence: At least 50% of those who suffer an attack will experience another. "Our whole concept of the disorder is shifting from thinking of it as time-limited to recognizing that it's much more chronic than we thought," says Brown's Dr. Shea. "For many people, depression won't be a one-shot deal." She adds that a few months of treatment with drugs or therapy, until fairly recently considered standard, often aren't enough to keep a patient well: "People shouldn't think of depression as something that can necessarily be cured in 16 weeks."

Therapy proponents argue that patients have a better chance of staying depression-free over time if they learn psychological techniques to help ward off relapses. "Pharmacology [drug therapy] is marvelous," says Hollon, "but it mostly suppresses symptoms. It's like taking aspirin. If you want to take it every day, it will do a very good job of stopping your headache. But if you learn to meditate and you reduce your overall stress level, maybe you won't get headaches to begin with. In that sense, cognitive therapy may be analagous to learning to meditate."

In a recent study published in the *Archives of General Psychiatry*, Hollon and colleague Mark Evans, a University of Minnesota psychologist, found that about 75% of depressed people in each of two groups treated either with medication or cognitive therapy felt well enough to stop treatment after three months. But over the next two years, 50% of those treated with medication relapsed into depressions, while only 20% of those treated with therapy did.

A growing number of doctors, however, are dealing with the threat of recurrence by keeping patients on medication for much longer periods of time—in some instances, many years beyond the six to nine months typically allotted for treating an episode of depression. Some 90% of those who stay on antidepressants remain symptom-free, but it has yet to be seen if prolonged antidepressant use carries undiscovered risks. "I'm a little nervous about the amount of time people are kept on drugs these days," says Hollon. "There probably aren't any really nasty complications lurking out there, but we're mucking around with complex physiology. You always wonder about the risk of side effects."

Clearly, there are complex questions remaining about depression that can only be answered through years of research. One point, however, is clear: Today, no one need stoically endure the lethargy and sense of futility that descend with an episode of depression. "I don't think long-term suffering is very therapeutic," sums up Dr. Zisook of UC-San Diego. "It doesn't help someone become a better person. And it's not something that people need to go through when we have treatments for it."

For more information on mood disorders, contact the following organizations: D/ART (Depression Awareness, Recognition, and Treatment), 800-421-4211; the National Depressive and Manic-Depressive Association, 800-826-3632; and the Depression and Related Affective Disorders Association, 410-955-4647.

ADDICTED

Why do people get hooked? Mounting evidence points to a powerful brain chemical called dopamine

By J. MADELEINE NASH

IMAGINE YOU ARE TAKING A SLUG OF WHISKEY. A puff of a cigarette. A toke of marijuana. A snort of cocaine. A shot of heroin. Put aside whether these drugs are legal or illegal. Concentrate, for now, on the chemistry. The moment you take that slug, that puff, that toke, that snort, that shot, trillions of potent molecules surge through your bloodstream and into your brain. Once there, they set off a cascade of chemical and electrical events, a kind of neurological chain reaction that ricochets around the skull and rearranges the interior reality of the mind.

Given the complexity of these events—and the inner workings of the mind in general—it's not surprising that scientists have struggled mightily to make sense of the mechanisms of addiction. Why do certain substances have the power to make us feel so good (at least at first)? Why do some people fall so easily into the thrall of alcohol, cocaine, nicotine and other addictive substances, while others can, literally, take them or leave them?

The answer, many scientists are convinced, may be simpler than anyone has dared imagine. What ties all these mood-altering drugs together, they say, is a remarkable ability to elevate levels of a common substance in the brain called dopamine. In fact, so overwhelming has evidence of the link between dopamine and drugs of abuse become that the distinction (pushed primarily by the tobacco industry and its supporters) between substances that are addictive and those that are merely habit-forming has very nearly been swept away.

The Liggett Group, smallest of the U.S.'s Big Five cigarette makers, broke ranks in March and conceded not only that tobacco is addictive but also that the company has known it all along. While RJR Nabisco and the others continue to battle in the courts-insisting that smokers are not hooked, just exercising free choice—their denials ring increasingly hollow in the face of the growing weight of evidence. Over the past year, several scientific groups have made the case that in dopamine-rich areas of the brain, nicotine behaves remarkably like cocaine. And late last week a federal judge ruled for the first time that the Food and Drug Administration has the right to regulate tobacco as a drug and cigarettes as drug-delivery devices.

Now, a team of researchers led by psychiatrist Dr. Nora Volkow of the Brookhaven National Laboratory in New York has published the strongest evidence to date that the surge of dopamine in addicts' brains is what triggers a cocaine high. In last week's edition of the journal *Nature* they described how powerful brain-imaging technology can be used to track the rise of dopamine and link it to feelings of euphoria.

Like serotonin (the brain chemical affected by such antidepressants as Prozac), dopamine is a neurotransmitter—a molecule that ferries messages from one neuron within the brain to another. Serotonin is associated with feelings of sadness and well-being, dopamine with pleasure and elation. Dopamine can be elevated by a hug, a kiss, a word of praise or a winning poker hand—as well as by the potent pleasures that come from drugs.

The idea that a single chemical could be associated with everything from snorting cocaine and smoking tobacco to getting good

PRIME SUSPECT

They don't yet know the precise mechanism by which it works, but scientists are increasingly convinced that dopamine plays a key role in a wide range of addictions, including those to heroin, nicotine, alcohol and marijuana

6. ❖ ENHANCING HUMAN ADJUSTMENT: LEARNING TO COPE EFFECTIVELY

DOPAMINE MAY BE LINKED TO GAMBLING, CHOCOLATE AND EVEN SEX

grades and enjoying sex has electrified scientists and changed the way they look at a wide range of dependencies, chemical and otherwise. Dopamine, they now believe, is not just a chemical that transmits pleasure signals but may, in fact, be the master molecule of addiction.

This is not to say dopamine is the only chemical involved or that the deranged thought processes that mark chronic drug abuse are due to dopamine alone. The brain is subtler than that. Drugs modulate the activity of a variety of brain chemicals, each of which intersects with many others. "Drugs are like sledgehammers," observes Dr. Eric Nestler of the Yale University School of Medicine. "They profoundly alter many pathways."

Nevertheless, the realization that dopamine may be a common end point of all those pathways represents a signal advance. Provocative, controversial, unquestionably incomplete, the dopamine hypothesis provides a basic framework for understanding how a genetically encoded trait—such as a tendency to produce too little dopamine—might intersect with environmental influences to create a serious behavioral disorder. Therapists have long known of patients who, in addition to having psychological problems, abuse drugs as well. Could their drug problems be linked to some inborn quirk? Might an inability to absorb enough dopamine, with its pleasure-giving properties, cause them to seek gratification in drugs?

Such speculation is controversial, for it suggests that broad swaths of the population may be genetically predisposed to drug abuse. What is not controversial is that the social cost of drug abuse, whatever its cause, is enormous. Cigarettes contribute to the death toll from cancer and heart disease. Alcohol is the leading cause of domestic violence and highway deaths. The needles used to inject heroin and cocaine are spreading AIDS. Directly or indirectly, addiction to drugs, cigarettes and alcohol is thought to account for a third of all hospital admissions, a quarter of all deaths and a majority of serious crimes. In the U.S. alone the combined medical and social costs of drug abuse are believed to exceed $240 billion.

FOR NEARLY A QUARTER-CENTURY the U.S. has been waging a war on drugs, with little apparent success. As scientists learn more about how dopamine works (and how drugs work on it), the evidence suggests that we may be fighting the wrong battle. Americans tend to think of drug addiction as a failure of character. But this stereotype is beginning to give way to the recognition that drug dependence has a clear biological basis. "Addiction," declares Brookhaven's Volkow, "is a disorder of the brain no different from other forms of mental illness."

That new insight may be the dopamine hypothesis' most important contribution in the fight against drugs. It completes the loop between the mechanism of addiction and programs for treatment. And it raises hope for more effective therapies. Abstinence, if maintained, not only halts the physical and psychological damage wrought by drugs but in large measure also reverses it.

Genes and social forces may conspire to turn people into addicts but do not doom them to remain so. Consider the case of Rafael Rios, who grew up in a housing project in New York City's drug-infested South Bronx. For 18 years, until he turned 31, Rios, whose father died of alcoholism, led a double life. He graduated from Harvard Law School and joined a prestigious Chicago law firm. Yet all the while he was secretly visiting a 'shooting gallery' once a day. His favored concoction: heroin spiked with a jolt of cocaine. Ten years ago, Rios succeeded in kicking his habit—for good, he hopes. He is now executive director of A Safe Haven, a Chicago-based chain of residential facilities for recovering addicts.

How central is dopamine's role in this familiar morality play? Scientists are still trying to sort that out. It is no accident, they say, that people are attracted to drugs. The major drugs of abuse, whether depressants like heroin or stimulants like cocaine, mimic the structure of neurotransmitters, the most mind-bending chemicals nature has ever concocted. Neurotransmitters underlie every thought and emotion, memory and learning; they carry the signals between all the nerve cells, or neurons, in the brain. Among some 50 neurotransmitters discovered to date, a good half a dozen, including dopamine, are known to play a role in addiction.

The neurons that produce this molecular messenger are surprisingly rare. Clustered in loose knots buried deep in the brain, they number a few tens of thousands of nerve cells out of an estimated total of 100 billion. But through long, wire-like projections known as axons, these cells influence neurological activity in many regions, including the nucleus accumbens, the primitive structure that is one of the brain's key pleasure centers. At a purely chemical level, every experience humans find enjoyable—whether listening to music, embracing a lover or savoring chocolate—amounts to little more than an explosion of dopamine in the nucleus accumbens, as exhilarating and ephemeral as a firecracker.

Dopamine, like most biologically important molecules, must be kept within strict bounds. Too little dopamine in certain areas of the brain triggers the tremors and paralysis of Parkinson's disease. Too much causes the hallucinations and bizarre thoughts of schizophrenia. A breakthrough in addiction research came in 1975, when psychologists Roy Wise and Robert Yokel at Concordia University in Montreal reported on the remarkable behavior of some drug-addicted rats. One day the animals were placidly dispensing cocaine and amphetamines to themselves by pressing a lever attached to their cages. The next they were angrily banging at the lever like someone trying to summon a stalled elevator. The reason? The scientists had injected the rats with a drug that blocked the action of dopamine.

In the years since, evidence linking dopamine to drugs has mounted. Amphetamines stimulate dopamine-producing cells to pump out more of the chemical. Cocaine keeps dopamine levels high by inhibiting the activity of a transporter molecule that would ordinarily ferry dopamine back into the cells that produce it. Nicotine, heroin and alcohol

HIGH AND LOWS
Number who used in the past month

Drug	Number
Heroin	200,000
Triggers release of dopamine; acts on other neurotransmitters	
Amphetamines	800,000
Stimulate excess release of dopamine	
Cocaine/Crack	1.5 million
Blocks dopamine absorption	
Marijuana	10 million
Binds to areas of brain involved in mood and memory; triggers release of dopamine	
Alcohol	11 million abusers
Triggers dopamine release; acts on other neurotransmitters	
Nicotine	61 million
Triggers release of dopamine	
Caffeine	130 million*
May trigger release of dopamine	

Sources: SAMHSA, National Coffee Association   *coffee drinkers

WHAT ELSE?

Preliminary evidence suggests that dopamine may be involved even when we form dependencies on things—like coffee or candy—that we don't think of as drugs at all

trigger a complex chemical cascade that raises dopamine levels. And a still unknown chemical in cigarette smoke, a group led by Brookhaven chemist Joanna Fowler reported last year, may extend the activity of dopamine by blocking a mopping-up enzyme, called MAO B, that would otherwise destroy it.

The evidence that Volkow and her colleagues present in the current issue of *Nature* suggests that dopamine is directly responsible for the exhilarating rush that reinforces the desire to take drugs, at least in cocaine addicts. In all, 17 users participated in the study, says Volkow, and they experienced a high whose intensity was directly related to how extensively cocaine tied up available binding sites on the molecules that transport dopamine around the brain. To produce any high at all, she and her colleagues found, cocaine had to occupy at least 47% of these sites; the "best" results occurred when it took over 60% to 80% of the sites, effectively preventing the transporters from latching onto dopamine and spiriting it out of circulation.

SCIENTISTS BELIEVE THE DOPAMINE system arose very early in the course of animal evolution because it reinforces behaviors so essential to survival. "If it were not for the fact that sex is pleasurable," observes Charles Schuster of Wayne State University in Detroit, "we would not engage in it." Unfortunately, some of the activities humans are neurochemically tuned to find agreeable—eating foods rich in fat and sugar, for instance—have backfired in modern society. Just as a surfeit of food and a dearth of exercise have conspired to turn heart disease and diabetes into major health problems, so the easy availability of addictive chemicals has played a devious trick. Addicts do not crave heroin or cocaine or alcohol or nicotine per se but want the rush of dopamine that these drugs produce.

Dopamine, however, is more than just a feel-good molecule. It also exercises extraordinary power over learning and memory. Think of dopamine, suggests P. Read Montague of the Center for Theoretical Neuroscience at Houston's Baylor College of Medicine, as the proverbial carrot, a reward the brain doles out to networks of neurons for making survival-enhancing choices. And while the details of how this system works are not yet understood, Montague and his colleagues at the Salk Institute in San Diego, California, and M.I.T. have proposed a model that seems quite plausible. Each time the outcome of an action is better than expected, they predicted, dopamine-releasing neurons should increase the rate at which they fire. When an outcome is worse, they should decrease it. And if the outcome is as expected, the firing rate need not change at all.

As a test of his model, Montague created a computer program that simulated the nectar-gathering activity of bees. Programmed with a dopamine-like reward system and set loose on a field of virtual "flowers," some of which were dependably sweet and some of which were either very sweet or not sweet at all, the virtual bees chose the reliably sweet flowers 85% of the time. In laboratory experiments real bees behave just like their virtual counterparts. What does this have to do with drug abuse? Possibly quite a lot, says Montague. The theory is that dopamine-enhancing chemicals fool the brain into thinking drugs are as beneficial as nectar to the bee, thus hijacking a natural reward system that dates back millions of years.

The degree to which learning and memory sustain the addictive process is only now being appreciated. Each time a neurotransmitter like dopamine floods a synapse, scientists believe, circuits that trigger thoughts and motivate actions are etched onto the brain. Indeed, the neurochemistry supporting addiction is so powerful that the people, objects and places associated with drug taking are also imprinted on the brain. Stimulated by food, sex or the smell of tobacco, former smokers can no more control the urge to light up than Pavlov's dogs could stop their urge to salivate. For months Rafael Rios lived in fear of catching a glimpse of bare arms—his own or someone else's. Whenever he did, he remembers, he would be seized by a nearly unbearable urge to find a drug-filled syringe.

Indeed, the brain has many devious tricks for ensuring that the irrational act of taking drugs, deemed "good" because it enhances dopamine, will be repeated. PET-scan images taken by Volkow and her colleagues reveal that the absorption of a cocaine-like chemical by neurons is profoundly reduced in cocaine addicts in contrast to normal subjects. One explanation: the addicts' neurons, assaulted by abnormally high levels of dopamine, have responded defensively and reduced the number of sites (or receptors) to which dopamine can bind. In the absence of drugs, these nerve cells probably experience a dopamine deficit, Volkow speculates, so while addicts begin by taking drugs to feel high, they end up taking them in order not to feel low.

PET-scan images of the brains of recovering cocaine addicts reveal other striking changes, including a dramatically impaired ability to process glucose, the primary energy source for working neurons. Moreover, this impairment—which persists for up to 100 days after withdrawal—is greatest in the prefrontal cortex, a dopamine-rich area of the brain that controls impulsive and irrational behavior. Addicts, in fact, display many of the symptoms shown by patients who have suffered strokes or injuries to the prefrontal cortex. Damage to this region, University of Iowa neurologist Antonio Damasio and his colleagues have demonstrated, destroys the emotional compass that controls behaviors the patient knows are unacceptable.

Anyone who doubts that genes influence behavior should see the mice in Marc Caron's lab. These tireless rodents race around their cages for hours on end. They lose weight because they rarely stop to eat, and then they drop from exhaustion because they are unable to sleep. Why? The mice, says Caron, a biochemist at Duke University's Howard Hughes Medical Institute

CRACK

Prolonged cocaine use deadens nerve endings in the brain's pleasure-regulation system. A brain scan of a cocaine abuser, shows a marked drop in the number of functioning dopamine receptors

laboratory, are high on dopamine. They lack the genetic mechanism that sponges up this powerful stuff and spirits it away. Result: there is so much dopamine banging around in the poor creatures' synapses that the mice, though drug-free, act as if they were strung out on cocaine.

For years scientists have suspected that genes play a critical role in determining who will become addicted to drugs and who will not. But not until now have they had molecular tools powerful enough to go after the prime suspects. Caron's mice are just the most recent example. By knocking out a single gene—the so-called dopamine-transporter gene—Caron and his colleagues may have created a strain of mice so sated with dopamine that they are oblivious to the allure of cocaine, and possibly alcohol and heroin as well. "What's exciting about our mice," says Caron, "is that they should allow us to test the hypothesis that all these drugs funnel through the dopamine system."

Several dopamine genes have already been tentatively, and controversially, linked to alcoholism and drug abuse. Inherited variations in these genes modify the efficiency

COKE'S HIGH IS DIRECTLY TIED TO DOPAMINE LEVELS

A.A.'S PATH TO RECOVERY STILL SEEMS THE BEST

with which nerve cells process dopamine, or so the speculation goes. Thus, some scientists conjecture, a dopamine-transporter gene that is superefficient, clearing dopamine from the synapses too rapidly, could predispose some people to a form of alcoholism characterized by violent and impulsive behavior. In essence, they would be mirror images of Caron's mice. Instead of being drenched in dopamine, their synapses would be dopamine-poor.

The dopamine genes known as D2 and D4 might also play a role in drug abuse, for similar reasons. Both these genes, it turns out, contain the blueprints for assembling what scientists call a receptor, a minuscule bump on the surface of cells to which biologically active molecules are attracted. And just as a finger lights up a room by merely flicking a switch, so dopamine triggers a sequence of chemical reactions each time it binds to one of its five known receptors. Genetic differences that reduce the sensitivity of these receptors or decrease their number could diminish the sensation of pleasure.

The problem is, studies that have purported to find a basis for addiction in variations of the D2 and D4 genes have not held up under scrutiny. Indeed, most scientists think addiction probably involves an intricate dance between environmental influences and multiple genes, some of which may influence dopamine activity only indirectly. This has not stopped some researchers from promoting the provocative theory that many people who become alcoholics and drug addicts suffer from an inherited condition dubbed the reward-deficiency syndrome. Low dopamine levels caused by a particular version of the D2 gene, they say, may link a breathtaking array of aberrant behaviors. Among them: severe alcoholism, pathological gambling, binge eating and attention-deficit hyperactivity disorder.

The more science unmasks the powerful biology that underlies addiction, the brighter the prospects for treatment become. For instance, the discovery by Fowler and her team that a chemical that inhibits the mopping-up enzyme MAO B may play a role in cigarette addiction has already opened new possibilities for therapy. A number of well-tolerated MAO B inhibitor drugs developed to treat Parkinson's disease could find a place in the antismoking arsenal. Equally promising, a Yale University team led by Eric Nestler and David Self has found that another type of compound—one that targets the dopamine receptor known as D1—seems to alleviate, at least in rats, the intense craving that accompanies withdrawal from cocaine. One day, suggests Self, a D1 skin patch might help cocaine abusers kick their habit, just as the nicotine patch attenuates the desire to smoke.

Like methadone, the compound that activates D1 appears to be what is known as a partial agonist. Because such medications stimulate some of the same brain pathways as drugs of abuse, they are often addictive in their own right, though less so. And while treating heroin addicts with methadone may seem like a cop-out to people who have never struggled with a drug habit, clinicians say they desperately need more such agents to tide addicts—particularly cocaine addicts—over the first few months of treatment, when the danger of relapse is highest.

REALISTICALLY, NO ONE BELIEVES better medications alone will solve the drug problem. In fact, one of the most hopeful messages coming out of current research is that the biochemical abnormalities associated with addiction can be reversed through learning. For that reason, all sorts of psychosocial interventions, ranging from psychotherapy to 12-step programs, can and do help. Cognitive therapy, which seeks to supply people with coping skills (exercising after work instead of going to a bar, for instance), appears to hold particular promise. After just 10 weeks of therapy, before-and-after PET scans suggest, some patients suffering from obsessive-compulsive disorder (which has some similarities with addiction) manage to resculpt not only their behavior but also activity patterns in their brain.

In late 20th century America, where drugs of abuse are being used on an unprecedented scale, the mounting evidence that treatment works could not be more welcome. Until now, policymakers have responded to the drug problem as though it were mostly a criminal matter. Only a third of the $15 billion the U.S. earmarks for the war on drugs goes to prevention and treatment. "In my view, we've got things upside down," says Dr. David Lewis, director of the Center for Alcohol and Addiction Studies at Brown University School of Medicine. "By relying so heavily on a criminalized approach, we've only added to the stigma of drug abuse and prevented high-quality medical care."

Ironically, the biggest barrier to making such care available is the perception that efforts to treat addiction are wasted. Yet treatment for drug abuse has a failure rate no differentから that for other chronic diseases. Close to half of recovering addicts fail to maintain complete abstinence after a year—about the same proportion of patients with diabetes and hypertension who fail to comply with their diet, exercise and medication regimens. What doctors who treat drug abuse should strive for, says Alan Leshner, director of the National Institute on Drug Abuse, is not necessarily a cure but long-term care that controls the progress of the disease and alleviates its worst symptoms. "The occasional relapse is normal," he says, "and just an indication that more treatment is needed."

Rafael Rios has been luckier than many. He kicked his habit in one lengthy struggle that included four months of in-patient treatment at a residential facility and a year of daily outpatient sessions. During that time, Rios checked into 12-step meetings continually, sometimes attending three a day. As those who deal with alcoholics and drug addicts know, such exertions of will power and courage are more common than most people suspect. They are the best reason yet to start treating addiction as the medical and public health crisis it really is.

—*With reporting by Alice Park/New York*

DON'T FACE STRESS ALONE

It's no news that stress can make you sick. But recent research says the solution isn't working less or playing more. It's having someone to confide in.

By Benedict Carey

THE CURE FOR EXCESSIVE STRESS SHOULD be excessive cash. A fat pile of Microsoft common that provides for limo service and trips to the Seychelles and nannies and someone to vacuum those tumbleweed pet hairs that breed in every corner of the house. Better still, a house that cleans itself. That way we'd have time to read Emerson, learn to play some baroque stringed instrument, and sample Eastern gurus like finger food, accumulating vast reserves of inner peace and healing energy....

We're fooling ourselves. Even stinking rich, most of us would often feel rushed, harassed, afraid that the maid's boyfriend had designs on our Swedish stereo components. We'd lose sleep, lose our tempers, and continue to wonder whether stress was killing us. Not because money doesn't buy

Almost half of Americans say they'd rather be alone when they're stressed. Only 18 percent would call a friend.

tranquility; it buys plenty. But because what we call stress is more than the sum of our chores and responsibilities and financial troubles. It's also a state of mind, a way of interpreting the world, a pattern of behavior.

Think of the people you know. There are those who are so consumed with work that they practically sleep with their cell phones, who go wild when they just have to wait in line at the checkout. And then there are those who breeze through the day as pleased as park rangers—despite having deadlines and kids and a broken-down car and charity work and scowling Aunt Agnes living in the spare bedroom. Back in the 1960s cardiologists Ray Rosenman and Meyer Friedman labeled these polar opposites Type A and Type B. They described Type As as "joyless strivers," people who go through life feeling harried, hostile, and combative. Type Bs, by contrast, are unhurried, even tempered, emotionally secure. In person Type As may be twitchy, prone to interrupt, resentful of conversational diversions. Type Bs are as placid as giraffes, well mannered, affectionately patient. In a landmark 1971 study Rosenman and Friedman found that Type As were about twice as likely to develop coronary artery disease as Type Bs. This was the first evidence of a phenomenon that we now take for granted: People consumed by stress often live short lives.

Often. But not always. Some Type As live long and prosper. Some Type Bs succumb to heart attacks before they turn 50. Rosenman and Friedman's theory represented a giant step in tracing a link between disease and personality. But it only partly explained why stress sometimes damages the heart. So the search has been under way to discover a more specific connection between personality and illness. In the past decade findings in fields as seemingly unrelated as sociology and immunology have begun to converge on a surprising answer. Of course it matters if your life is a high-wire act of clamoring demands and pressing deadlines. And yes, it does make a difference whether you're angry or retiring, effusive or shy, belligerent or thoughtful. But what really matters appears to be something much simpler: whether you have someone in your life who's emotionally on call, who's willing to sit up late and hear your complaints.

HUMAN EMOTIONS ARE a messy affair, fleeting, contradictory, and as hard to define as human beings themselves. So it's no wonder researchers have found themselves groping around the dim and convoluted catacombs of personality, trying to locate the core of the trouble with Type As. Some suspect the real villain may be a specific trait such as hostility, cynicism, or self-centeredness. And indeed, all of these characteristics are prevalent in many people who develop coronary disease. But none has proved terribly useful for predicting who will get sick. The search has been a little like being fitted for glasses: Lens two looks clearer than lens one at first, but then you're not so sure. Still, something's there, all right, and several studies conducted in the late eighties and early nineties have finally brought its ghostly shape into focus.

"If you look across all of these studies for a pattern," says psychologist Margaret Chesney, who has spent the past 20 years doing precisely that, "you see that the hostility questionnaires and the Type A interview and all the other measures—they're all picking up the same thing. It's this person who's often suspicious; who sees people as being in their way; who, when they meet someone new, asks, 'What do you do? Where did you go to school?'—not to make a connection but to assess the competition."

More details emerged in 1989 when psychologists Jerry Suls and Choi Wan of the State University of New York at Albany reviewed the Type A research to look for a common thread. They concentrated on studies whose authors had performed general psychological profiles as well as Type A assessments. As a rule, general psych profiles ask directly about fears, insecurities, childhood traumas, and so on, while the Type A diagnosis focuses on how pressured a person feels and how pleasantly he or she answers aggressive questions.

Suls and Wan had suspected that Type A behavior would be associated with emotional distress. But they found something strange. The Type As did show strains of insecurity and emotional isolation—but none of the anxiety and fear associated with the garden-variety neurotic. These are the sort of people who need counseling but consider therapists overpriced palm-readers. "The picture we're getting is of someone who has deep problems but doesn't admit them," says Suls. "So there are a couple of possibilities here. Either they're in denial. Or they really don't have rich inner lives. They never really think about these things."

They aren't Oprah Winfrey fans, in short. They're happy enough talking about work, fashion, sports—anything but the mushy personal stuff. "If you confront them with that," says Suls, "they get angry. They blow up." As one researcher puts it, "They never let their guard down. If you come close, they wonder, What is this person after?" Spare me the advice, Sigmund, can't you see I'm busy?

This evidence, admittedly raw, is still the subject of much debate, but it has even the most authoritative, skeptical, hard-line figures in the field talking like late-night radio shrinks. Just listen to founding father Rosenman, who has guarded the Type A franchise like a hawk, staring down dozens of psychologists whose work he deemed soft or flawed. "After 40 years of observing and treating thousands of patients, and doing all of the studies, I believe that what's underneath the inappropriate competitiveness of Type As is a deep-seated insecurity. I never would have said that before, but I keep coming back to it. It's different from anxiety in the usual sense, because Type As are not people who retreat. They constantly compete because it helps them suppress the insecurity they're afraid others will sense.

"If I felt this way, how would I cover it up? I'd distract myself, go faster and faster, and win over everybody else. I'd look at everyone as a threat, because they might expose me."

Avoiding exposure inevitably means avoiding close relationships. The person

The people most vulnerable to stress are those who are emotionally isolated. They might have the biggest Rolodex, but they're alone.

Rosenman is describing has friends, sure, but no genuine confidants, no one who's allowed so much as a whiff of frailty. That's why many researchers now believe that the symptom most common among those vulnerable to stress is emotional isolation. As Chesney puts it, "These people might have the biggest Rolodex, but they're alone. They're busy looking for more connections, charming more people. When they feel isolated they get busy. It's a defense mechanism."

According to Jonathan Schedler, a research psychologist affiliated with Harvard

43. Don't Face Stress Alone

They Touched a Nation

THANKS TO PUBLIC FIGURES who spoke out about their illnesses, we have all grown more comfortable in the past decade confronting health problems that were long shrouded in lonely silence.
—*Rita Rubin*

MUHAMMAD ALI

It was the most arresting moment of the 1996 Olympics in Atlanta: the former boxer, arm trembling, face frozen, raising the torch to the light the ceremonial flame. Calls flooded the National Parkinson's Foundation, which adopted a torch as its symbol.

ANNETTE FUNICELLO

In 1992, when the onetime Mickey Mouse Club girl publicly revealed her diagnosis, we all suddenly knew at least one person with MS: Annette. "She is everyone's extended family member," says Arney Rosenblat of the National Multiple Sclerosis Society.

LINDA ELLERBEE

Months after the journalist underwent a double mastectomy, she produced an emotionally charged special on breast cancer. "I can be fair and honest," she says of the disease. "But objective I cannot be."

RONALD REAGAN

Ever-folksy, the former president announced he had Alzheimer's disease in a handwritten letter addressed to "my fellow Americans" in 1994. He called his gesture "an opening of our hearts."

WILLIAM STYRON

The novelist told of his depression in the New York Times and later in *Darkness Visible: A Memoir of Madness*. "The overwhelming reaction made me feel that inadvertently I had helped unlock a closet from which many souls were eager to come out."

CHRISTOPHER REEVE

"You only have two choices," says the actor whose 1995 fall from a horse left him permanently paralyzed and who has raised millions for spinal injury research. "Either you vegetate and look out the window or activate and try to effect change."

GREG LOUGANIS

Mortified that he'd hid his HIV-positive status when his head wound bloodied the Olympic pool in 1988, the diver finally told his story during an interview with Barbara Walters in 1995.

---

ball: from "slow down, spend more time with your family, and don't sweat the little things" to "control your anger, read more poetry, and verbalize affection." Hardly the sort of wisdom that transforms lives.

If these interventions have anything in common, though, it is the presence of other people. This makes sense if you think of stress the way most doctors do, as a hormonal response to pressure. The body perceives a threat, mental or physical, and releases hormones that hike blood pressure and suppress immune response. According to the theory, some of us (the hostile, the troubled, the Type As) have a higher risk of heart disease or cancer because we secrete more of these hormones more frequently than the average joe. This stress response isn't easy to moderate, but one of the few things that seems to help is contact with a supportive person. In several lab experiments, for instance, psychologists have shown that having a friend in the room calms the cardiovascular response to distressing tasks such as public speaking. It's the secret of group therapy: We relax around our own. The simple grace of company can keep us healthy.

Humans are, after all, social by nature. So perhaps it makes sense that the healthiest among us might be the ones who find solace in companionship, who can defuse building pressure by opening up our hearts to someone else. As the late biologist and writer Lewis Thomas observed, human beings have survived by being useful to one another. We are as indispensable to each other as hummingbirds are to hibiscus.

And by finding ways to help each other out, the latest research hints, we forge the emotional connections that could very well sustain us. Thomas understood this. In a *New York Times* interview in 1993, just two weeks before his death, the reporter asked him, "Is there an art to dying?"

"There's an art to living," Thomas replied. "One of the very important things that has to be learned around the time dying becomes a real prospect is to recognize those occasions when we have been useful in the world. With the same sharp insight that we all have for acknowledging our failures, we ought to recognize when we have been useful, and sometimes uniquely useful. All of us have had such times in our lives, but we don't pay much attention to them. Yet the thing we're really good at as a species is usefulness. If we paid more attention to this biological attribute, we'd get a satisfaction that cannot be attained from goods or knowledge."

University, the tests researchers use to identify hostile personalities essentially measure something he calls interpersonal warmth. "It has to do with whether you see the people in your life as benevolent or malevolent, whether they offer nourishment or frustration," he says. "The fact is, humans are emotionally frail. We need real support from other people, and those who don't acknowledge it are going to feel besieged."

These notions could easily collapse into sentimentality. Yet scientific evidence for the physical benefits of social support is coming in from all sides. At Ohio State University, for example, immunologist Ron Glaser and psychologist Janice Kiecolt-Glaser have found that the biggest slump in immunity during exam periods occurs in medical students who report being lonely. Analyzing data from the Tecumseh Community Health Study, sociologist James House calculated that social isolation was as big a risk factor for illness and death as smoking was. And these were just the warm-up acts. In 1989 David Spiegel of Stanford Medical School measured the effect of weekly group therapy on women being treated for breast cancer. As expected, those who met in groups experienced less pain than those who didn't. But that wasn't all. The women in counseling survived an average of 37 months—nearly twice as long as those without the group support. Other researchers, including Friedman, have also lengthened some heart patients' lives through group therapy.

The reason remains anyone's guess. Perhaps, as Spiegel has suggested, being in a group makes patients more likely to take their medications, perform prescribed exercise, and so on. Patients may also benefit from advice offered in therapy, which can range from the commonsensical to the corn-

---

Benedict Carey has been a staff writer at the magazine since 1988.

PERSONALITY DISORDERS: COPING WITH THE BORDERLINE

Characterized by stormy relationships, self-mutilation, and rage, the borderline personality bewilders family, friends, and the psychiatric community itself.

by Patrick Perry

After a busy day at work, Bob was looking forward to a quick shower, light supper, and a concert with his new girlfriend, Amanda. But outside his apartment, he froze. On his door the word "CHEATER" had been spray-painted in large black letters. Embarrassed, he scanned the hallway, quietly unlocked the door, and slipped inside.

"Did anyone see who did this?" Bob asked the superintendent.

"Your neighbor said that she recognized the car in the parking lot," he answered. "This is the fourth time somebody's damaged your apartment. Shouldn't we call the police?"

"No," Bob said. "I'll handle it."

He knew who had been there. It was Jennifer.

When he first met Jennifer at a bookstore, he was immediately attracted to the pretty, outgoing 21-year-old. Their first few months together were fantastic. She always wanted to be with him, calling him two or three times a day at the office just to let him know she was thinking about him. Over time, Bob learned more about Jenny—the early sexual assault she had suffered, a broken home, and the barely visible scars on her wrists from a suicide attempt when she was just 17. She had been through a lot in her short life, yet seemed to survive it well.

When the accounting firm where Bob worked picked up a new client, Bob began working late hours. At first, Jenny understood, was even supportive. But as the weeks passed, she became more demanding, wanting to know why he "wanted" to be away from her and if "another woman" was involved. She telephoned him throughout the day, monitoring his every move. One night after work, he joined old fraternity buddies for a basketball game at the local Y. Jenny unexpectedly showed up. After delivering a barrage of jealous accusations in front of his teammates, she left. Bob thought the flat tire after the game was just a coincidence. On another late night at work, he found her parked alongside him in the garage, and she acted hurt when he questioned her motives.

Jenny's jealousy and demands continued, and soon Bob realized that

> **One moment calm and engaging, the next tempestuous and combative, borderlines bewilder those around them, straining relationships to the breaking point.**

something about the relationship just wasn't right. He decided to break it off. The decision wasn't mutual. Jenny began showing up at his office, at first begging for another chance. When he refused, she flew into a rage in front of his coworkers. When his appointment book came up missing, he chalked it up to forgetfulness until someone canceled his plane reservations to an important business conference and canceled his doctor's appointments. A late-night phone call from Jenny resulted in a trip to the emergency room and an all-night suicide vigil. Bob now realized that Jenny needed professional help. But when he spoke with her the next day about therapy, she became furious, blaming her hospitalization on him and men like him. He left, feeling ashamed and, for some reason, responsible.

For the next two months, Jenny phoned him at all hours of the night and at the office. She left scathing, often harassing messages on his answering machine. When the office disruptions threatened his job, Bob took out a restraining order against Jenny. Even then, Jenny persisted. On more than one occasion, he saw her peering through restaurant windows or parked outside his apartment building. His mailbox had been tampered with, his tires slashed, an anonymous basket of funeral flowers sent to his office, appointments cancelled, and a defamatory letter sent to his boss. Still, no one would suspect that the pretty, outgoing girl was capable of, much less responsible for, the havoc in his life.

When will it end? Bob thought. *Can I take much more of this?*

* * *

Rage, impulsivity, self-mutilation, guilt, overwhelming fears of abandonment, and volatile relationships—

44. Coping with the Borderline

Jenny's life is a tattered scrapbook of broken relationships, suicide attempts, uncontrollable anger, substance abuse, and violent mood swings. Jenny is a "borderline," short for someone with borderline personality disorder. Five million Americans fit the profile of the borderline personality disorder (BPD), according to the latest estimate. One moment calm and engaging, the next tempestuous and combative, borderlines bewilder those around them, straining relationships to the breaking point. It is this unpredictability and loss of control that baffles both people who love them and the psychiatric community that treats them. BPD is a mysterious malady of the personality that one psychiatrist defines as "a problem with who you are."

The case of Susan Smith, the South Carolina mother who murdered her two children by driving her car into a lake with the children left inside, brought national focus on the subject of personality disorders and the frightening consequences that often result when the disorders are left unchecked.

Unlike depression, a disease frequently episodic in nature and which most people can understand and empathize with, BPD is characterized by enduring and persistent ways of behavior and thought. As such, BPD lies in a unique classification of psychiatric illnesses called personality disorders. According to the current edition of the American Psychiatric Association's *Diagnostic and Statistical Manual of Mental Disorders, 4th Edition, (DSM-IV)*, a personality type is looked upon as a disorder when the traits, or personal habits, that constitute the personality are inflexible and damaging, causing serious distress or impaired function. The *DSM-IV* classifications of personality disorders include: borderline, antisocial, paranoid, narcissistic, avoidant, dependent, obsessive-compulsive, and passive-aggressive.

In her book *Imbroglio*, author Janice M. Cauwels, Ph.D., presents an in-depth look at BPD, exploring the causes and current theories and offering personal histories of patients suffering from the disorder. Dr. Cauwels discovered that many psychiatrists refuse to see these patients because borderlines are seen as provocateurs and expert manipulators. Dr. Cauwels cites a facetious report on BPD patients as "notorious for late-night irrelevant 'emergency' phone calls, no common sense, no redeeming qualities, no income, and no health insurance." The author also noted that one of the supreme ironies in BPD is that borderlines are the neediest people in the world, yet alienate all from whom they crave love.

BPD is the subject of mounting research, innumerable studies, and various theories. While therapists may differ on theory and origin, few would argue with the statement that BPD appears to be one of the most complicated forms of mental illness. The *Post* interviewed leading researchers and clinicians about this crippling mental disorder that affects not only the borderline patients but all who come into contact with them.

What Is Borderline Personality Disorder?

John W. Gunderson, M.D., is regarded as a leading authority on BPD. He is director of psychotherapy and psychosocial research at McLean Hospital in Massachusetts and professor of psychiatry at Harvard Medical School.

Post: How do you describe a borderline personality disorder?

JG: I think of it as a disorder primarily caused by some defect in early attachment that leads to the person searching for some type of protective, nurturing relationship which they feel makes up for what they unfairly did not get in their childhood. It sets in motion a sort of desperate search for some person who will take care of them and stay with them all the time.

Post: When does BPD begin to emerge?

JG: Usually in adolescence, but there's usually enough turmoil in normal adolescence that you're not safe identifying those who will have this disorder until it persists or emerges later in life.

Post: Do borderlines usually focus on one individual at a time?

JG: Yes.

Post: Is this individual a love interest or could it be just a friend?

JG: It could be a friend. It could be a teacher. Most borderline patients feel very secure and can function well, as long as they feel they have someone they believe cares about them and is accessible—someone who will be there. We all need to have caring relationships. What's different here is that the relationship generally evolves around the hope that there will be one person who will be able to provide all that they need. They get very panicky and have very severe, oftentimes behavioral, reactions when they feel that they're going to be alone. When borderlines feel the threat that somebody needed is going to leave or has lost interest in them, they engage in a lot of angry and manipulative behaviors to prevent the leaving. If they feel that it's futile and that they don't have anyone, they may behave in very desperate ways to become engaged with somebody new—promiscuity, substance abuse, fights. These behaviors—the fights and promiscuity—are often because of the disinhibiting influence of alcohol or other drugs that bring them once again into contact with someone with whom they can recreate the illusion of being loved.

Post: Many people remember the disturbing portrait of borderline disorder in the movie *Fatal Attraction*. What do you think of that movie's portrayal of a borderline patient?

JG: I think, more typically, borderline patients will become self-destructive as a way of evoking some kind of caretaking protective response from others. That's how they prevent people from leaving them.

Post: In the movie, the borderline character's rage grew, eventually leading her to destroy things dear to the man who was the focus of her obsession.

JG: That is a very extreme, dramatic example. Most of the time a borderline patient may start to feel enraged and may have poor control over that rage, and it comes out. It's usually verbal. These people feel that when they have been angry, they are bad, even though they initially felt anger was justified because they had been cruelly mistreated. It's usually hard for them to sustain being angry for long. They soon begin to feel they are evil, then turn the anger toward themselves in very self-destructive ways. Self-destructiveness takes the form of not simply trying to kill themselves, but trying to put themselves in a position where their life is at risk and whether they live or not is in the hands of somebody else. If they are saved, as is usually the case, that's affirmation they are meant to live and deserve to live. If they are not saved, that is an affirmation they are as evil as they thought and deserve to die. They put their lives at risk in a deliberate way where their fate depends upon external intervention.

Post: Could you give a description of how a borderline might react in frustrating situations that all of us encounter—when your car breaks down or you're stuck in a grocery line? Do they react the same way others do?

JG: Most of the time, yes. But consider a patient, for instance, who learns the night before that her boyfriend is going to move out. If then the next day she goes to a grocery store and a child is crying, she might feel inappropriately enraged at the child—so much so that she envisions very primitive things like cutting the kid's tongue out. She is frightened of that thought and says to herself, "This is crazy—I've got to get out of here," because borderlines fear they won't be able to control the anger. She leaves the store. At that point, she hasn't done her grocery shopping, so she feels ashamed of herself for that. She gets into the car and, in an admixture of frustration and guilt, slams into the car in front of her. Feeling that the car in front of her was going too slow and that this is unfair, she'll be enraged at the driver and create a big scene.

Post: What do you consider the two principal diagnostic hallmarks of borderline?

JG: Intolerance of aloneness and self-destructiveness.

Post: Many magazine and professional journal articles mention a relationship between sexual abuse and borderline disorder, particularly among female patients. Were the vast majority of borderline patients sexually abused as children?

JG: Yes, that's well-established, but a "vast majority" overstates it. You can safely say that a large percentage of borderline patients have had abusive experiences in their childhood, but abuse is neither necessary nor specific.

Post: You mean it doesn't matter if the abuse is sexual or if it's, for example, abandonment?

JG: It matters. But the degree of sexual abuse is linked to the high frequency of females with the disorder. With the antisocial personality, you see a familiar frequency of abuse in their childhood, but it's less frequently sexual.

Post: How often are borderlines also antisocial?

JG: About 25 percent.

Post: Is having both traits, borderline and antisocial, a particularly dangerous combination?

Diagnostic Criteria for Borderline Personality Disorder

A pervasive pattern of instability of interpersonal relationships, self-image, and affects, and marked impulsivity beginning by early adulthood and present in a variety of contexts, as indicated by five (or more) of the following:

❶ Frantic efforts to avoid real or imagined abandonment.
❷ A pattern of unstable and intense interpersonal relationships characterized by alternating between extremes of idealization and devaluation.
❸ Identity disturbance: markedly and persistently unstable self-image or sense of self.
❹ Impulsivity in at least two areas that are potentially self-damaging (e.g., spending, sex, substance abuse, reckless driving, binge eating).
❺ Recurrent suicidal behavior, gestures, or threats, or self-mutilating behavior.
❻ Affective instability due to a marked reactivity of mood (e.g., intense episodic dysphoria, irritability, or anxiety usually lasting a few hours and only rarely more than a few days).
❼ Chronic feelings of emptiness.
❽ Inappropriate, intense anger or difficulty controlling anger (e.g., frequent displays of temper, constant anger, recurrent physical fights).
❾ Transient, stress-related paranoid ideation or severe dissociative symptoms.

Source: Diagnostic and Statistical Manual of Mental Disorders, 4th Edition (DSM-IV™)

JG: "Dangerous" is a strong word because it implies that there's a high risk of violence to other people. I would not say that is the danger, primarily. The problem with the combination of BPD and antisocial disorder is that patients with both these traits are harder to treat and more apt to exploit others without great remorse.

Post: For example?

JG: A babysitter who steals from the employer. They are also, I think, at somewhat higher risk of being irresponsible caretakers. Violence in borderline patients is largely impulsive and under extreme circumstances. It's not something that recurs very often because it's usually followed by intense and suicidal self-accusations. That doesn't mean that such people are not capable of violence. That woman who drowned her children, for example.

Post: Susan Smith, the South Carolina mother who drove her two young children into a lake in a locked car and watched them drown?

JG: Yes. Chances of BPD are quite high in a number of such cases in the news where women have done very violent things to their kids. But that's a little different from antisocial as a recurrent pattern of disregard for social norms and the feelings of others.

Post: When I hear the term borderline, it's often associated with violence, as in the case of Susan Smith. Are cases like this exceptions to the rule when it comes to borderline personalities?

JG: Yes. Violence is usually an act of passion. It's done impulsively under the overriding influence of strong feelings and poor control over impulses. A repeated pattern of systematically being sadistic to others is not typical of borderline patients. It can happen, but that's not typical. Sadism would be much more likely in a purely antisocial person. Someone who really doesn't have any regard for the rights and feelings of others that isn't typical of borderlines.

Post: In what you've read about Susan Smith's history, what led you to label her a borderline personality?

JG: I didn't read very much of the story, so I may be in error. But borderlines have a tremendous dilemma once they become mothers, because an overriding fact of their lives is that they feel that they did not get adequate mothering. That doesn't mean it's true, but that's a very important and central part of their motivations and self-esteem. So they often dream and believe that the highest calling on earth is to become a mother—and a good mother. The problem is, they're psychologically handicapped. Are you a father?

Post: Yes.

JG: You probably know, then, that one's little blighters don't always behave. In fact, they disregard what you tell them to do repeatedly. It takes a lot of sustained limit-setting and frustration tolerance to keep your caretaking role in line, in the face of what could be extremely frustrating circumstances. This overwhelms mothers who are borderline

44. Coping with the Borderline

in a variety of ways. One is that the amount of care and attention children legitimately require can tax anybody. But for these women, it's accompanied by a feeling that they themselves are being deprived. It opens up to them how much they aren't getting. In fact, they are giving all the time; it is a depriving stance for everybody. But borderlines feel an enormous sense of deprivation when remaining in this stance for sustained periods of time. In addition, they can't get angry at the little blighters without feeling that they are as bad as, or the embodiment of, the evil mother they hated and renounced. That leads to suicide, because nothing is worse. Susan Smith, as I recall, felt herself to be in a bind where her hoped-for savior—the boyfriend—and his continued availability to her were dependent upon getting rid of the kids. So she sacrificed them—but then couldn't live with herself.

Post: Do borderline patients generally make good mothers?

JG: No, but not for a lack of wanting to. Borderline mothers don't have the psychological resources to manage the feelings normal mothers require in terms of the ability to satisfy personal needs and the ability to get angry in some kind of modulated, controlled, reasonable way—at least without feeling they'll lose control over the anger and do something violent, which they can do. But then they feel terrible about it, often withdrawing from their roles as mothers once it's happened.

Post: How do they withdraw?

JG: They will try to turn the primary care of the child over to someone else. They'll become chronic psychiatric patients. I've known a number of borderline women who found refuge in a psychiatric career because it gave a sort of legitimacy to their inability to mother. They could come back and spend shorter periods of time with the children without being overwhelmed, but they weren't expected to be there all the time. Sometimes they can arrange for someone else to take care of the children. These mothers have some strengths. They may be able to get employment so that they can help with the support in a responsible way, but away from some of the immediate emotional demands.

Post: Is the therapy used to treat borderlines primarily psychodynamic?

JG: I'm primarily psychodynamically oriented, but I have a strong conviction that individual psychodynamic therapy is not usually sufficient for such patients and that you need to integrate psychodynamic therapy with social therapies, like group and family work.

Post: If volatile, unstable relationships are characteristic of borderline people, do they generally end up alone?

JG: Borderline patients usually go from one intense relationship to another. It's the very intensity of their needs that usually makes relationships short-lived. Borderline patients do learn from experience, however. By the time many of them reach their 30s, they will either have modified their interpersonal behaviors enough to sustain relationships, or they will have gone into a more withdrawn situation where they try to avoid getting too involved with people. Instead they try to get their needs met by quite superficial involvements with lots of people. Involvement in self-help groups, churches, or employment situations provide sufficient social contact for them, but they don't get too close to anyone. That's one outcome.

A minority of borderline patients actually improve enough so that they can develop quite reasonably stable, and even relatively healthy, relationships. Those are people who usually have had a corrective relationship somewhere along the line, where they have gotten involved with someone over a long period of time and have become more comfortable with their feelings. Because their self-images have changed, they are less apt to feel that they are bad people. That can happen in the course of a good long-term therapy. Sometimes it may even happen, although I think not quite as completely, through the provision of a good relationship in the outside world.

Post: The *Post* featured an article on bipolar disorder in its March/April 1996 issue. We spoke with Dr. Kay Redfield Jamison, whose books examined a relationship between bipolar disease and creativity. What emerged was a roster of famous people who were highly creative. Are borderline patients also politicians, business leaders, mayors, teachers-of-the-year?

JG: That would be quite unusual, although Marilyn Monroe was probably borderline. Her whole life was tempestuous and maybe more typical of a borderline patient's life. Even when they have done something creative, they are likely to be embedded in a very inconsistent record of productivity, as well as involved in many tumultuous relationships. They would not make for good schoolteachers.

Post: Are borderlines masters at manipulation?

JG: Yes. Some more than others.

Post: Is that why therapists are reluctant to treat borderlines?

JG: Once again, I think it has less to do with their fears about the borderline patient actually hurting them in any physical way, but it may have to do with their apprehensions about being manipulated. Most therapists like to think the best about people, and so they're vulnerable to that kind of thing. But most often the apprehension will have more to do with their borderline patients fears of abandonment and their inability to be alone. The therapist often expects to be disrupted frequently in the middle of the night. Or that patients will want to go with them on vacation, be extremely jealous of the therapist's children, or park out in front of the yard. Those are the most common concerns of therapists.

Diagnosis and Treatment of BPD

BPD researcher, clinician, and author of the book Borderline Personality Disorder: A Multidimensional Approach, *Joel Paris, M.D., is senior psychiatrist, Institute of Community and Family Psychiatry, Sir Mortimer B. Davis-Jewish General Hospital, and professor of psychiatry at McGill University, Montreal.*

Post: How does BPD differ from other personality disorders?

JP: There are ten categories of personality disorder, of which borderline has been the subject of the most research. Borderline personality refers to people who can best be described as emotionally unstable in an extreme way. They tend to have many problems of a particular kind in their relationships. They get involved with other people quickly, but things also sour very quickly. They're impulsive in a number of ways, many of which are related to suicide.

The most characteristic feature of the condition is multiple suicide attempts. These attempts usually occur in the context of a problem in a relationship. These patients come into the emergency room, for example, after a fight with somebody, which leads them to take an overdose or to slash their wrists.

Post: One therapist said that he could diagnose a borderline personality in ten minutes. Are they difficult to diagnose?

JP: I can sometimes do it in ten minutes, but you may miss something. There is a feel about these people. For example, a patient that I saw this morning was dysphoric [depressed], miserable, angry, on edge, and impulsive: she couldn't stand how she felt. She immediately engaged me in a very complicated and unpleasant interaction.

Post: Wouldn't most people be initially hesitant with a stranger?

JP: That's right. Borderlines don't have very good boundaries. When most people see a psychiatrist, they open up slowly. Borderlines will give you deep stuff in minutes—which also makes you think about a borderline diagnosis.

Post: Are borderline personalities resistant to change?

JP: Resistant to change by definition, because all personality disorders are chronic and resistant to change over time. That is how they are defined.

Usually, borderline personalities are very demanding of therapy. The irony is, and this has been shown in research, that if you offer borderlines psychotherapy, about two thirds of them will drop out within a few months—another measure of their impulsivity and emotional instability. In other words, they get frustrated with the therapist. They might say to the therapist, "You're not helping me. You don't care," then storm out.

Post: What brings them to therapy in the first place?

JP: Suicide attempts or suicidal feelings are typical.

Post: Are pharmacological interventions successful?

JP: Borderlines don't respond to drugs very well, even though most of them are on medication. At this point in time, pharmacological treatment doesn't last long and is not very impressive. If I give Prozac to somebody with a classic depression, it's almost like magic. The patient often feels like a new person in a few weeks. But if I give borderline patients Prozac, they might feel a little better, yet in a few weeks we'll be back

Are you coping with someone who has Borderline Personality Disorder?

Do you find yourself:

■ Concealing what you really think or feel because you're afraid of the other person's reaction, and it just doesn't seem worth the horrible fight or hurt feelings that will surely follow? Has this become so automatic that you have a hard time even identifying what you think or feel?

■ Feeling like you're walking on eggshells much of the time, and that no matter what you say or do, it will be twisted and used against you?

■ Being blamed and criticized for everything wrong in the relationship, even when it makes no logical sense?

■ Being the focus of intense, even violent rages that make no logical sense, alternating with periods when the other person acts perfectly normal and loving?

■ Feeling like you're being manipulated, controlled, or even lied to sometimes?

■ Feeling like the person you care about sees you as either all good or all bad, with nothing in between? Wishing that the person would act like they used to, when they seemed to love you and think you were perfect and everything was wonderful?

■ Feeling like the other person is like "Dr. Jekyll and Mr. Hyde": one moment a loving, caring person; another moment someone who seems so vicious you barely recognize them? Wondering which one is "real"? Hoping that it's a phase that will go away—but it doesn't? Feeling like you're on an emotional roller coaster with high highs (things are incredible, fantastic) and very low lows (feelings of despair, depression, grief for the relationship you thought you had)?

■ Being afraid to ask for things in the relationship, because you will be told you're too demanding or there is something wrong with you? Being told that your needs are wrong or not important?

■ Wondering if you're losing your grip on reality because the other person is always putting down or denying your point of view? Plus, the other person often acts just fine in front of other people, so no one believes you when you explain what's going on?

■ Feeling that nothing you do is ever right, and when you do manage to do what the other person wants, suddenly they change their expectations? The rules keep changing, and no matter what you do, you can't win? Feeling helpless and trapped?

■ Being accused of doing things you never did and saying things you never said? Feeling misunderstood a great deal of the time, and when you try to explain, the other person doesn't believe you?

■ Being constantly put down, yet when you try to leave the relationship, the other person tries to prevent you from leaving in a variety of ways—anything from declarations of love and promises to change to outright implicit or explicit threats such as "you'll never see the children again" and "no one but me will ever love you"?

■ Having a hard time planning anything (social engagement, etc.) because of the other person's moodiness, impulsiveness, or unpredictability? Sometimes, even making excuses for their behavior to other people—or trying to convince yourself that this is normal behavior?

■ Reading the above list and thinking, *I had no idea that other people were going through the same thing and that there is a name for this:* Borderline Personality Disorder?

From BPD Central, an Internet resource for people who care about someone with borderline personality disorder. BPD Central is a three-star site of Mental Health Net (http://www.cmhc.com/).
Internet Address for BPD Central: http://members.aol.com/BPDCentral.
Copyright © 1996, Paul Mason, MS, and Randi Kreger. All rights reserved.

Editor's Note: *If you would like to share your experiences in living with a person with borderline personality disorder, please write to us. You may use fictitious name(s) to protect the anonymity of the patient. Send your responses to The Saturday Evening Post, P.O. Box 567, Indianapolis, IN 46206.*

to square one. Although drugs are given to many of these patients, we haven't discovered or haven't invented the right one yet.

Post: In your book *Borderline Personality Disorder,* you mentioned abnormally low levels of serotonin—a neurotransmitter affecting mood and behavior in the brain.

JP: Yes, that's a theory. There is indirect evidence supporting it. While it is a subject of intense research, I don't think neurotransmitters fully explain the disorder. If they were just deficient in serotonin, why don't they get better on Prozac?

Post: What about psychotherapy?

JP: This is a very interesting story. The term "borderline" was first used in the 1930s by an analyst who hypothesized that the reason these people don't get better is they are on the borderline of psychosis and neurosis. We are stuck with that term, even though we don't believe in the theory anymore. At the time, this analyst wrote that these people don't respond well to analysis. I think almost everyone since agrees. Nevertheless, a lot of psychotherapists have tried to use modified versions of psychoanalysis, so-called psychoanalytic therapies, with these patients. The problem is that there is no scientific evidence showing whether the therapies do or don't work.

What I wrote in my book was my own clinical experience, using therapy successfully in subgroup classes with high-functioning borderline patients—people, for example, who have good jobs or are attending a university, but whose personal lives are a mess. A lot of studies show that the better functioning you are, the more you get out of psychotherapy. If you are not functioning well anywhere in your life—are on welfare and have few friends—you tend not to do well in psychotherapy. The problem is that a lot of borderline patients are on welfare and also have many problems maintaining friendships.

Post: Structured environments seem to work best for these people?

JP: That is one of the main points in my book. Of course, they've got to have the ability to get into a structured environment. I work part-time in the McGill University health service, so a number of the cases I described were university students. Obviously, these are people who are able to structure themselves. They have higher IQs or other positive personality traits.

I also said in the book that modern society, where it's every man and woman for themselves and where there is such a high level of individualism, might be one factor making BPD more common.

Post: How would a lay person recognize these symptoms?

JP: It's not easy. When you are a psychiatrist, people tell you everything. You discover that you know your patients better than you know your friends. However, many people know someone who is chronically suicidal and has had many treatments for suicidal threats or attempts, usually involving overdoses or wrist cuttings. Attempted suicide is the most characteristic symptom of the disorder.

Post: If people have seven of the nine diagnostic criteria for BPD [see box, "Diagnostic Criteria for Borderline Personality Disorder] but lack the suicidal trait, would they fall outside the diagnosis?

> "Where other people in the life of borderline patients can go wrong is by trying to do too much. The borderline patient is asking you to be mother, father, lover—everything."

JP: No. If you have seven of the nine, you fit the profile. The way the *DSM-IV* is written, all nine have an equal weight, but they are not independent of each other. But I've never seen anyone who has met the criteria yet who didn't at least have some suicidal behavior.

Post: Is life with a borderline patient challenging?

JP: When you're the therapist, you start feeling that you must be a terrible therapist to have somebody hate you or telling you such things as "I'm going to kill myself, and it's your fault, Doctor." I like these patients very much who, with all of their pathology, can be quite engaging, but they are very good at making other people feel sorry for them,

44. Coping with the Borderline

guilty about them, and that people close to them haven't done enough to help. Friends and family should distinguish between empathy and sympathy. Empathy doesn't necessarily mean that you agree with the person's actions. There are times when a therapist has to say, "Well, you could kill yourself, but I would rather see you next week for the session."

Where other people in the life of borderline patients can go wrong is by trying to do too much. The borderline patient is asking you to be mother, father, lover—everything. People might think, *Gee, this person really needs me . . . I can understand her better than anyone else.* But after a while, the person gets mad at you, and you're caught.

Post: In your book, you write that the disease is self-limiting.

JP: That is what is called "burnout." Time wears the pathology down. That is true also of antisocial behavior and drug abuse.

The Prevalence of Childhood Sexual Abuse

Paul Soloff M.D., professor of psychiatry at the University of Pittsburgh, Western Psychiatric Institute and Clinic, is a leading researcher in the psychopharmacology, as well as psychobiology, of BPD.

Post: Is childhood abuse implicated in the incidence of borderline personality disorder?

PS: More recently, the literature has indicated high incidence of abuse—physical abuse or sexual abuse—in the histories of patients with borderline personality disorder. Not all, but many. Some of the percentages are as low as 20 percent, others as high as 70 percent, but always more than in control groups. So the sexual-physical trauma contributes to that interpersonal style of functioning that involves manipulative, dependent relationships. The patients have a chronic low sense of self-esteem, feel bad about themselves, feel like nobody could care for them.

Post: When do borderline patients most often come to the attention of the psychiatric community?

PS: Borderline patients most often come to our attention at times of crisis, usually in the face of a perceived rejection. I use the term "rejection sensitivity." That's one of the buzz words for the mood crashes, the depressive episodes that they have. At a time of perceived rejection, these are the patients who take pills on impulse, cut themselves, or burn themselves. When we see them, they are often in an emergency room with lacerated arms or an overdose of pills. When taking a patient's history, we discover there's a track record and that the patient may have done it many times before.

Post: Self-mutilation could take many forms, is that correct?

PS: Yes, it does, actually. The most common is wrist-cutting or burning with cigarettes. Part of what happens is that these patients usually use the cut or the burn. It has several meanings. One meaning is that the wrist cut or the burn deals with some intense feeling the patient is having. That's its primary purpose—to deal with some intense feeling. In psychiatry, we call that the primary gain. The symptom is doing something for the patient within himself or herself. It's handling this very strong feeling. But in psychiatry we also recognize that symptoms have a personal value to others—an interpersonal meaning. This is called the secondary gain. Now that's fairly easy to understand, because if you cut your wrist and you show it to somebody, what happens? Right away people pay attention. They either put you in the hospital, take care of you, nurture you, or criticize you, but you get a tremendous amount of attention. That's what happens with a borderline patient. Typically, you have a person who, feeling abandoned or alone, does something to himself to deal with that intense feeling. That's the primary gain. The secondary gain is that the patient usually makes sure that somebody else knows about it—the police, the family, or the doctors arrive. The person is the focus of attention. Think of these destructive actions as primitive efforts to obtain help, to force other people to take care of this person—that's a typical kind of borderline dynamic.

Post: Do borderline personalities want therapy?

PS: Patients want therapy. In fact, they're among our most demanding patients because these are people who are seeking care. They manipulate care. They force others to take care of them. That's not the problem. The problem is the forms of treatment that we have so far are not very good. The medications that we have help to palliate the impulsivity and the mood disorder, the mood disregulation. The psychotherapies are in no way curative; they are primarily supportive. You don't cure personality disorders. You help people deal with the symptoms and vulnerabilities that they have. You help them live better.

Post: What's it like to live with a borderline?

PS: I have not had that experience, but my patients certainly have, and I have talked to their spouses. Borderlines are very unstable and argumentative. A family disagreement can result in a trip to the emergency room with her overdosing or his smashing the windows. They're unpredictable in that sense. Borderlines are very rejection-sensitive, so that things you and I would take for granted—criticism, for example—a borderline patient might see as a rejection. Or a partner coming home late for dinner might be taken as rejection. It's the quality of feeling rejected that is important. Abandoned, rejected, that's the critical element here.

Post: Why do you think that three quarters of BPDs are women?

PS: That is part of cultural bias. In this country, three quarters of them are women. In general, that's not true in other countries. There are cultural ways of expressing distress. In this culture, women are taught to express stress by turning their aggression against themselves; men are taught to channel their aggression against others. Men do things that are very dramatic. Male borderlines would, for example, get into fights, stand on bridges, use handguns, create a disturbance—they'll usually end up in jail. Women will end up in mental hospitals: they cut themselves, they burn themselves, they take overdoses. So, the first thing we have to contend with is the cultural bias in symptom expression. What I am saying is that you can have exactly the same problem and, if you're a male, you do something dramatic; you won t cut your wrist. I had one patient who would punch policemen. Another would break picture windows in downtown department stores in broad daylight—smash windows one right after the other. They ended up in jail. They have exactly the same psychodynamic motivation as a woman who might take a handful of pills or cut her wrists when she's feeling rejected. So cultural expression of symptoms is a big part of it.

Comments by Janice M. Cauwels, Ph.D., writer, consultant, and author of Imbroglio

Post: What was the predominant feature of BPD you encountered in interviews with experts?

JC: The key feature of BPD to experts is that it is the most difficult psychiatric illness to treat. Physicians in other specialties don't like borderlines, either. While writing my book, for example, I mentioned the topic to a resident in allergy and immunology who had worked for a while in an emergency room. She launched into a tirade against the suicidal borderlines who had appeared or been brought in for treatment while she was on duty, apparently because they had been demanding and troublesome.

Borderlines appear to be very capricious and manipulative. They want to foist all their own responsibility for getting better onto their therapists, with whom they become intensely involved yet they often reject therapists' efforts to help.

Even competent therapists can become so emotionally involved with borderline patients, in turn, that they feel tossed around and make terrible mistakes in treatment. For this reason, knowledgeable therapists insist that ongoing consultation with a colleague about a borderline patient's case is always necessary. But even with such assistance no experienced therapist treats more than one or two borderlines at a time in private practice.

I observed a class on personality disorders in which several psychiatric residents explained that they disliked dealing with borderline instability, dishonesty, distortions, brief psychotic episodes, unbearable anger, demands, and constant threats of suicide. These residents felt scapegoated by the hospital staff for having such troublesome patients.

Writing *Imbroglio* was frustrating because of both the complexity of the subject matter and the objections of therapists to the forthcoming book. Most therapists believed that I had set myself an impossible task; some predicted that I would become a target of borderline rage; many, I think, feared that information about the illness would make their work more difficult by getting borderline patients all stirred up.

On the Power of Positive Thinking: The Benefits of Being Optimistic

Michael F. Scheier and Charles S. Carver

Michael F. Scheier is Professor of Psychology at Carnegie Mellon University. **Charles S. Carver** is Professor of Psychology at the University of Miami. Address correspondence to Michael F. Scheier, Department of Psychology, Carnegie Mellon University, Pittsburgh, PA 15213; e-mail: ms0a@andrew.cmu.edu.

If believing in something can make it so, then there really would be power in positive thinking. From the little train in the children's tale who said, "I think I can," to popular writers such as Norman Cousins and Norman Vincent Peale, to wise grandmothers everywhere—many people have espoused the benefits of positive thinking. But are these benefits real? Do people who think positively really fare better when facing challenge or adversity? Do they recover from illness more readily? If so, how and why do these things happen?

We and a number of other psychologists who are interested in issues surrounding stress, coping, and health have for several years focused our research attention on questions such as these. The primary purpose of this brief review is to provide a taste of the research conducted on this topic. We first document that positive thinking can be beneficial. We then consider why an optimistic orientation to life might confer benefits. After considering how individual differences in optimism might arise, we take up the question of whether optimism is always good and pessimism always bad. We close by discussing the similarities between our own approach and other related approaches.

CHARACTERIZING POSITIVE THINKING

Psychologists have approached the notion of positive thinking from a variety of perspectives. Common to most views, though, is the idea that positive thinking in some way involves holding positive expectancies for one's future. Such expectancies are thought to have built-in implications for behavior. That is, the actions that people take are thought to be greatly influenced by their expectations about the likely consequences of those actions. People who see desired outcomes as attainable continue to strive for those outcomes, even when progress is slow or difficult. When outcomes seem sufficiently unattainable, people withdraw their effort and disengage themselves from their goals. Thus, people's expectancies provide a basis for engaging in one of two very different classes of behavior: continued striving versus giving up.

People can hold expectancies at many levels of generality. Some theoretical views focus on expectancies that pertain to particular situations, or even to particular actions.[1] Such an approach allows for considerable variation in the positivity of one's thinking from one context to the next. Thus, a person who is quite optimistic about recovering successfully from a car accident may be far less optimistic about landing the big promotion that is up for grabs at work.

Our own research on positive and negative thinking began with a focus on situation-specific expectancies, but over the years we began to consider expectancies that are more general and diffuse. We believe that generalized expectancies constitute an important dimension of personality, that they are relatively stable across time and context. We refer to this dimension as optimism and construe it in terms of the belief that good, as opposed to bad, things will generally occur in one's life. We focus on this dimension for the rest of this article.

MEASURING OPTIMISM

We measure individual differences in optimism with the Life Orientation Test, or LOT.[2] The LOT consists of a series of items that assess the person's expectations regarding the favorability of future outcomes (e.g., "I hardly ever expect things to go my way," "In uncertain times, I usually expect the best"). LOT scores correlate positively with measures of internal control and self-esteem, correlate negatively with measures of depression and hopelessness, and are relatively unrelated to measures of social desirability.[2]

If dispositional optimism is in fact a personality characteristic, it should be relatively stable across time. We have reported a test–retest correlation of .79 across a 4-week period.[2] More recently, Karen Matthews has found a correlation of .69 between LOT scores assessed 3 years apart in a sample of 460 healthy, middle-aged women. Indeed, LOT scores seem to remain relatively stable even in the face of catastrophes. For example, Schulz, Tompkins, and Rau[3] tracked LOT scores in a group of stroke patients and their primary caregivers across a 6-month period. Although the LOT scores of both the patients and the support persons dropped over time (significantly so for the latter), the absolute magnitude of the drop was exceedingly small (less than 1 point on a 32-point scale). Thus, optimism as measured by the LOT seems to be a relatively enduring characteristic that changes little with the vagaries of life.

Factor analyses of the LOT routinely yield two separate factors,[2,4] comprised of positively worded (optimistic) items and negatively worded (pessimistic) items, respectively. Identification of two factors raises the question of whether it is better to view optimism and pessimism as opposite poles of a single dimension or as constituting two separate but correlated dimensions.[4] Though this is an interesting question, we have thus far taken the former view.

PSYCHOLOGICAL WELL-BEING

A growing number of studies have examined the effects of dispositional optimism on psychological well-being.[5] These studies have produced a remarkably consistent pattern of findings: Optimists routinely maintain higher levels of subjective well-being during times of stress than do people who are less optimistic. Let us briefly describe two illustrative cases.

One study[6] examined the development of postpartum depression in a group of women having their first children. Women in this study completed the LOT and a standard measure of depression in the third trimester of pregnancy. They completed the same depression measure again 3 weeks postpartum. Initial optimism was inversely associated with depression 3 weeks postpartum, even when the initial level of depression was controlled statistically. In other words, optimism predicted changes in depression over time. Optimistic women were less likely to become depressed following childbirth.

Conceptually similar findings have recently been reported in a study of undergraduate students' adjustment to their first semester of college.[7] A variety of factors were assessed when the students first arrived on campus, including dispositional optimism. Several measures of psychological well-being were obtained 3 months later. Optimism had a substantial effect on future psychological well-being: Higher levels of optimism upon entering college were associated with lower distress levels 3 months later. Notably, the effects of optimism in this study were distinct from those of the other personality factors measured, including self-esteem, locus of control, and desire for control. Thus, an optimistic orientation to life seemed to provide a benefit over and above that provided by these other personality characteristics.

PHYSICAL WELL-BEING

If the effects of optimism were limited to making people feel better, perhaps such findings would not be very surprising. The effects of optimism seem to go beyond this, however. There is at least some evidence that optimism also confers benefits on physical well-being.

Consider, for example, a study conducted on a group of men undergoing coronary artery bypass graft surgery.[8] Each patient was interviewed on the day prior to surgery, 6 to 8 days postsurgery, and again 6 months later. Optimism was assessed on the day prior to surgery by the LOT. A variety of medical and recovery variables were measured at several times, beginning before surgery and continuing through surgery and several months thereafter.

The data showed a number of effects for dispositional optimism. One notable finding concerns reactions to the surgery itself. Optimism was negatively related to physiological changes reflected in the patient's electrocardiogram and to the release of certain kinds of enzymes into the bloodstream. Both of these changes are widely taken as markers for myocardial infarction. The data thus suggest that optimists were less likely than pessimists to suffer heart attack during surgery.

Optimism was also a significant predictor of the rate of recovery during the immediate postoperative period. Optimists were faster to achieve selected behavioral milestones of recovery (e.g., sitting up in bed, walking around the room), and they were rated by medical staff as showing better physical recovery.

The advantages of an optimistic orientation were also apparent at the 6-month follow-up. Optimistic patients were more likely than pessimistic patients to have resumed vigorous physical exercise and to have returned to work full-time. Moreover, optimists returned to their activities more quickly than did pessimists. In sum, optimists were able to normalize their lifestyles more fully and more quickly than were pessimists. It is important to note that all of the findings just described were independent of the person's medical status at the outset of the study. Thus, it was not the case that optimists did better simply because they were less sick at the time of surgery.

HOW DOES OPTIMISM HELP?

If an understanding can be gained of why optimists do better than pessimists, then perhaps psychologists can begin to devise ways to help pessimists do better. One promising line of inquiry concerns differences between optimists and pessimists in how they cope with stress. Research from a variety of sources is beginning to suggest that optimists cope in more adaptive ways than do pessimists.[5] Optimists are more likely than pessimists to take direct action to solve their problems, are more planful in dealing with the adversity they confront, and are more focused in their coping efforts. Optimists are more likely to accept the reality of the stressful situations they encounter, and they also seem intent on growing personally from negative experiences and trying to make the best of bad situations. In contrast to these positive coping reactions, pessimists are more likely than optimists to react to stressful events by trying to deny that they exist or by trying to avoid dealing with problems. Pessimists are also more likely to quit trying when difficulties arise.

We now know that these coping differences are at least partly responsible for the differences in distress that optimists and pessimists experience in times of stress. When Aspinwall and Taylor[7] studied adjustment to college life, they collected information about the coping tactics the students were using to help themselves adjust to college, as well as measuring their optimism and eventual adjustment. Optimists were more likely than pessimists to rely on active coping techniques and less likely to engage in avoidance. These two general coping orientations were both related to later adjustment, in opposite directions. Avoidance coping was associated with poorer adjustment, whereas active coping was associated with better adjustment. Further analysis revealed that these two coping tendencies mediated the link between optimism and adjustment. Thus, optimists did better than pessimists at least partly because optimists used more effective ways of coping with problems.

A similar conclusion is suggested by a study of breast cancer patients that we and our colleagues recently completed. The women in this study reported on their distress and coping reactions before surgery, 10 days after surgery, and at 3-month, 6-month, and 12-month follow-ups. Throughout this period, optimism was associated with a coping pattern that involved accepting the reality of the situation, along with efforts to make the best of it. Optimism was inversely associated with attempts to act as though the problem was not real and with the tendency to give up on the life goals that were being threatened by the diagnosis of cancer. Further analyses suggested that these differences in coping served as paths by which the optimistic women remained less vulnerable to distress than the pessimistic women throughout the year.

ANTECEDENTS OF OPTIMISM

Where does optimism come from? Why do some people have it and others not? At present, not much is known about the origins of individual differences on this dimension. The determinants must necessarily fall in two broad categories, however: nature and nurture.

On the nature side, the available evidence suggests that individual differences in optimism-pessimism may be partly inherited. A translated version of the LOT was given to a sample of more than 500 same-sex pairs of middle-aged Swedish twins, and the heritability of optimism and pessimism was estimated to be about 25% using several different estimation procedures.[9] Thus, at least part of the variation in optimism and pessimism in the general population seems due to genetic influence.

On the environmental side, less is known. It is certainly reasonable to argue that optimism and pessimism are partly learned from prior experiences with success and failure. To the extent that one has been successful in the past, one should expect success in the future. Analogously, prior failure might breed the expectation of future failure. Children might also acquire a sense of optimism (or pessimism) from their parents, for example, through modeling. That is, parents who meet difficulties with positive expectations and who use adaptive coping strategies are explicitly or implicitly modeling those qualities for their children. Pessimistic parents also provide models for their children, although the qualities modeled are very different. Thus, children might become optimistic or pessimistic by thinking and acting in ways their parents do.

Parents might also influence children more directly by instructing them in problem solving. Parents who teach adaptive coping skills will produce children who are better problem solvers than children of parents who do not. To the extent that acquiring adaptive coping skills leads to coping success, the basis for an optimistic orientation is provided. We have recently begun a program of research designed to examine how coping strategies are transmitted from parent to child, with particular emphasis on the manner in which parental characteristics affect the kinds of coping strategies that are taught.

IS OPTIMISM ALWAYS GOOD? IS PESSIMISM ALWAYS BAD?

Implicit in our discussion thus far is the view that optimism is good for people. Is this always true? There are at least two ways in which an optimistic orientation might lead to poorer outcomes. First, it may be possible to be too optimistic, or to be optimistic in unproductive ways. For example, unbridled optimism may cause people to sit and wait for good things to happen, thereby decreasing the chance of success. We have seen no evidence of such a tendency among people defined as optimistic on the basis of the LOT, however. Instead, optimistic people seem to view positive outcomes as partially contingent on their continued effort.

Second, optimism might also prove detrimental in situations that are not amenable to constructive action. Optimists are prone to face problems with efforts to resolve them, but perhaps this head-on approach is maladaptive in situations that are uncontrollable or that involve major loss or a violation of one's world view. Data on this question are lacking, yet it is worth noting that the coping arsenal of optimists is not limited to the problem-focused domain. Optimists also use a host of emotion-focused coping responses, including tendencies to accept the reality of the situation, to put the situation in the best possible light, and to grow personally from their hardships. Given these coping options, optimists may prove to have a coping advantage even in the most distressing situations.

What about the reverse question? Can pessimism ever work in one's favor? Cantor and Norem[10] recently coined the term *defensive pessimism* to reflect a coping style in which people expect outcomes that are more negative than their prior reward histories in a given domain would suggest. Defensive pessimism may be useful because it helps to buffer the person against future failure, should failure occur. In addition, defensive pessimism may help the person perform better because the worry over anticipated failure prompts remedial action in preparation for the event.

Defensive pessimism does seem to work. That is, the performance of defensive pessimists tends to be better than the performance of real pessimists, whose negative expectations are anchored in prior failure. On the other hand, defensive pessimism never works better than optimism. Moreover, this style apparently has some hidden costs: People who use defensive pessimism in the short run report more psychological symptoms and a lower quality of life in the long run than do optimists.[10] Such findings call into serious question the adaptive value of defensive pessimism.

RELATIONSHIP TO OTHER APPROACHES

The concept of optimism, as discussed here, does not stand apart from the rest of personality psychology. There are easily noted family resemblances to several other personality constructs and approaches that have arisen in response to the same questions that prompted our line of theorizing. Two well-known examples are attributional style[11] and self-efficacy.[1] It may be useful to briefly note some similarities and differences between our conceptualization and these other approaches.

Attributional Style

Work on attributional style derives from the cognitive model[11] that was proposed to account for the phenomenon of learned helplessness[12] in humans. In this model, people's causal explanations for past events influence their expectations for controlling future events. The explanations thus influence subsequent feelings and behavior. As the attributional theory developed, it evolved toward a consideration of individual differences and began to focus on the possibility that an individual may have a stable tendency toward using one or another type of attribution. A tendency to attribute negative outcomes to causes that are stable, global, and internal has come to be known as pessimistic. A tendency to attribute negative events to causes that are unstable, specific, and external has come to be known as optimistic.

There is a clear conceptual link between this theory and the approach that we have taken. Both theories rely on the assumption that the consequences of optimism versus pessimism derive from differences in people's expectancies (at least in part). This assumption has been focal in our theory, and it is also important—albeit less focal—in the attributional approach. Moreover, despite differences in the types of measures used to assess optimism and attributional style, research findings relating attributional style to psychological and physical well-being have tended to parallel findings obtained for dispositional optimism.[13] Thus, the data converge on the conclusion that optimism is beneficial for mental and physical functioning.

Self-Efficacy

Self-efficacy expectancies are people's expectations of being either able or unable to execute desired behaviors successfully. Although there are obvious similarities between self-efficacy and optimism-pessimism, there are also two salient differences. One difference involves the extent to which the sense of personal agency is seen as the critical variable underlying behavior. Our approach to dispositional optimism intentionally deemphasizes the role of personal efficacy. Statements on self-efficacy make personal agency paramount.[1]

The second difference concerns the breadth of the expectancy on which the theory focuses. Efficacy theory holds that people's behavior is best predicted by focalized, domain-specific (or even act-specific) expectancies. Dispositional optimism, in contrast, is thought to be a very generalized tendency that has an influence in a wide variety of settings. Interestingly, relevant research[8] suggests that both types of expectancies (specific and general) are useful in predicting behavior.

CONCLUDING COMMENT

Our purpose in writing this article (perhaps in line with its subject matter) was to put a positive foot forward in presenting work on the benefits of optimism. In so doing, we may have created a false sense that the important questions about positive thinking have all been answered. Such is not the case. Understanding of the nature and effects of optimism is still in its infancy, and there is much more to learn. For example, although the effects of optimism seem attributable in part to differences in the ways optimists and pessimists cope with stress, this cannot be the complete answer. It is impossible to account fully for differences between optimists and pessimists on the basis of this factor alone.

Similarly, more work is needed to tease apart the effects of optimism from the effects of related variables. As noted earlier, a number of personality dimensions bear a conceptual resemblance to optimism-pessimism. Some of these dimensions, such as personal coherence, hardiness, and learned resourcefulness, have appeared in the literature only recently. Other dimensions, such as neuroticism, self-esteem, and self-mastery, have a longer scientific past. Given the existence of these related constructs, it is reasonable to ask whether their effects are distinguishable. This question cannot be resolved easily on the basis of one or two studies alone. An answer must await the gradual accumulation of evidence from many studies using different methodologies and assessing different outcomes.

There does seem to be a power to positive thinking. It surely is not as simple and direct a process as believing in something making it so. But believing that the future holds good things in store clearly has an effect on the way people relate to many aspects of life.

Acknowledgments—Preparation of this article was facilitated by National Science Foundation Grants BNS-9010425 and BNS-9011653, by National Institutes of Health Grant 1R01HL44432-01A1, and by American Cancer Society Grant PBR-56.

Notes

1. A. Bandura, *Social Foundations of Thought and Action: A Social Cognitive Theory* (Prentice Hall, Englewood Cliffs, NJ, 1986).
2. M. F. Scheier and C. S. Carver, Optimism, coping, and health: Assessment and implications of generalized outcome expectancies, *Health Psychology, 4,* 219–247 (1985).
3. R. Schulz, C. A. Tompkins, and M. T. Rau, A longitudinal study of the psychosocial impact of stroke on primary support persons, *Psychology and Aging, 3,* 131–141 (1988).
4. G. N. Marshall, C. B. Wortman, J. W. Kusulas, L. K. Hervig, and R. R. Vickers, Jr., Distinguishing optimism from pessimism: Relations to fundamental dimensions of mood and personality, *Journal of Personality and Social Psychology, 62,* 1067–1074 (1992).
5. See M. F. Scheier and C. S. Carver, Effects of optimism on psychological and physical well-being: Theoretical overview and empirical update. *Cognitive Therapy and Research, 16,* 201–228 (1992).
6. C. S. Carver and J. G. Gaines, Optimism, pessimism, and postpartum depression, *Cognitive Therapy and Research, 11,* 449–462 (1987).
7. L. G. Aspinwall and S. E. Taylor, Modeling cognitive adaptation: A longitudinal investigation of the impact of individual differences and coping on college adjustment and performance, *Journal of Personality and Social Psychology* (in press).
8. M. F. Scheier, K. A. Matthews, J. F. Owens, G. J. Magovern, Sr., R. Lefebvre, R. C. Abbott, and C. S. Carver, Dispositional optimism and recovery from coronary artery bypass surgery: The beneficial effects of optimism on physical and psychological well-being, *Journal of Personality and Social Psychology, 57,* 1024–1040 (1989).
9. R. Plomin, M. F. Scheier, C. S. Bergeman, N. L. Pedersen, J. R. Nesselroade, and G. E. McClearn, Optimism, pessimism and mental health: A twin/adoption analysis, *Personality and Individual Differences* (in press).
10. N. Cantor and J. K. Norem, Defensive pessimism and stress and coping, *Social Cognition, 7,* 92–112 (1989).
11. L. Y. Abramson, M. E. P. Seligman, and J. D. Teasdale, Learned helplessness in humans: Critique and reformulation, *Journal of Abnormal Psychology, 87,* 49–74 (1978).
12. M. E. P. Seligman, *Helplessness: On Depression, Development, and Death* (Freeman, San Francisco, 1975).
13. For a review, see C. Peterson and L. M. Bossio, *Health and Optimism: New Research on the Relationship Between Positive Thinking and Physical Well-Being* (Free Press, New York, 1991).

Recommended Reading

Scheier, M. F., and Carver, C. S. (1992). Effects of optimism on psychological and physical well-being: Theoretical overview and empirical update. *Cognitive Therapy and Research, 16,* 201–228.

Seligman, M. E. P. (1991). *Learned Optimism* (Knopf, New York).

Taylor, S. E. (1989). *Positive Illusions: Creative Self-Deception and the Healthy Mind* (Basic Books, New York).

Glossary

This glossary of psychology terms is included to provide you with a convenient and ready reference as you encounter general terms in your study of psychology and personal growth and behavior that are unfamiliar or require a review. It is not intended to be comprehensive, but taken together with the many definitions included in the articles themselves, it should prove to be quite useful.

Abnormal Irregular, deviating from the norm or average. Abnormal implies the presence of a mental disorder that leads to behavior that society labels as deviant. There is a continuum between normal and abnormal. These are relative terms in that they imply a social judgment. *See* Normal.

Accommodation Process in cognitive development; involves altering or reorganizing the mental picture to make room for a new experience or idea.

Acetylcholine A neurotransmitter involved in memory.

Achievement Drive The need to attain self-esteem, success, or status. Society's expectations strongly influence the achievement motive.

ACTH (Adrenocorticotropic Hormone) The part of the brain called the hypothalamus activates the release of the hormone ACTH from the pituitary gland when a stressful condition exists. ACTH in turn activates the release of adrenal corticoids from the cortex of the adrenal gland.

Action Therapy A general classification of therapy (as opposed to insight therapy) in which the therapist focuses on symptoms rather than on underlying emotional states. Treatment aims at teaching new behavioral patterns rather than at self-understanding. *See* Insight Therapy.

Actor-Observer Attribution The tendency to attribute the behavior of other people to internal causes and the behavior of yourself to external causes.

Acupuncture The technique for curing certain diseases and anesthetizing by inserting needles at certain points of the body; developed in China and now being studied and applied in the West.

Adaptation The process of responding to changes in the environment by altering one's responses to keep one's behavior appropriate to environmental demands.

Addiction Physical dependence on a drug. When a drug causes biochemical changes that are uncomfortable when the drug is discontinued, when one must take ever larger doses to maintain the intensity of the drug's effects, and when desire to continue the drug is strong, one is said to be addicted.

Adjustment How we react to stress; some change that we make in response to the demands placed upon us.

Adrenal Glands Endocrine glands involved in stress and energy regulation.

Affective Disorder Affect means feeling or emotion. An affective disorder is mental illness marked by a disturbance of mood (e.g., manic depression).

Afferent Neuron (Sensory) A neuron that carries messages from the sense organs toward the central nervous system.

Aggression Any act that causes pain or suffering to another. Some psychologists believe that aggressive behavior is instinctual to all species, including humans, while others believe that it is learned through the processes of observation and imitation.

Alienation Indifference to or loss of personal relationships. An individual may feel estranged from family members, or, on a broader scale, from society.

All-or-None Law The principle that states that a neuron only fires when a stimulus is above a certain minimum strength (threshold), and that when it fires, it does so at full strength.

Altered State of Consciousness (ASC) A mental state qualitatively different from a person's normal, alert, waking consciousness.

Altruism Behavior motivated by a desire to benefit another person. Altruistic behavior is aided by empathy and is usually motivated internally, not by observable threats or rewards.

Amphetamine A psychoactive drug that is a stimulant. Although used in treating mild depressions or, in children, hyperactivity, its medical uses are doubtful, and amphetamines are often abused. *See* Psychoactive Drug.

Anal Stage Psychosexual stage during which, according to Freud, the child experiences the first restrictions on his impulses.

Animism The quality of believing life exists in inanimate objects. According to Piaget, animism is characteristic of children's thinking until about age two.

Antisocial Personality Disorder Personality disorder in which individuals who engaged in antisocial behavior experience no guilt or anxiety about their actions; sometimes called sociopathy or psychopathy.

Anxiety An important term that has different meanings for different theories (psychoanalysis, behavior theory); a feeling state of apprehension, dread, or uneasiness. The state may be aroused by an objectively dangerous situation or by a situation that is not objectively dangerous. It may be mild or severe.

Anxiety Disorder Fairly long-lasting disruptions of the person's ability to deal with stress; often accompanied by feelings of fear and apprehension.

Applied Psychology The area of psychology that is most immediately concerned with helping to solve practical problems; includes clinical and counseling psychology, and industrial, environmental, and legal psychology.

Aptitude Tests Tests which are designed to predict what can be accomplished by a person in the future with the proper training.

Arousal A measure of responsiveness or activity; a state of excitement or wakefulness ranging from deepest coma to intense excitement.

Aspiration Level The level of achievement a person strives for. Studies suggest that people can use internal or external standards of performance.

Assertiveness Training Training which helps individuals stand up for their rights while not denying rights of other people.

Assimilation Process in cognitive development; occurs when something new is taken into the child's mental picture of the world.

Association Has separate meanings for different branches of psychology. Theory in cognitive psychology suggests that we organize information so that we can find our memories systematically, that one idea will bring another to mind. In psychoanalysis, the patient is asked to free associate (speak aloud all consecutive thoughts until random associations tend of themselves to form a meaningful whole). *See* Cognitive Psychology; Psychoanalysis.

Association Neurons Neurons that connect with other neurons.

Associationism A theory of learning suggesting that once two stimuli are presented together, one of them will remind a person of the other. Ideas are learned by association with sensory experiences and are not innate. Among the principles of associationism are contiguity (stimuli that occur close together are more likely to be associated than stimuli far apart), and repetition (the more frequently stimuli occur together, the more strongly they become associated).

Attachment Process in which the individual shows behaviors that promote the proximity or contact with a specific object or person.

Attention The tendency to focus activity in a particular direction and to select certain stimuli for further analysis while ignoring or possibly storing for further analysis all other inputs.

Attitude An overall tendency to respond positively or negatively to particular people or objects in a way that is learned through experience and that is made up of feelings (affects), thoughts (evaluations), and actions (conation).

Attribution The process of determining the causes of behavior in a given individual.

Autism A personality disorder in which a child does not respond socially to people.

Autonomic Nervous System The part of the nervous system (the other part is the central nervous system) that is for emergency functions and release of large amounts of energy (sympathetic division) and regulating functions such as digestion and sleep (parasympathetic division). *See* Biofeedback.

Aversion Therapy A counterconditioning therapy in which unwanted responses are paired with unpleasant consequences.

Avoidance Conditioning Situation in which a subject learns to avoid an aversive stimulus by responding appropriately before it begins.

Barbiturates Sedative-hypnotic, psychoactive drugs widely used to induce sleep and to reduce tension. Overuse can lead to addiction. *See* Addiction.

Behavior Any observable activity of an organism, including mental processes.

Behavior Therapy The use of conditioning processes to treat mental disorders. Various techniques may be used, including positive reinforcement in which rewards (verbal or tangible) are given to the patient for appropriate behavior, modeling in which patients unlearn fears by watching models exhibit fearlessness, and systematic desensitization in which the patient is taught to relax and visualize anxiety-producing items at the same time. *See* Insight Therapy; Systematic Desensitization.

Behaviorism A school of psychology stressing an objective approach to psychological questions, proposing that psychology be limited to observable behavior and that the subjectiveness of consciousness places it beyond the limits of scientific psychology.

217

Biofeedback The voluntary control of physiological processes by receiving information about those processes as they occur, through instruments that pick up these changes and display them to the subject in the form of a signal. Blood pressure, skin temperature, etc. can be controlled.

Biological (Primary) Motives Motives that have a physiological basis; include hunger, thirst, body temperature regulation, avoidance of pain, and sex.

Biological Response System System of the body that is particularly important in behavioral responding; includes the senses, endocrines, muscles, and the nervous system.

Biological Therapy Treatment of behavior problems through biological techniques; major biological therapies include drug therapy, psychosurgery, and electroconvulsive therapy.

Bipolar Disorder Affective disorder that is characterized by extreme mood swings from sad depression to joyful mania; sometimes called manic-depression.

Body Language Communication through position and movement of the body.

Brain Mapping A procedure for identifying the function of various areas of the brain; the surgeon gives a tiny electrical stimulation to a specific area and notes patient's reaction.

Brain Stimulation The introduction of chemical or electrical stimuli directly into the brain.

Brain Waves Electrical responses produced by brain activity that can be recorded directly from any portion of the brain or from the scalp with special electrodes. Brain waves are measured by an electroencephalograph (EEG). Alpha waves occur during relaxed wakefulness and beta waves during active behavior. Theta waves are associated with drowsiness and vivid visual imagery, delta waves with deep sleep.

Bystander Effect Phenomenon in which a single person is more likely to help in an emergency situation than a group of people.

Cannon-Bard Theory of Emotion Theory of emotion that states that the emotional feeling and the physiological arousal occur at the same time.

Catatonic Schizophrenia A type of schizophrenia that is characterized by periods of complete immobility and the apparent absence of will to move or speak.

Causal Attribution Process of determining whether a person's behavior is due to internal or external motives.

Cautious Shift Research suggests that the decisions of a group will be more conservative than that of the average individual member when dealing with areas for which there are widely held values favoring caution (e.g., physical danger or family responsibility). *See* Risky Shift.

Central Nervous System The part of the nervous system that interprets and stores messages from the sense organs, decides what behavior to exhibit, and sends appropriate messages to the muscles and glands; includes the brain and spinal cord.

Central Tendency In statistics, measures of central tendency give a number that represents the entire group or sample.

Cerebellum The part of the brain responsible for muscle and movement control and coordination of eye-body movement.

Cerebral Cortex The part of the brain consisting of the outer layer of cerebral cells. The cortex can be divided into specific regions: sensory, motor, and associative.

Chaining Behavior theory suggests that behavior patterns are built up of component parts by stringing together a number of simpler responses.

Character Disorder (or Personality Disorder) A classification of psychological disorders (as distinguished from neurosis or psychosis). The disorder has become part of the individual's personality and does not cause him or her discomfort, making that disorder more difficult to treat psychotherapeutically.

Chromosome *See* Gene.

Chunking The tendency to code memories so that there are fewer bits to store.

Classical Conditioning *See* Pavlovian Conditioning.

Client-Centered Therapy A nondirective form of psychotherapy developed by Carl Rogers in which the counselor attempts to create an atmosphere in which the client can freely explore herself or himself and her or his problems. The client-centered therapist reflects what the client says back to him, usually without interpreting it.

Clinical Psychology The branch of psychology concerned with testing, diagnosing, interviewing, conducting research and treating (often by psychotherapy) mental disorders and personality problems.

Cognitive Appraisal Intellectual evaluation of situations or stimuli. Experiments suggest that emotional arousal is produced not simply by a stimulus but by how one evaluates and interprets the arousal. The appropriate physical response follows this cognitive appraisal.

Cognitive Behavior Therapy A form of behavior therapy that identifies self-defeating attitudes and thoughts in a subject, and then helps the subject to replace these with positive, supportive thoughts.

Cognitive Dissonance People are very uncomfortable if they perceive that their beliefs, feelings, or acts are not consistent with one another, and they will try to reduce the discomfort of this dissonance.

Cognitive Psychology The study of how individuals gain knowledge of their environments. Cognitive psychologists believe that the organism actively participates in constructing the meaningful stimuli that it selectively organizes and to which it selectively responds.

Comparative Psychology The study of similarities and differences in the behavior of different species.

Compulsive Personality Personality disorder in which an individual is preoccupied with details and rules.

Concept Learning The acquisition of the ability to identify and use the qualities that objects or situations have in common. A class concept refers to any quality that breaks objects or situations into separate groupings.

Concrete-Operational Stage A stage in intellectual development, according to Piaget. The child at approximately seven years begins to apply logic. His or her thinking is less egocentric, reversible, and the child develops conservation abilities and the ability to classify. *See* Conservation.

Conditioned Reinforcer Reinforcement that is effective because it has been associated with other reinforcers. Conditioned reinforcers are involved in higher order conditioning.

Conditioned Response (CR) The response or behavior that occurs when the conditioned stimulus is presented (after the conditioned stimulus has been associated with the unconditioned stimulus).

Conditioned Stimulus (CS) An originally neutral stimulus that is associated with an unconditioned stimulus and takes on its capability of eliciting a particular reaction.

Conditioned Taste Aversion (CTA) Learning an aversion to particular tastes by associating them with stomach distress; usually considered a unique form of classical conditioning because of the extremely long interstimulus intervals involved.

Conduction The ability of a neuron to carry a message (an electrical stimulus) along its length.

Conflict Situation that occurs when we experience incompatible demands or desires.

Conformity The tendency of an individual to act like others regardless of personal belief.

Conscience A person's sense of the moral rightness or wrongness of behavior.

Consciousness Awareness of experienced sensations, thoughts, and feelings at any given point in time.

Consensus In causal attribution, the extent to which other people react the same way the subject does in a particular situation.

Conservation Refers to the child's ability to understand laws of length, mass, and volume. Before the development of this ability, a child will not understand that a particular property of an object (e.g., the quantity of water in a glass) does not change even though other perceivable features change.

Consistency In causal attribution, the extent to which the subject always behaves in the same way in a particular situation.

Consolidation The biological neural process of making memories permanent; possibly short-term memory is electrically coded and long-term memory is chemically coded.

Continuum of Preparedness Seligman's proposal that animals are biologically prepared to learn certain responses more readily than others.

Control Group A group used for comparison with an experimental group. All conditions must be identical for each group with the exception of the one variable (independent) that is manipulated. *See* Experimental Group.

Convergence Binocular depth cue in which we detect distance by interpreting the kinesthetic sensations produced by the muscles of the eyeballs.

Convergent Thinking The kind of thinking that is used to solve problems having only one correct answer. *See* Divergent Thinking.

Conversion Disorder Somatoform disorder in which a person displays obvious disturbance in the nervous system, however, a medical examination reveals no physical basis for the problem; often includes paralysis, loss of sensation, or blindness.

Corpus Callosum Nerve fibers that connect the two halves of the brain in humans. If cut, the halves continue to function although some functions are affected.

Correlation A measurement in which two or more sets of variables are compared and the extent to which they are related is calculated.

Correlation Coefficient The measure, in number form, of how two variables vary together. They extend from −1 (perfect negative correlation) to a +1 (perfect positive correlation).

Counterconditioning A behavior therapy in which an unwanted response is replaced by conditioning a new response that is incompatible with it.

Creativity The ability to discover or produce new solutions to problems, new inventions, or new works of art. Creativity is an ability independent of IQ and is opened-ended in that solutions are not predefined in their scope or appropriateness. *See* Problem Solving.

Critical Period A specific stage in an organism's development during which the acquisition of a particular type of behavior depends on exposure to a particular type of stimulation.

Cross-Sectional Study A research technique that focuses on a factor in a group of subjects as they are at one time, as in a study of fantasy play in subjects of three different age groups. *See* Longitudinal Study.

Culture-Bound The idea that a test's usefulness is limited to the culture in which it was written and utilized.

Curiosity Motive Motive that causes the individual to seek out a certain amount of novelty.

Cutaneous Sensitivity The skin's senses: touch, pain, pressure and temperature. Skin receptors respond in different ways and with varying degrees of sensitivity.

Decay Theory of forgetting in which sensory impressions leave memory traces that fade away with time.

Defense Mechanism A way of reducing anxiety that does not directly cope with the threat. There are many types, denial, repression, etc., all of which are used in normal function. Only when use is habitual or they impede effective solutions are they considered pathological.

Delusion A false belief that persists despite evidence showing it to be irrational. Delusions are often symptoms of mental illness.

Dependent Variable Those conditions that an experimenter observes and measures. Called "dependent" because they depend on the experimental manipulations.

Depersonalization Disorder Dissociative disorder in which individuals escape from their own personalities by believing that they don't exist or that their environment is not real.

Depression A temporary emotional state that normal individuals experience or a persistent state that may be considered a psychological disorder. Characterized by sadness and low self-esteem. *See* Self-Esteem.

Descriptive Statistics Techniques that help summarize large amounts of data information.

Developmental Norms The average time at which developmental changes occur in the normal individual.

Developmental Psychology The study of changes in behavior and thinking as the organism grows from the prenatal stage to death.

Deviation, Standard and Average Average deviation is determined by measuring the deviation of each score in a distribution from the mean and calculating the average of the deviations. The standard deviation is used to determine how representative the mean of a distribution is. *See* Mean.

Diagnostic and Statistical Manual of Mental Disorders (DSM) DSM-IV was published in 1994 by the American Psychiatric Association.

Diffusion of Responsibility As the number of witnesses to a help-requiring situation—and thus the degree of anonymity—increases, the amount of helping decreases and the amount of time before help is offered increases. *See* Bystander Effect.

Discrimination The ability to tell whether stimuli are different when presented together or that one situation is different from a past one.

Disorganized Schizophrenia A type of schizophrenia that is characterized by a severe personality disintegration; the individual often displays bizarre behavior.

Displacement The process by which an emotion originally attached to a particular person, object, or situation is transferred to something else.

Dissociative Disorders Disorders in which individuals forget who they are.

Distal Stimuli Physical events in the environment that affect perception. *See* Proximal Stimulus.

Distinctiveness In causal attribution, the extent to which the subject reacts the same way in other situations.

Divergent Thinking The kind of thinking that characterizes creativity (as contrasted with convergent thinking) and involves the development of novel resolutions of a task or the generation of totally new ideas. *See* Convergent Thinking.

DNA *See* Gene.

Double Bind A situation in which a person is subjected to two conflicting, contradictory demands at the same time.

Down's Syndrome Form of mental retardation caused by having three number 21 chromosomes (trisomy 21).

Dreams The thoughts, images, and emotions that occur during sleep. Dreams occur periodically during the sleep cycle and are usually marked by rapid movements of the eyes (REM sleep). The content of dreams tends to reflect emotions (sexual feelings, according to Freud) and experiences of the previous day. Nightmares are qualitatively different from other dreams, often occurring during deep or Stage 4 sleep.

Drive A need or urge that motivates behavior. Some drives may be explained as responses to bodily needs, such as hunger or sex. Others derive from social pressures and complex forms of learning, for example, competition, curiosity, achievement. *See* Motivation.

Drive Reduction Theory Theory of motivation that states that the individual is pushed by inner forces toward reducing the drive and restoring homeostasis.

Drug Dependence A state of mental or physical dependence on a drug, or both. Psychoactive drugs are capable of creating psychological dependence (anxiety when the drug is unavailable), although the relationship of some, such as marijuana and LSD, to physical dependence or addiction is still under study. *See* Psychoactive Drug; Addiction.

Drug Tolerance A state produced by certain psychoactive drugs in which increasing amounts of the substance are required to produce the desired effect. Some drugs produce tolerance but not withdrawal symptoms, and these drugs are not regarded as physically addicting.

Effectance Motive The striving for effectiveness in dealing with the environment. The effectance motive differs from the need for achievement in that effectance depends on internal feelings of satisfaction while the need for achievement is geared more to meeting others' standards.

Efferent Neuron (Motor) A neuron that carries messages from the central nervous system to the muscles and glands.

Ego A construct to account for the organization in a person's life and for making the person's behavior correspond to physical and social realities. According to Freud, the ego is the "reality principle" that is responsible for holding the id or "pleasure principle" in check. *See* Id.

Egocentrism Seeing things from only one's own point of view; also, the quality of a child's thought that prevents her or him from understanding that different people perceive the world differently. Egocentrism is characteristic of a stage that all children go through.

Electra Complex The libidinal feelings of a child toward a parent of the opposite sex. *See also* Oedipus Complex

Electroshock Therapy A form of therapy used to relieve severe depression. The patient receives electric current across the forehead, loses consciousness, and undergoes a short convulsion. When the patient regains consciousness, his or her mood is lifted.

Emotion A complex feeling-state that involves physiological arousal; a subjective feeling which might involve a cognitive appraisal of the situation and overt behavior in response to a stimulus.

Empathy The ability to appreciate how someone else feels by putting yourself in her or his position and experiencing her or his feelings. Empathy is acquired normally by children during intellectual growth.

Empiricism The view that behavior is learned through experience.

Encounter Groups Groups of individuals who meet to change their personal lives by confronting each other, discussing personal problems, and talking more honestly and openly than in everyday life.

Endocrine Glands Ductless glands that secrete chemicals called hormones into the blood stream.

Equilibration According to Piaget, the child constructs an understanding of the world through equilibration. Equilibration consists of the interaction of two complementary processes, assimilation (taking in input within the existing structures of the mind, e.g., putting it into mental categories that already exist) with accommodation (the changing of mental categories to fit new input that cannot be taken into existing categories) and is the process by which knowing occurs. One's developmental stage affects how one equilibrates.

Ethnocentrism The belief that one's own ethnic or racial group is superior to others.

Experiment Procedures executed under a controlled situation in order to test a hypothesis and discover relationships between independent and dependent variables.

Experimental Control The predetermined conditions, procedures, and checks built into the design of an experiment to ensure scientific control; as opposed to "control" in common usage, which implies manipulation.

Experimental Group In a scientific experiment, the group of subjects that is usually treated specially, as opposed to the control group, in order to isolate just the variable under investigation. *See* Control Group.

Experimental Psychology The branch of psychology concerned with the laboratory study of basic psychological laws and principles as demonstrated in the behavior of animals.

Experimenter Bias How the expectations of the person running an experiment can influence what comes out of the experiment. Experimenter bias can affect the way the experimenter sees the subjects' behavior, causing distortions of fact, and can also affect the way the experimenter reads data, also leading to distortions.

Extinction The elimination of behavior by, in classical conditioning, the withholding of the unconditional stimulus, and in operant conditioning, the withholding of the reinforcement.

Extrasensory Perception (ESP) The range of perceptions that are "paranormal," (such as the ability to predict events, reproduce drawings sealed in envelopes, etc.).

Fixed Interval (FI) Schedule Schedule of reinforcement in which the subject receives reinforcement for the first correct response given after a specified time interval.

Fixed Ratio (FR) Schedule Schedule of reinforcement in which the subject is reinforced after a certain number of responses.

Fixed-Action Pattern Movement that is characteristic of a species and does not have to be learned.

Forgetting The process by which material that once was available is no longer available. Theory exists that forgetting occurs because memories interfere with one another, either retroactively (new memories block old) or proactively (old memories block new); that forgetting occurs when the cues necessary to recall the information are not supplied, or when memories are too unpleasant to remain in consciousness. *See* Repression.

Formal Operational Stage According to Piaget, the stage at which the child develops adult powers of reasoning, abstraction, and symbolizing. The child can grasp scientific, religious, and political concepts and deduce their consequences as well as reason hypothetically ("what if?").

Frequency Theory of Hearing Theory of hearing that states that the frequency of vibrations at the basilar membrane determines the frequency of firing of neurons that carry impulses to the brain.

Frustration A feeling of discomfort or insecurity aroused by a blocking of gratification or by unresolved problems. Several theories hold that frustration arouses aggression. *See* Aggression.

Functionalism An early school of psychology stressing the ways behavior helps one adapt to the environment and the role that learning plays in this adaptive process.

Gene The unit of heredity that determines particular characteristics; a part of a molecule of DNA. DNA (dioxyribonucleic acid) is found mainly in the nucleus of living cells where it occurs in threadlike structures called chromosomes. Within the chromosomes, each DNA molecule is organized into specific units that carry the genetic information necessary for the development of a particular trait. These units are the genes. A gene can reproduce itself exactly, and this is how traits are carried between generations. The genotype is the entire structure of genes that are inherited by an organism from its parents. The environment interacts with this genotype to determine how the genetic potential will develop.

General Adaptation Syndrome (GAS) The way the body responds to stress, as described by Hans Selye. In the first stage, an alarm reaction, a person responds by efforts at self-control and shows signs of nervous depression (defense mechanisms, fear, anger, etc.) followed by a release of ACTH. In stage 2, the subject shows increased resistance to the specific source of stress and less resistance to other sources. Defense mechanisms may become neurotic. With stage 3 come exhaustion, stupor, even death.

Generalization The process by which learning in one situation is transferred to another, similar situation. It is a key term in behavioral modification and classical conditioning. *See* Pavlovian Conditioning.

Generalized Anxiety Disorder Disorder in which the individual lives in a state of constant severe tension; continuous fear and apprehension experienced by an individual.

Genetics The study of the transfer of the inheritance of characteristics from one generation to another.

Genotype The underlying genetic structure that an individual has inherited and will send on to descendants. The actual appearance of a trait (phenotype) is due to the interaction of the genotype and the environment.

Gestalt Psychology A movement in psychology begun in the 1920s, stressing the wholeness of a person's experience and proposing that perceiving is an active, dynamic process that takes into account the entire pattern of ("gestalt") of the perpetual field. *See* Associationism; Behaviorism.

Glia Cells in the central nervous system that regulate the chemical environment of the nerve cells. RNA is stored in glial cells.

Grammar The set of rules for combining units of a language.

Group Therapy A form of psychotherapy aimed at treating mental disorders in which interaction among group members is the main therapeutic mode. Group therapy takes many forms but essentially requires a sense of community, support, increased personal responsibility, and a professionally trained leader.

Growth The normal quantitative changes that occur in the physical and psychological aspects of a healthy child with the passage of time.

Gustation The sense of taste. Theory suggests that the transmission of sense information from tongue to brain occurs through patterns of cell activity and not just the firing of single nerve fibers. Also, it is believed that specific spatial patterns or places on the tongue correspond to taste qualities.

Habit Formation The tendency to make a response to a stimulus less variable, especially if it produced successful adaptation.

Hallucination A sensory impression reported by a person when no external stimulus exists to justify the report. Hallucinations are serious symptoms and may be produced by psychoses. *See* Psychosis.

Hallucinogen A substance that produces hallucinations, such as LSD, mescaline, etc.

Hierarchy of Needs Maslow's list of motives in humans, arranged from the biological to the uniquely human.

Higher Order Conditioning Learning to make associations with stimuli that have been previously learned (CSs).

Hippocampus Part of the cortex of the brain governing memory storage, smell, and visceral functions.

Homeostasis A set of processes maintaining the constancy of the body's internal state, a series of dynamic compensations of the nervous system. Many processes such as appetite, body temperature, water balance, and heart rate are controlled by homeostasis.

Hormones Chemical secretions of the endocrine glands that regulate various body processes (e.g., growth, sexual traits, reproductive processes, etc.).

Humanism Branch of psychology dealing with those qualities distinguishing humans from other animals.

Hypnosis A trancelike state marked by heightened suggestibility and a narrowing of attention that can be induced in a number of ways. Debate exists over whether hypnosis is a true altered state of consciousness and to what extent strong motivating instructions can duplicate so-called hypnosis.

Hypothalamus A part of the brain that acts as a channel that carries information from the cortex and the thalamus to the spinal cord and ultimately to the motor nerves or to the autonomic nervous system, where it is transmitted to specific target organs. These target organs release into the bloodstream specific hormones that alter bodily functions. *See* Autonomic Nervous System.

Hypothesis A hypothesis can be called an educated guess, similar to a hunch. When a hunch is stated in a way that allows for further testing, it becomes a hypothesis.

Iconic Memory A visual memory. Experiments suggest that in order to be remembered and included in long-term memory, information must pass through a brief sensory stage. Theory further suggests that verbal information is subject to forgetting but that memorized sensory images are relatively permanent.

Id According to Freud, a component of the psyche present at birth that is the storehouse of psychosexual energy called *libido*, and also of primitive urges to fight, dominate, or destroy.

Identification The taking on of attributes that one sees in another person. Children tend to identify with their parents or other important adults and thereby take on certain traits that are important to their development.

Illusion A mistaken perception of an actual stimulus.

Imitation The copying of another's behavior; learned through the process of observation. *See* Modeling.

Impression Formation The process of developing an evaluation of another person from your perceptions; first, or initial, impressions are often very important.

Imprinting The rapid, permanent acquisition by an organism of a strong attachment to an object (usually the parent). Imprinting occurs shortly after birth.

Independent Variable The condition in an experiment that is controlled and manipulated by the experimenter; it is a stimulus that will cause a response.

Inferential Statistics Techniques that help researchers make generalizations about a finding based on a limited number of subjects.

Inhibition Restraint of an impulse, desire, activity, or drive. People are taught to inhibit full expression of many drives (for example, aggression or sexuality) and to apply checks either consciously or unconsciously. In Freudian terminology, an inhibition is an unconsciously motivated blocking of sexual energy. In Pavlovian conditioning, inhibition is the theoretical process that operates during extinction, acting to block a conditioned response. *See* Pavlovian Conditioning.

Insight A sudden perception of useful or proper relations among objects necessary to solve the problem.

Insight Therapy A general classification of therapy in which the therapist focuses on the patient's underlying feelings and motivations and devotes most effort to increasing the patient's self-awareness or insight into his or her behavior. The other major class of therapy is action therapy. *See* Action Therapy.

Instinct An inborn pattern of behavior, relatively independent of environmental influence. An instinct may need to be triggered by a particular stimulus in the environment, but then it proceeds in a fixed pattern. The combination of taxis (orienting movement in response to a particular stimulus) and fixed-action pattern (inherited coordination) is the basis for instinctual activity. *See* Fixed-Action Pattern.

Instrumental Learning *See* Operant Conditioning.

Intelligence A capacity for knowledge about the world. This is an enormous and controversial field of study, and there is no agreement on a precise definition. However, intelligence has come to refer to higher-level abstract processes and may be said to comprise the ability to deal effectively with abstract concepts, the ability to learn, and the ability to adapt and deal with new situations. Piaget defines intelligence as the construction of an understanding. Both biological inheritance and environmental factors contribute to general intelligence. Children proceed through a sequence of identifiable stages in the development of conceptual thinking (Piaget). The degree to which factors such as race, sex, and social class affect intelligence is not known.

Intelligence Quotient (IQ) A measurement of intelligence originally based on tests devised by Binet and now widely applied. Genetic inheritance and environment affect IQ, although their relative contributions are not known. IQ can be defined in different ways; classically it is defined as a relation between chronological and mental ages.

Interference Theory of forgetting in which information that was learned before (proactive interference) or after (retroactive interference) the material of interest causes the learner to be unable to remember the material.

Interstimulus Interval The time between the start of the conditioned stimulus and the start of the unconditioned stimulus in Pavlovian conditioning. *See* Pavlovian Conditioning.

Intrauterine Environment The environment in the uterus during pregnancy can affect the physical development of the organism and its behavior after birth. Factors such as the mother's nutrition, emotional, and physical state significantly influence offspring. The mother's diseases, medications, hormones, and stress level all affect the pre- and postnatal development of her young.

Intrinsic Motivation Motivation inside of the individual; we do something because we receive satisfaction from it.

Introspection Reporting one's internal, subjective mental contents for the purpose of further study and analysis. *See* Structuralism.

James-Lange Theory of Emotion Theory of emotion that states that the physiological arousal and behavior come before the subjective experience of an emotion.

Labeling-of-Arousal Experiments suggest that an individual experiencing physical arousal that she or he cannot explain will interpret her or his feelings in terms of the situation she or he is in and will use environmental and contextual cues.

Language A set of abstract symbols used to communicate meaning. Language includes vocalized sounds or semantic units (words, usually) and rules for combining the units (grammar). There is some inborn basis for language acquisition, and there are identifiable stages in its development that are universal.

Language Acquisition Linguists debate how children acquire language. Some believe in environmental shaping, a gradual system of reward and punishment. Others emphasize the unfolding of capacities inborn in the brain that are relatively independent of the environment and its rewards.

Latency Period According to Freud, the psycho-sexual stage of development during which sexual interest has been repressed and thus is low or "latent" (dormant).

Law of Effect Thorndike's proposal that when a response produces satisfaction, it will be repeated; reinforcement.

Leadership The quality of exerting more influence than other group members. Research suggests that certain characteristics are generally considered essential to leadership: consideration, sensitivity, ability to initiate and structure, and emphasis on production. However, environmental factors may thrust authority on a person without regard to personal characteristics.

Learned Helplessness Theory suggests that living in an environment of uncontrolled stress reduces the ability to cope with future stress that is controllable.

Learned Social Motives Motives in the human that are learned, including achievement, affiliation, and autonomy.

Learning The establishment of connections between stimulus and response, resulting from observation, special training, or previous activity. Learning is relatively permanent.

Life Span Span of time from conception to death; in developmental psychology, a life span approach looks at development throughout an individual's life.

Linguistic Relativity Hypothesis Proposal by Whorf that the perception of reality differs according to the language of the observer.

Linguistics The study of language, its nature, structure, and components.

Locus of Control The perceived place from which come determining forces in one's life. A person who feels that he or she has some control over his or her fate and tends to feel more likely to succeed has an internal locus of control. A person with an external locus of control feels that control is outside himself or herself and therefore that his or her attempts to control his or her fate are less ensured.

Longitudinal Study A research method that involves following subjects over a considerable period of time (as compared with a cross-sectional approach); as in a study of fantasy play in children observed several times at intervals of two years. *See* Cross-Sectional Study.

Love Affectionate behavior between people, often in combination with interpersonal attraction. The mother-infant love relationship strongly influences the later capacity for developing satisfying love relationships.

Manic-Depressive Reaction A form of mental illness marked by alternations of extreme phases of elation (manic phase) and depression.

Maternalism Refers to the mother's reaction to her young. It is believed that the female is biologically determined to exhibit behavior more favorable to the care and feeding of the young than the male, although in humans maternalism is probably determined as much by cultural factors as by biological predisposition.

Maturation The genetically controlled process of physical and physiological growth.

Mean The measure of central tendency, or mathematical average, computed by adding all scores in a set and dividing by the number of scores.

Meaning The concept or idea conveyed to the mind, by any method. In reference to memory, meaningful terms are easier to learn than less meaningful, unconnected, or nonsense terms. Meaningfulness is not the same as the word's meaning.

Median In a set of scores, the median is that middle score that divides the set into equal halves.

Memory Involves the encoding, storing of information in the brain, and its retrieval. Several theories exist to explain memory. One proposes that we have both a short-term (STM) and a long-term memory (LTM) and that information must pass briefly through the STM to be stored in the LTM. Also suggested is that verbal information is subject to forgetting, while memorized sensory images are relatively permanent. Others see memory as a function of association—information processed systematically and the meaningfulness of the items. Debate exists over whether memory retrieval is actually a process of reappearance or reconstruction.

Mental Disorder A mental condition that deviates from what society considers to be normal.

Minnesota Multiphasic Personality Inventory (MMPI) An objective personality test that was originally devised to identify personality disorders.

Mode In a set of scores, the measurement at which the largest number of subjects fall.

Modeling The imitation or copying of another's behavior. As an important process in personality development, modeling may be based on parents. In therapy, the therapist may serve as a model for the patient.

Morality The standards of right and wrong of a society and their adoption by members of that society. Some researchers believe that morality develops in successive stages, with each stage representing a specific level of moral thinking (Kohlberg). Others see morality as the result of experiences in which the child learns through punishment and reward from models such as parents and teachers.

Motivation All factors that cause and regulate behavior that is directed toward achieving goals and satisfying needs. Motivation is what moves an organism to action.

Motor Unit One spinal motoneuron (motor nerve cell) and the muscle fibers it activates. The contraction of a muscle involves the activity of many motoneurons and muscle fibers. Normally we are aware only of our muscles contracting and not of the process producing the contraction, although biofeedback can train people to control individual motor units. *See* Biofeedback.

Narcotic A drug that relieves pain. Heroin, morphine, and opium are narcotics. Narcotics are often addicting.

Naturalistic Observation Research method in which behavior of people or animals in the normal environment is accurately recorded.

Negative Reinforcement Any event that, upon termination, strengthens the preceding behavior; taking from subject something bad will increase the probability that the preceding behavior will be repeated. Involves aversive stimulus.

Neuron A nerve cell. There are billions of neurons in the brain and spinal cord. Neurons interact at synapses or points of contact. Information passage between neurons is electrical and biochemical. It takes the activity of many neurons to produce a behavior.

Neurosis Any one of a wide range of psychological difficulties, accompanied by excessive anxiety (as contrasted with psychosis). Psychoanalytic theory states that neurosis is an expression of unresolved conflicts in the form of tension and impaired functioning. Most neurotics are in much closer contact with reality than most psychotics.

Nonverbal Behaviors Gestures, facial expressions, and other body movements. They are important because they tend to convey emotion. Debate exists over whether they are inborn or learned.

Norm An empirically set pattern of belief or behavior. Social norm refers to widely accepted social or cultural behavior to which a person tends to or is expected to conform.

Normal Sane, or free from mental disorder. Normal behavior is the behavior typical of most people in a given group, and "normality" implies a social judgment.

Normal Curve When scores of a large number of random cases are plotted on a graph, they often fall into a bell-shaped curve; there are as many cases above the mean as below on the curve.

Object Permanence According to Piaget, the stage in cognitive development when a child begins to conceive of objects as having an existence even when out of sight or touch and to conceive of space as extending beyond his or her own perception.

Oedipus Complex The conflicts of a child in a triangular relationship with his mother and father. According to Freud, a boy must resolve his unconscious sexual desire for his mother and the accompanying wish to kill his father and fear of his father's revenge in order that he proceed in his moral development. The analogous problem for girls is called the Electra complex.

Olfaction The sense of smell. No general agreement exists on how olfaction works, though theories exist to explain it. One suggests that the size and shape of molecules of what is smelled is a crucial cue. The brain processes involved in smell are located in a different and evolutionarily older part of the brain than the other senses.

Operant Conditioning The process of changing, maintaining, or eliminating voluntary behavior through the consequences of that behavior. Operant conditioning uses many of the techniques of Pavlovian conditioning but differs in that it deals with voluntary rather than reflex behaviors. The frequency with which a behavior is emitted can be increased if it is rewarded (reinforced) and decreased if it is not reinforced, or punished. Some psychologists believe that all behavior is learned through conditioning while others believe that intellectual and motivational processes play a crucial role. *See Pavlovian Conditioning.*

Operational Definitions If an event is not directly observable, then the variables must be defined by the operations by which they will be measured. These definitions are called operational definitions.

Organism Any living animal, human or subhuman.

Orienting Response A relatively automatic, "what's that?" response that puts the organism in a better position to attend to and deal with a new stimulus. When a stimulus attracts the attention, the body responds with movements of head and body toward the stimulus, changes in muscle tone, heart rate, blood flow, breathing, and changes in the brain's electrical activity.

Pavlovian Conditioning Also called classical conditioning, Pavlovian conditioning can be demonstrated as follows: in the first step, an *unconditioned stimulus* (UCS) such as food, loud sounds, or pain is paired with a neutral *conditioned stimulus* (CS) that causes no direct effect, such as a click, tone, or a dim light. The response elicited by the UCS is called the *unconditioned response* (UCR) and is a biological reflex of the nervous system (for example, eyeblinks or salivation). The combination of the neutral CS, the response-causing UCS, and the unlearned UCR is usually presented to the subject several times during conditioning. Eventually, the UCS is dropped from the sequence in the second step of the process, and the previously neutral CS comes to elicit a response. When conditioning is complete, presentation of the CS alone will result in a *conditioned response* (CR) similar but not always the same as the UCR.

Perception The field of psychology studying ways in which the experience of objects in the world is based upon stimulation of the sense organs. In psychology, the field of perception studies what determines sensory impressions, such as size, shape, distance, direction, etc. Physical events in the environment are called distal stimuli while the activity at the sense organ itself is called a proximal stimulus. The study of perceiving tries to determine how an organism knows what distal stimuli are like since proximal stimuli are its only source of information. Perception of objects remains more or less constant despite changes in distal stimuli and is therefore believed to depend on relationships within stimuli (size *and* distance, for example). Perceptual processes are able to adjust and adapt to changes in the perceptual field.

Performance The actual behavior of an individual that is observed. We often infer learning from observing performance.

Peripheral Nervous System The part of the human nervous system that receives messages from the sense organs and carries messages to the muscles and glands; nerves outside of the brain and spinal cord.

Persuasion The process of changing a person's attitudes, beliefs, or actions. A person's susceptibility to persuasion depends on the persuader's credibility, subtlety, and whether both sides of an argument are presented.

Phenotype The physical features or behavior patterns by which we recognize an organism. Phenotype is the result of interaction between genotype (total of inherited genes) and environment. *See Genotype.*

Phobia A neurosis consisting of an irrationally intense fear of specific persons, objects, or situations and a wish to avoid them. A phobic person feels intense and incapacitating anxiety. The person may be aware that the fear is irrational, but this knowledge does not help.

Pituitary Gland Is located in the brain and controls secretion of several hormones: the antidiuretic hormone that maintains water balance; oxytocin, which controls blood pressure and milk production; and ACTH, which is produced in response to stress, etc. *See ACTH.*

Placebo A substance that in and of itself has no real effect but which may produce an effect in a subject because the subject expects or believes that it will.

Positive Reinforcement Any event that, upon presentation, strengthens the preceding behavior; giving a subject something good will increase the probability that the preceding behavior will be repeated.

Prejudice An attitude in which one holds a negative belief about members of a group to which he or she does not belong. Prejudice is often directed at minority ethnic or racial groups and may be reduced by contact with these perceived "others."

Premack Principle Principle that states that of any two responses, the one that is more likely to occur can be used to reinforce the response that is less likely to occur.

Prenatal Development Development from conception to birth. It includes the physical development of the fetus as well as certain of its intellectual and emotional processes.

Preoperational Stage The development stage at which, according to Piaget, come the start of language, the ability to imitate actions, to symbolize, and to play make-believe games. Thinking is egocentric in that a child cannot understand that others perceive things differently.

Primary Reinforcement Reinforcement that is effective without having been associated with other reinforcers; sometimes called unconditioned reinforcement.

Probability (p) In inferential statistics, the likelihood that the difference between the experimental and control groups is due to the independent variable.

Problem Solving A self-directed activity in which an individual uses information to develop answers to problems, to generate new problems, and sometimes to transform the process by creating a unique, new system. Problem solving involves learning, insight, and creativity.

Projective Test A type of test in which people respond to ambiguous, loosely structured stimuli. It is assumed that people will reveal themselves by putting themselves into the stimuli they see. The validity of these tests for diagnosis and personality assessment is still at issue.

Propaganda Information deliberately spread to aid a cause. Propaganda's main function is persuasion.

Prosocial Behavior Behavior that is directed toward helping others.

Proximal Stimulus Activity at the sense organ.

Psychoactive Drug A substance that affects mental activities, perceptions, consciousness, or mood. This type of drug has its effects through strictly physical effects and through expectations.

Psychoanalysis There are two meanings to this word: it is a theory of personality development based on Freud and a method of treatment also based on Freud. Psychoanalytic therapy uses techniques of free association, dream analysis, and analysis of the patient's relationship (the "transference") to the analyst. Psychoanalytic theory maintains that the personality develops through a series of psychosexual stages and that the personality consists of specific components energized by the life and death instincts.

Psychogenic Pain Disorder Somatoform disorder in which the person complains of severe, long-lasting pain for which there is no organic cause.

Psycholinguistics The study of the process of language acquisition as part of psychological development and of language as an aspect of behavior. Thinking may obviously depend on language, but their precise relationship still puzzles psycholinguists, and several different views exist.

Psychological Dependence Situation when a person craves a drug even though it is not biologically necessary for his or her body.

Psychophysiological Disorders Real medical problems (such as ulcers, migraine headaches, and high blood pressure) that are caused or aggravated by psychological stress.

Psychosexual Stages According to Freud, an individual's personality develops through several stages. Each stage is associated with a particular bodily source of gratification (pleasure). First comes the oral stage when most pleasures come from the mouth. Then comes the anal stage when the infant derives pleasure from holding and releasing while learning bowel control. The phallic stage brings pleasure from the genitals, and a crisis (Oedipal) occurs in which the child gradually suppresses sexual desire for the opposite-sex parent, identifies with the same-sex parent and begins to be interested in the outside world. This latency period lasts until puberty, after which the genital stage begins and mature sexual relationships develop. There is no strict timetable, but, according to Freudians, the stages do come in a definite order. Conflicts experienced and not adequately dealt with remain with the individual.

Psychosis The most severe of mental disorders, distinguished by a person being seriously out of touch with objective reality. Psychoses may result from physical factors (organic) or may have no known physical cause (functional). Psychoses take many forms, of which the most common are schizophrenia and psychotic depressive reactions, but all are marked by personality disorganization and a severely reduced ability to perceive reality. Both biological and environmental factors are believed to influence the development of psychosis, although the precise effect of each is not presently known. *See Neurosis.*

Psychosomatic Disorders A variety of body reactions that are closely related to psychological events. Stress, for example, brings on many physical changes and can result in illness or even death if prolonged and severe. Psychosomatic disorders can affect any part of the body.

Psychotherapy Treatment involving interpersonal contacts between a trained therapist and a patient in which the therapist tries to produce beneficial changes in the patient's emotional state, attitudes, and behavior.

Punishment Any event that decreases the probability of the preceding behavior being repeated. You can give something bad (positive punishment) to decrease the preceding behavior.

Rational-Emotive Therapy A cognitive behavior modification technique in which a person is taught to identify irrational, self-defeating beliefs and then to overcome them.

Rationalization Defense mechanism in which individuals make up logical excuses to justify their behavior rather than exposing their true motives.

Reaction Formation Defense mechanism in which a person masks an unconsciously distressing or unacceptable trait by assuming an opposite attitude or behavior pattern.

Reactive Schizophrenia A type of schizophrenia in which the disorder appears as a reaction to some major trauma or terribly stressful encounter; sometimes called acute schizophrenia.

Reality Therapy A form of treatment of mental disorders pioneered by William Glasser in which the origins of the patient's problems are considered irrelevant and emphasis is on a close, judgmental bond between patient and therapist aimed to improve the patient's present and future life.

Reflex An automatic movement that occurs in direct response to a stimulus.

Rehearsal The repeating of an item to oneself and the means by which information is stored in the short-term memory (STM). Theory suggests that rehearsal is necessary for remembering and storage in the long-term memory (LTM).

Reinforcement The process of affecting the frequency with which a behavior is emitted. A reinforcer can reward and thus increase the behavior or punish and thus decrease its frequency. Reinforcers can also be primary, satisfying basic needs such as hunger or thirst, or secondary, satisfying learned and indirect values, such as money.

Reliability Consistency of measurement. A test is reliable if it repeatedly gives the same results. A person should get nearly the same score if the test is taken on two different occasions.

REM (Rapid-Eye Movement) Type of sleep in which the eyes are rapidly moving around; dreaming occurs in REM sleep.

Repression A defense mechanism in which a person forgets or pushes into the unconscious something that arouses anxiety. *See* Anxiety; Defense Mechanism.

Reticular Formation A system of nerve fibers leading from the spinal column to the cerebral cortex that functions to arouse, alert, and make an organism sensitive to changes in the environment. *See* Cerebral Cortex.

Retina The inside coating of the eye, containing two kinds of cells that react to light: the rods that are sensitive only to dim light and the cones that are sensitive to color and form in brighter light. There are three kinds of cones, each responsive to particular colors in the visible spectrum (range of colors).

Risky Shift Research suggests that decisions made by groups will involve considerably more risk than individuals in the group would be willing to take. This shift in group decision depends heavily on cultural values. *See* Cautious Shift.

RNA (Ribonucleic Acid) A chemical substance that occurs in chromosomes and that functions in genetic coding. During task-learning, RNA changes occur in the brain.

Rod Part of the retina involved in seeing in dim light. *See* Retina.

Role Playing Adopting the role of another person and experiencing the world in a way one is not accustomed to.

Role Taking The ability to imagine oneself in another's place or to understand the consequences of one's actions for another person.

Schachter-Singer Theory of Emotion Theory of emotion that states that we interpret our arousal according to our environment and label our emotions accordingly.

Schizoid Personality Personality disorder characterized by having great trouble developing social relationships.

Schizophrenia The most common and serious form of psychosis in which there exists an imbalance between emotional reactions and the thoughts associated with these feelings. it may be a disorder of the process of thinking. *See* Psychosis.

Scientific Method The process used by psychologists to determine principles of behavior that exist independently of individual experience and that are untouched by unconscious bias. It is based on a prearranged agreement that criteria, external to the individual and communicable to others, must be established for each set of observations referred to as fact.

Secondary Reinforcement Reinforcement that is only effective after it has been associated with a primary reinforcer.

Self-Actualization A term used by humanistic psychologists to describe what they see as a basic human motivation: the development of all aspects of an individual into productive harmony.

Self-Esteem A person's evaluation of oneself. If someone has confidence and satisfaction in oneself, self-esteem is considered high.

Self-Fulfilling Prophecy A preconceived expectation or belief about a situation that evokes behavior resulting in a situation consistent with the preconception.

Senses An organism's physical means of receiving and detecting physical changes in the environment. Sensing is analyzed in terms of reception of the physical stimulus by specialized nerve cells in the sense organs, transduction or converting the stimulus's energy into nerve impulses that the brain can interpret, and transmission of those nerve impulses from the sense organ to the part of the brain that can interpret the information they convey.

Sensitivity Training Aims at helping people to function more effectively in their jobs by increasing their awareness of their own and others' feelings and exchanging "feedback" about styles of interacting. Sensitivity groups are unlike therapy groups in that they are meant to enrich the participants' lives. Participants are not considered patients or ill. Also called T-groups.

Sensorimotor Stage According to Piaget, the stage of development beginning at birth during which perceptions are tied to objects that the child manipulates. Gradually the child learns that objects have permanence even if they are out of sight or touch.

Sensory Adaptation Tendency of the sense organs to adjust to continuous, unchanging stimulation by reducing their functioning; a stimulus that once caused sensation no longer does.

Sensory Deprivation The blocking out of all outside stimulation for a period of time. As studied experimentally, it can produce hallucinations, psychological disturbances, and temporary disorders of the nervous system of the subject.

Sex Role The attitudes, activities, and expectations considered specific to being male or female, determined by both biological and cultural factors.

Shaping A technique of behavior shaping in which behavior is acquired through the reinforcement of successive approximations of the desired behavior.

Sleep A periodic state of consciousness marked by four brain-wave patterns. Dreams occur during REM sleep. Sleep is a basic need without which one may suffer physical or psychological distress. *See* Brain Waves; Dreams.

Sleeper Effect The delayed impact of persuasive information. People tend to forget the context in which they first heard the information, but they eventually remember the content of the message sufficiently to feel its impact.

Social Comparison Theory proposed by Festinger that states that we have a tendency to compare our behavior to others to ensure that we are conforming.

Social Facilitation Phenomenon in which the presence of others increases dominant behavior patterns in an individual; Zajonc's theory of social facilitation states that the presence of others enhances the emission of the dominant response of the individual.

Social Influence The process by which people form and change the attitudes, opinions, and behavior of others.

Social Learning Learning acquired through observation and imitation of others.

Social Psychology The study of individuals as affected by others and of the interaction of individuals in groups.

Socialization A process by which a child learns the various patterns of behavior expected and accepted by society. Parents are the chief agents of a child's socialization. Many factors have a bearing on the socialization process, such as the child's sex, religion, social class, and parental attitudes.

Sociobiology The study of the genetic basis of social behavior.

Sociophobias Excessive irrational fears and embarrassment when interacting with other people.

Somatic Nervous System The part of the peripheral nervous system that carries messages from the sense organs and relays information that directs the voluntary movements of the skeletal muscles.

Somatoform Disorders Disorders characterized by physical symptoms for which there are no obvious physical causes.

Somesthetic Senses Skin senses; includes pressure, pain, cold, and warmth.

Species-Typical Behavior Behavior patterns common to members of a species. Ethologists state that each species inherits some patterns of behavior (e.g., birdsongs).

Stanford-Binet Intelligence Scale Tests that measure intelligence from two years of age through adult level. The tests determine one's intelligence quotient by establishing one's chronological and mental ages. *See* Intelligence Quotient.

State-Dependent Learning Situation in which what is learned in one state can only be remembered when the person is in that state.

Statistically Significant in inferential statistics, a finding that the independent variable did influence greatly the outcome of the experimental and control group.

Stereotype The assignment of characteristics to a person mainly on the basis of the group, class, or category to which he or she belongs. The tendency to categorize and generalize is a basic human way of organizing information. Stereotyping, however, can reinforce misinformation and prejudice. See Prejudice.

Stimulus A unit of the environment that causes a response in an individual; more specifically, a physical or chemical agent acting on an appropriate sense receptor.

Stimulus Discrimination Limiting responses to relevant stimuli.

Stimulus Generalization Responses to stimuli similar to the stimulus that had caused the response.

Stress Pressure that puts unusual demands on an organism. Stress may be caused by physical conditions but generally involves emotions. Stimuli that cause stress are called stressors, and an organism's response is the stress reaction. A three-stage general adaptation syndrome is hypothesized involving both emotional and physical changes. See General Adaptation Syndrome.

Structuralism An early school of psychology that stressed the importance of conscious experience as the subject matter of psychology and maintained that experience should be analyzed into its component parts by use of introspection. See Introspection.

Sublimation Defense mechanism in which a person redirects his socially undesirable urges into socially acceptable behavior.

Subliminal Stimuli Stimuli that do not receive conscious attention because they are below sensory thresholds. They may influence behavior, but research is not conclusive on this matter.

Substance-Induced Organic Mental Disorders Organic mental disorders caused by exposure to harmful environmental substances.

Suggestibility The extent to which a person responds to persuasion. Hypnotic susceptibility refers to the degree of suggestibility observed after an attempt to induce hypnosis has been made. See Hypnosis; Persuasion.

Superego According to Freud, the superego corresponds roughly to conscience. The superego places restrictions on both ego and id and represents the internalized restrictions and ideals that the child learns from parents and culture. See Conscience; Ego; Id.

Sympathetic Nervous System The branch of the autonomic nervous system that is more active in emergencies; it causes a general arousal, increasing breathing, heart rate, and blood pressure.

Synapse A "gap" where individual nerve cells (neurons) come together and across which chemical information is passed.

Syndrome A group of symptoms that occur together and mark a particular abnormal pattern.

Systematic Desensitization A technique used in behavior therapy to eliminate a phobia. The symptoms of the phobia are seen as conditioned responses of fear, and the procedure attempts to decondition the fearful response until the patient gradually is able to face the feared situation. See Phobia.

TAT (Thematic Apperception Test) Personality and motivation test that requires the subject to devise stories about pictures.

Taxis An orienting movement in response to particular stimuli in the environment. A frog, for example, always turns so its snout points directly at its prey before it flicks its tongue. See Orienting Response.

Theory A very general statement that is more useful in generating hypotheses than in generating research. See Hypothesis.

Therapeutic Community The organization of a hospital setting so that patients have to take responsibility for helping one another in an attempt to prevent patients from getting worse by being in the hospital.

Token Economy A system for organizing a treatment setting according to behavioristic principles. Patients are encouraged to take greater responsibility for their adjustment by receiving tokens for acceptable behavior and fines for unacceptable behavior. The theory of token economy grew out of operant conditioning techniques. See Operant Conditioning.

Traits Distinctive and stable attributes that can be found in all people.

Tranquilizers Psychoactive drugs that reduce anxiety. See Psychoactive Drug.

Trial and Error Learning Trying various behaviors in a situation until the solution is hit upon; past experiences lead us to try different responses until we are successful.

Unconditioned Response (UR) An automatic reaction elicited by a stimulus.

Unconditioned Stimulus (US) Any stimulus that elicits an automatic or reflexive reaction in an individual; it does not have to be learned in the present situation.

Unconscious In Freudian terminology, a concept (not a place) of the mind. The unconscious encompasses certain inborn impulses that never rise into consciousness (awareness) as well as memories and wishes that have been repressed. The chief aim of psychoanalytic therapy is to free repressed material from the unconscious in order to make it susceptible to conscious thought and direction. Behaviorists describe the unconscious as an inability to verbalize. See Repression.

Undifferentiated Schizophrenia Type of schizophrenia that does not fit into any particular category, or fits into more than one category.

Validity The extent to which a test actually measures what it is designed to measure.

Variability In statistics, measures of variability communicate how spread out the scores are; the tendency to vary the response to a stimulus, particularly if the response fails to help in adaptation.

Variable Any property of a person, object, or event that can change or take on more than one mathematical value.

Weber's Law States that the difference threshold depends on the ratio of the intensity of one stimulus to another rather than an absolute difference.

Wechsler Adult Intelligence Scale (WAIS) An individually administered test designed to measure adults' intelligence, devised by David Wechsler. The WAIS consists of eleven subtests, of which six measure verbal and five measure performance aspects of intelligence. See Wechsler Intelligence Scale for Children.

Wechsler Intelligence Scale for Children (WISC) Similar to the Wechsler Adult Intelligence Scale, except that it is designed for people under fifteen. Wechsler tests can determine strong and weak areas of overall intelligence. See Wechsler Adult Intelligence Scale (WAIS).

Whorfian Hypothesis The linguistic relativity hypothesis of Benjamin Whorf; states that language influences thought.

Withdrawal Social or emotional detachment; the removal of oneself from a painful or frustrating situation.

Yerkes-Dodson Law Prediction that the optimum motivation level decreases as the difficulty level of a task increases.

Source for the Glossary:
The majority of terms in this glossary are condensed from *The Encyclopedic Dictionary of Psychology,* Terry F. Pettijohn. © 1991 Dushkin/McGraw-Hill, Guilford, CT 06437. The remaining terms were developed by the Annual Editions staff.

Index

addiction: dopamine and, 199–202; as genetic, 28, 34–35
adolescence, society and extended, 85–88
adolescents: marijuana use by, 75–79; shyness in, 112, 114–115
adrenarche, development of sexual attraction and, 80–84
adulthood: extended adolescence and, 85–88; premarital sex in, 135–139
aging, 89–91
agoraphobia, 189
alife, 201
alcohol abuse: effect of, on prenatal development, 62–67
alcoholism, genetic influences on, 28, 34–35
Alka Seltzer, 181
Alzheimer's disease, 41, 42, 43
amygdala, 45, 101, 114
Anafranil, 190
anger, heart disease and, 117–122
anoxia, near-death experiences and, 96
antisocial personalities, 142–151; borderline personality disorder and, 208
anxiety: guided imagery and, 17–18; panic attacks and, 172–178; primary psychopath and, 144, 146
anxiety disorders, 189
apes, 15
apologies, importance of, 123–125
Arcus, Doreen, 111, 112, 116
Aristotle, 101
attention deficit disorder, as genetic, 34
attraction: biological factors involved in physical beauty and, 126–130; development of sexual, and andrenarche, 80–84
avocados, 154
axons, 43

beauty, biology of physical, 126–130
bed nucleus of the stria terminalis (BNST), 114
bees, computer simulated, 201
behavior therapy, for panic attacks, 173–176
Behavioral Activation System (BAS), 146
Behavioral Inhibition System (BIS), 146
behaviorism, 9–12
Benson, Herbert, 58
Biondi, Matt, 102
bipolar disorder, 194
birthweight, low, and prenatal substance abuse, 63–64
"blood," folk concept of, and race, 154
body fat, as genetic, 34
body language, physical attractiveness and, 128, 129–130
borderline personality disorder (BPD), 206–212
brain, 41–44, 114; neurochemistry in, and psychological disorders, 188–190; neurochemistry in, and violence, 45–49; sex differences in, 50–53
Brazil, race in, 154–155
brief therapy, 180
bulimia, 177
Bundy, Ted, 143, 145
Bushmen, 153, 164, 166

Canada, Geoffrey, 69–70
Carter, Jimmy, 102
cataracts, 90
catastrophic thinking, panic attacks and, 173
Cauwels, Janice M., 207, 212
cell death, 42–43
cerebellum, 101
Chagnon, Napoleon A., 165
change, possibility of, 172–178
children: effect of media violence on, 157–163; effect of prenatal exposure to drugs on, 62–67; resilient, 68–71; sociopathy and, 149–151
Cleckley, Hervey, 142–143, 144, 147–148
Clinton, Bill, 102
cholecystokinin (CCK), 189
chlopromazine, 189
Civilization and Its Discontents (Freud), 164, 166
Clark, David, 93, 173–175
client, effectiveness of therapy and, 181, 184
clinical depression, 193. *See also* depression
Clinton, Bill, 92
clomipramine hydrochlorine, 190
clozapine, 189
Cobain, Kurt, 92
cognitive therapy, for panic attacks, 173–176
cognitive-development model, of moral development, 108
cohabitation, 136, 137
computers: alife and, 201; cybertherapy and, 191–192
Comstock, George, 158, 162
conditioning, 161
conscience, apologies and, 123–124
"contextual" conditioning, 114
corpus callosum, 51
Cosmides, Leda, 165
crime, psychopathy and, 142–151
criminal justice, media violence and, 162–163
cults, 19–21, 168–169
cybertherapy, 191–192
cyclical bi-directional model, media violence and, 162

Damasio, Antonio, 101, 146–147
Davidson, Richard, 39–40
daydreams, 17–18
de Klerk, F. W., 124, 125
dehydroepiandrosterone (DHEA), 81
delayed gratification, 100, 104
depression, 43, 173, 178, 193–198; suicide and, 92–94
Descartes, René, 101
desipramine, 189
DHEA (dehydroepiandrosterone), 81
Diener, Edward, 38, 39
dieting, change and, 176–178
DiPietro, Loretta, 90
discipline, desire of students for, and school violence, 72–74
disgust, 101
dopamine, 39–40, 44, 189; addiction and, 199–202
drug abuse, effect of, on prenatal development, 62–67
drug use, by teens, 75–79
Durkheim, Emile, 93

dystymia, 193, 196

eating disorders, 104, 177
education, desire of students for discipline, and school violence, 72–74
Einstein, Albert, 17
emotion, primary psychopathy and, 144
empathy, 102, 108, 123
environment. *See* nature vs. nurture
episodic dyscontrol, neurochemistry and, 45–49
Eron, Leonard, 160–161
eugenics, 27, 29
evil, 9
evolutionary psychology, 164–167
excitocity, 42
exercise, aging and, 90

false-belief test, self-awareness and, 16
families, extended, 149
fantasy, 17–18
feminism, 166
fear: primary psychopathy and, 144, 145; surfers and, 144
"fear quotient" theory, 144
fetal alcohol syndrome (FAS), 64–65
fluoxetine, 43–44, 48, 189–190
Fogel, Alan, 15
folk taxonomies, 154
Foster, Vincent, 92
Fowles, Don, 146
Frank, Jerome, 40
Freud, Sigmund, 12–16, 57, 164, 166
friendships, enduring power of, 105–107

GABA (gamma-aminobutyric acid), 189
Gage, Phineas, 146
Galston, William, 139
gamma-aminobutyric acid (GABA), 189
gender differences. *See* sex differences
genes: brain and, 41–42; depression and, 195; influence of neurochemistry in brain on violence and, 48; panic and, 173. *See also* nature vs. nurture
Gibbs, Sherenia, 70
glutamate, 42
Gnosticism, 169
gonadarche, development of sexual attraction and, 80–81
Goodwin, Frederick K., 93, 94
Gould, Stephen Jay, 13
gratification, delayed, 100, 104
Gray, Jeffrey, 146
Green, A. C., 137
Greenspan, Stanley, 25
Greyson, Bruce, 95–97
Grossman, Jennifer, 136, 139
gun culture, 161
Gunderson, John W., 207–212
Gur, Ruben C., 51, 52–53

Haldol, 189
haloperidol, 189
happiness, 38–40
Harlow, Harry, 10, 11–12
Hauser, Marc D., 15
health, prayer and, 57–59
heart disease, anger and, 117–122

Heaven's Gate, 19, 20, 168, 169
Heritage Village, 90
Hernnstein, Richard, 157, 159
hippocampus, 58, 114
Holmes, Leonard, 191
homosexuality, nature vs. nurture and, 28–29, 34
hostility, heart disease and, 117–122
Huesmann, L. Rowell, 160–161
Hugh Grant Effect, 115
Huntington's disease, 41–42
hypo-descent, 154
hypothalamus, 58, 114
hysterical psychopath, 147, 148

idiopathic psychopathy, 142
imipramine, 189
indigenous peoples, 164–165
infants, development of rational thinking skills in, and spoken language, 54–56
infatuation, 132
inhibitions, 147
inhibitory defect, psychopathy and, 146
intelligence: emotions and, 100–104; race and, 155
Internet, 166; cults and, 169; cybertherapy on, 191–192
intimacy, 131–134
Israel, shyness in, 112–113

Japan, shy children in, 112–113
Johnson, Lyndon, 102

Kagan, Jerome, 24, 25, 38, 101, 111–112
Karpman, Benjamin, 142
Kennedy, John F., 102
ketamine, near-death experiences and, 96
Kevorkian, Jack, 93, 94
Kinsey, Alfred, 10
Koch, Robert, 142
Kohlberg, Lawrence, 108
Kraepelin, Emil, 142
Kramer, Peter, 196–197
Krantz, David, 119
Krasnegor, Norman, 52
!Kung San, 153, 164, 166

language. See spoken language
Ledoux, Joseph, 101
Letterman, David, 111
LeVay, Simon, 28–29
licensing parents, 150–151
Licensing Parents (Westman), 150
Life Orientation Test (LOT), 213–214, 215
limbic system, 51, 58, 101
Litwin, Dorothy, 191
Locke, John, 94
LOT (Life Orientation Test), 213–214, 215
love, 131–134; limbic system and, 101
lust, 132
Lykken, David, 38–39, 40

mammals, self-awareness and, 14–15
manic depression. See bipolar disorder
marijuana, 75–79
Maslow, Abraham, interview with, 8–12
McHugh, James, 138
McHugh, Paul, 100, 101, 104
media: premarital sex and, 136–137; psychopathy and, 143; violence and, 86–87, 157–163
meditation, 176
metamotivation, 11
Milgram, Stanley, 109

mirror self-recognition test, of self-awareness, 14–15
"mismatch theory," technology and, 164–167
monkeys, 15
moral development, 144; nature vs. nurture in, 108–109
Munson, Ronald, 50, 52
murder, sociopathy and, 148, 149

Nadel, Ethan, 90
National Crime Victimization Survey (NCVS), 148
National Research Council (NRC), 148
natural weight, 177
nature vs. nurture: in moral development, 108–109; public policy and, 26–30; in shyness, 24–25; twin studies and, 28–29, 31–37, 38–39. See also genes
near-death experiences, 95–97
negligible cause model, of media violence, 159
neurobehavioral theories, 146
neurochemistry, violence and, 45–49
neuroprotective drugs, 42
neurotransmitters, 43, 102, 188–189, 195–196. See also specific neurotransmitter
New Trier Township High School, 76–79
NMDA receptor, 43
nonlocal mind, 34
norepinephrine, 47, 195–196

Oates, Joyce Carol, 92
obsessive-compulsive disorder (OCD), 188, 190
optimism, 102, 213–216; as genetic, 34
oral language. See spoken language
Order of the Solar Temple, 168
osteoporosis, 90

Pannen, Donald, 106
panic attacks, 172–178
panic disorders, 188, 189
paralysis, anxiety as, 176
Parent Alliance for Drug and Alcohol Awareness (PADAA), 79
parents: licensing of, 149, 150, 151; shyness in children and, 112, 115; single, 150; sociopathy and, 149–150
Parkinson's disease, 42
peak experience, 8, 11
personalities, psychopathic, 142–151
personality disorders, borderline, 206–212
PET (positron emission topography) scans, 173, 190
phenylethylamine (PEA), 132
physical beauty, biological factors of, 126–130
Pilkonis, Philip, 111, 112
Pinel, Phillipe, 142
Pinker, Steven, 16
placebo effect, 58; effectiveness of therapy and, 181
Plomin, Robert, 24
Porges, Stephen, 14
pornography, 159
positive thinking, optimism and, 213–216
post-traumatic stress disorder (PTSD), 173, 188, 190
prayers, health and, 57–59
pregnancy, effect of substance abuse during, 62–67
premarital sex, adult, 135–139
prenatal substance abuse, effects of, 62–67

primary cause model, media violence and, 158–159
primary psychopathy, 142, 144, 145, 146, 147
primates, self-awareness of, 15
progressive relaxation, 175, 176
Prozac, 43–44, 48, 189–190
Prusank, Diane, 106
psychodynamic therapy, for borderline personality disorder, 209
psychopathy, 142–151
psychotherapy, 211
puberty, development of sexual attraction and, 80–84
punishment, apologies and, 123

race myth, 159
race, physical appearance and, 152–156
Rachman, S. J., 173
rational thinking skills, development of, in infants, and spoken language, 54–56
Rawlins, William, 106–107
Reagan, Ronald, 102
Reed, Ralph, 139
regret, 123–124
religiosity: as genetic, 34; health and, 57–59
reparation, apology and, 123–125
reptiles, 14
resilient children, 68–71
Richard III, 143
Richelson, Elliot, 195–196, 197
Rip van Winkle study, 160–161
risperidone, 189
Romanoski, Alan, 194, 195
Rules, The, 139
Rush, A. John, 194, 195, 197
Rush, Benjamin, 142, 144

Salovey, Peter, 100, 104
Sambia, of Papua New Guinea, 82
Schiffren, Lisa, 138
Schindler, Oscar, 143
schizophrenia, 24–25, 35, 43–44, 188, 189
school violence, desire of students for discipline and, 72–74
scorpion flies, 126, 127
Scott, Kody, 144, 145
seasonal affective disorder (SAD), 194
secondary psychopath, 146
selective serotonin re-uptake inhibitors (SSRSs), 43–44, 189–190. See also Prozac
self-actualization, 8, 9, 11, 12
self-awareness, 13–16
self-destruction, borderline personality disorder and, 207–208, 209–210
self-efficacy, optimism and, 216
self-recognition, self-awareness and, 14–15
Seligman, Martin, 102
senescence, 89–91
serotonin, 45, 47, 93, 94, 189, 195–196, 199
sex, adult premarital, 135–139
sex differences, in brain, 50–53
sexual abuse, borderline personality disorder and, 208, 211–212
sexual attraction, development of, and adrenarche, 80–84
sexual orientation, as genetic, 34
Shaywitz, Sally and Bennett, 51, 52, 53
Shea, Tracie, 196
Shrink-Link, 191, 192
shyness, 24–25, 113–117
sibling society, extended adolescence and, 85–88
Singer, Jerome, 17, 18
Smith, Susan, 207, 208

smoking, effect of, on prenatal development, 62–67
Snidman, Nancy, 111, 113–114
socialization, 144, 148–150
sociopathy, 142–151
spoken language, development of rational thinking skills in infants and, 54–56
St. Louis Park, Minnesota, 71
statutory rape laws, 138
stress, 24–25, 100, 101, 203–205; heart disease and, 117–122
stroke, 43
students, desire of, for discipline, and school violence, 72–74
Styron, William, 193, 194
substance abuse: effects of, on prenatal development, 62–67; as genetic, 34
suicide, 92–94; borderline personality disorder and, 209–210
symmetry, physical attractiveness and, 126–128
symptomatic psychopathy, 142
synergy, 8, 11

talking, to infants and development of rational thinking, 54–56

tamarins, 15
Tanner stages, 81
technology: communications and, 116; evolutionary psychology and, 166–167
teenagers. *See* adolescents
telomerase, 91
temperament, happiness and, 38–40
temporal lobe, 46
therapeutic relationship, effectiveness of therapy and, 181
therapy, effectiveness of, 178–187
thinking skills, development of rational, in infants, and spoken language, 54–56
Thorazine, 189
Tinetti, Mary, 90–91
tipos, 154–155
Tooby, John, 165
twin studies: happiness and, 38–39; homosexuality and, 28–29; nature vs. nurture and, 31–37
Type A behavior, 118, 119

Unabomber, 164, 165
underendowment, psychopathy and, 146
Unification Church, 169
Uniform Crime Report (UCR), 148, 150

unipolar depression, 193. *See also* depression

victimization, 148
violence: borderline personality disorder and, 208; desire of students for discipline and school, 72–74; media and, 157–163; nature vs. nurture and, 27; neurochemistry and, 45–49
Vissarion, 169

weight, as genetic, 34
weight-to-hip ratio (WHR), physical attractiveness and, 128, 129–130
Werner, Emmy, 68, 69
Whitehead, Alfred North, 11
Wilson, James Q., 157, 159
Witelson, Sandra, 51, 53

Xanax, 189

Yanomamö people, 164–165

Zimbardo, Philip, 110, 111, 112–113, 115
Zisook, Sidney, 195, 198

Credits/Acknowledgments

Cover design by Charles Vitelli.

1. Becoming a Person: Seeking Self-Identity
Facing overview—© 1997 by PhotoDisc, Inc.
2. Determinants of Behavior: Motivation, Environment, and Physiology
Facing overview—WHO photo.
3. Problems Influencing Personal Growth
Facing overview—© 1997 by Cleo Freelance Photography.

4. Relating to Others
Facing overview—© 1997 by Cleo Freelance Photography.
5. Dynamics of Personal Adjustment: The Individual and Society
Facing overview—© 1997 by Cleo Freelance Photography.
6. Enhancing Human Adjustment: Learning to Cope Effectively
Facing overview—WHO photo by Jean Mohr.

PHOTOCOPY THIS PAGE!!!*

ANNUAL EDITIONS ARTICLE REVIEW FORM

■ NAME: _____ DATE: _____

■ TITLE AND NUMBER OF ARTICLE: _____

■ BRIEFLY STATE THE MAIN IDEA OF THIS ARTICLE: _____
_____

■ LIST THREE IMPORTANT FACTS THAT THE AUTHOR USES TO SUPPORT THE MAIN IDEA:
_____
_____
_____
_____

■ WHAT INFORMATION OR IDEAS DISCUSSED IN THIS ARTICLE ARE ALSO DISCUSSED IN YOUR TEXTBOOK OR OTHER READINGS THAT YOU HAVE DONE? LIST THE TEXTBOOK CHAPTERS AND PAGE NUMBERS:
_____
_____
_____
_____
_____

■ LIST ANY EXAMPLES OF BIAS OR FAULTY REASONING THAT YOU FOUND IN THE ARTICLE:
_____
_____
_____
_____

■ LIST ANY NEW TERMS/CONCEPTS THAT WERE DISCUSSED IN THE ARTICLE, AND WRITE A SHORT DEFINITION:
_____
_____
_____
_____

*Your instructor may require you to use this ANNUAL EDITIONS Article Review Form in any number of ways: for articles that are assigned, for extra credit, as a tool to assist in developing assigned papers, or simply for your own reference. Even if it is not required, we encourage you to photocopy and use this page; you will find that reflecting on the articles will greatly enhance the information from your text.

We Want Your Advice

ANNUAL EDITIONS revisions depend on two major opinion sources: one is our Advisory Board, listed in the front of this volume, which works with us in scanning the thousands of articles published in the public press each year; the other is you—the person actually using the book. Please help us and the users of the next edition by completing the prepaid article rating form on this page and returning it to us. Thank you for your help!

ANNUAL EDITIONS: PERSONAL GROWTH AND BEHAVIOR 98/99
Article Rating Form

Here is an opportunity for you to have direct input into the next revision of this volume. We would like you to rate each of the 45 articles listed below, using the following scale:

1. Excellent: should definitely be retained
2. Above average: should probably be retained
3. Below average: should probably be deleted
4. Poor: should definitely be deleted

Your ratings will play a vital part in the next revision. So please mail this prepaid form to us just as soon as you complete it.
Thanks for your help!

Rating	Article	Rating	Article
	1. The Last Interview of Abraham Maslow		21. The Mystery of Suicide
	2. Evolutionary Necessity or Glorious Accident? Biologists Ponder the Self		22. Is There Life after Death?
	3. How Useful Is Fantasy?		23. The EQ Factor
	4. The Stability of Personality: Observations and Evaluations		24. The Enduring Power of Friendship
	5. Is It Nature or Nurture?		25. Born to Be Good?
	6. Politics of Biology		26. Are You Shy?
	7. Nature's Clones		27. Hotheads and Heart Attacks
	8. Forget Money: Nothing Can Buy Happiness, Some Researchers Say		28. Go Ahead, Say You're Sorry
	9. Revealing the Brain's Secrets		29. The Biology of Beauty
	10. Violence and the Brain		30. The Future of Love
	11. Man's World, Woman's World? Brain Studies Point to Differences		31. Was It Good for Us?
	12. Studies Show Talking with Infants Shapes Basis of Ability to Think		32. Psychopathy, Sociopathy, and Crime
	13. Faith & Healing		33. Mixed Blood
	14. Clipped Wings		34. Media, Violence, Youth, and Society
	15. Invincible Kids		35. The Evolution of Despair
	16. Students Want More Discipline, Disruptive Classmates Out		36. The Lure of the Cult
	17. Kids & Pot and High Times at New Trier High		37. What You Can Change and What You Cannot Change
	18. Rethinking Puberty: The Development of Sexual Attraction		38. No More Bells and Whistles
	19. A World of Half-Adults		39. Targeting the Brain
	20. Older, Longer		40. Upset? Try Cybertherapy
			41. Defeating Depression
			42. Addicted
			43. Don't Face Stress Alone
			44. Personality Disorders: Coping with the Borderline
			45. On the Power of Positive Thinking: The Benefits of Being Optimistic

(Continued on next page)

ABOUT YOU

Name _____ Date _____

Are you a teacher? ❏ Or a student? ❏

Your school name _____

Department _____

Address _____

City _____ State _____ Zip _____

School telephone # _____

YOUR COMMENTS ARE IMPORTANT TO US!

Please fill in the following information:
For which course did you use this book? _____
Did you use a text with this ANNUAL EDITION? ❏ yes ❏ no
What was the title of the text? _____
What are your general reactions to the Annual Editions concept?

Have you read any particular articles recently that you think should be included in the next edition?

Are there any articles you feel should be replaced in the next edition? Why?

Are there any World Wide Web sites you feel should be included in the next edition? Please annotate.

May we contact you for editorial input?

May we quote your comments?

ANNUAL EDITIONS: PERSONAL GROWTH AND BEHAVIOR 98/99

BUSINESS REPLY MAIL
First Class   Permit No. 84   Guilford, CT

Postage will be paid by addressee

**Dushkin/McGraw·Hill
Sluice Dock
Guilford, CT 06437**

No Postage
Necessary
if Mailed
in the
United States